T0092061

Automata Theory

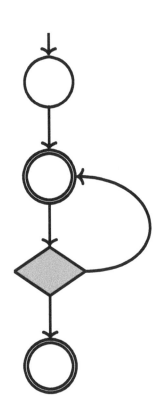

Automata Theory

An Algorithmic Approach

Javier Esparza and Michael Blondin

The MIT Press
Cambridge, Massachusetts
London, England

© 2023 Javier Esparza and Michael Blondin

This work is subject to a Creative Commons CC-BY-ND-NC license.

Subject to such license, all rights are reserved.

The MIT Press would like to thank the anonymous peer reviewers who provided comments on drafts of this book. The generous work of academic experts is essential for establishing the authority and quality of our publications. We acknowledge with gratitude the contributions of these otherwise uncredited readers.

This book was set in Times New Roman by Westchester Publishing Services. Printed and bound in the United States of America.

Library of Congress Cataloging-in-Publication Data

Names: Esparza, Javier, author. | Blondin, Michael, author.
Title: Automata theory : an algorithmic approach / Javier Esparza and
    Michael Blondin.
Description: Cambridge : The MIT Press, 2023. | Includes bibliographical
    references and index. | Summary: "The book presents automata theory
    from a fresh viewpoint inspired by its main modern application: program
    verification"—Provided by publisher.
Identifiers: LCCN 2022052126 (print) | LCCN 2022052127 (ebook) |
    ISBN 9780262048637 | ISBN 9780262376938 (epub) |
    ISBN 9780262376945 (adobe pdf)
Subjects: LCSH: Machine theory.
Classification: LCC QA267 .E87 2023 (print) | LCC QA267 (ebook) |
    DDC 005.13/1—dc23/eng20230711
LC record available at https://lccn.loc.gov/2022052126
LC ebook record available at https://lccn.loc.gov/2022052127

10   9   8   7   6   5   4   3   2   1

To the memory of Wilfried Brauer, a noble spirit who also wrote one.

Contents

Preface

Why This Book?

There are excellent textbooks on automata theory, ranging from course books for under-graduates to research monographs for specialists. Why another one?

During the 1960s and 1970s, the main application of automata theory was the develop-ment of lexicographic analyzers, parsers, and compilers. Analyzers and parsers determine whether an input string conforms to a given syntax, while compilers transform strings con-forming to a syntax into equivalent strings conforming to another. With these applications in mind, it was natural to look at automata as abstract machines that accept, reject, or transform input strings, and this view deeply influenced the textbook presentation of automata theory. The expressive power of machines (which languages are recognized by finite automata or pushdown automata), equivalences between models (are nondeterministic and determinis-tic automata equivalent?), or closure properties (are context-free languages closed under intersection?) received much attention, while *constructions* on automata, like the powerset or product constructions, often played a subordinate role.

This can already be observed in the article "Finite Automata and Their Decision Prob-lems" by Rabin and Scott, a foundational paper published in the IBM *Journal of Research and Development* in 1959. The paper introduces a large part of the theory of finite automata taught in current undergraduate courses: deterministic finite automata (DFAs) and nondeter-ministic finite automata (NFAs), the powerset construction, closure of the regular languages under boolean operations and others, decision algorithms for emptiness and finiteness of the language recognized by a given automaton, and uniqueness of the minimal DFA for a given language. Much of the presentation style of this paper survives in today's textbooks, and the style is not algorithmically oriented. For example, the powerset construction is not introduced as an algorithm that, given an NFA as input, produces an equivalent DFA as output but as a mathematical definition (definition 11): a DFA whose states are all the sub-sets of states of the original automaton. The simple but computationally important fact that only the states of the DFA reachable from the initial state need to be constructed is not mentioned. Another example can be found in section 4, which studies the emptiness problem for DFAs. It contains a corollary (corollary 7.1) stating that, "given an automaton A, there is an effective procedure whereby in a finite number of steps it can be decided whether $\mathcal{L}(A)$ is empty." The effective procedure, which is only sketched, consists of checking for all words of length up to the number of states of A whether they are accepted; this procedure has exponential complexity, while the problem can be solved in linear time.

We claim that this presentation style, summarized by the slogan *automata are abstract machines*, is no longer adequate. In particular, during the second half of the 1980s and in the 1990s, program verification emerged as a new and exciting application of automata theory. Automata were used to describe the *behavior* of hardware and software systems, not their syntax, and this shift from syntax to semantics had important consequences. While automata for lexical or syntactical analysis typically have at most some thousands of states, automata for semantic descriptions can easily have tens of millions. In order to handle automata of this size, it became imperative to pay special attention to efficient constructions and algorithmic issues, and research in this direction made great progress. Moreover, *automata on infinite words*, a class of automata models originally introduced in the 1960s to solve abstract problems in logic, became the model of choice to specify and verify liveness properties of software. These automata run over words of infinite length, and so they can hardly be seen as machines accepting or rejecting an input; they could only do so after infinite time!

This book intends to reflect this evolution of automata theory. The modern change of focus, from expressivity to algorithmic questions, is captured by the new slogan *automata as data structures*. Hash tables and Fibonacci heaps are adequate data structures for representing sets when one needs the operations of a dictionary and a priority queue, respectively. Similarly, automata are the right data structure for representing sets and relations when the required operations are union, intersection, complement, projections, and joins. From this point of view, it is the algorithmic implementation of the operations that gets the limelight, and it constitutes the spine of this book.

The shape of the book is also very influenced by two further design decisions. First, automata-theoretic constructions are best explained by means of examples, and examples are best presented with the help of pictures. Automata on words are blessed with a graphical representation of instantaneous appeal. We have invested much effort into finding illustrative, nontrivial examples whose graphical representation still fits in one page. Second, students learning directly from a book often find solved exercises more illustrative than any written explanation and essential to self-evaluate their progress. This book contains a large number of solved exercises, ranging from mechanic applications of algorithms to relatively involved proofs.

Acknowledgments

First and foremost, we thank Orna Kupferman and Moshe Vardi. This book grew out of a joint attempt to write a research monograph on the automata-theoretic approach to model checking and automatic synthesis. The project started in the early 2000s, but, like so many projects without a deadline, it was postponed multiple times. In 2007, the first author moved to the Technical University of Munich and started to teach a new master course on automata theory. The initial version of the course was focused on automata on infinite words, and it heavily relied on course material by Orna and Moshe. The course notes assumed familiarity with automata on finite words, as taught in a standard introductory course to theoretical computer science. However, students had difficulties in refreshing their knowledge on automata—which usually had not been presented in an algorithmic way—and connecting it to the new algorithmic approach. Addressing these issues required producing additional notes on automata on finite words. With a new student cohort demanding better notes year after year, the notes grew step by step, until they covered pattern matching, applications to verification, decision procedures for several logics, and binary decision diagrams. The final result is the book you have in your hands, which would not exist without Orna and Moshe's initial push.

Special thanks go to Jörg Kreiker, Jan Kretínský, Michael Luttenberger, Salomon Sickert, and Stefan Schwoon for their contributions to several chapters and for many discussions. In particular, Jan contributed a lot to chapter 4 on pattern matching, and Stefan Schwoon graciously allowed us to use his unpublished lecture notes in chapter 12 on emptiness checking of Büchi automata.

We also express our gratitude to many colleagues and students who helped us in various ways. Udi Boker patiently answered many questions, and his work strongly influenced chapter 10 on the relations between different classes of ω-automata. Breno Faria helped to draw many (former) figures; he was funded by a program at the Computer Science Department of the Technical University of Munich. Noé Canva, François Ladouceur, and Alex Sansfaçon-Buchanan proofread the book while taking a dedicated master's course at the Université de Sherbrooke. Philipp Czerner, Debarghya Ghoshdastidar, Kush Grover, Roland Guttenberg, Marijana Lazic, Mikhail Raskin, Salomon Sickert, Chana Weil-Kennedy, and Markus Wenzel proofread chapters at the Technical University of Munich. Hardik Arora, Joe Bedard, Fabio Bove, Birgit Engelmann, Tabea Frisch, Tobias Forner, Moritz Fuchs, Matthias Heizmann, Barbara König, Stefan Krusche, Siyun Liang, Philipp Müller, Batikan Bora Ormanci, Martin Perzl, Marcel Ruegenberg, Franz Saller, Hayk Shoukourian, Ala Sleimi, Alexander Simon Treml, Radu Vintan, Theresa Wasserer, Yi Wei, and Daniel Weißauer spotted mistakes and provided very helpful comments. We also wish to express our gratitude to all those who have assisted in making this publication possible, notably Elisabeth Swayze and Matthew Valades from the MIT Press and the production team at Westchester Publishing Services led by Madhulika Jain.

0 Overview

0.1 Introduction

Courses on data structures show how to represent sets of objects in a computer so that operations like insertion, deletion, lookup, and many others can be efficiently implemented. Typical representations are hash tables, search trees, or heaps.

This textbook also deals with the problem of representing and manipulating sets of objects but with respect to a different family of operations: the *boolean operations of set theory* (union, intersection, and complement with respect to some universe set), some *tests* that check basic properties (whether a set is empty, contains all elements of the universe, or is contained in another set), and operations on *relations* between objects, like joins and projections. Table 0.1 defines the operations we would like to support, where U denotes some universe of objects, X, Y are subsets of U, x is an element of U, and $R, S \subseteq U \times U$ are binary relations on U. Note that many other operations, like set difference, can be reduced to the ones in the table and that operations on n-ary relations for $n \geq 3$ can be reduced to operations on binary relations.

We want a data structure that is able to represent infinite subsets of an infinite universe set, like infinite sets of natural numbers. For example, the constraint $x > 5$ is a finite representation of the infinite set $\{6, 7, 8, \ldots\}$, and the logical formula $\exists y\, 3y = x$ is a finite representation of the set of multiples of 3—that is, of the set $\{0, 3, 6, 9, \ldots\}$. It is easy to see that no data structure can finitely represent *every* infinite set.[1] Because of this limitation, every good data structure for infinite sets must find a reasonable compromise between *expressivity* (which sets it can finitely represent) and *manipulability* (which operations can be carried out and at which cost). This book introduces the compromise offered by *finite automata*, which, as shown by more than sixty years of research on the theory of formal languages, is the best

---

1. An infinite universe, like the set of natural numbers, has uncountably many subsets. However, a data structure only has a countable number of instances; indeed, an instance of a data structure—say, a tree—can always be encoded as a string, and there are only a countable number of strings over a finite alphabet. So, loosely speaking, we do not have enough instances for all sets.

Table 0.1
Operations and tests for manipulation of sets and relations.

Operation on sets	Returns
Complement(X)	$U \setminus X$
Intersection(X, Y)	$X \cap Y$
Union(X, Y)	$X \cup Y$

Test on sets	Returns
Member(x, X)	**true** if $x \in X$, **false** otherwise
Empty(X)	**true** if $X = \emptyset$, **false** otherwise
Universal(X)	**true** if $X = U$, **false** otherwise
Included(X, Y)	**true** if $X \subseteq Y$, **false** otherwise
Equal(X, Y)	**true** if $X = Y$, **false** otherwise

Operation on relations	Returns
Projection_1(R)	$\pi_1(R) = \{x : \exists y \, (x, y) \in R\}$
Projection_2(R)	$\pi_2(R) = \{y : \exists x \, (x, y) \in R\}$
Join(R, S)	$R \circ S = \{(x, z) : \exists y \in X \, (x, y) \in R \wedge (y, z) \in S\}$
Post(X, R)	$post_R(X) = \{y \in U : \exists x \in X \, (x, y) \in R\}$
Pre(X, R)	$pre_R(X) = \{y \in U : \exists x \in X \, (y, x) \in R\}$

one available for many practical purposes. Finite automata, as we will call them throughout the book, represent and manipulate sets whose elements are encoded as *words* (i.e., as
sequences of symbols).[2]

Any kind of object can be represented by a word, at least in principle. Natural numbers,
for instance, are represented as sequences of digits, that is, as words over the alphabet of
digits. Vectors and lists can also be represented as words by concatenating the word representations of their elements. As a matter of fact, whenever a computer stores an object in a
file, the computer is representing it as a word over some alphabet, like ASCII or Unicode.
So, automata are a very general data structure. However, while any object can be represented by a word, not every object can be represented by a *finite* word, that is, a word of
finite length. Typical examples are real numbers and nonterminating executions of a program. When objects cannot be represented by finite words, computers usually only represent
some approximation: a float instead of a real number or a finite prefix instead of a nonterminating computation. In the second part of the book, we show how to represent sets of
infinite objects *exactly* using *automata on infinite words*. While the theory of automata on
finite words is often considered a "gold standard" of theoretical computer science—a powerful and beautiful theory with lots of important applications in many fields—automata on

---

2. There are generalizations of word automata in which objects are encoded as trees. The theory of tree automata
is also very well developed but not the subject of this book.

infinite words are more demanding, and their theory does not achieve the same degree of "perfection." The structure of part II reflects this: we follow the same steps as in part I, always comparing the solutions for infinite words with the "gold standard."

0.2 Outline and Structure

Part I presents data structures and algorithms for regular languages of finite words.

Chapter 1 introduces the classical data structures for the representation of regular languages: regular expressions, deterministic finite automata (DFAs), nondeterministic finite automata (NFAs), and nondeterministic automata with ε-transitions. We refer to all of them as *automata*. The chapter presents some examples showing how to use automata to finitely represent sets of words, numbers, or program states and describes conversion algorithms between the representations. All algorithms are well known (and can also be found in other textbooks) with the exception of the algorithm for the elimination of ϵ-transitions.

Chapter 2 addresses the issue of finding small representations for a given set. It shows that there is a unique minimal representation of a language as a DFA and introduces the classical minimization algorithms. It also presents algorithms to reduce the size of NFAs.

Chapter 3 describes algorithms that implement boolean operations on sets, like union, intersection, and complement, using automata as data structure. It then presents implementations of test operations on sets, like testing inclusion or equality between sets.

Chapter 4 presents a first, classical application of the techniques and results of chapter 3: pattern matching. Even this well-known problem gets a new twist when examined from the automata-as-data-structures point of view. The chapter presents the Knuth–Morris–Pratt algorithm as the design of a new data structure, lazy DFAs, for which the membership operation can be performed very efficiently.

Chapter 5 shows how to implement operations on relations, in particular the join operation using length-preserving transducers (i.e., automata over an alphabet consisting of pairs of letters), as data structure. It discusses in detail how to encode relations as words.

Chapter 6 presents specific data structures, that is, automata, for the important special case in which the universe U of objects is finite. In this case, all objects can be encoded by words of the same length, and the set and relation operations can be optimized. In particular, one can then use minimal DFAs as data structure and directly implement algorithms for all operations, without having to introduce extra minimization operations after each intermediate step. The second part of the chapter introduces (ordered) binary decision diagrams as a class of automata that can represent finite sets even more succinctly than minimal DFAs.

Chapter 7 applies nearly all of the constructions and algorithms of previous chapters to the problem of verifying safety properties of sequential and concurrent programs with bounded-range variables. In particular, the chapter shows how to model concurrent programs as networks of automata, how to express safety properties using automata or regular expressions, and how to automatically verify them using the algorithmic constructions of previous chapters.

Chapter 8 presents first-order logic (FOL) and monadic-second order logic (MSOL) on words as languages for the declarative specification of regular languages. Intuitively, logic formulas are used to specify a language by describing a property that a word may satisfy or not, and defining the language as the set of words that satisfy the property. The chapter shows that FOL cannot describe all regular languages and that MSOL does.

Chapter 9 introduces Presburger arithmetic, a language to define sets of (tuples of) natural numbers. As in the previous chapter, formulas of Presburger arithmetic describe properties that a tuple of numbers may satisfy or not. The chapter presents an algorithm to compute an automaton encoding all the tuples satisfying a given formula.

Part II presents data structures and algorithms for regular languages of infinite words, also called ω-regular languages.

Chapter 10 introduces ω-regular expressions and several classes of ω-automata: deterministic and nondeterministic Büchi, co-Büchi, Rabin, Street, parity, and Muller automata. It explains the advantages and disadvantages of each class, in particular whether the automata in the class can be determinized, and presents conversion algorithms between the classes.

Chapter 11 presents implementations of the set operations (union, intersection, and complementation) for Büchi and generalized Büchi automata. In particular, it presents in detail a complementation algorithm for Büchi automata.

Chapter 12 presents different implementations of the emptiness test for Büchi and generalized Büchi automata (i.e., the problem of deciding whether the automaton recognizes the empty language). The first part of the chapter presents two linear-time implementations based on depth-first-search (DFS): the algorithm known as nested-DFS and a modification of Tarjan's algorithm for the computation of strongly connected components. The second part presents further implementations based on breadth-first-search.

Chapter 13 applies the algorithms of previous chapters to the problem of verifying liveness properties of programs. After an introductory example, the chapter presents linear temporal logic (LTL) as property specification formalism and shows how to algorithmically translate a formula into an equivalent generalized Büchi automaton recognizing the language of all words satisfying the formula. It then uses the operations implemented in chapter 12 to derive an algorithm for the automatic verification of LTL properties.

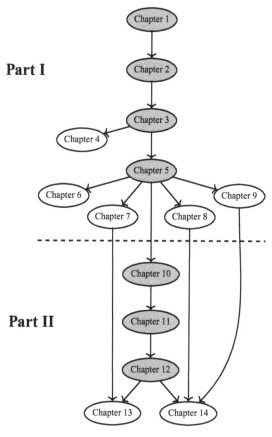

Figure 0.1
Chapter dependencies.

Chapter 14 extends the logic approach to regular languages studied in chapters 8 and 9 to ω-words. The first part of the chapter introduces monadic second-order logic on ω-words and shows how to construct a Büchi automaton recognizing the set of ω-words satisfying a given formula. The second part introduces linear arithmetic, the first-order theory of the real numbers with addition, and shows how to construct a Büchi automaton recognizing the encodings of all the real numbers satisfying a given formula.

Dependencies between chapters are depicted graphically in figure 0.1. The "spine" of the book, containing chapters 1–3, chapter 5, and chapters 10–12, presents the implementations of the operations on sets and relations. The rest of the chapters contain applications, which, in the case of chapter 4 and chapter 6, also introduce some special automata classes.

Chapters 1–5 are an introduction to finite automata at bachelor level, similar in content to the ones found in introductory books to the theory of computation, but with more examples and greater emphasis on algorithms. (A few sections, marked with "★" in the table of contents, require background that bachelor students typically do not yet have, for example, in computational complexity theory; they can be skipped.) This material can be complemented with any subset of the applications presented in chapters 6–9.

A master course, like the ones we teach at the Technical University of Munich and the Université de Sherbrooke, can cover the full spine (presenting chapters 1–5 at higher speed) and a selection of applications.

0.3   On the Exercises

Each chapter ends with exercises. About a third of the solutions appear only in a version intended for instructors. The rest (and hence the majority) of the solutions appear in an appendix at the end of the book. Each exercise is marked by its difficulty, (dominant) type, and solution availability, with these symbols:

Difficulty	Symbol
Standard	☆
Harder	⯪
Challenging	★

Type	Symbol
Construction	▣
Algorithm design	🖌
Algorithm execution	⚙
Proofs	■
Extra material	☛

Solution	Symbol
Available in appendix	🔓
Not available in appendix	🔒

I AUTOMATA ON FINITE WORDS

1 Automata Classes and Conversions

In section 1.2, we define basic notions, like words and languages, and introduce regular expressions, a textual notation for the finite representation of languages. Section 1.3 introduces increasingly larger classes of finite automata: deterministic, nondeterministic, with ε-transitions, and with transitions labeled by regular expressions. Section 1.4 presents conversion algorithms that transform a regular expression into an equivalent automaton, an automaton into an equivalent regular expression, or an automaton of one kind into an equivalent automaton of another.

1.1 Alphabets, Letters, Words, and Languages

An *alphabet* is a finite nonempty set. The elements of an alphabet are called *letters* or *symbols*. A finite, possibly empty, sequence of letters is a *word*. A word $a_1 a_2 \cdots a_n$ has *length n*. The empty word is the only word of length 0 and it is written ε. The concatenation of two words $u = a_1 \cdots a_n$ and $v = b_1 \ldots b_m$ is the word $uv = a_1 \cdots a_n b_1 \cdots b_m$, sometimes also denoted by $u \cdot v$. Observe that $\varepsilon \cdot w = w = w \cdot \varepsilon$. For every word w, we define $w^0 = \varepsilon$ and $w^{k+1} = ww^k$ for every $k \geq 0$.

Remark 1.1 The formal definition of a word differs from the one used in daily life, according to which this sentence has twenty-two words. This is so because in (modern) natural languages, words are defined as sequences of letters with a special symbol on each side, the blank, except at the beginning or end of a sentence. On the contrary, the mathematical definition treats all symbols the same. It sees a whole English text, say *Hamlet*, as one single word of length (about) 186,400 over a sixty-seven-symbol alphabet containing twenty-six lower case letters, twenty-six upper case letters, the blank, and fourteen punctuation marks. This word is a concatenation of the form

$$w_1 \, u \, w_2 \, u \, \cdots u \, w_n,$$

where $n \approx 32{,}000$, the word u has length 1 and consists of just a blank, and $w_1, \ldots, w_n$ are English words, possibly with punctuation marks at the end. In particular, we have

$$w_1 = \text{ACT} \quad w_2 = \text{I} \qquad\qquad w_3 = \text{SCENE} \quad w_4 = \text{I.} \qquad w_5 = \text{ELSINORE.}$$

$$w_6 = \text{A} \qquad w_7 = \text{platform} \quad w_8 = \text{before} \qquad w_9 = \text{the} \quad w_{10} = \text{castle.}$$

Given an alphabet Σ, we denote by Σ^* the set of all words over Σ. A set $L \subseteq \Sigma^*$ of words is a *language* over Σ. We define three operations on languages over a given alphabet Σ:

- The *complement* of a language L is the language $\Sigma^* \setminus L$, which we often denote $\overline{L}$. Notice that the notation $\overline{L}$ implicitly assumes that the alphabet Σ is fixed. For example, consider the language $L = \{a^n : n \geq 0\}$. If $\Sigma = \{a\}$, then $\overline{L} = \emptyset$, but if $\Sigma = \{a, b\}$, then $\overline{L}$ contains all words over $\{a, b\}$ with at least one occurrence of b.
- The *concatenation* of two languages L_1 and L_2 is $L_1 \, L_2 = \{w_1 w_2 : w_1 \in L_1, w_2 \in L_2\}$ also denoted by $L_1 \cdot L_2$. Observe that $\emptyset \, L = L \, \emptyset = \emptyset$, because no word is the concatenation of a word of $\emptyset$ and a word of L, since $\emptyset$ contains no words.
- The *iteration* of a language L is the language $L^* = \bigcup_{i \geq 0} L^i$, where $L^0 = \{\varepsilon\}$ and $L^{i+1} = L^i \cdot L$ for every $i \geq 0$.

Example 1.2 Here is an assorted collection of languages, where $\Sigma = \{a, b\}$.

- $\{ab, a\}\{ab, b\} = \{abab, abb, aab, ab\}$.
- $\{a\}^* = \{\varepsilon, a, aa, aaa, \dots\}$.
- $\{a, b\}^3 = \{a, b\}\{a, b\}\{a, b\} = \{aaa, aab, aba, abb, baa, bab, bba, bbb\}$.
- $\{a, b, \varepsilon\}^2 = \{\varepsilon, a, b, aa, ab, ba, bb\}$.
- $(\{a, b\}\{a, b\})^*$ is the set of all words over Σ of even length.
- $\overline{\{a, b\}\{a, b\}}$ is the set of all words over Σ of length different from 2.
- $\{\varepsilon\}^* = \{\varepsilon\}$.
- $\emptyset^* = \{\varepsilon\}$. (Indeed, $\emptyset^0 = \{\varepsilon\}$ by definition, and $\emptyset^i = \emptyset$ for every $i \geq 1$.)

1.2   Regular Expressions: A Language to Describe Languages

Finite languages can be described by explicit enumeration of the words they contain, but this no longer works for infinite languages. We introduce *regular expressions*, a language to describe languages. They are a suitable notation for the concise description of many infinite languages.

Definition 1.3 *Regular expressions r over an alphabet Σ are generated by the following grammar, where $a \in \Sigma$:*

$$r ::= \emptyset \mid \varepsilon \mid a \mid r_1 r_2 \mid r_1 + r_2 \mid r^*$$

The set of all regular expressions over Σ is written $\mathcal{RE}(\Sigma)$.

Remark 1.4 Definition 1.3 assumes that the reader is familiar with the Backus–Naur form and some standard conventions concerning parentheses. For a definition from scratch, let $\Gamma = \{\emptyset, \varepsilon, (,), +, {}^*\}$ and let Σ be an alphabet disjoint from Γ. We denote by $\mathcal{RE}(\Sigma) \subseteq (\Sigma \cup \Gamma)^*$ the language over the alphabet $\Sigma \cup \Gamma$ defined inductively as follows:

- $\emptyset, \varepsilon \in \mathcal{RE}(\Sigma)$ and $\Sigma \subseteq \mathcal{RE}(\Sigma)$.
- If $r_1, r_2 \in \mathcal{RE}(\Sigma)$, then $(r_1 r_2) \in \mathcal{RE}(\Sigma)$ and $(r_1 + r_2) \in \mathcal{RE}(\Sigma)$.
- If $r \in \mathcal{RE}(\Sigma)$ then $(r)^* \in \mathcal{RE}(\Sigma)$.

Intuitively, a regular expression can be seen as a "recipe" for generating words. For example, the regular expression $(ab)^*c$ corresponds to the recipe "concatenate as many copies of ab as you wish (including zero copies), and then add c at the end." This recipe produces words like abc, $ababc$, or just c. The expression $a^* + b^*$ corresponds to "choose one of these two: concatenate as many copies of a as you want (including zero); or, concatenate as many copies of b as you want (including zero)." It produces words like aa or $bbbb$ but not ab. Observe the difference with the recipe $(a + b)^*$, "concatenate as many letters as you want (including zero), where each letter can be an a or a b." This recipe can produce ab, and in fact, it can produce *any* word.

Let us give a precise definition of the language generated by a regular expression.

Definition 1.5 *The language $\mathcal{L}(r) \subseteq \Sigma^*$ of a regular expression $r \in \mathcal{RE}(\Sigma)$ is defined inductively by*

$$\mathcal{L}(\emptyset) = \emptyset \qquad\qquad \mathcal{L}(r_1 r_2) = \mathcal{L}(r_1) \cdot \mathcal{L}(r_2)$$

$$\mathcal{L}(\varepsilon) = \{\varepsilon\} \qquad\qquad \mathcal{L}(r_1 + r_2) = \mathcal{L}(r_1) \cup \mathcal{L}(r_2)$$

$$\mathcal{L}(a) = \{a\} \qquad\qquad \mathcal{L}(r^*) = \mathcal{L}(r)^*$$

A language L is regular *if there is a regular expression r such that $L = \mathcal{L}(r)$.*

When there is no risk of confusion, we write "the language r" instead of "the language $\mathcal{L}(r)$." In the same vein, we call $r_1 r_2$ the *concatenation* of r_1 and r_2, $r_1 + r_2$ the *union* of r_1 and r_2, and r^* the *iteration* of r. Sometimes, we write $r_1 \cdot r_2$ instead of $r_1 r_2$ and r^k instead of $\underbrace{rr \cdots r}_{k \text{ times}}$.

Example 1.6 Let $\Sigma = \{0, 1\}$. Some languages expressible by regular expressions are:

- The set of all words: $(0 + 1)^*$. We often use Σ as an abbreviation of $(0 + 1)$ and so Σ^* as an abbreviation of $(0 + 1)^*$.
- The set of all words of length at most 4: $(0 + 1 + \varepsilon)^4$.
- The set of all words that begin and end with 0: $0\Sigma^*0$.

Table 1.1
Some equivalence laws for regular expressions.

Laws for union

$r + (s + t) \equiv (r + s) + t$	(associativity)
$r + s \equiv s + r$	(commutativity)
$\emptyset + r \equiv r$	(left neutrality)
$r + \emptyset \equiv r$	(right neutrality)
$r + r \equiv r$	(idempotence)

Laws for concatenation

$r(st) \equiv (rs)t$	(associativity)
$\varepsilon r \equiv r$	(left neutrality)
$r\varepsilon \equiv r$	(right neutrality)
$\emptyset r \equiv \emptyset$	(left annihilation)
$r\emptyset \equiv \emptyset$	(right annihilation)

Laws for iteration

$\emptyset^* \equiv \varepsilon^* \equiv \varepsilon$	
$r^* \equiv \varepsilon + rr^*$	(expansion)
$(r^*)^* \equiv r^*$	(idempotence)

Other laws

$r(s + t) \equiv rs + rt$	(left distributivity)
$(r + s)t \equiv rt + st$	(right distributivity)
$(r + s)^* \equiv (r^*s^*)^*$	

- The set of all words containing at least one pair of 0s exactly five letters apart: $\Sigma^* 0 \Sigma^4 0 \Sigma^*$.

- The set of all words containing an even number of 0s: $1^* + (1^*01^*01^*)^*$.

- The set of all words containing an even number of 0s and an even number of 1s: $(00 + 11 + (01 + 10)(00 + 11)^*(01 + 10))^*$.

Two regular expressions r_1 and r_2 are *equivalent*, denoted $r_1 \equiv r_2$, if $\mathcal{L}(r_1) = \mathcal{L}(r_2)$. For example, we have $a(b + c) \equiv ab + ac$ because $\mathcal{L}(a(b + c)) = \{ab, ac\} = \mathcal{L}(ab + ac)$. Table 1.1 presents a list of useful *equivalence laws*, valid for arbitrary regular expressions r, s, and t.

1.3   Automata Classes

We introduce deterministic finite automata, abstract machines that receive a word as input, and either reject or accept it. Then we present several generalizations of this basic model: nondeterministic finite automata, nondeterministic automata with ε-transitions, and nondeterministic automata with transitions labeled by regular expressions.

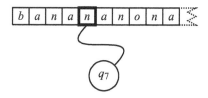

Figure 1.1
Tape with reading head.

1.3.1 Deterministic Finite Automata

Intuitively, a deterministic automaton can be seen as the control unit of a machine that reads an input from a *tape* divided into *cells* by means of a *reading head* (see figure 1.1). Initially, the automaton is in the initial control state, the tape contains the word to be read, and the reading head is positioned on the first cell of the tape.

At each step, the machine reads the contents of the cell occupied by the reading head, updates the current control state according to a *transition function*, and advances the head one cell to the right. The machine accepts a word if the state reached after reading it completely belongs to a set of *final* states.

Definition 1.7 *A deterministic automaton (DA) is a tuple $A = (Q, \Sigma, \delta, q_0, F)$, where*

- *Q is a nonempty set of states,*
- *Σ is an alphabet,*
- *$\delta \colon Q \times \Sigma \to Q$ is a transition function,*
- *$q_0 \in Q$ is the initial state, and*
- *$F \subseteq Q$ is the set of final states.*

A run of A on input $a_0 a_1 \cdots a_{n-1}$ is a sequence $q_0 \xrightarrow{a_0} q_1 \xrightarrow{a_1} \cdots \xrightarrow{a_{n-1}} q_n$, such that $q_i \in Q$ for all $0 \le i \le n$, and $\delta(q_i, a_i) = q_{i+1}$ for all $0 \le i < n$. A run is accepting if $q_n \in F$. The automaton A accepts a word $w \in \Sigma^*$ if it has an accepting run on input w. The language recognized by A is the set $\mathcal{L}(A) = \{w \in \Sigma^* : w \text{ is accepted by } A\}$.

A deterministic finite automaton (DFA) is a DA with a finite set of states.

Notice that a DA has exactly one run on a given word. Given a DA, we often say "the word w leads from q_0 to q," meaning that the unique run of the DA on the word w ends at the state q, and write $q_0 \xrightarrow{w} q$.

Graphically, nonfinal states of a DFA are represented by circles and final states by double circles (see example 1.8). The transition function is represented by labeled directed edges: if $\delta(q, a) = q'$, then we draw an edge from q to q' labeled by a. We also draw an edge into the initial state to denote that the DFA starts there.

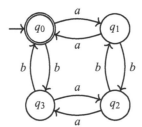

Figure 1.2
A DFA.

Example 1.8   Figure 1.2 shows the graphical representation of the DFA $A = (Q, \Sigma, \delta, q_0, F)$, where $Q = \{q_0, q_1, q_2, q_3\}$, $\Sigma = \{a, b\}$, $F = \{q_0\}$, and δ is given by

$$\delta(q_0, a) = q_1 \qquad \delta(q_1, a) = q_0 \qquad \delta(q_2, a) = q_3 \qquad \delta(q_3, a) = q_2,$$

$$\delta(q_0, b) = q_3 \qquad \delta(q_1, b) = q_2 \qquad \delta(q_2, b) = q_1 \qquad \delta(q_3, b) = q_0.$$

The runs of A on *aabb* and *abbb* are

$$q_0 \xrightarrow{a} q_1 \xrightarrow{a} q_0 \xrightarrow{b} q_3 \xrightarrow{b} q_0,$$

$$q_0 \xrightarrow{a} q_1 \xrightarrow{b} q_2 \xrightarrow{b} q_1 \xrightarrow{b} q_2.$$

The first one is accepting, but the second one is not. It is not difficult to see that the DFA recognizes the language of all words over alphabet $\{a, b\}$ that contain an even number of as and an even number of bs. Indeed, the DFA is in the states on the left if it has read an even number of as, and in the states on the right if it has read an odd number of as. The same holds for bottom and top states w.r.t. the number of bs.

Trap states.   Consider the DFA depicted in figure 1.3 over alphabet $\{a, b, c\}$. It recognizes the language $\{\varepsilon, ab, ba\}$. The colored state on the right is often called a *trap state* or a *garbage collector*: if a run reaches this state, it gets trapped in it, and so the run cannot be accepting. DFAs often have a trap state with several ingoing transitions, and this makes it difficult to find a nice graphical representation. So, when drawing DFAs, we often omit the trap state. For instance, we only draw the uncolored part of the automaton depicted in figure 1.3. Note that no information is lost: if a state q has no outgoing transition labeled by a, then we know that $\delta(q, a) = q_t$, where q_t is the unique trap state.

1.3.2   Using DFAs as Data Structures

We think of regular expressions as word *generators* and of DFAs (and the automata classes we will introduce soon) as word *acceptors*. These mental images are useful to guide our intuition, but there is a more general and fruitful view: DFAs are *finite representations* of

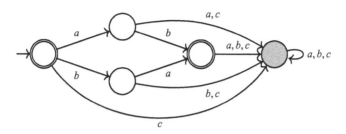

Figure 1.3
A DFA with a trap state.

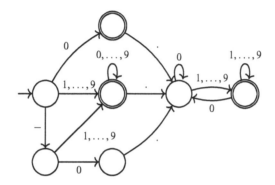

Figure 1.4
A DFA for decimal numbers.

possibly infinite languages. In applications, a suitable encoding is used to represent objects (like numbers, programs, relations, and tuples) as words. Via this encoding, a DFA is a finite representation of a possibly infinite set of objects. Let us see four examples of DFAs representing interesting sets, which also illustrate the theory and applications described in the coming chapters.

Example 1.9 The DFA of figure 1.4 (drawn without the trap state) recognizes the strings over alphabet $\{-, \cdot, 0, 1, \ldots, 9\}$ that encode real numbers with a finite decimal part. We wish to exclude 002, -0, or 3.10000000 but accept 37, 10.503, or -0.234 as correct encodings. An English description of the correct encodings is rather long:

• a string encoding a number consists of an integer part, followed by a possibly empty fractional part;

• the integer part consists of an optional minus sign, followed by a nonempty sequence of digits;

• if the first digit of the integer part is 0, then it is the only digit of the integer part;

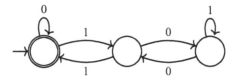

Figure 1.5
A DFA for the multiples of 3 encoded in binary.

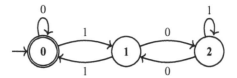

Figure 1.6
Same DFA, after naming the states.

- if the fractional part is nonempty, then it starts with ".", followed by a nonempty sequence of digits that does not end with 0; and

- if the integer part is −0, then the fractional part is nonempty.

In chapters 2 and 3, we will see how to obtain this DFA algorithmically, by applying constructions to small automata corresponding to each of the items in the above description. In chapter 4, we will describe how to use a DFA to find occurrences of decimal numbers in a given text.

Example 1.10 The DFA of figure 1.5 recognizes the binary encodings of the multiples of 3. For instance, it recognizes 11, 110, 1001, and 1100 (which are, respectively, the binary encodings of 3, 6, 9, and 12) but not, say, 10 or 111 (which, respectively, encode 2 and 7). Observe that if the DFA accepts a word, say 110, then it also accepts the words $0110, 00110, \ldots$ which encode the same number. We let ε encode 0, and so in particular, the DFA accepts ε.

To see why the DFA recognizes this language, let us call the left, middle, and right state **0**, **1**, and **2**, respectively, as depicted in figure 1.6.
Given a word w, let n_w denote the number encoded by w. Further, let $r_w \in \{0, 1, 2\}$ be the remainder of dividing n_w by 3, and let $\mathbf{r}_w \in \{\mathbf{0}, \mathbf{1}, \mathbf{2}\}$ be the corresponding state of the DFA. For example, if $w = 1000$, then $n_w = 8$, $r_w = 2$, and $\mathbf{r}_w = \mathbf{2}$. A word w encodes a multiple of 3 iff $r_w = 0$ and is accepted by the DFA iff $\mathbf{0} \xrightarrow{w} \mathbf{0}$. So, it suffices to show that $\mathbf{0} \xrightarrow{w} \mathbf{r}_w$ holds for every word w. We claim that this is the case. Consider first the particular case $w = 1000$. We have

$$\mathbf{0} \xrightarrow{1} \mathbf{1} \xrightarrow{0} \mathbf{2} \xrightarrow{0} \mathbf{1} \xrightarrow{0} \mathbf{2},$$

and so, since $r_w = 2$, we indeed get $\mathbf{0} \xrightarrow{w} \mathbf{r}_w$.

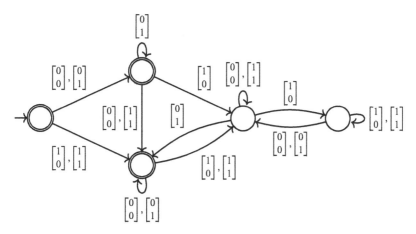

Figure 1.7
A DFA for the solutions of $2x - y \leq 2$.

To prove the claim for every word w, we proceed by induction on the length of w. For $w = \varepsilon$, we have $r_\varepsilon = 0$ and $\mathbf{0} \xrightarrow{\varepsilon} \mathbf{0}$, and we are done. Assume now that $|w| > 0$ and $w = w'0$ (the case $w = w'1$ is similar).

Assume further that $\mathbf{0} \xrightarrow{w'} \mathbf{2}$ (again, the cases $\mathbf{0} \xrightarrow{w'} \mathbf{0}$ and $\mathbf{0} \xrightarrow{w'} \mathbf{1}$ are analogous). We have $n_{w'0} = 2n_{w'}$, because adding a 0 to a binary number amounts to doubling it. Thus, $r_{w'0}$ is the remainder of dividing $2 \cdot r_{w'}$ by 3. Since $r_{w'} = 2$ by induction hypothesis, we have $r_{w'0} = 1$. Finally, since $\mathbf{0} \xrightarrow{w'} \mathbf{2} \xrightarrow{0} \mathbf{1}$, we get $\mathbf{0} \xrightarrow{w'0} \mathbf{1}$, and so $\mathbf{0} \xrightarrow{w'0} \mathbf{r}_{w'0}$.

Finding this DFA seems to require some ingenuity, but actually that is not the case. By definition, the multiples of 3 are the numbers x satisfying the formula $\exists y\, 3y = x$. In chapter 9, we present an algorithm that takes a formula like this as input and returns a DFA recognizing the encodings of the numbers that satisfy it.

Example 1.11 The inequality $2x - y \leq 2$ has infinitely many nonnegative integer solutions, like $(x, y) = (0, 0)$ or $(x, y) = (7, 20)$. Let us encode solutions as words over the alphabet $\{[0, 0], [0, 1], [1, 0], [1, 1]\}$. We explain the encoding by example. Consider the word

$$\begin{bmatrix} 1 \\ 0 \end{bmatrix} \begin{bmatrix} 0 \\ 1 \end{bmatrix} \begin{bmatrix} 1 \\ 0 \end{bmatrix} \begin{bmatrix} 1 \\ 0 \end{bmatrix} \begin{bmatrix} 0 \\ 1 \end{bmatrix} \begin{bmatrix} 0 \\ 1 \end{bmatrix}$$

where we have written the letters vertically. The top row 101100 encodes the number $1 \cdot 2^0 + 0 \cdot 2^1 + 1 \cdot 2^2 + 1 \cdot 2^3 + 0 \cdot 2^4 + 0 \cdot 2^5 = 13$, and the bottom row 010011 the number $2^1 + 2^4 + 2^5 = 50$. That is, each row represents a number in binary, starting with the least significant bit. Using an algorithm presented in Chapter 9, we can algorithmically construct the DFA of Figure 1.7 (drawn without the trap state), which recognizes the set of solutions of $2x - y \leq 2$. In other words, the DFA accepts a word if and only if its corresponding pair of numbers satisfies the inequality.

Example 1.12   Consider the following program foo with two boolean variables x and y:

```
1    while x = 1 do
2        if y = 1 then
3            x ← 0
4        y ← 1 − x
5    end
```

A configuration of the program is a triple $[\ell, n_x, n_y]$, where $\ell \in \{1, 2, 3, 4, 5\}$ is the current value of the program counter, and $n_x, n_y \in \{0, 1\}$ are the current values of x and y. The initial configurations are

$$[1, 0, 0], [1, 0, 1], [1, 1, 0], [1, 1, 1],$$

that is, all configurations in which control is at line 1. The DFA of figure 1.8 recognizes all reachable configurations of the program. For instance, the DFA accepts $[5, 0, 1]$, indicating that it is possible to reach the last line of the program with values $x = 0$ and $y = 1$. The DFA shows, for example, that after termination, the value of x is always 0.

Chapter 7 describes different algorithms that, given such a program, automatically construct a DFA for its reachable configurations. As we will see, this allows for the automatic detection of bugs.

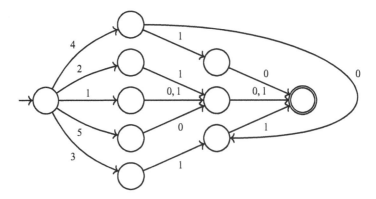

Figure 1.8
A DFA for the reachable configurations of program foo.

1.3.3 Nondeterministic Finite Automata

In a deterministic automaton, the next state is completely determined by the current state and the letter read by the head. In particular, this implies that the automaton has exactly one run for each word. Nondeterministic automata have the possibility to choose the next state out of a set of candidates (possibly empty), and so they may have zero, one, or many runs on the same word. Such an automaton is said to accept a word if *at least one* of these runs is accepting.

Definition 1.13 *A nondeterministic automaton (NA) is a tuple* $A = (Q, \Sigma, \delta, Q_0, F)$, *where*

- Q, Σ, *and* F *are as for DAs;*
- Q_0 *is a nonempty set of* initial states; *and*
- $\delta: Q \times \Sigma \to \mathcal{P}(Q)$ *is a* transition relation.

A run of A *on input* $a_0 a_1 \cdots a_n$ *is a sequence* $p_0 \xrightarrow{a_0} p_1 \xrightarrow{a_1} \cdots \xrightarrow{a_{n-1}} p_n$, *such that* $p_i \in Q$ *for every* $0 \le i \le n$, $p_0 \in Q_0$, *and* $p_{i+1} \in \delta(p_i, a_i)$ *for every* $0 \le i < n$. *A run is* accepting *if* $p_n \in F$.

A word $w \in \Sigma^*$ *is* accepted *by* A *if at least one run of* A *on* w *is accepting. The* language recognized *by* A *is the set* $\mathcal{L}(A) = \{w \in \Sigma^* : w \text{ is accepted by } A\}$.

A nondeterministic finite automaton (NFA) is an NA with a finite set of states.

We often identify the transition function δ of a DA with the set of triples (q, a, q') such that $q' = \delta(q, a)$ and the transition relation δ of an NFA with the set of triples (q, a, q') such that $q' \in \delta(q, a)$. Consequently, we often write $(q, a, q') \in \delta$, meaning $q' = \delta(q, a)$ for a DA or $q' \in \delta(q, a)$ for an NA.

If an NA has several initial states, then, by definition, its language is the union of the sets of words accepted by runs starting at each initial state.

Example 1.14 Figure 1.9 depicts an NFA $A = (Q, \Sigma, \delta, Q_0, F)$ where $Q = \{q_0, q_1, q_2, q_3\}$, $\Sigma = \{a, b\}$, $Q_0 = \{q_0\}$, $F = \{q_3\}$, and the transition relation δ is given by

$$\delta(q_0, a) = \{q_1\} \quad \delta(q_1, a) = \{q_1\} \quad \delta(q_2, a) = \emptyset \quad \delta(q_3, a) = \{q_3\},$$

$$\delta(q_0, b) = \emptyset \quad \delta(q_1, b) = \{q_1, q_2\} \quad \delta(q_2, b) = \{q_3\} \quad \delta(q_3, b) = \{q_3\}.$$

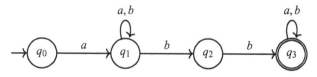

Figure 1.9
An NFA.

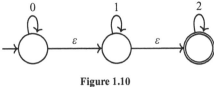

Figure 1.10
An NFA-ε.

Automaton A has no run for any word starting with letter b. It has exactly one run for aa and four runs for $abbb$, namely,

$$q_0 \xrightarrow{a} q_1 \xrightarrow{b} q_1 \xrightarrow{b} q_1 \xrightarrow{b} q_1 \qquad q_0 \xrightarrow{a} q_1 \xrightarrow{b} q_1 \xrightarrow{b} q_1 \xrightarrow{b} q_2,$$
$$q_0 \xrightarrow{a} q_1 \xrightarrow{b} q_1 \xrightarrow{b} q_2 \xrightarrow{b} q_3 \qquad q_0 \xrightarrow{a} q_1 \xrightarrow{b} q_2 \xrightarrow{b} q_3 \xrightarrow{b} q_3.$$

Two of these runs are accepting; the other two are not. Language $\mathcal{L}(A)$ is the set of words that start with a and contain two consecutive bs.

After a DA reads a word, we know whether it belongs to the language or not. This is no longer the case for NAs: if a run on the word is not accepting, then we do not know anything; there might be a different run leading to a final state. Hence, NAs are not very useful as language acceptors. However, they are very important. From an operational point of view, it is often easier to find an NFA for a given language than to find a DFA. Moreover, as we will see later in this chapter, NFAs can be *automatically* transformed into DFAs. From a data structure point of view, there are two further reasons to study NAs. First, many sets can be represented far more compactly as NFAs than as DFAs. So, using NFAs may save memory. Second, in chapter 5, we will describe how to implement operations on relations, and we will see that the implementation of the projection operation (see table 0.1 of section 0.1) may return an NFA, even if its input is a DFA. Therefore, NFAs are not only convenient but also necessary to obtain a data structure implementing all operations of table 0.1.

1.3.4   Nondeterministic Finite Automata with ε-Transitions

Recall that the state of an NA can only change by reading a letter. We consider NAs with ε-transitions that may also change their state "spontaneously" by executing an "internal" transition without reading any input. To emphasize this, we label these transitions with the empty word ε (see figure 1.10).

Definition 1.15 *A nondeterministic automaton with ε-transitions (NA-ε) is a tuple $A = (Q, \Sigma, \delta, Q_0, F)$, where*

- *Q, Σ, Q_0, and F are as for NAs, and*
- *$\delta \colon Q \times (\Sigma \cup \{\varepsilon\}) \to \mathcal{P}(Q)$ is a transition relation.*

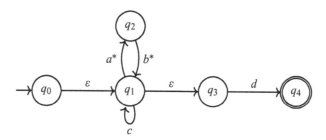

Figure 1.11
An NFA with transitions labeled by regular expressions.

The runs and accepting runs of an NA-ε are defined as for NAs. We say that A accepts a word $a_1 \cdots a_n \in \Sigma^*$ if there exist numbers $k_0, k_1, \ldots, k_n \geq 0$ such that A has an accepting run on the word

$$\varepsilon^{k_0} a_1 \varepsilon^{k_1} \cdots \varepsilon^{k_{n-1}} a_n \varepsilon^{k_n} \in (\Sigma \cup \{\varepsilon\})^*.$$

A nondeterministic finite automaton with ε-transitions *(NFA-ε) is an NA-ε with a finite set of states.*

Notice that, unlike for NAs, the number of accepting runs of an NA-ε on a word may be infinite. This is the case when some cycle of the NA-ε only contains ε-transitions, and some final state is reachable from the cycle.

NA-εs are useful as intermediate representations. In particular, later in this chapter, we will see how to automatically transform a regular expression into an NFA in two steps; first we convert the expression into an NFA-ε, and then we convert the NFA-ε into an NFA.

1.3.5   Nondeterministic Finite Automata with Regular Expressions

We generalize the notion of NA-ε even further. Both letters and the empty word ε are instances of regular expressions. Now we allow *arbitrary* regular expressions as transition labels (see figure 1.11). A run leading to a final state accepts all the words of the regular expression obtained by concatenating all the labels of the transitions of the run into a single regular expression. For example,

$$q_0 \xrightarrow{\varepsilon} q_1 \xrightarrow{a^*} q_2 \xrightarrow{b^*} q_1 \xrightarrow{a^*} q_2 \xrightarrow{b^*} q_1 \xrightarrow{\varepsilon} q_3 \xrightarrow{d} q_4$$

is a run of the automaton of figure 1.11 leading to an accepting state, and so the automaton accepts, among others, all words of the regular expression $\varepsilon a^* b^* a^* b^* \varepsilon d \equiv a^* b^* a^* b^* d$.

We call these automata *NA-reg*. They are useful to formulate conversion algorithms between automata and regular expressions, because they generalize both. Indeed, a regular expression can be seen as a NA-reg with only one transition leading from the initial state to a final state and labeled by the regular expression.

Definition 1.16 *A nondeterministic automaton with regular expression transitions (NA-reg) is a tuple* $A = (Q, \Sigma, \delta, Q_0, F)$, *where*

- *Q, Σ, Q_0, and F are as for NAs, and*
- *$\delta \colon Q \times \mathcal{RE}(\Sigma) \to \mathcal{P}(Q)$ is a relation such that $\delta(q,r) = \emptyset$ for all but a finite number of pairs $(q,r) \in Q \times \mathcal{RE}(\Sigma)$.*

Accepting runs are defined as for NAs. Automaton A accepts a word $w \in \Sigma^*$ if A has an accepting run on $r_1 \cdots r_k$ such that $w \in \mathcal{L}(r_1) \cdots \mathcal{L}(r_k)$.

A nondeterministic finite automaton with regular expression transitions (NFA-reg) *is an NA-reg with a finite set of states.*

1.3.6   A Normal Form for Automata

For any of the automata classes we have introduced, if a state is not reachable from any initial state, then removing it does not change the language accepted by the automaton. We say that an automaton is in normal form if each state is reachable from an initial one.

Definition 1.17 *Let $A = (Q, \Sigma, \delta, Q_0, F)$ be an automaton. A state $q \in Q$ is* reachable from *state $q' \in Q$ if either $q = q'$, or there exists a run $q' \xrightarrow{a_1} \cdots \xrightarrow{a_n} q$ on some word $a_1 \cdots a_n \in \Sigma^*$. Automaton A is in* normal form *if every state is reachable from some initial state.*

Obviously, for every automaton, there is an equivalent automaton of the same kind in normal form. In this book, we follow this convention:

Unless otherwise stated, we assume that automata are in normal form. In particular, we assume that if an automaton A is an input to an algorithm, then A is in normal form. If the output of an algorithm is an automaton, then the algorithm is expected to produce an automaton in normal form. This condition is a proof obligation when showing that the algorithm is correct.

1.4   Conversion Algorithms

We show that all our data structures represent exactly the same class of languages—namely, the regular languages. The solid edges of figure 1.12 show the relations between the formalisms that follow immediately from the definitions: DFAs are a special case of NFAs, which are a special case of NFA-εs, which are a special case of NFA-regs; further, regular expressions can also be seen as a special case of NFA-regs. Indeed, a regular expression r "is" the NFA-reg A_r having two states, one initial and the other final, and a single transition labeled r leading from the initial to the final state.

In the next sections, we present four conversion algorithms corresponding to the dashed arrows of figure 1.12. A dashed arrow from a source to a target node indicates that for every instance of the source, there is an equivalent instance of the target. The algorithms allow us to convert any representation of a language into any other.

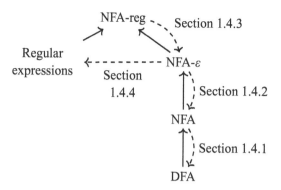

Figure 1.12
Our data structures for languages.

1.4.1   From NFA to DFA

The *powerset construction* transforms an NFA A into a DFA B recognizing the same language. We first give an informal idea of the construction. Recall that an NFA may have many different runs on a word w, possibly leading to different states, while a DFA has exactly one run on w. Denote by Q_w the set of states q such that some run of A on w leads from some initial state to q. Intuitively, B "keeps track" of the set Q_w: its states are *sets of states* of A, with Q_0 as initial state (A starts at some initial state), and its transition function is defined to ensure that the run of B on w leads from Q_0 to Q_w (see below). It is then easy to ensure that A and B recognize the same language: it suffices to choose the final states of B as the sets of states of A containing *at least one* final state, because for every word w:

$\qquad$ B accepts w
iff $\quad Q_w$ is a final state of B
iff $\quad Q_w$ contains at least a final state of A
iff $\quad$ some run of A on w leads to a final state of A
iff $\quad A$ accepts w.

Let us now define the transition function Δ of B. "Keeping track of the set Q_w" amounts to satisfying $\Delta(Q_w, a) = Q_{wa}$ for every word w. Since we have $Q_{wa} = \bigcup_{q \in Q_w} \delta(q, a)$, we define

$$\Delta(Q', a) = \bigcup_{q \in Q'} \delta(q, a) \qquad\qquad \text{for every } Q' \subseteq Q.$$

Note that we may have $Q' = \emptyset$; in this case, $\emptyset$ is a state of B, and since $\Delta(\emptyset, a) = \emptyset$ for every $a \in \Delta$, it is a "trap" state.

Summarizing, given $A = (Q, \Sigma, \delta, Q_0, F)$, we define the DFA $B = (\mathcal{Q}, \Sigma, \Delta, q_0, \mathcal{F})$ as follows:

- $\mathcal{Q} = \mathcal{P}(Q)$,
- $\Delta(Q', a) = \bigcup_{q \in Q'} \delta(q, a)$ for every $Q' \subseteq Q$ and every $a \in \Sigma$,
- $q_0 = Q_0$, and
- $\mathcal{F} = \{Q' \in \mathcal{Q} : Q' \cap F \neq \emptyset\}$.

Observe, however, that B may not be in normal form: many states may not be reachable from Q_0. For instance, assume A happens to be a DFA with states $\{q_0, \ldots, q_{n-1}\}$. Then B has 2^n states, but only the singletons $\{q_0\}, \ldots, \{q_{n-1}\}$ are reachable. The conversion procedure of algorithm 1 constructs only the reachable states.

The algorithm is written in pseudocode, with abstract sets as data structure. Like nearly all the algorithms presented in the next chapters, it is a *workset algorithm*. These maintain a set of objects, the *workset*, waiting to be processed. The elements of the workset are unordered, and the workset contains at most one copy of an element (i.e., if an element already in the workset is added to it again, the workset does not change). For most algorithms in this book, the workset can be implemented as a hash table.

In *NFAtoDFA*, the workset is called $\mathcal{W}$, in other algorithms just W (we use a calligraphic font to emphasize that in this case, the objects of the workset are sets). Workset algorithms repeatedly pick an object from the workset (instruction **pick Q from $\mathcal{W}$**) and process it. Picking an object removes it from the workset. Processing an object may generate new objects that are added to the workset. The algorithm terminates when the workset is empty. Since objects removed from the list may generate new objects, workset algorithms may potentially fail to terminate. Even if the set of all objects is finite, the algorithm may not

---

Algorithm 1 Conversion from NFA to DFA.

NFAtoDFA(A)
Input: NFA $A = (Q, \Sigma, \delta, Q_0, F)$
Output: DFA $B = (\mathcal{Q}, \Sigma, \Delta, q_0, \mathcal{F})$ with $\mathcal{L}(B) = \mathcal{L}(A)$

```
1    Q, Δ, F ← ∅; q₀ ← Q₀
2    W = {Q₀}
3    while W ≠ ∅ do
4        pick Q' from W
5        add Q' to Q
6        if Q' ∩ F ≠ ∅ then add Q' to F
7        for all a ∈ Σ do
8            Q'' ← ⋃_{q∈Q'} δ(q, a)
9            if Q'' ∉ Q then add Q'' to W
10           add (Q', a, Q'') to Δ
```

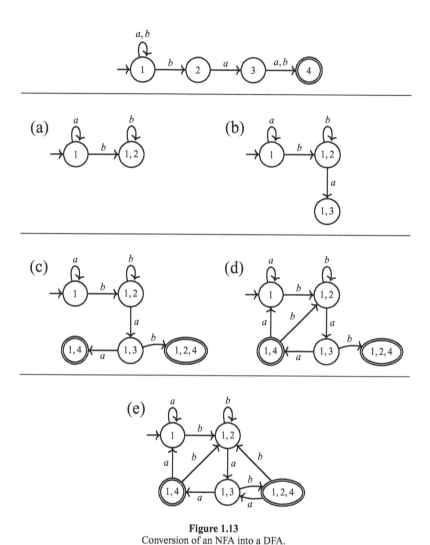

Figure 1.13
Conversion of an NFA into a DFA.

terminate because an object is added to and removed from the workset infinitely many times. Termination is guaranteed by making sure that no object that has been removed from the workset once is ever added to it again. For this, objects picked from the workset are stored (in *NFAtoDFA*, they are stored in $\mathcal{Q}$), and objects are added to the workset only if they have not been stored yet.

Example 1.18 Consider the NFA A at the top of figure 1.13. The rest of the figure depicts some snapshots of the run of *NFAtoDFA* on A. The states of the resulting DFA are labeled with the corresponding sets of states of A. The algorithm picks states from the workset in order $\{1\}, \{1,2\}, \{1,3\}, \{1,4\}, \{1,2,4\}$. Snapshots (a)–(d) are taken right after it picks the states $\{1,2\}, \{1,3\}, \{1,4\}$, and $\{1,2,4\}$, respectively. Snapshot (e) is taken at the end. Notice that out of the $2^4 = 16$ subsets of states of A, only five are constructed, because the remaining ones are not reachable from $\{1\}$.

Complexity.   If A has n states, then the output of *NFAtoDFA(A)* can have up to 2^n states. To show that this bound is essentially reachable, consider the family $\{L_n\}_{n \geq 1}$ of languages over $\Sigma = \{a, b\}$ given by $L_n = (a+b)^* a(a+b)^{(n-1)}$. That is, L_n contains the words of length at least n whose nth letter *starting from the end* is an a. The language L_n is accepted by the NFA with $n+1$ states shown in figure 1.14a: intuitively, the automaton chooses one of the as in the input word and checks that it is followed by exactly $n-1$ letters before the word ends. Applying the powerset construction, however, yields a DFA with 2^n states. The DFA for L_3

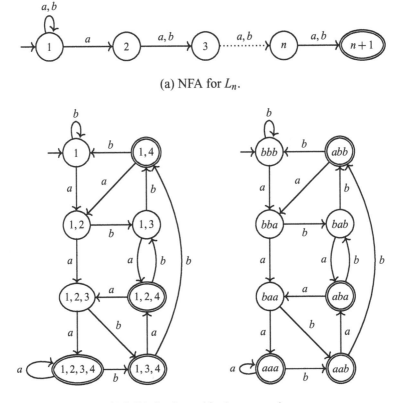

(a) NFA for L_n.

(b) DFA for L_3 and its interpretation.

Figure 1.14
Top: An NFA for L_n. *Bottom*: A DFA for L_3.

is shown on the left of figure 1.14b. The states of the DFA have a natural interpretation: they "store" the last n letters read by the automaton. If the DFA is in the state storing $a_1 a_2 \cdots a_n$ and reads letter a_{n+1}, then it moves to the state storing $a_2 \cdots a_{n+1}$. States are final if the first letter they store is an a. The interpreted version is shown on the right of figure 1.14b.

We can also easily prove that *any* DFA recognizing L_n must have at least 2^n states. For the sake of contradiction, suppose there is a DFA $A_n = (Q, \Sigma, \delta, q_0, F)$ such that $|Q| < 2^n$ and $\mathcal{L}(A_n) = L_n$. Let us extend δ to words—that is, to the mapping $\hat{\delta}: Q \times \{a, b\}^* \to Q$, where $\hat{\delta}(q, \varepsilon) = q$ and $\hat{\delta}(q, w\sigma) = \delta(\hat{\delta}(q, w), \sigma)$ for all $w \in \Sigma^*$ and $\sigma \in \Sigma$. Since $|Q| < 2^n$, there must exist two words uav_1 and ubv_2 of length n for which $\hat{\delta}(q_0, uav_1) = \hat{\delta}(q_0, ubv_2)$. This means that $\hat{\delta}(q_0, uav_1u) = \hat{\delta}(q_0, ubv_2u)$; that is, either both uav_1u and ubv_2u are accepted by A_n, or neither is. Since, however, $|av_1u| = |bv_2u| = n$, this contradicts the assumption that A_n consists of exactly the words with an a at the nth position from the end.

1.4.2 From NFA-ε to NFA

Let A be an NFA-ε over an alphabet Σ. In this section, we use a to denote an element of Σ and α, β to denote elements of $\Sigma \cup \{\varepsilon\}$.

Loosely speaking, the conversion first adds to A new transitions that make all ε-transitions redundant, without changing the language: every word accepted by A before adding the new transitions is accepted after adding them by a run without ε-transitions. The conversion then removes all ε-transitions, delivering an NFA that recognizes the same language as A.

The new transitions are *shortcuts*: if A has transitions (q, α, q') and (q', β, q'') such that $\alpha = \varepsilon$ or $\beta = \varepsilon$, then the shortcut $(q, \alpha\beta, q'')$ is added. (Note that either $\alpha\beta = a$ for some $a \in \Sigma$, or $\alpha\beta = \varepsilon$.) Shortcuts may generate further shortcuts: for example, if $\alpha\beta = a$ and A has a further transition (q'', ε, q'''), then a new shortcut (q, a, q''') is added. We call the process of adding all possible shortcuts *saturation*. Obviously, saturation does not change the language of A. If A has a run accepting a *nonempty* word before saturation, for example,

$$q_0 \xrightarrow{\varepsilon} q_1 \xrightarrow{\varepsilon} q_2 \xrightarrow{a} q_3 \xrightarrow{\varepsilon} q_4 \xrightarrow{b} q_5 \xrightarrow{\varepsilon} q_6,$$

then after saturation, it has a run accepting the same word, and visiting no ε-transitions, namely,

$$q_0 \xrightarrow{a} q_4 \xrightarrow{b} q_6.$$

However, removing ε-transitions immediately after saturation may not preserve the language. The NFA-ε of figure 1.15a accepts ε. After saturation, we get the NFA-ε of figure 1.15b. Removing all ε-transitions yields an NFA that no longer accepts ε. To solve this problem, if A accepts ε from some initial state, then we mark that state as final, which clearly does not change the language. To decide whether A accepts ε, we check if some state reachable from some initial state by a sequence of ε-transitions is final. Figure 1.15c shows the result. Observe that, in general, after removing ε-transitions, the automaton may not be

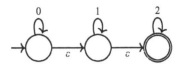

(a) NFA-ε accepting $\mathcal{L}(0^*1^*2^*)$.

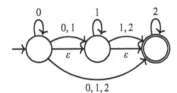   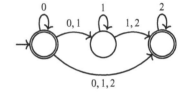

(b) After saturation.   (c) After marking the initial state final and removing all ε-transitions.

Figure 1.15
Conversion of an NFA-ε into an NFA by shortcutting ε-transitions.

in normal form, because some states may no longer be reachable. So the naive procedure runs in four phases: saturation, ε-check, removal of all ε-transitions, and normalization.

We show that it is possible to carry all four steps in a single pass. We present a work-set algorithm *NFAεtoNFA*, in algorithm 2, that carries the ε-check while saturating and generates only the reachable states. Furthermore, the algorithm avoids constructing some redundant shortcuts. For instance, for the NFA-ε of figure 1.15a, the algorithm does not construct the transition leading from the state in the middle to the state on the right labeled by 2.

The correctness proof is easy, but the different cases require some care, and so we devote a proposition to it.

Proposition 1.19 *Let A be an NFA-ε, and let B = NFAεtoNFA(A). It is the case that B is an NFA and $\mathcal{L}(A) = \mathcal{L}(B)$.*

Proof To show that the algorithm terminates, observe first that every transition that leaves W is never added to W again. Indeed, when a transition (q_1, α, q_2) leaves W, it is added to either δ' or δ'', and a transition enters W only if it does not belong to either δ' or δ''. Further, every execution of the while loop removes a transition from the workset. Thus, the algorithm eventually exits the loop and terminates.

To show that B is an NFA, we have to prove that it only has non-ε-transitions and that it is in normal form (i.e., that every state of Q' is reachable from some state of $Q_0' = Q_0$ in B). For the first part, observe that transitions are only added to δ' in line 7, and none of them

---

Algorithm 2   Conversion from NFA-ε to NFA.

$NFA\varepsilon toNFA(A)$
Input: NFA-ε $A = (Q, \Sigma, \delta, Q_0, F)$
Output: NFA $B = (Q', \Sigma, \delta', Q_0', F')$ with $\mathcal{L}(B) = \mathcal{L}(A)$

```
 1   Q'_0 ← Q_0
 2   Q' ← Q_0; δ' ← ∅; F' ← F ∩ Q_0
 3   δ'' ← ∅; W ← {(q, α, q') ∈ δ : q ∈ Q_0}
 4   while W ≠ ∅ do
 5       pick (q_1, α, q_2) from W
 6       if α ≠ ε then
 7           add q_2 to Q'; add (q_1, α, q_2) to δ'; if q_2 ∈ F then add q_2 to F'
 8           for all q_3 ∈ δ(q_2, ε) do
 9               if (q_1, α, q_3) ∉ δ' then add (q_1, α, q_3) to W
10           for all a ∈ Σ, q_3 ∈ δ(q_2, a) do
11               if (q_2, a, q_3) ∉ δ' then add (q_2, a, q_3) to W
12       else  /* α = ε */
13           add (q_1, α, q_2) to δ''; if q_2 ∈ F then add q_1 to F'
14           for all β ∈ Σ ∪ {ε}, q_3 ∈ δ(q_2, β) do
15               if (q_1, β, q_3) ∉ δ' ∪ δ'' then add (q_1, β, q_3) to W
```

---

is an ε-transition because of the guard in line 6. For the second part, we need the following invariant, which can be easily proved by inspection: for every transition (q_1, α, q_2) added to W, if $\alpha = \varepsilon$, then $q_1 \in Q_0$, and if $\alpha \neq \varepsilon$, then q_2 is reachable in B (after termination). Since new states are added to Q' only at line 7, applying the invariant, we get that every state of Q' is reachable in B from some state in Q_0.

It remains to prove $\mathcal{L}(A) = \mathcal{L}(B)$. For the inclusion $\mathcal{L}(A) \supseteq \mathcal{L}(B)$, we have to show that after the addition of a new transition to δ' or a new final state to F', the recognized language is the same as before. For transitions, this follows from the fact that every transition added to δ' is either a transition of A or a shortcut, which is shown by inspection. For final states, observe that the algorithm only adds new final states at line 13. Further, at that line q_1 only becomes final if there is a transition $q_1 \xrightarrow{\varepsilon} q_2$ for some final state q_2. So every word accepted by a run ending at q_1 was already accepted before making q_1 final. For the inclusion $\mathcal{L}(A) \subseteq \mathcal{L}(B)$, we first claim that $\varepsilon \in \mathcal{L}(A)$ implies $\varepsilon \in \mathcal{L}(B)$. Let $q_0 \xrightarrow{\varepsilon} q_1 \xrightarrow{\varepsilon} \cdots \xrightarrow{\varepsilon} q_n$ be a run of A such that $q_n \in F$. If $n = 0$ (i.e., $q_n = q_0$), then we are done. If $n > 0$, then we prove by induction on n that a transition (q_0, ε, q_n) is eventually added to W (and so eventually picked from it), which implies that q_0 is eventually added to F' at line 13. If $n = 1$, then (q_0, ε, q_n) is added to W at line 3. If $n > 1$, then by hypothesis, $(q_0, \varepsilon, q_{n-1})$ is eventually added to W and picked from it at some later point. So (q_0, ε, q_n) is added to W at line 15, and the claim is proved. We now show that for every $w \in \Sigma^+$, if $w \in \mathcal{L}(A)$, then $w \in \mathcal{L}(B)$. Let $w = a_1 a_2 \cdots a_n$ with $n \geq 1$. Automaton A has a run

$$q_0 \xrightarrow{\varepsilon} \cdots \xrightarrow{\varepsilon} q_{m_1} \xrightarrow{a_1} q_{m_1+1} \xrightarrow{\varepsilon} \cdots \xrightarrow{\varepsilon} q_{m_n} \xrightarrow{a_n} q_{m_n+1} \xrightarrow{\varepsilon} \cdots \xrightarrow{\varepsilon} q_m$$

such that $q_m \in F$. We have just proved that a transition $(q_0, \varepsilon, q_{m_1})$ is eventually added to W. So, (q_0, a_1, q_{m_1+1}) is eventually added at line 15, $(q_0, a_1, q_{m_1+2}), \ldots, (q_0, a_1, q_{m_2})$ are eventually added at line 9, and $(q_{m_2}, a_2, q_{m_2+1})$ is eventually added at line 11. Iterating this argument, the following is a run of B:

$$q_0 \xrightarrow{a_1} q_{m_2} \xrightarrow{a_2} \cdots \xrightarrow{a_{n-1}} q_{m_n} \xrightarrow{a_n} q_m.$$

Moreover, state q_m is added to F' at line 7, and so $w \in \mathcal{L}(B)$. $\qquad\square$

Complexity. The algorithm processes pairs of transitions (q_1, α, q_2) and (q_2, β, q_3), where (q_1, α, q_2) comes from W and (q_2, β, q_3) from δ (lines 8, 10, and 14). As every transition is removed from W at most once, the algorithm processes at most $|Q| \cdot |\Sigma| \cdot |\delta|$ pairs. Indeed, for a fixed transition $(q_2, \beta, q_3) \in \delta$, there are $|Q|$ possibilities for q_1 and $|\Sigma|$ possibilities for α. Thus, the runtime is dominated by the processing of the pairs, and so it belongs to $\mathcal{O}(|Q| \cdot |\Sigma| \cdot |\delta|)$.

1.4.3 From NFA-reg to NFA-ε

We present an algorithm that, given an NFA-reg, constructs an equivalent NFA-ε. In a first step, we preprocess the regular expressions labeling the transitions of the NFA-reg by exhaustively applying the following rewrite rules:

$$r \cdot \emptyset \rightsquigarrow \emptyset \qquad\qquad r + \emptyset \rightsquigarrow r \qquad\qquad \emptyset^* \rightsquigarrow \varepsilon$$

$$\emptyset \cdot r \rightsquigarrow \emptyset \qquad\qquad \emptyset + r \rightsquigarrow r$$

Since the left- and right-hand sides of each rule denote the same language, the regular expressions before and after preprocessing denote the same language. Moreover, if r is a regular expression obtained after preprocessing, then either $r = \emptyset$, or r does not contain any occurrence of the $\emptyset$ symbol, since otherwise, one of the above rules can be applied. A transition of an NFA-reg labeled by $\emptyset$ can be removed without changing its language. Indeed, any regular expression accepted by means of a run containing such a transition is of the form $r_1 \emptyset r_2$, whose language is empty. After removing such transitions, we are left with an NFA-reg whose labels contain no occurrence of the $\emptyset$ symbol. This concludes the first step.

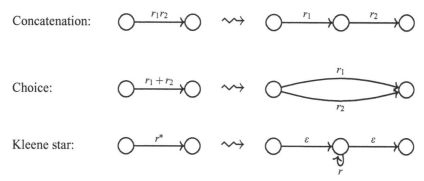

Figure 1.16
Three rules for converting an NFA-reg into an NFA-ε.

In the second step, we exhaustively apply the transformation rules of figure 1.16.

It is readily seen that each rule preserves the recognized language (i.e., the NFA-regs before and after the application of the rule recognize the same language). The two ε-transitions of the rule for Kleene iteration guarantee that the automata before and after applying the rule are equivalent, even if the source and target states of the transition labeled by r^* have other incoming or outgoing transitions. If the source state has no other outgoing transitions, then we can omit the first ε-transition. If the target state has no other incoming transitions, then we can omit the second.

Since each rule splits a regular expression into its constituents, we eventually reach an NFA-reg to which no rule can be applied. Since, due to the preprocessing, the initial regular expressions do not contain any occurrence of $\emptyset$, the transitions of this NFA-reg can only be labeled with letters from Σ, or with ε, and so the NFA-reg is an NFA-ε.

Observe that if we start with an NFA-reg consisting of an initial state q_0, a final state q_f, different from q_0, and one transition $q_0 \xrightarrow{r} q_f$, then the final NFA-ε also has q_0 and q_f as unique initial and final states. Moreover, no transition leads to q_0, and no transition leaves q_f.

Example 1.20   Consider the regular expression $(a^*b^* + c)^*d$. Figure 1.17 depicts the result of applying the transformation rules.

Complexity.   Given a regular expression r, define $\ell(r)$ inductively as follows: $\ell(\emptyset) = \ell(\varepsilon) = \ell(a) = 0$, $\ell(r_1 \cdot r_2) = \ell(r_1 + r_2) = \ell(r_1) + \ell(r_2) + 1$, and $\ell(r^*) = \ell(r) + 1$. Further, given an NFA-reg $A = (Q, \Sigma, \delta, Q_0, F)$, define $\ell(A) = \sum_{(q,r,q') \in \delta} \ell(r)$. The application of a rule transforms A into an automaton A' such that $\ell(A') = \ell(A) - 1$; moreover, if $\ell(A') = 0$, then A' is an NFA-ε. So we obtain an NFA-ε after $\ell(A)$ applications, with at most $|Q| + \ell(A)$ states. Further, the conversion runs in linear time.

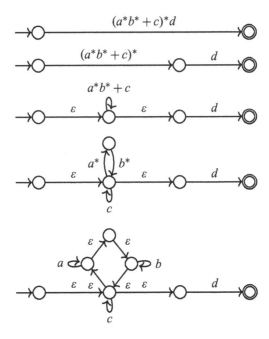

Figure 1.17
The result of converting $(a^*b^* + c)^*d$ into an NFA-ε.

1.4.4 From NFA-ε to Regular Expressions

Given an NFA-ε A, we transform it into an equivalent regular expression. For this, we convert A into an equivalent NFA-reg A_r with two states and a single transition labeled by a regular expression r.

As in the previous section, it is convenient to apply some preprocessing to guarantee that the NFA-ε has a single initial state with no incoming transitions and a single final state with no outgoing transitions. We proceed as follows (see figure 1.18):

• If A has several initial states, or if an initial state has an incoming transition, then add a new initial state q_0, add ε-transitions leading from q_0 to each initial state, and replace the set of initial states by $\{q_0\}$.

• If A has several final states, or if a final state has an outgoing transition, then add a new state q_f, add ε-transitions leading from each final state to q_f, and replace the set of final states by $\{q_f\}$.

After preprocessing, the algorithm runs in phases. Each phase has two steps. The first step yields an automaton with at most one transition between any two given states:

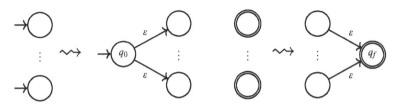

Figure 1.18
Rule 1: Preprocessing.

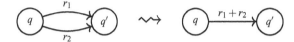

Figure 1.19
Rule 2: at most one transition between two states.

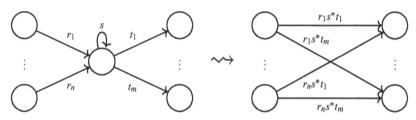

Figure 1.20
Rule 3: removing a state.

- Repeat exhaustively: replace a pair of transitions (q, r_1, q') and (q, r_2, q') by a single transition $(q, r_1 + r_2, q')$. (See figure 1.19.)

The second step, depicted in figure 1.20, reduces the number of states by 1, until the only states left are the initial and final ones:

- Pick a nonfinal and noninitial state q, and *shortcut* it: if q has a self-loop (q, s, q), then replace each pair of transitions (q', r, q), (q, t, q''), where $q' \neq q \neq q''$, but possibly $q' = q''$, by a shortcut (q', rs^*t, q''). Otherwise, replace it by (q', rt, q''). After shortcutting all pairs, remove q. (Notice that there is at most one self-loop on q, as otherwise we would have two or more transitions leading from q to q, contradicting that rule 2 was applied exhaustively.)

At the end of the last phase, we are left with an NFA-reg having exactly two states, the unique initial state q_0 and the unique final state q_f. Moreover, q_0 has no incoming transitions and q_f has no outgoing transitions, because it was initially so, and the application of the rules cannot change it. After applying rule 2 exhaustively one last time, the NFA-reg has

---

Algorithm 3 Conversion from NFA-ε to regular expression.

NFA-εtoRE(A)
Input: NFA-ε $A = (Q, \Sigma, \delta, Q_0, F)$
Output: regular expression r with $\mathcal{L}(r) = \mathcal{L}(A)$

1   **apply** *Rule 1*
2   let q_0 and q_f be the initial and final states of A
3   **while** $Q \setminus \{q_0, q_f\} \neq \emptyset$ **do**
4   **apply** exhaustively *Rule 2*
5   **pick** q **from** $Q \setminus \{q_0, q_f\}$
6   **apply** *Rule 3* to q
7   **apply** exhaustively *Rule 2*
8   **return** the label of the (unique) transition

---

exactly one transition from q_0 to q_f, and we are done. The complete procedure is described in algorithm 3.

Example 1.21 An example of the execution of *NFA-εtoRE* will be given shortly at the beginning of the forthcoming "Tour of Conversions" in the next section.

Complexity. The running time of the algorithm depends on the data structure used to store regular expressions. If they are stored as strings or trees (following the syntax tree of the expression), then the complexity can be exponential. To see this, consider, for $n \geq 1$, the NFA $A_n = (Q, \Sigma, \delta, Q_0, F)$, where

$$Q = \{q_0, \ldots, q_{n-1}\},$$

$$\Sigma = \{a_{ij} : 0 \leq i, j < n\},$$

$$Q_0 = Q,$$

$$\delta = \{(q_i, a_{ij}, q_j) : 0 \leq i, j < n\},$$

$$F = Q.$$

That is, all states are initial and final, there is one transition between each pair of states, and each transition is labeled by a different letter. By symmetry, the running time of the algorithm is independent of the order in which states are eliminated. Consider the order $q_0, q_2, \ldots, q_{n-1}$. It is easy to see that after eliminating state q_i, the NFA-reg contains some transitions labeled by regular expressions with 3^i occurrences of letters. This exponential blowup cannot be avoided: it can be shown that every regular expression recognizing the same language as A_n contains at least 2^{n-1} occurrences of letters.

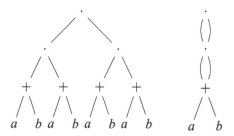

Figure 1.21
Compact representation of regular expressions.

Regular expressions can also be stored as acyclic directed graphs by sharing common subexpressions in the syntax tree. For example, the regular expression $((a+b)(a+b))$ $((a+b)(a+b))$ can be represented by the syntax tree with fifteen nodes on the left of figure 1.21 or, more compactly, by the acyclic directed graph with five nodes on the right. If the algorithm is implemented using acyclic directed graphs, then it works in polynomial time, because the label of a new transition is obtained by concatenating or starring already computed labels.

1.5   A Tour of Conversions

We present an example chaining the conversions of this chapter.

(1) We begin with a DFA A that recognizes the language of words over $\{a, b\}$ with an even number of as and an even number of bs. We convert it into a regular expression via *NFA-εtoRE*. In the following drawing, parts (b) to (f) depict snapshots of the run of *NFA-εtoRE(A)*. Snapshot (b) is taken right after applying rule 1. Snapshots (c) to (e) are taken after each execution of the body of the **while** loop. Snapshot (f) shows the final expression r.

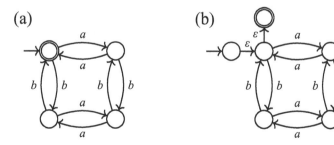

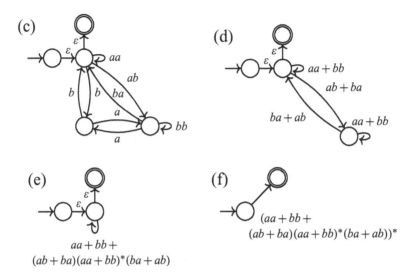

(2) We convert r into an NFA-ε by repeatedly applying the three rules of figure 1.16. The following drawing gives four snapshots (a)–(d) of these applications.

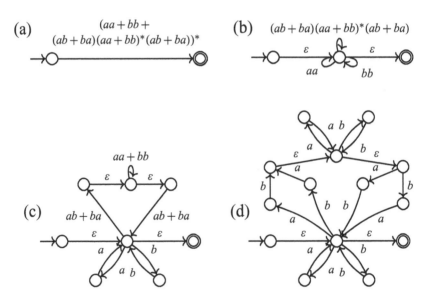

(3) We convert the resulting NFA-ε into an NFA via *NFA-εtoNFA*.

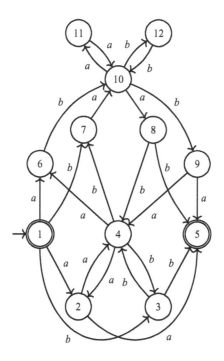

(4) Finally, we transform the resulting NFA back into a DFA by means of the powerset construction.

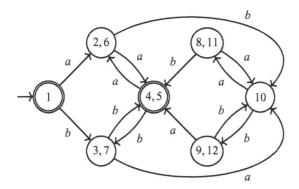

Note that we do not end up with the initial four-state DFA but rather with a "more complicated one" recognizing the same language. A last step, allowing us to close the circle, is presented in the next chapter.

1.6 Exercises

☆ 🔲 **Exercise 1.** Give a regular expression for the language of all words over $\Sigma = \{a, b\}$

(a) beginning and ending with the same letter.
(b) having two occurrences of a at distance 3.
(c) with no occurrence of the subword aa.

☆ 🔲 **Exercise 2.** Give a regular expression for the language of all words over $\Sigma = \{a, b\}$

(a) containing exactly two occurrences of aa (that may "overlap," e.g., aaa belongs to the language).
(b) that can be obtained from $abaab$ by deleting letters.

★ ■ **Exercise 3.** Show that the language of the regular expression $r = (a + \varepsilon)(b^* + ba)^*$ is the language A of all words over $\{a, b\}$ that do not contain any occurrence of aa.

★ ■ **Exercise 4.** Prove or disprove the following claim: the regular expressions $(1 + 10)^*$ and $1^*(101^*)^*$ represent the same language (namely, the language of words where each occurrence of 0 is preceded by a 1).

☆ ■ **Exercise 5.**

(a) Prove that for all languages A and B, the following holds: $A \subseteq B \implies A^* \subseteq B^*$.
(b) Prove that the regular expressions $((a + ab)^* + b^*)^*$ and Σ^* represent the same language, where $\Sigma = \{a, b\}$ and where Σ^* stands for $(a + b)^*$.

☆ ■ **Exercise 6.** Prove that every regular expression r is equivalent to a regular expression s of the form $s = s_1 + \ldots + s_n$ for some $n \geq 1$, where $s_1, \ldots, s_n$ do not contain any occurrence of "+."

★ 🔲 **Exercise 7.** For each of the following properties, provide a syntax that describes the regular expressions r satisfying the property.

(a) $\mathcal{L}(r) = \emptyset$,
(b) $\mathcal{L}(r) = \{\varepsilon\}$,
(c) $\varepsilon \in \mathcal{L}(r)$,
(d) $(\mathcal{L}(r) = \mathcal{L}(rr)) \implies (\mathcal{L}(r) = \mathcal{L}(r^*))$.

☆ 🔲 **Exercise 8.** Use the solution to exercise 7 to define inductively the predicates *IsEmpty*(r), *IsEpsilon*(r), and *HasEpsilon*(r) over regular expressions given by

- *IsEmpty*(r) $\Leftrightarrow$ ($\mathcal{L}(r) = \emptyset$),
- *IsEpsilon*(r) $\Leftrightarrow$ ($\mathcal{L}(r) = \{\varepsilon\}$),
- *HasEpsilon*(r) $\Leftrightarrow$ ($\varepsilon \in \mathcal{L}(r)$).

⭐■ **Exercise 9.** Let us extend the syntax and semantics of regular expressions as follows. If r and s are regular expressions over Σ, then $\bar{r}$ and $r \cap s$ are also valid expressions, where $\mathcal{L}(\bar{r}) = \overline{\mathcal{L}(r)}$ and $\mathcal{L}(r \cap s) = \mathcal{L}(r) \cap \mathcal{L}(s)$. We say that an extended regular expression is *star-free* if it does not contain any occurrence of the Kleene star operation (e.g., expressions $\overline{ab}$ and $(\bar{\emptyset}ab\bar{\emptyset}) \cap (\bar{\emptyset}ba\bar{\emptyset})$ are star-free, but expression ab^* is not).

A language $L \subseteq \Sigma^*$ is called *star-free* if there exists a star-free extended regular expression r such that $L = \mathcal{L}(r)$; for example, Σ^* is star-free, because $\Sigma^* = \mathcal{L}\left(\bar{\emptyset}\right)$.

Show that the languages of the regular expressions (a) $(01)^*$ and (b) $(01 + 10)^*$ are star-free.

☆▣ **Exercise 10.** Let $L \subseteq \{a, b\}^*$ be the language described by the regular expression $a^*b^*a^*a$.

(a) Give an NFA-ε that accepts L.

(b) Give an NFA that accepts L.

(c) Give a DFA that accepts L.

⭐■ **Exercise 11.** Let $|w|_\sigma$ denote the number of occurrences of letter σ in word w. For every $k \geq 2$, let $L_{k,\sigma} = \{w \in \{a, b\}^* : |w|_\sigma \bmod k = 0\}$.

(a) Give a DFA with k states that accepts $L_{k,\sigma}$.

(b) Show that any NFA accepting $L_{m,a} \cap L_{n,b}$ has at least $m \cdot n$ states.

Hint: Consider using the pigeonhole principle.

☆✏ **Exercise 12.** For every language L, let L_{pref} and L_{suff} be respectively the languages of all prefixes and suffixes of words in L. For example, if $L = \{abc, d\}$, then $L_{\text{pref}} = \{abc, ab, a, \varepsilon, d\}$ and $L_{\text{suff}} = \{abc, bc, c, \varepsilon, d\}$.

(a) Given an NFA A, construct NFAs A_{pref} and A_{suff} that recognize $\mathcal{L}(A)_{\text{pref}}$ and $\mathcal{L}(A)_{\text{suff}}$.

(b) Let $r = (ab + b)^*cd$. Give a regular expression r_{pref} such that $\mathcal{L}(r_{\text{pref}}) = \mathcal{L}(r)_{\text{pref}}$.

(c) More generally, give an algorithm that takes an arbitrary regular expression r as input and returns a regular expression r_{pref} such that $\mathcal{L}(r_{\text{pref}}) = \mathcal{L}(r)_{\text{pref}}$.

☆⚙ **Exercise 13.** Consider the regular expression $r = (a + ab)^*$.

(a) Convert r into an equivalent NFA-ε A.

(b) Convert A into an equivalent NFA B.

(c) Convert B into an equivalent DFA C.

(d) By inspection of C, give an equivalent minimal DFA D.

(e) Convert D into an equivalent regular expression r'.

(f) Prove formally that $\mathcal{L}(r) = \mathcal{L}(r')$.

Exercise 14. The *reverse* of a word w, denoted by w^R, is defined as follows: $\varepsilon^R = \varepsilon$ and $(a_1 a_2 \cdots a_n)^R = a_n \cdots a_2 a_1$. The *reverse* of a language L is the language $L^R = \{w^R : w \in L\}$.

(a) Give a regular expression for the reverse of the language of $((a + ba)^* ba(a + b))^* ba$.

(b) Give an algorithm that takes as input a regular expression r and returns a regular expression r^R such that $\mathcal{L}\left(r^R\right) = \mathcal{L}(r)^R$.

(c) Give an algorithm that takes an NFA A and returns an NFA A^R such that $\mathcal{L}\left(A^R\right) = \mathcal{L}(A)^R$.

(d) Does your construction in (c) work for DFAs? More precisely, does it preserve determinism?

Exercise 15. Prove or disprove: every regular language is recognized by an NFA

(a) having one single initial state,

(b) having one single final state,

(c) whose initial states have no incoming transitions,

(d) whose final states have no outgoing transitions,

(e) all of the above,

(f) whose states are all initial,

(g) whose states are all final.

Which of the above hold for DFAs? Which ones for NFA-ε?

Exercise 16. Given a regular expression r, construct an NFA A that satisfies $\mathcal{L}(A) = \mathcal{L}(r)$ and the following properties:

- initial states have no incoming transitions,
- accepting states have no outgoing transitions,
- all input transitions of a state (if any) carry the same label,
- all output transitions of a state (if any) carry the same label.

Apply your construction on $r = (a(b + c))^*$.

Exercise 17. Convert this NFA-ε to an NFA using the algorithm *NFAεtoNFA*:

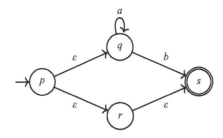

☆■ **Exercise 18.** Show that every finite language L (i.e., every language containing finitely many words) is regular. Do so by defining a DFA that recognizes L.

★▨ **Exercise 19.** Let $\Sigma_n = \{1, 2, \ldots, n\}$, and let L_n be the set of all words $w \in \Sigma_n$ such that at least one letter of Σ_n does not appear in w. So, for instance, $1221, 32, 1111 \in L_3$ and $123, 2231 \notin L_3$.

(a) Give an NFA for L_n with $\mathcal{O}(n)$ states and transitions.

(b) Give a DFA for L_n with 2^n states.

(c) Show that any DFA for L_n has at least 2^n states.

(d) Do the bounds of (a), (b), and (c) also hold for $\overline{L_n}$?

☆▨ **Exercise 20.** Let M_n be the language of the following regular expression:

$$(0 + 1)^* 0 (0 + 1)^{n-1} 0 (0 + 1)^*.$$

These are the words containing at least one pair of 0s at distance n. For example, $101101, 001001, 000000 \in M_3$ and $101010, 000111, 011110 \notin M_3$.

(a) Give an NFA for M_n with $\mathcal{O}(n)$ states and transitions.

(b) Give a DFA for M_n with $\Omega(2^n)$ states.

(c) Show that any DFA for M_n has at least 2^n states.

★☛ **Exercise 21.** Recall that an NFA A accepts a word w if at least one of the runs of A on w is accepting. This is sometimes called the *existential* accepting condition. Consider the variant where A accepts word w if *all* runs of A on w are accepting (in particular, if A has no run on w, then it trivially accepts w). This is called the *universal* accepting condition. Note that a DFA accepts the same language with both the existential and the universal accepting conditions.

Intuitively, we can imagine an automaton with universal accepting condition as executing all runs in parallel. After reading a word w, the automaton is simultaneously in all states reached by all runs labeled by w and accepts if all those states are accepting.

Consider the language by $L_n = \{ww : w \in \{0, 1\}^n\}$.

(a) Give an automaton of size $\mathcal{O}(n)$ with universal accepting condition that recognizes L_n.

(b) Prove that every NFA (and so in particular every DFA) recognizing L_n has at least 2^n states.

(c) Give an algorithm that transforms an automaton with universal accepting condition into a DFA recognizing the same language. This shows that automata with universal accepting condition recognize the regular languages.

★☛ **Exercise 22.** The existential and universal accepting conditions can be combined, yielding *alternating automata*. The states of an alternating automaton are partitioned into *existential* and *universal* states. An existential state q accepts a word w, denoted $w \in \mathcal{L}(q)$, if either $w = \varepsilon$ and $q \in F$, or $w = aw'$ and *there exists* a transition (q, a, q') such that $w' \in \mathcal{L}(q')$. A universal state q accepts a word w if either $w = \varepsilon$ and $q \in F$, or $w = aw'$ and $w' \in \mathcal{L}(q')$ *for every* transition (q, a, q'). The language recognized by an alternating automaton is the set of words accepted by its initial state.

Give an algorithm that transforms an alternating automaton into a DFA recognizing the same language.

☆ 🖳 **Exercise 23.** In algorithm *NFAεtoNFA*, no transition that has been added to the workset, processed, *and* removed from the workset is ever added to the workset again. However, transitions may be added to the workset more than once. Give an NFA-ε and a run of *NFAεtoNFA* where this happens.

☆ ⚙ **Exercise 24.** Execute algorithm *NFAεtoNFA* on the following NFA-ε over $\Sigma = \{a_1, \ldots, a_n\}$ to show that the algorithm may increase the number of transitions quadratically:

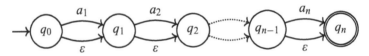

☆ 🖊 **Exercise 25.** We say that $u = a_1 \cdots a_n$ is a *scattered subword* of $w \in \Sigma^*$, denoted $u \preceq w$, if there are words $w_0, \ldots, w_n \in \Sigma^*$ such that $w = w_0 a_1 w_1 a_2 \cdots a_n w_n$. The *upward closure* and *downward closure* of a language L are the following languages:

$$\uparrow L = \{u \in \Sigma^* : w \preceq u \text{ for some } w \in L\},$$

$$\downarrow L = \{u \in \Sigma^* : u \preceq w \text{ for some } w \in L\}.$$

(a) Give regular expressions for the upward and downward closures of $\{a^n b^n : n \geq 0\}$.

(b) Give algorithms that take a regular expression r as input and return regular expressions for $\uparrow \mathcal{L}(r)$ and $\downarrow \mathcal{L}(r)$.

(c) Give algorithms that take an NFA A as input and return NFAs for $\uparrow \mathcal{L}(A)$ and $\downarrow \mathcal{L}(A)$.

★ ■ **Exercise 26.** An *atomic expression* over alphabet Σ^* is an expression of the form $\emptyset$, ε, $(a + \varepsilon)$, or $(a_1 + \ldots + a_n)^*$, where $a, a_1, \ldots, a_n \in \Sigma$. A *product* is a concatenation $e_1 e_2 \cdots e_n$ of atomic expressions. A *simple regular expression* is a sum $p_1 + \ldots + p_n$ of products.

(a) Prove that the language of a simple regular expression is downward-closed (i.e., it is equal to its downward closure) (see exercise 25).

(b) Prove that any downward-closed language can be represented by a simple regular expression.

Hint: Since every downward-closed language is regular, it can be represented by a regular expression. Prove that this expression is equivalent to a simple regular expression.

★ ▣ **Exercise 27.** Let L be a regular language over Σ. Show that the following languages are also regular by constructing automata:

(a) $\sqrt{L} = \{w \in \Sigma^* : ww \in L\}$,

(b) $\mathrm{Cyc}(L) = \{vu \in \Sigma^* : uv \in L\}$.

★ ▣ **Exercise 28.** For every $n \in \mathbb{N}$, let msbf(n) be the set of *most-significant-bit-first* encodings of n, that is, the words that start with an arbitrary number of leading zeros, followed by n written in binary. For example, msbf$(3) = \mathcal{L}(0^*11)$, msbf$(9) = \mathcal{L}(0^*1001)$, and msbf$(0) = \mathcal{L}(0^*)$. Similarly, let LSBF$(n)$ denote the set of *least-significant-bit-first* encodings of n, that is, the set containing for each word $w \in$ msbf(n) its reverse. For example, LSBF$(6) = \mathcal{L}(0110^*)$ and LSBF$(0) = \mathcal{L}(0^*)$.

(a) Construct and compare DFAs recognizing the set of even numbers w.r.t. the unary encoding (where n is encoded by the word 1^n), the msbf-encoding, and the LSBF-encoding.

(b) Do the same for the set of numbers divisible by 3.

(c) Give regular expressions corresponding to the languages of (b).

★ ■ **Exercise 29.** Consider this DFA over alphabet $\{[0,0],[0,1],[1,0],[1,1]\}$:

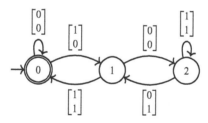

A word w encodes a pair of natural numbers $(X(w), Y(w))$, where $X(w)$ and $Y(w)$ are obtained by reading the top and bottom rows in MSBF encoding. For instance, the following word encodes $(44, 19)$:

$$w = \begin{bmatrix} 1 \\ 0 \end{bmatrix} \begin{bmatrix} 0 \\ 1 \end{bmatrix} \begin{bmatrix} 1 \\ 0 \end{bmatrix} \begin{bmatrix} 1 \\ 0 \end{bmatrix} \begin{bmatrix} 0 \\ 1 \end{bmatrix} \begin{bmatrix} 0 \\ 1 \end{bmatrix}$$

Show that the above DFA recognizes the set of words w such that $X(w) = 3 \cdot Y(w)$, that is, the solutions of the equation $x - 3y = 0$.

★ ☞ **Exercise 30.** Algorithm *NFAtoRE* transforms a finite automaton into a regular expression representing the same language by iteratively eliminating states of the automaton. In this exercise, we present an algebraic reformulation of the algorithm. We represent an NFA as a system of *language equations* with as many variables as states and solve the system by eliminating variables. A language equation over an alphabet Σ and a set V of variables is an equation of the form $r_1 = r_2$, where r_1 and r_2 are regular expressions over $\Sigma \cup V$. For instance, $X = aX + b$ is a language equation. A solution of a system of equations is a mapping that assigns to each variable X a regular expression over Σ, such that the languages of the left- and right-hand sides of each equation are equal. For instance, a^*b is a solution of $X = aX + b$ because $\mathcal{L}(a^*b) = \mathcal{L}(aa^*b + b)$.

(a) Arden's lemma states that, given two languages $A, B \subseteq \Sigma^*$, the smallest language $X \subseteq \Sigma^*$ satisfying $X = AX + B$ is the language A^*B. Moreover, if $\varepsilon \notin A$, then the solution is unique. Prove Arden's lemma.

(b) Consider the following system of equations, where variables X and Y represent languages (regular expressions) over the alphabet $\Sigma = \{a, b, c, d, e, f\}$:

$$X = aX + bY + c$$

$$Y = dX + eY + f.$$

Find the unique solution with the help of Arden's lemma.

Hint: As a first step, consider X not as a variable but as a constant language, and solve the equation for Y using Arden's lemma.

(c) We can associate to any NFA $A = (Q, \Sigma, \delta, \{q_0\}, F)$ a system of linear equations as follows. We take Q as variables, which we call here $X, Y, Z, \ldots$, with X as initial state. The system has the following equation for each state Y:

$$Y = \begin{cases} \displaystyle\sum_{(Y,a,Z) \in \delta} aZ & \text{if } Y \notin F, \\[2em] \left(\displaystyle\sum_{(Y,a,Z) \in \delta} aZ \right) + \varepsilon & \text{if } Y \in F. \end{cases}$$

Consider the DFA (1)(a) from the Tour of Conversions on page 35.

Let X, Y, Z, W be the states of the automaton, and read from top to bottom and from left to right. The associated system of linear equations is

$$X = aY + bZ + \varepsilon \qquad\qquad Y = aX + bW$$

$$Z = bX + aW \qquad\qquad W = bY + aZ.$$

Compute the solution of this system by iteratively eliminating variables. Start with Y, then eliminate Z, and finally W. Compare with the elimination procedure depicted in step (1) of the Tour of Conversions on page 35.

⭐ 🖳 **Exercise 31.** Consider a deck of cards (with arbitrary many cards) in which black and colored cards alternate, the top card is black, and the bottom card is colored. The set of possible decks is given by the regular expression $(BR)^*$. Cut the deck at any point into two piles, and then perform a perfect riffle shuffle to yield a new deck (where cards strictly alternate). For example, we can cut a deck with six cards 123456 (with 1 as the top card) into two piles 12 and 3456, and the riffle yields 345162 (we start the riffle with the first pile). Give a regular expression over the alphabet $\{B, R\}$ describing the possible configurations of the decks after the riffle.

Hint: After the cut, the last card of the first pile can be black or colored. In the first case, the two piles belong to $(BR)^*B$ and $R(BR)^*$ and in the second case to $(BR)^*$ and $(BR)^*$. Let $Rif(r_1, r_2)$ be the language of all decks obtained by performing a riffle on decks taken from $\mathcal{L}(r_1)$ and $\mathcal{L}(r_2)$. We are looking for a regular expression for

$$Rif\big((BR)^*B, R(BR)^*\big) + Rif\big((BR)^*, (BR)^*\big).$$

Use exercise 30 to set up a system of equations over the variables $X = Rif((BR)^*B, R(BR)^*)$ and $Y = Rif((BR)^*, (BR)^*)$, and solve it.

⭐ ■ **Exercise 32.** Let L be an arbitrary language over a one-letter alphabet. Prove that L^* is regular.

⭐ ■ **Exercise 33.** In contrast to exercise 32, show that there exists a language L over a two-letter alphabet such that L^* is not necessarily regular.

⭐ ■ **Exercise 34.** Let $K_n = (V_n, E_n)$ be the complete directed graph of n nodes— that is, with nodes $V_n = \{1, \ldots, n\}$ and edges $E_n = \{(i, j) : 1 \le i, j \le n\}$. A path of K_n is a sequence of nodes, and a circuit is a path that begins and ends in the same node. Let $A_n = (Q_n, \Sigma_n, \delta_n, q_{0n}, F_n)$ be the DFA defined by $Q_n = \{1, \ldots, n\} \cup \{\bot\}$, $\Sigma_n = \{a_{i,j} : 1 \le i, j \le n\}$, $q_{0n} = 1$, $F_n = \{1\}$, and

$$\delta_n(q, a_{i,j}) = \begin{cases} \bot & \text{if } q = \bot \text{ or } q \ne i, \\ j & \text{otherwise (if } q = i). \end{cases}$$

The language accepted by A_n consists of all words encoding circuits of K_n from node 1 to itself. For example, the following DFA A_3 accepts $a_{1,3}a_{3,2}a_{2,1}$, which encodes the circuit 1321 of K_3.

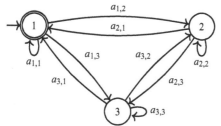

The *size* of a regular expression r, denoted $|r|$, is defined recursively as 1 if $r \in \{\varepsilon, \emptyset\} \cup \Sigma_n$; $|r_1| + |r_2|$ if $r = r_1 + r_2$ or $r = r_1 r_2$; and $|s|$ if $r = s^*$. Similarly, we define the *length* of r, denoted $\text{len}(r)$, as 1 if $r \in \{\varepsilon, \emptyset\} \cup \Sigma_n$; $\max(\text{len}(r_1), \text{len}(r_2))$ if $r = r_1 + r_2$; $\text{len}(r_1) + \text{len}(r_2)$ if $r = r_1 r_2$; and $\text{len}(s)$ if $r = s^*$. Note that $|r| \geq \text{len}(r)$.

A *path expression* r is a regular expression over Σ_n that encodes paths of K_n. We seek to show that any path expression for $\mathcal{L}(A_n)$, and hence any regular expression, must have length $\Omega(2^n)$. As a consequence, this means that DFAs can be exponentially more succinct than regular expressions.

(a) Let π be a circuit of K_n and let r be a path expression. We say that r *covers* π if $\mathcal{L}(r)$ contains a word uwv such that w encodes π. Furthermore, we say that r *covers* π^* if $\mathcal{L}(r)$ covers π^k for every $k \geq 0$. It can be shown that if r covers $\pi^{2 \cdot \text{len}(r)}$, then it covers π^*.

From this, show that if r covers π^* and no proper subexpression of r does, then $r = s^*$ for some expression s, and every word of $\mathcal{L}(s)$ encodes a circuit starting at a node of π.

(b) For every $1 \leq k \leq n+1$, let $[k]$ denote the permutation of $\{1, 2, \ldots, n+1\}$ that cyclically shifts every index k position to the right. More formally, node i is renamed to $i + k$ if $i + k \leq n+1$ and to $i + k - (n+1)$ otherwise. Let $\pi[k]$ be the result of applying the permutation to π. For example, if $n = 4$ and $\pi = 24142$, we obtain

$$\pi[1] = 35253, \quad \pi[2] = 41314, \quad \pi[3] = 52425, \quad \pi[4] = 13531, \quad \pi[5] = 24142 = \pi.$$

Let π be a circuit of K_n. Show that $\pi[k]$ is a circuit of K_{n+1} that does not pass through node k.

(c) Let us define a circuit g_n of K_n inductively:

$$g_1 = 11,$$

$$g_{n+1} = 1 \, (g_n[1])^{2^n} \, (g_n[2])^{2^n} \, \cdots \, (g_n[n+1])^{2^n} \qquad \text{for every } n \geq 1.$$

In particular, we have

$$g_1 = 11,$$

$$g_2 = 1 \, (22)^2 \, (11)^2,$$

$$g_3 = 1 \, (2 \, (33)^2 \, (22)^2)^4 \, (3 \, (11)^2 \, (33)^2 \, 3)^4 \, (1 \, (22)^2 \, (11)^2)^4.$$

Prove, using (a)–(b), that every path expression r covering g_n is such that $|r| \geq 2^{n-1}$.

(d) Show that any regular expression r_n such that $\mathcal{L}(r_n) = \mathcal{L}(A_n)$ is such that $|r_n| \geq 2^{n-1}$.

★■ **Exercise 35.** Let us introduce weakly acyclic DFAs, NFAs, and regular expressions:

• A DFA $A = (Q, \Sigma, \delta, q_0, F)$ is *weakly acyclic* if $\delta(q, w) = q$ implies $\delta(q, a) = q$ for every letter a occurring in w.

- An NFA $A = (Q, \Sigma, \delta, Q_0, F)$ is *weakly acyclic* if $q \in \delta(q, w)$ implies $\delta(q, a) = \{q\}$ for every letter a occurring in w.

- *Weakly acyclic* regular expressions over an alphabet Σ are regular expressions generated by

$$r ::= \emptyset \mid \Gamma^* \mid \Lambda^* a r \mid r + r \qquad\qquad \text{where } \Gamma, \Lambda \subseteq \Sigma \text{ and } a \in \Sigma \setminus \Lambda.$$

Finally, a regular language is *weakly acyclic* if it is recognized by some weakly acyclic DFA. Show the following statements:

(a) An NFA $A = (Q, \Sigma, \delta, q_0, F)$ is weakly acyclic iff it satisfies any of the following three conditions:

(i) the binary relation $\preceq\, \subseteq Q \times Q$, given by $q \preceq q'$ iff $\delta(q, w) = \{q'\}$ for some word w, is a partial order;

(ii) each strongly connected component of the underlying directed graph of A contains a single state; and

(iii) the underlying directed graph of A does not contain any simple cycle beyond self-loops.

(b) If A is a weakly acyclic NFA, then $B = NFAtoDFA(A)$ is a weakly acyclic DFA.

(c) For every weakly acyclic regular expression r, there is a weakly acyclic DFA that accepts $\mathcal{L}(r)$.

(d) For every weakly acyclic NFA A, there is a weakly acyclic regular expression for $\mathcal{L}(A)$.

Since every weakly acyclic DFA is also a weakly acyclic NFA by definition, we conclude that a language is *weakly acyclic* iff it is recognized by a weakly acyclic DFA iff it is recognized by a weakly acyclic NFA iff it is the language of a weakly acyclic regular expression.

2 Minimization and Reduction

In the previous chapter, we showed through a chain of conversions that the two DFAs of figure 2.1 recognize the same language. Obviously, the automaton on the left is better as a data structure for this language, since it has smaller size.

A DFA (respectively, NFA) is *minimal* if no other DFA (respectively, NFA) recognizing the same language has fewer states. We show that every regular language has a unique minimal DFA up to isomorphism (i.e., up to renaming of the states). Moreover, we present an efficient algorithm that "minimizes" a given DFA (i.e., converts it into the unique minimal DFA). In particular, the algorithm converts the DFA on the right of figure 2.1 into the one on the left.

From a data structure point of view, the existence of a unique minimal DFA has two important consequences. First, as mentioned earlier, the minimal DFA is the one that can be stored with a minimal amount of memory. Second, the uniqueness of the minimal DFA makes it a *canonical* representation of a regular language. Canonicity leads to a fast equality check: in order to decide if two regular languages are equal, we can construct their minimal DFAs and check if they are isomorphic.

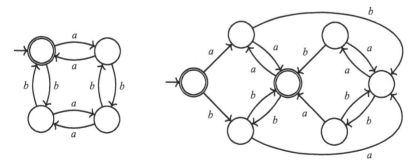

Figure 2.1
Two DFAs for the same language.

In the second part of the chapter, we observe that, unfortunately, computing a minimal NFA is a computationally hard problem, for which no efficient algorithm is likely to exist. Moreover, the minimal NFA is not necessarily unique. However, we show that a generalization of the minimization algorithm for DFAs can be used to at least reduce the size of an NFA while preserving its language.

2.1   Minimal DFAs

We start with a simple but very useful definition.

Definition 2.1   *Given a language $L \subseteq \Sigma^*$ and a word $w \in \Sigma^*$, the* residual of L with respect to w *is the language $L^w = \{u \in \Sigma^* : wu \in L\}$. A language $L' \subseteq \Sigma^*$ is a* residual *of L if $L' = L^w$ for at least one $w \in \Sigma^*$.*

The language L^w satisfies the following property:

$$wu \in L \iff u \in L^w. \tag{2.1}$$

Moreover, L^w is the only language satisfying this property. In other words, if a language L' satisfies $wu \in L \iff u \in L'$ for every word u, then $L' = L^w$.

Example 2.2   Let $\Sigma = \{a, b\}$ and $L = \{a, ab, ba, aab\}$. We compute L^w for all words w by increasing length of w.

- $|w| = 0$: $L^\varepsilon = \{a, ab, ba, aab\}$.
- $|w| = 1$: $L^a = \{\varepsilon, b, ab\}$ and $L^b = \{a\}$.
- $|w| = 2$: $L^{aa} = \{b\}$, $L^{ab} = \{\varepsilon\}$, $L^{ba} = \{\varepsilon\}$ and $L^{bb} = \emptyset$.
- $|w| \geq 3$: $L^w = \begin{cases} \{\varepsilon\} & \text{if } w = aab, \\ \emptyset & \text{otherwise.} \end{cases}$

Observe that residuals with respect to different words can be equal. In fact, even though Σ^* contains infinitely many words, L has only six residuals, namely, the languages $\emptyset$, $\{\varepsilon\}$, $\{a\}$, $\{b\}$, $\{\varepsilon, b, ab\}$, and $\{a, ab, ba, aab\}$.

Example 2.3   Languages containing infinitely many words can have finitely many residuals. For example, $(a + b)^*$ contains infinitely many words, but it has a single residual: indeed, we have $L^w = (a + b)^*$ for every $w \in \{a, b\}^*$. Another example is the language of the two DFAs depicted in figure 2.1. Recall that it is the language of all words over $\{a, b\}$ with an even number of as and an even number of bs. Let us call this language EE in the following.[1] The language has four residuals, namely, the languages EE, EO, OE, and OO, where E stands for "even" and O for "odd." For example, EO contains the words with an even

---

1. Here, EE is a two-letter name for a language, not a concatenation of two languages!

number of as and an odd number of bs. In particular, we have $(EE)^{\varepsilon} = EE$, $(EE)^a = OE$, $(EE)^b = EO$, and $(EE)^{ab} = OO$.

Example 2.4 The languages of examples 2.2 and 2.3 have finitely many residuals, but this is not the case for every language. In general, proving that the number of residuals of a language is finite or infinite can be complicated. To show that a language L has an infinite number of residuals, one can use the following general proof strategy:

- Define an infinite set $W = \{w_0, w_1, w_2, \ldots\} \subseteq \Sigma^*$.
- Prove that $L^{w_i} \neq L^{w_j}$ holds for every $i \neq j$. For this, show that for every $i \neq j$, there exists a word $w_{i,j}$ that belongs to exactly one of the sets L^{w_i} and L^{w_j}.

As an example, we apply this strategy to two languages:

- Let $L = \{a^n b^n : n \geq 0\}$. Let $W = \{a^k : k \geq 0\}$. For every two distinct words $a^i, a^j \in W$, we have $b^i \in L^{a^i}$ since $a^i b^i \in L$, and $b^i \notin L^{a^j}$ since $a^j b^i \notin L$. Thus, L has infinitely many residuals.
- Let $L = \{ww : w \in \{0, 1\}^*\}$. Let $W = \{0^n 1 : n \geq 0\}$. For every two distinct words $u = 0^i 1, v = 0^j 1 \in W$, where without loss of generality (w.l.o.g.) $i < j$, we have $u \in L^u$ since $uu \in L$, and $u \notin L^v$ since $vu \notin L$. Thus, L has infinitely many residuals.

There is a close connection between the states of a (not necessarily finite) DA and the residuals of the language it recognizes. In order to formulate it, we introduce the following definition:

Definition 2.5 *Let $A = (Q, \Sigma, \delta, q_0, F)$ be a DA and let $q \in Q$. The language recognized by q, denoted by $\mathcal{L}_A(q)$ (or just $\mathcal{L}(q)$ if there is no risk of confusion), is the language recognized by A with q as initial state, that is, the language recognized by the DA $A_q = (Q, \Sigma, \delta, q, F)$.*

For every transition $q \xrightarrow{a} q'$ of an automaton, deterministic or not, if a word w is accepted from q', then the word aw is accepted from q. For deterministic automata, the converse also holds: since $q \xrightarrow{a} q'$ is the unique transition leaving q labeled by a, if aw is accepted from q, then w is accepted from q'. So, we have $aw \in \mathcal{L}(q)$ iff $w \in \mathcal{L}(q')$ and, comparing with (2.1), we obtain

$$\text{For every transition } q \xrightarrow{a} q' \text{ of a DA: } \mathcal{L}(q') = \mathcal{L}(q)^a. \tag{2.2}$$

More generally, we can establish the following:

Lemma 2.6 *Let $A = (Q, \Sigma, \delta, q_0, F)$ be a DA and let $L = \mathcal{L}(A)$.*

(a) Every residual of L is recognized by some state of A. More formally, for every $w \in \Sigma^*$, there is at least one state $q \in Q$ such that $\mathcal{L}_A(q) = L^w$.

(b) Every state of A recognizes a residual of L. More formally, for every $q \in Q$, there is at least one word $w \in \Sigma^*$ such that $\mathcal{L}_A(q) = L^w$.

Proof

(a) Let $w \in \Sigma^*$, and let q be the state reached by the unique run of A on w, that is, $q_0 \xrightarrow{w} q$. We prove $\mathcal{L}_A(q) = L^w$. By (2.1), it suffices to show that every word u satisfies

$$wu \in L \iff u \in \mathcal{L}_A(q).$$

Since A is a DFA, for every word $wu \in \Sigma^*$, the unique run of A on wu is of the form $q_0 \xrightarrow{w} q \xrightarrow{u} q'$. Hence, A accepts wu iff q' is a final state, which is the case iff $u \in \mathcal{L}_A(q)$. Thus, $\mathcal{L}_A(q) = L^w$.

(b) Since A is in normal form, q can be reached from q_0 by at least a word w. The proof that $\mathcal{L}_A(q) = L^w$ holds is exactly as above.   □

Example 2.7   Figure 2.2 shows the result of labeling the states of the DFAs of figure 2.1 with the languages they recognize. These languages are residuals of *EE*.

We use the notion of a residual to define the *canonical deterministic automaton* of a given language L. The states of the canonical DA are themselves languages. Furthermore, "each state recognizes itself" (i.e., the language recognized from the state L is the language L itself). This single property completely determines the initial state, transitions, and final states of the canonical DA:

• The canonical DA for a language L must recognize L. So, the initial state of the canonical DA recognizes L. Since each state "recognizes itself," the initial state is necessarily the language L itself.

• Since each state K recognizes the language K, by (2.2), all transitions of the canonical DA are of the form $K \xrightarrow{a} K^a$.

• A state q of a DA is final iff it recognizes the empty word. Thus, a state K of the canonical DA is final iff $\varepsilon \in K$.

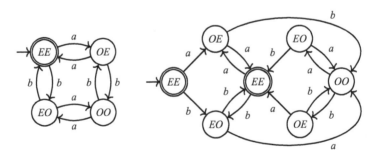

Figure 2.2
Languages of the states from the DFAs of figure 2.1.

We formalize this construction and prove its correctness.

Definition 2.8   *The* canonical DA *for language* $L \subseteq \Sigma^*$ *is the DA* $C_L = (Q_L, \Sigma, \delta_L, q_{0L}, F_L)$, *where*

- Q_L *is the set of residuals of* L, *that is,* $Q_L = \{L^w : w \in \Sigma^*\}$;
- $\delta_L(K, a) = K^a$ *for every* $K \in Q_L$ *and* $a \in \Sigma$;
- $q_{0L} = L$; *and*
- $F_L = \{K \in Q_L : \varepsilon \in K\}$.

Example 2.9   Figure 2.3 illustrates the canonical DA A for the language $\{a, ab, ba, aab\}$. As the language has six residuals, A has six states. Note that every state "recognizes itself." For example, the language recognized from the state $\{\varepsilon, b, ab\}$ is $\{\varepsilon, b, ab\}$. The final states are the residuals containing ε, that is, the two residuals $\{\varepsilon, b, ab\}$ and $\{\varepsilon\}$.

Example 2.10   Let us reconsider the language EE recognized by the two automata depicted in figure 2.2. Its canonical DA is the one shown on the left of the figure. It has four states, corresponding to the four residuals of EE. Since, for instance, $EE^a = OE$, the canonical DA has a transition $EE \xrightarrow{a} OE$. The initial state is EE. Since the empty word has an even number of a and b (namely, zero in both cases), we have $\varepsilon \in EE$, and $\varepsilon \notin EO \cup OE \cup OO$. Thus, the only final state is EE.

Proposition 2.11   *The canonical DA for language* $L \subseteq \Sigma^*$ *recognizes* L.

Proof   Let C_L be the canonical DA for L. We show that $\mathcal{L}(C_L) = L$. Let $w \in \Sigma^*$. We prove, by induction on $|w|$, that $w \in L$ iff $w \in \mathcal{L}(C_L)$. If $|w| = 0$, then $w = \varepsilon$, and we have

$$\varepsilon \in L \iff L \in F_L \qquad \text{(by definition of } F_L)$$
$$\iff q_{0L} \in F_L \qquad \text{(by } q_{0L} = L)$$
$$\iff \varepsilon \in \mathcal{L}(C_L) \qquad \text{(as } q_{0L} \text{ is the initial state of } C_L).$$

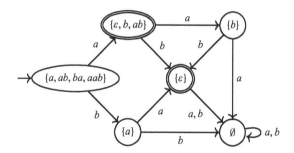

Figure 2.3
Canonical DA for the language $\{a, ab, ba, aab\} \subseteq \{a, b\}^*$.

If $|w| > 0$, then $w = aw'$ for some $a \in \Sigma$ and $w' \in \Sigma^*$, and we have

$$aw' \in L \iff w' \in L^a \qquad\qquad \text{(by definition of } L^a)$$
$$\iff w' \in \mathcal{L}(C_{L^a}) \qquad\qquad \text{(by induction hypothesis)}$$
$$\iff aw' \in \mathcal{L}(C_L) \qquad\qquad \text{(by } \delta_L(L, a) = L^a). \qquad\qquad \square$$

We now prove that if L is a regular language, then C_L is the unique minimal DFA recognizing L (up to isomorphism). The informal argument goes as follows. Since every DFA for L has *at least* one state for each residual, and C_L has *exactly* one state for each residual, C_L has a minimal number of states. Further, every other minimal DFA for L also has exactly one state for each residual. It remains to show that all these minimal DFAs are isomorphic. For this, we observe that, if we know which state recognizes which residual, we can infer the initial state, the transitions, and the final states. In other words, the transitions, initial states, and final states of a minimal DFA are completely determined by the residual recognized by each state. Indeed, if state q recognizes residual R, then the a-transition from q necessarily leads to the state recognizing R^a; further, q is initial iff $R = L$, and q is final iff $\varepsilon \in R$. A more formal proof looks as follows:

Theorem 2.12 *If language L is regular, then the canonical DFA C_L is the unique minimal DFA up to isomorphism that recognizes L.*

Proof Let L be a regular language, and let $A = (Q, \Sigma, \delta, q_0, F)$ be an arbitrary DFA recognizing L. By lemma 2.6, the number of states of A is greater than or equal to the number of states of C_L, and so C_L is a minimal automaton for L. It remains to prove uniqueness of the minimal automaton up to isomorphism. Assume A is minimal. Let $\mathcal{L}_A$ be the mapping that assigns to each state q of A the language $\mathcal{L}(q)$ recognized from q. By lemma 2.6(b), $\mathcal{L}_A$ assigns to each state of A a residual of L, and so $\mathcal{L}_A \colon Q \to Q_L$. We prove that $\mathcal{L}_A$ is an isomorphism between A and C_L. First, $\mathcal{L}_A$ is bijective because it is surjective by lemma 2.6(a), and $|Q| = |Q_L|$ since A is minimal by assumption. Moreover, if $\delta(q, a) = q'$, then $\mathcal{L}_A(q') = (\mathcal{L}_A(q))^a$, and so $\delta_L(\mathcal{L}_A(q), a) = \mathcal{L}_A(q')$. Moreover, $\mathcal{L}_A$ maps the initial state of A to the initial state of C_L: $\mathcal{L}_A(q_0) = L = q_{0L}$. Finally, $\mathcal{L}_A$ maps final to final states and nonfinal to nonfinal states: $q \in F$ iff $\varepsilon \in \mathcal{L}_A(q)$ iff $\mathcal{L}_A(q) \in F_L$. $\qquad\qquad \square$

The following simple corollary is useful to establish that a DFA is minimal:

Corollary 2.13 *A DFA is minimal if and only if different states recognize different languages, that is, $\mathcal{L}(q) \neq \mathcal{L}(q')$ holds for every two states $q \neq q'$.*

Proof $\Rightarrow$) By theorem 2.12, the number of states of a minimal DFA is equal to the number of residuals of its language. Since every state recognizes some residual, each state must recognize a different residual.

$\Longleftarrow$) If all states of a DFA A recognize different languages, then, since every state recognizes some residual, the number of states of A is less than or equal to the number of residuals. Thus, A has at most as many states as $C_{\mathcal{L}(A)}$, and so it is minimal. $\qquad \square$

2.1.1 The Master Automaton

The master automaton over an alphabet Σ is a deterministic automaton with an infinite number of states but no initial state. As in the case of canonical DAs, the states are languages—in this case, *all* regular languages.

Definition 2.14 *The* master automaton *over the alphabet Σ is the tuple $M = (Q_M, \Sigma, \delta_M, F_M)$, where*

- *Q_M is the set of all regular languages over Σ,*
- *$\delta: Q_M \times \Sigma \to Q_M$ is given by $\delta(L, a) = L^a$ for every $q \in Q_M$ and $a \in \Sigma$, and*
- *$L \in F_M$ iff $\varepsilon \in L$.*

Figure 2.4 depicts a small fragment of the master automaton for the alphabet $\Sigma = \{a, b\}$.

Given two states L and L' of the master automaton, we say that L' is *reachable* from L if there is a word $a_1 \cdots a_n \in \Sigma^*$ and languages $L_1, \ldots, L_{n-1}$ such that $L \xrightarrow{a_1} L_1 \xrightarrow{a_2} L_2 \cdots L_{n-2} \xrightarrow{a_{n-1}} L_{n-1} \xrightarrow{a_n} L'$. By definition of the canonical automaton definition (2.8) and theorem 2.12, for every regular language L, the fragment of the master automaton containing the states reachable from L and the transitions between them is the canonical DFA for L. So, in a sense, the master automaton "contains" all minimal DFAs for all regular languages: in order to find the canonical DFA for L, just search for state L of the master automaton, and "copy" the fragment reachable from there. For example, the reader can check that the minimal DFA for the language $a\Sigma + b(\varepsilon + \Sigma^2 \Sigma^*)$ is indeed the seven-state DFA obtained by taking all the states reachable from this regular expression in figure 6.1—namely, the language itself; the languages $\varepsilon + \Sigma^2 \Sigma^*$, $\Sigma \Sigma^*$, and Σ^* (moving upward); and the languages Σ, ε, and $\emptyset$ (moving downward).

The master automaton is a beautiful mathematical object, a sort of God's view of the universe of regular languages. It enjoys many interesting properties (see exercises 55 and 56), and in chapter 6 we use it to define decision diagrams, a data structure with many applications.

2.2 Minimizing DFAs

We present an algorithm that converts a given DFA into the unique minimal DFA recognizing the same language. The algorithm first partitions the states of the DFA into *blocks*, where a block contains all states recognizing the same residual. We call this partition the *language partition*. Then, the algorithm "merges" the states of each block into a single state,

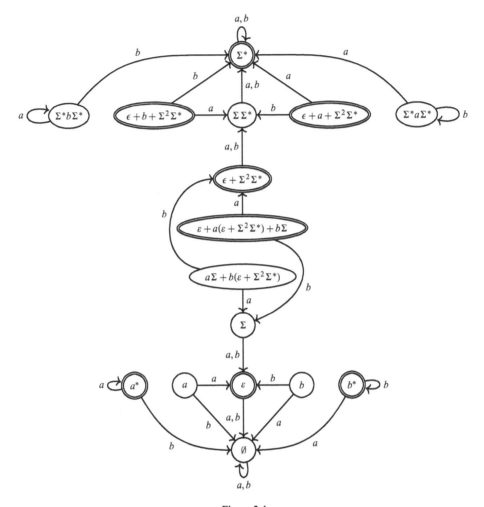

Figure 2.4
A fragment of the master automaton over $\Sigma = \{a, b\}$. We use Σ as an abbreviation of $(a + b)$.

an operation usually called *quotienting* with respect to the partition. Intuitively, this yields a DFA where distinct states recognize different residuals. These two steps are described in sections 2.2.1 and 2.2.2.

For the rest of this section, we fix a DFA $A = (Q, \Sigma, \delta, q_0, F)$ recognizing a regular language L.

2.2.1   Computing the Language Partition

We need some basic notions on partitions. A *partition* of Q is a finite set $P = \{B_1, \dots, B_n\}$ of nonempty subsets of Q, called *blocks*, such that $Q = B_1 \cup \dots \cup B_n$, and $B_i \cap B_j = \emptyset$ for every $1 \leq i < j \leq n$. The block containing a state q is denoted by $[q]_P$. A partition P' *refines* or *is a refinement of* another partition P if every block of P' is contained in some block of P. If P' refines P and $P' \neq P$, then P is *coarser* than P'.

The *language partition*, denoted by P_ℓ, puts two states in the same block iff they recognize the same language (i.e, the same residual). To compute P_ℓ, we iteratively refine an initial partition P_0 while maintaining the following

Invariant: *States in different blocks recognize different languages.*

Partition P_0 consists of two blocks containing the final and the nonfinal states, respectively (or just one of the two if all states are final or all states are nonfinal). That is, $P_0 = \{F, Q \setminus F\}$ if F and $Q \setminus F$ are nonempty, $P_0 = \{F\}$ if $Q \setminus F$ is empty, and $P_0 = \{Q \setminus F\} = \{Q\}$ if F is empty. Notice that P_0 satisfies the invariant, because every state of F accepts the empty word, but no state of $Q \setminus F$ does.

A partition is refined by splitting a block into two blocks. To find a block to split, we first observe the following:

Fact 2.15 If $\mathcal{L}(q_1) = \mathcal{L}(q_2)$, then $\mathcal{L}(\delta(q_1, a)) = \mathcal{L}(\delta(q_2, a))$ for every $a \in \Sigma$.

By contraposition, if $\mathcal{L}(\delta(q_1, a)) \neq \mathcal{L}(\delta(q_2, a))$, then $\mathcal{L}(q_1) \neq \mathcal{L}(q_2)$, or, rephrasing in terms of blocks: if $\delta(q_1, a)$ and $\delta(q_2, a)$ belong to different blocks, but q_1 and q_2 belong to the same block B, then B can be split, because q_1 and q_2 can be put in different blocks while respecting the invariant.

Definition 2.16 *Let B, B' be (not necessarily distinct) blocks of a partition P, and let $a \in \Sigma$. The pair (a, B') splits B if there are $q_1, q_2 \in B$ such that $\delta(q_1, a) \in B'$ and $\delta(q_2, a) \notin B'$. The result of the split is the partition $Ref_P[B, a, B'] = (P \setminus \{B\}) \cup \{B_0, B_1\}$, where*

$$B_0 = \{q \in B : \delta(q, a) \notin B'\} \text{ and } B_1 = \{q \in B : \delta(q, a) \in B'\}.$$

A partition is unstable *if it contains blocks B, B' such that (a, B') splits B for some $a \in \Sigma$ and is* stable *otherwise.*

The partition refinement algorithm *LanPar(A)*, described in algorithm 4, iteratively refines the initial partition of A until it becomes stable. The algorithm terminates as each iteration increases the number of blocks by 1, and a partition has at most $|Q|$ blocks.

Observe that if all states of a DFA are nonfinal, then every state recognizes $\emptyset$, and if all are final, then every state recognizes Σ^*. In both cases, all states recognize the same language, and the language partition is $\{Q\}$.

Example 2.17 Figure 2.5 illustrates a run of *LanPar* on the DFA depicted on the right of figure 2.1. States that belong to the same block have the same color and pattern. The initial partition, shown in (a), consists of the solid and hatched states. In (b), the solid block and the letter a split the hatched block into the crosshatched block (hatched states with

---

Algorithm 4 Partition refinement algorithm.

LanPar(A)
Input: DFA $A = (Q, \Sigma, \delta, q_0, F)$
Output: The language partition P_ℓ

1   **if** $F = \emptyset$ or $Q \setminus F = \emptyset$ **then return** $\{Q\}$
2   **else** $P \leftarrow \{F, Q \setminus F\}$
3   **while** P is unstable **do**
4   pick $B, B' \in P$ and $a \in \Sigma$ such that (a, B') splits B
5       $P \leftarrow Ref_P[B, a, B']$
6   **return** P

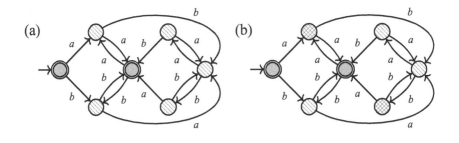

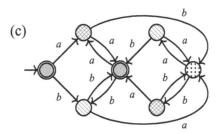

Figure 2.5
Computing the language partition of a DFA in steps (a), (b), and (c).

an a-transition to the solid block) and the rest (hatched states with an a-transition to other blocks), which stay hatched. In the final step (c), the crosshatched block and the letter b split the hatched block into the dotted block (hatched states with a b-transition into the crosshatched block) and the rest, which stay hatched.

We prove the correctness of *LanPar* in two steps. First, we show that it computes the *coarsest stable refinement of* P_0, denoted by *CSR*; in other words, we show that, after termination, the partition P is coarser than every other stable refinement of P_0. Then, we prove that CSR is equal to P_ℓ.

Lemma 2.18   *LanPar(A) computes CSR.*

Proof   *LanPar*(A) clearly computes a stable refinement of P_0. We prove that, after termination, P is coarser than any other stable refinement of P_0 or, equivalently, that every stable refinement of P_0 refines P. Actually, we prove that this holds not only after termination but at any time.

Let P' be an arbitrary stable refinement of P_0. Initially, $P = P_0$, and so P' refines P. Now, we show that if P' refines P, then P' also refines $Ref_P[B, a, B']$. For this, let q_1 and q_2 be two states belonging to the same block of P'. We show that they belong to the same block of $Ref_P[B, a, B']$. Assume the contrary. Since the only difference between P and $Ref_P[B, a, B']$ is the splitting of B into B_0 and B_1, exactly one of q_1 and q_2, say q_1, belongs to B_0, and the other belongs to B_1. Therefore, there exists a transition $(q_2, a, q'_2) \in \delta$ such that $q'_2 \in B'$. Since P' is stable and q_1, q_2 belong to the same block of P', there is also a transition $(q_1, a, q'_1) \in \delta$ such that $q'_1 \in B'$. This contradicts $q_1 \in B_0$.   □

Theorem 2.19   *CSR is equal to P_ℓ.*

Proof   We show that (a) P_ℓ refines P_0, (b) P_ℓ is stable, and (c) every stable refinement P of P_0 refines P_ℓ.

(a) Trivial.

(b) By fact 2.15, if two states q_1 and q_2 belong to the same block of P_ℓ, then $\delta(q_1, a)$ and $\delta(q_2, a)$ also belong to the same block, for every letter a. Hence, no block can be split.

(c) Let q_1, q_2 be states belonging to the same block B of P. We prove that they belong to the same block of P_ℓ—that is, that $\mathcal{L}(q_1) = \mathcal{L}(q_2)$. By symmetry, it suffices to prove that, for every word w, if $w \in \mathcal{L}(q_1)$, then $w \in \mathcal{L}(q_2)$. We proceed by induction on the length of w. If $w = \varepsilon$, then $q_1 \in F$, and since P refines P_0, we have $q_2 \in F$, and so $w \in \mathcal{L}(q_2)$. If $w = aw'$, then there exists $(q_1, a, q'_1) \in \delta$ such that $w' \in \mathcal{L}(q'_1)$. Let B' be the block containing q'_1. Since P is stable, B' does not split B, and so there is $(q_2, a, q'_2) \in \delta$ such that $q'_2 \in B'$. By induction hypothesis, $w' \in \mathcal{L}(q'_1)$ iff $w' \in \mathcal{L}(q'_2)$. Therefore, $w' \in \mathcal{L}(q'_2)$, which implies $w \in \mathcal{L}(q_2)$.   □

2.2.2   Quotienting

It remains to define the quotient of A with respect to a partition. It is convenient to define it not only for DFAs but more generally for NFAs. The states of the quotient are the blocks of the partition. The quotient has a transition (B, a, B') from block B to block B' if A contains some transition (q, a, q') for some states q and q' belonging to B and B', respectively. Formally:

Definition 2.20   *The* quotient *of an NFA A with respect to a partition P is the NFA* $A/P = (Q_P, \Sigma, \delta_P, Q_{0P}, F_P)$ *where*

- Q_P *is the set of blocks of P;*
- $(B, a, B') \in \delta_P$ *if* $(q, a, q') \in \delta$ *for some* $q \in B$, $q' \in B'$;
- Q_{0P} *is the set of blocks of P that contain at least one state from* Q_0; *and*
- F_P *is the set of blocks of P that contain at least one state of F.*

Example 2.21   The right-hand side of figure 2.6 depicts the result of quotienting the DFA on the left-hand side with respect to its language partition. The quotient has as many states as colored patterns, and it has a transition between two colored patterns (say, an *a*-transition from solid to crosshatched) if the DFA on the left has such a transition.

We show that A/P_ℓ, the quotient of a DFA A with respect to the language partition, is the minimal DFA for L. The main part of the argument is contained in the forthcoming lemma. Loosely speaking, it says that any refinement of the language partition (i.e., any partition in which states of the same block recognize the same language) "is good" for quotienting, because the quotient recognizes the same language as the original automaton. Moreover, if the partition not only refines but is equal to the language partition, then the quotient is a DFA.

Lemma 2.22   *Let A be an NFA, and let P be a partition of the states of A. If P refines* P_ℓ, *then* $\mathcal{L}_A(q) = \mathcal{L}_{A/P}(B)$ *for every state q of A, where B is the block of P containing q. In particular,* $\mathcal{L}(A/P) = \mathcal{L}(A)$. *Moreover, if A is a DFA and* $P = P_\ell$, *then* A/P *is a DFA.*

Proof   Let P be a refinement of P_ℓ. We prove that for every $w \in \Sigma^*$, it is the case that $w \in \mathcal{L}_A(q)$ iff $w \in \mathcal{L}_{A/P}(B)$. We proceed by induction on $|w|$.

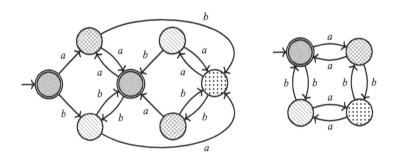

Figure 2.6
Quotient of a DFA with respect to its language partition.

If $|w| = 0$, then $w = \varepsilon$ and we have

$$\varepsilon \in \mathcal{L}_A(q) \iff q \in F$$

$$\iff B \subseteq F \qquad \text{(since } P \text{ refines } P_\ell \text{ and so also } P_0\text{)}$$

$$\iff B \in F_P$$

$$\iff \varepsilon \in \mathcal{L}_{A/P}(B).$$

If $|w| > 0$, then $w = aw'$ for some $a \in \Sigma$. Therefore, $w \in \mathcal{L}_A(q)$ iff there is a transition $(q, a, q') \in \delta$ such that $w' \in \mathcal{L}_A(q')$. Let B' be the block containing q'. By definition of A/P, we have $(B, a, B') \in \delta_P$, and hence

$$aw' \in \mathcal{L}_A(q)$$

$$\iff w' \in \mathcal{L}_A(q') \qquad \text{(by definition of } q'\text{)}$$

$$\iff w' \in \mathcal{L}_{A/P}(B') \qquad \text{(by induction hypothesis)}$$

$$\iff aw' \in \mathcal{L}_{A/P}(B) \qquad \text{(by } (B, a, B') \in \delta_P\text{)}.$$

For the second part, we show that $(B, a, B_1), (B, a, B_2) \in \delta_{P_\ell}$ implies $B_1 = B_2$. By definition, there exist $(q, a, q_1), (q', a, q_2) \in \delta$ for some $q, q' \in B$, $q_1 \in B_1$, and $q_2 \in B_2$. Since q and q' belong to the same block of the language partition, we have $\mathcal{L}_A(q) = \mathcal{L}_A(q')$. Since A is a DFA, we get $\mathcal{L}_A(q_1) = \mathcal{L}_A(q_2)$. Since $P = P_\ell$, the states q_1 and q_2 belong to the same block, and so $B_1 = B_2$. □

Proposition 2.23 *The quotient A/P_ℓ is the minimal DFA for L.*

Proof By lemma 2.22, A/P_ℓ is a DFA, and its states recognize residuals of L. Moreover, two states of A/P_ℓ recognize different residuals by definition of the language partition. Thus, A/P_ℓ has as many states as residuals. □

2.2.3 Hopcroft's Algorithm

Algorithm *LanPar* leaves open the choice of an adequate refinement triple $[B, a, B']$. While every exhaustive sequence of refinements leads to the same result, and so the choice does not affect the correctness of the algorithm, it affects its runtime. Hopcroft's algorithm is a modification of *LanPar*, which carefully selects the next triple. When properly implemented, Hopcroft's algorithm runs in time $\mathcal{O}(mn \log n)$ for a DFA with n states over a m-letter alphabet. A full analysis of the algorithm is beyond the scope of this book, and so we limit ourselves to presenting its main ideas.

It is convenient to start by describing an intermediate algorithm, not as efficient as the final one. The intermediate algorithm maintains a workset of pairs (a, B'), called *splitters*.

Initially, the workset contains all pairs (a, B') where a is an arbitrary letter and B' is a block of the original partition (i.e., either $B' = F$ or $B' = Q \setminus F$). At every step, the algorithm chooses a splitter from the workset and uses it to split every block of the current partition (if possible). Whenever a block B is split by (a, B') into two new blocks B_0 and B_1, the algorithm adds to the workset all pairs (b, B_0) and (b, B_1) for every letter $b \in \Sigma$.

It is not difficult to see that the intermediate algorithm is correct. The only point requiring a moment of thought is that it suffices to use each splitter at most once. A priori, a splitter (a, B') could be required at some point of the execution and then later again. To discard this, observe that, by the definition of split, if (a, B') splits a block B into B_0 and B_1, then it does not split any subset of B_0 or B_1. So, after (a, B') is used to split all blocks of a partition, since all future blocks are strict subsets of the current blocks, (a, B') is not useful anymore.

Hopcroft's algorithm improves on the intermediate algorithm by observing that when a block B is split into B_0 and B_1, it is not always necessary to add both (b, B_0) and (b, B_1) to the workset. The fundamental for this is the following:

Proposition 2.24 *Let $A = (Q, \Sigma, \delta, q_0, F)$, let P be a partition of Q, and let B be a block of P. Suppose we refine B into B_0 and B_1. Then, for every $a \in \Sigma$, refining all blocks of P with respect to any two of the splitters (a, B), (a, B_0), and (a, B_1) gives the same result as refining them with respect to all three of them.*

Proof Let C be a block of P. Every refinement sequence with respect to two of the splitters (there are six possible cases) yields the same partition of C—namely, $\{C_0, C_1, C_2\}$, where C_0, C_1, and C_2 contain the states $q \in Q$ that respectively satisfy $\delta(q, a) \in B_0$, $\delta(q, a) \in B_1$, and $\delta(q, a) \notin B$. □

Now, assume that (a, B') splits a block B into B_0 and B_1. For every $b \in \Sigma$, if (b, B) is in the workset, then adding both (b, B_0) and (b, B_1) is redundant, because we only need two of the three. In this case, Hopcroft's algorithm chooses to replace (b, B) in the workset by (b, B_0) and (b, B_1) (i.e., to remove (b, B) and to add (b, B_0) and (b, B_1)). If (b, B) is not in the workset, then in principle, we could have two possible cases.

• If (b, B) was already removed from the workset and used to refine, then we only need to add one of (b, B_0) and (b, B_1). Hopcroft's algorithm adds the *smaller* of the two (i.e., (b, B_0) if $|B_0| \le |B_1|$ and (b, B_1) otherwise).

• If (b, B) has not been added to the workset yet, then it looks as if we would still have to add both (b, B_0) and (b, B_1). However, a more detailed analysis shows that this is not the case, it suffices to add only one of (b, B_0) and (b, B_1). Hopcroft's algorithm adds again the smaller of the two.

These considerations lead to algorithm 5, where $(b, \min\{B_0, B_1\})$ denotes the smaller of (b, B_0) and (b, B_1).

Algorithm 5 Hopcroft's algorithm.

Hopcroft(A)
Input: DFA $A = (Q, \Sigma, \delta, q_0, F)$
Output: The language partition P_ℓ

```
1    if F = ∅ or Q \ F = ∅ then return {Q}
2    else P ← {F, Q \ F}
3    W ← {(a, min{F, Q \ F}) : a ∈ Σ}
4    while W ≠ ∅ do
5        pick (a, B′) from W
6        for all B ∈ P split by (a, B′) do
7            replace B by B₀ and B₁ in P
8            for all b ∈ Σ do
9                if (b, B) ∈ W then replace (b, B) by (b, B₀) and (b, B₁) in W
10               else add (b, min{B₀, B₁}) to W
11   return P
```

We sketch an argument showing that the main **while** loop is executed at most $\mathcal{O}(mn \log n)$ times, where $m = |\Sigma|$ and $n = |Q|$. Fix a state $q \in Q$ and a letter $a \in \Sigma$. It is easy to see that at every moment during the execution of *Hopcroft*, the workset contains at most one splitter (a, B) such that $q \in B$ (in particular, if (a, B) is in the workset and B is split at line 9, then q goes to either B_0 or to B_1). We call this splitter (if present) the a-q-splitter and define its size as the size of the block B. So, during the execution of the algorithm, there are alternating phases in which the workset contains one or zero a-q-splitters, respectively. Let us call them one-phases and zero-phases. It is easy to see that during a one-phase, the size of the a-q-splitter (defined as the number of states in the block) can only decrease (at line 9). Moreover, if at the end of a one-phase, the a-q-splitter has size k, then, because of line 10, at the beginning of the next one-phase, it has size at most $k/2$. Thus, the number of a-q-splitters added to the workset throughout the execution of the algorithm is $\mathcal{O}(\log n)$, and therefore the total number of splitters added to the workset is $\mathcal{O}(mn \log n)$. Hence, the **while** loop is executed $\mathcal{O}(mn \log n)$ times. If the algorithm is carefully implemented (which is nontrivial), then it also runs in time $\mathcal{O}(mn \log n)$.

2.3 Reducing NFAs

There is no canonical minimal NFA for a given regular language. The simplest witness of this fact is the language aa^*, which is recognized by the two nonisomorphic, minimal NFAs of figure 2.7. Moreover, computing any of the minimal NFAs equivalent to a given NFA

Figure 2.7
Two minimal NFAs for aa^*.

is computationally hard. Indeed, the problem can be shown to be PSPACE-complete. For readers not familiar with complexity theory, "PSPACE-complete" informally means that there is most likely no minimization algorithm that uses less than exponential time and a polynomial amount of memory. The proof is deferred to a forthcoming optional subsection.

Despite this intractability, we can reuse part of the theory for the DFA case to obtain an efficient procedure to possibly reduce the size of a given NFA.

2.3.1   The Reduction Algorithm

For the rest of the section, we fix an NFA $A = (Q, \Sigma, \delta, Q_0, F)$ recognizing a language L. Recall that definition 2.20 and the first part of lemma 2.22 were defined for NFAs. Thus, $\mathcal{L}(A) = \mathcal{L}(A/P)$ holds for every refinement P of P_ℓ, and so *any* refinement of P_ℓ can be used to reduce A. The largest reduction is obtained for $P = P_\ell$, but P_ℓ is hard to compute for NFAs. On the other extreme, the partition that puts each state in a separate block is always a refinement of P_ℓ, but it does not provide any reduction.

To find a reasonable trade-off, we examine again lemma 2.18, which proves that *Lan-Par(A)* computes *CSR* for deterministic automata. Its proof only uses the following property of stable partitions: if q_1 and q_2 belong to the same block of a stable partition and there is a transition $(q_2, a, q_2') \in \delta$ such that $q_2' \in B'$ for some block B', then there is also a transition $(q_1, a, q_1') \in \delta$ such that $q_1' \in B'$. We extend the definition of stability to NFAs so that stable partitions still satisfy this property: we just replace condition

$$\delta(q_1, a) \in B' \text{ and } \delta(q_2, a) \notin B'$$

of definition 2.16 by

$$\delta(q_1, a) \cap B' \neq \emptyset \text{ and } \delta(q_2, a) \cap B' = \emptyset.$$

Definition 2.25   [Refinement and stability for NFAs] *Let B, B' be (not necessarily distinct) blocks of a partition P, and let $a \in \Sigma$. The pair (a, B') splits B if there are $q_1, q_2 \in B$ such that $\delta(q_1, a) \cap B' \neq \emptyset$ and $\delta(q_2, a) \cap B' = \emptyset$. The result of the split is the partition $Ref_P^{NFA}[B, a, B'] = (P \setminus \{B\}) \cup \{B_0, B_1\}$, where*

$$B_0 = \{q \in B : \delta(q, a) \cap B' = \emptyset\} \text{ and } B_1 = \{q \in B : \delta(q, a) \cap B' \neq \emptyset\}.$$

A partition is unstable *if it contains blocks B and B' such that B' splits B and is* stable *otherwise.*

Using this definition, we generalize *LanPar(A)* to NFAs in the obvious way: allow NFAs as inputs, and replace Ref_P by Ref_P^{NFA} as new notion of refinement. Lemma 2.18 still holds: the algorithm still computes *CSR*, but with respect to the new notion of refinement. The procedure is described in algorithm 6. Notice that in the special case of DFAs, it reduces to *LanPar(A)*, because Ref_P and Ref_P^{NFA} coincide for DFAs.

Algorithm 6   Coarsest stable refinement for NFAs.

CSR(A)
Input: NFA $A = (Q, \Sigma, \delta, Q_0, F)$
Output: The partition *CSR* of A

1   **if** $F = \emptyset$ or $Q \setminus F = \emptyset$ **then** $P \leftarrow \{Q\}$
2   **else** $P \leftarrow \{F, Q \setminus F\}$
3   **while** P is unstable **do**
4   pick $B, B' \in P$ and $a \in \Sigma$ such that (a, B') splits B
5       $P \leftarrow Ref_P^{NFA}[B, a, B']$
6   **return** P

Observe that line 1 of CSR(A) is different from line 1 of algorithm *LanPar*. If all states of an NFA are nonfinal, then every state recognizes $\emptyset$, but if all are final, we can no longer conclude that every state recognizes Σ^*, as was the case for DFAs. In fact, all states might recognize different languages.

In the case of DFAs, we had theorem 2.19, which states that *CSR* is equal to P_ℓ. The theorem does not hold anymore for NFAs, as we will see later. However, part (c) of the proof, which showed that *CSR* refines P_ℓ, still holds, with exactly the same proof. Hence:

Theorem 2.26   *The partition CSR refines P_ℓ.*

Now, lemma 2.22 and theorem 2.26 lead to the final result:

Corollary 2.27   *Let A be an NFA. It is the case that $\mathcal{L}(A/CSR) = \mathcal{L}(A)$.*

Example 2.28   Consider the NFA as depicted on the left of figure 2.8.

CSR is the partition indicated by colored patterns. A possible run of CSR(A) is graphically represented on the right as a tree. Initially, we have the partition with two blocks shown at the top of the figure: the block $\{1, \dots, 14\}$ of nonfinal states and the block $\{15\}$ of final states. The first refinement uses $(a, \{15\})$ to split the block of nonfinal states, yielding the blocks $\{1, \dots, 8, 11, 12, 13\}$ (no a-transition to $\{15\}$) and $\{9, 10, 14\}$ (an a-transition to $\{15\}$). The leaves of the tree are the blocks of *CSR*.

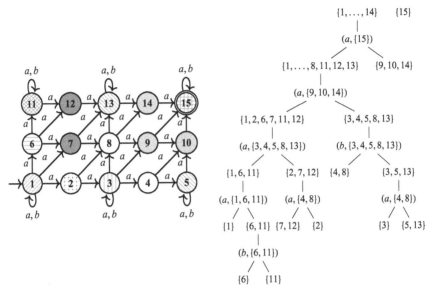

Figure 2.8
An NFA A and a run of CSR(A).

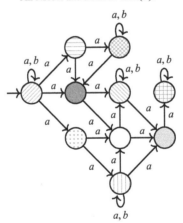

Figure 2.9
The quotient of the NFA of Figure 2.8.

In this example, we have $CSR \neq P_\ell$. For instance, states 3 and 5 recognize the same language, that is, $(a + b)^* aa(a + b)^*$, but they belong to different blocks of CSR. The quotient automaton is shown in figure 2.9.

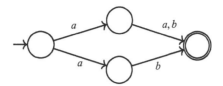

Figure 2.10
An NFA A such that A/P_ℓ is not minimal.

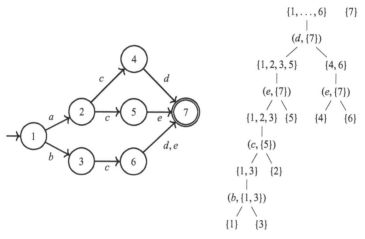

Figure 2.11
An NFA such that $CSR \neq P_\ell$.

Remark 2.29 If A is an NFA, then A/P_ℓ might not be a minimal NFA for L. The NFA of figure 2.10 is an example: all states accept different languages, and so $A/P_\ell = A$, but the NFA is not minimal, since, for instance, the state at the bottom can be removed without changing the language.

It is not difficult to show that if two states q_1 and q_2 belong to the same block of CSR, then they not only recognize the same language but also satisfy the following far stronger property: for every $a \in \Sigma$ and $q_1' \in \delta(q_1, a)$, there exists $q_2' \in \delta(q_2, a)$ such that $\mathcal{L}(q_1') = \mathcal{L}(q_2')$. This can be used to show that two states belong to different blocks of CSR. For instance, consider states 2 and 3 of the NFA on the left of figure 2.11. They recognize the same language, but state 2 has a c-successor—namely, state 4—that recognizes $\{d\}$, while state 3 has no such successor. So, states 2 and 3 belong to different blocks of CSR. A possible run of the CSR algorithm is shown on the right of the figure. Here, CSR has as many blocks as states.

2.3.2 ★ Minimality Is PSPACE-Complete

We show that NFA minimality is PSPACE-complete and hence computationally hard. Readers not familiar with complexity theory can directly move to the next section.

In chapter 3, we will show that the *universality problem* for NFAs is PSPACE-complete: given an NFA A over an alphabet Σ, decide whether $\mathcal{L}(A) = \Sigma^*$. Using this result, we can easily prove that deciding the existence of a small NFA equivalent to a given one is PSPACE-complete.

Theorem 2.30 *The following problem is PSPACE-complete: given an NFA A and $k \geq 1$, decide if there exists an NFA equivalent to A with at most k states.*

Proof To prove membership in PSPACE, observe first that if A has at most k states, then we can answer "yes." So, assume that A has more than k states. Since PSPACE = co-PSPACE, it suffices to give a procedure to decide if no NFA with at most k states is equivalent to A. For this, we construct all NFAs with at most k states (over the same alphabet as A), reusing the same space for each of them, and check that none of them is equivalent to A. Since NPSPACE = PSPACE, it suffices to exhibit a nondeterministic algorithm that, given an NFA B with at most k states, checks that B is not equivalent to A (and runs in polynomial space). The algorithm nondeterministically guesses a word, one letter at a time, while maintaining the sets of states in both A and B reached from the initial states by the word guessed so far. The algorithm stops when it observes that the current word is accepted by exactly one of A and B.

PSPACE-hardness is easily proved by a reduction from the universality problem. If an NFA is universal, then it is equivalent to an NFA with one state, and so, to decide if a given NFA A is universal, we can proceed as follows: check first if A accepts all words of length 1. If not, then A is not universal. Otherwise, check if some NFA with one state is equivalent to A. If not, then A is not universal. Otherwise, if such an NFA, say B, exists, then, since A accepts all words of length 1, B is the NFA with one final state and a loop for each alphabet letter. Therefore, A is universal. □

2.4 A Characterization of Regular Languages

In this last section, we present a useful by-product of the results of section 2.1.

Theorem 2.31 *A language L is regular iff it has finitely many residuals.*

Proof If L is not regular, then no DFA recognizes it. Since, by proposition 2.11, the canonical automaton C_L recognizes L, then C_L necessarily has infinitely many states, and so L has infinitely many residuals. If L is regular, then some DFA A recognizes it. By lemma 2.6, the number of states of A is greater than or equal to the number of residuals of L, and so L has finitely many residuals. □

This theorem provides a technique for proving that a given language $L \subseteq \Sigma^*$ is not regular: exhibit an infinite set of words $W \subseteq \Sigma^*$ such that $L^w \neq L^v$ for every distinct words $w, v \in W$. In example 2.4, we showed using this technique that the languages $\{a^n b^n : n \geq 0\}$ and $\{ww : w \in \Sigma^*\}$ have infinitely many residuals, and so they are not regular. We provide a third example.

Example 2.32 Let $L = \{a^{n^2} : n \geq 0\}$. Let $W = L$. For every two distinct words $a^{i^2}, a^{j^2} \in W$, word a^{2i+1} belongs to the a^{i^2}-residual of L, because $a^{i^2+2i+1} = a^{(i+1)^2}$, but not to the a^{j^2}-residual, since a^{j^2+2i+1} is only a square number for $i = j$.

2.5 Exercises

☆ ▣ **Exercise 36.** For each language $L \subseteq \{a, b, c\}^*$ below, say whether L has finitely many residuals, and, if so, describe the residuals.

(a) $(ab + ba)^*$,

(b) $(aa)^*$,

(c) $\{a^n b^n c^n : n \geq 0\}$.

☆ ▣ **Exercise 37.** Consider the most-significant-bit-first (MSBF) encoding of natural numbers over alphabet $\Sigma = \{0, 1\}$. Recall that every number has infinitely many encodings, because all the words of 0^*w encode the same number as w. Construct the minimal DFAs accepting the following languages, where Σ^4 denotes all words of length 4:

(a) $\{w : \text{MSBF}^{-1}(w) \bmod 3 = 0\} \cap \Sigma^4$.

(b) $\{w : \text{MSBF}^{-1}(w) \text{ is a prime}\} \cap \Sigma^4$.

☆ ■ **Exercise 38.** Prove or disprove the following statements:

(a) A subset of a regular language is regular.

(b) A superset of a regular language is regular.

(c) If L_1 and $L_1 L_2$ are regular languages, then L_2 is regular.

(d) If L_2 and $L_1 L_2$ are regular languages, then L_1 is regular.

☆ ⚙ **Exercise 39.** Consider the following DFA A:

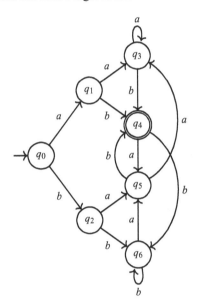

(a) Compute the language partition of A.

(b) Construct the quotient of A with respect to its language partition.

(c) Give a regular expression for $\mathcal{L}(A)$.

☆ ⚙ **Exercise 40.** Consider the following DFA A:

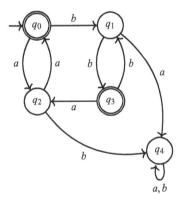

(a) Compute the language partition of A.

(b) Construct the quotient of A with respect to its language partition.

(c) Give a regular expression for $\mathcal{L}(A)$.

★ 📇 **Exercise 41.** Consider the language partition algorithm *LanPar*. Since every execution of its while loop increases the number of blocks by 1, the loop can be executed at most $|Q| - 1$ times. Show that this bound is tight, that is, give a family of DFAs for which the loop is executed $|Q| - 1$ times.

Hint: There exists a family with a one-letter alphabet.

☆ ⚙ **Exercise 42.** For each of the two following NFAs:

(a) Compute the coarsest stable refinement (CSR).

(b) Construct the quotient with respect to the CSR.

(c) Say whether the obtained automaton is minimal.

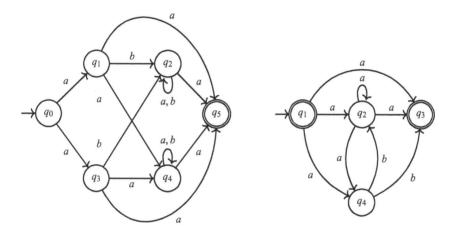

★ ■ **Exercise 43.** Let A_1 and A_2 be DFAs with n_1 and n_2 states such that $\mathcal{L}(A_1) \neq \mathcal{L}(A_2)$. Show that there exists a word w of length at most $n_1 + n_2 - 2$ such that $w \in (\mathcal{L}(A_1) \setminus \mathcal{L}(A_2)) \cup (\mathcal{L}(A_2) \setminus \mathcal{L}(A_1))$.

Hint: Consider the NFA obtained by putting A_1 and A_2 "side by side" and CSR(A).

★ 📇 **Exercise 44.** Let $\Sigma = \{a, b\}$. Let A_k be the minimal DFA such that $\mathcal{L}(A_k) = \{ww : w \in \Sigma^k\}$.

(a) Construct A_2.

(b) Construct a DFA that accepts $\mathcal{L}(A_k)$.

(c) How many states does A_k contain for $k > 2$?

★ ■ **Exercise 45.** For every language $L \subseteq \Sigma^*$ and word $w \in \Sigma^*$, let $^wL = \{u \in \Sigma^* : uw \in L\}$. A language $L' \subseteq \Sigma^*$ is an *inverse residual* of L if $L' = {}^wL$ for some $w \in \Sigma^*$.

(a) Determine the inverse residuals of the first two languages of exercise 36: $(ab + ba)^*$ and $(aa)^*$.

(b) Show that a language is regular iff it has finitely many inverse residuals.

(c) Does a language always have as many residuals as inverse residuals?

★ ✔ **Exercise 46.** Design an efficient algorithm $Res(r, a)$, where r is a regular expression over an alphabet Σ and $a \in \Sigma$, which returns a regular expression satisfying $\mathcal{L}(Res(r, a)) = \mathcal{L}(r)^a$.

☆ ■ **Exercise 47.** A DFA $A = (Q, \Sigma, \delta, q_0, F)$ is said *reversible* if no letter can enter a nontrap state from two distinct states, that is, for every $p, q \in Q$ and $\sigma \in \Sigma$, if $\delta(p, \sigma) = \delta(q, \sigma)$, then $p = q$.

(a) Give a reversible DFA that accepts $L = \{ab, ba, bb\}$.

(b) Show that the minimal DFA that accepts L is not reversible.

(c) Is there a unique minimal reversible DFA that accepts L? Justify.

★ ☞ **Exercise 48.** A DFA with *negative transitions* (DFA-n) is a DFA whose transitions are partitioned into *positive* and *negative* transitions. A run of a DFA-n is accepting if

- it ends in a final state *and* the number of occurrences of negative transitions is even, *or*
- it ends in a nonfinal state *and* the number of occurrences of negative transitions is odd.

The intuition is that taking a negative transition "inverts the polarity" of the acceptance condition.

(a) Show that the language accepted by a DFA-n is regular.

(b) Give a DFA-n for a regular language L that has fewer states than the minimal DFA for L.

(c) Show that the minimal DFA-n for a language is not necessarily unique.

★ ■ **Exercise 49.** We say that a residual of a regular language L is *composite* if it is the union of other residuals of L and that it is *prime* otherwise. Show that every regular language L is recognized by an NFA whose number of states is equal to the number of prime residuals of L.

☆ ■ **Exercise 50.** Let $L_{u,v}$ be the language of words over $\{0, 1\}$ that contain the same number of occurrences of u and v. Say whether $L_{u,v}$ is regular for the following choices of u and v.

(a) $u = 0$ and $v = 1$.

(b) $u = 01$ and $v = 10$.

(c) $u = 00$ and $v = 11$.

(d) $u = 001$ and $v = 110$.

(e) $u = 001$ and $v = 100$.

☆ 🔳 **Exercise 51.** Consider the alphabet $\Sigma = \{up, down, left, right\}$. A word over Σ corresponds to a line in a grid consisting of concatenated segments drawn in the direction specified by the letters. In the same way, a language corresponds to a set of lines. For example, the set of all *staircases* can be specified as the set of lines given by the regular language $(up\ right)^*$.

(a) Specify the set of all *skylines* as a regular language (i.e., formalize the intuitive notion of skyline). The left drawing is a skyline, while the two others are not.

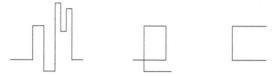

(b) Show that the set of all *rectangles* is not regular.

☆ 🔳 **Exercise 52.** An NFA $A = (Q, \Sigma, \delta, Q_0, F)$ is *reverse-deterministic* if $(q_1, a, q) \in \delta$ and $(q_2, a, q) \in \delta$ implies $q_1 = q_2$, that is, no state has two input transitions labeled by the same letter. Furthermore, we say that A is *trimmed* if every state accepts at least one word, that is, if $L_A(q) \neq \emptyset$ for every $q \in Q$. Let A be a reverse-deterministic trimmed NFA with a single final state q_f. Show that $NFAtoDFA(A)$ is minimal.

Hint: States of NFAtoDFA(A) accept different languages; use corollary 2.13.

☆ 🔳 **Exercise 53.** Let $Rev(A)$ be the algorithm of exercise 14 that, given an NFA A as input, returns a trimmed NFA A^R such that $\mathcal{L}(A^R) = \mathcal{L}(A)^R$, where L^R denotes the reverse of L. Recall that an NFA is trimmed if every state accepts at least one word (see exercise 52). Prove that, for every NFA A, the following DFA is the unique minimal DFA that accepts $\mathcal{L}(A)$:

$$NFAtoDFA(Rev(NFAtoDFA(Rev(A)))).$$

☆ 🔳 **Exercise 54.**

(a) Let $\Sigma = \{a, b\}$. Find a language $L \subseteq \Sigma^*$ that has infinitely many residuals and that satisfies $|L^w| > 0$ for all $w \in \Sigma^*$.

(b) Let $\Sigma = \{a\}$. Find a language $L \subseteq \Sigma^*$, such that $L^w = L^{w'} \implies w = w'$ for all words $w, w' \in \Sigma^*$.

☆ 🔳 **Exercise 55.** Recall the master automaton M defined in section 2.1.1. Does M have

(a) other states than $\emptyset$ and Σ^* that can only reach themselves?

(b) states that cannot be reached from any other state?

(c) states that can reach all other states?

(d) states with infinitely many immediate predecessors?
(i.e., states L such that $L' \xrightarrow{a} L$ for infinitely many states L'?)

(e) two states having the same successor for every letter of Σ?

(f) bottom strongly connected components with infinitely many states?
(A bottom strongly connected component is a maximal set of states S such that for every state $s \in S$, the set of states reachable from S is exactly S.)

(g) bottom strongly connected components with arbitrarily many states?

★ ■ **Exercise 56.** Recall the master automaton M defined in section 2.1.1. A *symmetry* is a bijection f on the states of the master automaton such that $L \xrightarrow{a} L'$ iff $f(L) \xrightarrow{a} f(L')$. Loosely speaking, after applying f, we still obtain the same graph. Show that the bijection given by $f(L) = \overline{L}$ is a symmetry.

★ ■ **Exercise 57.** Recall that weakly acyclic DFAs were introduced in exercise 35. Show that weakly acyclic DFAs are closed under minimization, that is, prove that the unique minimal DFA equivalent to a given weakly acyclic DFA is also weakly acyclic.

3 Operations on Sets: Implementations

Recall that, in this book, we see automata as data structures over some universe of objects U. In this chapter, we explain how to implement important operations on such data structures.

As a motivating example, let us consider the case where U is the set of natural numbers. Let A be the automaton, over alphabet $\Sigma = \{0, 1\}$, depicted on the left of figure 3.1. The words read by A are seen as numbers encoded in binary with their most significant bit appearing first, for example, the word 1100 corresponds to number 12. Observe that A accepts infinitely many numbers. In particular, it accepts words $\{11, 111, 1111, \ldots\}$, which respectively correspond to numbers $\{3, 7, 15, \ldots\}$. Nonetheless, automaton A does not accept all numbers. For example, it rejects word 100, which corresponds to number 4.

Suppose we ask ourselves whether *all* multiples of 3 are accepted by A. For example, we see that numbers 0, 3, 6, 9, and 12 are accepted by A, as they are respectively represented by words ε, 11, 110, 1001, and 1100 (with possibly leading zeros). Such a brute-force approach quickly gets tedious when carried manually. Further, it is not clear how many numbers must be checked (even if done with a computer). In fact, if A accepts all multiples of 3, then there are infinitely many numbers to check! Thus, we need a better approach.

Let B be the automaton depicted on the right of figure 3.1. This automaton accepts the set of all multiples of 3 (see example 1.10 if you want to know why). Hence, our question can be rephrased as does $\mathcal{L}(B) \subseteq \mathcal{L}(B)$ hold?" or "does $\mathcal{L}(A) \cap \mathcal{L}(B) = \mathcal{L}(B)$?. So, in order to answer our question, it suffices to implement inclusion, or both intersection and equality.

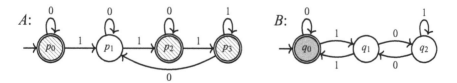

Figure 3.1
Two automata representing sets of numbers, represented in binary with their most significant bit first.

As we shall see in section 3.1.6, A does not accept all multiples of 3. Moreover, a counter-example can be obtained *automatically*, that is, an algorithm can produce a word from B that is not accepted by A.

Such algorithms have important applications. For example, in chapter 7 we will use automata to represent the behavior of concurrent programs. In that setting, counterexamples are bugs, and it is certainly desirable to detect bugs automatically.

In the remainder of this chapter, we provide implementations of inclusion, intersection, and other operations. More precisely, we show that automata as a data structure support the following operations, where U is the universe of objects, $X, Y \subseteq U$ and $x \in U$:

Operation	Returns
Member(x, X)	**true** if $x \in X$, **false** otherwise
Complement(X)	$U \setminus X$
Intersection(X, Y)	$X \cap Y$
Union(X, Y)	$X \cup Y$
Empty(X)	**true** if $X = \emptyset$, **false** otherwise
Universal(X)	**true** if $X = U$, **false** otherwise
Included(X, Y)	**true** if $X \subseteq Y$, **false** otherwise
Equal(X, Y)	**true** if $X = Y$, **false** otherwise

Let us fix an alphabet Σ. We assume that there exists a bijection between U and Σ^*—that is, we assume that each object of the universe is encoded by a word and that each word is the encoding of some object. Under this assumption, the operations on sets and elements become operations on languages and words, as in our motivating example. For instance, the first two operations become the following:

Operation	Returns
Member(w, L)	**true** if $w \in L$, **false** otherwise
Complement(L)	$\overline{L}$

The assumption that each word encodes some object may seem too strong. Indeed, the language E of encodings is usually only a subset of Σ^*. For example, not every word over the alphabet $\{0, \ldots, 9, ., -\}$ encodes a decimal number. However, once we have implemented the operations under this strong assumption, we can easily modify them so that they work under a much weaker assumption that almost always holds: the assumption that the language E of encodings is regular. For instance, assume that E is a regular subset of Σ^* and that L is the language of encodings of a set X. We implement **Complement**(X) so that it returns not $\overline{L}$ but rather **Intersection**$(\overline{L}, E)$.

For each operation, we present an implementation that, given automata representations of the operands, returns an automaton representing the result (or a boolean value, when that is the return type). Sections 3.1 and 3.2 respectively consider the cases in which the representation is a DFA and an NFA.

3.1 Implementation on DFAs

In order to evaluate the complexity of the operations, we must first provide our assumptions on the complexity of basic operations on a DFA $A = (Q, \Sigma, \delta, q_0, F)$. We assume that dictionary operations (lookup, add, remove) on Q and δ can be performed in constant time using hashing. We further assume that, given a state q, we can decide in constant time if $q = q_0$, and if $q \in F$, and that given a state q and a letter $a \in \Sigma$, we can find the unique state $\delta(q, a)$ in constant time.

3.1.1 Membership

To check membership for a word w, we just execute the run of the DFA on w. It is convenient for future use to have an algorithm $MemDFA[A](w, q)$ that checks whether word w is accepted from state q in A, that is, whether $w \in \mathcal{L}_A(q)$. Operation **Member**(w, L) can then be implemented by $MemDFA[A](w, q_0)$, where A is the automaton representing L. Writing $head(aw) = a$ and $tail(aw) = w$ for $a \in \Sigma$ and $w \in \Sigma^*$, the procedure is described in algorithm 7.

Algorithm 7 Membership for DFAs.

$MemDFA[A](w, q)$
Input: DFA $A = (Q, \Sigma, \delta, q_0, F)$, state $q \in Q$, word $w \in \Sigma^*$
Output: true if $w \in \mathcal{L}(q)$, **false** otherwise

1   **if** $w = \varepsilon$ **then return** $q \in F$
2   **else return** $MemDFA[A](tail(w), \delta(q, head(w)))$

The complexity of the algorithm is $\mathcal{O}(|w|)$.

3.1.2 Complementation

Implementing the complement operations on DFAs is easy. Recall that a DFA has exactly one run for each word, and the run is accepting iff it reaches a final state. Thus, if we swap final and nonfinal states, the run on a word becomes accepting iff it was nonaccepting, and so the new DFA accepts the word iff the old one did not accept it. So, we get the linear-time procedure $CompDFA$ described in algorithm 8.

Observe that complementation of DFAs preserves minimality. By construction, each state of $CompDFA(A)$ recognizes the complement of the language recognized by the same state in A. Thus, if the states of A recognize pairwise different languages, so do the states of

---

Algorithm 8 DFA complementation.

CompDFA(A)
Input: DFA $A = (Q, \Sigma, \delta, q_0, F)$
Output: DFA $B = (Q', \Sigma, \delta', q'_0, F')$ with $\mathcal{L}(B) = \overline{\mathcal{L}(A)}$

1   $Q' \leftarrow Q; \delta' \leftarrow \delta; q'_0 \leftarrow q_0; F' = \emptyset$
2   **for all** $q \in Q$ **do**
3   **if** $q \notin F$ **then add** q **to** F'

CompDFA(A). Apply now corollary 2.13, stating that a DFA is minimal iff their states recognize different languages.

3.1.3 Binary Boolean Operations

Instead of specific implementations for union and intersection, we give a generic implementation for all binary boolean operations. Given two DFAs A_1 and A_2 and a binary boolean operation like union, intersection, or difference, the implementation returns a DFA recognizing the result of applying the operation to $\mathcal{L}(A_1)$ and $\mathcal{L}(A_2)$. The DFAs for different boolean operations always have the same states and transitions; they differ only in the set of final states. We call this DFA with a yet unspecified set of final states the *pairing* of A_1 and A_2, denoted by $[A_1, A_2]$. Formally:

Definition 3.1 *Let* $A_1 = (Q_1, \Sigma, \delta_1, q_{01}, F_1)$ *and* $A_2 = (Q_2, \Sigma, \delta_2, q_{02}, F_2)$ *be DFAs. The pairing* $[A_1, A_2]$ *of* A_1 *and* A_2 *is the tuple* (Q, Σ, δ, q_0) *where*

- $Q = \{[q_1, q_2] : q_1 \in Q_1, q_2 \in Q_2\}$,
- $\delta = \{([q_1, q_2], a, [q'_1, q'_2]) : (q_1, a, q'_1) \in \delta_1, (q_2, a, q'_2) \in \delta_2\}$,
- $q_0 = [q_{01}, q_{02}]$.

The run of $[A_1, A_2]$ *on a word of* Σ^* *is defined as for DFAs.*

It follows immediately from this definition that the run of $[A_1, A_2]$ over a word $w = a_1 a_2 \cdots a_n$ is also a "pairing" of the runs of A_1 and A_2 over w. Formally,

$$q_{01} \xrightarrow{a_1} q_{11} \xrightarrow{a_2} \cdots \xrightarrow{a_n} q_{n1}$$

$$q_{02} \xrightarrow{a_1} q_{12} \xrightarrow{a_2} \cdots \xrightarrow{a_n} q_{n2}$$

are the runs of A_1 and A_2 on w if and only if

$$\begin{bmatrix} q_{01} \\ q_{02} \end{bmatrix} \xrightarrow{a_1} \begin{bmatrix} q_{11} \\ q_{12} \end{bmatrix} \xrightarrow{a_2} \cdots \xrightarrow{a_n} \begin{bmatrix} q_{n1} \\ q_{n2} \end{bmatrix}$$

is the run of $[A_1, A_2]$ on w.

DFAs for different boolean operations are obtained by adding an adequate set of final states to $[A_1, A_2]$. For intersection, $[A_1, A_2]$ must accept w iff A_1 accepts w *and* A_2 accepts w. This is achieved by declaring a state $[q_1, q_2]$ final iff $q_1 \in F_1$ *and* $q_2 \in F_2$. For union, we replace *and* by *or*. For difference, $[A_1, A_2]$ must accept w iff A_1 accepts w *and* A_2 does *not* accept w, and so we declare $[q_1, q_2]$ final iff $q_1 \in F_1$ *and not* $q_2 \in F_2$.

Example 3.2   The top of figure 3.2 depicts two DFAs over alphabet $\Sigma = \{a\}$. They recognize the words whose length is a multiple of 2 and 3, respectively. We denote these languages by *Mult*(2) and *Mult*(3). The remainder of the figure illustrates the pairing of the two DFAs (for clarity, the states carry labels x, y instead of $[x, y]$) and three DFAs recognizing *Mult*(2) $\cap$ *Mult*(3), *Mult*(2) $\cup$ *Mult*(3), and *Mult*(2) \ *Mult*(3), respectively.

Example 3.3   The tour of conversions of chapter 1 started with a DFA for the language of all words over $\{a, b\}$ containing an even number of as and an even number of bs. This language is the intersection of the language of all words containing an even number of as, and the language of all words containing an even number of bs. Figure 3.3 shows DFAs for these two languages and the DFA for their intersection.

We can now formulate a generic algorithm that, given two DFAs recognizing languages L_1, L_2 and a binary boolean operation, returns a DFA recognizing the result of "applying"

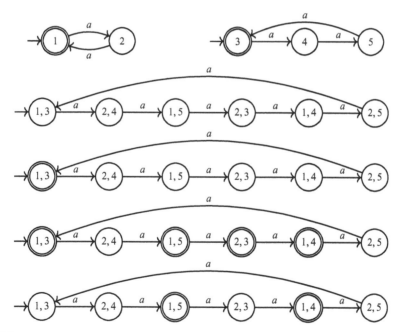

Figure 3.2
Two DFAs, their pairing, and DFAs for the intersection, union, and difference of their languages.

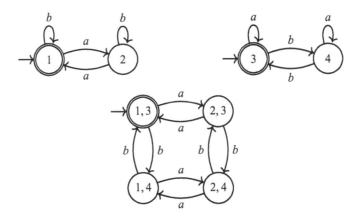

Figure 3.3
Two DFAs and a DFA for their intersection.

the boolean operation to L_1, L_2. First, let us formally define what this means. Given an alphabet Σ and a binary boolean operator $\odot\colon \{\textbf{true}, \textbf{false}\} \times \{\textbf{true}, \textbf{false}\} \to \{\textbf{true}, \textbf{false}\}$, we lift $\odot$ to a function $\widehat{\odot}\colon 2^{\Sigma^*} \times 2^{\Sigma^*} \to 2^{\Sigma^*}$ on languages as follows:

$$L_1 \widehat{\odot} L_2 = \{w \in \Sigma^* : (w \in L_1) \odot (w \in L_2)\}.$$

Algorithm 9 Boolean combination of two DFAs.

$BinOp[\odot](A_1, A_2)$
Input: DFAs $A_1 = (Q_1, \Sigma, \delta_1, q_{01}, F_1)$, $A_2 = (Q_2, \Sigma, \delta_2, q_{02}, F_2)$
Output: DFA $A = (Q, \Sigma, \delta, q_0, F)$ with $\mathcal{L}(A) = \mathcal{L}(A_1) \widehat{\odot} \mathcal{L}(A_2)$

1   $Q, \delta, F \leftarrow \emptyset$
2   $q_0 \leftarrow [q_{01}, q_{02}]$
3   $W \leftarrow \{q_0\}$
4   **while** $W \neq \emptyset$ **do**
5   **pick** $[q_1, q_2]$ **from** W
6   **add** $[q_1, q_2]$ **to** Q
7   **if** $(q_1 \in F_1) \odot (q_2 \in F_2)$ **then add** $[q_1, q_2]$ **to** F
8   **for all** $a \in \Sigma$ **do**
9           $q_1' \leftarrow \delta_1(q_1, a); q_2' \leftarrow \delta_2(q_2, a)$
10   **if** $[q_1', q_2'] \notin Q$ **then add** $[q_1', q_2']$ **to** W
11   **add** $([q_1, q_2], a, [q_1', q_2'])$ **to** δ

That is, to decide whether w belongs to $L_1 \widehat{\odot} L_2$, we evaluate $(w \in L_1)$ and $(w \in L_2)$ to **true** or **false** and then apply $\widehat{\odot}$ to the results. For instance, $L_1 \cap L_2 = L_1 \widehat{\wedge} L_2$. The generic algorithm, parameterized by $\odot$, is described in algorithm 9.

Popular choices of boolean language operations are summarized in the left column of the following table, while the right column shows the corresponding boolean operation needed to instantiate $BinOp[\odot]$.

Language operation	$b_1 \odot b_2$
Union	$b_1 \vee b_2$
Intersection	$b_1 \wedge b_2$
Set difference ($L_1 \setminus L_2$)	$b_1 \wedge \neg b_2$
Symmetric difference ($L_1 \setminus L_2 \cup L_2 \setminus L_1$)	$b_1 \leftrightarrow \neg b_2$

The output of $BinOp$ is a DFA with $\mathcal{O}(|Q_1| \cdot |Q_2|)$ states, regardless of the boolean operation being implemented. To show that the bound is reachable, let $\Sigma = \{a\}$, and, for every $n \geq 1$, let $Mult(n)$ denote the language of words whose length is a multiple of n. As in figure 3.3, the minimal DFA recognizing $Mult(n)$ is a cycle of n states, with the initial state being also the only final state. For any two relatively prime numbers n_1 and n_2 (i.e., two numbers without a common divisor), we have $Mult(n_1) \cap Mult(n_2) = Mult(n_1 \cdot n_2)$. Therefore, any DFA for $Mult(n_1 \cdot n_2)$ has at least $n_1 \cdot n_2$ states. In fact, if we denote the minimal DFA for $Mult(k)$ by A_k, then $BinOp[\wedge](A_{n_1}, A_{n_2}) = A_{n_1 \cdot n_2}$.

Note, however, that in general, minimality is *not* preserved: the product of two minimal DFAs may not be minimal. In particular, given any regular language L, the minimal DFA for $L \cap \overline{L}$ has one state, but the result of the product construction is a DFA with the same number of states as the minimal DFA for L.

3.1.4 Emptiness

A DFA recognizes the empty language iff it has no final states (recall our normal form, where all states must be reachable). This leads to algorithm 10.

Algorithm 10 DFA emptiness check.

Empty(A)
Input: DFA $A = (Q, \Sigma, \delta, q_0, F)$
Output: true if $\mathcal{L}(A) = \emptyset$, **false** otherwise

1   **return** $F = \emptyset$

The runtime depends on the implementation. If we keep a boolean indicating whether the DFA has some final state, then the complexity is $\mathcal{O}(1)$. If checking $F = \emptyset$ requires a linear scan over Q, then the complexity is $\mathcal{O}(|Q|)$.

3.1.5   Universality

A DFA in normal form recognizes Σ^* iff all its states are final. This leads to algorithm 11, which again has complexity $\mathcal{O}(1)$ or $\mathcal{O}(|Q|)$, depending on the implementation.

Algorithm 11   DFA universality check.

UnivDFA(A)
Input: DFA $A = (Q, \Sigma, \delta, q_0, F)$
Output: true if $\mathcal{L}(A) = \Sigma^*$, **false** otherwise

1   **return** $F = Q$

3.1.6   Inclusion

The following lemma characterizes the inclusion of regular languages.

Lemma 3.4   *Let $A_1 = (Q_1, \Sigma, \delta_1, Q_{01}, F_1)$ and $A_2 = (Q_2, \Sigma, \delta_2, Q_{02}, F_2)$ be DFAs. It is the case that $\mathcal{L}(A_1) \subseteq \mathcal{L}(A_2)$ iff every state $[q_1, q_2]$ of the pairing $[A_1, A_2]$ satisfying $q_1 \in F_1$ also satisfies $q_2 \in F_2$.*

Proof   Let $L_1 = \mathcal{L}(A_1)$ and $L_2 = \mathcal{L}(A_2)$. We have

$$L_1 \not\subseteq L_2 \iff L_1 \setminus L_2 \neq \emptyset$$

$$\iff \text{at least one state } [q_1, q_2] \text{ of the DFA for } L_1 \setminus L_2 \text{ is final}$$

$$\iff \text{there exist } q_1 \in Q_1, q_2 \in Q_2 \text{ s.t. } q_1 \in F_1 \text{ and } q_2 \notin F_2. \qquad \square$$

The condition of the lemma can be checked by slightly modifying *BinOp*. The resulting algorithm checks inclusion on the fly, as described in algorithm 12.

Recall the example from the beginning of the chapter. We were interested in determining whether all multiples of 3 are accepted by automaton A of figure 3.1. Let us show that this is not the case by algorithmically testing whether $\mathcal{L}(B) \subseteq \mathcal{L}(A)$. We execute *InclDFA(B, A)*. The algorithm internally constructs a fragment of the automaton C depicted in figure 3.4. Note that the state $[q_0, p_1]$ of C is such that q_0 is final in B and p_1 is nonfinal in A. Therefore, the algorithm returns **false**, which means that A does not accept all multiples of 3. A counterexample can be obtained from C by taking any word w that leads to $[q_0, p_1]$. For example, $w = 11110$ corresponds to number 30, which is rejected by A. In fact, this is the shortest counterexample since A accepts 0, 3, 6, 9, 12, 15, 18, 21, 24, 27 (and more multiples of 3 such as 33, 36, and 39 but not 42).

Algorithm 12 DFA inclusion check.

$InclDFA(A_1, A_2)$
Input: DFAs $A_1 = (Q_1, \Sigma, \delta_1, q_{01}, F_1)$, $A_2 = (Q_2, \Sigma, \delta_2, q_{02}, F_2)$
Output: true if $\mathcal{L}(A_1) \subseteq \mathcal{L}(A_2)$, **false** otherwise

```
1   Q ← ∅; W ← {[q01, q02]}
2   while W ≠ ∅ do
3       pick [q1, q2] from W
4       add [q1, q2] to Q
5       if (q1 ∈ F1) and (q2 ∉ F2) then return false
6       for all a ∈ Σ do
7           q1′ ← δ1(q1, a); q2′ ← δ2(q2, a)
8           if [q1′, q2′] ∉ Q then add [q1′, q2′] to W
9   return true
```

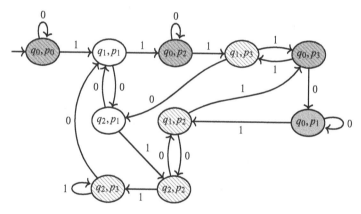

Figure 3.4
Underlying automaton of $IncDFA(B, A)$, where colors and patterns correspond to those of the final states of figure 3.1.

3.1.7 Equality

For equality, just observe that $\mathcal{L}(A_1) = \mathcal{L}(A_2)$ holds iff the symmetric difference of $\mathcal{L}(A_1)$ and $\mathcal{L}(A_2)$ is empty. The algorithm is obtained by replacing line 6 of $IncDFA(A_1, A_2)$ by

> **if** $((q_1 \in F_1)$ **and** $q_2 \notin F_2))$ **or** $((q_1 \notin F_1)$ **and** $(q_2 \in F_2))$, **then return false**.

Let us call this algorithm $EqDFA$. An alternative procedure consists of minimizing A_1 and A_2 and checking whether the results are isomorphic DFAs. In fact, the isomorphism check is not even necessary: one can just apply algorithm CSR (Algorithm 6 of chapter 2) to the NFA $A_1 \cup A_2 := (Q_1 \cup Q_2, \Sigma, \delta_1 \cup \delta_2, \{q_{01}, q_{02}\}, F_1 \cup F_2)$. It is easy to see that, in this particular case, CSR still computes the language partition, and so we have $\mathcal{L}(A_1) = \mathcal{L}(A_2)$ iff after termination, the initial states of A_1 and A_2 belong to the same block.

If Hopcroft's algorithm is used for computing CSR, then the equality check can be performed in time $\mathcal{O}(n \log n)$, where n is the sum of the number of states of A_1 and A_2. This complexity is lower than that of *EqDFA*. However, *EqDFA* has two important advantages:

- It works on-the-fly. That is, $\mathcal{L}(A_1) = \mathcal{L}(A_2)$ can be tested while constructing A_1 and A_2. This allows to stop early if a difference in the languages is detected. On the contrary, minimization algorithms cannot minimize a DFA while constructing it. All states and transitions must be known before the algorithm can start.

- It is easy to modify *EqDFA* so that it returns a witness whenever $\mathcal{L}(A_1) \neq \mathcal{L}(A_2)$, that is, a word in the symmetric difference of $\mathcal{L}(A_1)$ and $\mathcal{L}(A_2)$. This is more difficult to achieve with the minimization algorithm. Moreover, to the best of our knowledge, it cancels the complexity advantage. This may seem surprising, since, as shown in exercise 43, the shortest word in the symmetric difference of $\mathcal{L}(A_1)$ and $\mathcal{L}(A_2)$ has length $n_1 + n_2 - 2$, where n_1 and n_2 are the numbers of states of A_1 and A_2, respectively. However, this word is computed by tracking for each pair of states the shortest word in the symmetric difference of their languages. Since there are $\mathcal{O}(n_1 \cdot n_2)$ pairs, this takes time $\mathcal{O}(n_1 \cdot n_2)$. There could be a more efficient way to compute the witness, but we do not know any.

3.2   Implementation on NFAs

For NFAs, we make the same assumptions on the complexity of basic operations as for DFAs. For DFAs, however, we had the assumption that, given a state q and a letter $a \in \Sigma$, we can find in constant time the unique state $\delta(q, a)$. This assumption no longer makes sense for NFA, since $\delta(q, a)$ is a set.

3.2.1   Membership

Membership testing is slightly more involved for NFAs than for DFAs. An NFA may have many runs on the same word, and examining all of them one after the other in order to see if at least one is accepting is a bad idea: the number of runs may be exponential in the length of the word. The algorithm described in algorithm 13 does better. For each prefix of the word, it computes the *set of states* in which the automaton may be after having read the prefix.

Example 3.5   Consider the NFA depicted on the left of figure 3.5. Let $w = aaabba$. The successive values of W—that is, the sets of states A can reach after reading the prefixes of w—are shown on the right of the figure. Since the final set contains final states, the algorithm returns **true**.

Algorithm 13 Membership for NFAs.

MemNFA[A](w)
Input: NFA $A = (Q, \Sigma, \delta, Q_0, F)$, word $w \in \Sigma^*$
Output: true if $w \in \mathcal{L}(A)$, **false** otherwise

```
1   W ← Q_0
2   while w ≠ ε do
3       U ← ∅
4       for all q ∈ W do
5           add δ(q, head(w)) to U
6       W ← U
7       w ← tail(w)
8   return (W ∩ F ≠ ∅)
```

For the complexity, observe first that the **while** loop is executed $|w|$ times. The **for** loop is executed at most $|Q|$ times. Each execution takes at most time $\mathcal{O}(|Q|)$, because $\delta(q, head(w))$ contains at most $|Q|$ states. So the overall running time is $\mathcal{O}(|w| \cdot |Q|^2)$.

3.2.2 Complementation

Recall that an NFA A may have multiple runs on a word w. Moreover, it accepts w if *at least one* is accepting. In particular, an NFA can accept w because of an accepting run ρ_1 but have another nonaccepting run ρ_2 on w. It follows that the complement operation for DFAs cannot be extended to NFAs: after exchanging final and nonfinal states, the run ρ_1 becomes

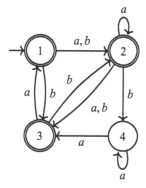

Prefix read	W
ε	$\{1\}$
a	$\{2\}$
aa	$\{2, 3\}$
aaa	$\{1, 2, 3\}$
$aaab$	$\{2, 3, 4\}$
$aaabb$	$\{2, 3, 4\}$
$aaabba$	$\{1, 2, 3, 4\}$

Figure 3.5
An NFA A and the run of *MemNFA[A](aaabba)*.

nonaccepting, but p_2 becomes accepting. So, the resulting NFA still accepts w (because p_2 accepts), and so it does not recognize the complement of $\mathcal{L}(A)$.

For this reason, complementation for NFAs is carried out by converting to a DFA and complementing the result, as described in algorithm 14.

Algorithm 14 NFA complementation.

CompNFA(A)
Input: NFA A
Output: DFA $\overline{A}$ with $\mathcal{L}\left(\overline{A}\right) = \overline{\mathcal{L}(A)}$
  1 $\overline{A} \leftarrow CompDFA\left(NFAtoDFA(A)\right)$

Since determinizing an NFA may cause an exponential blowup in the number of states, the number of states of $\overline{A}$ is $\mathcal{O}(2^{|Q|})$.

3.2.3 Union and Intersection

Let us see that, on NFAs, it is no longer possible to uniformly implement all binary boolean operations. The pairing operation can be defined exactly as in definition 3.1. Observe that if for some letter a states q_1 and q_2 have n_1 and n_2 successors, then the state $[q_1, q_2]$ of the pairing has $n_1 \times n_2$ successors. The runs of a pairing $[A_1, A_2]$ of NFAs on a given word are defined as for DFAs. The difference with respect to the DFA case is that the pairing may have *multiple* runs or *no run at all* on a word. But we still have that

$$q_{01} \xrightarrow{a_1} q_{11} \xrightarrow{a_2} \cdots \xrightarrow{a_n} q_{n1}$$

$$q_{02} \xrightarrow{a_1} q_{12} \xrightarrow{a_2} \cdots \xrightarrow{a_n} q_{n2}$$

are runs of A_1 and A_2 on w if and only if

$$\begin{bmatrix} q_{01} \\ q_{02} \end{bmatrix} \xrightarrow{a_1} \begin{bmatrix} q_{11} \\ q_{12} \end{bmatrix} \xrightarrow{a_2} \cdots \xrightarrow{a_n} \begin{bmatrix} q_{n1} \\ q_{n2} \end{bmatrix}$$

is a run of $[A_1, A_2]$ on w.

Let us now discuss the cases of intersection, union, and set difference.

Intersection. Let $[q_1, q_2]$ be a final state of $[A_1, A_2]$ if q_1 is a final state of A_1 *and* q_2 is a final state of A_2. It is still the case that $[A_1, A_2]$ has an accepting run on w iff A_1 has an accepting run on w *and* A_2 has an accepting run on w. Thus, with this choice of final states, automaton $[A_1, A_2]$ recognizes $\mathcal{L}(A_1) \cap \mathcal{L}(A_2)$. So, we obtain algorithm 15.

Notice that we overload the symbol and denote the output by $A_1 \cap A_2$. Automaton $A_1 \cap A_2$ is often called the *product* of A_1 and A_2. It is readily seen that, as operation on NFAs, $\cap$ is

---

Algorithm 15 NFA intersection.

$IntersNFA(A_1, A_2)$
Input: NFA $A_1 = (Q_1, \Sigma, \delta_1, Q_{01}, F_1)$, $A_2 = (Q_2, \Sigma, \delta_2, Q_{02}, F_2)$
Output: NFA $A_1 \cap A_2 = (Q, \Sigma, \delta, Q_0, F)$ with $\mathcal{L}(A_1 \cap A_2) = \mathcal{L}(A_1) \cap \mathcal{L}(A_2)$

```
1    Q, δ, F ← ∅; Q₀ ← Q₀₁ × Q₀₂
2    W ← Q₀
3    while W ≠ ∅ do
4        pick [q₁, q₂] from W
5        add [q₁, q₂] to Q
6        if (q₁ ∈ F₁) and (q₂ ∈ F₂) then add [q₁, q₂] to F
7        for all a ∈ Σ do
8            for all q₁′ ∈ δ₁(q₁, a), q₂′ ∈ δ₂(q₂, a) do
9                if [q₁′, q₂′] ∉ Q then add [q₁′, q₂′] to W
10               add ([q₁, q₂], a, [q₁′, q₂′]) to δ
```

---

associative and commutative in the following sense:

$$\mathcal{L}((A_1 \cap A_2) \cap A_3) = \mathcal{L}(A_1) \cap \mathcal{L}(A_2) \cap \mathcal{L}(A_3) = \mathcal{L}(A_1 \cap (A_2 \cap A_3))$$

$$\mathcal{L}(A_1 \cap A_2) = \mathcal{L}(A_1) \cap \mathcal{L}(A_2) \qquad\qquad = \mathcal{L}(A_2 \cap A_1).$$

For the complexity, observe that in the worst case, the algorithm must examine all pairs $(q_1, a, q_1') \in \delta_1$, $(q_2, a, q_2') \in \delta_2$ of transitions, but every pair is examined at most once. So, the running time is $\mathcal{O}(|\delta_1||\delta_2|)$.

Example 3.6 Consider the two NFAs of figure 3.6 over alphabet $\{a, b\}$. The top one recognizes the words containing at least two non-overlapping occurrences of aa. The bottom one recognizes the words containing at least one occurrence of aa. The result of applying *IntersNFA* is the NFA of figure 2.8. Observe that the NFA has fifteen states (i.e., all pairs of states are reachable).

Note that in this example, the intersection of the two languages is equal to the language of the first NFA. So, there is an NFA with five states that recognizes the intersection, which means that the output of *IntersNFA* is far from optimal in this case. Even after applying the reduction algorithm for NFAs, we only obtain the ten-state automaton of figure 2.9.

Union. It could seem that the argumentation for intersection still holds if we replace *and* by *or*, and so that the algorithm obtained from *IntersNFA* by substituting **and** for **or** correctly computes an NFA for $\mathcal{L}(A_1) \cup \mathcal{L}(A_2)$. It could seem that the algorithm obtained by substituting **or** for **and** in line 6 of *IntersNFA* correctly computes an NFA for $\mathcal{L}(A_1) \cup \mathcal{L}(A_2)$. However, this is not true! Assume that A_1 accepts a word but A_2 has no run on it at all.

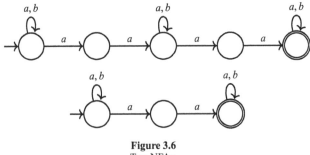

Figure 3.6
Two NFAs.

In this case, the pairing $[A_1, A_2]$ also has no run on the word, and so the NFA returned by the algorithm does not accept it. If both A_1 and A_2 have at least one run for each word, then the algorithm is indeed correct. However, there is a much simpler algorithm. It suffices to put A_1 and A_2 "side by side": take the union of its states, transitions, initial states, and final states (where we assume these to be disjoint). The resulting procedure is described in algorithm 16.

Algorithm 16 NFA union.

$UnionNFA(A_1, A_2)$
Input: NFA $A_1 = (Q_1, \Sigma, \delta_1, Q_{01}, F_1)$, $A_2 = (Q_2, \Sigma, \delta_2, Q_{02}, F_2)$
Output: NFA $A_1 \cup A_2 = (Q, \Sigma, \delta, Q_0, F)$ with $\mathcal{L}(A_1 \cup A_2) = \mathcal{L}(A_1) \cup \mathcal{L}(A_2)$

1 $Q \leftarrow Q_1 \cup Q_2$
2 $\delta \leftarrow \delta_1 \cup \delta_2$
3 $Q_0 \leftarrow Q_{01} \cup Q_{02}$
4 $F \leftarrow F_1 \cup F_2$

Set difference. The generalization of the procedure for DFAs fails. Let $[q_1, q_2]$ be a final state of $[A_1, A_2]$ if q_1 is a final state of A_1 and q_2 is not a final state of A_2. Then, $[A_1, A_2]$ has an accepting run on w if and only if A_1 has an accepting run on w and A_2 has a nonaccepting run on w. But "A_2 has a nonaccepting run on w" is not equivalent to "A_2 has no accepting run on w": this only holds in the DFA case. An algorithm producing an NFA $A_1 \setminus A_2$ recognizing $\mathcal{L}(A_1) \setminus \mathcal{L}(A_2)$ can be obtained from the algorithms for complement and intersection through the equality $\mathcal{L}(A_1) \setminus \mathcal{L}(A_2) = \mathcal{L}(A_1) \cap \overline{\mathcal{L}(A_2)}$.

3.2.4 Emptiness and Universality

Emptiness for NFAs is decided using the same algorithm as for DFAs: just check if the NFA has at least one final state.

Universality requires a new algorithm. An NFA whose states are all final is not universal if it has no run at all on some word. Moreover, an NFA may be universal even if some states are nonfinal: for every word having a run that leads to a nonfinal state, there may be another run leading to a final state. An example is the NFA of figure 3.5, which, as we shall show in this section, is universal.

A language L is universal if and only if $\overline{L}$ is empty, and so universality of an NFA A can be checked by applying the emptiness test to $\overline{A}$. However, complementation requires to compute an equivalent DFA by means of the powerset construction, which involves a worst-case exponential blow-up in the number of states. So the algorithm runs in exponential time and space in the worst case.

Since the universality problem is PSPACE-complete, it is unlikely that a superpolynomial blowup can be avoided. The forthcoming optional section 3.2.6 provides a proof for readers familiar with complexity theory. But one can still improve on the powerset construction. Let us see how.

A subsumption test. We show that it is not necessary to completely construct the automaton $\overline{A}$. First, the universality check of a DFA only examines the states of the DFA, not the transitions. So, instead of $NFAtoDFA(A)$, we can use a modified version that only stores the states of the DFA but not its transitions. Second, let us see that it is not necessary to store all states.

Definition 3.7 *Let A be an NFA, and let $B = NFAtoDFA(A)$. A state Q' of B is minimal if no state Q'' satisfies $Q'' \subset Q'$.*

Proposition 3.8 *Let A be an NFA and let $B = NFAtoDFA(A)$. Automaton A is universal iff every minimal state of B is final.*

Proof Since A and B recognize the same language, A is universal iff B is universal. So, A is universal iff every state of B is final. But a state of B is final iff it contains some final state of A, and so every state of B is final iff every minimal state of B is final. □

Example 3.9 Figure 3.7 depicts an NFA on the left and the equivalent DFA obtained through the application of $NFAtoDFA$ on the right. Since all states of the DFA are final, the NFA is universal. Only the colored states $\{1\}$, $\{2\}$, and $\{3, 4\}$ are minimal.

Proposition 3.8 establishes that it suffices to construct and store the minimal states of B. Procedure $UnivNFA(A)$, described in algorithm 17, constructs the states of B as in $NFAtoDFA(A)$ but introduces at line 8 a *subsumption test*: it checks if some state $Q'' \subseteq \delta(Q', a)$ has already been constructed. If so, either $\delta(Q', a)$ has already been constructed (case $Q'' = \delta(Q', a)$) or is nonminimal (case $Q'' \subset \delta(Q', a)$). In both cases, the state is not added to the workset.

The next proposition shows that $UnivNFA(A)$ constructs *all* minimal states of B. If $UnivNFA(A)$ would first generate all states of $\overline{A}$ and then would remove all nonminimal

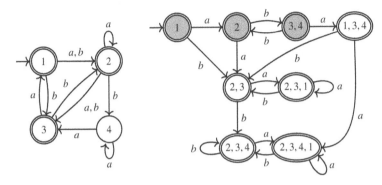

Figure 3.7
An NFA (left) and the result of converting it into a DFA (right). The minimal states of the latter are colored.

Algorithm 17 NFA universality check.

UnivNFA(*A*)
Input: NFA $A = (Q, \Sigma, \delta, Q_0, F)$
Output: true if $\mathcal{L}(A) = \Sigma^*$, **false** otherwise

```
1   Q ← ∅;
2   W ← {Q₀}
3   while W ≠ ∅ do
4     pick Q′ from W
5     if Q′ ∩ F = ∅ then return false
6     add Q′ to Q
7     for all a ∈ Σ do
8       Q″ ← ⋃_{q∈Q′} δ(q, a)
9       if W ∪ Q contains no Q‴ ⊆ Q″ then add Q″ to W
10  return true
```

---

states, the proof would be trivial. But the algorithm removes nonminimal states whenever they appear, and we must show that this does not prevent the future generation of other minimal states.

Proposition 3.10 *Let $A = (Q, \Sigma, \delta, Q_0, F)$ be an NFA, and let $B = NFAtoDFA(A)$. After termination of UnivNFA(A), the set $\mathcal{Q}$ contains all minimal states of B.*

Proof Let $\mathcal{Q}_t$ be the value of $\mathcal{Q}$ after termination of *UnivNFA*(*A*). We show that no path of *B* leads from a state of $\mathcal{Q}_t$ to a minimal state of *B* not in $\mathcal{Q}_t$. Since $\{q_0\} \in \mathcal{Q}_t$ and all states of *B* are reachable from $\{q_0\}$, it follows that each minimal state of *B* belongs to $\mathcal{Q}_t$.

Suppose there is a path $\pi = Q_1 \xrightarrow{a_1} Q_2 \xrightarrow{a_2} \cdots \xrightarrow{a_n} Q_n$ of B such that $Q_1 \in \mathcal{Q}_t$, $Q_n \notin \mathcal{Q}_t$, and Q_n are minimal. Assume further that π is as short as possible. This implies $Q_2 \notin \mathcal{Q}_t$ (otherwise $Q_2 \xrightarrow{a_2} \cdots \xrightarrow{a_n} Q_n$ is a shorter path satisfying the same properties), and so Q_2 is never added to the workset. On the other hand, since $Q_1 \in \mathcal{Q}_t$, the state Q_1 is eventually added to and picked from the workset. When Q_1 is processed at line 7, the algorithm considers $Q_2 = \delta(Q_1, a_1)$ but does not add it to the workset in line 8. Thus, at that moment, either the workset or $\mathcal{Q}$ contains a state $Q_2' \subset Q_2$. This state is eventually added to $\mathcal{Q}$ (if it is not already there), and so $Q_2' \in \mathcal{Q}_t$. So, B has a path $\pi' = Q_2' \xrightarrow{a_2} \cdots Q_{n-1}' \xrightarrow{a_n} Q_n'$ for some states $Q_3', \ldots, Q_n'$. Since $Q_2' \subset Q_2$, we have $Q_2' \subset Q_2, Q_3' \subseteq Q_3, \ldots, Q_n' \subseteq Q_n$ (note that we may have $Q_3' = Q_3$). By minimality of Q_n, we get $Q_n' = Q_n$, and so π' leads from Q_2', which belongs to $\mathcal{Q}_t$, to Q_n, which is minimal and not in $\mathcal{Q}_t$. This contradicts the assumption that π is as short as possible. $\square$

Observe that the complexity of the subsumption test may be considerable, because the new set $\delta(Q', a)$ must be compared with every set in $\mathcal{W} \cup \mathcal{Q}$. Good use of data structures (hash tables or radix trees) is advisable.

3.2.5 Inclusion and Equality

Recall lemma 3.4: given two DFAs A_1, A_2, the inclusion $\mathcal{L}(A_1) \subseteq \mathcal{L}(A_2)$ holds if and only if every state $[q_1, q_2]$ of $[A_1, A_2]$ having $q_1 \in F_1$ also has $q_2 \in F_2$. This lemma no longer holds for NFAs. To see why, let A be any NFA having two runs for some word w, one of them leading to a final state q_1, the other to a nonfinal state q_2. We have $\mathcal{L}(A) \subseteq \mathcal{L}(A)$, but the pairing $[A, A]$ has a run on w leading to $[q_1, q_2]$.

To obtain an algorithm for checking inclusion, we observe that $L_1 \subseteq L_2$ holds if and only if $L_1 \cap \overline{L_2} = \emptyset$. This condition can be checked using the constructions for intersection and for the emptiness check. However, as in the case of universality, we can apply a subsumption check.

Definition 3.11 *Let A_1, A_2 be NFAs, and let $B_2 = NFAtoDFA(A_2)$. A state $[q_1, Q_2]$ of $[A_1, B_2]$ is minimal if no other state $[q_1', Q_2']$ satisfies $q_1' = q_1$ and $Q_2' \subseteq Q_2$.*

Proposition 3.12 *Let $A_1 = (Q_1, \Sigma, \delta_1, Q_{01}, F_1)$ and $A_2 = (Q_2, \Sigma, \delta_2, Q_{02}, F_2)$ be NFAs, and let $B_2 = NFAtoDFA(A_2)$. It is the case that $\mathcal{L}(A_1) \subseteq \mathcal{L}(A_2)$ iff every minimal state $[q_1, Q_2]$ of $[A_1, B_2]$ having $q_1 \in F_1$ also has $Q_2 \cap F_2 \neq \emptyset$.*

Proof Since A_2 and B_2 recognize the same language, we have

$$\mathcal{L}(A_1) \subseteq \mathcal{L}(A_2)$$

$$\Longleftrightarrow \mathcal{L}(A_1) \cap \overline{\mathcal{L}(A_2)} = \emptyset$$

$$\Longleftrightarrow \mathcal{L}(A_1) \cap \overline{\mathcal{L}(B_2)} = \emptyset$$

$\Longleftrightarrow$ $[A_1, B_2]$ has no state $[q_1, Q_2]$ s.t. $q_1 \in F_1$ and $Q_2 \cap F_2 = \emptyset$

$\Longleftrightarrow$ $[A_1, B_2]$ has no *minimal* state $[q_1, Q_2]$ s.t. $q_1 \in F_1$ and $Q_2 \cap F_2 = \emptyset$.   □

This leads to algorithm 18 for checking inlcusion.

Algorithm 18 NFA inclusion check.

InclNFA(A_1, A_2)
Input: NFAs $A_1 = (Q_1, \Sigma, \delta_1, Q_{01}, F_1)$, $A_2 = (Q_2, \Sigma, \delta_2, Q_{02}, F_2)$
Output: true if $\mathcal{L}(A_1) \subseteq \mathcal{L}(A_2)$, **false** otherwise

```
1   Q ← ∅;
2   W ← {[q₀₁, Q₀₂] : q₀₁ ∈ Q₀₁}
3   while W ≠ ∅ do
4       pick [q₁, Q′₂] from W
5       if (q₁ ∈ F₁) and (Q′₂ ∩ F₂ = ∅) then return false
6       add [q₁, Q′₂] to Q
7       for all a ∈ Σ do
8           Q″₂ ← ⋃_{q₂∈Q′₂} δ₂(q₂, a)
9           for all q′₁ ∈ δ₁(q₁, a) do
10              if W ∪ Q contains no [q‴₁, Q‴₂] s.t. q‴₁ = q′₁ and Q‴₂ ⊆ Q″₂ then
11                  add [q′₁, Q″₂] to W
12  return true
```

Observe that, in unfavorable cases, the overhead of the subsumption test may not be compensated by a reduction in the number of states. Without the test, the number of pairs that can be added to the workset is at most $|Q_1| \cdot 2^{|Q_2|}$. For each of them, we have to execute the **for** loop $\mathcal{O}(|Q_1|)$ times, each of them taking time $\mathcal{O}(|Q_2|^2)$. So, the algorithm runs in time and space $|Q_1|^2 \cdot 2^{\mathcal{O}(|Q_2|)}$.

As was the case for universality, the inclusion problem is PSPACE-complete, and so it is unlikely that the exponential factor can be avoided (see the optional section 3.2.6). There is, however, an important case with polynomial complexity. When A_2 is a DFA, the number of pairs that can be added to the workset is at most $|Q_1| \cdot |Q_2|$. The **for** loop is still executed $\mathcal{O}(|Q_1|)$ times, but each iteration takes constant time. Thus, the algorithm runs in time and space $\mathcal{O}(|Q_1|^2 \cdot |Q_2|)$.

Equality. Equality of two languages is decided by checking that each of them is included in the other. The equality problem is also PSPACE-complete. The only point worth observing is that, unlike the inclusion case, we do not get a polynomial algorithm when A_2 is a DFA.

3.2.6 ★ Universality and Inclusion Are PSPACE-Complete

In this subsection, we show that the universality and inclusion problems for NFAs are PSPACE-complete.

Theorem 3.13 *The universality problem for NFAs is PSPACE-complete.*

Proof We only sketch the proof. To prove that the problem is in PSPACE, we show that it belongs to NPSPACE and apply Savitch's theorem. The polynomial-space nondeterministic algorithm for universality looks as follows. Given an NFA $A = (Q, \Sigma, \delta, Q_0, F)$, it guesses a run of $B = NFAtoDFA(A)$ leading from $\{q_0\}$ to a nonfinal set of states—that is, to a set of states of A containing no final state (if such a run exists). The algorithm does not store the whole run, only the current state of B, and so it only needs linear space in the size of A.

We prove PSPACE-hardness with a reduction from the acceptance problem for linearly bounded automata. A linearly bounded automaton is a deterministic Turing machine that always halts and only uses the part of the tape containing the input. A configuration of the Turing machine on an input of length k is encoded as a word of length k. The run of the machine on an input can be encoded as a word $c_0 \# c_1 \cdots \# c_n$, where the c_is are the encodings of the configurations.

Let Σ be the alphabet used to encode the run of the machine. Given an input x, the machine accepts if there exists a word w of $(\Sigma \cup \{\#\})^*$ (we assume $\# \notin \Sigma$) satisfying the following properties:

(a) w has the form $c_0 \# c_1 \ldots \# c_n$, where the c_is are configurations;

(b) c_0 is the initial configuration;

(c) c_n is an accepting configuration; and

(d) for every $0 \leq i < n$: configuration c_{i+1} is the successor of c_i according to the transition relation of the machine.

The reduction shows how to construct in polynomial time, given a linearly bounded automaton M and an input x, an NFA $A_{M,x}$ accepting all the words of Σ^* that do *not* satisfy at least one of the conditions (a)–(d) above. Thus:

- If M accepts x, then there is a word $w_{M,x}$ encoding the accepting run of M on x, and so $\mathcal{L}\left(A_{M,x}\right) = \Sigma^* \setminus \{w_{M,x}\}$.
- If M rejects x, then no word encodes an accepting run of M on x, and so $\mathcal{L}\left(A_{M,x}\right) = \Sigma^*$.

Therefore, M rejects x iff $\mathcal{L}\left(A_{M,x}\right) = \Sigma^*$, and we are done. $\square$

Proposition 3.14 *The inclusion problem for NFAs is PSPACE-complete.*

Proof We first prove membership in PSPACE. Since PSPACE = co-PSPACE = NPSPACE, it suffices to give a polynomial space nondeterministic algorithm that decides noninclusion.

Given NFAs A_1 and A_2, the algorithm guesses $w \in \mathcal{L}(A_1) \setminus \mathcal{L}(A_2)$ letter by letter, maintaining the sets Q_1' and Q_2' of states that A_1 and A_2 reached by the word guessed so far. When the guessing ends, the algorithm checks that Q_1' contains some final state of A_1, but Q_2' does not.

Hardness follows from the fact that A is universal iff $\Sigma^* \subseteq \mathcal{L}(A)$, and so the universality problem, which is PSPACE-complete by Theorem 3.13, is a subproblem of the inclusion problem.   □

3.3   Exercises

☆ ⚙ **Exercise 58.** Consider the following languages over alphabet $\Sigma = \{a, b\}$:

- L_1 is the set of all words where between any two occurrences of bs, there is at least one a;
- L_2 is the set of all words where every maximal sequence of consecutive as has odd length;
- L_3 is the set of all words where a occurs only at even positions;
- L_4 is the set of all words where a occurs only at odd positions;
- L_5 is the set of all words of odd length; and
- L_6 is the set of all words with an even number of as.

Construct an NFA for the language

$$(L_1 \setminus L_2) \cup \overline{(L_3 \bigtriangleup L_4)} \cap L_5 \cap L_6,$$

where $L \bigtriangleup L'$ denotes the symmetric difference of L and L', while sticking to the following rules:

- Start from NFAs for $L_1, \ldots, L_6$.
- Any further automaton must be constructed from already existing automata via an algorithm introduced in the chapter (e.g., *Comp*, *BinOp*, *UnionNFA*, *NFAtoDFA*, etc.).

☆ ■ **Exercise 59.** Prove or disprove: the minimal DFAs recognizing a language L and its complement $\overline{L}$ have the same number of states.

☆ ▣ **Exercise 60.** Give a regular expression for the words over $\{0, 1\}$ that do not contain 010 as a subword.

★ ⚙ **Exercise 61.** In example 1.9, we presented an automaton that recognizes words over alphabet $\Sigma = \{-, \cdot, 0, 1, \ldots, 9\}$ that encode real numbers with a finite decimal part, for example, 37, 10.503, and -0.234 are accepted, but 002, -0, and 3.10000000 are not. This language is described by these four properties:

(a) a word encoding a number consists of an integer part, followed by a possibly empty fractional part; the integer part consists of an optional minus sign, followed by a nonempty sequence of digits;

(b) if the first digit of the integer part is 0, then it is the only digit of the integer part;

(c) if the fractional part is nonempty, then it starts with "," followed by a nonempty sequence of digits that does not end with 0; and

(d) if the integer part is -0, then the fractional part is nonempty.

We seek to obtain the automaton presented in example 1.9 in a more modular and algorithmic way. More precisely, give an automaton for each of the above properties, construct the pairing of these automata, and minimize the resulting automaton.

☆ ⚙ **Exercise 62.** The following automaton A accepts a set of numbers encoded in binary 🔒 with their most significant bit appearing first (as in the example from the beginning of the chapter). Say whether A accepts *all* odd numbers. This can be answered by inspection. Instead, answer the question algorithmically.

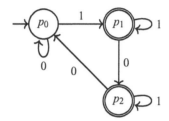

★ 🖳 **Exercise 63.** Find a family of NFAs $\{A_n\}_{n\geq 1}$ with $\mathcal{O}(n)$ states such that *every* NFA 🔓 recognizing the complement of $\mathcal{L}(A_n)$ has at least 2^n states. *Hint: See exercise 21.*

☆ ⚙ **Exercise 64.** Consider again the regular expressions $(1+10)^*$ and $1^*(101^*)^*$ of 🔒 exercise 4.

• Construct NFAs for these expressions and use *InclNFA* to check if their languages are equal.

• Construct DFAs for the expressions and use *InclDFA* to check if their languages are equal.

• Construct minimal DFAs for the expressions and check whether they are isomorphic.

☆ ■ **Exercise 65.** Consider the variant of *IntersNFA* in which line 7 🔓

$$\textbf{if } (q_1 \in F_1) \textbf{ and } (q_2 \in F_2) \textbf{ then add } [q_1, q_2] \textbf{ to } F$$

is replaced by

$$\textbf{if } (q_1 \in F_1) \textbf{ or } (q_2 \in F_2) \textbf{ then add } [q_1, q_2] \textbf{ to } F$$

Let $A_1 \otimes A_2$ be the result of applying this variant to two NFAs A_1 and A_2. An NFA $A = (Q, \Sigma, \delta, Q_0, F)$ is *complete* if $\delta(q, a) \neq \emptyset$ for all $q \in Q$ and all $a \in \Sigma$.

• Prove the following: if A_1 and A_2 are complete NFAs, then $\mathcal{L}(A_1 \otimes A_2) = \mathcal{L}(A_1) \cup \mathcal{L}(L_2)$.

• Give NFAs A_1 and A_2 that are *not complete* and such that $\mathcal{L}(A_1 \otimes A_2) = \mathcal{L}(A_1) \cup \mathcal{L}(L_2)$.

★ 🖵 **Exercise 66.** The *even part* of a word $w = a_1 a_2 \cdots a_n$ over alphabet Σ is the word $a_2 a_4 \cdots a_{2 \cdot \lfloor n/2 \rfloor}$. Given an NFA A, construct an NFA A' such that $\mathcal{L}(A')$ is the even parts of the words of $\mathcal{L}(A)$.

☆ 🖵 **Exercise 67.** Let $L_i = \{w \in \{a\}^* : \text{the length of } w \text{ is divisible by } i\}$.

(a) Construct an NFA for $L := L_4 \cup L_6$ with a single initial state and at most eleven states.

(b) Construct the minimal DFA for L.

☆ 🖌 **Exercise 68.** Modify algorithm *Empty* so it returns a witness when the automaton is nonempty, that is, a word accepted by the automaton. Explain how could you further return a *shortest* witness. What is the complexity of your procedure?

☆ ⚙ **Exercise 69.** Use the algorithm *UnivNFA* to test whether the following NFA is universal.

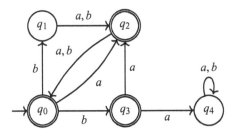

★ 🖵 **Exercise 70.** Let Σ be an alphabet. We define the *shuffle operator* $|||: \Sigma^* \times \Sigma^* \to \mathcal{P}(\Sigma^*)$ inductively as follows, where $a, b \in \Sigma$ and $w, v \in \Sigma^*$:

$$w \,|||\, \varepsilon = \{w\},$$

$$\varepsilon \,|||\, w = \{w\},$$

$$aw \,|||\, bv = \{au : u \in w \,|||\, bv\} \cup \{bu : u \in aw \,|||\, v\}.$$

For example, we have

$$b \,|||\, d = \{bd, db\},$$

$$ab \,|||\, d = \{abd, adb, dab\},$$

$$ab \,|||\, cd = \{cabd, acbd, abcd, cadb, acdb, cdab\}.$$

Given DFAs recognizing languages $L_1, L_2 \subseteq \Sigma^*$, construct an NFA recognizing their *shuffle*

$$L_1 \,|||\, L_2 = \bigcup_{u \in L_1, v \in L_2} u \,|||\, v.$$

★ ▣ **Exercise 71.** The *perfect shuffle* of two languages $L, L' \in \Sigma^*$ is a variant of the shuffle introduced in exercise 70, defined as

$$L \; \widetilde{|||} \; L' = \{w \in \Sigma^* : \exists a_1, \ldots, a_n, b_1, \ldots, b_n \in \Sigma \text{ s.t. } a_1 \cdots a_n \in L \text{ and}$$

$$b_1 \cdots b_n \in L' \text{ and}$$

$$w = a_1 b_1 \cdots a_n b_n\}.$$

Give an algorithm that returns a DFA accepting $\mathcal{L}(A) \; \widetilde{|||} \; \mathcal{L}(B)$ from two given DFAs A and B.

★ ▣ **Exercise 72.** Let Σ_1, Σ_2 be two alphabets. A *homomorphism* is a map $h : \Sigma_1^* \to \Sigma_2^*$ such that $h(\varepsilon) = \varepsilon$ and $h(uv) = h(u)h(v)$ for every $u, v \in \Sigma_1^*$. Observe that if $\Sigma_1 = \{a_1, \ldots, a_n\}$, then h is completely determined by the values $h(a_1), \ldots, h(a_n)$. Let $h : \Sigma_1^* \to \Sigma_2^*$ be a homomorphism.

(a) Construct an NFA for the language $h(\mathcal{L}(A)) = \{h(w) : w \in \mathcal{L}(A)\}$ where A is an NFA over Σ_1.

(b) Construct an NFA for $h^{-1}(\mathcal{L}(A)) = \{w \in \Sigma_1^* : h(w) \in \mathcal{L}(A)\}$ where A is an NFA over Σ_2.

(c) Recall that the language $\{0^n 1^n : n \in \mathbb{N}\}$ is not regular. Use the preceding results to show that $\{(01^k 2)^n 3^n : k, n \in \mathbb{N}\}$ is also not regular.

★ ▣ **Exercise 73.** Let L_1 and L_2 be regular languages over alphabet Σ. The *left quotient* of L_1 by L_2 is the language

$$L_2 \backslash L_1 = \{v \in \Sigma^* : \exists u \in L_2 \text{ s.t. } uv \in L_1\}.$$

Note that $L_2 \backslash L_1$ is different from the set difference $L_2 \setminus L_1$.

(a) Given NFAs A_1 and A_2, construct an NFA A s.t. $\mathcal{L}(A) = \mathcal{L}(A_1) \backslash \mathcal{L}(A_2)$.

(b) Do the same for the *right quotient*, defined as $L_1 / L_2 = \{u \in \Sigma^* : \exists v \in L_2 \text{ s.t. } uv \in L_1\}$.

(c) Determine the inclusions between L_1, $(L_1/L_2)L_2$, and $(L_1 L_2)/L_2$.

☆ ✔ **Exercise 74.** Given alphabets Σ and Δ, a *substitution* is a map $f : \Sigma \to 2^{\Delta^*}$ assigning to each letter $a \in \Sigma$ a language $L_a \subseteq \Delta^*$. A substitution f can be canonically extended to a map $2^{\Sigma^*} \to 2^{\Delta^*}$ by defining $f(\varepsilon) = \varepsilon$, $f(wa) = f(w)f(a)$, and $f(L) = \bigcup_{w \in L} f(w)$. Note that a homomorphism can be seen as the special case of a substitution in which all L_as are singletons.

Let $\Sigma = \{\text{Name}, \text{Tel}, :, \#\}$, let $\Delta = \{A, \ldots, Z, 0, 1, \ldots, 9, :, \#\}$, and let f be the substitution:

$$f(\text{Name}) = (A + \cdots + Z)^*$$

$$f(:) = \{:\}$$

$$f(\text{Tel}) = 0049(1 + \ldots + 9)(0 + 1 + \ldots + 9)^{10} +$$

$$00420(1 + \ldots + 9)(0 + 1 + \ldots + 9)^8$$

$$f(\#) = \{\#\}$$

(a) Draw a DFA recognizing $L = \text{Name}:\text{Tel}(\#\text{Tel})^*$.

(b) Sketch an NFA recognizing $f(L)$.

(c) Give an algorithm that takes as input an NFA A, a substitution f, and for every $a \in \Sigma$ an NFA recognizing $f(a)$ and returns an NFA recognizing $f(\mathcal{L}(A))$.

★ ▇ **Exercise 75.** Let A_1 and A_2 be two NFAs with n_1 and n_2 states. Let

$$B = NFAtoDFA(IntersNFA(A_1, A_2)),$$

$$C = IntersDFA(NFAtoDFA(A_1), NFAtoDFA(A_2)).$$

A superficial analysis shows that B and C have $\mathcal{O}(2^{n_1 \cdot n_2})$ and $\mathcal{O}(2^{n_1 + n_2})$ states, respectively, wrongly suggesting that C might be more compact than B. Show that, in fact, B and C are isomorphic and hence have the same number of states.

★ ☛ **Exercise 76.** Let $A = (Q, \Sigma, \delta, q_0, F)$ be a DFA. A word $w \in \Sigma^*$ is a *synchronizing word* of A if reading w from any state of A leads to a common state, that is, if there exists $q \in Q$ such that for every $p \in Q$, $p \xrightarrow{w} q$. A DFA is *synchronizing* if it has a synchronizing word.

(a) Show that the following DFA is synchronizing:

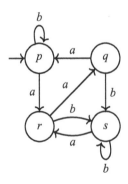

(b) Give a DFA that is not synchronizing.

(c) Give an exponential time algorithm to decide whether a DFA is synchronizing.

Hint: Use the powerset construction.

(d) Show that a DFA $A = (Q, \Sigma, \delta, q_0, F)$ is synchronizing iff for every $p, q \in Q$, there exist $w \in \Sigma^*$ and $r \in Q$ such that $p \xrightarrow{w} r$ and $q \xrightarrow{w} r$.

(e) Give a polynomial time algorithm to test whether a DFA is synchronizing.

Hint: Use (d).

(f) Show that (d) implies that every synchronizing DFA with n states has a synchronizing word of length at most $(n^2 - 1)(n - 1)$.

Hint: You might need to reason in terms of pairing.

(g) Show that the upper bound obtained in (f) is not tight by finding a synchronizing word of length $(4 - 1)^2$ for the following DFA:

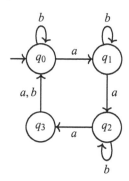

★ 🎓 **Exercise 77.**

(a) Prove that the following problem is PSPACE-complete:

Given: DFAs $A_1, \ldots, A_n$ over the same alphabet Σ;
Decide: whether $\bigcap_{i=1}^{n} \mathcal{L}(A_i) = \emptyset$.

Hint: Reduce from the acceptance problem for deterministic linearly bounded automata.

(b) Prove that if the DFAs are acyclic, but the alphabet is arbitrary, then the problem is coNP-complete. Here, acyclic means that the graph induced by transitions has no cycle, apart from a self-loop on a trap state. *Hint: Reduce from 3-SAT.*

(c) Prove that if Σ is a one-letter alphabet, then the problem is coNP-complete.

☆ ■ **Exercise 78.** Let $A = (Q, \Sigma, \delta, Q_0, F)$ be an NFA. Show that, with the universal accepting condition of exercise 21, automaton $A' = (Q, \Sigma, \delta, q_0, Q \setminus F)$ recognizes the complement of $\mathcal{L}(A)$.

☆ 🎓 **Exercise 79.** Recall the model of alternating automata introduced in exercise 22.

(a) Show that alternating automata can be complemented by exchanging existential and universal states, as well as final and nonfinal states. More precisely, let $A = (Q_1, Q_2, \Sigma, \delta, q_0, F)$ be an alternating automaton, where Q_1 and Q_2 are respectively the sets of existential and universal states and where $\delta: (Q_1 \cup Q_2) \times \Sigma \to \mathcal{P}(Q_1 \cup Q_2)$. Show that the alternating automaton $\overline{A} = (Q_2, Q_1, \Sigma, \delta, q_0, Q \setminus F)$ recognizes the complement of the language recognized by A.

(b) Give linear time algorithms that take two alternating automata recognizing languages L_1 and L_2 and that deliver a third alternating automaton recognizing $L_1 \cup L_2$ and $L_1 \cap L_2$.

Hint: The algorithms are very similar to UnionNFA.

(c) Show that testing emptiness for alternating automata is PSPACE-complete.

Hint: Use exercise 77.

☆ ■ **Exercise 80.** Recall that weakly acyclic DFAs were introduced in exercise 35. Show that if A is a weakly acyclic DFA, then *CompDFA(A)* is also weakly acyclic, and, that for every binary boolean operator $\odot$, if A_1 and A_2 are weakly acyclic DFAs, then *BinOp*$[\odot](A_1, A_2)$ is also weakly acyclic.

4 Application I: Pattern Matching

As a first example of a practical application of automata, we consider the *pattern matching problem*. Given $w, w' \in \Sigma^*$, we say that w' *is a factor of* w if there are words $w_1, w_2 \in \Sigma^*$ such that $w = w_1 w' w_2$. If w_1 and $w_1 w'$ have lengths i and j, respectively, we say that w' is the $[i,j]$-*factor* of w. The *pattern matching problem* is as follows: given a word $t \in \Sigma^+$ (called the *text*) and a regular expression p over Σ (called the *pattern*), determine the smallest $j \geq 0$ such that a $[i,j]$-factor of t belongs to $\mathcal{L}(p)$. We call j the *first occurrence of p in t*.

Example 4.1 Let $t = aabab$ and $p = a(aba)^*b$. The $[1,3]$-, $[3,5]$-, and $[0,5]$-factors of t are ab, ab, and $aabab$, respectively. All of these factors belong to $\mathcal{L}(p)$. The first occurrence of p in t is 3.

Usually, one is interested in finding not only the ending position j of the $[i,j]$-factor but also the starting position i. Adapting the algorithms to also provide this information is left as an exercise.

4.1 The General Case

We present two different solutions to the pattern matching problem, using nondeterministic and deterministic automata, respectively.

Solution 1. Some word of $\mathcal{L}(p)$ occurs in t iff some prefix of t belongs to $\mathcal{L}(\Sigma^* p)$. Thus, we construct an NFA A_p for the regular expression $\Sigma^* p$ by first using the rules of figure 1.16 and then removing all ε-transitions by means of *NFAεtoNFA*. Let us call the resulting algorithm *RegtoNFA*. Once A_p is constructed, we simulate it on t as in *MemNFA[A](q_0,t)*. Recall that the simulation algorithm reads the text letter by letter, maintaining the set of states reachable from the initial state by the prefix read so far. So the simulation reaches a set of states containing a final state iff the prefix read so far belongs to $\mathcal{L}(\Sigma^* p)$. The pseudocode is described in algorithm 19.

Let us estimate the complexity of *PatternMatchingNFA* for a text of length n over a k-letter alphabet Σ, where $k \leq n$, and a pattern of length m. *RegtoNFA* is the concatenation

---

Algorithm 19 NFA-based pattern matching.

PatternMatchingNFA(t, p)
Input: text $t = a_1 \cdots a_n \in \Sigma^+$, pattern p
Output: the first occurrence of p in t, or $\bot$ if no such occurrence exists

```
1   A ← RegtoNFA(Σ*p)
2   S ← Q₀
3   for all k = 0 to n − 1 do
4       if S ∩ F ≠ ∅ then return k
5       S ← δ(S, aₖ₊₁)
6   return ⊥
```

1 $A \leftarrow RegtoNFA(\Sigma^* p)$
2 $S \leftarrow Q_0$
3 **for all** $k = 0$ to $n - 1$ **do**
4   **if** $S \cap F \neq \emptyset$ **then return** k
5     $S \leftarrow \delta(S, a_{k+1})$
6 **return** $\bot$

---

of *RegtoNFAε* and *NFAεtoNFA*. Since $\Sigma^* p$ has size $\mathcal{O}(k + m)$, *RegtoNFAε* takes time $\mathcal{O}(k + m)$ and outputs an NFA-ε with $\mathcal{O}(k + m)$ states and $\mathcal{O}(k + m)$ transitions. When applied to this output, *NFAεtoNFA* takes time $\mathcal{O}(k(k + m)^2)$ and outputs an NFA with $\mathcal{O}(m)$ states and $\mathcal{O}(km^2)$ transitions. The **for all** loop is executed at most n times, and for an automaton with $\mathcal{O}(m)$ states, each line of the loop's body takes a time of at most $\mathcal{O}(m^2)$. So the loop runs in time $\mathcal{O}(k(k + m)^2 + nm^2)$.

If k can be considered a constant—for example, when searching in standard English books, where the alphabet always consists of twenty-six letters, fourteen punctuation marks, and the blank symbol—then this reduces to $\mathcal{O}(nm^2)$ time. If the alphabet is implicitly defined by the text and can be of similar size, then, since $k \leq n$, we obtain $\mathcal{O}(n(n + m)^2 + nm^2)$ time, which for the typical case $n > m$ reduces to $\mathcal{O}(n^3)$.

Solution 2. We proceed as in the previous case, but constructing a DFA for $\Sigma^* p$ instead of an NFA, as described in algorithm 20.

Algorithm 20 DFA-based pattern matching.

PatternMatchingDFA(t, p)
Input: text $t = a_1 \cdots a_n \in \Sigma^+$, pattern p,
Output: the first occurrence of p in t, or $\bot$ if no such occurrence exists.

1 $A \leftarrow NFAtoDFA(RegtoNFA(\Sigma^* p))$
2 $q \leftarrow q_0$
3 **for all** $k = 0$ to $n - 1$ **do**
4   **if** $q \in F$ **then return** k
5     $q \leftarrow \delta(q, a_{k+1})$
6 **return** $\bot$

Note that there is a trade-off: while the conversion to a DFA can take (much) longer than the conversion to an NFA, the membership check for a DFA is faster. The complexity of *PatternMatchingDFA* for a word of length n and a pattern of length m can be easily estimated: *RegtoNFA(p)* runs in time $\mathcal{O}(k(k+m)^2 + nm^2)$, but it outputs an NFA with only $\mathcal{O}(m)$ states. The equivalent DFA produced by *NFAtoDFA* has $2^{\mathcal{O}(m)}$ states and $k \cdot 2^{\mathcal{O}(m)}$ transitions. However, transitions for letters that do not appear in p necessarily go to a trap state and do not need to be explicitly constructed. Since p has at most m different letters, the DFA can be constructed in time $m \cdot 2^{\mathcal{O}(m)} = 2^{\mathcal{O}(m)}$. Since the loop is executed at most n times, and each line of the body takes constant time, the overall runtime is $\mathcal{O}(n) + 2^{\mathcal{O}(|\Sigma|+m)}$. For a fixed alphabet, this reduces to $\mathcal{O}(n) + 2^{\mathcal{O}(m)}$.

4.2   The Word Case

We study the special but very common case of the pattern matching problem in which we wish to know if a given word appears in a text. In this case, the pattern p is the word itself. For the rest of the section, we consider an arbitrary but fixed text $t = a_1 \cdots a_n$ and an arbitrary but fixed word pattern $p = b_1 \cdots b_m$. We do not assume that the alphabet has fixed size but only that it has size $\mathcal{O}(n+m)$.

It is easy to find a faster algorithm for this special case, without any use of automata theory: just move a "window" of length m over the text t, one letter at a time, and check after each move whether the content of the window is p. The number of moves is $n - m + 1$, and a check requires $\mathcal{O}(m)$ letter comparisons, giving a runtime of $\mathcal{O}(nm)$, independently of the size of the alphabet. In the rest of the section, we present a faster algorithm with time complexity $\mathcal{O}(m+n)$. Notice that in many applications n is very large, and so, even for a relatively small m, the difference between nm and $m+n$ can be significant.

Example 4.2   Figure 4.1a depicts an NFA A_p, recognizing $\Sigma^* p$ for the case $p = nano$.

In general, the obvious NFA recognizing $\Sigma^* p$ is $A_p = (Q, \Sigma, \delta, \{q_0\}, F)$, where $Q = \{0, 1, \ldots, m\}$, $q_0 = 0$, $F = \{m\}$, and

$$\delta = \{(i, b_{i+1}, i+1) : 0 \le i < m\} \cup \{(0, a, 0) : a \in \Sigma\}.$$

Clearly, A_p can reach state k whenever the word read so far ends with $b_0 \cdots b_k$. We define the *hit* and *miss* letters for each state of A_p. Intuitively, the hit letter makes A_p "progress" toward reading p, while the miss letters "throw it back."

Definition 4.3   *A letter $a \in \Sigma$ is a hit for state i of A_p if $\delta(i, a) = \{i+1\}$; otherwise, it is a miss for i.*

Example 4.4   Figure 4.1b depicts the DFA B_p obtained by applying *NFAtoDFA* on A_p. It has as many states as A_p, and there is a natural correspondence between the states of A_p and

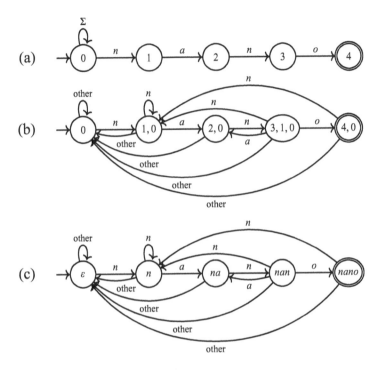

Figure 4.1
NFA A_p and DFA B_p for $p = nano$.

B_p: each state of A_p is the largest element of *exactly one* state of B_p. For example, 3 is the largest element of $\{3, 1, 0\}$, and 4 is the largest element of $\{4, 0\}$.

Definition 4.5 *The* head *of a state $S \subseteq \{0, \ldots, m\}$ of B_p, denoted by $h(S)$, is the largest element of S. The* tail *of S, denoted by $t(S)$, is the set $t(S) = S \setminus \{h(S)\}$. The* hit *for a state S of B_p is defined as the hit of the state $h(S)$ in A_p.*

If we label a state with head k by the word $b_1 \cdots b_k$, as shown in figure 4.1c, then we see that the states of B_p keep track of how close the automaton is to finding *nano*. For instance:

- if B_p is in state n and reads an a (a hit for this state), then it "makes progress" and moves to state na;
- if B_p is in state nan and reads an a (a miss for this state), then it is "thrown back" to state na. Not to state ε, because if the next two letters are n and o, then B_p should accept!

Automaton B_p has another property that will be very important later on: for each state $S \neq \{0\}$ of B_p, the tail of S is again a state of B_p. For instance, the tail of $\{3, 1, 0\}$ is $\{1, 0\}$,

---

Algorithm 21   Conversion from NFA to DFA.

NFAtoDFA(A)
Input: NFA $A = (Q, \Sigma, \delta, Q_0, F)$
Output: DFA $B = (\mathcal{Q}, \Sigma, \Delta, Q_0, \mathcal{F})$ with $\mathcal{L}(B) = \mathcal{L}(A)$

```
 1   Q, Δ, F ← ∅
 2   W = {Q₀}
 3   while W ≠ ∅ do
 4       pick S from W
 5       add S to Q
 6       if S ∩ F ≠ ∅ then add S to F
 7       for all a ∈ Σ do
 8           S' ← δ(S, a)
 9           if S' ∉ Q then add S' to W
10           add (S, a, S') to Δ
```

---

which is also a state of B_p. We show that this property and the ones above hold in general and not only in the special case $p = nano$. Formally, we prove the following invariant of *NFAtoDFA* when applied to a word pattern p. Algorithm *NFAtoDFA* is recalled in algorithm 21 for convenience.

Proposition 4.6   *Let p be a pattern of length m. For every $k \geq 0$, let S_k be the kth set picked from the workset during the execution of NFAtoDFA(A_p). We have:*

(a) $h(S_k) = k$ (which implies $k \leq m$), and
(b) either $k = 0$ and $t(S_k) = \emptyset$, or $k > 0$ and $t(S_k) \in \mathcal{Q}$.

Proof   We first prove by induction on k that (a), (b), and the following fact (c) hold for every $0 \leq k \leq m$: before the kth iteration of the while loop, the workset only contains S_k. Then, we prove that S_m is the last state added to the workset and hence that the mth iteration is the last one.

For $k = 0$, we have $S_0 = \{0\}$, which implies (a) and (b); further, (c) follows because of line 2. Assume now $k > 0$. By induction hypothesis, we have $h(S_k) = k$ by (a) and $t(S_k) = S_l$ for some $l < k$ by (b); further, by (c), at the start of the kth iteration the, workset only contains S_k. At the start of the kth iteration the algorithm picks S_k from the workset, which becomes empty, and examines the sets $\delta(S_k, a)$ for every action a. We consider two cases:

• Letter a is a miss for S_k. By definition, it is also a miss for its head $h(S_k) = k$. So we have $\delta(k, a) = \emptyset$, and hence $\delta(S_k, a) = \delta(t(S_k), a) = \delta(S_l, a)$. So $\delta(S_k, a)$ was already explored by the algorithm during the lth iteration of the loop, and $\delta(S_k, a)$ is not added to the workset at line 9.

• Letter a is a hit for S_k. We have $\delta(k, a) = \{k + 1\}$. Since $\delta(S_k, a) = \delta(h(S_k), a) \cup \delta(t(S_k), a)$, we get $\delta(S_k, a) = \{k + 1\} \cup \delta(S_l, a)$. Since state $k + 1$ has not been explored before, the set $\{k + 1\} \cup \delta(S_l, a)$ becomes the $(k + 1)$th state added to the workset, that is, $S_{k+1} = \{k + 1\} \cup \delta(S_l, a)$. Therefore, $h(S_{k+1}) = k + 1$, which yields (a). Further, $t(S_{k+1}) = t(S_l, a)$, and so $t(S_{k+1}) \in Q$, which gives (b).

Let us now prove (c). For every $0 \le k < m$, exactly one letter is a hit for S_k. Therefore, at the end of the kth iteration, S_{k+1} is the only state added to the workset, and so the workset only contains $k + 1$. Thus, (c) follows from the fact that the end of the kth iteration, is also the beginning of the $(k + 1)$th iteration.

It still remains to prove that S_m is the last state added to the workset. For this, observe that there is no hit letter for S_m. Therefore, during the mth iteration, no state is added to the workset. So, at the end of the mth iteration, the workset is empty, and the algorithm terminates. □

By proposition 4.6, the DFA B_p has $m + 1$ states for a pattern of length m. So, *NFAtoDFA* does not incur in any exponential blowup for word patterns. Even more: since, for any two distinct prefixes p_1 and p_2 of p, the residuals $(\Sigma^* p)^{p_1}$ and $(\Sigma^* p)^{p_2}$ are also distinct, any DFA for $\Sigma^* p$ has at least $m + 1$ states. Thus:

Corollary 4.7 *Automaton B_p is the minimal DFA recognizing $\Sigma^* p$.*

Since B_p is a DFA with $m + 1$ states, it has $(m + 1) \cdot |\Sigma|$ transitions. Transitions of B_p labeled by letters that do not appear in p always lead to state 0, and so they do not need to be explicitly stored. The remaining $\mathcal{O}(m)$ transitions for each state can easily be constructed and stored using space and time of $\mathcal{O}(m^2)$, leading to a $\mathcal{O}(n + m^2)$ algorithm. To achieve a time of $\mathcal{O}(n + m)$, we introduce an even more compact data structure: the *lazy DFA for* $\Sigma^* p$, which, as we shall see, can be constructed in space and time $\mathcal{O}(m)$.

4.2.1 Lazy DFAs

Recall that a DFA can be seen as the control unit of a machine that reads an input from a tape divided into cells by means of a reading head. At each step, the machine reads the contents of the cell occupied by the reading head, updates the current state according to the transition function, and moves the head one cell to the right. It accepts a word if the state reached after reading it is final.

In *lazy* DFAs, the machine advances the head one cell to the right *or keeps it on the same cell* (see figure 4.2). Which of the two takes place is a function of the current state and the current letter read by the head. Formally, a lazy DFA only differs from a DFA in the transition function, which has the form $\delta \colon Q \times \Sigma \to Q \times \{R, N\}$, where R stands for "*move Right*" and N stands for "*No move*." A transition of a lazy DFA is a quadruple of the form

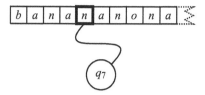

Figure 4.2
Tape with reading head.

(q, a, q', d), where $d \in \{R, N\}$ is the move of the head. Intuitively, a transition (q, a, q', N) means that state q *delegates* processing the letter a to state q'.

A lazy DFA C_p for $\Sigma^* p$. Recall that each state S_k of B_p, except the last one, has a hit letter and all other letters are misses. In particular, if letter a is a miss, then $\delta_B(S_k, a) = \delta(t(S_k), a)$, and so:

When B_p is in state S_k and reads a miss, it moves to the same state it would move to if it were in state $t(S_k)$.

Using this fact, we construct a lazy DFA C_p with the same states as B_p and with transition function $\delta_C(S_k, a)$ given by:

- If a is a hit for S_k, then C_p behaves as B_p, that is:

$$\delta_C(S_k, a) = (S_{k+1}, R).$$

- If a is a miss for S_k and $k > 0$, then S_k "delegates" to $t(S_k)$, that is:

$$\delta_C(S_k, a) = (t(S_k), N).$$

- If a is a miss for S_k and $k = 0$, then $t(S_k)$ is not a state, and so S_k cannot "delegate"; instead, C_p behaves as B_p:

$$\delta_C(S_0, a) = (S_0, R).$$

Note that, in the case of a miss, C_p always delegates *to the same state, independently of the letter being read*. So, we can "summarize" the transitions for all misses into a single transition $\delta_C(S_k, miss) = (t(S_k), N)$.

Example 4.8 Figure 4.3 depicts the DFA and the lazy DFA for $p = nano$, where we write k instead of S_k in the states of the lazy DFA. Consider the behavior of B_p and C_p from state S_3 if they read the letter n. While B_p moves to S_1 (what it would do if it were in state S_1), C_p delegates to S_1, which delegates to S_0, which moves to S_1. That is, the move of B_p is simulated in C_p by a chain of delegations, followed by a move of the head to the right (in the worst case, the chain of delegations reaches S_0, who cannot delegate to anybody). The final destination is the same in both cases.

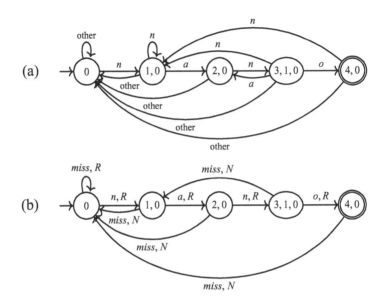

Figure 4.3
DFA and lazy DFA for $p = nano$.

Observe that C_p may require more steps than B_p to read the text. However, we can easily show that the number of steps is at most $2n$. For every letter, the automaton C_p does a number of N-steps, followed by one R-step. Call this step sequence a *macrostep*, and let S_{j_i} be the state reached after the ith macrostep, with $j_0 = 0$. Since the ith macrostep leads from $S_{j_{i-1}}$ to S_{j_i}, and N-steps never move forward along the spine, the number of steps of the ith macrostep is bounded by $j_{i-1} - j_i + 2$. Hence, the total number of steps is bounded by

$$\sum_{i=1}^{n} (j_{i-1} - j_i + 2) = j_0 - j_n + 2n = 0 - j_n + 2n \leq 2n.$$

Computing C_p in time $\mathcal{O}(m)$: The Knuth–Morris–Pratt algorithm. Let $Miss(i)$ be the head of the state reached from S_i by the miss transition of the lazy DFA. For instance, for $p = nano$, we have $Miss(3) = 1$ and $Miss(i) = 0$ otherwise (see figure 4.3). Clearly, if we can compute $Miss(0), \ldots, Miss(m)$ *together* in time $\mathcal{O}(m)$, then we can construct C_p in time $\mathcal{O}(m)$.

Consider the auxiliary function $miss(S_i)$ which returns the target state of the miss transition, instead of its head, that is, $Miss(i) = h(miss(S_i))$. We obtain some equations for $miss$ and then transform them into equations for $Miss$. By definition, for every $i > 0$, in the case of a miss, the state S_i delegates to $t(S_i)$, that is, $miss(S_i) = t(S_i)$. Since $t(S_1) = \{0\} = S_0$, this already gives $miss(S_1) = S_0$. For $i > 1$, using $S_{i-1} = \{i-1\} \cup t(S_{i-1})$, we get

$$t(S_i) = t(\delta_B(S_{i-1}, b_i)) = t(\delta(i-1, b_i) \cup \delta(t(S_{i-1}, b_i))) =$$

$$t(\{i\} \cup \delta(t(S_{i-1}), b_i)) = \delta_B(t(S_{i-1}), b_i),$$

yielding

$$miss(S_i) = \delta_B(miss(S_{i-1}), b_i). \tag{4.1}$$

Moreover, we have

$$\delta_B(S_j, b) = \begin{cases} S_{j+1} & \text{if } b = b_{j+1} \text{ (hit),} \\ S_0 & \text{if } b \neq b_{j+1} \text{ (miss) and } j = 0, \\ \delta_B(t(S_j), b) & \text{if } b \neq b_{j+1} \text{ (miss) and } j \neq 0. \end{cases} \tag{4.2}$$

Combining (4.1) and (4.2), and recalling that $miss(S_0) = S_0$, we obtain

$$miss(S_i) = \begin{cases} S_0 & \text{if } i = 0 \text{ or } i = 1, \\ \delta_B(miss(S_{i-1}), b_i) & \text{if } i > 1, \end{cases} \tag{4.3}$$

$$\delta_B(S_j, b) = \begin{cases} S_{j+1} & \text{if } b = b_{j+1} \text{ (hit),} \\ S_0 & \text{if } b \neq b_{j+1} \text{ (miss) and } j = 0, \\ \delta_B(miss(S_j), b) & \text{if } b \neq b_{j+1} \text{ (miss) and } j \neq 0. \end{cases} \tag{4.4}$$

Let $Miss(i) = h(miss(S_i))$ and $\Delta_B(i, b) = h(\delta_B(S_i, b))$. Equations (4.3) and (4.4) on sets of states become equations on numbers:

$$Miss(i) = \begin{cases} 0 & \text{if } i = 0 \text{ or } i = 1, \\ \Delta_B(Miss(i-1), b_i) & \text{if } i > 1, \end{cases} \tag{4.5}$$

$$\Delta_B(j, b) = \begin{cases} j+1 & \text{if } b = b_{j+1}, \\ 0 & \text{if } b \neq b_{j+1} \text{ and } j = 0, \\ \Delta_B(Miss(j), b) & \text{if } b \neq b_{j+1} \text{ and } j \neq 0. \end{cases} \tag{4.6}$$

Equations (4.5) and (4.6) lead to the procedures described in algorithm 22. Given a word p of length m, $CompMiss(p)$ computes $Miss(i)$ for every index $i \in \{0, \ldots, m\}$. $CompMiss(p)$ calls $DeltaB(j, b)$, which in turn calls $Miss(j)$.

It remains to prove that $CompMiss(p)$ runs in time $\mathcal{O}(m)$. This amounts to showing that all calls to $DeltaB$ together take time $\mathcal{O}(m)$. During the execution of $CompMiss(p)$, function $DeltaB(j, b)$ is called with $j = Miss(1), b = b_2; j = Miss(2), b = b_3; \ldots; j = Miss(m-1), b = b_m$. Let n_i be the number of iterations of the **while** loop, at line 1 of $DeltaB$, executed during the call with arguments $j = Miss(i-1)$ and $b = b_i$. We show that $\sum_{i=2}^{m} n_i < m$. To this end, we claim that $n_i \leq Miss(i-1) - (Miss(i) - 1)$ holds. Indeed, since each iteration of the loop decreases j by at least 1 (line 1 of $DeltaB$), the number of iterations is at most equal to the

---

Algorithm 22 Algorithm *CompMiss(p)*.

CompMiss(p)
Input: pattern $p = b_1 \cdots b_m$

  1    $Miss(0) \leftarrow 0;\ Miss(1) \leftarrow 0$
  2   **for** $i \leftarrow 2, \ldots, m$ **do**
  3        $Miss(i) \leftarrow DeltaB(Miss(i-1), b_i)$

DeltaB(j, b)
Input: head $j \in \{0, \ldots, m\}$, letter b
Output: head of the state $\delta_B(S_j, b)$

  1   **while** $b \neq b_{j+1}$ **and** $j \neq 0$ **do** $j \leftarrow Miss(j)$
  2   **if** $b = b_{j+1}$ **then return** $j + 1$
  3   **else return** 0

---

value of j before the loop minus its value after the loop. The value of j before the loop is $Miss(i-1)$, and so it suffices to show that the final value is at least $Miss(i) - 1$. This follows from the fact that the call to *DeltaB* returns either $j + 1$ or 0 (lines 2 and 3 of *DeltaB*), and the returned value is assigned to $Miss(i)$ (line 3 of *CompMiss*). This concludes the proof of the claim, and we get

$$\sum_{i=2}^{m} n_i \leq \sum_{i=2}^{m} (Miss(i-1) - Miss(i) + 1) = Miss(1) - Miss(m) + m - 1 < m.$$

4.3 Exercises

☆ ✔ **Exercise 81.** Use ideas from the main text to design an algorithm for the pattern matching problem that *identifies* a matched $[i, j]$-factor of the text, where position j is minimal and where position i is as close to j as possible, that is, maximal w.r.t. j. Run your algorithm on text $t = caabac$ and pattern $p = a^+(b + c)a^+ + bac$. What is the complexity of your algorithm?

☆ ■ **Exercise 82.** The pattern matching problem deals with finding the first $[i, j]$-factor of t that belongs to $\mathcal{L}(p)$. Show that the first such $[i, j]$-factor w.r.t. j is not necessarily the first one w.r.t. to i.

☆ ✔ **Exercise 83.** Suppose we have an algorithm that solves the pattern matching problem—that is, one that finds the first $[i, j]$-factor (w.r.t. j) of a text t that matches a pattern p. How can we use it as a black box to find the *last* $[i, j]$-factor w.r.t. i?

☆ ✔ **Exercise 84.** Use the ideas of exercises 81 and 83 to obtain an algorithm that solves the pattern matching problem, but this time by finding the first $[i,j]$-factor w.r.t. i (instead of j).

☆ ⚙ **Exercise 85.**

(a) Build the automata B_p and C_p for the word pattern $p = mammamia$.

(b) How many transitions are taken when reading $t = mami$ in B_p and C_p?

★ ■ **Exercise 86.** We have shown that lazy DFAs for a word pattern may need more than n steps to read a text of length n but not more than $2n + m$, where m is the length of the pattern. Find a text t and a word pattern p such that the run of B_p on t takes at most n steps and the run of C_p takes at least $2n - 1$ steps.

Hint: A simple pattern of the form a^k is sufficient.

☆ ✔ **Exercise 87.** Give an algorithm that, given a text t and a word pattern p, counts the number of occurrences of p in t. Try to obtain a complexity of $\mathcal{O}(|t| + |p|)$.

★ ☞ **Exercise 88.** Two-way DFAs are an extension of lazy automata where the reading head is also allowed to move left. Formally, a *two-way DFA (2DFA)* is a tuple $A = (Q, \Sigma, \delta, q_0, F)$, where $\delta : Q \times (\Sigma \cup \{\vdash, \dashv\}) \to Q \times \{L, N, R\}$. Given a word $w \in \Sigma^*$, A starts in q_0 with its reading tape initialized with $\vdash w \dashv$ and its reading head pointing on $\vdash$. When reading a letter, A moves the head according to δ (*Left*, *No* move, *Right*). Moving left on $\vdash$ or right on $\dashv$ does not move the reading head. A accepts w if, and only if, it reaches $\dashv$ in a state of F.

(a) Let $n \in \mathbb{N}$. Give a 2DFA that accepts $(a + b)^* a(a + b)^n$.

(b) Give a 2DFA that does not terminate on any input.

(c) Describe an algorithm to test whether a given 2DFA A accepts a given word w.

(d) Let $A_1, A_2, \ldots, A_n$ be DFAs over a common alphabet. Give a 2DFA B such that

$$\mathcal{L}(B) = \mathcal{L}(A_1) \cap \mathcal{L}(A_2) \cap \cdots \cap \mathcal{L}(A_n).$$

★ ▣ **Exercise 89.** In order to make pattern matching robust to typos, we further wish to include "similar words" in our results. For this, we consider as "similar" words with a small Levenshtein distance (also known as the edit distance). We may transform a word w into a new word w' using the following operations, where $a_i, b \in \Sigma$:

(R) *Replace:* $w = a_1 \cdots a_{i-1} a_i a_{i+1} \cdots a_l \to w' = a_1 \cdots a_{i-1}\, b\, a_{i+1} \cdots a_l,$

(D) *Delete:* $w = a_1 \cdots a_{i-1} a_i a_{i+1} \cdots a_l \to w' = a_1 \cdots a_{i-1}\, \varepsilon\, a_{i+1} \cdots a_l,$

(I) *Insert:* $w = a_1 \cdots a_{i-1} a_i a_{i+1} \cdots a_l \to w' = a_1 \cdots a_{i-1} a_i\, b\, a_{i+1} \cdots a_l.$

The *Levenshtein distance* of w and w', denoted $\Delta(w, w')$, is the minimal number of operations (R), (D), and (I) needed to transform w into w'. We write $\Delta_{L,i} = \{w \in \Sigma^* : \exists w' \in L$ s.t. $\Delta(w, w') \leq i\}$ to denote the language of all words with Levenshtein distance at most i to some word of L.

(a) Compute $\Delta(abcde, accd)$.

(b) Prove the following statement: If L is a regular language, then $\Delta_{L,n}$ is a regular language.

(c) Let p be the pattern *abba*. Construct an NFA-ε locating the pattern or variations of it with Levenshtein distance 1.

5 Operations on Relations: Implementations

In this chapter, we show how to implement operations on *relations* over a (possibly infinite) universe U. Even though we will encode elements from U as words, when implementing relations, it is convenient to think of U as an abstract universe and not as the set of all words over an alphabet. The reason is that for some operations we will encode an object not by a single word but by (infinitely) many words. In the case of operations on sets, this is not necessary, and one can safely identify the object and its encoding as a word.

We are interested in several operations. A first group contains the operations we already studied for sets but lifted to relations. For instance, given objects x, y and a relation R, we consider the operation **Membership**$((x, y), R)$ that returns **true** if $(x, y) \in R$, and **false** otherwise, or **Complement**(R), which returns $\overline{R} = (U \times U) \setminus R$. Their implementations will be very similar to those of the language case. A second group contains three fundamental operations proper to relations. Given relations $R, R_1, R_2 \subseteq U \times U$:

Operation	Returns
Projection_1(R)	$\pi_1(R) = \{x : \exists y \text{ s.t. } (x, y) \in R\}$
Projection_2(R)	$\pi_2(R) = \{y : \exists x \text{ s.t. } (x, y) \in R\}$
Join(R_1, R_2)	$R_1 \circ R_2 = \{(x, z) : \exists y \text{ s.t. } (x, y) \in R_1 \wedge (y, z) \in R_2\}$

Finally, given $X \subseteq U$, we are interested in two derived operations:

Operation	Returns
Post(X, R)	$post_R(X) = \{y : \exists x \in X \text{ s.t. } (x, y) \in R\}$
Pre(X, R)	$pre_R(X) = \{y : \exists x \in X \text{ s.t. } (y, x) \in R\}$

Example 5.1 Let $R = \{(a, a), (b, a), (ab, ba)\}$, $S = \{(ba, b)\}$ and $X = \{a, b, ab\}$. We have

$$\pi_1(R) = \{a, b, ab\}, \pi_2(R) = \{a, ba\} \text{ and } R \circ S = \{(ab, b)\}.$$

Furthermore, $post_R(X) = \{a, ba\}$ and $pre_R(X) = \{a, b\}$.

5.1   Encodings

We encode elements of U as words over an alphabet Σ. It is convenient to assume that Σ contains a padding letter # and that an element $x \in U$ is encoded not only by a word $s_x \in \Sigma^*$ but by *all* the words of the language $\{s_x \#^n : n \geq 0\}$. That is, an element x has a shortest encoding s_x, and other encodings are obtained by appending to s_x an arbitrary number of padding letters. We assume that the shortest encodings of two distinct elements are also distinct and that, for every $x \in U$, the last letter of s_x differs from #. It follows that the sets of encodings of two distinct elements are disjoint.

The advantage of this assumption is that for any two elements x and y, there exists a number n (and in fact infinitely many) such that both x and y have encodings of length n. We say that a pair of words (w_x, w_y) encodes the pair (x, y) if w_x encodes x, w_y encodes y, and $|w_x| = |w_y|$. Note that if (w_x, w_y) encodes (x, y), then so does $(w_x \#^k, w_y \#^k)$ for every $k \geq 0$. If s_x and s_y are the shortest encodings of x and y, and $|s_x| \leq |s_y|$, then the shortest encoding of (x, y) is $(s_x \#^{|s_y| - |s_x|}, s_y)$.

Example 5.2   We encode the number 6 not only by its small end binary representation 011 but by *any* word of $\mathcal{L}(0110^*)$. In this case, we have $\Sigma = \{0, 1\}$ with 0 as a padding letter. Note, however, that taking 0 as a padding letter requires to take the empty word as the shortest encoding of the number 0 (otherwise, the last letter of the encoding of 0 is the padding letter).

In the rest of this chapter, we use this particular encoding of natural numbers without further notice. We call it the *least-significant-bit-first* (LSBF) encoding and write, for example, LSBF(6) to denote the language $\mathcal{L}(0110^*)$.

If we encode an element of U by more than one word, then we have to define when is an element accepted or rejected by an automaton. Does it suffice that the automaton accepts (rejects) *some* encoding, or does it have to accept (reject) *all* of them? Several definitions are possible, leading to different implementations of the operations. We choose the following option:

Definition 5.3   *Suppose an encoding of the universe U over Σ^* has been fixed. Let A be an NFA. We say that*

- *A accepts $x \in U$ if it accepts all encodings of x,*
- *A rejects $x \in U$ if it accepts no encoding of x, and*
- *A recognizes a set $X \subseteq U$ if*

$$\mathcal{L}(A) = \{w \in \Sigma^* : w \text{ encodes some element of } X\}.$$

A set is regular *(with respect to the fixed encoding) if it is recognized by some NFA.*

Observe that if A recognizes $X \subseteq U$, then, as one would expect, A accepts every $x \in X$ and rejects every $x \notin X$. Furthermore, with this definition, an NFA may neither accept nor reject a given x. An NFA is *well formed* if it recognizes some set of objects and *ill-formed* otherwise.

5.2   Transducers and Regular Relations

Assume an encoding of the universe U over alphabet Σ has been fixed.

Definition 5.4   *A* transducer *over Σ is an NFA over the alphabet $\Sigma \times \Sigma$.*

Transducers are also called *Mealy machines*. According to this definition, a transducer accepts sequences of pairs of letters, but it is convenient to look at it as a machine accepting pairs of words:

Definition 5.5   *Let T be a transducer over Σ. Given words $u = a_1 a_2 \cdots a_n$ and $v = b_1 b_2 \cdots b_n$, we say that T accepts the pair (u, v) if it accepts the word $(a_1, b_1) \cdots (a_n, b_n) \in (\Sigma \times \Sigma)^*$.*

In other words, we identify the set

$$\bigcup_{i \geq 0} (\Sigma^i \times \Sigma^i) \text{ with } (\Sigma \times \Sigma)^* = \bigcup_{i \geq 0} (\Sigma \times \Sigma)^i.$$

We now define when a transducer accepts a pair $(x, y) \in U \times U$, which allows us to define the relation recognized by a transducer. The definition is analogous to definition 5.3.

Definition 5.6   *Let T be a transducer. We say that*

- *T accepts a pair $(x, y) \in U \times U$ if it accepts all encodings of (x, y),*
- *T rejects a pair $(x, y) \in U \times U$ if it accepts no encoding of (x, y), and*
- *T recognizes a relation $R \subseteq U \times U$ if*

$$\mathcal{L}(T) = \{(w_x, w_y) \in (\Sigma \times \Sigma)^* : (w_x, w_y) \text{ encodes some pair of } R\}.$$

A relation is regular *if it is recognized by some transducer.*

It is important to emphasize that not every transducer recognizes a relation, because it may recognize only some, but not all, of the encodings of a pair (x, y). As for NFAs, we say a transducer is *well formed* if it recognizes some relation and *ill-formed* otherwise.

Example 5.7   The *Collatz function* is the function $f : \mathbb{N} \to \mathbb{N}$ defined as follows:

$$f(n) = \begin{cases} 3n + 1 & \text{if } n \text{ is odd,} \\ n/2 & \text{if } n \text{ is even.} \end{cases}$$

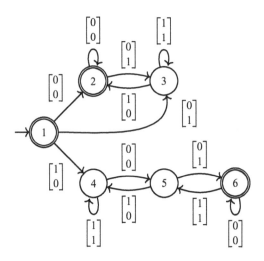

Figure 5.1
A transducer for Collatz's function.

Figure 5.1 depicts a transducer that recognizes $\{(n, f(n)) : n \in \mathbb{N}\}$ using the LSBF encoding and $\Sigma = \{0, 1\}$.

The elements of $\Sigma \times \Sigma$ are drawn as column vectors with two components. The transducer accepts, for instance, the pair $(7, 22)$ because it accepts all pairs of words of the form $(111000^k, 011010^k)$, that is, it accepts

$$\begin{bmatrix}1\\0\end{bmatrix}\begin{bmatrix}1\\1\end{bmatrix}\begin{bmatrix}1\\1\end{bmatrix}\begin{bmatrix}0\\0\end{bmatrix}\begin{bmatrix}0\\1\end{bmatrix}\begin{bmatrix}0\\0\end{bmatrix}^k \quad \text{for every } k \geq 0.$$

Moreover, we have $\mathrm{LSBF}(7) = \mathcal{L}\,(1110^*)$ and $\mathrm{LSBF}(22) = \mathcal{L}\,(011010^*)$.

Why "transducer"? In engineering, a transducer is a device that converts signals in one form of energy into signals of a different form. Two examples of transducers are microphones and loudspeakers. We can look at a transducer T over an alphabet Σ as a device that transforms an input word into an output word. If we choose Σ as the union of an input and an output alphabet, and ensure that in every transition

$$q \xrightarrow{(a,b)} q'$$

the letters a and b are an input and an output letter, respectively, then the transducer transforms a word over the input alphabet into a word over the output alphabet. Observe that the same word can be transformed into different ones.

When looking at transducers from this point of view, it is customary to write a pair $(a, b) \in \Sigma \times \Sigma$ as a/b and read it as "the transducer reads an a and writes a b." In some exercises, we use this notation. However, in section 5.4 we extend the definition of a transducer and consider transducers that recognize relations of arbitrary arity. For such transducers, the metaphor of a converter is less appealing: while in a binary relation, it is natural and canonical to interpret the first and second components of a pair as "input" and "output," there is no such canonical interpretation for a relation of arity 3 or more. In particular, there is no canonical extension of the a/b notation. For this reason, while we keep the name "transducer" for historical reasons, we use the notation

$$q \xrightarrow{(a_1,...,a_n)} q'$$

for transitions, or the column notation, as in example 5.7.

Determinism.   A transducer is *deterministic* if it is a DFA. In particular, a state of a deterministic transducer over alphabet $\Sigma \times \Sigma$ has exactly $|\Sigma|^2$ outgoing transitions. The transducer of figure 5.1 is deterministic in this sense, when an appropriate trap state is added.

There is another possibility to define determinism of transducers, which corresponds to the converter interpretation $(a, b) \mapsto a/b$ described in the previous paragraph. If the letter a/b is interpreted as "the transducer receives the input a and produces the output b," then it is natural to call a transducer deterministic if for every state q and every letter a, there is exactly one transition of the form $(q, a/b, q')$. Note that these two definitions of determinism are *not* equivalent.

We do not give separate implementations of the operations for deterministic and nondeterministic transducers. The new operations (projection and join) can only be reasonably implemented on nondeterministic transducers, and so the deterministic case does not add anything new to the discussion of chapter 3.

5.3   Implementing Operations on Relations

In chapter 3, we made two assumptions on the encoding of objects from the universe U as words:

- every word is the encoding of some object, and
- every object is encoded by exactly one word.

We have relaxed the second assumption and allowed for multiple (and, in fact, infinitely many) encodings of an object. Fortunately, as long as the first assumption still holds, the implementations of the boolean operations remain correct, in the following sense: if the input automata are well formed, then the output automaton is also well formed. Consider, for instance, the complementation operation on DFAs. Since every word encodes some object, the set of all words can be partitioned in equivalence classes, each of them containing all the encodings of an object. If the input automaton A is well formed, then for every object from the universe, A either accepts all words in an equivalence class or none of them. The complement automaton then satisfies the same property but accepts a class iff the original automaton does not accept it.

Note that membership of an object x in a set represented by a well-formed automaton can be checked by taking any encoding w_x of x and checking if the automaton accepts w_x.

5.3.1 Projection

Given a transducer T recognizing a relation $R \subseteq X \times X$, we construct an automaton over Σ recognizing the set $\pi_1(R)$. The initial idea is very simple: loosely speaking, we go through all transitions and replace their labels (a, b) by a. This transformation yields an NFA that has an accepting run on a word w iff T has an accepting run on some pair (w, w'). Formally, this step is carried out in lines 1–4 of algorithm 23 (line 5 is explained below).

However, this initial idea is not fully correct. Consider $R = \{(1, 4)\}$ over $\mathbb{N}$. A transducer T recognizing relation R recognizes the language

$$\{(10^{n+2}, 0010^n) : n \geq 0\},$$

and hence the NFA constructed after lines 1–4 recognizes $\{10^{n+2} : n \geq 0\}$. However, it does not recognize the number 1, because it does not accept *all* of its encodings: the encodings 1 and 10 are rejected.

Algorithm 23 Projection onto the first component of a binary relation.

Proj_1(T)
Input: transducer $T = (Q, \Sigma \times \Sigma, \delta, Q_0, F)$
Output: NFA $A = (Q', \Sigma, \delta', Q'_0, F')$ with $\mathcal{L}(A) = \pi_1(\mathcal{L}(T))$

1   $Q' \leftarrow Q; \ Q'_0 \leftarrow Q_0; \ F'' \leftarrow F$
2   $\delta' \leftarrow \emptyset$
3   **for all** $(q, (a, b), q') \in \delta$ **do**
4   **add** (q, a, q') **to** δ'
5   $F' \leftarrow PadClosure((Q', \Sigma, \delta', Q'_0, F''), \#)$

This problem can be easily repaired. We introduce an auxiliary construction that "completes" a given NFA: the *padding closure* of an NFA is another NFA that accepts a word w if and only if the first NFA accepts $w\#^n$ for some $n \geq 0$. Formally, the padding closure augments the set of final states and returns a new such set. The procedure constructing the padding closure is described in algorithm 24.

Projection onto the second component is implemented in the same fashion. The complexity of *Proj_i* is clearly $\mathcal{O}(|\delta| + |Q|)$, since every transition is examined at most twice, once in line 3 and possibly a second time at line 5 of *PadClosure*.

Algorithm 24   Closure with respect to a padding symbol #.

PadClosure$(A, \#)$
Input: NFA $A = (\Sigma, Q, \delta, q_0, F)$
Output: new set F' of final states

1   $W \leftarrow F; F' \leftarrow \emptyset$
2   **while** $W \neq \emptyset$ **do**
3   **pick** q **from** W
4   **add** q **to** F'
5   **for all** $(q', \#, q) \in \delta$ **do**
6   **if** $q' \notin F'$ **then add** q' **to** W
7   **return** F'

Observe that projections do *not* preserve determinism, because two transitions leaving a state and labeled by two different (pairs of) letters (a, b) and (a, c) become after projection two transitions labeled with the same letter a. In practice, the projection of a transducer is hardly ever deterministic. Since, typically, a sequence of operations manipulating transitions contains at least one projection, deterministic transducers are relatively uninteresting.

Example 5.8   Figure 5.2 depicts the NFAs obtained by projecting the transducer for the Collatz function onto the first and second components. States 4 and 5 of the NFA on the left are made final by *PadClosure*, because they can both reach the final state 6 through a chain of 0s (recall that 0 is the padding symbol). The same happens to state 3 for the NFA on the right, which can reach the final state 2 with 0.

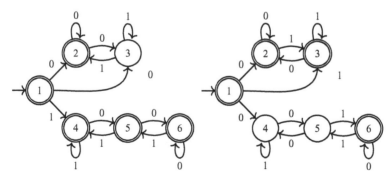

Figure 5.2
Projection of the transducer for the Collatz function onto the first component (left) and second component (right).

Recall that the original transducer recognizes $R = \{(n, f(n)) : n \in \mathbb{N}\}$, where f denotes the Collatz function. Therefore, we have $\pi_1(R) = \{n : n \in \mathbb{N}\} = \mathbb{N}$ and $\pi_2(R) = \{f(n) : n \in \mathbb{N}\}$, and a moment of thought shows that $\pi_2(R) = \mathbb{N}$ as well. So, both NFAs should be universal, and the reader can easily check that this is indeed the case. Observe that both projections are nondeterministic, although the transducer is deterministic.

5.3.2 Join, Post and Pre

We give an implementation of the **Join** operation and then show how to modify it to obtain implementations of **Pre** and **Post**.

Given transducers T_1 and T_2 recognizing relations R_1 and R_2, we construct a transducer $T_1 \circ T_2$ recognizing $R_1 \circ R_2$. We first construct a transducer T with the following property: T accepts (w, w') iff there is a word w'' such that T_1 accepts (w, w'') and T_2 accepts (w'', w'). The intuitive idea is to slightly modify the pairing operation. Recall that the pairing $[A_1, A_2]$ of two NFAs A_1 and A_2 has a transition $[q, r] \xrightarrow{a} [q', r']$ iff

$$A_1 \text{ has a transition } q \xrightarrow{a} q' \text{ and } A_2 \text{ has a transition } r \xrightarrow{a} r'.$$

Similarly, T has a transition $[q, r] \xrightarrow{(a,b)} [q', r']$ if *there is a letter c such that*

$$T_1 \text{ has a transition } q \xrightarrow{(a,c)} q' \text{ and } A_2 \text{ has a transition } r \xrightarrow{(c,b)} r'.$$

So, loosely speaking, the transducer T can output b on input a if there is a letter c such that T_1 can output c on input a, and T_2 can output b on input c. It follows that T has a run

$$[q_{01}, q_{02}] \xrightarrow{(a_1, b_1)} [q_{11}, q_{12}] \xrightarrow{(a_2, b_2)} \cdots \xrightarrow{(a_n, b_n)} [q_{n1}, q_{n2}]$$

iff T_1 and T_2 respectively have runs

$$q_{01} \xrightarrow{(a_1, c_1)} q_{11} \xrightarrow{(a_2, c_2)} \cdots \xrightarrow{(a_n, c_n)} q_{n1},$$

$$q_{02} \xrightarrow{(c_1, b_1)} q_{12} \xrightarrow{(c_2, b_2)} \cdots \xrightarrow{(c_n, b_n)} q_{n2}.$$

Formally, if $T_1 = (Q_1, \Sigma \times \Sigma, \delta_1, Q_{01}, F_1)$ and $T_2 = (Q_2, \Sigma \times \Sigma, \delta_2, Q_{02}, F_2)$, then $T = (Q, \Sigma \times \Sigma, \delta, Q_0, F')$ is the transducer generated by lines 1–9 of algorithm 25. However, transducer T does not necessarily recognize $R_1 \circ R_2$ yet. The issue is similar to the one of the projection operation. Consider the relations on numbers $R_1 = \{(2, 4)\}$ and $R_2 = \{(4, 2)\}$. Transducers T_1 and T_2 recognize

$$\{(010^{n+1}, 0010^n) : n \geq 0\} \text{ and } \{(0010^n, 010^{n+1}) : n \geq 0\}.$$

Therefore, T recognizes $\{(010^{n+1}, 010^{n+1}) : n \geq 0\}$. According to our definition, T does not accept the pair $(2, 2) \in \mathbb{N} \times \mathbb{N}$, because it does not accept *all* of its encodings: the encoding $(01, 01)$ is missing. To fix this, we add a padding closure again at line 10, this time using $(\#, \#)$ as a padding symbol.

Algorithm 25 Join operation.

$Join(T_1, T_2)$

Input: transducers $T_1 = (Q_1, \Sigma \times \Sigma, \delta_1, Q_{01}, F_1), T_2 = (Q_2, \Sigma \times \Sigma, \delta_2, Q_{02}, F_2)$

Output: transducer $T_1 \circ T_2 = (Q, \Sigma \times \Sigma, \delta, Q_0, F)$

```
1   Q, δ, F' ← ∅; Q₀ ← Q₀₁ × Q₀₂
2   W ← Q₀
3   while W ≠ ∅ do
4       pick [q₁, q₂] from W
5       add [q₁, q₂] to Q
6       if q₁ ∈ F₁ and q₂ ∈ F₂ then add [q₁, q₂] to F'
7       for all (q₁, (a, c), q₁') ∈ δ₁, (q₂, (c, b), q₂') ∈ δ₂ do
8           add ([q₁, q₂], (a, b), [q₁', q₂']) to δ
9           if [q₁', q₂'] ∉ Q then add [q₁', q₂'] to W
10  F ← PadClosure((Q, Σ × Σ, δ, Q₀, F'), (#, #))
```

The transducer $T_1 \circ T_2$ has $\mathcal{O}(|Q_1| \cdot |Q_2|)$ states.

Example 5.9 Recall that the transducer T of figure figure 5.1 recognizes the relation $\{(n, f(n)) : n \in \mathbb{N}\}$, where f is the Collatz function. Figure 5.3 depicts the transducer $T \circ T$ as computed by $Join(T, T)$. For example, the transition leading from $[2, 3]$ to $[3, 2]$, labeled by $(0, 0)$, is the result of "pairing" the transition from 2 to 3 labeled by $(0, 1)$ and the one from 3 to 2 labeled by $(1, 0)$. Observe that $T \circ T$ is not deterministic since, for instance, $[1, 1]$ is the source of two transitions labeled by $(0, 0)$, even though T is deterministic.

This transducer recognizes the relation $\{(n, f(f(n))) : n \in \mathbb{N}\}$. A little calculation gives

$$f(f((n))) = \begin{cases} n/4 & \text{if } n \equiv 0 \pmod 4 \\ 3n/2 + 1 & \text{if } n \equiv 2 \pmod 4 \\ 3n/2 + 1/2 & \text{if } n \equiv 1 \pmod 4 \text{ or } n \equiv 3 \pmod 4. \end{cases}$$

The three (shaded) components of the transducer reachable from state $[1, 1]$ correspond to these three cases.

Post and Pre. Note that $\textbf{Post}(X, R) = \textbf{Projection\_2}(\textbf{Join}(Id_X, R))$ and $\textbf{Pre}(X, R) = \textbf{Projection\_1}(\textbf{Join}(R, Id_x))$, where $Id_X = \{(x, x) : x \in X\}$. Thus, operations **Post** and **Pre** can be applied by chaining the previous implementations. However, it is possible to implement them directly.

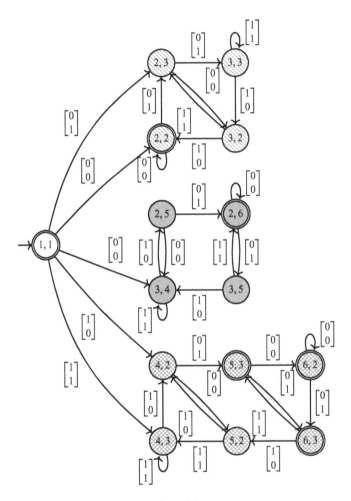

Figure 5.3
A transducer for $f(f(n))$.

Given an NFA $A_1 = (Q_1, \Sigma, \delta_1, Q_{01}, F_1)$ recognizing a regular set $X \subseteq U$ and a transducer $T_2 = (Q_2, \Sigma \times \Sigma, \delta_2, q_{02}, F_2)$ recognizing a regular relation $R \subseteq U \times U$, we construct an NFA B recognizing the set $post_R(X)$. It suffices to slightly modify the join operation. The algorithm $Post(A_1, T_2)$ is the result of replacing lines 7–8 of *Join* by

7   **for all** $(q_1, c, q_1') \in \delta_1$, $(q_2, (c, b), q_2') \in \delta_2$ **do**
8   **add** $([q_1, q_2], b, [q_1', q_2'])$ to δ

As for the join operation, the resulting NFA has to be postprocessed, closing it with respect to the padding symbol.

In order to construct an NFA recognizing $pre_R(X)$, we replace lines 7–8 by

7   **for all** $(q_1, (a, c), q'_1) \in \delta_1, (q_2, c, q'_2) \in \delta_2$ **do**
8   **add** $([q_1, q_2], a, [q'_1, q'_2])$ **to** δ

Observe that both *post* and *pre* are computed with the same complexity as the pairing construction—namely, the product of the number of states of transducer and NFA.

Example 5.10   Let us construct an NFA recognizing the image of multiples of 3 under the Collatz function—that is, the set $\{f(3n) : n \in \mathbb{N}\}$. For this, we first need an automaton recognizing the set Y of all LSBF encodings of the multiples of 3. Such a DFA is depicted in figure 5.4a. For instance, this DFA recognizes 0011 (encoding of 12) and 01001 (encoding of 18) but not 0101 (encoding of 10). We now compute $post_R(Y)$, where, as usual, $R = \{(n, f(n)) : n \in \mathbb{N}\}$. The result is the NFA shown in figure 5.4c.

For instance, $[1, 1] \xrightarrow{1} [1, 3]$ is generated by $1 \xrightarrow{0} 1$ of the DFA and $1 \xrightarrow{(0,1)} 3$ of the transducer for the Collatz function. State $[2, 3]$ becomes final due to the closure with respect to the padding symbol 0.

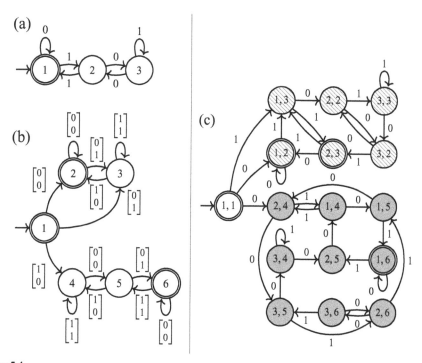

Figure 5.4
Left: (a) DFA for multiples of 3, (b) transducer for the Collatz function f. Right: (c) NFA computing f for multiples of 3.

The NFA of figure 5.4c is not difficult to interpret. The multiples of 3 are the union of the sets $\{6k : k \in \mathbb{N}\}$, all whose elements are even, and the set $\{6k + 3 : k \in \mathbb{N}\}$, all whose elements are odd. Applying f to them yields the sets $\{3k : k \in \mathbb{N}\}$ and $\{18k + 10 : k \in \mathbb{N}\}$. The first of them is again the set of all multiples of 3, and it is recognized by the upper part of the NFA. In fact, this upper part is a DFA, and if we minimize it, we obtain exactly the DFA described above. The lower part of the NFA recognizes the second set. The lower part is minimal; it is easy to find for each state a word recognized by it but not by the others.

It is interesting to observe that an explicit computation of the set $\{f(3k) : k \in \mathbb{N}\}$) in which we apply f to each multiple of 3 does not terminate, because the set is infinite. In a sense, our solution "speeds up" the computation by an infinite factor!

5.4   Relations of Higher Arity

The implementations described in the previous sections can be easily extended to relations of higher arity over the universe U. We briefly describe the generalization. Let us fix an encoding of U over the alphabet Σ with padding symbol #. A tuple $(w_1, \ldots, w_k)$ of words over Σ encodes the tuple $(x_1, \ldots, x_k) \in U^k$ if w_i encodes x_i for every $1 \le i \le k$, and $|w_1| = \cdots = |w_k|$. A k-*transducer* over Σ is an NFA over alphabet Σ^k. Acceptance of a k-transducer is defined as for standard transducers.

Boolean operations are defined as for NFAs. The projection operation can be generalized to projection over an arbitrary subset of components. For this, given an index set $I = \{i_1, \ldots, i_n\} \subseteq \{1, \ldots, k\}$, let x_I denote the projection of a tuple $x = (x_1, \ldots, x_k) \in U^k$ over I, defined as the tuple $(x_{i_1}, \ldots, x_{i_n}) \in U^n$. Given a relation $R \subseteq U \times U$, we define:

Operation	Returns
Projection_I(R):	$\pi_I(R) = \{x_I : x \in R\}$

The operation is implemented analogously to the case of a binary relation. Given a k-transducer T recognizing R, the n-transducer recognizing **Projection_I(R)** is computed as follows:

- Replace every transition $(q, (a_1, \ldots, a_k), q')$ of T by $(q, (a_{i_1}, \ldots, a_{i_n}), q')$.
- Compute the padding closure: for every transition $(q, (\#, \ldots, \#), q')$, if q' is a final state, then add q to the set of final states.

The join operation can also be generalized. Given tuples $x = (x_1, \ldots, x_n)$ and $y = (y_1, \ldots, y_m)$ respectively of arities n and m, we write $x \cdot y$ to denote the tuple $(x_1, \ldots, x_n, y_1, \ldots, y_m)$ of arity $n + m$. Given relations $R_1 \subseteq U^{k_1}$ and $R_2 \subseteq U^{k_2}$ respectively of arities k_1 and k_2, and index sets $I_1 \subseteq \{1, \ldots, k_1\}$ and $I_2 \subseteq \{1, \ldots, k_2\}$ *of the same cardinality ℓ,* we define:

Operation	Returns
Join_I(R_1, R_2)	$\{x_{\overline{I_1}} \cdot y_{\overline{I_2}} : \exists x \in R_1, y \in R_2 \text{ s.t. } x_{I_1} = y_{I_2}\}$

The arity of **Join_I**(R_1, R_2) is $k_1 + k_2 - \ell$. The operation is implemented similarly to the case of binary relations. We proceed in two steps. The first step constructs a transducer according to the following rule:

If the transducer for R_1 has a transition (q, a, q'), the transducer for R_2 has a transition (r, b, r'), and if $a_{I_1} = b_{I_2}$, then add a transition $([q, r], a_{\overline{I_1}} \cdot b_{\overline{I_2}}, [q', r'])$ to the transducer for **Join_I**(R_1, R_2).

In the second step, we compute the padding closure of the result. The generalization of the **Pre** and **Post** operations is analogous.

5.5 Exercises

☆ ✎ **Exercise 90.** In phone dials, letters are mapped into digits as follows:

$$\text{ABC} \mapsto 2 \quad \text{DEF} \mapsto 3 \quad \text{GHI} \mapsto 4 \quad \text{JKL} \mapsto 5$$
$$\text{MNO} \mapsto 6 \quad \text{PQRS} \mapsto 7 \quad \text{TUV} \mapsto 8 \quad \text{WXYZ} \mapsto 9$$

This map can be used to assign a telephone number to a given word. For instance, the number for AUTOMATON is 288662866.

Consider the problem of, given a telephone number (for simplicity, we assume that it contains neither 1 nor 0), finding the set of English words that are mapped into it. For instance, the set of words mapping to 233 contains at least ADD, BED, and BEE. Let N be a given DFA over alphabet $\{A, \ldots, Z\}$ that recognizes the set of all English words. Given a number n, explain how to construct an NFA recognizing the set of all words mapped to n.

☆ ✎ **Exercise 91.** As we have seen, the application of the **Post** and **Pre** operations to transducers requires to compute the padding closure in order to guarantee that the resulting automaton accepts either all or none of the encodings of an object. The padding closure has been defined for encodings where padding occurs *on the right*—that is, w belongs to the padding closure of an NFA A iff $w\#^k \in \mathcal{L}(A)$ for some $k \in \mathbb{N}$. However, in some natural encodings, like the *most-significant-bit-first* encoding of natural numbers, padding occurs *on the left*. Give an algorithm for computing the padding closure of an NFA when padding occurs on the left (i.e., where we consider $\#^k w$).

★ ✎ **Exercise 92.** Let val: $\{0, 1\}^* \to \mathbb{N}$ be the function such that val(w) is the number represented by $w \in \{0, 1\}^*$ with the "least-significant bit-first" encoding.

(a) Give a transducer that doubles numbers, that is, a transducer accepting)

$$L_1 = \{[x, y] \in (\{0, 1\} \times \{0, 1\})^* : \mathrm{val}(y) = 2 \cdot \mathrm{val}(x)\}.$$

(b) Give an algorithm that takes $k \in \mathbb{N}$ as input and that produces a transducer A_k accepting

$$L_k = \left\{[x, y] \in (\{0, 1\} \times \{0, 1\})^* : \mathrm{val}(y) = 2^k \cdot \mathrm{val}(x)\right\}.$$

Hint: Use (a) and consider operations seen in the chapter.

(c) Give a transducer for the addition of two numbers, that is, a transducer accepting

$$\{[x, y, z] \in (\{0, 1\} \times \{0, 1\} \times \{0, 1\})^* : \mathrm{val}(z) = \mathrm{val}(x) + \mathrm{val}(y)\}.$$

(d) For every $k \in \mathbb{N}_{>0}$, let

$$X_k = \{[x, y] \in (\{0, 1\} \times \{0, 1\})^* : \mathrm{val}(y) = k \cdot \mathrm{val}(x)\}.$$

Suppose you are given transducers A and B accepting respectively X_a and X_b for some $a, b \in \mathbb{N}_{>0}$. Sketch an algorithm that builds a transducer C accepting X_{a+b}.

Hint: Use (b) and (c).

(e) Let $k \in \mathbb{N}_{>0}$. Using (b) and (d), how can you build a transducer accepting X_k?

(f) Show that the following language has infinitely many residuals and hence is not regular:
$$\{[x, y] \in (\{0, 1\} \times \{0, 1\})^* : \mathrm{val}(y) = \mathrm{val}(x)^2\}.$$

★ 🖳 **Exercise 93.** Let $U = \mathbb{N}$ be the universe of natural numbers, and consider MSBF encodings. Give transducers for the sets of pairs $(n, m) \in \mathbb{N}^2$ such that

(a) $m = n + 1$,

(b) $m = \lfloor n/2 \rfloor$,

(c) $n \leq 2m$.

☆ ■ **Exercise 94.** Let U be some universe of objects, and let us fix an encoding of U over Σ^*. Prove or disprove: if a relation $R \subseteq U \times U$ is regular, then the following language is regular:

$$L_R = \{w_x w_y : (w_x, w_y) \text{ encodes a pair } (x, y) \in R\}.$$

☆ 🖳 **Exercise 95.** Let A be an NFA over alphabet Σ.

(a) Show how to construct a transducer T over alphabet $\Sigma \times \Sigma$ such that $(w, v) \in \mathcal{L}(T)$ iff $wv \in \mathcal{L}(A)$ and $|w| = |v|$.

(b) Give an algorithm that takes an NFA A as input and returns an NFA $A_{\div 2}$ such that $\mathcal{L}(A_{\div 2}) = \{w \in \Sigma^* : \exists v \in \Sigma^* \text{ s.t. } wv \in \mathcal{L}(A) \text{ and } |w| = |v|\}$.

☆ ✐ **Exercise 96.** We have defined transducers as NFAs whose transitions are labeled by
pairs of symbols $(a, b) \in \Sigma \times \Sigma$. With this definition, transducers can only accept pairs of
words $(a_1 \cdots a_n, b_1 \cdots b_n)$ of the same length, which is not suitable for many applications.

An *ε-transducer* is an NFA whose transitions are labeled by elements of $(\Sigma \cup \{\varepsilon\}) \times (\Sigma \cup \{\varepsilon\})$. An ε-transducer accepts a pair (w, w') of words if it has a run

$$q_0 \xrightarrow{(a_1, b_1)} q_1 \xrightarrow{(a_2, b_2)} \cdots \xrightarrow{(a_n, b_n)} q_n \text{ with } a_i, b_i \in \Sigma \cup \{\varepsilon\}$$

such that $w = a_1 \cdots a_n$ and $w' = b_1 \cdots b_n$. Note that $|w| \leq n$ and $|w'| \leq n$. The relation
accepted by the ε-transducer T is denoted by $\mathcal{L}(T)$. The following figure depicts an ε-transducer over alphabet $\{a, b\}$ that, intuitively, duplicates the letters of a word, for example,
on input *aba*, it outputs *aabbaa*.

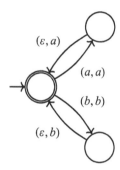

Give an algorithm $Post^\varepsilon(A, T)$ that, given an NFA A and an ε-transducer T, both over a
common alphabet Σ, returns an NFA recognizing the language

$$post_{T_\varepsilon}(A) = \{w : \exists\, w' \in \mathcal{L}(A) \text{ such that } (w', w) \in \mathcal{L}(T)\}.$$

Hint: View ε as an additional letter.

★ ■ **Exercise 97.** In exercise 96, we have shown how to compute preimages and postimages of relations described by ε-transducers. In this exercise, we show that, unfortunately,
and unlike standard transducers, ε-transducers are not closed under intersection.

(a) Construct ε-transducers T_1 and T_2 recognizing the relations

$$R_1 = \{(a^n b^m, c^{2n}) : n, m \geq 0\} \text{ and } R_2 = \{(a^n b^m, c^{2m}) : n, m \geq 0\}.$$

(b) Show that no ε-transducer recognizes $R_1 \cap R_2$.

☆ 🖾 **Exercise 98.** Consider transducers whose transitions are labeled by elements of
$(\Sigma \cup \{\varepsilon\}) \times \Sigma^*$. Intuitively, at each transition, these transducers read one letter or no letter,
and write a string of arbitrary length. These transducers can be used to perform operations
on strings like, for instance, capitalizing all the words in the string: if the transducer reads,

say, "singing in the rain," it writes "Singing In The Rain." Sketch ε-transducers for the following operations, each of which is informally defined by means of two or three examples. In each example, when the transducer reads the string on the left, it writes the string on the right.

```
        Company\Code\index.html        Company\Code
      Company\Docs\Spec\specs.doc      Company\Docs\Spec

   International Business Machines      IBM
  Principles Of Programming Languages   POPL

              Oege  De   Moor          Oege De Moor
     Kathleen  Fisher   AT&T Labs      Kathleen Fisher AT&T Labs

                   Eran Yahav          Yahav, E.
                   Bill Gates          Gates, B.

                 004989273452          +49 89 273452
                (00)4989273452         +49 89 273452
                       273452          +49 89 273452
```

⭐ 🖳 **Exercise 99.** This exercise deals with transducers "normalizing" representations of numbers.

(a) Give a transducer that removes left-trailing zeros from a fractional number. For example, the number 00123.45 should be written as 123.45. More precisely, the transducer should "remove" these zeros by replacing them by the delete symbol "x," for example,

$$00123.450 \mapsto \text{xx}123.450$$

$$00.000 \mapsto \text{x}0.000$$

$$98701.2304 \mapsto 98701.2304$$

(b) Give a transducer that now handles trailing zeros from both sides, for example,

$$00123.450 \mapsto \text{xx}123.45\text{x}$$

$$00.000 \mapsto \text{x}0.0\text{xx}$$

$$98701.2304 \mapsto 98701.2304$$

(c) Give a transducer that achieves the task of (b) but that further handles negative and integral numbers, for example,

$$-00123.450 \mapsto -\text{xx}123.45\text{x}$$

$$-00.000 \mapsto \text{x}0\text{xxxxx}$$

$$98701.2304 \mapsto 98701.2304$$

$$00042.0 \mapsto \text{xxx42xx}$$

$$9000 \mapsto 9000$$

☆ ☞ **Exercise 100.** Transducers can be used to capture the behavior of simple programs. For example, consider this program P and its control-flow diagram:

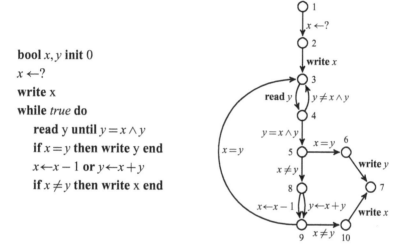

bool x, y **init** 0

$x \leftarrow ?$

write x

while *true* **do**

    read y **until** $y = x \wedge y$

    if $x = y$ **then write** y **end**

    $x \leftarrow x - 1$ **or** $y \leftarrow x + y$

    if $x \neq y$ **then write** x **end**

Program P communicates with the environment through its two boolean variables, both initialized to 0. The instruction **end** finishes the execution of P. The I/O-relation of P is the set of pairs $(w_I, w_O) \in \{0, 1\}^* \times \{0, 1\}^*$ such that there is an execution of P during which P reads the sequence w_I of values and writes the sequence w_O.

Let $[i, x, y]$ denote the configuration of P in which P is at node i of the control-flow diagram, and the values of its two boolean variables are x and y, respectively. The initial configuration of P is $[1, 0, 0]$. By executing the first instruction, P moves nondeterministically to one of the configurations $[2, 0, 0]$ and $[2, 1, 0]$; no input symbol is read and no output symbol is written. Similarly, by executing its second instruction, the program P moves from $[2, 1, 0]$ to $[3, 1, 0]$ while reading nothing and writing 1.

(a) Give an ε-transducer recognizing the I/O-relation of P.

(b) Can an overflow error occur? That is, can a configuration be reached in which the value of x or y is not 0 or 1?

(c) Can node 10 of the control-flow graph be reached?

(d) What are the possible values of x upon termination, that is, upon reaching **end**?

(e) Is there an execution during which P reads 101 and writes 01?

(f) Let I and O be regular sets of inputs and outputs, respectively. Think of O as a set of dangerous outputs that we want to avoid. We wish to prove that the inputs from I are safe, that is, when P is fed inputs from I, none of the dangerous outputs can occur. Describe an algorithm that decides, given I and O, whether there are $i \in I$ and $o \in O$ such that (i, o) belongs to the I/O-relation of P.

6 Finite Universes and Decision Diagrams

In chapter 2, we proved that every regular language has a unique minimal DFA. A natural question is whether the operations on languages and relations, described in chapters 3 and 5, can be implemented using minimal DFAs and minimal deterministic transducers as data structure.

The implementations described in the first part of chapter 3 accept and return DFAs but do not preserve minimality: even if the arguments are minimal DFAs, the result may be nonminimal (the only exception was complementation). So, in order to return the minimal DFA, an extra minimization operation must be applied. The situation is worse for the projection and join operations of chapter 5, because they do not even preserve determinism: the result of projecting a deterministic transducer or joining two of them may be nondeterministic. In order to return a minimal DFA, it is necessary to first determinize, at exponential cost in the worst case, and then minimize.

In this chapter, we present implementations that *directly* yield the minimal DFA, with no need for an extra minimization step, for the special case in which the universe of objects is finite. The fundamental feature of this case is that all objects can be encoded by words over a suitable alphabet Σ *of a fixed length*. For instance, if the universe consists of sixty-four-bit unsigned integers, that is, natural numbers in the range $\{0, \ldots, 2^{64} - 1\}$, then its objects can be encoded by words over $\Sigma = \{0, 1\}$ of length 64. Number 0 is encoded by the word 0^{64}, number 1 by $0^{63}1$, number 2 by $0^{62}10$, and so on until number $2^{64} - 1$, encoded by 1^{64}. A first consequence is that, since all encodings have the same length, we can represent a tuple of n objects by a word of the same length over alphabet Σ^n, without having to pad shorter words up to the length of the longest one, as we did in chapter 5.

In the first part of this chapter, we give a first implementation of the operations on languages and relations using minimal DFAs as data structure. But we can even do better. We introduce a very restricted class of automata with transitions labeled by regular expressions. This class still has a unique minimal automaton for each fixed-length language, which can have fewer states than the minimal DFA. We reimplement the operations using these new minimal automata. The resulting data structure, called *decision diagrams*, is a slight generalization of binary decision diagrams, or BDDs, a fundamental data structure introduced by R. E. Bryant in 1986. Bryant introduced binary decision diagrams as a compact representation of boolean functions and have been extensively used in many areas of computer science, particularly in the synthesis and verification of logical circuits. We will provide an example of such an application in section 6.4.1.

6.1   Fixed-Length Languages and the Master Automaton

Let us introduce fixed-length languages.

Definition 6.1   *A language $L \subseteq \Sigma^*$ has* length $n \geq 0$ *if every word of L has length n. If L has length n for some $n \geq 0$, then we say that L is a* fixed-length language, *or that it has* fixed-length.

Some remarks are in order:

- According to this definition, the empty language has length n for *all $n \geq 0$* (the assertion "every word of L has length n" is vacuously true).
- There are exactly two languages of length 0: the empty language $\emptyset$ and the language $\{\varepsilon\}$ containing only the empty word.
- Every fixed-length language contains only finitely many words, and so it is regular.

In chapter 2, we introduced the master automaton, an object "encompassing" all minimal DFAs of all regular languages (definition 2.14). We now consider the fragment of the master automaton obtained by retaining the states corresponding to fixed-length languages and the transitions between them. Given a language L and a letter $a \in \Sigma$, recall that L^a, the *residual* of L with respect to a, is the set of all words w such that $aw \in L$ (definition 2.1). The fixed-length master automaton is defined exactly as the master automaton but replacing the set of all regular languages by the smaller set of all fixed-length languages:

Definition 6.2   *The* fixed-length master automaton *over the alphabet Σ is the tuple $M = (Q_M, \Sigma, \delta_M, F_M)$, where*

- Q_M *is the set of all fixed-length languages over Σ,*
- $\delta \colon Q_M \times \Sigma \to Q_M$ *is given by $\delta(L, a) = L^a$ for every $q \in Q_M$ and $a \in \Sigma$, and*
- $L \in F_M$ *iff $\varepsilon \in L$.*

Example 6.3   Figure 6.1 depicts a small part of the fixed-length master automaton for the alphabet $\Sigma = \{a, b\}$.

We make some observations:

- The set of transitions of M is well defined, because if L is a fixed-length language, then so is L^a.

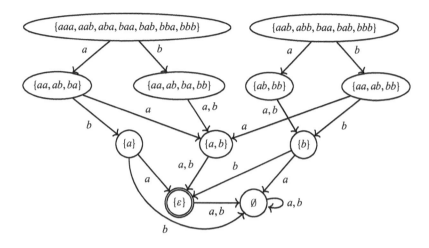

Figure 6.1
A fragment of the fixed-length master automaton over $\Sigma = \{a, b\}$.

- M has a single final state—namely, $\{\varepsilon\}$. Indeed, by definition 6.2, the final states of M are the fixed languages containing ε, and the only such language is $\{\varepsilon\}$.

- For every $k \geq 1$, every transition of M starting at a language of length k leads to a state of length $k - 1$. This allows us to organize the states of M in *layers*, according to their lengths. (Recall that $\emptyset$ has all lengths, and so it could be in any layer, but we assign it to layer 0.)

- M is almost acyclic. More precisely, the only cycles of M are the self-loops leading from $\emptyset$ to itself for every letter $a \in \Sigma$.

We proved in chapter 2 that the minimal DFA for a regular language L is the fragment of the master automaton with the state L as the initial state. In particular, the language recognized from the state L is L. The fixed-length master automaton inherits this property; for example, the reader can check that the language recognized from state $\{ab, bb\}$ of figure 6.1 is indeed $\{ab, bb\}$.

6.2   A Data Structure for Fixed-Length Languages

The previous observations allow us to define a data structure for representing *finite sets of fixed-length languages*, all of them *of the same length*. Loosely speaking, the structure representing the languages $\mathcal{L} = \{L_1, \ldots, L_m\}$ is the fragment of the fixed-length master automaton containing the states recognizing $L_1, \ldots, L_n$ and their descendants. It is a DFA with multiple initial states, and, for this reason, we call it *the multi-DFA for $\mathcal{L}$*. Formally:

Definition 6.4   *Let $\mathcal{L} = \{L_1, \ldots, L_n\}$ be a set of languages of the same length over a common alphabet Σ. The* multi-DFA $A_{\mathcal{L}}$ *is the tuple* $A_{\mathcal{L}} = (Q_{\mathcal{L}}, \Sigma, \delta_{\mathcal{L}}, Q_{0\mathcal{L}}, F_{\mathcal{L}})$, *where*

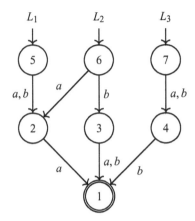

Figure 6.2
The multi-DFA for set $\mathcal{L} = \{L_1, L_2, L_3\}$, where $L_1 = \{aa, ba\}$, $L_2 = \{aa, ba, bb\}$, and $L_3 = \{ab, bb\}$.

- $Q_{\mathcal{L}}$ *is the set of states of the fixed-length master automaton reachable from at least one of the states* $L_1, \ldots, L_n$,
- $Q_{0\mathcal{L}} = \{L_1, \ldots, L_n\}$,
- $\delta_{\mathcal{L}}$ *is the projection of* δ_M *onto* $Q_{\mathcal{L}}$, *and*
- $F_{\mathcal{L}} = F_M \cap Q_{\mathcal{L}}$.

Example 6.5 Figure 6.2 depicts the multi-DFA for $\mathcal{L} = \{L_1, L_2, L_3\}$, where $L_1 = \{aa, ba\}$, $L_2 = \{aa, ba, bb\}$, and $L_3 = \{ab, bb\}$. For clarity, the state for the empty language has been omitted, as well as the transitions leading to it.

In order to manipulate multi-DFAs, we represent them as a *table of nodes*. Let $\Sigma = \{a_1, \ldots, a_m\}$. A *node* is a pair $\langle q, s \rangle$, where q is a *state identifier* and $s = (q_1, \ldots, q_m)$ is the *successor tuple* of the node. Along the chapter, we denote the state identifiers of the states for $\emptyset$ and $\{\varepsilon\}$ by $q_\emptyset$ and q_ε, respectively.

A multi-DFA is represented by a table containing a node for each state, with the exception of the nodes $q_\emptyset$ and q_ε. The table for the multi-DFA of figure 6.2, where state identifiers are numbers, is as follows:

Ident.	a-succ	b-succ
2	1	0
3	1	1
4	0	1
5	2	2
6	2	3
7	4	4

The procedure *make*. The algorithms on multi-DFAs use a procedure $make(s)$ that returns the identifier of the state of T having s as successor tuple, if such a state exists, and that, otherwise, adds a new node $\langle q, s \rangle$ to T, where q is a fresh state identifier, different from all other state identifiers in T, and returns q. If s is the tuple whose components all equal $q_\emptyset$, then $make(s)$ returns $q_\emptyset$. The procedure assumes that all the states of the tuple s (with the exception of $q_\emptyset$ and q_ε) appear in T.[1] For instance, if T is the table above, then $make(2, 2)$ returns 5, and $make(3, 2)$ adds a new row, say $\langle 8, (3, 2) \rangle$, and returns 8.

6.3   Operations on Fixed-Length Languages

All operations assume that input fixed-length languages are given as multi-DFAs represented as a table of nodes. Nodes are pairs of state identifier and successor tuple. The key to all implementations is the fact that if L is a language of length $n \geq 1$, then L^a is a language of length $n - 1$. This allows to design recursive algorithms that directly compute the result when the inputs are languages of length 0 and reduce the problem of computing the result for languages of length $n \geq 1$ to the same problem for languages of smaller length.

Fixed-length membership.   The operation is implemented as for DFAs, and the complexity is linear in the size of the input.

Fixed-length union and intersection.   Implementing a boolean operation on multi-DFAs corresponds to possibly extending the multi-DFA and returning the state corresponding to the result of the operation. This is best explained by means of an example. Consider again the multi-DFA of figure 6.2. An operation like **Union**(L_1, L_2) gets the initial states 5 and 6 as input and returns the state recognizing $L_1 \cup L_2$. Since $L_1 \cup L_2 = L_2$, the operation returns state 6. However, if we take **Intersection**(L_2, L_3), then the multi-DFA does not contain any state recognizing it. In this case, the operation extends the multi-DFA for $\{L_1, L_2, L_3\}$ to the multi-DFA for $\{L_1, L_2, L_3, L_2 \cap L_3\}$, depicted in figure 6.3, and returns state 8. Thus, **Intersection**(L_2, L_3) not only returns a state but also has a side effect on the multi-DFA underlying the operations.

Given two fixed-length languages L_1, L_2 *of the same length*, we present an algorithm that returns the state of the fixed-length master automaton recognizing $L_1 \cap L_2$ (the algorithm for $L_1 \cup L_2$ is analogous). The following properties lead to the recursive algorithm $inter(q_1, q_2)$ shown in algorithm 26:

- if $L_1 = \emptyset$ or $L_2 = \emptyset$, then $L_1 \cap L_2 = \emptyset$;
- if $L_1 = \{\varepsilon\}$ and $L_2 = \{\varepsilon\}$, then $L_1 \cap L_2 = \{\varepsilon\}$; and
- if $L_1, L_2 \notin \{\emptyset, \{\varepsilon\}\}$, then $(L_1 \cap L_2)^a = L_1^a \cap L_2^a$ for every $a \in \Sigma$.

---

1. Note that the procedure makes use of the fact that no two states have the same successor tuple.

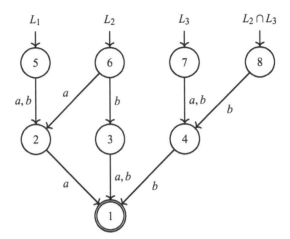

Figure 6.3
The multi-DFA for $\{L_1, L_2, L_3, L_1 \cup L_2, L_2 \cap L_3\}$.

Assume that the states q_1 and q_2 recognize languages L_1 and L_2 of the same length. We say that q_1 and q_2 have the same length. The algorithm returns the state identifier $q_{L_1 \cap L_2}$. If $q_1 = q_\emptyset$, then $L_1 = \emptyset$, which implies $L_1 \cap L_2 = \emptyset$. So, the algorithm returns the state identifier $q_\emptyset$. If $q_2 = q_\emptyset$, then the algorithm also returns $q_\emptyset$. If $q_1 = q_\varepsilon = q_2$, then the algorithm returns q_ε. This deals with all the cases in which $q_1, q_2 \in \{q_\emptyset, q_\varepsilon\}$ (and some more, which does no harm). If $q_1, q_2 \notin \{q_\emptyset, q_\varepsilon\}$, then the algorithm computes the state identifiers $r_1, \ldots, r_m$ recognizing the languages $(L_1 \cap L_2)^{a_1}, \ldots, (L_1 \cap L_2)^{a_m}$ and returns $make(r_1, \ldots, r_m)$, creating a new node if no node of T has $(r_1, \ldots, r_m)$ as successor tuple. But how does the algorithm compute the state identifier of $(L_1 \cap L_2)^{a_i}$? By the above identity, we have $(L_1 \cap L_2)^{a_i} = L_1^{a_i} \cap L_2^{a_i}$, so the algorithm computes the state identifier of $L_1^{a_i} \cap L_2^{a_i}$ by a recursive call $inter(q_1^{a_i}, q_2^{a_i})$.

The only remaining point is the role of table G. The algorithm uses memoization to avoid recomputing the same object. Table G is initially empty. When $inter(q_1, q_2)$ is computed for the first time, the result is memoized in $G(q_1, q_2)$. In any subsequent call, the result is not recomputed but just read from G. For the complexity, let n_1 and n_2 be the number of states of T reachable from states q_1 and q_2. It is easy to see that every call to $inter$ receives as arguments states reachable from q_1 and q_2, respectively. Thus, $inter$ is called with at most $n_1 \cdot n_2$ possible arguments, and hence the complexity is $\mathcal{O}(n_1 \cdot n_2)$.

Algorithm $inter$ is generic: in order to obtain an algorithm for another binary operator, it suffices to change lines 2 and 3. For example, the symmetric difference of L_1 and L_2 is implemented by changing lines 2 and 3 to

2   **if** $(q_1 = q_\emptyset$ **and** $q_2 = q_\varepsilon)$ **or** $(q_1 = q_\varepsilon$ **and** $q_2 = q_\emptyset)$ **then return** q_ε
3   **else if** $(q_1 = q_\varepsilon$ **and** $q_2 = q_\varepsilon)$ **or** $(q_1 = q_\emptyset$ **and** $q_2 = q_\emptyset)$ **then return** $q_\emptyset$

Algorithm 26 Algorithm *inter*.

---

inter(q_1, q_2)
Input: states q_1, q_2 of the same length
Output: state recognizing $\mathcal{L}(q_1) \cap \mathcal{L}(q_2)$

```
1    if G(q₁,q₂) is not empty then return G(q₁,q₂)
2    if q₁ = q∅ or q₂ = q∅ then return q∅
3    else if q₁ = qε and q₂ = qε then return qε
4    else /* q₁,q₂ ∉ {q∅,qε} */
5        for all i = 1,...,m do rᵢ ← inter(q₁ᵃⁱ,q₂ᵃⁱ)
6        G(q₁,q₂) ← make(r₁,...,rₘ)
7        return G(q₁,q₂)
```

For intersection, we can easily obtain a more efficient version. For instance, we know that *inter*(q_1, q_2) and *inter*(q_2, q_1) return the same state, and so we can improve line 1 by checking not only if $G(q_1, q_2)$ is nonempty but also if $G(q_2, q_1)$ is. Moreover, *inter*(q, q) always returns q, so there is no need to compute anything either.

Example 6.6 Consider the multi-DFA at the top of figure 6.4 but without the colored states. State 0 for $\emptyset$ is again not shown. The tree at the bottom of the figure graphically describes the run of *inter*$(12, 13)$, that is, we compute the node for the intersection of the languages recognized from states 12 and 13. A node $q, q' \mapsto q''$ of the tree stands for a recursive call to *inter* with arguments q and q' that returns q''. For instance, the node $2, 4 \mapsto 2$ indicates that *inter* is called with arguments 2 and 4 and that the call returns state 2. Let us see why the result is 2. The call *inter*$(2, 4)$ produces two recursive calls, first *inter*$(1, 1)$ (the a-successors of 2 and 4) and then *inter*$(0, 1)$. The first call returns 1 and the second 0. Therefore, *inter*$(2, 4)$ returns a state with 1 as a-successor and 0 as b-successor. Since this state already exists (it is state 2), *inter*$(2, 4)$ returns 2. On the other hand, *inter*$(9, 10)$ creates and returns a new state: its two "children calls" return 5 and 6, and so a new state with states 5 and 6 as a- and b-successors must be created.

Solid colored nodes of the tree correspond to calls that have already been computed and for which *inter* just looks up the result in G. Hatched colored nodes correspond to calls that are not computed by the more efficient version. For instance, this version immediately returns 4 as result of *inter*$(4, 4)$.

Fixed-length complement. Observe that if a set $X \subseteq U$ is encoded by a language L of length n, then the set $U \setminus X$ is encoded by the *fixed-length complement* $\Sigma^n \setminus L$, which we denote by $\overline{L}^n$. In particular, since the empty language has all lengths, we have, for example, $\overline{\emptyset}^2 = \Sigma^2$, $\overline{\emptyset}^3 = \Sigma^3$, and $\overline{\emptyset}^0 = \Sigma^0 = \{\varepsilon\}$.

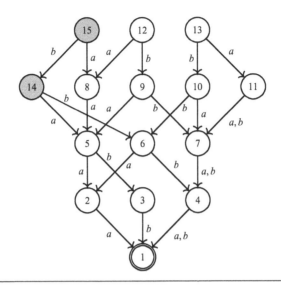

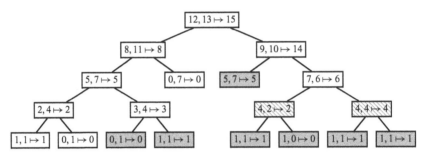

Figure 6.4
An execution of *inter*.

Given the state of the fixed-length master automaton recognizing L, we compute the state recognizing $\overline{L}^n$ with the help of these properties:

- if L has length 0 and $L = \emptyset$, then $\overline{L}^0 = \{\varepsilon\}$;
- if L has length 0 and $L = \{\varepsilon\}$, then $\overline{L}^0 = \emptyset$; and
- if L has length $n \geq 1$, then $\left(\overline{L}^n\right)^a = \overline{L^a}^{(n-1)}$ (observe that $w \in \left(\overline{L}\right)^a$ iff $aw \notin L$ iff $w \notin L^a$ iff $w \in \overline{L^a}$).

We obtain the procedure described in algorithm 27. If the fixed-length master automaton has n states reachable from q, then the operation has complexity $\mathcal{O}(n)$.

Example 6.7 Consider the multi-DFA at the top of figure 6.5 without the colored states. The tree of recursive calls at the bottom of the figure graphically describes the run of

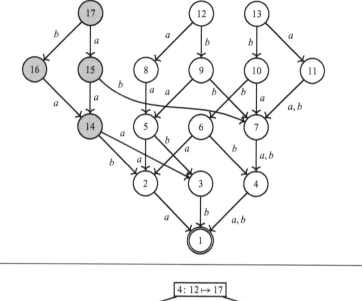

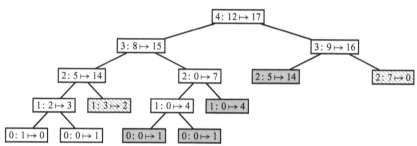

Figure 6.5
An execution of *comp*.

comp(4, 12)—that is, we compute the node for the complement of the language recognized from state 12, which has length 4. For instance, *comp*(1, 2) generates two recursive calls, first *comp*(0, 1) (the *a*-successor of 2) and then *comp*(0, 0). The calls return 0 and 1, respectively, and so *comp*(1, 2) returns 3. Observe how the call *comp*(2, 0) returns 7, the state accepting $\{a, b\}^2$.

Solid colored nodes correspond again to calls for which *comp* just looks up the result in *G*. Hatched colored nodes correspond to calls whose result is directly computed by a more efficient version of *comp* that applies the following rule: if *comp*(*i, j*) returns *k*, then *comp*(*i, k*) returns *j*.

Fixed-length emptiness. A fixed-language language *L* is empty iff the node representing *L* has $q_\emptyset$ as state identifier. Hence, emptiness can be checked in constant time.

Algorithm 27 Algorithm *comp*.

$comp(n, q)$
Input: length n, state q of length n
Output: state recognizing $\overline{\mathcal{L}(q)}^n$

1   **if** $G(n, q)$ is not empty **then return** $G(n, q)$
2   **if** $n = 0$ **and** $q = q_\emptyset$ **then return** q_ε
3   **else if** $n = 0$ **and** $q = q_\varepsilon$ **then return** $q_\emptyset$
4   **else** $/* n \geq 1 */$
5   **for all** $i = 1, \ldots, m$ **do** $r_i \leftarrow comp(n - 1, q^{a_i})$
6       $G(n, q) \leftarrow make(r_1, \ldots, r_m)$
7   **return** $G(n, q)$

Algorithm 28 Algorithm *univ*.

$univ(q)$
Input: state q
Output: **true** if $\mathcal{L}(q)$ is fixed-length universal,
                   false otherwise

1   **if** $G(q)$ is not empty **then return** $G(q)$
2   **if** $q = q_\emptyset$ **then return false**
3   **else if** $q = q_\varepsilon$ **then return true**
4   **else** $/* q \neq q_\emptyset$ and $q \neq q_\varepsilon */$
5       $G(q) \leftarrow \mathbf{and}(univ(q^{a_1}), \ldots, univ(q^{a_m}))$
6   **return** $G(q)$

Fixed-length universality.   A language L of length n is *fixed-length universal* if $L = \Sigma^n$. The universality of a language of length n recognized by a state q can be checked in time $\mathcal{O}(n)$. It suffices to check for all states reachable from q, with the exception of $q_\emptyset$, that no transition leads to $q_\emptyset$. More systematically, we use the following properties that lead to algorithm 28:

- if $L = \emptyset$, then L is not universal;
- if $L = \{\varepsilon\}$, then L is universal; and
- if $\emptyset \neq L \neq \{\varepsilon\}$, then L is universal iff L^a is universal for every $a \in \Sigma$.

For a better algorithm, see exercise 103.

Algorithm 29 Algorithm $eq2$.

$eq2(q_1, q_2)$
Input: states q_1, q_2 of different tables, of the same length
Output: true if $\mathcal{L}(q_1) = \mathcal{L}(q_2)$, **false** otherwise

```
1     if G(q₁,q₂) is not empty then return G(q₁,q₂)
2     if q₁ = q∅₁ and q₂ = q∅₂ then G(q₁,q₂) ← true
3     else if q₁ = q∅₁ and q₂ ≠ q∅₂ then G(q₁,q₂) ← false
4     else if q₁ ≠ q∅₁ and q₂ = q∅₂ then G(q₁,q₂) ← false
5     else /* q₁ ≠ q∅₁ and q₂ ≠ q∅₂ */
6         G(q₁,q₂) ← and(eq2(q₁ᵃ¹,q₂ᵃ¹), . . . , eq2(q₁ᵃᵐ,q₂ᵃᵐ))
7     return G(q₁,q₂)
```

Fixed-length equality. Since minimal DFAs are unique, two languages are equal iff the nodes representing them have the same state identifier. This leads to a constant time algorithm. This solution, however, assumes that the two input nodes come from the same table. If they come from two different tables T_1 and T_2, then, since state identifiers can be assigned in both tables in different ways, it is necessary to check if the DFAs rooted at the states q_1 and q_2 are isomorphic. This is done by $eq2$ described in algorithm 29, which assumes that q_i belongs to a table T_i and that both tables assign state identifiers $q_{\emptyset 1}$ and $q_{\emptyset 2}$ to $\emptyset$.

Fixed-length inclusion. Given $L_1, L_2 \subseteq \Sigma^n$, in order to check $L_1 \subseteq L_2$, we compute $L_1 \cap L_2$ and check whether it is equal to L_1 using the equality check. The complexity is dominated by the complexity of computing the intersection.

6.4   Determinization and Minimization

Let L be a fixed-length language, and let $A = (Q, \Sigma, \delta, Q_0, F)$ be an NFA recognizing L. The forthcoming procedure $det\&min(A)$ returns the state of the fixed-length master automaton recognizing L. In other words, $det\&min(A)$ simultaneously determinizes and minimizes A.

The algorithm actually solves a more general problem. Given a set $S \subseteq Q$ of states, all recognizing languages *of the same length*, the language $\mathcal{L}(S) = \cup_{q \in S}\mathcal{L}(q)$ has also this common length. The heart of the algorithm is a procedure $state(S)$ that returns the state recognizing $\mathcal{L}(S)$. Since $L = \mathcal{L}(\{q_0\})$, the algorithm $det\&Min(A)$ just calls $state(\{q_0\})$.

We make the assumption that for every state q of A, there is a path leading from q to some final state. This assumption can be enforced by suitable preprocessing, but usually it is not necessary; in applications, NFAs for fixed-length languages usually satisfy the property by construction. With this assumption, $\mathcal{L}(S)$ satisfies the following properties:

Algorithm 30   Algorithm *det&min*.

---

det&min(*A*)
Input: NFA $A = (Q, \Sigma, \delta, Q_0, F)$
Output: master state recognizing $\mathcal{L}(A)$

 1   **return** *state*(Q_0)

state(*S*)
Input: set $S \subseteq Q$ recognizing languages of the same length
Output: state recognizing $\mathcal{L}(S)$

 1   **if** $G(S)$ is not empty **then return** $G(S)$
 2   **else if** $S = \emptyset$ **then return** $q_\emptyset$
 3   **else if** $S \cap F \neq \emptyset$ **then return** q_ε
 4   **else** $/* S \neq \emptyset$ and $S \cap F = \emptyset * /$
 5   **for all** $i = 1, \ldots, m$ **do** $S_i \leftarrow \delta(S, a_i)$
 6        $G(S) \leftarrow make(state(S_1), \ldots, state(S_m))$
 7   **return** $G(S)$

- if $S = \emptyset$, then $\mathcal{L}(S) = \emptyset$;
- if $S \cap F \neq \emptyset$, then $\mathcal{L}(S) = \{\varepsilon\}$ (since the states of S recognize fixed-length languages, the states of F recognize $\{\varepsilon\}$; since all the states of S recognize languages of the same length and $S \cap F \neq \emptyset$, we have $\mathcal{L}(S) = \{\varepsilon\}$); and
- if $S \neq \emptyset$ and $S \cap F = \emptyset$, then $\mathcal{L}(S) = \bigcup_{i=1}^{n} a_i \cdot \mathcal{L}(S_i)$, where $S_i = \delta(S, a_i) := \bigcup_{q \in S} \delta(q, a_i)$.

These properties lead to the recursive procedure of algorithm 30. The procedure *state*(*S*) uses a table G of results, initially empty. When *state*(*S*) is computed for the first time, the result is memoized in $G(S)$, and any subsequent call directly reads the result from G.

The algorithm has exponential complexity, as, in the worst case, it may call *state*(*S*) for every set $S \subseteq Q$. To show that an exponential blowup is unavoidable, consider the family $\{L_n\}_{n \geq 0}$, where $L_n = \{ww' : w, w' \in \{0, 1\}^n, w \neq w'\}$. While L_n can be recognized by an NFA of size $\mathcal{O}(n^2)$, its minimal DFA has $\mathcal{O}(2^n)$ states: for all $u, v \in \Sigma^n$ if $u \neq v$, then $L_n^u \neq L_n^v$, as $v \in L_n^u$ but $v \notin L_n^v$.

Example 6.8   Figure 6.6 shows an NFA (top left) and the result of applying *det&min* to it (top right). The run of *det&min* is shown at the bottom of the figure, where, for the sake of readability, sets of states are written without curly brackets (e.g., β, γ instead of $\{\beta, \gamma\}$). Observe, for instance, that the algorithm assigns to $\{\gamma\}$ the same node as to $\{\beta, \gamma\}$, because both have the states 2 and 3 as *a*-successor and *b*-successor, respectively.

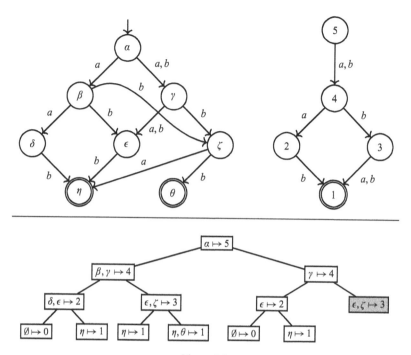

Figure 6.6
Run of *det&min* on an NFA for a fixed-length language.

6.4.1   An Application: Equivalence of Digital Circuits

A *carry-ripple adder* is a digital circuit that adds two n-bits binary numbers $x_n \cdots x_1$ and $y_n \cdots y_1$, producing a $(n+1)$-bit number $s_{n+1}s_n \cdots s_1$. The circuit implements the simple algorithm that repeatedly adds the bits x_i and y_i, together with a carry-bit c_{i-1}^{in}, producing the sum-bit s_i and the carry-bit c_i^{out} (where $c_0^{in} := 0$ and $s_{n+1} := c_n$). So, the adder consists of a cascade of one-bit *full adders*, each of which implements one step of the algorithm.

A full adder has three inputs x, y, c^{in}; two outputs s, c^{out}; and the following specification: s must be set to 1 iff exactly one or exactly three of the inputs are 1, and c^{out} must be set to 1 iff at least two of the inputs are 1.

When asked to implement a full adder, some students produce the circuit depicted on the left of figure 6.7. It corresponds to the logical formulas

$$s = c^{in} \oplus x \oplus y,$$

$$c^{out} = ((c^{in} \wedge x) \vee (c^{in} \wedge y)) \vee (x \wedge y),$$

where $\oplus$ denotes the exclusive-or operator. It is a natural seven-gate implementation, which deals with the three possible cases for the carry-bit separately: c^{in} and x are 1, c^{in} and y are 1,

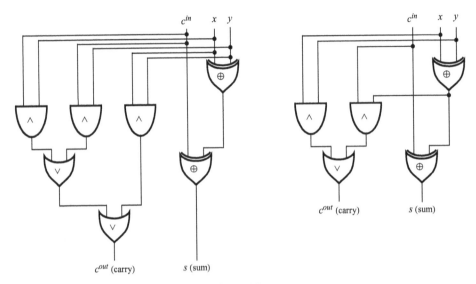

Figure 6.7
Two implementations of a full adder.

and x and y are 1. However, there is a more economic and efficient five-gate implementation, depicted on the right of figure 6.7. It corresponds to the formulas

$$s = c^{in} \oplus x \oplus y,$$

$$c^{out} = (x \wedge y) \vee (c^{in} \wedge (x \oplus y)).$$

Verifying that the two circuits indeed compute the same boolean function reduces to checking the logical equivalence of the two boolean formulas

$$\varphi_1 := (c^{in} \wedge x) \vee (c^{in} \wedge y) \vee (x \wedge y) \quad \text{and} \quad \varphi_2 := (x \wedge y) \vee (c^{in} \wedge (x \oplus y)).$$

In this simple example, equivalence can be checked by computing the truth tables of φ_1 and φ_2; since they have three variables, there are only eight truth assignments. However, a formula with n variables has 2^n truth assignments, and so this approach does not scale to circuits with hundreds of input signals. A much better algorithm encodes assignments as words and constructs a multi-DFA for the languages of satisfying assignments of φ_1 and φ_2.

Let us encode an assignment $c^{in} := b_1$, $x := b_2$ and $y := b_3$ as the word $b_1 b_2 b_3 \in \Sigma^3$, where $\Sigma = \{0, 1\}$. Figure 6.8 depicts the multi-DFA produced to construct nodes for φ_1 and φ_2. It has been constructed by starting with the smallest subformulas of φ_1, iteratively constructing nodes for increasingly large subformulas, ending with a node for φ_1 itself, and then proceeding in the same way for φ_2. More precisely, we first construct nodes for the smallest subformulas of φ_1—namely, c^{in}, x, and y. Their languages of satisfying assignments are $1\Sigma\Sigma$, $\Sigma 1 \Sigma$, and $\Sigma \Sigma 1$, respectively, corresponding to nodes 4, 6, and 9. Then,

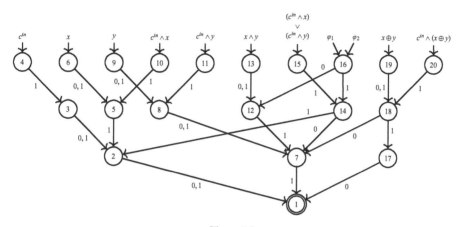

Figure 6.8
Multi-DFA produced when computing the sets of satisfying assignments of the formulas φ_1 and φ_2.

we repeatedly apply the algorithms for union, intersection, and symmetric difference to construct nodes for increasingly larger subformulas; for example, node 10 is obtained by applying the intersection algorithm to nodes 4 and 6. We compute in this way nodes 10, 11, 13, 15, and, finally, node 16 for φ_1. We proceed in the same way for φ_2. For example, node 19 is the result of applying the algorithm for symmetric difference to nodes 6 and 9. In this way, we compute nodes 19, 20, and finally node 16. Since φ_1 and φ_2 point to the same node, they have the same satisfying assignments, and hence they are equivalent.

6.5   Operations on Fixed-Length Relations

Fixed-length relations can be manipulated very similarly to fixed-length languages. Boolean operations are as for fixed-length languages. Nonetheless, the projection, join, *pre*, and *post* operations can be implemented more efficiently than in chapter 5.

   We start with an observation on encodings. In chapter 5, we assumed that if an element of X is encoded by word $w \in \Sigma^*$, then it is also encoded by $w\#$, where $\#$ is the padding symbol. This ensures that every pair $(x, y) \in X \times X$ has an encoding (w_x, w_y) such that w_x and w_y have the same length. Since, in the fixed-length case, all shortest encodings have the same length, the padding symbol is no longer necessary. So, in this section, we assume that each word or pair has exactly one encoding.

   The basic definitions on fixed-length languages extend easily to fixed-length relations. A word relation $R \subseteq \Sigma^* \times \Sigma^*$ has length $n \geq 0$ if for all pairs $(w_1, w_2) \in R$, the words w_1 and w_2 have length n. If R has length n for some $n \geq 0$, then we say that R has *fixed length*.

   Recall that a transducer T accepts a pair $(u, v) \in \Sigma^* \times \Sigma^*$ if $u = a_1 \cdots a_n$, $v = b_1 \cdots b_n$, and T accepts the word $(a_1, b_1) \cdots (a_n, b_n) \in (\Sigma \times \Sigma)^*$. A fixed-length transducer accepts a relation $R \subseteq U \times U$ if it recognizes the word relation $\{(w_x, w_y) : (x, y) \in R\}$.

Given a relation $R \subseteq \Sigma^* \times \Sigma^*$ and $a, b \in \Sigma$, we define $R^{[a,b]} = \{(w_1, w_2) \in \Sigma^* \times \Sigma^* : (aw_1, bw_2) \in R\}$. Note that, in particular, $\emptyset^{[a,b]} = \emptyset$ and that if R has fixed length, then so does $R^{[a,b]}$. The *fixed-length master transducer* over alphabet Σ is the tuple $MT = (Q_M, \Sigma \times \Sigma, \delta_M, F_M)$, where

- Q_M is the set of all fixed-length relations,
- $F_M = \{(\varepsilon, \varepsilon)\}$, and
- $\delta_M : Q_M \times (\Sigma \times \Sigma) \to Q_M$ is given by $\delta_M(R, [a, b]) = R^{[a,b]}$ for all $q \in Q_M$ and $a, b \in \Sigma$.

As in the language case, the minimal deterministic transducer recognizing a fixed-length relation R is the fragment of the fixed-length master transducer containing the states reachable from R.

Like minimal DFAs, minimal deterministic transducers are represented as tables of nodes. However, a remark is in order: since a state of a deterministic transducer has $|\Sigma|^2$ successors, one for each letter of $\Sigma \times \Sigma$, a row of the table has $|\Sigma|^2$ entries, too large when the table is only sparsely filled. Sparse transducers over $\Sigma \times \Sigma$ are better encoded as NFAs over Σ by introducing auxiliary states:

a transition $q \xrightarrow{[a,b]} q'$ is "simulated" by two transitions $q \xrightarrow{a} r \xrightarrow{b} q'$,

where r is an auxiliary state with exactly one input and one output transition.

Fixed-length projection. The implementation of the projection operation of chapter 5 may yield a nondeterministic transducer, even if the initial transducer is deterministic. So we need a different implementation. We observe that projection can be reduced to *pre* or *post*: the projection of a binary relation R onto its first component is equal to $pre_R(\Sigma^*)$ and the projection onto the second component to $post_R(\Sigma^*)$. Thus, we defer dealing with projection until the implementation of *pre* and *post* has been discussed.

Fixed-length join. We give a recursive definition of the join $R_1 \circ R_2$ of two fixed-length relations R_1, R_2. Given a fixed-length relation R, let $[a, b]R = \{(aw_1, bw_2) : (w_1, w_2) \in R\}$. We have the following properties:

- $\emptyset \circ R = R \circ \emptyset = \emptyset$,
- $\{[\varepsilon, \varepsilon]\} \circ \{[\varepsilon, \varepsilon]\} = \{[\varepsilon, \varepsilon]\}$, and
- $R_1 \circ R_2 = \displaystyle\bigcup_{a,b,c \in \Sigma} [a, b] \cdot \left(R_1^{[a,c]} \circ R_2^{[c,b]}\right)$.

This leads to algorithm 31, where *union* is defined similarly to *inter*. The complexity is exponential in the worst case: if $t(n)$ denotes the worst-case complexity for two states of length n, then we have $t(n) \in \mathcal{O}(t(n-1)^2)$, since *union* has quadratic worst-case complexity. This exponential blowup is unavoidable. We prove it later for projections (see example 6.9), which is a special case of *pre* and *post*, which in turn can be seen as variants of join.

Algorithm 31 Algorithm *join*.

$join(r_1, r_2)$
Input: states r_1, r_2 of a transducer table, of the same length
Output: state recognizing $\mathcal{L}(r_1) \circ \mathcal{L}(r_2)$

1   **if** $G(r_1, r_2)$ is not empty **then return** $G(r_1, r_2)$
2   **if** $r_1 = q_\emptyset$ or $r_2 = q_\emptyset$ **then return** $q_\emptyset$
3   **else if** $r_1 = q_\varepsilon$ and $r_2 = q_\varepsilon$ **then return** q_ε
4   **else** $/ * q_\emptyset \neq r_1 \neq q_\varepsilon$ and $q_\emptyset \neq r_2 \neq q_\varepsilon * /$
5   **for all** $(a_i, a_j) \in \Sigma \times \Sigma$ **do**
6         $r_{i,j} \leftarrow union\left(join\left(r_1^{[a_i,a_1]}, r_2^{[a_1,a_j]} \right), \ldots, join\left(r_1^{[a_i,a_m]}, r_2^{[a_m,a_j]} \right) \right)$
7       $G(r_1, r_2) = make(r_{1,1}, \ldots, r_{m,m})$
8   **return** $G(r_1, r_2)$

Fixed-length *pre* and *post*. Recall that in the fixed-length case, we do not need any padding symbol. Given a fixed-length language L and a fixed-length relation R, $pre_R(L)$ admits an inductive definition that we now derive. We have the following:

- if $R = \emptyset$ or $L = \emptyset$, then $pre_R(L) = \emptyset$;
- if $R = \{[\varepsilon, \varepsilon]\}$ and $L = \{\varepsilon\}$, then $pre_R(L) = \{\varepsilon\}$; and
- if $\emptyset \neq R \neq \{[\varepsilon, \varepsilon]\}$ and $\emptyset \neq L \neq \{\varepsilon\}$, then $pre_R(L) = \bigcup_{a,b \in \Sigma} a \cdot pre_{R^{[a,b]}}(L^b)$, where $R^{[a,b]} = \{w \in (\Sigma \times \Sigma)^* : [a,b]w \in R\}$.

The first two properties are obvious. For the last one, observe that all pairs of R have length at least 1, and so every word of $pre_R(L)$ also has length at least 1. Now, given $a \in \Sigma$ and $w_1 \in \Sigma^*$, we have

$$aw_1 \in pre_R(L) \iff \exists bw_2 \in L \text{ s.t. } [aw_1, bw_2] \in R$$

$$\iff \exists b \in \Sigma, \exists w_2 \in L^b \text{ s.t. } [w_1, w_2] \in R^{[a,b]}$$

$$\iff \exists b \in \Sigma \text{ s.t. } w_1 \in pre_{R^{[a,b]}}(L^b)$$

$$\iff aw_1 \in \bigcup_{b \in \Sigma} a \cdot pre_{R^{[a,b]}}(L^b).$$

These properties lead to the recursive procedure of algorithm 32, which accepts as inputs a state of the transducer table for a fixed-length relation R and a state of the automaton table for a language L, and returns the state of the automaton table recognizing $pre_R(L)$. The transducer table is not changed by the algorithm.

Algorithm 32   Algorithm *pre*.

$pre(r, q)$
Input: state r of a transducer table and state q of an automaton table, of the same length
Output: state recognizing $pre_{\mathcal{L}(r)}(\mathcal{L}(q))$

1   **if** $G(r, q)$ is not empty **then return** $G(r, q)$
2   **if** $r = r_\emptyset$ **or** $q = q_\emptyset$ **then return** $q_\emptyset$
3   **else if** $r = r_\varepsilon$ **and** $q = q_\varepsilon$ **then return** q_ε
4   **else**
5   **for all** $a_i \in \Sigma$ **do**
6              $q'_i \leftarrow union\left(pre\left(r^{[a_i,a_1]}, q^{a_1}\right), \ldots, pre\left(r^{[a_i,a_m]}, q^{a_m}\right)\right)$
7          $G(q, r) \leftarrow make(q'_1, \ldots, q'_m)$
8   **return** $G(q, r)$

Algorithm 33   Algorithm pro_1.

$pro_1(r)$
Input: state r of a transducer table
Output: state recognizing $proj_1(\mathcal{L}(r))$

1   **if** $G(r)$ is not empty **then return** $G(r)$
2   **if** $r = r_\emptyset$ **then return** $q_\emptyset$
3   **else if** $r = r_\varepsilon$ **then return** q_ε
4   **else**
5   **for all** $a_i \in \Sigma$ **do**
6              $q'_i \leftarrow union\left(pro_1\left(r^{[a_i,a_1]}\right), \ldots, pro_1\left(r^{[a_i,a_m]}\right)\right)$
7          $G(r) \leftarrow make(q'_1, \ldots, q'_m)$
8   **return** $G(r)$

As promised, we can now implement the operation that projects a fixed-length relation R onto its first component. We provide a dedicated procedure for $pre_R(\Sigma^*)$, described in algorithm 33.

Algorithm pro_1 has exponential worst-case complexity. As for *join*, the reason is the quadratic blowup introduced by *union* when the recursion depth increases by 1. The next example shows that projection is inherently exponential. Slight modifications of this example show that *join*, *pre*, and *post* are inherently exponential as well.

Example 6.9   Consider the relation $R \subseteq \Sigma^{2n} \times \Sigma^{2n}$ given by

$$R = \left\{\left(w_1 x w_2 y w_3, 0^{|w_1|} 10^{|w_2|} 10^{|w_3|}\right) : x \neq y, |w_2| = n, |w_1 w_3| = n - 2\right\}.$$

That is, R contains all pairs of words of length $2n$ whose first word has a position $i \leq n$ such that the letters at positions i and $i + n$ are distinct and whose second word contains only 0s except for two 1s at the same two positions. It is easy to see that the minimal deterministic transducer for R has $\mathcal{O}(n^2)$ states (intuitively, it memorizes the letter x above the first 1, reads $n - 1$ letters of the form $[z, 0]$, and then reads $[z, 1]$, where $y \neq x$). On the other hand, we have

$$proj_1(R) = \{ww' : w, w' \in \Sigma^n \text{ and } w \neq w'\},$$

whose minimal DFA, as shown when discussing *det&min*, has $\mathcal{O}(2^n)$ states. Thus, any algorithm for projection has complexity $\Omega(2^{\sqrt{n}})$.

6.6 Decision Diagrams

Binary decision diagrams, BDDs for short, are a very popular data structure for the representation and manipulation of boolean functions. In this section, we show that they can be seen as minimal automata of a certain kind.

Given a boolean function $f(x_1, \ldots, x_n) \colon \{0, 1\}^n \to \{0, 1\}$, let L_f denote the set of strings $b_1 b_2 \cdots b_n \in \{0, 1\}^n$ such that $f(b_1, \ldots, b_n) = 1$. The minimal DFA recognizing L_f is very similar to the BDD representing f but not completely equal. We modify the constructions of the last section to obtain an exact match.

Consider the DFA depicted in figure 6.9. It is a minimal DFA for some language of length 4 that can be described as follows: after reading an a, accept any word of length 3; after reading ba, accept any word of length 2; and after reading bb, accept any two-letter word whose last letter is a b. Following this description, the language can also be more compactly described by the automaton of figure 6.10 with regular expressions as transitions.

We call such an automaton a *decision diagram (DD)*. The intuition behind this name is that, if we view states as points at which a decision is made—namely, which should be the next state—then states q_1, q_3, q_4, and q_5 do not correspond to any real decision; whatever the next letter, the next state is the same. As we shall see, the states of a minimal DD will always correspond to "real" decisions.

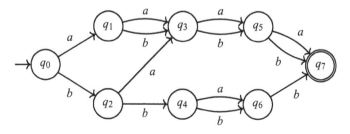

Figure 6.9
A minimal DFA for some language of length 4.

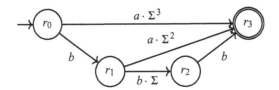

Figure 6.10
Compact presentation of the DFA from figure 6.9.

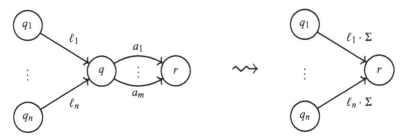

Figure 6.11
Decision diagram reduction rule.

The forthcoming section 6.6.1 shows that the minimal DD for a fixed-length language is unique and can be obtained by repeatedly applying to the minimal DFA the reduction rule of figure 6.11.

The converse direction also works: the minimal DFA can be recovered from the minimal DD by "reversing" the rule. This already allows us to use DDs as a data structure for fixed-length languages but only through conversion to minimal DFAs: to compute an operation using minimal DDs, expand them to minimal DFAs, conduct the operation, and convert the result back. The forthcoming section 6.6.2 shows how to do better by directly defining the operations on minimal DDs, bypassing the minimal DFAs.

6.6.1 Decision Diagrams and Kernels

A *decision diagram (DD)* is an automaton $A = (Q, \Sigma, \delta, Q_0, F)$ whose transitions are labeled by regular expressions of the form

$$a\Sigma^n = a \underbrace{\Sigma\,\Sigma\,\Sigma \cdots \Sigma\,\Sigma}_{n}$$

and that satisfies the following *determinacy condition*: for all $q \in Q$ and $a \in \Sigma$, there is exactly one $k \in \mathbb{N}$ such that $\delta(q, a\Sigma^k) \neq \emptyset$, and for this k, there is a state q' such that $\delta(q, a\Sigma^k) = \{q'\}$. Observe that DFAs are DDs in which $k = 0$ for every state and every letter.

We introduce the notion of kernel, as well as kernel of a fixed-length language.

Definition 6.10 *A fixed-length language $L \subseteq \Sigma^*$ is a* kernel *if $L = \emptyset$, $L = \{\varepsilon\}$, or $L^a \neq L^b$ for some $a, b \in \Sigma$. The* kernel *of a fixed-length language L, denoted by $\langle L \rangle$, is the unique kernel satisfying $L = \Sigma^k \langle L \rangle$ for some $k \geq 0$.*

Observe that the number k is also unique for every language but $\emptyset$. Indeed, for the empty language, we have $\langle \emptyset \rangle = \emptyset$ and so $\emptyset = \Sigma^k \langle \emptyset \rangle$ for every $k \geq 0$.

Example 6.11 Let $\Sigma = \{a, b, c\}$. The language $L_1 = \{aab, abb, bab, cab\}$ is a kernel because $L_1^a = \{ab, bb\} \neq \{ab\} = L_1^b$. The language $L_2 = \{aa, ba\}$ is also a kernel since $L_2^a = \{a\} \neq \emptyset = L_2^c$. However, if we change the alphabet to $\Sigma' = \{a, b\}$, then L_2 is no longer a kernel, and we have $\langle L_2 \rangle = \{a\}$.

For the language $L_3 = \{aa, ab, ba, bb\}$ over Σ', we have $L_3 = (\Sigma')^2$, and so $k = 2$ and $\langle L_3 \rangle = \{\varepsilon\}$.

The mapping that assigns to every nonempty fixed-length language L the pair $(k, \langle L \rangle)$ is a bijection. In other words, L is completely determined by k and $\langle L \rangle$. Thus, a representation of kernels can be extended to a representation of all fixed-length languages. Let us now see how to represent kernels.

The *master decision diagram* has the set of all kernels as states, the kernel $\{\varepsilon\}$ as a unique final state, and a transition $(K, a\Sigma^k, \langle K^a \rangle)$ for every kernel K and $a \in \Sigma$, where k is equal to the length of K^a minus the length of $\langle K^a \rangle$. For $K = \emptyset$, which has all lengths, we take $k = 0$.

Example 6.12 Figure 6.12 shows a fragment of the master decision diagram over alphabet $\{a, b\}$. In comparison to the fixed-length master automaton of figure 2.4, the languages $\{a, b\}$, $\{ab, bb\}$, and $\{aa, ab, ba, bb\}$ are not states of the master since they are not kernels.

The DD A_K for a kernel K is the fragment of the master decision diagram containing the states reachable from K. It is readily seen that A_K recognizes K. A DD is minimal if no other DD for the same language has fewer states. Observe that, since every DFA is also a DD, the minimal DD for a language has at most as many states as its minimal DFA.

The following proposition shows that the minimal DD of a kernel has very similar properties to the minimal DFAs of a regular language. In particular, A_K is always a minimal DD for the kernel K. However, because of a technical detail, it is not the unique minimal DD: the label of the transitions of the master leading to $\emptyset$ can be changed from a to $a\Sigma^k$ for any $k \geq 0$, and from b to $b\Sigma^k$ for any $k \geq 0$, without changing the language. To recover unicity, we redefine minimality: a DD is *minimal* if no other DD for the same language has fewer states, and every transition leading to a state from which no word is accepted is labeled by a or b.

Proposition 6.13 *The following statements hold.*

(a) Let A be a DD such that $\mathcal{L}(A)$ is a kernel. It is the case that A is minimal if and only if (i) every state of A recognizes a kernel, and (ii) distinct states of A recognize distinct kernels.

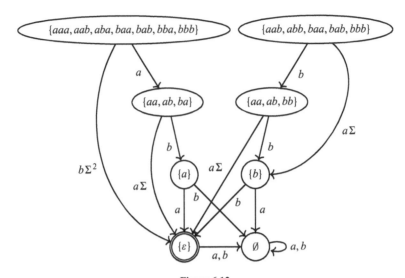

Figure 6.12
A fragment of the master decision diagram.

(b) For every $K \neq \emptyset$, A_K is the unique minimal DD recognizing K.

(c) The result of exhaustively applying the reduction rule to the minimal DFA recognizing a fixed-length language L is the minimal DD recognizing $\langle L \rangle$.

Proof

(a) $\Rightarrow$) For (i), assume A contains a state q such that $\mathcal{L}(q)$ is not a kernel. We prove that A is not minimal. Since $\mathcal{L}(A)$ is a kernel, q is neither initial nor final. Let k be the smallest number such that A contains a transition $(q, a\Sigma^k, q')$ for some letter a and some state q'. We have $\mathcal{L}(q)^a = \Sigma^k \mathcal{L}(q')$, and since $\mathcal{L}(q)$ is not a kernel, $\mathcal{L}(q)^a = \mathcal{L}(q)^b$ for every $b \in \Sigma$. So, we have $\mathcal{L}(q) = \bigcup_{a \in \Sigma} a\Sigma^k \mathcal{L}(q') = \Sigma^{k+1} \mathcal{L}(q')$. Now we perform the following two operations: first, we replace every transition $(q'', b\Sigma^l, q)$ of A by a transition $(q'', b\Sigma^{l+k+1}, q')$; then, we remove q and any other state no longer reachable from the initial state (recall that q is neither initial nor final). The resulting DD recognizes the same language as A and has at least one state less. Therefore, A is not minimal.

For (ii), observe that the quotienting operation can be defined for DDs as for DFAs, and so we can merge states that recognize the same kernel without changing the language. If two distinct states of A recognize the same kernel, then the quotient has fewer states than A, and so A is not minimal.

$\Leftarrow$) We show that two DDs A and A' that satisfy (i) and (ii) and recognize the same language are isomorphic, which, together with $\Rightarrow$), proves that they are minimal. It suffices to prove that if two states q and q' of A and A' satisfy $\mathcal{L}(q) = \mathcal{L}(q')$, then for every $a \in \Sigma$, the (unique) transitions $(q, a\Sigma^k, r)$ and $(q', a\Sigma^{k'}, r')$ satisfy $k = k'$ and $\mathcal{L}(r) = \mathcal{L}(r')$. Let $\mathcal{L}(q) = K = \mathcal{L}(q')$. By (i), both $\mathcal{L}(r)$ and $\mathcal{L}(r')$ are kernels. Thus, we necessarily have $\mathcal{L}(r) = \langle K^a \rangle = \mathcal{L}(q')$, because the only solution to the equation $K = a\Sigma^\ell K'$, where ℓ and K' are unknowns and K' must be a kernel, is $K' = \langle K^a \rangle$.

(b) Automaton A_K recognizes K, and it satisfies conditions (i) and (ii) of (a) by definition. So, it is a minimal DD. Uniqueness follows from the proof of direction $\Leftarrow$) of (a).

(c) Let B be a DD obtained by exhaustively applying the reduction rule to A. By (a), it suffices to prove that B satisfies (i) and (ii). For (ii), observe that, since every state of A recognizes a different language, so does every state of B (the reduction rule preserves the recognized languages). For (i), assume that some state q does not recognize a kernel. Without loss of generality, we can choose $\mathcal{L}(q)$ of minimal length, and therefore the target states of all outgoing transitions of q recognize kernels. It follows that all of them necessarily recognize $\langle \mathcal{L}(q) \rangle$. Since B contains at most one state recognizing $\langle \mathcal{L}(q) \rangle$, all outgoing transitions of q have the same target, and so the reduction rule can be applied to q, contradicting the hypothesis that it has been applied exhaustively. □

6.6.2 Operations on Kernels

We use *multi-DDs* to represent sets of fixed-length languages of the same length. A set $\mathcal{L} = \{L_1, \ldots, L_m\}$ is represented by the states of the master decision diagram recognizing $\langle L_1 \rangle, \ldots, \langle L_m \rangle$ *and* by the common length of $L_1, \ldots, L_m$. Observe that the states and the length completely determine $\mathcal{L}$.

Example 6.14 Figure 6.13 shows the multi-DD for the set $\mathcal{L} = \{L_1, L_2, L_3\}$ previously depicted in figure 6.2. Recall that we have $L_1 = \{aa, ba\}$, $L_2 = \{aa, ba, bb\}$, and $L_3 = \{ab, bb\}$. The multi-DD is the result of applying the reduction rule to the multi-DFA of figure 6.2. Observe that, while L_1, L_2, and L_3 have the same length, $\langle L_2 \rangle$ has a different length than $\langle L_1 \rangle$ and $\langle L_3 \rangle$.

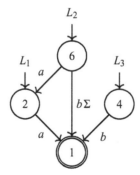

Figure 6.13
The multi-DD for $\{L_1, L_2, L_3\}$, where $L_1 = \{aa, ba\}$, $L_2 = \{aa, ba, bb\}$, and $L_3 = \{ab, bb\}$.

Multi-DDs are represented as a table of kernodes. A *kernode* is a triple $\langle q, \ell, s \rangle$, where q is a *state identifier*, ℓ is a *length*, and $s = (q_1, \ldots, q_m)$ is the *successor tuple* of the kernode. The table for the multi-DD of figure 6.13 is the following:

Ident.	Length	*a*-succ	*b*-succ
2	1	1	0
4	1	0	1
6	2	2	1

This example explains the role of the new *length* field. If we only know that the *a*- and *b*-successors of, say, state 6 are states 2 and 1, we cannot infer which expressions label the transitions from 6 to 2 and from 6 to 1: they could be a and $b\Sigma$, $a\Sigma$ and $b\Sigma^2$, or $a\Sigma^n$ and $b\Sigma^{n+1}$ for any $n \geq 0$. However, once we know that state 6 accepts a language of length 2, we can deduce the correct labels: since states 2 and 1 accept languages of length 1 and 0, respectively, the labels are a and $b\Sigma$.

The procedure *kmake(ℓ, s)*.   All algorithms call a procedure *kmake(ℓ, s)* with the following specification. Let K_i be the kernel recognized by the ith component of s. A call to *kmake(ℓ, s)* returns the kernode for $\langle L \rangle$, where L is the unique language of length ℓ such that $\langle L^{a_i} \rangle = K_i$ for every $a_i \in \Sigma$.

If $K_i \neq K_j$ for some i and j, then *kmake(ℓ, s)* behaves like *make(s)*: if the current table already contains a kernode $\langle q, \ell, s \rangle$, then *kmake($\ell, s$)* returns q, and if no such kernode exists, then *kmake(ℓ, s)* creates a new kernode $\langle q, \ell, s \rangle$ with a fresh identifier q and returns q.

If $K_1, \ldots, K_m$ are all equal to some kernel K, then we have $L = \bigcup_{i=1}^{m} a_i \Sigma^k K$ for some k, and hence $\langle L \rangle = \langle \Sigma^{\ell+1} K \rangle = K$. So, *kmake($\ell, s$)* returns the kernode for K. For instance, if T is the table above, then *kmake(3, (2, 2))* returns 3, while *make(2, 2)* creates a new node having 2 as *a*-successor and *b*-successor.

Algorithms.   The algorithms for operations on kernels are modifications of the algorithms of the previous section. We show how to modify the algorithms for intersection, complement, and simultaneous determinization and minimization. In the previous section, the state of the fixed-length master automaton for a language L was the language L itself and was obtained by recursively computing the states for $L^{a_1}, \ldots, L^{a_m}$ and then applying *make*. Now, the state of the master for L is $\langle L \rangle$ and can be obtained by recursively computing states for $\langle L^{a_1} \rangle, \ldots, \langle L^{a_m} \rangle$ and applying *kmake*.

Fixed-length intersection.   Given kernels K_1 and K_2 of languages L_1 and L_2, we compute the state recognizing $K_1 \sqcap K_2 = \langle L_1 \cap L_2 \rangle$.[2] We have the following obvious property: if $K_1 = \emptyset$ or $K_2 = \emptyset$, then $K_1 \sqcap K_2 = \emptyset$. Assume $K_1 \neq \emptyset \neq K_2$. If the lengths of K_1 and K_2 are ℓ_1 and

---

2. Operation $\sqcap$ is well defined as $\langle L_1 \rangle = \langle L_1' \rangle$ and $\langle L_2 \rangle = \langle L_2' \rangle$ implies $\langle L_1 \cap L_2 \rangle = \langle L_1' \cap L_2' \rangle$.

ℓ_2, then since $\langle \Sigma^k L \rangle = \langle L \rangle$ holds for every k and L, we have

$$K_1 \sqcap K_2 = \begin{cases} \langle \Sigma^{l_2 - l_1} K_1 \cap K_2 \rangle & \text{if } \ell_1 < \ell_2, \\ \langle K_1 \cap \Sigma^{l_1 - l_2} K_2 \rangle & \text{if } \ell_1 > \ell_2, \\ \langle K_1 \cap K_2 \rangle & \text{if } \ell_1 = \ell_2, \end{cases}$$

which allows us to obtain the state for $K_1 \sqcap K_2$ by computing states for

$$\langle (\Sigma^{\ell_1 - \ell_2} K_1 \cap K_2)^a \rangle, \langle (K_1 \cap \Sigma^{\ell_2 - \ell_1} K_2)^a \rangle \text{ or } \langle (K_1 \cap K_2)^a \rangle$$

for every $a \in \Sigma$ and applying *kmake*.

These states can be computed recursively by means of the following rules, which lead to the procedure of algorithm 34:

if $\ell_1 < \ell_2$, then $\langle (\Sigma^{\ell_2 - \ell_1} K_1 \cap K_2)^a \rangle = \langle \Sigma^{\ell_2 - \ell_1 - 1} K_1 \cap K_2^a \rangle = K_1 \sqcap \langle K_2^a \rangle$;

if $\ell_1 > \ell_2$, then $\langle (K_1 \cap \Sigma^{\ell_1 - \ell_2} K_2)^a \rangle = \langle K_1^a \cap \Sigma^{\ell_1 - \ell_2 - 1} K_2 \rangle = \langle K_1^a \rangle \sqcap K_2$; and

if $\ell_1 = \ell_2$, then $\langle (K_1 \cap K_2)^a \rangle \qquad = \langle K_1^a \cap K_2^a \rangle \qquad = \langle K_1^a \rangle \sqcap \langle K_2^a \rangle$.

Example 6.15 Figure 6.14 shows a run of *kinter* on the two languages represented by the multi-DFA at the top of figure 6.4. The multi-DD for the same languages is shown at the

---

Algorithm 34 Algorithm *kinter*.

---

kinter(q_1, q_2)
Input: states q_1, q_2 recognizing $\langle L_1 \rangle, \langle L_2 \rangle$
Output: state recognizing $\langle L_1 \cap L_2 \rangle$

```
1    if G(q1, q2) is not empty then return G(q1, q2)
2    if q1 = q∅ or q2 = q∅ then return q∅
3    if q1 ≠ q∅ and q2 ≠ q∅ then
4        if ℓ1 < ℓ2 /* lengths of the kernodes for q1, q2 */ then
5            for all i = 1, ..., m do ri ← kinter(q1, q2^ai)
6            G(q1, q2) ← kmake(ℓ2, r1, ..., rm)
7        else if ℓ1 > ℓ2 then
8            for all i = 1, ..., m do ri ← kinter(q1^ai, q2)
9            G(q1, q2) ← kmake(ℓ1, r1, ..., rm)
10       else /* ℓ1 = ℓ2 */
11           for all i = 1, ..., m do ri ← kinter(q1^ai, q2^ai)
12           G(q1, q2) ← kmake(ℓ1, r1, ..., rm)
13   return G(q1, q2)
```

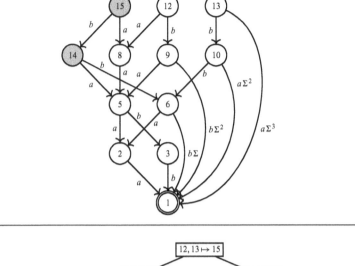

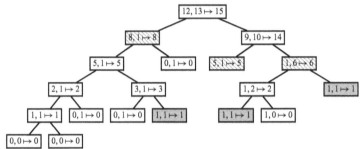

Figure 6.14
An execution of *kinter*.

top of figure 6.14, and the rest of the figure describes the run of *kinter* on it. Recall that solid colored nodes correspond to calls whose result has already been memoized and need not be executed. The meaning of the hatched colored nodes is explained below.

The algorithm can be improved by noting that two further properties hold:

$$\text{If } K_1 = \{\varepsilon\}, \text{ then } L_1 \cap L_2 = L_2, \text{ and so } K_1 \sqcap K_2 = K_2.$$

$$\text{If } K_2 = \{\varepsilon\}, \text{ then } L_1 \cap L_2 = L_1, \text{ and so } K_1 \sqcap K_2 = K_1.$$

These properties imply that $kinter(q_\varepsilon, q) = q = kinter(q, q_\varepsilon)$ for every state q. Thus, we can improve *kinter* by explicitly checking if one of the arguments is q_ε. The hatched colored nodes in figure 6.14 correspond to calls whose result is immediately returned with the help of this check. Observe how this improvement has a substantial effect, reducing the number of calls from nineteen to only five.

Algorithm 35 Algorithm *kcomp*.

$kcomp(q)$
Input: state q recognizing a kernel K
Output: state recognizing $\widehat{K}$
1   **if** $G(q)$ is not empty **then return** $G(q)$
2   **if** $q = q_{\emptyset}$ **then return** q_{ε}
3   **else if** $q = q_{\varepsilon}$ **then return** $q_{\emptyset}$
4   **else**
5   **for all** $i = 1, \ldots, m$ **do** $r_i \leftarrow kcomp(q^{a_i})$
6       $G(q) \leftarrow kmake(r_1, \ldots, r_m)$
7   **return** $G(q)$

Fixed-length complement. Given the kernel K of a fixed-language L of length n, we wish to compute the state of the master decision diagram recognizing $\langle \overline{L}^n \rangle$, where n is the length of L. The superscript n is only necessary because $\emptyset$ has all possible lengths, and so $\overline{\emptyset}^n = \Sigma^n \neq \Sigma^m = \overline{L}^m$ for $n \neq m$. But now we have $\langle \overline{\emptyset}^n \rangle = \{\varepsilon\}$ for all $n \geq 0$, and so the superscript is not needed anymore. We define the operator $\widehat{}$ on kernels by $\widehat{K} = \langle \overline{L} \rangle$.[3] We obtain the state for $\widehat{K}$ by recursively computing states for $\langle \widehat{K}^a \rangle$ by means of the following properties, which lead to algorithm 35:

- If $K = \emptyset$, then $\widehat{K} = \{\varepsilon\}$, and if $K = \{\varepsilon\}$, then $\widehat{K} = \emptyset$.
- If $\emptyset \neq K \neq \{\varepsilon\}$, then $\langle \widehat{K}^a \rangle = \widehat{K^a}$.

6.6.3   Determinization and Minimization

The algorithm *kdet&min* that converts an NFA recognizing a fixed-language L into the minimal DD recognizing $\langle L \rangle$ differs from *det&min* essentially in one letter: it uses *kmake* instead of *make*. It is described in algorithm 36.

Example 6.16   Figure 6.15 shows again the NFA of figure 6.6 and the minimal DD for the kernel of its language. The run of *kdet&min*(A) is at the bottom of the figure. For the difference with *det&min*(A), consider the call *kstate*$(\{\varepsilon, \zeta\})$. Since the two recursive calls *kstate*$(\{\eta\})$ and *kstate*$(\{\eta, \theta\})$ return both state 1 with length 1, *kmake*$(1, 1)$ does not create a new state, as *make*$(1, 1)$ would return state 1. The same occurs at the top call *kstate*$(\{\alpha\})$.

---

3. The operator is well defined because $\langle L \rangle = \langle L' \rangle$ implies $\langle \overline{L} \rangle = \langle \overline{L'} \rangle$.

Algorithm 36   Algorithm *kdet&min*.

---

kdet&min(A)
Input: NFA $A = (Q, \Sigma, \delta, Q_0, F)$
Output: state of a multi-DFA recognizing $\mathcal{L}(A)$
  1   **return** *kstate*(Q_0)
kstate(S)
Input: set S of states of length ℓ
Output: state recognizing $\mathcal{L}(R)$
  1   **if** $G(S)$ is not empty **then return** $G(S)$
  2   **else if** $S = \emptyset$ **then return** $q_\emptyset$
  3   **else if** $S \cap F \neq \emptyset$ **then return** q_ε
  4   **else** $/ * S \neq \emptyset$ and $S \cap F = \emptyset * /$
  5   **for all** $i = 1, \ldots, m$ **do** $S_i \leftarrow \delta(S, a_i)$
  6       $G(S) \leftarrow kmake(\ell, kstate(S_1), \ldots, kstate(S_m));$
  7   **return** $G(S)$

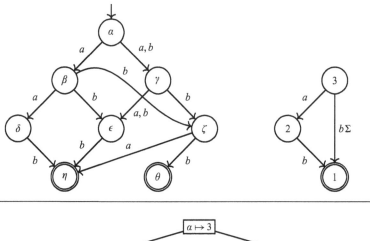

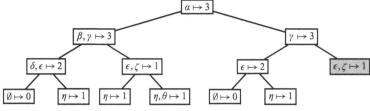

Figure 6.15
Run of *kdet&min* on an NFA for a fixed-length language.

6.7   Exercises

⭐ ■ **Exercise 101.** Prove that the minimal DFA for a language of length 4 over a two-letter alphabet has at most twelve states, and give a language for which the minimal DFA has twelve states.

☆ ✔ **Exercise 102.** Give an *efficient* algorithm that receives as input the minimal DFA of a fixed-length language and returns the number of words it contains.

☆ ✔ **Exercise 103.** The algorithm for fixed-length universality given in table 28 has a best-case runtime equal to the length of the input state q. Give an improved algorithm that only needs $\mathcal{O}(|\Sigma|)$ time for inputs q such that $\mathcal{L}(q)$ is not fixed-size universal.

⭐ ■ **Exercise 104.** Let $\Sigma = \{0, 1\}$. Let $f: \Sigma^6 \to \Sigma$ be the boolean function defined by $f(x_1, x_2, \ldots, x_6) = (x_1 \wedge x_2) \vee (x_3 \wedge x_4) \vee (x_5 \wedge x_6)$.

(a) Construct the minimal DFA recognizing $\{x_1 \cdots x_6 \in \Sigma^6 : f(x_1, \ldots, x_6) = 1\}$. For example, the DFA accepts 111000 because $f(1, 1, 1, 0, 0, 0) = 1$ but not 101010.

(b) Show that the minimal DFA recognizing $\{x_1 x_3 x_5 x_2 x_4 x_6 : f(x_1, \ldots, x_6) = 1\}$ has at least fifteen states. Variables are ordered differently, for example, the DFA accepts neither 111000 nor 101010.

(c) More generally, consider function $f(x_1, \ldots, x_{2n}) = \bigvee_{1 \le k \le n}(x_{2k-1} \wedge x_{2k})$ and languages

$$L_n = \{x_1 x_2 \cdots x_{2n-1} x_{2n} : f(x_1, \ldots, x_{2n}) = 1\},$$

$$K_n = \{x_1 x_3 \cdots x_{2n-1} x_2 x_4 \cdots x_{2n} : f(x_1, \ldots, x_{2n}) = 1\}.$$

Show that the size of the minimal DFA grows linearly for L_n and exponentially for K_n.

☆ ⚙ **Exercise 105.** Let $L_1 = \{abb, bba, bbb\}$ and $L_2 = \{aba, bbb\}$.

(a) Suppose you are given a fixed-length language L described explicitly by a set instead of an automaton. Give an algorithm that outputs the state q of the fixed-length master automaton for L.

(b) Use the previous algorithm to build the states of the fixed-length master automaton for L_1 and L_2.

(c) Compute the state of the fixed-length master automaton representing $L_1 \cup L_2$.

(d) Identify the kernels $\langle L_1 \rangle$, $\langle L_2 \rangle$, and $\langle L_1 \cup L_2 \rangle$.

⭐ ✔ **Exercise 106.**

(a) Give an algorithm to compute $\mathcal{L}(p) \cdot \mathcal{L}(q)$ given states p and q of the fixed-length master automaton.

(b) Give an algorithm to compute both the length and size of $\mathcal{L}(q)$ given a state q of the fixed-length master automaton.

(c) The length and size of $\mathcal{L}(q)$ could be obtained in constant time if they were simply stored in the fixed-length master automaton table. Give a new implementation of *make* for this representation.

★ 🔲 **Exercise 107.** Let $k \in \mathbb{N}_{>0}$. Let flip : $\{0,1\}^k \to \{0,1\}^k$ be the function that inverts the bits of its input, for example, flip$(010) = 101$. Let val : $\{0,1\}^k \to \mathbb{N}$ be such that val(w) is the number represented by w with the "least significant bit first" encoding.

(a) Describe the minimal transducer that accepts

$$L_k = \left\{ [x,y] \in (\{0,1\} \times \{0,1\})^k : \mathrm{val}(y) = \mathrm{val}(\mathrm{flip}(x)) + 1 \bmod 2^k \right\}.$$

(b) Build the state r of the fixed-length master transducer for L_3 and the state q of the fixed-length master automaton for $\{010, 110\}$.

(c) Adapt the algorithm *pre* seen in the chapter to compute *post*(r, q).

☆ ✎ **Exercise 108.** We define the *language* of a boolean formula φ over variables $x_1, \ldots, x_n$ as

$$\mathcal{L}(\varphi) = \{a_1 \cdots a_n \in \{0,1\}^n : \text{assignment } x_1 \mapsto a_1, \ldots, x_n \mapsto a_n \text{ satisfies } \varphi\}.$$

(a) Give a polynomial-time algorithm that takes as input a DFA A recognizing a language of length n and returns a boolean formula φ such that $\mathcal{L}(\varphi) = \mathcal{L}(A)$.

(b) Give an exponential-time algorithm that takes a boolean formula φ as input and returns a DFA A recognizing $\mathcal{L}(\varphi)$.

★ ✎ **Exercise 109.** Given $X \subseteq \{0, 1, \ldots, 2^k - 1\}$, where $k \geq 1$, let A_X be the minimal DFA recognizing the "least-significant-bit-first" encodings of length k of the elements of X.

(a) Let $X + 1 = \{x + 1 \bmod 2^k : x \in X\}$. Give an algorithm that on input A_X produces A_{X+1}.

(b) Let $A_X = (Q, \{0, 1\}, \delta, q_0, F)$. What is the set of numbers recognized by the automaton $A' = (Q, \{0, 1\}, \delta', q_0, F)$, where $\delta'(q, b) = \delta(q, 1 - b)$?

★ ◼ **Exercise 110.** Recall that weakly acyclic languages and DFAs have been introduced in exercise 35. Recall that the relation $\preceq$ on the states of a weakly acyclic DFA, defined by $q \preceq q'$ iff $\delta(q, w) = q'$ for some word w, is a partial order. Show that:

(a) Every fixed-length language is weakly acyclic.

(b) If L is weakly acyclic, then L^w is also weakly acyclic for every $w \in \Sigma^*$.

Given weakly acyclic languages L and L', let $L \preceq_{\mathcal{L}} L'$ denote that $L = (L')^w$ for some word w. Show that:

(c) $\preceq_{\mathcal{L}}$ is a partial order on the set of all weakly acyclic languages.

(d) $\preceq_{\mathcal{L}}$ has no infinite descending chains.

(e) The only two minimal languages w.r.t. $\preceq_{\mathcal{L}}$ are $\emptyset$ and Σ^*.

Recall that, by exercise 57, the minimal DFA recognizing a given weakly acyclic language is weakly acyclic. We define the *weakly acyclic master automaton* over alphabet Σ as $M = (Q_M, \Sigma, \delta_M, F_M)$, where

- Q_M is the set of all weakly acyclic languages over Σ;
- $\delta \colon Q_M \times \Sigma \to Q_M$ is given by $\delta(L, a) = L^a$ for every $q \in Q_M$ and $a \in \Sigma$; and
- $L \in F_M$ iff $\varepsilon \in L$.

Prove the following result, which generalizes the corresponding one for fixed-length languages:

(f) For every weakly acyclic language L, the language recognized from the state L of the weakly acyclic master automaton M is L.

★ ✔ Exercise 111. Recall that exercise 110 establishes that weakly acyclic languages can be represented by a weakly acyclic master automaton. A state q of the weakly acyclic master automaton can be represented by a table as follows. A *node* is a triple $\langle q, s, b \rangle$, where

- q is a *state identifier*;
- $s = (\alpha_1, \ldots, \alpha_m)$ is the *successor tuple* of the node, where for every $1 \leq i \leq m$, the component α_i is either a state identifier or the special symbol SELF; and
- $b \in \{0, 1\}$ indicates whether the state is accepting ($b = 1$) or not ($b = 0$).

For example, if $\Sigma = \{a, b\}$ and q is an accepting state satisfying $\delta(q, a) = q'$ and $\delta(q, b) = q$, then q is represented by the triple $\langle q, s, b \rangle$, where $s = (q', \text{SELF})$ and $b = 1$. The state identifiers of the states for the languages $\emptyset$ and Σ^* are denoted respectively by $q_\emptyset$ and q_{Σ^*}.

Given a table T that represents a fragment of the weakly acyclic master automaton, the procedure *make*(s, b) returns the state identifier of the unique state of T having s as successor tuple and b as boolean flag, if such a state exists; otherwise, it adds a new node $\langle q, s, b \rangle$ to T, where q is a fresh identifier, and it returns q.

(a) Give an algorithm to compute $\mathcal{L}(q_1) \cap \mathcal{L}(q_2)$ given states q_1 and q_2 of the weakly acyclic master automaton.

(b) Give an algorithm to compute $\mathcal{L}(q_1) \cup \mathcal{L}(q_2)$ given states q_1 and q_2 of the weakly acyclic master automaton.

(c) Give an algorithm to compute $\overline{\mathcal{L}(q)}$ given a state q of the weakly acyclic master automaton.

☆ ☛ Exercise 112. Recall that we can associate a language to a boolean formula as done in exercise 108. Show that the following problem is NP-hard:

Given: a boolean formula φ.

Decide: whether the minimal DFA for $\mathcal{L}(\varphi)$ has more than one state.

7 Application II: Verification

A significant part of the development of computer systems consists of finding and fixing bugs. For many systems, code inspection and testing are not enough to catch every bug. In particular, this is the case for concurrent systems. A concurrent system consists of multiple computing units communicating by some means, like shared memory or message-passing. The order in which different units of a concurrent system execute instructions depends on many factors, like the particular hardware on which the system is running, the specific state of the memory, the relative speed of communication channels, and others. These factors are not under the control of the designer, and so a concurrent system that is repeatedly started in the same initial configuration can potentially execute in many different ways. A bug that is only revealed in a few of these executions is very hard to find and to reproduce.

One of the main applications of automata theory is the algorithmic verification or falsification of correctness properties of hardware and software systems, in particular of concurrent ones. Given a system (such as a digital circuit, a program, or a communication protocol) and a property (such as "after termination, the values of variables x and y are equal" or "every sent message is eventually received"), we wish to *automatically* determine whether the system satisfies the property or not. We apply the theory developed in the previous chapters to this question.

7.1 The Automata-Theoretic Approach to Verification

We consider discrete systems for which a notion of *configuration* is definable.[1] At every time moment, the system is in a configuration. Moves from one configuration to the next take place instantaneously and are determined by the system dynamics. If the semantics allows a move from a configuration c to another one c', then c' is a *legal successor* of c. A configuration may have several successors, in which case the system is said to be

---

1. We speak of the "configurations" of a system and not of its "states," as it is sometimes done in the literature, in order to avoid confusion with the states of automata.

nondeterministic. There is a distinguished set of *initial* configurations. An *execution* is a finite or an infinite sequence of configurations starting at some initial configuration and in which every other configuration is a legal successor of its predecessor in the sequence. A *full* execution is either an infinite execution or an execution whose last configuration has no successors.

In this chapter, we are only interested in finite executions (see chapter 13 for an extension to infinite executions). The set of executions can then be seen as a language $E \subseteq C^*$, where the alphabet C is the set of possible configurations of the system. We call C^* the set of *potential executions* of the system.

Example 7.1 Consider program 1, which has two boolean variables x and y. A configuration of the program is a triple $[\ell, n_x, n_y]$, where $\ell \in \{1, 2, 3, 4, 5\}$ is the current value of the program counter, and $n_x, n_y \in \{0, 1\}$ are the current values of x and y. The set C of all possible configurations contains $5 \cdot 2 \cdot 2 = 20$ elements. The initial configurations are $[1, 0, 0]$, $[1, 0, 1]$, $[1, 1, 0]$, $[1, 1, 1]$—that is, all configurations in which control is at line 1.

The sequence

$$[1, 1, 1]\ [2, 1, 1]\ [3, 1, 1]\ [4, 0, 1]\ [1, 0, 1]\ [5, 0, 1]$$

is a full execution, while

$$[1, 1, 0]\ [2, 1, 0]\ [4, 1, 0]\ [1, 1, 0]$$

is also an execution but not a full one. All words of

$$([1, 1, 0]\ [2, 1, 0]\ [4, 1, 0])^*$$

are executions, and hence the language E of all executions is infinite.

```
1    while x = 1 do
2        if y = 1 then
3            x ← 0
4        y ← 1 − x
5    end
```

Program 1 A simple boolean program.

Assume we wish to determine whether the system has an execution satisfying some property of interest. If we can construct automata for the language $E \subseteq C^*$ of executions and the language $P \subseteq C^*$ of potential executions satisfying the property, then we can solve the problem by checking whether the language $E \cap P$ is empty, which can be decided using the algorithms of chapter 3. This is the main insight behind the automata-theoretic approach to verification.

The requirement that the language E of executions is regular is satisfied by all systems with finitely many reachable configurations (i.e., finitely many configurations c such that some execution leads from some initial configuration to c). A *system automaton* recognizing the executions of the system can be easily obtained from the *configuration graph*: the graph having the reachable configurations as nodes and arcs from each configuration to its successors. There are two possible constructions, both very simple.

- In the first construction, the states are the reachable configurations of the program plus a new state i, which is also the initial state. All states are final. For every transition $c \to c'$ of the graph, there is a transition $c \xrightarrow{c'} c'$ in the system automaton. Moreover, there is a transition $i \xrightarrow{c} c$ for every initial configuration.

It is easy to see that this construction produces a deterministic automaton. Since the label of a transition is also its target state, for any two transitions $c \xrightarrow{c'} c_1$ and $c \xrightarrow{c'} c_2$ we necessarily have $c_1 = c' = c_2$, and so the automaton is deterministic.

- In the second construction, the states are the reachable configurations of the program plus a new state f. The initial states are all the initial configurations, and all states are final. For every transition $c \to c'$ of the graph, there is a transition $c \xrightarrow{c} c'$ in the system automaton. Moreover, there is a transition $c \xrightarrow{c} f$ for every configuration c having no successor.

Example 7.2 Figure 7.1 depicts the configuration graph of program 1, together with the system automata produced by the two constructions above. Let us algorithmically decide whether the system has a full execution such that initially $y = 1$, finally $y = 0$, and y never increases. Let $[\ell, x, 0]$ and $[\ell, x, 1]$ stand for the sets of configurations where $y = 0$ and $y = 1$, respectively, and the values of ℓ and x are arbitrary. Similarly, let $[5, x, 0]$ stand for the set of configurations where $\ell = 5$, $y = 0$, and x is arbitrary. The set of potential executions satisfying the property is given by the regular expression

$$[\ell, x, 1] \ [\ell, x, 1]^* \ [\ell, x, 0]^* \ [5, x, 0],$$

which is recognized by the *property automaton* at the top of figure 7.2. Its intersection with the system automaton in the middle of figure 7.1 (we could also use the other one) is shown at the bottom of figure 7.2. A solid colored state of the pairing labeled by $[\ell, x, y]$ is the result of pairing the solid colored state of the property NFA and the state $[\ell, x, y]$ of the system DFA. Since labels of the transitions of the pairing are always equal to the target state, they are omitted for the sake of readability.

Since the intersection has no hatched colored state, the intersection is empty, and so the program has no execution satisfying the property.

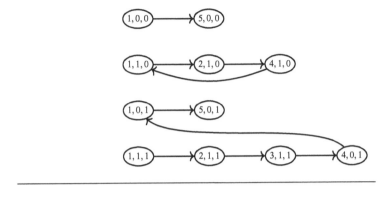

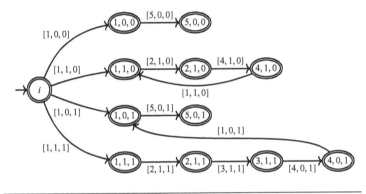

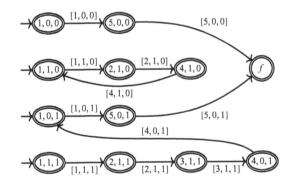

Figure 7.1
Top: the configuration graph of program 1. *Middle and bottom:* two system automata arising from the configuration graph.

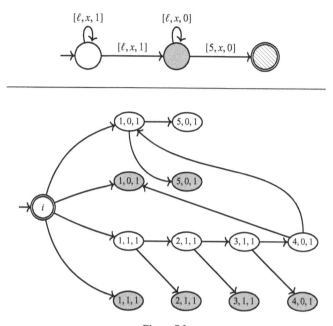

Figure 7.2
Top: property automaton. *Bottom:* product automaton.

Example 7.3   Let us determine whether the assignment "$y \leftarrow 1 - x$" on line 4 of program 1 is redundant and can be safely removed. This is the case if the assignment never changes the value of y. The potential executions of the program in which the assignment changes the value of y at some point correspond to the regular expression

$$[\ell,x,y]^* \; ([4,x,0] \, [1,x,1] + [4,x,1] \, [1,x,0]) \; [\ell,x,y]^*.$$

A property automaton for this expression can be easily constructed, and its intersection with the system automaton is again empty. So, the property holds, and the assignment is indeed redundant.

7.2   Programs as Networks of Automata

We can also model program 1 as a *network of communicating automata*. The key idea is to model the two variables x and y and the control flow of the program as three indepen-dent processes. The processes for x and y maintain their current values, and the control flow process maintains the current value of the program counter. The execution of, say, the assignment "$x \leftarrow 0$" in line 3 of the program is modeled as the execution of a joint action between the control flow process and the process for variable x: the control flow process

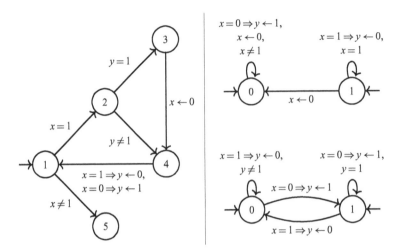

Figure 7.3
A network of three automata modeling program 1. All states are final, so the double circles are drawn as simple circles for clarity.

updates the current control position to 4, and simultaneously, the process for x updates the current value of x to 0.

The processes for the variables and the control flow are represented by finite automata whose states are all final. The three automata for program 1 are shown in figure 7.3. Since all states are final, we do not use the graphical representation with a double circle. The automata for x and y have two states, one for each possible value of the variables. The control-flow automaton has five states, one for each control location. The alphabet of the automaton for x contains the assignments and the boolean conditions of the program involving x and similarly for y. So, for example, the alphabet for x contains $x \leftarrow 0$ but not $y = 1$. However, a single assignment may produce several alphabet letters. For instance, the assignment "$y \leftarrow 1 - x$" at line 4 produces two alphabet letters, corresponding to two possible actions: if the automaton for x is currently at state 0 (i.e., if x currently has value 0), then the automaton for y must move to state 1, otherwise to state 0. We let "$x = 0 \Rightarrow y \leftarrow 1$" and "$x = 1 \Rightarrow y \leftarrow 0$" denote these two alphabet letters. Observe also that the execution of "$y \leftarrow 1 - x$" is modeled as a joint action of all three automata: intuitively, the action "$x = 0 \Rightarrow y \leftarrow 1$" can be executed only if the automaton for x is currently at state 0 and the control-flow automaton is currently at state 4.

Let us give a formal definition of networks of automata. In the definition, we do not require all states to be final, because, as we shall see later, a more general definition proves to be useful.

Definition 7.4   *A network of automata is a tuple* $\mathcal{A} = \langle A_1, \ldots, A_n \rangle$ *of NFAs, not necessarily over a common alphabet. Let* $A_i = (Q_i, \Sigma_i, \delta_i, Q_{0i}, F_i)$ *for every* $i \in \{1, \ldots, n\}$, *and let*

$\Sigma = \Sigma_1 \cup \cdots \cup \Sigma_n$. *A letter of* Σ *is called an* action. *A* configuration *of* $\mathcal{A}$ *is a tuple* $[q_1, \ldots, q_n]$ *of states such that* $q_i \in Q_i$ *for every* $i \in \{1, \ldots, n\}$. *A configuration is* initial *if* $q_i \in Q_{0i}$ *for every* $i \in \{1, \ldots, n\}$ *and* final *if* $q_i \in F_i$ *for every* $i \in \{1, \ldots, n\}$.

Observe that each NFA of a network has its own alphabet Σ_i. The alphabets $\Sigma_1, \ldots, \Sigma_n$ are not necessarily disjoint; in fact, usually they are not. We define when is an action enabled at a configuration and what happens when it occurs.

Definition 7.5 *Let* $\mathcal{A} = \langle A_1, \ldots, A_n \rangle$ *be a network of automata, where* $A_i = (Q_i, \Sigma_i, \delta_i, Q_{0i}, F_i)$. *Given an action* $a \in \Sigma$, *we say that* A_i participates *in* a *if* $a \in \Sigma_i$. *An action* a *is* enabled *at a configuration* $[q_1, \ldots, q_n]$ *if* $\delta_i(q_i, a) \neq \emptyset$ *for every* $i \in \{1, \ldots, n\}$ *such that* A_i *participates in* a. *If* a *is enabled, then it can* occur, *and its occurrence leads to any element of* $Q_1' \times \cdots \times Q_n'$, *where*

$$Q_i' = \begin{cases} \delta(q_i, a) & \textit{if } A_i \textit{ participates in } a, \\ \{q_i\} & \textit{otherwise.} \end{cases}$$

We call $Q_1' \times \cdots \times Q_n'$ *the set of* successor configurations *of* $[q_1, \ldots, q_n]$ *with respect to action* a. *We write* $[q_1, \ldots, q_n] \xrightarrow{a} [q_1', \ldots, q_n']$ *to denote that* $[q_1, \ldots, q_n]$ *enables* a *and* $[q_1', \ldots, q_n'] \in Q_1' \times \cdots \times Q_n'$.

The language accepted by a network is defined in the standard way:

Definition 7.6 *A* run *of* $\mathcal{A}$ *on input* $a_0 a_1 \cdots a_{n-1} \in \Sigma^*$ *is a sequence*

$$c_0 \xrightarrow{a_0} c_1 \xrightarrow{a_1} \cdots \xrightarrow{a_{n-1}} c_n,$$

where $c_0, \ldots, c_n$ *are configurations of* $\mathcal{A}$, *the configuration* c_0 *is initial, and* c_{i+1} *is a successor of* c_i *with respect to* a_i *for every* $0 \le i < n$. *A run is* accepting *if* c_n *is a final configuration. Network* $\mathcal{A}$ *accepts* $w \in \Sigma^*$ *if it has an accepting run on input* w. *The* language recognized *by* $\mathcal{A}$, *denoted by* $\mathcal{L}(\mathcal{A})$, *is the set of words accepted by* $\mathcal{A}$.

Example 7.7 Let A_x, A_y, and A_P be the three automata of figure 7.3 for the variables x and y and the control flow, respectively. We have

$$\Sigma_x = \{x = 1; x \neq 1; x \leftarrow 0; x = 0 \Rightarrow y \leftarrow 1; x = 1 \Rightarrow y \leftarrow 0\},$$

$$\Sigma_y = \{y = 1; y \neq 1; x = 0 \Rightarrow y \leftarrow 1; x = 1 \Rightarrow y \leftarrow 0\}, \text{ and}$$

$$\Sigma_P = \Sigma_x \cup \Sigma_y.$$

The automata participating in the action $x \leftarrow 0$ are A_P and A_x, and all three automata participate in "$x = 1 \Rightarrow y \leftarrow 0$." Observe that A_P participates in all actions. If we define $\mathcal{A} = \langle A_P, A_x, A_y \rangle$, then the configurations of $\mathcal{A}$ are the configurations of program 1. The configuration $[3, 1, 1]$ enables the action $x \leftarrow 0$, and we have $[3, 1, 1] \xrightarrow{x \leftarrow 0} [4, 0, 1]$. One of the runs of $\mathcal{A}$ is

$$[1,1,1] \xrightarrow{x=1} [2,1,1] \xrightarrow{y=1} [3,1,1] \xrightarrow{x\leftarrow 0} [4,0,1] \xrightarrow{x=0\Rightarrow y\leftarrow 1} [5,0,1]$$

and so the word $(x=1)(y=1)(x\leftarrow 0)(x=0\Rightarrow y\leftarrow 1)$ belongs to $\mathcal{L}(\mathcal{A})$.

7.2.1 Parallel Composition of Languages

We introduce a useful characterization of the language of a network of automata. Given $L_1 \subseteq \Sigma_1^*, \ldots, L_n \subseteq \Sigma_n^*$, the *parallel composition* of $L_1, \ldots, L_n$ is the language $L_1 \parallel L_2 \parallel \cdots \parallel L_n \subseteq (\Sigma_1 \cup \cdots \cup \Sigma_n)^*$ defined as follows: $w \in L_1 \parallel \cdots \parallel L_n$ iff $proj_{\Sigma_i}(w) \in L_i$ for every $1 \le i \le n$, where $proj_{\Sigma_i}(w)$ is the word obtained from w by only keeping letters from Σ_i.

Example 7.8   Let $L_1 = \{aa, bc\}$ be a language over alphabet $\Sigma_1 = \{a, b, c\}$ and $L_2 = \{ada, dc\}$ a language over alphabet $\Sigma_2 = \{a, c, d\}$. We have $L_1 \parallel L_2 = \{ada, bdc, dbc\}$.

Notice that, strictly speaking, parallel composition is an operation that depends not only on the languages $L_1, \ldots, L_n$, but also on their alphabets. Take, for example, $L_1 = \{a\}$ and $L_2 = \{ab\}$. If we look at them as languages over the alphabet $\{a, b\}$, then $L_1 \parallel L_2 = \emptyset$, but if we look at L_1 as a language over $\{a\}$ and L_2 as a language over $\{a, b\}$, then $L_1 \parallel L_2 = \{ab\}$. Thus, the correct notation would be $L_1 \parallel_{\Sigma_1,\Sigma_2} L_2$, but we abuse language and assume that when a language is defined, its alphabet is clear from the context.

Proposition 7.9   *The parallel composition of languages satisfies the following:*

(a) Parallel composition is associative, commutative, and idempotent, that is, $(L_1 \parallel L_2) \parallel L_3 = L_1 \parallel (L_2 \parallel L_3)$ (associativity), $L_1 \parallel L_2 = L_2 \parallel L_1$ (commutativity), and $L \parallel L = L$ (idempotence).

(b) If L_1 and L_2 are over a common alphabet $\Sigma_1 = \Sigma_2$, then $L_1 \parallel L_2 = L_1 \cap L_2$.

(c) If $\mathcal{A} = \langle A_1, \ldots, A_n \rangle$ is a network of automata, then $\mathcal{L}(\mathcal{A}) = \mathcal{L}(A_1) \parallel \cdots \parallel \mathcal{L}(A_n)$.

Proof   See exercise 115.   □

By property (b), two automata A_1 and A_2 over a common alphabet satisfy $\mathcal{L}(A_1 \parallel A_2) = \mathcal{L}(A_1) \cap \mathcal{L}(A_2)$. Intuitively, in this case, every action must be jointly executed by A_1 and A_2, or, in other words, the automata move in lockstep. At the other extreme, if the input alphabets of A_1 and A_2 are pairwise disjoint, then, intuitively, the automata do not communicate at all and move independently of each other.

7.2.2 Asynchronous Product

Given a network of automata $\mathcal{A} = \langle A_1, \ldots A_n \rangle$, we can compute an NFA recognizing the same language. This NFA, called the *asynchronous product* of $\mathcal{A}$ and denoted by $A_1 \otimes \cdots \otimes A_n$, is the output of algorithm 37.

Algorithm 37 Asynchronous product.

$AsyncProduct(A_1, \ldots, A_n)$

Input: a network of automata $\mathcal{A} = \langle A_1, \ldots, A_n \rangle$, where
      $A_i = (Q_i, \Sigma_i, \delta_i, Q_{0i}, F_i)$ for every $i \in \{1, \ldots, n\}$
Output: NFA $A_1 \otimes \cdots \otimes A_n = (Q, \Sigma, \delta, Q_0, F)$ recognizing $\mathcal{L}(\mathcal{A})$

```
1   Q, δ, F ← ∅
2   Q₀ ← Q₀₁ × ··· × Q₀ₙ
3   W ← Q₀
4   while W ≠ ∅ do
5     pick [q₁, . . . , qₙ] from W
6     add [q₁, . . . , qₙ] to Q
7     if ⋀ⁿᵢ₌₁ qᵢ ∈ Fᵢ then add [q₁, . . . , qₙ] to F
8     for all a ∈ Σ₁ ∪ . . . ∪ Σₙ do
9       for all i ∈ [1..n] do
10        if a ∈ Σᵢ then Q'ᵢ ← δᵢ(qᵢ, a) else Q'ᵢ = {qᵢ}
11        for all [q'₁, . . . , q'ₙ] ∈ Q'₁ × . . . × Q'ₙ do
12          if [q'₁, . . . , q'ₙ] ∉ Q then add [q'₁, . . . , q'ₙ] to W
13          add ([q₁, . . . , qₙ], a, [q'₁, . . . , q'ₙ]) to δ
14  return Q, Σ₁ ∪ ··· ∪ Σₙ, δ, Q₀, F
```

The algorithm follows closely definitions 7.5 and 7.6. Starting at the initial configurations, *AsyncProduct* repeatedly picks a configuration from the workset, stores it, constructs its successors, and adds them (if not yet stored) to the workset. Line 10 is the crucial one. Assume we are in the middle of the execution of $AsyncProduct(A_1, A_2)$, currently processing a configuration $[q_1, q_2]$ and an action a at line 8. There are three cases.

- Assume that a belongs to $\Sigma_1 \cap \Sigma_2$, and the a-transitions leaving q_1 and q_2 are $q_1 \xrightarrow{a} q_1', q_1 \xrightarrow{a} q_1''$ and $q_2 \xrightarrow{a} q_2', q_1 \xrightarrow{a} q_2''$. Then, we obtain $Q_1' = \{q_1', q_1''\}$ and $Q_2' = \{q_2', q_2''\}$, and the loop at lines 11–13 adds the transitions

$$[q_1, q_2] \xrightarrow{a} [q_1', q_2'], \qquad [q_1, q_2] \xrightarrow{a} [q_1'', q_2'],$$
$$[q_1, q_2] \xrightarrow{a} [q_1', q_2''], \qquad [q_1, q_2] \xrightarrow{a} [q_1'', q_2''],$$

corresponding to the four possible "joint a-moves" that A_1 and A_2 can execute from $[q_1, q_2]$.

- Assume that a only belongs to Σ_1, the a-transitions leaving q_1 are as before, and, since $a \notin \Sigma_2$, there are no a-transitions leaving q_2. Then, $Q_1' = \{q_1', q_1''\}$, $Q_2' = \{q_2\}$, and the loop adds transitions $[q_1, q_2] \xrightarrow{a} [q_1', q_2]$ and $[q_1, q_2] \xrightarrow{a} [q_1'', q_2]$, which correspond to A_1 making a move while A_2 stays put.

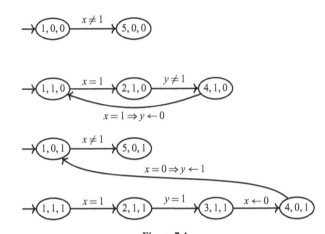

Figure 7.4
Asynchronous product of the automata of figure 7.3.

- Assume that a belongs to $\Sigma_1 \cap \Sigma_2$, the a-transitions leaving q_1 are as before, and there are no a-transitions leaving q_2 (which is possible even if $a \in \Sigma_2$, because A_2 is an NFA). Then, $Q'_1 = \{q'_1, q''_1\}$, $Q'_2 = \emptyset$, and the loop adds no transitions. This corresponds to the fact that, since a-moves must be jointly executed by A_1 and A_2, and A_2 is not currently able to do any a-move, no joint a-move can happen.

Example 7.10   The asynchronous product $A_P \otimes A_x \otimes A_y$, where A_P, A_x, A_y are the three automata of figure 7.3, is shown in figure 7.4. Its states are the reachable configurations of the program. Since all states are final, we draw all states as simple instead of double circles.

Finally, while we have defined the asynchronous product of $A_1 \otimes \cdots \otimes A_n$ as an automaton over alphabet $\Sigma = \Sigma_1 \cup \cdots \cup \Sigma_n$, the algorithm can be easily modified to return a system automaton recognizing the set of executions of the program. We provide a procedure $SysAut(A_1, \ldots, A_n)$ in algorithm 38 for the first of the two constructions on page 165 (the one in which the automaton has an extra initial state i). Giving an algorithm for the second construction is left as an exercise (see exercise 114). To obtain $SysAut$, we first modify line 13 of $AsyncProduct$ so that, instead of transition $[q_1, \ldots, q_n] \xrightarrow{a} [q'_1, \ldots, q'_n]$, it adds

$$[q_1, \ldots, q_n] \xrightarrow{[q_1, \ldots, q_n]} [q'_1, \ldots, q'_n] \text{ (see line 14 of } SysAut).$$

It only remains to add the initial state and its outgoing transitions, which happens in lines 1 to 4.

7.2.3   State- and Action-Based Properties

We have defined executions as sequences of configurations of the program and modeled properties as sets of potential executions. This is called the *state-based* approach. One

---

Algorithm 38 Generation of the system automaton with an extra initial state.

$SysAut(A_1, \ldots, A_n)$
Input: a network of automata $\langle A_1, \ldots A_n \rangle$, where
$\quad\quad\quad A_1 = (Q_1, \Sigma_1, \delta_1, Q_{01}, Q_1), \ldots, A_n = (Q_n, \Sigma_n, \delta_n, Q_{0n}, Q_n)$
Output: a system automaton $S = (Q, \Sigma, \delta, Q_0, F)$

```
 1   Q, δ, Q₀, F ← ∅
 2   add i to Q; add i to Q₀; add i to F
 3   for all [q₁,…,qₙ] ∈ Q₀₁ × ⋯ × Q₀ₙ do
 4       add (i, [q₁,…,qₙ], [q₁,…,qₙ]) to δ
 5   W ← Q₀₁ × ⋯ × Q₀ₙ
 6   while W ≠ ∅ do
 7       pick [q₁,…,qₙ] from W
 8       add [q₁,…,qₙ] to Q; add [q₁,…,qₙ] to F
 9       for all a ∈ Σ₁ ∪ … ∪ Σₙ do
10           for all i ∈ [1..n] do
11               if a ∈ Σᵢ then Q′ᵢ ← δᵢ(qᵢ, a) else Q′ᵢ = {qᵢ}
12           for all [q′₁,…,q′ₙ] ∈ Q′₁ × … × Q′ₙ do
13               if [q′₁,…,q′ₙ] ∉ Q then add [q′₁,…,q′ₙ] to W
14               add ([q₁,…,qₙ], [q′₁,…,q′ₙ], [q′₁,…,q′ₙ]) to δ
15   return (Q, Σ, δ, Q₀, F)
```

---

can also define executions as sequences of *instructions*. The set of executions of a network $\langle A_1, \ldots, A_n \rangle$ is then defined directly as the language of $AsyncProduct(A_1, \ldots, A_n)$. For example, the execution of our running example is the language of the NFA shown in figure 7.4. The property "no terminating execution of the program contains an occurrence of the action $(x = 0 \Rightarrow y \leftarrow 1)$" holds iff this language and the regular language

$$\Sigma_P^* \, (x = 0 \Rightarrow y \leftarrow 1) \, \Sigma_P^* \, (x \neq 1)$$

have an empty intersection, which is not the case. In this context, program instructions are called *actions*, and we speak of *action-based verification*.

7.3   Concurrent Programs

Networks of automata can also elegantly model *concurrent programs*—that is, programs consisting of several sequential programs, usually called *processes*, communicating in some way. A popular communication mechanism includes *shared variables*, where processes communicate by writing a value to a variable, which can then be read by other processes.

As an example, we consider (a simplified version of) Lamport-Burns' mutual exclusion algorithm for two processes, called process 0 and process 1, whose code is described in algorithm 39.

Algorithm 39 Lamport-Burns' mutual exclusion algorithm.

Process 0   Process 1

$\quad$ **repeat** $\qquad\qquad\qquad\qquad\qquad$ **repeat**

nc_0 : $\quad$ $b_0 \leftarrow 1$ $\qquad\qquad$ nc_1 : $\quad$ $b_1 \leftarrow 1$

t_0 $\quad$: $\quad$ **while** $b_1 = 1$ **do skip** $\qquad$ t_1 $\quad$: $\quad$ **if** $b_0 = 1$ **then**

c_0 $\quad$: $\quad$ $b_0 \leftarrow 0$ $\qquad\qquad$ q_1 $\quad$: $\quad\quad$ $b_1 \leftarrow 0$

$\quad$ **forever** $\qquad\qquad\qquad\qquad$ q_1' $\quad$: $\quad\quad$ **while** $b_0 = 1$ **do skip**

$\qquad\qquad\qquad\qquad\qquad\qquad\qquad\qquad$ **goto** nc_1

$\qquad\qquad\qquad\qquad\qquad\qquad$ c_1 $\quad$: $\quad$ $b_1 \leftarrow 0$

$\qquad\qquad\qquad\qquad\qquad\qquad$ **forever**

The processes communicate through the shared boolean variables b_0 and b_1, which initially hold the value 0. Process i reads and writes variable b_i and reads variable b_{1-i}. The algorithm should guarantee that the processes are never simultaneously at control points c_0 and c_1 (their *critical sections*) and that they will not reach a deadlock. Other properties the algorithm should satisfy will be discussed later. Initially, process 0 is in its noncritical section (local state nc_0); it can also be trying to enter its critical section (t_0) or be already in its critical section (c_0). The process can move from nc_0 to t_0 at any time by setting b_0 to 1, it can move from t_0 to c_0 only if the current value of b_1 is 0, and it can move from c_0 to nc_0 at any time by setting b_0 to 0.

Process 1 is a bit more complicated. The local states nc_1, t_1, and c_1 play the same role as in process 0. The local states q_1 and q_1' model a "polite" behavior: intuitively, if process 1 sees that process 0 is trying to enter or in the critical section, it moves to an "after you" local state q_1 and sets b_1 to 0 to signal that it is no longer trying to enter its critical section (local state q_1'). It can then return to its noncritical section if the value of b_0 is 0.

A configuration of this program is a tuple $[n_{b_0}, n_{b_1}, \ell_0, \ell_1]$, where $n_{b_0}, n_{b_1} \in \{0, 1\}$, $\ell_0 \in \{nc_0, t_0, c_0\}$, and $\ell_1 \in \{nc_1, t_1, q_1, q_1', c_1\}$. We define executions of the program by *interleaving*. We assume that, if at the current configuration both processes can do an action, then one of the two will occur before the other, but which one occurs before is decided nondeterministically. So, loosely speaking, if two processes can execute two sequences of actions independently of each other (because, say, they involve disjoint sets of variables), then the sequences of actions of the two processes running in parallel are the interleaving of the sequences of the processes.

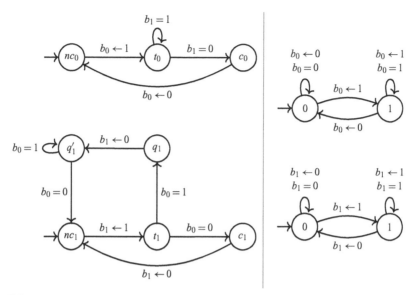

Figure 7.5
A network of four automata modeling the Lamport–Burns mutex algorithm for two processes. The automata on the left model the control flow of the processes and the automata on the right the two shared variables. All states are final.

For example, at the initial configuration $[0, 0, nc_0, nc_1]$, both processes can set their variables to 1. Hence, there are two possible transitions:

$$[0, 0, nc_0, nc_1] \rightarrow [1, 0, t_0, nc_1] \text{ and } [0, 0, nc_0, nc_1] \rightarrow [0, 1, nc_0, t_1].$$

Since the other process can still set its variable, we also have transitions

$$[1, 0, t_0, nc_1] \rightarrow [1, 1, t_0, t_1] \text{ and } [1, 0, t_0, nc_1] \rightarrow [1, 1, t_0, t_1].$$

In order to model a shared-variable program as a network of automata, we model each process and variable by an automaton. The network of automata modeling Lamport-Burns' algorithm is shown in figure 7.5 and its asynchronous product in figure 7.6.

7.3.1 Expressing and Checking Properties

We use Lamport-Burns' algorithm to present some more examples of properties and how to check them automatically.

The mutual exclusion property can be easily formalized: it holds if the asynchronous product does not contain any configuration of the form $[v_0, v_1, c_0, c_1]$, where $v_0, v_1 \in \{0, 1\}$. The property can be easily checked on-the-fly while constructing the asynchronous product, and an inspection of figure 7.6 shows that it holds. Notice that in order to check mutual exclusion, we do not need to construct the NFA for the executions of the program. This

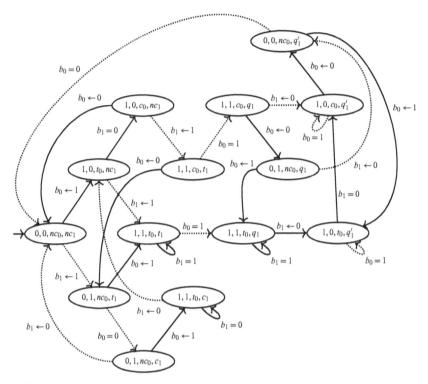

Figure 7.6
Asynchronous product of the network of figure 7.5. Solid (respectively, dotted) transitions correspond to moves by process 0 (respectively, process 1).

is always the case if we only wish to check the reachability of a configuration or set of configurations.

Other properties of interest for the algorithm are as follows:

• **Deadlock freedom**. The algorithm is deadlock-free if every configuration of the asynchronous product has at least one successor. Again, the property can be checked on-the-fly, and it holds.

• **Bounded overtaking**. The property states that after process 0 signals its interest in accessing the critical section by moving to t_0, process 1 can enter the critical section at most once before process 0 enters the critical section.[2] Bounded overtaking can be checked using the NFA recognizing the executions of the network. The NFA can be easily obtained from the asynchronous product by renaming the transitions as shown in example 7.2. Let NC_i, T_i, C_i

---

2. More precisely, this is the bounded overtaking property for process 0. We would like it to hold for both process 0 and process 1.

be the sets of configurations in which process i is in its noncritical section, is trying to access its critical section, and is in its critical section, respectively. Let Σ stand for the set of all configurations. The regular expression

$$r = \Sigma^* \, T_0 \, (\Sigma \setminus C_0)^* \, C_1 \, (\Sigma \setminus C_0)^* \, NC_1 \, (\Sigma \setminus C_0)^* \, C_1 \, \Sigma^*$$

represents potential executions of the algorithm that violate the property.

7.4   Coping with the State-Explosion Problem

Recall that the automata-theoretic approach to the verification of networks of automata reduces the verification problem to the question of deciding whether given an automaton A_E and a regular expression r_V, the language $\mathcal{L}(A_E) \cap \mathcal{L}(r_V)$ is empty or not. Automaton A_E recognizes the language E of executions of the system, and r_V is a regular expression for the set V of potential executions that violate the property.

When the system is modeled as a network of automata, A_E is essentially the asynchronous product of the network (after the minor modifications mentioned at the end of section 7.2.2; see also exercise 114). The main problem of the approach is the number of states of A_E. If the network has n components, each of them with at most k states, then A_E can have as many as k^n states. Thus, in the worst case, the number of states of A_E grows exponentially in the size of the network. This is called the *state-explosion problem*.

The existence of a polynomial-time algorithm for the verification problem is very unlikely. Indeed, the problem is PSPACE-complete. For readers not familiar with complexity theory, "PSPACE-complete" informally means that there is most likely no verification algorithm that uses less than exponential time and a polynomial amount of memory. The proof is deferred to a forthcoming optional subsection, which may be skipped.

Despite this result, the automata-theoretic approach is successfully applied to many hardware and software systems. This is possible thanks to numerous clever ideas that improve its performance in practice. We introduce three of them in the rest of the section.

7.4.1   ★ Verification Is PSPACE-Complete

Theorem 7.11   *The following problem is PSPACE-complete.*

Given: a network of automata $\mathcal{A} = \langle A_1, \ldots, A_n \rangle$ over alphabets $\Sigma_1, \ldots, \Sigma_n$, a regular expression r_V over the set of configurations of $\mathcal{A}$.

Decide: whether $\mathcal{L}(A_1 \otimes \cdots \otimes A_n) \cap \mathcal{L}(r_V) \neq \emptyset$.

Proof   To prove that the problem is in PSPACE, we show that it lies in NPSPACE and apply Savitch's theorem. Let $B = \mathit{IntersNFA}(A_1 \otimes \cdots \otimes A_n, A_V)$. The states of B are tuples $[q_1, \ldots, q_n, q]$, where q_i is a state of A_i for every $1 \leq i \leq n$, and q is a state of V. The polynomial-space nondeterministic algorithm guesses a run of B, one state at a time, leading to a final state. Notice that storing a state of B only requires linear space.

To prove PSPACE-hardness, consider the special case of the problem in which all the alphabets $\Sigma_1, \ldots, \Sigma_n$ are equal. By proposition 7.9(b) and (c), in this case, we have $\mathcal{L}(A_1 \otimes \cdots \otimes A_n) = \bigcap_{i=1}^{n} \mathcal{L}(A_i)$, and the problem reduces to checking whether the intersection $\bigcap_{i=1}^{n} \mathcal{L}(A_i)$ is empty. This problem was shown to be PSPACE-hard in exercise 77 by a reduction from the acceptance problem for deterministic linearly bounded automata. $\square$

7.4.2   On-the-Fly Verification

Given a program with a set E of executions and a regular expression describing the set V of potential executions violating a property, we can check if $E \cap V = \emptyset$ holds in four steps:

(a) model the program as a network of automata $\langle A_1, \ldots, A_n \rangle$, and construct $A_E = SysAut(A_1, \ldots, A_n)$ with $\mathcal{L}(A_E) = E$;

(b) transform the regular expression into an NFA A_V using the algorithm of section 1.4.3;

(c) construct an NFA $A_{E \cap V}$ recognizing $E \cap V$; and

(d) check the emptiness of $A_{E \cap V}$.

Observe that A_E may have *more* states than $A_{E \cap V}$. Indeed, if a state of A_E is not reachable by any word of V, then it does not appear in $A_{E \cap V}$. The difference in size between A_E and $A_{E \cap V}$ can be large, and so it is better to *directly* construct $A_{E \cap V}$, bypassing the construction of A_E. Further, it is inefficient to first construct $A_{E \cap V}$ and then check if its language is empty. It is better to check for emptiness *on-the-fly*, while constructing $A_{E \cap V}$. This is done by *CheckViol* as described in algorithm 40.

Algorithm *CheckViol* is designed for state-based properties. For action-based properties, the algorithm is even simpler. Recall that, in the action-based approach, the potential executions of a network $\langle A_1, \ldots, A_n \rangle$ violating the property are specified by a regular expression r_V over the alphabet $\Sigma = \Sigma_1 \cup \cdots \cup \Sigma_n$ of actions. Therefore, both the asynchronous product $A_1 \otimes \cdots \otimes A_n$ and the NFA A_V computed from r_V have Σ as an alphabet. Furthermore, recall that if two NFAs A_1 and A_2 have the same alphabet, then $\mathcal{L}(A_1 \otimes A_2) = \mathcal{L}(A_1) \cap \mathcal{L}(A_2)$ (by proposition 7.9b and c). So, we have $\mathcal{L}(\mathcal{A}) \cap \mathcal{L}(A_V) = \mathcal{L}(A_1 \otimes \cdots \otimes A_n \otimes A_V)$. Thus, we can test the emptiness of $\mathcal{L}(\mathcal{A}) \cap \mathcal{L}(V)$ by constructing the asynchronous product $A_1 \otimes \cdots \otimes A_n \otimes A_V$, checking on-the-fly if its language is empty. If we rename A_V as A_{n+1}, then it suffices to change line 7 of *AsyncProduct* to

$$\textbf{if } \bigwedge_{i=1}^{n+1} q_i \in F_i \textbf{ then return true.}$$

Intuitively, in the construction above, we consider A_V as another component of the asynchronous product. This has another small advantage. Let us consider again the language

$$\Sigma_P^* \ (x = 0 \Rightarrow y \leftarrow 1) \ \Sigma_P^* \ (x \neq 1).$$

Algorithm 40 Algorithm to check violation of a property.

$CheckViol(A_1, \ldots, A_n, r_V)$

Input: a network $\mathcal{A} = \langle A_1, \ldots A_n \rangle$, where $A_i = (Q_i, \Sigma_i, \delta_i, Q_{0i}, F_i)$

  a regular expression r_V over the configurations of $\mathcal{A}$

Output: true if $\mathcal{L}(A_1 \otimes \cdots \otimes A_n) \cap \mathcal{L}(r_V)$ is nonempty, **false** otherwise

1   $(Q_V, \Sigma_V, \delta_V, Q_{0V}, F_V) \leftarrow REtoNFA(r_V)$
2   $Q \leftarrow \emptyset;\ Q_0 \leftarrow Q_{01} \times \cdots \times Q_{0n} \times Q_{0V}$
3   $W \leftarrow Q_0$
4   **while** $W \neq \emptyset$ **do**
5   **pick** $[q_1, \ldots, q_n, q]$ **from** W
6   **add** $[q_1, \ldots, q_n, q]$ **to** Q
7   **for all** $a \in \Sigma_1 \cup \ldots \cup \Sigma_n$ **do**
8   **for all** $i \in [1..n]$ **do**
9   **if** $a \in \Sigma_i$ **then** $Q'_i \leftarrow \delta_i(q_i, a)$ **else** $Q'_i = \{q_i\}$
10   **for all** $[q'_1, \ldots, q'_n] \in Q'_1 \times \ldots \times Q'_n$ **do**
11          $Q' \leftarrow \delta_V(q, [q'_1, \ldots, q'_n])$
12   **for all** $q' \in Q'$ **do**
13   **if** $\bigwedge_{i=1}^{n} q'_i \in F_i$ **and** $q' \in F_V$ **then return true**
14   **if** $[q'_1, \ldots, q'_n, q'] \notin Q$ **then add** $[q'_1, \ldots, q'_n, q']$ **to** W
15 **return false**

In order to check whether some execution of the program belongs to it, we are only interested in the actions "$x = 0 \Rightarrow y \leftarrow 1$" and "$x \neq 1$." Thus, we can replace A_V by an automaton A'_V with only these two actions as an alphabet and recognizing only the word $(x = 0 \Rightarrow y \leftarrow 1)$ $(x \neq 1)$. Note that A'_V only participates in these two actions. Intuitively, A'_V is an *observer* of the network $\langle A_1, \ldots, A_n \rangle$ that only monitors occurrences of "$x = 0 \Rightarrow y \leftarrow 1$" and "$x \neq 1$."

7.4.3 Compositional Verification

Consider the asynchronous product $A_1 \otimes A_2$ of two NFAs over alphabets Σ_1 and Σ_2. Intuitively, A_2 does not see the actions of $\Sigma_1 \setminus \Sigma_2$; they are "internal" actions of A_1. Therefore, A_1 can be replaced by any other automaton A'_1 satisfying $\mathcal{L}(A'_1) = proj_{\Sigma_2}(\mathcal{L}(A_1))$ without A_2 "noticing," meaning that the sequences of actions that A_2 can execute with A_1 and A'_1 as partners are the same. Formally,

$$proj_{\Sigma_2}(A_1 \otimes A_2) = proj_{\Sigma_2}(A'_1 \otimes A_2).$$

In particular, we have $\mathcal{L}(A_1 \otimes A_2) \neq \emptyset$ iff $\mathcal{L}(A'_1 \otimes A_2) \neq \emptyset$, and so instead of checking emptiness of $A_1 \otimes A_2$, one can also check the emptiness of $A'_1 \otimes A_2$.

It is easy to construct an automaton recognizing $proj_{\Sigma_2}(\mathcal{L}(A_1))$: it suffices to replace all transitions of A_1 labeled with letters of $\Sigma_1 \setminus \Sigma_2$ by ε-transitions. This automaton has the same size as A_1, and so substituting it for A_1 has no immediate advantage. However, after removing the ε-transitions and reducing the resulting NFA, we may obtain an automaton A_1' smaller than A_1.

This idea can be extended to the problem of checking emptiness of a product $A_1 \otimes \cdots \otimes A_n$ with an arbitrary number of components. Exploiting the associativity of $\otimes$, we rewrite the product as $A_1 \otimes (A_2 \otimes \cdots \otimes A_n)$ and replace A_1 by a hopefully smaller automaton A_1' over the alphabet $\Sigma_2 \cup \cdots \cup \Sigma_n$. In a second step, we rewrite $A_1' \otimes A_2 \otimes A_3 \otimes \cdots \otimes A_n$ as $(A_1' \otimes A_2) \otimes (A_3 \otimes \cdots \otimes A_n)$ and, applying again the same procedure, replace $A_1' \otimes A_2$ by a new automaton A_2' over the alphabet $\Sigma_3 \cup \cdots \cup \Sigma_n$. The procedure continues until we are left with a single automaton A_n' over Σ_n, whose emptiness can be checked directly on-the-fly. We call this approach *compositional verification* because it exploits the structure of the system as a network of components.

To see this idea in action, consider the network of automata depicted on the left of figure 7.7. It models a 3-bit counter consisting of an array of three 1-bit counters, where each counter communicates with its neighbors. We call the components of the network $\langle A_0, A_1, A_2 \rangle$ instead of $\langle A_1, A_2, A_3 \rangle$ to better reflect that A_i stands for the ith bit. Each NFA but the last one has three states, two of which are marked with 0 and 1 ("a" stands for "auxiliary"). The alphabets are

$$\Sigma_0 = \{inc, inc_1, 0, \ldots, 7\},$$

$$\Sigma_1 = \{inc_1, inc_2, 0, \ldots, 7\},$$

$$\Sigma_2 = \{inc_2, 0, \ldots, 7\}.$$

Intuitively, the system interacts with its environment by means of the "visible" actions $Vis = \{inc, 0, 1, \ldots, 7\}$. More precisely, inc models a request of the environment to increase the counter by 1, and $i \in \{0, \ldots, 7\}$ models a query of the environment asking whether i is the current value of the counter. A configuration of the form $[b_2, b_1, b_0] \in \{0, 1\}^3$ indicates that the current value of the counter is $4b_2 + 2b_1 + b_0$ (configurations are represented as triples of states of A_2, A_1, A_0, in that order).

Here is a run of the network starting and ending at configuration $[0, 0, 0]$:

$$[0, 0, 0] \xrightarrow{inc} [0, 0, 1]$$

$$\xrightarrow{inc} [0, 0, a] \xrightarrow{inc_1} [0, 1, 0]$$

$$\xrightarrow{inc} [0, 1, 1]$$

$$\xrightarrow{inc} [0, 1, a] \xrightarrow{inc_1} [0, a, 0] \xrightarrow{inc_2} [1, 0, 0]$$

$$\xrightarrow{inc} [1, 0, 1]$$

$$\xrightarrow{inc} [1,0,a] \xrightarrow{inc_1} [1,1,0]$$

$$\xrightarrow{inc} [1,1,1]$$

$$\xrightarrow{inc} [1,1,a] \xrightarrow{inc_1} [1,a,0] \xrightarrow{inc_2} [0,0,0] \cdots.$$

The right-hand side of figure 7.7 illustrates the asynchronous product of the network (all states are final, but we have drawn them as simple instead of double ellipses for simplicity). The asynchronous product has eighteen states.

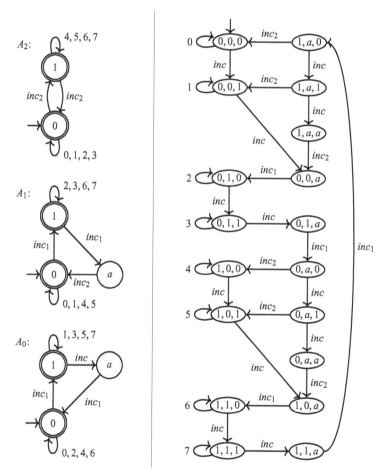

Figure 7.7
A network modeling a 3-bit counter and its asynchronous product.

Assume we wish to check some property whose violations are given by the language of an automaton A_V over the alphabet *Vis* of visible actions. For this, we construct an automaton A_0' such that $\mathcal{L}\left(A_0'\right) = proj_{Vis}(\mathcal{L}\,(A_2 \otimes A_1 \otimes A_0))$ and check emptiness of $A_0' \otimes A_V$. If we compute A_0' by first constructing the asynchronous product $A_2 \otimes A_1 \otimes A_0$, replacing invisible actions by ε, and removing ε-transitions, then the maximum size of all intermediate automata involved is at least 18, because that is the number of states of $A_2 \otimes A_1 \otimes A_0$. Let us instead apply the procedure above, starting with A_2. We first construct an automaton A_2' over the alphabet $\Sigma_1 \cup \Sigma_0 \cup Vis$ such that $\mathcal{L}\left(A_2'\right) = proj_{\Sigma_1 \cup \Sigma_0 \cup Vis}(\mathcal{L}\,(A_2))$. Since $\Sigma_2 \subseteq (\Sigma_1 \cap \Sigma_0)$, we take $A_2' = A_2$. In the next step, we compute the product $A_2' \otimes A_1$, shown on the left of figure 7.8, and replace it by an automaton A_1' such that $\mathcal{L}\left(A_1'\right) = proj_{\Sigma_0 \cup Vis}(\mathcal{L}\,(A_1))$. Since $inc_2 \notin \Sigma_0 \cup Vis$, we can replace inc_2 by ε and remove ε-transitions, leading to the automaton A_1' shown on the right of figure 7.8.

In the next step, we construct $A_1' \otimes A_0$, shown on the left of figure 7.9, and replace it by an automaton A_0' such that $\mathcal{L}\left(A_0'\right) = proj_{Vis}(\mathcal{L}\,(A_0))$. Since $inc_1 \notin Vis$, we replace inc_1 by ε and eliminate ε-transitions. The result is shown on the left of the figure. The important fact is that we have never had to construct an automaton with more than twelve states, saving six states with respect to the method that directly computes $A_2 \otimes A_1 \otimes A_0$. While saving six states is, of course, irrelevant in practice, in larger examples, the savings can be significant. In particular, it can be the case that an asynchronous product $A_0 \otimes \cdots \otimes A_n$ is too large to be stored in memory, but each of the intermediate automata constructed by the compositional approach fits in it.

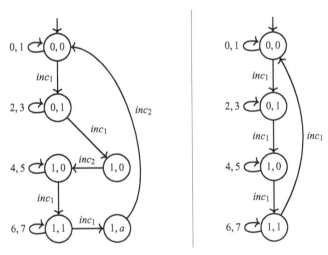

Figure 7.8
Asynchronous product $A_2 \otimes A_1$ and reduced automaton A_1'.

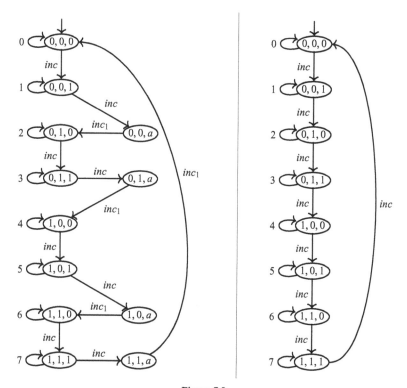

Figure 7.9
The asynchronous product $A_1' \otimes A_0$ and the reduced automaton A_0'.

7.4.4 Symbolic State-Space Exploration

Recall that many program properties, like deadlock-freedom or mutual exclusion, can be checked by computing the set of reachable configurations of the program. In breadth-first search, this is done by iteratively computing the set of configurations reachable in at most $0, 1, 2, \ldots$ steps from the set I of initial configurations until a fixed point is reached. Let C denote the set of all possible configurations of the program, and let $S \subseteq C \times C$ be the *step relation*, defined by $(c, c') \in S$ iff the program can reach c' from c in one step. Note that c may or may not be a reachable configuration. For example, $[4, 0, 0] \to [1, 0, 1]$ is a step of program 1, even though $[4, 0, 0]$ is not reachable. Algorithm 41 computes the configurations reachable from I.

The algorithm can be implemented using different data structures, which can be *explicit* or *symbolic*. Explicit data structures store separately each configuration of I and each pair of configurations of S; typical examples are lists and hash tables. Their distinctive feature is that the memory needed to store a set is proportional to the number of its elements. Symbolic data structures, on the contrary, do not store a set by storing each of its elements; they

---

Algorithm 41   Computation of configurations reachable from I.

Reach(I, R)
Input: set I of initial configurations; step relation S
Output: set of configurations reachable from I

```
1   OldP ← ∅; P ← I
2   while P ≠ OldP do
3       OldP ← P
4       P ← Union(P, Post(P, S))
5   return P
```

---

store a representation of the set itself. A prominent example of a symbolic data structure are finite automata and transducers: given an encoding of configurations as words over some alphabet Σ, the set I and the step relation S are represented by an automaton and a transducer, respectively, recognizing the encodings of its elements. Their sizes can be much smaller than the sizes of I or S. For instance, if I is the set of all possible configurations, then its encoding is often Σ^*, which is represented by a very small automaton. Symbolic data structures are only useful if all the operations required by the algorithm can be implemented without having to switch to an explicit data structure. This is the case of automata and transducers: **Union**, **Post**, and the equality check in the condition of the while loop operation are implemented by the algorithms of chapters 3 and 5 or, if they are of fixed length, by the algorithms of chapter 6.

Symbolic data structures are interesting when the set of reachable configurations can be very large or even infinite. When the set is small, the overhead of symbolic data structures usually offsets the advantage of a compact representation. Despite this, and in order to illustrate the method, we apply it to the five-line program 1, shown with its flow graph in figure 7.10.

An edge of the flow graph leading from node ℓ to node ℓ' can be associated a step relation $S_{\ell, \ell'}$ containing all pairs of configurations $([\ell, x_0, y_0], [\ell', x_0', y_0'])$ such that if at control point ℓ, the current values of the variables are x_0 and y_0, then the program can take a step after which the new control point is ℓ', and the new values are x_0', y_0'. For instance, for the edge leading from node 4 to node 1, we have

$$S_{4,1} = \left\{ ([4, x_0, y_0], [1, x_0', y_0']) : x_0' = x_0, y_0' = 1 - x_0 \right\},$$

and, for the edge leading from 1 to 2, we have

$$S_{1,2} = \left\{ ([1, x_0, y_0], [2, x_0', y_0']) : x_0 = 1 = x_0', y_0' = y_0 \right\}.$$

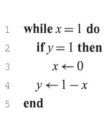

```
1   while x = 1 do
2     if y = 1 then
3       x ← 0
4     y ← 1 − x
5   end
```

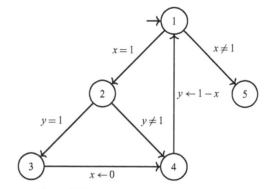

Figure 7.10
Flow graph of program 1.

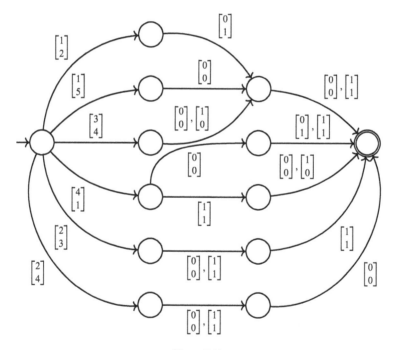

Figure 7.11
Transducer for the program of figure 7.10.

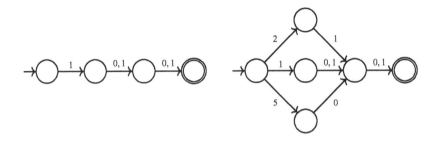

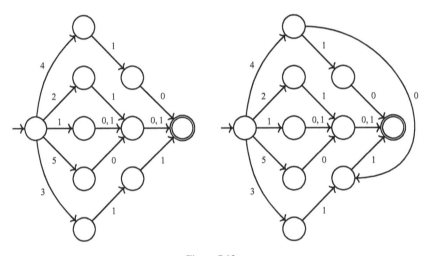

Figure 7.12
Minimal DFAs for the reachable configurations of the program of figure 7.10.

It is convenient to assign a relation to every pair of nodes of the control graph, even to those not connected by any edge. If no edge leads from a to b, then we define $S_{a,b} = \emptyset$. The complete step relation of the program is then described by

$$S = \bigcup_{\ell,\ell' \in \mathcal{L}} S_{\ell,\ell'},$$

where $\mathcal{L}$ is the set of control points.

The fixed-length transducer for the step relation S is shown in figure 7.11; a configuration $[\ell, x_0, y_0]$ is encoded by the word $\ell x_0 y_0$ of length 3.

Consider, for instance, the transition labeled by $[4, 1]$. Using it, the transducer can recognize four pairs of configurations describing the action of the instruction "$y \leftarrow 1 - x$", namely,

$$\left\{ \begin{bmatrix} 400 \\ 101 \end{bmatrix}, \begin{bmatrix} 401 \\ 101 \end{bmatrix}, \begin{bmatrix} 410 \\ 110 \end{bmatrix}, \begin{bmatrix} 411 \\ 110 \end{bmatrix} \right\}.$$

Figure 7.12 depicts minimal DFAs for the set I and for the sets obtained after each iteration of the while loop.

7.4.4.1 Variable Orders

We have defined a configuration of program 1 as a triple $[\ell, n_x, n_y]$, and we have encoded it as the word $\ell n_x n_y$. We could also have encoded it as the word $n_x \ell n_y$, $n_x \ell n_y$, or any other permutation, since in all cases, the information contents is the same. Of course, when encoding a set of configurations, all elements of the set must be encoded using the same *variable order*. While the information contents is independent of the variable order, the *size* of the automaton encoding a set is not. The following example gives an extreme case.

Example 7.12 Consider the set of tuples $X_k = \{[x_1, x_2, \ldots, x_{2k}] : x_1, \ldots, x_{2k} \in \{0, 1\}\}$ and the subset $Y_k \subseteq X_k$ of tuples satisfying $x_1 = x_{k+1}, x_2 = x_{k+2}, \ldots, x_k = x_{2k}$. Consider two possible encodings of a tuple $[x_1, x_2, \ldots, x_{2k}]$: by the word $x_1 x_2 \cdots x_{2k}$ and by the word $x_1 x_{k+1} x_2 x_{k+2} \ldots x_k x_{2k}$. In the first case, the encoding of Y_k for $k = 3$ is the language

$$L_1 = \{000000, 001001, 010010, 011011, 100100, 101101, 110110, 111111\},$$

and, in the second case, the language

$$L_2 = \{000000, 000011, 001100, 001111, 110000, 110011, 111100, 111111\}.$$

Figure 7.13 depicts the minimal DFAs for the languages L_1 and L_2. It is readily seen that the minimal DFA for L_1 has at least 2^k states: since for every word $w \in \{0, 1\}^k$, the residual L_1^w

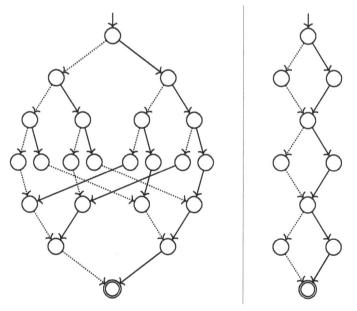

Figure 7.13
Minimal DFAs for the languages L_1 and L_2. For the sake of readability, 0 and 1 are respectively represented by solid and dotted arcs.

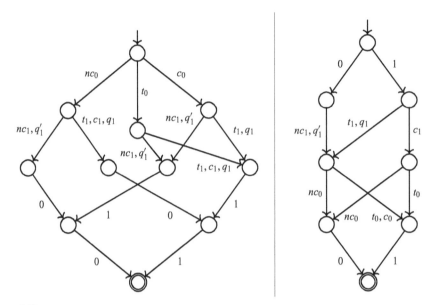

Figure 7.14
Minimal DFAs for the reachable configurations of Lamport–Burns's algorithm. On the left, a configuration $\langle s_0, s_1, v_0, v_1 \rangle$ is encoded by the word $s_0 s_1 v_0 v_1$, on the right, by $v_1 s_1 s_0 v_0$.

is equal to $\{w\}$, the language L_1 has a different residual for each word of length k, and so the minimal DFA has at least 2^k states (the exact number is $2^{k+1} + 2^k - 2$). On the other hand, it is easy to see that the minimal DFA for L_2 has only $3k + 1$ states. So, a good variable order can lead to an exponentially more compact representation.

We can also appreciate the effect of the variable order in Lamport–Burns' algorithm. The set of reachable configurations, where a configuration is described by the control point of the first process, the control point of the second process, the variable of first process, and finally the variable of the second process, is

$\langle nc_0, nc_1, 0, 0 \rangle$	$\langle t_0, nc_1, 1, 0 \rangle$	$\langle c_0, nc_1, 1, 0 \rangle$
$\langle nc_0, t_1, 0, 1 \rangle$	$\langle t_0, t_1, 1, 1 \rangle$	$\langle c_0, t_1, 1, 1 \rangle$
$\langle nc_0, c_1, 0, 1 \rangle$	$\langle t_0, c_1, 1, 1 \rangle$	
$\langle nc_0, q_1, 0, 1 \rangle$	$\langle t_0, q_1, 1, 1 \rangle$	$\langle c_0, q_1, 1, 1 \rangle$
$\langle nc_0, q_1', 0, 0 \rangle$	$\langle t_0, q_1', 1, 0 \rangle$	$\langle c_0, q_1', 1, 0 \rangle$

If we encode a tuple $\langle s_0, s_1, v_0, v_1 \rangle$ as the word $v_0 s_0 s_1 v_1$, then the set of reachable configurations is recognized by the minimal DFA on the left of figure 7.14. However, if we encode it as the word $v_1 s_1 s_0 v_0$, then we get the minimal DFA illustrated on the right.

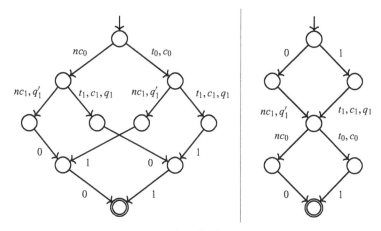

Figure 7.15
Minimal DFAs for the reachable configurations of Lamport's algorithm plus $\langle c_0, c_1, 1, 1 \rangle$.

The same example can be used to visualize how, by adding configurations to a set, the size of its minimal DFA can decrease. If we add the "missing" configuration $\langle c_0, c_1, 1, 1 \rangle$ to the set of reachable configurations (filling the "hole" in the list above), two states of the DFAs of figure 7.14 can be merged, yielding the minimal DFAs of figure 7.15. Further note that the set of all configurations, reachable or not, contains 120 elements but is recognized by a five-state DFA.

7.5 Safety and Liveness Properties

Apart from the state-explosion problem, the automata-theoretic approach to automatic veri-fication as described in this chapter has a second limitation: it assumes that the violations of the property can be witnessed by finite executions. In other words, if an execution violates the property, then we can detect the violation after finite time. Not all properties satisfy this assumption. A typical example is the property "if a process requests access to the critical section, then it eventually enters the critical section" (without specifying how long it may take). After a finite time, we can only tell that the process has not entered the critical sec-tion *yet*, but we cannot say that the property has been violated: the process might still enter the critical section in the future. A violation of the property can only be witnessed by an *infinite* execution, in which we observe that the process requests access, but the access is never granted.

Properties that are violated by finite executions are called *safety properties*. Intuitively, they correspond to properties of the form "nothing bad ever happens." Typical examples are "the system never deadlocks" or, more generally, "the system never enters a set of bad states." Clearly, every interesting system must also satisfy properties of the form "something good eventually happens" because otherwise, the system that does nothing would already satisfy all properties. Properties of this kind are called *liveness properties* and can only be witnessed by *infinite* executions. Fortunately, the automata-theoretic approach can be extended to liveness properties. This requires to develop a theory of automata on infinite words, which is the subject of the second part of this book. The application of this theory to the verification of liveness properties is presented in chapter 13. As an appetizer, some exercises of this chapter already start to discuss them.

7.6   Exercises

☆ 🁢 **Exercise 113.** Exhibit a family $\{P_n\}_{n \geq 1}$ of sequential programs (like program 1) satisfying the following conditions:

- P_n has $\mathcal{O}(n)$ boolean variables, $\mathcal{O}(n)$ lines, and exactly one initial configuration; and
- P_n has at least 2^n reachable configurations.

☆ ✔ **Exercise 114.** When applied to program 1, algorithm *SysAut* outputs the system automaton shown in the middle of figure 7.1. Give an algorithm *SysAut′* that outputs the automaton depicted at the bottom.

☆ ■ **Exercise 115.** Prove the following statements:

(a) Parallel composition is

- associative: $(L_1 \parallel L_2) \parallel L_3 = L_1 \parallel (L_2 \parallel L_3)$,
- commutative: $L_1 \parallel L_2 = L_2 \parallel L_1$, and
- idempotent: $L \parallel L = L$.

(b) If $L_1, L_2 \subseteq \Sigma^*$, then $L_1 \parallel L_2 = L_1 \cap L_2$.

(c) It is the case that $\mathcal{L}(\mathcal{A}) = \mathcal{L}(A_1) \parallel \cdots \parallel \mathcal{L}(A_n)$ for any network of automata $\mathcal{A} = \langle A_1, \ldots, A_n \rangle$.

☆ 🁢 **Exercise 116.** Let $\Sigma = \{request, answer, working, idle\}$.

(a) Build a regular expression and an automaton recognizing all words with the property P_1: "for every occurrence of *request*, there is a later occurrence of *answer*."

(b) Property P_1 does not imply that every occurrence of *request* has "its own" *answer*: for instance, the sequence *request request answer* satisfies P_1, but both requests must necessarily be mapped to the same answer. If words were infinite and there were infinitely many requests, would P_1 guarantee that every *request* has its own *answer*?

More precisely, let $w = w_1 w_2 \cdots$ satisfy P_1 and contain infinitely many occurrences of *request*, and let $f : \mathbb{N} \to \mathbb{N}$ be such that $w_{f(i)}$ is the *i*th *request* of w. Is there always an injective function $g\colon \mathbb{N} \to \mathbb{N}$ satisfying $w_{g(i)} = answer$ and $f(i) < g(i)$ for all $i \in \{1, \ldots, k\}$?

(c) Build an automaton recognizing all words with the property P_2: "there is an occurrence of *answer* before which only *working* and *request* occur."

(d) Using automata-theoretic constructions, prove that all words accepted by the following automaton A satisfy P_1, and give a regular expression for all words accepted by A that violate P_2.

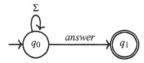

★ 🔳 **Exercise 117.** Consider two processes (process 0 and process 1) being executed through the following generic mutual exclusion algorithm:

```
1   while true do
2       enter(process_id)
3       critical section
4       leave(process_id)
5       for arbitrarily many iterations do
6           noncritical section
7   end
```

(a) Consider the following implementations of enter and leave:

```
1   x ← 0
2   proc enter(i)
3       while x = 1 − i do
4           pass
5   proc leave(i)
6       x ← 1 − i
```

(i) Design a network of automata capturing the executions of the two processes.

(ii) Build the asynchronous product of the network.

(iii) Show that both processes cannot reach their critical sections at the same time.

(iv) If a process wants to enter its critical section, is it always the case that it can eventually enter it?   *Hint: Reason in terms of infinite executions.*

(b) Consider the following alternative implementations of enter and leave:

```
1   x0 ← false
2   x1 ← false
3   proc enter(i)
4       xi ← true
5       while x1−i do
6           pass
7   proc leave(i)
8       xi ← false
```

(i) Design a network of automata capturing the executions of the two processes.

(ii) Say whether a deadlock can occur, that is, can both processes get stuck trying to enter their critical sections?

★ ▣ **Exercise 118.** Consider a circular railway divided into eight tracks: $0 \to 1 \to \ldots \to 7 \to 0$. Three trains, modeled by three automata T_1, T_2, and T_3, circulate on the railway. Each automaton T_i is defined as follows:

- states: $\{q_{i,0}, \ldots, q_{i,7}\}$;
- alphabet: $\{enter[i,j] : 0 \leq j \leq 7\}$, where $enter[i,j]$ models that train i enters track j;
- transition relation: $\{(q_{i,j}, enter[i, j \oplus 1], q_{i,j \oplus 1}) : 0 \leq j \leq 7\}$, where $\oplus$ denotes addition mod 8;
- initial state: $q_{i,2i}$ (i.e., initially the trains occupy tracks 2, 4, and 6).

Describe automata $C_0, \ldots, C_7$, called *local controllers*, that ensure that two trains can never be on the same track or adjacent tracks, that is, there must always be at least one empty track between two trains. Each controller C_j can only have knowledge of the state of tracks $j \ominus 1$, j, and $j \oplus 1$; there must be no deadlocks; and every train must eventually visit every track. More formally, the network of automata $\mathcal{A} = \langle C_0, \ldots, C_7, T_1, T_2, T_3 \rangle$ must satisfy the following specification:

(a) C_j only knows the state of local tracks: C_j has alphabet $\{enter[i, j \ominus 1], enter[i,j], enter[i,j \oplus 1] : 1 \leq i \leq 3\}$;

(b) no deadlock and each train eventually visits every segment: $\mathcal{L}(\mathcal{A})|_{\Sigma_i} = (enter[i, 2i] \, enter[i, 2i \oplus 1] \cdots enter[i, 2i \oplus 7])^*$ for each $i \in \{1, 2, 3\}$; and

(c) no two trains on the same or adjacent tracks: for every word $w \in \mathcal{L}(\mathcal{A})$, it is the case that $w = u \, enter[i,j] \, enter[i',j'] \, v$ and $i' \neq i$ implies $|j - j'| \notin \{0, 1, 7\}$.

8 Automata and Logic

A regular expression can be seen as a set of instructions (a "recipe") for generating the words of a language. For instance, the expression $aa(a+b)^*b$ can be interpreted as the recipe "write two as, repeatedly choose one a or b and write it, an arbitrary number of times, and then write a b." We say that regular expressions are an *operational* formalism.

Languages can also be described in *declarative* style, as the set of words that satisfy a property. For instance, "the words over $\{a, b\}$ containing an even number of as and an even number of bs" is a declarative description. It describes the property but does not give a recipe to construct the words that satisfy it.

For some languages, declarative descriptions can be simpler than operational ones. For instance, the regular expression

$$(aa + bb + (ab + ba)(aa + bb)^*(ba + ab))^*$$

is an operational description of the language "even number of as and even number of bs," and most people will agree that it is far less intuitive than the declarative description. In particular, the expression does not consist of the conjunction of two smaller regular expressions, one for "even number of as" and the other for "even number of bs." Another example in which a declarative description is arguably simpler is "the words over $\{a, b\}$ that do not contain any occurrence of aba." This description is immediately understood by a human, who also has no problem to formulate it as the negation of the simpler property "the words over $\{a, b\}$ that contain some occurrence of aba." However, the operational description

$$(b + aa^*bb)^*(\varepsilon + aa^*(b + \varepsilon))$$

is substantially harder to understand and produce.

In this chapter, we first present a logical formalism for the declarative description of regular languages. We use logical formulas to describe properties of words and logical operators to construct complex properties out of simpler ones. In particular, the formalism allows us to combine properties using conjunction, disjunction, and negation. We then show how to automatically translate a formula describing a property of words into an automaton recognizing the words satisfying the property. As a consequence, we obtain an algorithm to convert declarative into operational descriptions and vice versa.

8.1 Predicate Logic on Words: An Informal Introduction

In declarative style, a language is defined indirectly as the set of words satisfying a given property, called the *membership predicate*. A word belongs to the language if and only if it satisfies the membership predicate. For example, the membership predicates of the languages discussed in the previous section are "to have an even number of *a*s and an even number of *b*s," and "to not contain any occurrence of *aba*."

The standard mathematical framework for expressing membership predicates is *predicate logic*, also called—for reasons explained in section 8.5—*first-order logic*. Starting from very few natural "atomic formulas," predicate logic allows one to build more complex formulas through boolean combinations and quantification. Formulas of predicate logic represent predicates in the same sense that regular expressions represent languages. We consider a version of predicate logic usually called "predicate logic on words," because its atomic formulas represent predicates on words.[1]

Before introducing predicate logic on words, let us become familiar with it at an intuitive level. (Readers acquainted with predicate logic can move directly to section 8.5.) For the time being, it suffices to know that the symbols $\wedge$, $\vee$, $\neg$, $\rightarrow$, $\exists x$, and $\forall x$ roughly correspond to the English expressions "and," "or," "not," "implies," "there exists an x such that," and "every x satisfies."

We start by fixing an alphabet, for example, $\Sigma = \{a, b\}$. Predicate logic on words has two types of atomic formulas:

- Formulas of the form $Q_a(x)$ or $Q_b(x)$, where x is a variable ranging over the positions of the word.

The intended meaning of $Q_a(x)$ is "the letter at position x is an a," and the meaning of $Q_b(x)$ is analogous. For instance, the predicate "all letters of the word are as" is expressed by the formula $\forall x\, Q_a(x)$. The language of all words satisfying the formula, called just the language of the formula, is $\mathcal{L}(a^*)$.

- Formulas of the form $x < y$, where x and y range over the positions of the word.

The intended meaning is "position x is smaller than (lies to the left of) position y." For example, the predicate "if some letter is an a, then all subsequent letters are also as" is expressed by the formula

$$\forall x\, \forall y\, ((Q_a(x) \wedge x < y) \rightarrow Q_a(y)).$$

---

1. Chapter 9 presents a different predicate logic expressing properties of tuples of numbers.

The language of the formula is $\mathcal{L}(b^*a^*)$. Notice, however, that this is so because $\Sigma = \{a, b\}$. If $\Sigma = \{a, b, c\}$, then the language of the formula is $\mathcal{L}((b+c)^*a^*)$.

Example 8.1 Other examples of formulas are

- $\forall x \, Q_a(x) \vee \forall x \, Q_b(x)$.

The formula expresses the predicate "either all letters are as or all letters are bs." The same predicate is also expressed by $\neg \exists x \, \exists y \, (Q_a(x) \wedge Q_b(y))$. The language of both formulas is $\mathcal{L}(a^* + b^*)$.

- $\forall x \, \forall y \, (Q_a(x) \wedge x < y \wedge Q_a(y)) \rightarrow \exists z \, (x < z \wedge z < y \wedge Q_b(z))$.

The formula expresses the predicate "between every two as, there is at least one b," which corresponds to the language $\mathcal{L}((b+ab)^*(\epsilon+a))$. For $\Sigma = \{a, b\}$, this predicate is equivalent to "after every a there is a b, unless that a is the last letter," which corresponds to the formula $\forall x \, \forall y \, (Q_a(x) \wedge x < y \wedge \neg \exists z \, (x < z \wedge z < y)) \rightarrow Q_b(y)$.

While our intuitive understanding of the meaning of "and," "implies," and so on can bring us a long way, it is not precise enough for formal reasoning. For example, faced with the question whether the empty word ε satisfies $\forall x \, Q_a(x)$, some people answer "yes," others "no." Some people argue that the question whether the empty word satisfies the formula $\exists x \, Q_a(x) \rightarrow \forall x \, Q_a(x)$ does not make sense. Some formulas truly seem to make no sense, for example $\exists x \, \forall x \, Q_a(x)$ or $\exists x \, Q_a(y)$, which raises the problem of defining which formulas make sense. Such problems can only be solved by formally specifying which sequences of symbols are formulas and, for every formula, which are the words that satisfy it. These specifications are called the *syntax* and the *semantics* of predicate logic on words.

8.2 Syntax and Semantics

We introduce the syntax and semantics of predicate logic on words over a given alphabet Σ. Readers familiar with logic only need to look at the forthcoming definition 8.2 (syntax) and definitions 8.3 and 8.5 (semantics).

8.2.1 Syntax

The following definition determines which sequences of symbols are formulas of predicate logic on words.

Definition 8.2 *Let $V = \{x, y, z, \ldots\}$ be an infinite set of variables, and let $\Sigma = \{a, b, c, \ldots\}$ be a finite alphabet. The formulas of predicate logic on words over Σ, also called the first-order formulas over Σ and denoted $FO(\Sigma)$, are the expressions generated by the grammar*

$$\varphi ::= Q_a(x) \mid x < y \mid \neg\varphi \mid (\varphi \vee \varphi) \mid \exists x \, \varphi$$

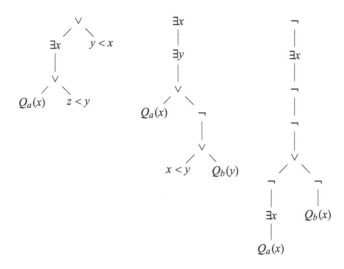

Figure 8.1
Syntax trees of (8.1), (8.2), and (8.3).

where $a \in \Sigma$ and $x, y \in V$. Expressions of the form $Q_a(x)$ and $x < y$ are called atomic formulas.

In the rest of the section, we introduce or recall several notions, using the following three formulas as running examples.

$$\varphi_1 := (\exists x \, (Q_a(x) \lor z < y) \lor y < x) \tag{8.1}$$

$$\varphi_2 := \exists x \, \exists y \, (Q_a(x) \lor \neg(x < y \lor Q_b(y))) \tag{8.2}$$

$$\varphi_3 := \neg \exists x \, \neg\neg(\neg \exists x \, Q_a(x) \lor \neg Q_b(x)) \tag{8.3}$$

Syntax tree of a formula. We assume that the reader is familiar with the notion and just show the syntax trees of (8.1), (8.2), and (8.3) in figure 8.1.

Free and bound variables. The *occurrences* of a variable x in a formula are the leaves of the syntax tree containing x. For example, x occurs twice in all of (8.1), (8.2), and (8.3), while y occurs two, two, and zero times, respectively. An occurrence of a variable x is *bound* if it is in the scope of some $\exists x$, that is, if the unique path of the syntax tree leading from the root to the occurrence of x traverses a node labeled by $\exists x$; otherwise, the occurrence of x is *free*. Observe that the same variable can occur bound and free in a formula; for example, x occurs bound and free in (8.1). A variable is *free* in φ if it has at least one free occurrence in φ and *bound* otherwise. The set of *free variables* of φ, denoted *free*(φ), can also be defined inductively as follows:

$$free(Q_a(x)) = \{x\}, \qquad\qquad free(x < y) = \{x, y\},$$

$$free(\neg\varphi) = free(\varphi), \qquad free(\varphi_1 \vee \varphi_2) = free(\varphi_1) \cup free(\varphi_2), \qquad (8.4)$$

$$free(\exists x\ \varphi) = free(\varphi) \setminus \{x\}.$$

For the formulas (8.1), (8.2), and (8.3), we get $free(\varphi_1) = \{x, y, z\}$ and $free(\varphi_2) = free(\varphi_3) = \emptyset$. A formula without free variables is called a *sentence*, and so (8.2) and (8.3) are sentences, but (8.1) is not.

We use the following abbreviations:

$$(\varphi_1 \wedge \varphi_2) := \neg(\neg\varphi_1 \vee \neg\varphi_2), \quad (\varphi_1 \to \varphi_2) := (\neg\varphi_1 \vee \varphi_2), \quad \forall x\ \varphi := \neg\exists x\ \neg\varphi.$$

For example, (8.3) can be rewritten as $\forall x\ (\exists x\ Q_a(x) \wedge Q_b(x))$.

8.2.2 Semantics

The semantics of $FO(\Sigma)$ is the definition that determines whether a given word over Σ satisfies a given sentence or not. In logical jargon, this definition allows us to *interpret* the sentence on the word. The definition is inductive, that is, the set of words satisfying a sentence is defined as a function of the sets of words satisfying its subformulas. However, we have to overcome the fact that the subformulas of a sentence may not be sentences themselves. So, we give a semantics not only for sentences but also for formulas with free variables.

Interpretations. While a sentence can be interpreted on just a word (e.g., we intuitively see that aaa satisfies $\forall x\ Q_a(x)$ and aba does not), formulas with free variables usually cannot. For example, whether aba satisfies $Q_a(x)$ or not depends on the position x is referring to. If $x \mapsto 1$ or $x \mapsto 3$, then aba satisfies the formula, but if $x \mapsto 2$, then it does not. Generally, we interpret a formula, with or without free variables, over a pair $(w, \mathcal{V})$, where w is a word and $\mathcal{V}$ is a mapping that assigns to every free variable of the formula, and perhaps to others, a position in the word, that is, a value in the range $\{1, \ldots, |w|\}$. We call $\mathcal{V}$ a *valuation*. Formally, we define valuations as partial mappings $V \to \mathbb{N}$, that is, mappings that may be defined only for a subset of V. In particular, the *totally undefined valuation* $\perp: V \to \mathbb{N}$ is the partial map that is undefined for every variable of V.[2]

Definition 8.3 *An* interpretation *of a formula φ of $FO(\Sigma)$ is a pair $(w, \mathcal{V})$, where $w \in \Sigma^*$ and $\mathcal{V}: V \to \mathbb{N}$ is a partial mapping such that $\mathcal{V}(x)$ is defined and satisfies $1 \le \mathcal{V}(x) \le |w|$ for every $x \in free(\varphi)$. We call $\mathcal{V}$ a* valuation.

We often write the map $\mathcal{V}$ extensionally, that is, enumerating the value assigned to each variable for which the map is defined. For example, if $\mathcal{V}$ is the valuation that is defined only for the variables x and y and satisfies $\mathcal{V}(x) = 5$ and $\mathcal{V}(y) = 3$, then we write $(w, \{x \mapsto 5, y \mapsto$

---

2. A partial mapping $f: V \to \mathbb{N}$ is just a set of pairs of $V \times \mathbb{N}$, containing one pair for each $x \in V$ such that $f(x)$ is defined; the totally undefined map corresponds to the empty set of pairs.

3}) instead of $(w, \mathcal{V})$. With this convention, $(ab, \{x \mapsto 1\})$ is an interpretation of formulas like $Q_a(x)$, $\exists x \, Q_a(x)$, or $\exists x \, \exists y \, (Q_a(x) \land Q_b(y))$ but not of $x < y$ or $Q_a(y)$. In particular, the definition of interpretation requires that all free variables are assigned values but does not forbid that other variables are assigned values as well.

Remark 8.4

• Since ε has no positions, it is not possible to assign values to them. Thus, a formula with at least one free variable has no interpretation of the form $(\varepsilon, \mathcal{V})$.

• If φ is a sentence and $w \neq \varepsilon$, then $(w, \mathcal{V})$ is an interpretation of φ for every valuation $\mathcal{V} \colon V \to \{1, \ldots, |w|\}$, including the totally undefined valuation $\bot$. However, if $w = \varepsilon$, then $(w, \mathcal{V})$ is an interpretation if and only if $\mathcal{V} = \bot$. Indeed, if $\mathcal{V}(x)$ is defined, then by the definition of an interpretation we have $1 \leq \mathcal{V}(x) \leq |\epsilon| = 0$, which is not possible.

Models.   The pairs $(ab, \{x \mapsto 1\})$ and $(ab, \{x \mapsto 2\})$ are interpretations of $Q_a(x)$. Intuitively, the first interpretation satisfies $Q_a(x)$, but the second does not. In logical jargon, the interpretations of a formula that satisfy it are called the *models* of the formula. We formally define which interpretations $(w, \mathcal{V})$ of a formula φ are models of φ.

Given a word w and a number $1 \leq i \leq |w|$, let $w[i]$ denote the letter of w at position i, and let $\mathcal{V}[i/x]$ denote the partial mapping that assigns i to x and coincides with $\mathcal{V}$ on all other variables (in particular, $\mathcal{V}[i/x](x)$ is always defined and satisfies $\mathcal{V}[i/x](x) = i$, even if $\mathcal{V}(x)$ is undefined).

Definition 8.5   *Let φ be a formula of $FO(\Sigma)$, and let $(w, \mathcal{V})$ be an interpretation of φ. We say that $(w, \mathcal{V})$ satisfies φ, or is a model of φ, if one of the following conditions holds:*

• $\varphi = Q_a(x)$ *and* $w[\mathcal{V}(x)] = a$,

• $\varphi = x < y$ *and* $\mathcal{V}(x) < \mathcal{V}(y)$,

• $\varphi = \neg\varphi'$ *and* $(w, \mathcal{V}) \not\models \varphi'$,

• $\varphi = (\varphi_1 \lor \varphi_2)$ *and* $(w, \mathcal{V}) \models \varphi_1$ *or* $(w, \mathcal{V}) \models \varphi_2$, *and*

• $\varphi = \exists x \, \varphi$, $w \neq \varepsilon$ *and* $(w, \mathcal{V}[i/x]) \models \varphi$ *holds for some i such that $1 \leq i \leq |w|$.*

Two formulas φ_1, φ_2 are equivalent, *denoted $\varphi_1 \equiv \varphi_2$, if they have the same interpretations and the same models.*

Example 8.6   Let $\Sigma = \{a, b\}$. We show that, unsurprisingly, $(ab, \bot) \models \exists x \, \neg Q_a(x)$. We use definition 8.5 to deduce that $(ab, \bot)$ satisfies $\exists x \, \neg Q_a(x)$ iff $b \neq a$, which is true:

$$(ab, \bot) \models \exists x \, \neg Q_a(x)$$

$$\Longleftrightarrow (ab, \{x \mapsto 1\}) \models \neg Q_a(x) \text{ or } (ab, \{x \mapsto 2\}) \models \neg Q_a(x)$$

$$\Longleftrightarrow (ab, \{x \mapsto 1\}) \not\models Q_a(x) \text{ or } (ab, \{x \mapsto 2\}) \not\models Q_a(x)$$

$$\Longrightarrow (ab)[1] \neq a \text{ or } (ab)[2] \neq a$$

$$\Longrightarrow a \neq a \text{ or } b \neq a$$

$$\Longrightarrow \text{true.}$$

Remark 8.7

• Only interpretations can be models. For example, the question of whether $(\varepsilon, \perp)$ is a model $Q_a(x)$ is ill-posed, as $(\varepsilon, \perp)$ is not an interpretation of $Q_a(x)$.

• If $free(\varphi) \subseteq free(\psi)$, then every interpretation of ψ is also an interpretation of φ. Indeed, every interpretation of ψ assigns values to all free variables of ψ, and so it also assigns values to all free variables of φ.

• Definition 8.5 silently uses three facts:

1. An interpretation of $\neg\varphi'$ is also an interpretation of φ', because $free(\neg\varphi') = free(\varphi')$.

2. An interpretation of $(\varphi_1 \vee \varphi_2)$ is also an interpretation of φ_1 and φ_2, because $free(\varphi_1 \vee \varphi_2) = free(\varphi_1) \cup free(\varphi_2)$.

3. If $w \neq \varepsilon$ and $(w, \mathcal{V})$ is an interpretation of $\exists x\, \varphi$, then $(w, \mathcal{V}[i/x])$ is an interpretation of φ for every $i \in \{1, \ldots, |w|\}$.

Since $w \neq \varepsilon$, the set $i \in \{1, \ldots, |w|\}$ is nonempty, and so it is possible to assign to x at least one value. For $w = \varepsilon$, the pair $(w, \perp)$ is an interpretation of $\exists x Q_a(x)$, but there are no interpretations $(w, \mathcal{V}[i/x])$ such that $1 \leq i \leq 0$.

For the previously introduced abbreviations, it follows from definition 8.5 that

$$(w, \mathcal{V}) \models (\varphi_1 \wedge \varphi_2) \text{ iff } (w, \mathcal{V}) \models \varphi_1 \text{ and } (w, \mathcal{V}) \models \varphi_2, \text{ and}$$

$$(w, \mathcal{V}) \models (\varphi_1 \rightarrow \varphi_2) \text{ iff } (w, \mathcal{V}) \not\models \varphi_1 \text{ or } (w, \mathcal{V}) \models \varphi_2 .$$

Let us now consider the abbreviation $\forall x\, \varphi = \neg\exists x\, \neg\varphi$. We have

$$(w, \mathcal{V}) \models \forall x\, \varphi$$

$$\Longleftrightarrow (w, \mathcal{V}) \models \neg\exists x\, \neg\varphi$$

$$\Longleftrightarrow (w, \mathcal{V}) \not\models \exists x\, \neg\varphi$$

$$\Longleftrightarrow w = \varepsilon \text{ or } (w, \mathcal{V}[i/x]) \models \varphi \text{ for every } i \in \{1, \ldots, |w|\}.$$

Remark 8.8   Recall that if $(\varepsilon, \mathcal{V})$ is an interpretation of a formula, then the formula is a sentence and $\mathcal{V}$ is the totally undefined valuation (i.e., $\mathcal{V} = \perp$). By definition 8.5, $(\varepsilon, \perp)$ satisfies no sentences of the form $\exists x\, \varphi$ and every sentence of the form $\forall x\, \varphi$. For example, $(\varepsilon, \perp)$ satisfies neither $\exists x\, Q_a(x)$ nor $\exists x\, \forall z\, Q_a(z)$, but it satisfies both $\forall x\, Q_a(x)$ and $\forall x\, \exists z\, Q_a(z)$. Intuitively, "there exists a position x in the word such that φ" is always false for ε, because the empty word has no positions at all, while "for every position in the word φ holds" is vacuously true for ε.

Using definition 8.5, it is possible to prove many standard equivalence rules, like $\neg\neg\varphi \equiv \varphi$ for every φ; $(\varphi_1 \vee (\varphi_2 \vee \varphi_3)) \equiv ((\varphi_1 \vee \varphi_2) \vee \varphi_3)$ for every $\varphi_1, \varphi_2, \varphi_3$; $\exists x\, \exists y\, \varphi \equiv \exists y\, \exists x\, \varphi$ for every φ; or $\exists x\, (\varphi_1 \vee \varphi_2) \equiv (\exists x\, \varphi_1 \vee \exists x\, \varphi_2)$ for every φ_1, φ_2. We implicitly use them to lighten notation. For example, instead of $(\varphi_1 \vee (\varphi_2 \vee \varphi_3))$ or $((\varphi_1 \vee \varphi_2) \vee \varphi_3)$, as we would have to write according to the syntax, we simply write $(\varphi_1 \vee \varphi_2 \vee \varphi_3)$ or even $\varphi_1 \vee \varphi_2 \vee \varphi_3$.

The following lemma is easy to prove by induction on the structure of formulas. It corresponds to our intuition that bound variables are "internal" variables of a formula that are "invisible outside of it."

Lemma 8.9 *Let w be a word, and let $(w, \mathcal{V})$ and $(w, \mathcal{V}')$ be two interpretations of a formula φ. If $\mathcal{V}$ and $\mathcal{V}'$ assign the same values to all free variables of φ, then either $(w, \mathcal{V}) \models \varphi$ and $(w, \mathcal{V}') \models \varphi$ or $(w, \mathcal{V}) \not\models \varphi$ and $(w, \mathcal{V}') \not\models \varphi$. In particular, for every word w and every sentence φ, either all interpretations $(w, \mathcal{V})$ of φ are models, or none of them is a model.*

Example 8.10 Let w be a word of length at least 2. It is the case that $(w, \{x \mapsto 1\})$ and $(w, \{x \mapsto 2\})$ are interpretations of $\exists x\, Q_a(x)$ that assign the same values to all free variables, because $\exists x\, Q_a(x)$ is a sentence. We have

$$(w, \{x \mapsto 1\}) \models \exists x\, Q_a(x)$$

$$\Longleftrightarrow (w, \{x \mapsto 1\}[1/x]) \models Q_a(x) \text{ or } (w, \{x \mapsto 1\}[2/x]) \models Q_a(x)$$

$$(\text{by def. of } (w, \mathcal{V}) \models \exists x\, \varphi)$$

$$\Longleftrightarrow (w, \{x \mapsto 2\}[1/x]) \models Q_a(x) \text{ or } (w, \{x \mapsto 2\}[2/x]) \models Q_a(x)$$

$$(\text{since } \{x \mapsto 1\}[i/x] = \{x \mapsto i\} = \{x \mapsto 2\}[i/x])$$

$$\Longleftrightarrow (w, \{x \mapsto 2\}) \models \exists x\, Q_a(x).$$

The second part of lemma 8.9 justifies the following definition, which takes us to our final destination: a precise definition of when a given word over Σ satisfies a given sentence of $FO(\Sigma)$.

Definition 8.11 *Let φ be a sentence of $FO(\Sigma)$. A word $w \in \Sigma^*$ satisfies φ or is a model of φ, denoted $w \models \varphi$, if every interpretation $(w, \mathcal{V})$ of φ satisfies φ or, equivalently (by lemma 8.9), if some interpretation $(w, \mathcal{V})$ of φ satisfies φ.*

Example 8.12 Consider the two sentences $\exists x\, Q_a(x)$ and $\forall x\, \exists x\, Q_a(x)$. Are they equivalent? This is the kind of question that challenges our intuition. If you accept definition 8.5, then there is only one right answer. By remark 8.8, we have $\varepsilon \not\models \exists x\, Q_a(x)$ and $\varepsilon \models \forall x\, \exists x\, Q_a(x)$, and so the two formulas are not equivalent. However, they are "almost" equivalent: every word $w \neq \varepsilon$ satisfies $\exists x\, Q_a(x)$ iff it satisfies $\forall x\, \exists x\, Q_a(x)$. This is an easy consequence of lemma 8.9. Indeed,

$$w \models \forall x \, \exists x \, Q_a(x)$$

$$\Longleftrightarrow (w, \perp) \models \forall x \, \exists x \, Q_a(x)$$

(by lemma 8.9 and as $\forall x \, \exists x \, Q_a(x)$ is a sentence)

$$\Longleftrightarrow (w, \perp[1/x]) \models \exists x \, Q_a(x) \text{ and } \cdots \text{ and } (w, \perp[|w|/x]) \models \exists x \, Q_a(x)$$

(by $w \neq \varepsilon$ and def. of $(w, \mathcal{V}) \models \forall x \, \varphi$)

$$\Longleftrightarrow (w, \{x \mapsto 1\}) \models \exists x \, Q_a(x) \text{ and } \cdots \text{ and } (w, \{x \mapsto |w|\}) \models \exists x \, Q_a(x)$$

$$\Longleftrightarrow w \models \exists x \, Q_a(x)$$

(by lemma 8.9 and as $\exists x \, Q_a(x)$ is a sentence).

8.3   Macros and Examples

Expressing predicates in first-order logic on words is akin to writing programs in a low-level language. The language has a very small syntax and is therefore easy to learn, but expressing even simple predicates may be tedious, is error prone, and requires writing long formulas. All these problems are palliated by the use of *macros*. Formally, a macro is an expression of the form $m(x_1, \ldots, x_n) = \varphi$, where φ is a formula with free variables $x_1, \ldots, x_n$. Intuitively, macros play the same role as procedures in programming: they are defined once and can be used multiple times in other formulas, where they stand for the formula φ. Here are two examples:

- "x is the first position."

$$\text{first}(x) := \neg \exists y \, y < x$$

Observe that x is the only free variable of first(x).

- "x is the last position."

$$\text{last}(x) := \neg \exists y \, x < y$$

Sometimes we use infix notation for macros and write "$x_1 \, m \, x_2$" instead of $m(x_1, x_2)$. The following examples illustrate this.

- "x and y are the same position."

$$x = y := \neg (x < y \lor y < x)$$

We could also call this macro equal(x, y).

- "y is the successor position of x," or "y is the position to the right of x."

$$y = x + 1 := (x < y \land \neg \exists z \, (x < z \land z < y))$$

Recall that here the expression $y = x + 1$ is just a name; we could also call the macro $\text{succ}(x, y)$. We prefer $y = x + 1$ because the name can be generalized, as shown by the next example.

- "y is two positions to the right of x."

$$y = x + 2 := \exists z\, (z = x + 1 \wedge y = z + 1)$$

The macros $y = x + 3$, $y = x + 4$, and so on are defined similarly.

- "y is at most k positions to the right of x."

$$y < x + k := \exists z\, (z = x + k \wedge y < z)$$

Observe that k is a constant, that is, $y < x + k$ stands for the infinite family of macros $y < x + 1$, $y < x + 2$, $y < x + 3$, and so on. Further, remember that $y < x + k$ is just the name of a formula. For example, unravelling all macros, we have

$$(y < x + 2) = \exists z\, (z = x + 2 \wedge y < z) = \exists z\, (\exists u\, (u = x + 1 \wedge z = u + 1) \wedge y < z).$$

In particular, one should not confuse the atomic formula $x < y$ and the macro $x < y + 2$. The latter is only an abbreviation, for which we could have chosen any other name.

- "x is to the left of the kth position."

$$x < k := \neg \exists y\, x = y + k - 1$$

- "The length of the word is smaller than k."

$$last < k := \forall x\, (last(x) \to x < k)$$

Example 8.13 Using the macros above, we can express some predicates on words by rather short sentences:

- "The last letter is a b and before it, there are only as."

$$(\exists x\, Q_b(x) \wedge \forall x\, (last(x) \to Q_b(x) \wedge \neg last(x) \to Q_a(x)))$$

- "Every a is immediately followed by a b."

$$\forall x\, (Q_a(x) \to \exists y\, (y = x + 1 \wedge Q_b(y)))$$

- "Every a is immediately followed by a b, unless it is the last letter."

$$\forall x\, (Q_a(x) \to \forall y\, (y = x + 1 \to Q_b(y)))$$

Observe the difference: The previous sentence states that if the letter at position x is an a, then the word has a successor position y, and the letter at y is a b. This sentence only states that for every position y, if y happens to be the successor of x, then the letter at that position is a b. It does not state that the successor position of x exists.

- "Between every a and every later b there is a c."

$$\forall x \, \forall y \, ((Q_a(x) \wedge Q_b(y) \wedge x < y) \rightarrow \exists z \, (x < z \wedge z < y \wedge Q_c(z)))$$

- Finally, we formalize the second predicate from the introduction to the chapter: "no occurrence of aba."

$$\neg \exists x \, \exists y \, \exists z \, (y = x + 1 \wedge z = y + 1 \wedge Q_a(x) \wedge Q_b(y) \wedge Q_a(z))$$

8.4 Expressive Power of $FO(\Sigma)$

Now that we have defined which words satisfy which sentences, we can associate to a sentence the language of all words that satisfy it. Intuitively, this language is the "meaning" of the sentence.

Definition 8.14 *The language of a sentence $\varphi \in FO(\Sigma)$ is the set $\mathcal{L}(\varphi) := \{ w \in \Sigma^* \mid w \models \varphi \}$. We also say that φ expresses $\mathcal{L}(\varphi)$. A language $L \subseteq \Sigma^*$ is FO-definable if $L = \mathcal{L}(\varphi)$ for some formula φ of $FO(\Sigma)$.*

The languages of the predicates from example 8.13 are FO-definable by definition. Which languages are FO-definable? Are all FO-definable languages regular? Are all regular languages FO-definable? These are questions concerning the *expressive power* of first-order logic on words.

We study which languages are FO-definable when the alphabet Σ contains exactly one letter. We show that in this case, a language is FO-definable iff it is finite or co-finite. A language is *co-finite* if its complement is finite. It follows from this result that all FO-definable languages over a one-letter alphabet are regular. Indeed, we know that all finite languages are regular and, since the regular languages are closed under complement, so are all co-finite languages. However, it also follows that even very simple regular languages, like $\{ a^n : n \text{ is even} \}$, are not FO-definable. Thus, first-order logic on words is not expressive enough as a declarative language.

Let $\Sigma = \{ a \}$. The proof that a language is FO-definable iff it is finite or co-finite proceeds in three steps (readers not interested in the proof can move directly to section 8.5):

1. We define a fragment of $FO(\{ a \})$, called QF, standing for *quantifier-free*. Formulas of QF contain no quantifiers, existential or universal, and no occurrences of $Q_a(x)$.

2. We show that languages over $\{ a \}$ are QF-definable iff they are finite or co-finite.

3. We prove that languages over $\{ a \}$ are FO-definable iff they are QF-definable. That is, we show that for every formula of $FO(\{ a \})$, there exists an equivalent formula of QF.

The fragment QF. Formulas of QF are boolean combinations of some of the macros introduced in section 8.3:

Definition 8.15 *The formulas of QF are the formulas of FO({a}) generated by the grammar*

$$f ::= x < k \mid x < y + k \mid last < k \mid \neg f \mid (f \vee f) \mid (f \wedge f),$$

where $k \in \mathbb{N}$.

Observe that the *sentences* of QF are especially simple. They cannot contain any occurrence of $x < k$ or $x < y + k$ because, loosely speaking, QF does not have quantification, and so it cannot bind free occurrences of variables. So, sentences of QF are boolean combinations of expressions of the form $last < k$. For example,

$$\varphi := ((last < 3 \wedge \neg\, last < 2) \vee \neg\, last < 7)$$

is a sentence of QF. Its language is $\mathcal{L}\left(aa + a^7 a^*\right)$, whose complement is the finite set $\{\varepsilon, a, a^3, a^4, a^5, a^6\}$. So the language of φ is co-finite.

One-letter languages are QF-definable iff they are finite or co-finite. We prove the following proposition:

Proposition 8.16 *A language over a one-letter alphabet is QF-definable iff it is finite or co-finite.*

Proof ⇒) We show that, for every sentence f of QF, the language $\mathcal{L}(f)$ is finite or co-finite. Let f be a sentence of QF, that is, a boolean combination of formulas of the form $last < k$. We proceed by induction on the structure of f. If $f = last < k$, then $\mathcal{L}(f)$ is finite. If $f = \neg f'$, then by induction hypothesis, $\mathcal{L}(f')$ is finite or co-finite, and so $\mathcal{L}(f) = \overline{\mathcal{L}(f')}$ is co-finite or finite, respectively. If $f = (f_1 \vee f_2)$, then by induction hypothesis, $\mathcal{L}(f_1)$ and $\mathcal{L}(f_2)$ are finite or co-finite; if $\mathcal{L}(f_1)$ and $\mathcal{L}(f_2)$ are finite, then so is $\mathcal{L}(f)$, and otherwise, $\mathcal{L}(f)$ is co-finite. The case of $f = (f_1 \wedge f_2)$ is similar.

⇐) Let $\Sigma = \{a\}$. The empty language is expressed by $last < 1$. A nonempty finite language $\{a^{k_1}, \ldots, a^{k_n}\}$ is expressed by the formula

$$((\neg last < k_1 - 1 \wedge last < k_1 + 1) \vee \cdots \vee (\neg last < k_n - 1 \wedge last < k_n + 1)).$$

A co-finite language L is expressed by $\neg f$, where f is the formula for the finite language $\overline{L}$ (i.e., where $\mathcal{L}(f) = \overline{L}$). $\square$

One-letter languages are FO-definable iff they are QF-definable. We show that when Σ contains only one letter, every first-order formula over Σ has an equivalent formula in the QF-fragment. The main difficulty is that first-order formulas are closed under quantification (i.e., if φ is a formula so is $\exists x \, \varphi$), but formulas of QF are not.

Theorem 8.17 *Every formula of FO({a}) is equivalent to a formula of QF.*

Proof sketch Let φ be a formula of $FO(\{a\})$. Observe that, since the alphabet only contains one letter, every formula of $FO(\{a\})$ is equivalent to a formula without occurrences of $Q_a(x)$. So, we can assume that φ has no occurrence of $Q_a(x)$. We proceed by induction on the structure of φ. If $\varphi(x, y) = x < y$, then $\varphi \equiv x < y + 0$. If $\varphi = \neg \psi$, then by induction hypothesis, there is a formula f of QF equivalent to ψ, and so $\varphi \equiv \neg f$. The cases $\varphi = (\varphi_1 \vee \varphi_2)$ and $\varphi = (\varphi_1 \wedge \varphi_2)$ are similar.

Consider now the case $\varphi = \exists x \, \psi$. By induction hypothesis, ψ is equivalent to a formula f of QF. Further, we can assume that f is in disjunctive normal form, that is, $f = (f_1 \vee \cdots \vee f_n)$, where each f_i is a conjunction of atomic formulas of QF or their negations. Repeatedly applying the equivalence $\exists x \, (\varphi_1 \vee \varphi_2) \equiv (\exists x \, \varphi_1 \vee \exists x \, \varphi_2)$, we obtain

$$\varphi \equiv \exists x \, (f_1 \vee \cdots \vee f_n) \equiv (\exists x \, f_1 \vee \exists x \, f_2 \vee \cdots \vee \exists x \, f_n).$$

Thus, it suffices to find a formula g_i of QF equivalent to $\exists x \, f_i$ for every $1 \leq i \leq n$, since then $\varphi \equiv (g_1 \vee \cdots \vee g_n)$.

We sketch how to construct g_i with the help of this representative example:

$$f_i = ((x < y + 3) \wedge \neg(x < z + 4) \wedge (z < y + 2) \wedge (y < x + 1)).$$

We start by classifying the conjuncts of f_i with some occurrence of x into

- *lower bounds* of the form $\neg(x < k)$, $\neg(x < y + k)$, or $y < x + k$; and
- *upper bounds* of the form $x < k$, $x < y + k$, or $\neg(y < x + k)$.

In our example, the lower bounds are $\neg(x < z + 4)$ and $y < x + 1$, and the only upper bound is $x < y + 3$. The remaining conjunct, $z < y + 2$, has no occurrence of x.

Assume that the lower bounds of f_i are $\ell_1, \ldots, \ell_p$, the upper bounds are $u_1, \ldots, u_q$, and the conjuncts with no occurrence of x are $e_1, \ldots, e_r$. Applying standard logical equivalences, we have

$$\exists x \, f_i \equiv \exists x \left(\bigwedge_{j=1}^{p} \ell_j \wedge \bigwedge_{k=1}^{q} u_k \wedge \bigwedge_{\ell=1}^{r} e_\ell \right) \equiv \bigwedge_{\ell=1}^{r} e_\ell \wedge \exists x \left(\bigwedge_{j=1}^{p} \bigwedge_{k=1}^{q} (\ell_j \wedge u_k) \right).$$

In our example, this yields

$$\exists x \, f_i \equiv z < y + 2 \wedge \exists x \big((\neg x < z + 4 \wedge x < y + 3) \wedge (y < x + 1 \wedge x < y + 3) \big).$$

Observe that $\bigwedge_{\ell=1}^{r} e_\ell$ is already a formula of QF. So it remains to find a formula of QF equivalent to $\exists x \bigwedge_{j=1}^{p} \bigwedge_{k=1}^{q} (\ell_j \wedge u_k)$. Intuitively, each conjunct $\ell_j \wedge u_k$ expresses that x must lie in an interval determined by ℓ_j and u_k. The key insight is that, since we consider *all* combinations of upper and lower bounds, there exists an x that simultaneously lies in all intervals iff each interval is nonempty. Let us see how this works in our example. Since there is one upper bound and two lower bounds, we have to consider two conjuncts:

- $\neg(x < z + 4) \wedge (x < y + 3)$.

This expresses that x must lie in the interval $[z + 4, y + 3)$ (closed on the left, open on the right). The interval is nonempty iff $z + 2 \leq y$ or, equivalently, if $\neg(y < z + 2)$.

- $(y < x + 1) \wedge (x < y + 3)$.

This expresses that x must lie in the interval $(y - 1, y + 3)$ (open on both sides). The interval is always nonempty.

So, in our example, we finally obtain

$$\exists x\, f_i = \exists x\, ((x < y + 3) \wedge \neg(x < z + 4) \wedge (z < y + 2) \wedge (y < x + 1))$$
$$\equiv ((z < y + 2) \wedge \neg(y < z + 2))$$
$$=: g_i. \qquad \square$$

As the set of words of even length is neither finite nor co-finite, we have

Corollary 8.18   *The language Even* $= \{a^{2n} : n \geq 0\}$ *is not FO-definable.*

8.5   Monadic Second-Order Logic on Words

In a nutshell, monadic second-order logic on words extends first-order logic on words with variables $X, Y, Z, \ldots$ ranging over *sets* of positions, and with a new kind of atomic formulas of the form $x \in X$, with intended meaning "position x belongs to the set X of positions." The logic allows to quantify over both kinds of variables.

Variables $x, y, z, \ldots$ ranging over positions are called *first-order variables*, and variables $X, Y, Z, \ldots$ ranging over *sets* of positions are called *second-order variables*. One could further introduce variables ranging over *sets of sets* of positions, called *third-order* variables, and so on. Further, sets can be seen as unary relations, and one could have variables for unary, binary, and ternary relations, and so forth, called *monadic*, *dyadic*, and *triadic* second-order variables, respectively. Thus, monadic second-order logic is the extension of first-order logic that allows variables ranging over sets of positions, and no variables ranging over binary relations, or relations of higher arity.

Before introducing the syntax and semantics of the logic, let us informally argue that monadic second-order logic can express the language *Even* of words of even length. The formula expressing *Even* states that the set containing exactly all even positions also contains the last position (if there is one, observe that the empty word has even length but no positions):

$$\text{EvenLength} := \forall X\, \forall x\, ((\text{Even}(X) \wedge \text{last}(x)) \rightarrow x \in X).$$

It remains to define the macro $\text{Even}(X)$. To express that X contains exactly the even positions, we state that a position belongs to X iff it is the second position or if it is the second successor of another position in X:

$$\text{second}(x) := \exists y \ (\text{first}(y) \wedge x = y + 1),$$

$$\text{Even}(X) := \forall x \ (x \in X \leftrightarrow (\text{second}(x) \vee \exists y \ (x = y + 2 \wedge y \in X))) .$$

8.6   Syntax and Semantics

We introduce the syntax and semantics of monadic second-order logic on words. They extend those of first-order logic presented in section 8.2.

8.6.1   Syntax

We add the new atomic formula $x \in X$ to the syntax of first-order logic, as well as quantification over second-order variables.

Definition 8.19 *Let* $V_1 = \{x, y, z, \ldots\}$ *and* $V_2 = \{X, Y, Z, \ldots\}$ *be two infinite sets of* first-order *and* second-order *variables. Let* $\Sigma = \{a, b, c, \ldots\}$ *be a finite alphabet. The set* $MSO(\Sigma)$ *of* monadic second-order formulas *over* Σ *is the set of expressions generated by the following grammar:*

$$\varphi ::= Q_a(x) \mid x < y \mid x \in X \mid \neg\varphi \mid \varphi \vee \varphi \mid \exists x \ \varphi \mid \exists X \ \varphi .$$

The abbreviations $\varphi_1 \wedge \varphi_2$, $\varphi_1 \rightarrow \varphi_2$, and $\forall x \ \varphi$ are defined as for $FO(\Sigma)$. Furthermore, we introduce

$$x \notin X := \neg \ x \in X$$

$$\forall X \ \varphi := \neg \exists X \ \neg\varphi \qquad\qquad \text{``}\varphi \text{ holds for every set } X\text{''}$$

$$\exists x \in X \ \varphi := \exists x \ (x \in X \wedge \varphi) \qquad \text{``some position } x \text{ in } X \text{ satisfies } \varphi\text{''}$$

$$\forall x \in X \ \varphi := \forall x \ (x \in X \rightarrow \varphi) \qquad \text{``every position } x \text{ in } X \text{ satisfies } \varphi\text{.''}$$

To define the free variables of a formula, we extend the definition of the first-order case (see [8.4]), with

$$free(x \in X) = \{x, X\} \quad \text{and} \quad free(\exists X \ \varphi) = free(\varphi) \setminus \{X\}.$$

A formula φ of $MSO(\Sigma)$ is a *sentence* if $free(\varphi) = \emptyset$, that is, if it has neither first-order nor second-order free variables.

8.6.2   Semantics

Interpretations of monadic second-order formulas assign positions to first-order variables and sets of positions to second-order variables.

Definition 8.20   *An* interpretation *of a formula φ of MSO(Σ) is a triple $(w, \mathcal{V}_1, \mathcal{V}_2)$ where $w \in \Sigma^*$ and*

- *$\mathcal{V}_1 \colon V_1 \to \mathbb{N}$ is a partial mapping such that $\mathcal{V}_1(x)$ is defined and satisfies $1 \leq \mathcal{V}_1(x) \leq |w|$ for every $x \in free(\varphi) \cap V_1$, and*
- *$\mathcal{V}_2 \colon V_2 \to 2^{\mathbb{N}}$ is a partial mapping such that $\mathcal{V}_2(X)$ is defined and satisfies $\mathcal{V}_2(X) \subseteq \{1, \ldots, |w|\}$ for every $X \in free(\varphi) \cap V_2$.*

We call $\mathcal{V}_1$ and $\mathcal{V}_2$ valuations.

As in the first-order case, we often write the mappings $\mathcal{V}_1$ and $\mathcal{V}_2$ extensionally. For example, the triple $(aba, \{x \mapsto 1\}, \{X \mapsto \{1, 3\}, Y \mapsto \emptyset\})$ is an interpretation of $Q_a(X)$, of $x \in X$, and of $(x \in X \vee x \in Y)$.

Remark 8.21   Recall that the only interpretation of a sentence $(w, \mathcal{V})$ of $FO(\Sigma)$ with $w = \varepsilon$ is $(\varepsilon, \bot)$. The interpretations of a sentence of $MSO(\Sigma)$ over the empty word are the triples $(\varepsilon, \bot, \mathcal{V}_2)$ such that for every second-order variable X, either $\mathcal{V}_2(X)$ is undefined or $\mathcal{V}_2(X) = \emptyset$.

Let us formally define when an interpretation $(w, \mathcal{V}_1, \mathcal{V}_2)$ of a formula φ satisfies φ. We use the same notations as in definition 8.5. Additionally, given $S \subseteq \{1, \ldots, |w|\}$, we let $\mathcal{V}_2[S/X]$ denote the valuation of V_2 that assigns S to X and the same value as $\mathcal{V}_2$ to every other second-order variable (with the convention that $\{1, \ldots, |w|\} = \emptyset$ for $w = \varepsilon$).

Definition 8.22   *Let φ be a formula of MSO(Σ), and let $(w, \mathcal{V}_1, \mathcal{V}_2)$ be an interpretation of φ. We say that $(w, \mathcal{V}_1, \mathcal{V}_2)$ satisfies φ, or is a* model *of φ, if one of the following conditions holds:*

- *$\varphi = Q_a(x)$ and $w[\mathcal{V}_1(x)] = a$;*
- *$\varphi = x < y$ and $\mathcal{V}_1(x) < \mathcal{V}_1(y)$;*
- *$\varphi = x \in X$ and $\mathcal{V}_1(x) \in \mathcal{V}_2(X)$;*
- *$\varphi = \neg \varphi'$ and $(w, \mathcal{V}_1, \mathcal{V}_2) \not\models \varphi'$;*
- *$\varphi = (\varphi_1 \vee \varphi_2)$ and $(w, \mathcal{V}_1, \mathcal{V}_2) \models \varphi_1$ or $(w, \mathcal{V}_1, \mathcal{V}_2) \models \varphi_2$;*
- *$\varphi = \exists x\, \varphi$, $w \neq \varepsilon$, and $(w, \mathcal{V}_1[i/x], \mathcal{V}_2) \models \varphi$ holds for some $i \in \{1, \ldots, |w|\}$;*
- *$\varphi = \exists X\, \varphi$ and $(w, \mathcal{V}_1, \mathcal{V}_2[S/X]) \models \varphi$ holds for some $S \subseteq \{1, \ldots, |w|\}$.*

We say that two formulas φ_1, φ_2 are equivalent, *denoted $\varphi_1 \equiv \varphi_2$, if they have the same models.*

Remark 8.23

- Note that the set S from definition 8.22 may be empty. Therefore, for instance, any interpretation $(w, \bot, \mathcal{V}_2)$ of $\exists X\, \forall x\, \neg(x \in X)$ such that $\mathcal{V}_2(X) = \emptyset$ is a model.

• Recall that every interpretation $(\varepsilon, \mathcal{V})$ of a formula $\forall x\ \varphi$ of $FO(\Sigma)$ is a model, and no interpretation $(\varepsilon, \mathcal{V})$ of $\exists x\ \varphi$ is a model (remark 8.8). Does this also hold for all formulas $\forall X\ \varphi$ and $\exists X\ \varphi$? The answer is no. For example, let us show that $\varepsilon \not\models \forall X\ \exists x\ x \in X$. From definition 8.22, we get

$$\varepsilon \not\models \forall X\ \exists x\ x \in X$$

$$\Longleftrightarrow (\varepsilon, \bot, \bot) \not\models \forall X\ \exists x\ x \in X \qquad\qquad \text{(by lemma 8.9)}$$

$$\Longleftrightarrow (\varepsilon, \bot, \{X \mapsto \emptyset\}) \not\models \exists x\ x \in X \qquad\qquad \text{(by lemma 8.9)}$$

$$\Longleftrightarrow \text{true}$$

Analogously, we have $\varepsilon \models \forall X\ \forall x\ x \in X$. Further, $\varepsilon \models \exists X\ \forall x\ x \notin X$ and $\varepsilon \not\models \exists X\ \exists x\ x \in X$.

It is easy to see that lemma 8.9 extends to monadic second-order logic: if two interpretations $(w, \mathcal{V}_1, \mathcal{V}_2)$ and $(w, \mathcal{V}_1', \mathcal{V}_2')$ of a formula assign the same values to all free variables, then either both satisfy φ or none satisfy the formula. Thus, we can define the following:

Definition 8.24 *Let φ be a sentence of $MSO(\Sigma)$. A word $w \in \Sigma^*$ satisfies φ, denoted $w \models \varphi$, if every interpretation $(w, \mathcal{V})$ of φ satisfies φ or, equivalently, if some interpretation $(w, \mathcal{V})$ of φ satisfies φ.*

The language $\mathcal{L}(\varphi)$ of a sentence φ of $MSO(\Sigma)$ is the set $\mathcal{L}(\varphi) = \{w \in \Sigma^* : w \models \varphi\}$. A language $L \subseteq \Sigma^*$ is MSO-definable if $L = \mathcal{L}(\varphi)$ for some formula φ of $MSO(\Sigma)$.

8.7   Macros and Examples

As for first-order logic, macros are essential to turn monadic second-order logic into a flexible language. Here are a few macros expressing standard properties of sets:

$$X = \emptyset := \forall x\ x \notin X$$

$$X = Y \cup Z := \forall x\ (x \in X \leftrightarrow (x \in Y \vee x \in Z))$$

$$X = Y \cap Z := \forall x\ (x \in X \leftrightarrow (x \in Y \wedge x \in Z))$$

$$X = Y \uplus Z := (X = Y \cup Z \wedge \exists W\ (W = Y \cap Z \wedge W = \emptyset))$$

$$|X| = 1 := \exists x \forall y \in X\ y = x$$

$$|X| = k + 1 := \exists Y\ \exists Z\ (X = Y \uplus Z \wedge |Y| = k \wedge |Z| = 1)$$

Example 8.25   We use the macros to give sentences of $MSO(\Sigma)$ for two predicates.

Even number of *as* and even number of *bs*. This is the first predicate discussed in the introduction of the chapter. We give a formalization valid for every Σ such that $a, b \in \Sigma$. We first define formulas expressing that x is the first (last) position in X, and that x and y are neighbor positions in X:

$$\text{Is\_first\_in}(x, X) := x \in X \wedge \forall y \, (y < x \rightarrow y \notin X))$$

$$\text{Is\_last\_in}(x, X) := x \in X \wedge \forall y \, (x < y \rightarrow y \notin X))$$

$$\text{Neighbors}(x, y, X) := x \in X \wedge y \in X \wedge \forall z \, ((x < z \wedge z \wedge y) \rightarrow z \notin X) \, .$$

Now we express that X can be partitioned into two disjoint sets of positions X_o and X_e, such that the set X_o contains the first, third, fifth, ... position of X, the set X_e contains the second, fourth, sixth, ... position of X, and the rightmost position of X belongs to X_e. This holds iff X has even size.

$$\text{EvenSize}(X) := \exists X_o \, \exists X_e$$

$$X = X_o \uplus X_e$$

$$\wedge \, \forall x \, (\text{Is\_first\_in}(x, X) \rightarrow x \in X_o)$$

$$\wedge \, \forall x \, \forall y \, (\text{Neighbors}(x, y, X) \rightarrow (x \in X_o \leftrightarrow y \in X_e))$$

$$\wedge \, \forall x \, (\text{Is\_last\_in}(x, X) \rightarrow x \in X_e)$$

Given a letter $\sigma \in \Sigma$, we define

$$\text{Even\_number\_of\_}\sigma := \exists X \, ((x \in X \leftrightarrow Q_\sigma(x)) \wedge \text{EvenSize}(X))$$

The formula we are looking for is

$$\text{Even\_number\_of\_a} \wedge \text{Even\_number\_of\_b}.$$

The formula is longer than the regular expression at the beginning of the chapter, but it is easier to find for a human. Moreover, it is now trivial to find another formula for "even number of *as*, *bs* and *cs*," while finding another regular expression is not.

A formula for $c^*(ab)^*d^*$. Let $\Sigma = \{a, b, c, d\}$. We construct a formula with language $\mathcal{L}(c^*(ab)^*d^*)$. The membership predicate for this language can be informally formulated as follows:

There is a block of consecutive positions X such that (1) before X, there are only *cs*; (2) after X, there are only *ds*; (3) in X, *bs* and *as* alternate; (4) the first letter in X is an *a*; and (5) the last letter in X is a *b*.

This predicate is a conjunction of five smaller predicates. We give formulas expressing each of the conjuncts.

- "X is a block of consecutive positions."

Intuitively, X is a block of consecutive positions if it does not contain a "hole" or, equivalently, if all positions between two positions of X also belong to X.

$$\mathrm{Block}(X) := \forall x \in X \; \forall y \in X$$

$$(x < y \rightarrow \forall z \, ((x < z \wedge z < y) \rightarrow z \in X))$$

- "Before X, there are only cs."

$$\mathrm{Before}(x, X) := \forall y \in X \; x < y$$

$$\mathrm{Before\_only\_c}(X) := \forall x \; (\mathrm{Before}(x, X) \rightarrow Q_c(x))$$

- "After X, there are only ds."

$$\mathrm{After}(x, X) := \forall y \in X \; y < x$$

$$\mathrm{After\_only\_d}(X) := \forall x \; (\mathrm{After}(x, X) \rightarrow Q_d(x))$$

- "as and bs alternate in X."

$$\mathrm{Alternate}(X) := \forall x \in X \; \forall y \in X$$

$$\left(y = x + 1 \rightarrow \left((Q_a(x) \rightarrow Q_b(y)) \wedge (Q_b(x) \rightarrow Q_a(y)) \right) \right)$$

- "The first letter in X is an a."

$$\mathrm{Is\_first\_in}(x, X) := x \in X \wedge \forall y \, (y < x \rightarrow y \notin X)$$

$$\mathrm{First\_is\_a}(X) := \forall x \, (\mathrm{Is\_first\_in}(x, X) \rightarrow Q_a(x))$$

- "The last letter in X is a b."

$$\mathrm{Is\_last\_in}(x, X) := x \in X \wedge \forall y \, (x < y \rightarrow y \notin X)$$

$$\mathrm{Last\_is\_b}(X) := \forall x \, (\mathrm{Is\_last\_in}(x, X) \rightarrow Q_b(x))$$

Putting everything together, we get the formula

$$\exists X \big(\mathrm{Block}(X) \wedge \mathrm{Before\_only\_c}(X) \wedge \mathrm{After\_only\_d}(X) \wedge$$

$$\mathrm{Alternate}(X) \wedge \mathrm{First\_is\_a}(X) \wedge \mathrm{Last\_is\_b}(X) \big).$$

Note that the empty word is a model of the formula, because the empty set of positions satisfies all conjuncts.

8.8   All Regular Languages Are Expressible in $MSO(\Sigma)$

We show that, contrary to first-order logic, monadic second-order logic on words can express all regular languages.

Proposition 8.26   *If $L \subseteq \Sigma^*$ is regular, then L is expressible in $MSO(\Sigma)$.*

For the proof, we present a *generic* procedure that, given a regular language over Σ, represented by a DFA A, constructs a formula φ_A of $MSO(\Sigma)$ such that $\mathcal{L}(\varphi_A) = \mathcal{L}(A)$.

Imagine we are given A. There is an obvious way to express the membership predicate of $\mathcal{L}(A)$: a word belongs to $\mathcal{L}(A)$ iff the last state of its run on A is accepting. Thus, it suffices to find a formula of $MSO(\Sigma)$ expressing "the last state of the run of A is accepting." For this, we introduce the *visit record* of a word. The visit record of a word w is a mapping that assigns to each state q the set of positions of w after which the run reaches q. It is the inverse of the mapping that assigns to each letter of w the state reached by A after reading it. Formally:

Definition 8.27   *Let $A = (Q, \Sigma, \delta, q_0, F)$ be a DFA, and let $w = a_1 \cdots a_m$ be a nonempty word over Σ. The* visit record *of w is the mapping $R_w \colon Q \to 2^{\{1,\dots,m\}}$ that assigns to each state $q \in Q$ the set of positions defined as follows:*

$$R_w(q) = \left\{ i \in \{1, \dots, m\} : \hat{\delta}(q_0, a_1 \cdots a_i) = q \right\}.$$

Example 8.28   Figure 8.2 shows a DFA, its run on the word $w = aabbb$, and the visit record R_w. Observe that each position belongs to the visit record of exactly one state. In other words, $R_w(q_0)$, $R_w(q_1)$, and $R_w(q_2)$ form a partition of the set of positions $\{1, 2, \dots, 5\}$.

For every nonempty word, "the run of A on the word is accepting" is equivalent to the predicate "the last position of the word belongs to the visit record of an accepting state." Let us examine this predicate. Assume the states of A are $\{q_0, q_1, \dots, q_n\}$, and imagine we are

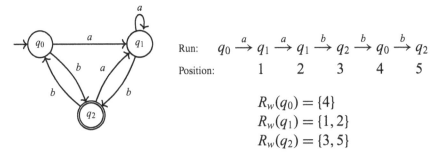

Figure 8.2
Example of a run and a visit record.

able to define a macro expressing the visit record—that is, a macro VisitRecord($X_0, \ldots X_n$) such that an interpretation $(w, \perp, \mathcal{V}_2)$ is a model if and only if $\mathcal{V}_2$ assigns to $X_0, \ldots, X_n$ the visit record $R_w(q_0), \ldots, R_w(q_n)$. The predicate is then expressed by the sentence

$$\psi_A := \forall X_0 \cdots \forall X_n \; \forall x \left((\text{VisitRecord}(X_0, \ldots, X_n) \wedge \text{last}(x)) \rightarrow \bigvee_{q_i \in F} x \in X_i \right)$$

and hence, for every nonempty word w, we have $w \in \mathcal{L}(\psi_A)$ iff $w \in \mathcal{L}(A)$. It remains to take care of the empty word, which has no visit record. Since the only first-order quantifier of ψ_A is universal, we have $\varepsilon \models \psi_A$ for every DFA A, independently of whether $\varepsilon \in \mathcal{L}(A)$ holds or not, and so we cannot define $\varphi_A := \psi_A$. This is easy to fix by defining φ_A as follows: if $\varepsilon \in \mathcal{L}(A)$, then $\varphi_A := \psi_A$, and otherwise, $\varphi_A := \psi_A \wedge \varphi$, where φ is any sentence satisfied by every word but ε (e.g., $\varphi = \exists x \, \neg(x < x)$). After this adjustment, we have $\mathcal{L}(\varphi_A) = \mathcal{L}(A)$. For example 8.28, we get

$$\varphi_A := \forall X_0 \forall X_1 \forall X_2 \; \forall x$$

$$\left(((\text{VisitRecord}(X_0, X_1, X_2) \wedge \text{last}(x)) \rightarrow x \in X_2) \wedge \exists x \, \neg(x < x) \right).$$

It remains to construct the macro VisitRecord($X_0, \ldots, X_n$). For this, note that the visit record R_w can also be defined inductively: we first define which component $R_w(q)$ of the record contains position 1, and then, assuming we know which component contains position i, we define which component contains position $i+1$.

Lemma 8.29 *Let $A = (Q, \Sigma, \delta, q_0, F)$ be a DFA, and let $w = a_1 \cdots a_m$ be a nonempty word over Σ. The visit record R_w is the unique mapping $Q \rightarrow 2^{\{1,\ldots,m\}}$ satisfying the following properties for every $q, q' \in Q$ and every $1 \leq i < m$:*

(a) $1 \in R_w(q)$ iff $q = \delta(q_0, a_1)$, and

(b) if $i \in R_w(q)$ then $i+1 \in R_w(q')$ iff $q' = \delta(q, a_i)$.

The proof of the lemma follows immediately from definition 8.27. For example 8.28, we get

$$1 \in R_w(q) \text{ iff } q = \delta(q_0, a) = q_1$$

$$2 \in R_w(q) \text{ iff } q = \delta(q_1, a) = q_1$$

$$3 \in R_w(q) \text{ iff } q = \delta(q_1, b) = q_2$$

$$\vdots$$

Intuitively, conditions (a) and (b) of lemma 8.29 state that the initial position belongs to the right component of the visit record and that the visit record "respects" the transition relation of A. We give macros Init($X_0, \ldots, X_n$) and Respect($X_0, \ldots, X_n$) expressing these predicates, where we assume the states of A to be $\{q_0, q_1, \ldots, q_n\}$. Given $0 \leq i \leq n$, let us define the following auxiliary macro expressing that position x belongs to X_j iff $j = i$:

$$\text{InX}_i(x) := \left(x \in X_i \wedge \bigwedge_{j \neq i} x \notin X_j \right).$$

For condition (a), we take

$$\text{Init}(X_0, \ldots, X_n) := \forall x \bigwedge_{a \in \Sigma} \left((\text{first}(x) \wedge Q_a(x)) \rightarrow \text{InX}_{\delta(0,a)}(x) \right),$$

where we abuse language, and write $\delta(0, a)$ for the index of the state $\delta(q_0, a)$. In words, $\text{Init}(X_0, \ldots, X_n)$ expresses that if the letter at position 1 is an a, then position 1 belongs to $X_{\delta(0,a)}$ and to no other set.

Example 8.30   For the DFA of figure 8.2 with states $\{q_0, q_1, q_2\}$, we get

$$\text{Init}(X_0, X_1, X_2) = \forall x \left((\text{first}(x) \wedge Q_a(x)) \rightarrow \text{InX}_1(x) \right)$$

$$\wedge \left((\text{first}(x) \wedge Q_b(x)) \rightarrow \text{InX}_2(x) \right).$$

For condition (b), we define

$$\text{Respect}(X_0, \ldots, X_n) := \forall x \, \forall y \left(y = x + 1 \rightarrow \bigwedge_{\substack{a \in \Sigma, \\ i \in \{0, \ldots, n\}}} (Q_a(x) \wedge x \in X_i) \rightarrow \text{InX}_{\delta(i,a)}(y) \right).$$

The formula expresses that if a position x belongs to X_i, and the letter at this position is an a, then its successor position $x + 1$ belongs to $X_{\delta(i,a)}$, and to no other set.

Example 8.31   For the DFA of figure 8.2, this yields:

$$\text{Respect}(X_0, X_1, X_2) = \forall x \, \forall y$$

$$\left(y = x + 1 \rightarrow \left(\begin{array}{ccc} (Q_a(x) \wedge x \in X_0) & \rightarrow & \text{InX}_1(y) \\ \wedge (Q_b(x) \wedge x \in X_0) & \rightarrow & \text{InX}_2(y) \\ \wedge (Q_a(x) \wedge x \in X_1) & \rightarrow & \text{InX}_1(y) \\ \wedge (Q_b(x) \wedge x \in X_1) & \rightarrow & \text{InX}_2(y) \\ \wedge (Q_a(x) \wedge x \in X_2) & \rightarrow & \text{InX}_1(y) \\ \wedge (Q_b(x) \wedge x \in X_2) & \rightarrow & \text{InX}_0(y) \end{array} \right) \right).$$

Finally, we are done by setting

$$\text{VisitRecord}(X_0, \ldots X_n) := \text{Init}(X_0, \ldots, X_n) \wedge \text{Respect}(X_0, \ldots, X_n).$$

8.9   All Languages Expressible in $MSO(\Sigma)$ Are Regular

It remains to prove that MSO-definable languages are regular—that is, for every sentence $\varphi \in MSO(\Sigma)$, the language $\mathcal{L}(\varphi)$ is regular. The proof is by induction on the structure of φ. Since definition 8.11 only defines $\mathcal{L}(\varphi)$ for sentences, we must overcome the obstacle that the subformulas of a sentence are not necessarily sentences.

For this, we define the language of a formula for every formula, sentence or not, in an appropriate way. Recall that the interpretations of a formula φ are triples $(w, \mathcal{V}_1, \mathcal{V}_2)$ where $\mathcal{V}_1$ assigns positions to the free first-order variables of φ and possibly to others, and $\mathcal{V}_2$ assigns sets of positions to the free second-order variables of φ and possibly to others. For example, if $\Sigma = \{a, b\}$ and $free(\varphi) = \{x, y, X, Y\}$, then two possible interpretations are

$$\left(aab, \begin{Bmatrix} x \mapsto 1 \\ y \mapsto 3 \end{Bmatrix}, \begin{Bmatrix} X \mapsto \{2,3\} \\ Y \mapsto \{1,2\} \end{Bmatrix} \right) \text{ and } \left(ba, \begin{Bmatrix} x \mapsto 2 \\ y \mapsto 1 \end{Bmatrix}, \begin{Bmatrix} X \mapsto \emptyset \\ Y \mapsto \{1\} \end{Bmatrix} \right).$$

Given an interpretation $(w, \mathcal{V}_1, \mathcal{V}_2)$, we encode each assignment of the form $x \mapsto k$ or $X \mapsto \{k_1, \ldots, k_\ell\}$ as a bitstring of the same length as w: the string for $x \mapsto k$ contains exactly a 1 at position k and 0s everywhere else; the string for $X \mapsto \{k_1, \ldots, k_\ell\}$ contains 1s at positions $k_1, \ldots, k_\ell$ and 0s everywhere else. After fixing an order on the variables, an interpretation $(w, \mathcal{V}_1, \mathcal{V}_2)$ can then be encoded as a tuple $(w, v_1, \ldots, v_n)$, where n is the number of variables, $w \in \Sigma^*$, and $v_1 \cdots v_n \in \{0,1\}^*$. In particular, for the two interpretations above, we respectively get the encodings

w:	a	a	b		w:	b	a
x:	1	0	0		x:	0	1
y:	0	0	1	and	y:	1	0
X:	0	1	1		X:	0	0
Y:	1	1	0		Y:	1	0

As all of $w, v_1, \ldots, v_n$ have the same length, we can encode the tuple $(w, v_1, \ldots, v_n)$ as a word over the alphabet $\Sigma \times \{0,1\}^n$. The encodings above yield the words

$$\begin{bmatrix} a \\ 1 \\ 0 \\ 0 \\ 1 \end{bmatrix} \begin{bmatrix} a \\ 0 \\ 0 \\ 1 \\ 1 \end{bmatrix} \begin{bmatrix} b \\ 0 \\ 1 \\ 1 \\ 0 \end{bmatrix} \text{ and } \begin{bmatrix} b \\ 0 \\ 1 \\ 0 \\ 1 \end{bmatrix} \begin{bmatrix} a \\ 1 \\ 0 \\ 0 \\ 0 \end{bmatrix} \text{ over the alphabet } \Sigma \times \{0,1\}^4.$$

We can define the language of φ as the set of encodings of the models of φ. However, since an interpretation must assign values to all free variables of a formula but can assign values to others, a formula may have models encoded over alphabets $\Sigma \times \{0,1\}^k$ for arbitrarily large values of k. For example, both $(ab, \perp, \perp)$ and $(a, \{y \mapsto 1\}, \{Y \mapsto \{1,2\}\})$ are models of the formula $\exists x \, Q_a(x)$, but the first is encoded as a word over $\{a, b\}$, while the second is encoded as a word over $\{a, b\} \times \{0, 1\}^2$.

This problem has a simple solution: consider only the *minimal* interpretations of the formula that assign values to exactly the free variables of the formula and to no others. Since, by lemma 8.9, the values assigned to bound variables do not influence whether an interpretation is a model or not, we do not lose any information, and all minimal interpretations are encoded as words over the same alphabet.

We still need to fix the encoding of the interpretations $(w, \mathcal{V}_1, \mathcal{V}_2)$ such that $w = \varepsilon$. Recall that, since we cannot assign values to first-order variables, only formulas without free first-order variables can have such interpretations, and they are of the form $(\varepsilon, \bot, \{X_1 \mapsto \emptyset, \ldots, X_k \mapsto \emptyset\})$. We encode all these interpretations by the empty word.

Definition 8.32 *Let φ be a formula with sets $\{x_1, \ldots, x_{k_1}\}$ and $\{X_1, \ldots, X_{k_2}\}$ of free first-order and second-order variables, respectively, where $k_1, k_2 \geq 0$. Let $(w, \mathcal{V}_1, \mathcal{V}_2)$ be a minimal interpretation of φ. The encoding $\mathrm{enc}(w, \mathcal{V}_1, \mathcal{V}_2)$ of $(w, \mathcal{V}_1, \mathcal{V}_2)$ is the word over alphabet $\Sigma \times \{0, 1\}^{k_1 + k_2}$ defined as follows:*

- *if $w = \varepsilon$, then $\mathrm{enc}(w, \mathcal{V}_1, \mathcal{V}_2) = \varepsilon$;*
- *if $w \neq \varepsilon$, then $\mathrm{enc}(w, \mathcal{V}_1, \mathcal{V}_2) = (w, v_1, \ldots, v_{k_1}, u_1, \ldots, u_{k_2})$, where*
  - *for every $1 \leq i \leq k_1$ and $1 \leq j \leq |w|$: $v_i[j] = 1$ iff $\mathcal{V}_1(x_i) = j$; and*
  - *for every $1 \leq i \leq k_2$, $1 \leq j \leq |w|$: $u_i[j] = 1$ iff $j \in \mathcal{V}_2(X_i)$.*

The language of φ, denoted $\mathcal{L}(\varphi)$, is the set of encodings of all minimal models of φ.

We have thus associated to every formula φ a language $\mathcal{L}(\varphi)$ over alphabet $\Sigma \times \{0, 1\}^n$, where $n \geq 0$ is the number of free variables of φ. We prove by induction on the structure of φ that $\mathcal{L}(\varphi)$ is regular. We do so by exhibiting an NFA accepting $\mathcal{L}(\varphi)$. For simplicity, in the rest of the section, we assume $\Sigma = \{a, b\}$. The extension to larger alphabets is straightforward. Recall that $\mathit{free}(\varphi)$ denotes the set of free variables of φ.

Case $\varphi = Q_a(x)$. We have $\mathit{free}(\varphi) = \{x\}$, and hence the minimal models of φ are encoded as words over $\Sigma \times \{0, 1\}$. By definition 8.22, the language $\mathcal{L}(\varphi)$ is given by

$$
\mathcal{L}(\varphi) = \left\{ \begin{bmatrix} a_1 \\ \beta_1 \end{bmatrix} \cdots \begin{bmatrix} a_k \\ \beta_k \end{bmatrix} : \begin{array}{l} k \geq 1; \\ a_1 \ldots a_k \in \Sigma^k, \beta_1 \ldots \beta_k \in \{0, 1\}^k; \text{ and} \\ \beta_i = 1 \text{ for a single index } i \in \{1, \ldots, k\} \\ \text{such that } a_i = a. \end{array} \right\}
$$

Observe that $k \geq 1$ because, by definition, no triple $(\varepsilon, \mathcal{V}_1, \mathcal{V}_2)$ is an interpretation of $Q_a(x)$. The language $\mathcal{L}(\varphi)$ is recognized by this automaton:

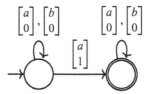

Case $\varphi = x < y$. We have $free(\varphi) = \{x, y\}$, and hence the minimal models of φ are encoded as words over $\Sigma \times \{0, 1\}^2$. By definition Definition 8.22, the language $\mathcal{L}(\varphi)$ is given by

$$\mathcal{L}(\varphi) = \left\{ \begin{bmatrix} a_1 \\ \beta_1 \\ \gamma_1 \end{bmatrix} \cdots \begin{bmatrix} a_k \\ \beta_k \\ \gamma_k \end{bmatrix} : \begin{array}{l} k \geq 1; \\ a_1 \ldots a_k \in \Sigma^k, \beta_1 \ldots \beta_k, \gamma_1 \ldots \gamma_k \in \{0, 1\}^k; \\ \beta_i = 1 \text{ for a single index } i \in \{1, \ldots, k\}; \\ \gamma_j = 1 \text{ for a single index } j \in \{1, \ldots, k\}; \text{ and} \\ i < j. \end{array} \right\}$$

It is recognized by this automaton:

Case $\varphi = x \in X$. We have $free(\varphi) = \{x, X\}$, and hence the minimal interpretations of φ are encoded as words over $\Sigma \times \{0, 1\}^2$. By definition 8.22, the language $\mathcal{L}(\varphi)$ is given by

$$\mathcal{L}(\varphi) = \left\{ \begin{bmatrix} a_1 \\ \beta_1 \\ \gamma_1 \end{bmatrix} \cdots \begin{bmatrix} a_k \\ \beta_k \\ \gamma_k \end{bmatrix} : \begin{array}{l} k \geq 1; \\ a_1 \ldots a_k \in \Sigma^k, \beta_1 \ldots \beta_k, \gamma_1 \ldots \gamma_k \in \{0, 1\}^k; \\ \beta_i = 1 \text{ for a single index } i \in \{1, \ldots, k\}; \text{ and} \\ \beta_i = 1 \text{ implies } \gamma_i = 1 \text{ for all } i \in \{1, \ldots, k\}. \end{array} \right\}$$

It is recognized by

Case $\varphi = \neg\psi$. We have $free(\varphi) = free(\psi)$, and by induction hypothesis, there exists an automaton A_ψ such that $\mathcal{L}(A_\psi) = \mathcal{L}(\psi)$.

By definition 8.22, $\mathcal{L}(\varphi)$ is the set of encodings of the minimal interpretations of ψ that do not satisfy ψ. Observe that, in general, $\mathcal{L}(\varphi)$ is *not* equal to $\overline{\mathcal{L}(\psi)}$, as one might first think. Consider, for example, the instance $\varphi = \neg\psi = \neg Q_a(x)$. The word

$$\begin{bmatrix} a \\ 1 \end{bmatrix} \begin{bmatrix} a \\ 1 \end{bmatrix} \begin{bmatrix} a \\ 1 \end{bmatrix}$$

belongs neither to $\mathcal{L}(\psi)$ nor $\mathcal{L}(\varphi)$, because it is not the encoding of any interpretation: the bitstring for x contains more than one 1. What holds is $\mathcal{L}(\varphi) = \overline{\mathcal{L}(\psi)} \cap Enc(\psi)$, where $Enc(\psi)$ is the language of the encodings of all minimal interpretations of ψ, whether they are models of ψ or not. We construct a DFA A_ψ^{enc} recognizing $Enc(\psi)$, after which we can take $A_\varphi = A_\psi \cap A_\psi^{enc}$.

Assume ψ has k_1 and k_2 free first-order and second-order variables, respectively. By definition 8.20, which defines the interpretations of a formula ψ, and definition 8.32, which defines their encodings, we have that a word w over $\Sigma \times \{0,1\}^{k_1+k_2}$ belongs to $Enc(\psi)$ if

- $w = \varepsilon$ and $k_1 = 0$, or
- $w \neq \varepsilon$, and each of the bitstrings obtained by projecting w onto the second, third, ..., $(k_1 + 1)$th component of the alphabet contains exactly one occurrence of the letter 1.

We define a DFA A_ψ^{enc} recognizing $Enc(\psi)$. For clarity, it is convenient to separate the definition into the cases $k_1 > 0$, that is, ψ has at least one free first-order variable, and $k_1 = 0$. Recall that if $k_1 > 0$, then ψ has no interpretations on the empty word, but if $k_1 = 0$, then the triple $(\varepsilon, \perp, \{X_1 \mapsto \emptyset, \ldots, X_{k_2} \mapsto \emptyset\})$ is a minimal interpretation. If $k_1 > 0$, then A_ψ^{enc} is defined as follows:

- The states are all the strings of $\{0,1\}^{k_1}$, plus a trap state.

  The intended meaning of a state, say state 101 for the case $k_1 = 3$, is "the automaton has already read the 1s in the first and the third bitstrings, but not yet read the 1 of the second."

- The initial state is 0^{k_1}.

  Initially, the automaton has not read any 1 for any first-order variable.

- Transitions are defined according to the intended meaning of the states.

  For example, if the automaton is in state 100 and reads the letter $[a, 0, 0, 1]$, then the automaton moves to state 101, indicating that it has now also read the 1 in the third bitstring. However, if the automaton reads the letter $[a, 1, 1, 0]$, then it moves to the nonaccepting trap state, because the first bitstring contains at least two 1s, and so the word does not encode an interpretation. All transitions leaving the trap state lead to the trap state.

- The only final state is 1^{k_1}.

At this point, the 1s in all bitstrings have been read.

If $k_1 = 0$, then A_ψ^{enc} has a single state, which is both initial and final, and, for every letter of $\Sigma \times \{0,1\}^{k_2}$, the corresponding transition leads from this state to itself.

Example 8.33 The formula $x < y$ has two free first-order variables. The states of $A_{x<y}^{enc}$ are $\{00, 01, 10, 11\}$. The automaton is depicted in figure 8.3.

Since an interpretation can assign the same position to x and y, we have two transitions leading from 00 to 11. While such interpretations are not models of $x < y$, their encodings must be recognized by A_ψ^{enc}.

Remark 8.34

- A_ψ^{enc} only depends on $free(\psi)$. For example, $A_{Q_a(x)}^{enc} = A_{\exists y\, x<y}^{enc}$.
- The number of states of A_ψ^{enc} grows exponentially in the number of free variables of ψ. This makes negations expensive, even when the automaton A_ψ is deterministic.

Case $\varphi = (\varphi_1 \vee \varphi_2)$. We have $free(\varphi) = free(\varphi_1) \cup free(\varphi_2)$, and by induction hypothesis, there are automata $A_{\varphi_1}, A_{\varphi_2}$ such that $\mathcal{L}\left(A_{\varphi_1}\right) = \mathcal{L}(\varphi_1)$ and $\mathcal{L}\left(A_{\varphi_2}\right) = \mathcal{L}(\varphi_2)$.

If $free(\varphi_1) = free(\varphi_2)$, then we can take $A_\varphi = A_{\varphi_1} \cup A_{\varphi_2}$. But, this needs not be the case. If $free(\varphi_1) \neq free(\varphi_2)$, then $\mathcal{L}(\varphi_1)$ and $\mathcal{L}(\varphi_2)$ are languages over different alphabets Σ_1 and Σ_2, or over the same alphabet but with different intended meanings. Thus, we cannot just compute their union. For example, if $\varphi_1 = Q_a(x)$ and $\varphi_2 = Q_b(y)$, then both $\mathcal{L}(\varphi_1)$ and

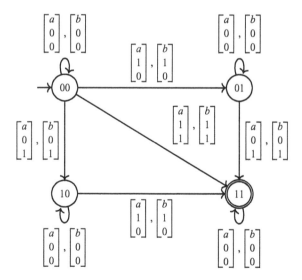

Figure 8.3
Automaton $A_{x<y}^{enc}$.

$\mathcal{L}(\varphi_2)$ are languages over $\Sigma \times \{0, 1\}$, but in $(aba, 100) \in \mathcal{L}(\varphi_1)$, the bitstring 100 encodes the position of x, whereas in $(aba, 010) \in \mathcal{L}(\varphi_2)$, the bitstring 010 encodes the position of y.

This problem is solved by extending $\mathcal{L}(\varphi_1)$ and $\mathcal{L}(\varphi_2)$ to languages L_1 and L_2 over $\Sigma \times \{0, 1\}^2$. In our example, L_1 contains the encodings of all interpretations $(w, \{x \mapsto n_1, y \mapsto n_2\})$ such that the projection $(w, \{x \mapsto n_1\})$ belongs to $\mathcal{L}(Q_a(x))$, and similarly, L_2 contains the encodings of all interpretations such that $(w, \{y \mapsto n_2\})$ belongs to $\mathcal{L}(Q_b(y))$.

Let us transform the two-state automaton $A_{Q_a(x)}$ recognizing $\mathcal{L}(Q_a(x))$, that is, the automaton

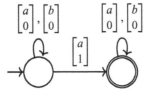

into an automaton A_1 recognizing L_1. For this, it suffices to "split" every transition of $A_{Q_a(x)}$ labeled by $[a, \beta] \in \Sigma \times \{0, 1\}$ into two transitions, labeled by $[a, \beta, 0]$ and $[a, \beta, 1]$. This yields the automaton

After constructing A_2 in a similar manner, we take $A_\varphi = A_1 \cup A_2$.

We can use the same procedure to construct an automaton for the case $\varphi = \varphi_1 \wedge \varphi_2$. We only need to modify the very last step and set $A_\varphi = A_1 \cap A_2$.

Case $\varphi = \exists x \, \psi$. We have $free(\varphi) = free(\psi) \setminus \{x\}$, and by induction hypothesis, there is an automaton A_ψ such that $\mathcal{L}(A_\psi) = \mathcal{L}(\psi)$. We define $A_{\exists x \, \psi}$ as the result of the projection operation, where we project onto all variables but x. The operation simply corresponds to removing in each letter of each transition of A_ψ the component for variable x. For example, the automaton $A_{\exists x \, Q_a(x)}$ is obtained by removing the second component in all labels of the automaton for $A_{Q_a(x)}$:

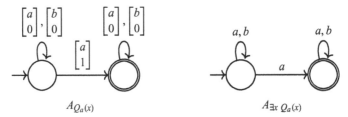

$A_{Q_a(x)}$ · · · $A_{\exists x \, Q_a(x)}$

Observe that the automaton for $\exists x\, Q_a(x)$ is nondeterministic even though $A_{Q_a(x)}$ is a DFA, because the projection maps $[a, 0]$ and $[a, 1]$ to the same letter.

Case $\varphi = \exists X\, \varphi$. We proceed exactly as in the previous case.

Size of A_φ. The procedure for constructing A_φ proceeds bottom-up on the syntax tree of φ. It first constructs automata for the atomic formulas in the leaves of the tree and then proceeds upward: given automata for the children of a node in the tree, it constructs an automaton for the node itself.

The automaton for a node labeled by a negation can be exponentially larger than the automaton for its only child. This yields an upper bound for the size of A_φ equal to a tower of exponentials, where the height of the tower is the largest number of negations in any path from the root of the tree to one of its leaves. It can be shown that this very large upper bound is essentially tight: there are formulas φ for which the smallest automaton recognizing $\mathcal{L}(\varphi)$ reaches the upper bound. In other words, monadic second-order logic on words allows us to express some regular languages in an extremely succinct form.

We conclude the section with an example illustrating all of the parts of the inductive procedure.

Example 8.35 Consider the language $a^*b \subseteq \Sigma^*$ over $\Sigma = \{a, b\}$, recognized by this NFA:

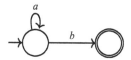

We derive the NFA by giving a formula φ such that $\mathcal{L}(\varphi) = \mathcal{L}(a^*b)$ and then transforming φ into an automaton. (We shall see that the procedure is quite laborious.) The formula states that the last letter is a b and all other letters are as:

$$\varphi = \exists x\, (\mathrm{last}(x) \wedge Q_b(x)) \wedge \forall x\, (\neg\mathrm{last}(x) \rightarrow Q_a(x)).$$

We first replace the abbreviations in φ by their definitions, yielding

$$\psi = \exists x\, (\mathrm{last}(x) \wedge Q_b(x)) \wedge \neg\exists x\, (\neg\mathrm{last}(x) \wedge \neg Q_a(x)).$$

We transform ψ into an NFA by constructing automata for larger and larger subformulas of ψ, starting with the atomic formulas. For readability, we let $[\psi']$ denote the automaton for a subformula ψ', instead of $A_{\psi'}$.

An automaton for $\mathrm{last}(x)$. We first compute an automaton for $\mathrm{last}(x) := \neg\exists y\, (x < y)$. Recall that the automaton $[x < y]$ for $x < y$ is

$$\begin{bmatrix} a \\ 0 \\ 0 \end{bmatrix}, \begin{bmatrix} b \\ 0 \\ 0 \end{bmatrix} \qquad \begin{bmatrix} a \\ 0 \\ 0 \end{bmatrix}, \begin{bmatrix} b \\ 0 \\ 0 \end{bmatrix} \qquad \begin{bmatrix} a \\ 0 \\ 0 \end{bmatrix}, \begin{bmatrix} b \\ 0 \\ 0 \end{bmatrix}$$

$$\begin{bmatrix} a \\ 1 \\ 0 \end{bmatrix}, \begin{bmatrix} b \\ 1 \\ 0 \end{bmatrix} \qquad \begin{bmatrix} a \\ 0 \\ 1 \end{bmatrix}, \begin{bmatrix} b \\ 0 \\ 1 \end{bmatrix}$$

$[x < y]$

Applying the projection operation, we get an automaton for $\exists y\ (x < y)$:

$$\begin{bmatrix} a \\ 0 \end{bmatrix}, \begin{bmatrix} b \\ 0 \end{bmatrix} \qquad \begin{bmatrix} a \\ 0 \end{bmatrix}, \begin{bmatrix} b \\ 0 \end{bmatrix} \qquad \begin{bmatrix} a \\ 0 \end{bmatrix}, \begin{bmatrix} b \\ 0 \end{bmatrix}$$

$$\begin{bmatrix} a \\ 1 \end{bmatrix}, \begin{bmatrix} b \\ 1 \end{bmatrix} \qquad \begin{bmatrix} a \\ 0 \end{bmatrix}, \begin{bmatrix} b \\ 0 \end{bmatrix}$$

$[\exists y\ (x < y)]$

It remains to compute the automaton for $\neg \exists y\ (x < y)$. Recall that computing the automaton for the negation of a formula requires more than complementing the automaton. First, we need an automaton recognizing the set $Enc(\exists y\ (x < y))$ of encodings of the minimal interpretations of $\exists y\ (x < y)$. Since x is a free variable of the formula, we get

$$\begin{bmatrix} a \\ 0 \end{bmatrix}, \begin{bmatrix} b \\ 0 \end{bmatrix} \qquad \begin{bmatrix} a \\ 0 \end{bmatrix}, \begin{bmatrix} b \\ 0 \end{bmatrix}$$

$$\begin{bmatrix} a \\ 1 \end{bmatrix}, \begin{bmatrix} b \\ 1 \end{bmatrix}$$

$A^{enc}_{\exists y\ (x < y)}$

Second, we determinize and complement the automaton for $\exists y\ (x < y)$:

$$\begin{bmatrix} a \\ 0 \end{bmatrix}, \begin{bmatrix} b \\ 0 \end{bmatrix} \qquad \Sigma \times \{0, 1\}$$

$$\begin{bmatrix} a \\ 1 \end{bmatrix}, \begin{bmatrix} b \\ 1 \end{bmatrix} \qquad \Sigma \times \{0, 1\}$$

Finally, we compute the intersection of the last two automata, which yields

$$\begin{bmatrix} a \\ 0 \end{bmatrix}, \begin{bmatrix} b \\ 0 \end{bmatrix} \qquad \begin{bmatrix} a \\ 0 \end{bmatrix}, \begin{bmatrix} b \\ 0 \end{bmatrix}$$

$$\begin{bmatrix} a \\ 1 \end{bmatrix}, \begin{bmatrix} b \\ 1 \end{bmatrix} \qquad \begin{bmatrix} a \\ 0 \end{bmatrix}, \begin{bmatrix} b \\ 0 \end{bmatrix}$$

The last state is useless and can be removed, finally yielding the following NFA for last(x):

$$[\text{last}(x)]$$

An automaton for $\exists x$ (last(x) $\wedge$ $Q_b(x)$). Next, we compute an automaton for $\exists x$ (last(x) $\wedge$ $Q_b(x)$)), the first conjunct of ψ. We start with an NFA for $Q_b(x)$:

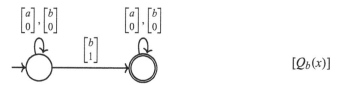

$$[Q_b(x)]$$

The automaton for $\exists x$ (last(x) $\wedge$ $Q_b(x)$) is the result of intersecting $[Q_b(x)]$ and $[\text{last}(x)]$ and projecting onto the first component. This yields

$$[\exists x\,(\text{last}(x) \wedge Q_b(x))]$$

An automaton for $\neg\exists x$ ($\neg$last(x) $\wedge$ $\neg Q_a(x)$). Now we compute an automaton for $\neg\exists x$ ($\neg$last(x) $\wedge$ $\neg Q_a(x)$), the second conjunct of ψ. We first obtain an automaton for $\neg Q_a(x)$ by intersecting the complement of $[Q_a(x)]$ and the automaton for $Enc(Q_a(x))$. The automaton for $Q_a(x)$ is

$$[Q_a(x)]$$

After determinization and complementation, we get

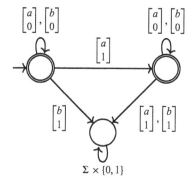

For the automaton recognizing $Enc(Q_a(x))$, note that

$$Enc(Q_a(x)) = Enc(\exists y\ (x < y)),$$

because both formulas have the same free variables and so the same interpretations. But we have already computed an automaton recognizing $Enc(\exists y\ (x < y))$, and so

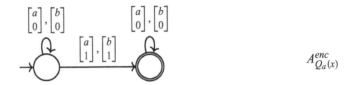

$$A^{enc}_{Q_a(x)}$$

The intersection of the last two automata yields a three-state automaton for $\neg Q_a(x)$, but after eliminating a useless state, we get

$$[\neg Q_a(x)]$$

Note that this is the same automaton we obtained for $Q_b(x)$, which is fine, because over alphabet $\{a, b\}$, the formulas $Q_b(x)$ and $\neg Q_a(x)$ are equivalent.

To compute an automaton for $\neg\mathrm{last}(x)$, we observe that $\neg\mathrm{last}(x)$ is equivalent to $\exists y\ (x < y)$, for which we have already computed an NFA, and so

$$[\neg\mathrm{last}(x)]$$

Intersecting the automata for $\neg\mathrm{last}(x)$ and $\neg Q_a(x)$, and subsequently projecting onto the first component, we obtain an automaton for the sentence $\exists x\ (\neg\mathrm{last}(x) \land \neg Q_a(x))$:

$$[\exists x\ (\neg\mathrm{last}(x) \land \neg Q_a(x))]$$

Determinizing, complementing, and removing a useless state yields the following NFA for $\neg\exists x\ (\neg\mathrm{last}(x) \land \neg Q_a(x))$:

$[\neg \exists x \, (\neg\mathrm{last}(x) \wedge \neg Q_a(x))]$

Summarizing, the automata for the two conjuncts of ψ are

and

whose intersection yields a three-state automaton, which after removal of a useless state becomes

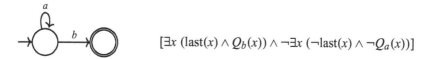

$[\exists x \, (\mathrm{last}(x) \wedge Q_b(x)) \wedge \neg \exists x \, (\neg\mathrm{last}(x) \wedge \neg Q_a(x))]$

This ends the derivation.

8.10 Exercises

☆ 🖳 **Exercise 119.** Give formulations in plain English of the languages described by the following formulas of $FO(\{a, b\})$, and give a corresponding regular expression:

(a) $\exists x \, \mathit{first}(x)$

(b) $\forall x \, \mathit{false}$

(c) $[\neg \exists x \exists y \, (x < y \wedge Q_a(x) \wedge Q_b(y))] \wedge [\forall x \, (Q_b(x) \rightarrow \exists y \, x < y \wedge Q_a(y))] \wedge [\exists x \, \neg \exists y \, x < y]$

★ 🖳 **Exercise 120.** Let $\Sigma = \{a, b\}$.

(a) Give a formula $\varphi_n(x, y)$ from $FO(\Sigma)$, of size $\mathcal{O}(n)$, that holds iff $y = x + 2^n$. Note that the abbreviation $y = x + k$ of page 202 has length $\mathcal{O}(k)$ and hence cannot be directly used.

(b) Give a sentence from $FO(\Sigma)$, of size $\mathcal{O}(n)$, for the language $L_n = \{ww : w \in \Sigma^* \text{ and } |w| = 2^n\}$.

(c) Show that the minimal DFA accepting L_n has at least 2^{2^n} states.

Hint: Consider residuals.

★ ■ **Exercise 121.** The *nesting depth* $d(\varphi)$ of a formula φ of $FO(\{a\})$ is defined inductively as follows:

• $d(Q_a(x)) = d(x < y) = 0$,

- $d(\neg\psi) = d(\psi)$,
- $d(\varphi_1 \vee \varphi_2) = \max\{d(\varphi_1), d(\varphi_2)\}$, and
- $d(\exists x\ \psi) = 1 + d(\psi)$.

Prove that every formula φ from $FO(\{a\})$ of nesting depth n is equivalent to a formula f of QF having the same free variables as φ, and such that every constant k appearing in f satisfies $k \leq 2^n$. _Hint: Modify suitably the proof of theorem 8.17._

☆ 🔲 **Exercise 122.** Consider the extension of $FO(\Sigma)$ where addition of variables is allowed. Give a sentence of this logic for palindromes, that is, for language $\{w \in \Sigma^* : w = w^R\}$.

☆ 🖝 **Exercise 123.** Let Σ be a finite alphabet. A language $L \subseteq \Sigma^*$ is *star-free* if it can be expressed by a star-free regular expression, that is, a regular expression where the Kleene star operation is forbidden, but complementation is allowed. For example, Σ^* is star-free since $\Sigma^* = \overline{\emptyset}$, but $(aa)^*$ is not. In this exercise we show that every star-free language can be expressed by a sentence of $FO(\Sigma)$.

(a) Give star-free regular expressions and $FO(\Sigma)$ sentences for the following star-free languages:

(i) Σ^+,

(ii) $\Sigma^* A \Sigma^*$ for some $A \subseteq \Sigma$,

(iii) A^* for some $A \subseteq \Sigma$,

(iv) $\{w \in \Sigma^* : w$ does not contain $aa\}$, and

(v) $(ab)^*$.

(b) Show that finite and co-finite languages are star-free.

(c) Show that for every sentence $\varphi \in FO(\Sigma)$, there exists a formula $\varphi^+(x, y)$, with two free variables x and y, such that for every $w \in \Sigma^+$ and for every $1 \leq i \leq j \leq w$,

$$w \models \varphi^+(i, j) \ \text{ iff } \ w_i w_{i+1} \cdots w_j \models \varphi.$$

(d) Give a polynomial-time algorithm that decides whether ε satisfies a given sentence of $FO(\Sigma)$.

(e) Show that any star-free language can be expressed by an $FO(\Sigma)$ sentence.
Hint: Use (c).

☆ 🔲 **Exercise 124.** Give a formula Odd_card(X) from $MSO(\Sigma)$ expressing that the set of positions X has odd cardinality. _Hint: Follow the pattern of_ Even(X).

☆ 🔲 **Exercise 125.** Give formulas of $MSO(\{a, b\})$ that define the following languages:

(a) aa^*b^*,

(b) the set of words with an odd number of occurrences of a, and

(c) the set of words such that every two bs with no other b in between are separated by a block of as of odd length.

⭐ 🔳 **Exercise 126.** Given a formula φ from $MSO(\Sigma)$ and a second-order variable X not occurring in φ, show how to construct a formula φ^X with X as an additional free variable expressing "the projection of the word onto the positions of X satisfies φ." Formally, φ^X must satisfy the following property: for every interpretation $\mathcal{V}$ of φ^X, we have $(w, \mathcal{V}) \models \varphi^X$ iff $(w|_{\mathcal{V}(X)}, \mathcal{V}) \models \varphi$, where $w|_{\mathcal{V}(X)}$ denotes the result of deleting from w the letters at all positions that do not belong to $\mathcal{V}(X)$.

⭐ 🖌 **Exercise 127.**

(a) Given two sentences $\varphi_1, \varphi_2 \in MSO(\Sigma)$, construct a sentence $\text{Conc}(\varphi_1, \varphi_2)$ satisfying $\mathcal{L}(\text{Conc}(\varphi_1, \varphi_2)) = \mathcal{L}(\varphi_1) \cdot \mathcal{L}(\varphi_2)$.

(b) Given a sentence φ of $MSO(\Sigma)$, construct a sentence $\text{Star}(\varphi)$ satisfying

$$\mathcal{L}(\text{Star}(\varphi)) = \mathcal{L}(\varphi)^* .$$

(c) Give an algorithm *RegtoMSO* that takes a regular expression r as input and constructs a sentence φ of $MSO(\Sigma)$ such that $\mathcal{L}(\varphi) = \mathcal{L}(r)$, without first constructing an automaton.

Hint: Use exercise 126.

☆ ⬛ **Exercise 128.** Consider the logic $PureMSO(\Sigma)$ with syntax

$$\varphi ::= X \subseteq Q_a \mid X < Y \mid X \subseteq Y \mid \neg\varphi \mid \varphi \vee \varphi \mid \exists X\, \varphi.$$

Note that formulas of $PureMSO(\Sigma)$ do not contain first-order variables. The satisfaction relation of $PureMSO(\Sigma)$ is given by

$$
\begin{aligned}
(w, \mathcal{V}) &\models X \subseteq Q_a &\text{iff}\quad & w[p] = a \text{ for every } p \in \mathcal{V}(X), \\
(w, \mathcal{V}) &\models X < Y &\text{iff}\quad & p < p' \text{ for every } p \in \mathcal{V}(X), p' \in \mathcal{V}(Y), \\
(w, \mathcal{V}) &\models X \subseteq Y &\text{iff}\quad & \mathcal{V}(X) \subseteq \mathcal{V}(Y),
\end{aligned}
$$

with the rest as for $MSO(\Sigma)$.

Prove that $MSO(\Sigma)$ and $PureMSO(\Sigma)$ have the same expressive power for sentences—that is, show that for every sentence ϕ of $MSO(\Sigma)$, there is an equivalent sentence ψ of $PureMSO(\Sigma)$ and vice versa.

⭐ ⬛ **Exercise 129.** Recall the syntax of $MSO(\Sigma)$:

$$\varphi := Q_a(x) \mid x < y \mid x \in X \mid \neg\varphi \mid \varphi \vee \varphi \mid \exists x\, \varphi \mid \exists X\, \varphi.$$

We have introduced $y = x + 1$ ("y is the successor position of x") as an abbreviation:

$$(y = x + 1) := (x < y) \wedge \neg\exists z\, (x < z \wedge z < y).$$

Consider now the variant $MSO'(\Sigma)$ in which, instead of an abbreviation, $y = x + 1$ is part of the syntax and replaces $x < y$. In other words, the syntax of $MSO'(\Sigma)$ is

$$\varphi := Q_a(x) \mid y = x + 1 \mid x \in X \mid \neg\varphi \mid \varphi \vee \varphi \mid \exists x\, \varphi \mid \exists X\, \varphi.$$

Prove that $MSO'(\Sigma)$ has the same expressive power as $MSO(\Sigma)$.

☆ ▣ **Exercise 130.**

(a) Give a macro Block_between(X, i, j) of $MSO(\Sigma)$ expressing "X contains the positions between i and j (inclusively)."

(b) Let $0 \leq m < n$. Give a formula $\mathrm{Mod}^{m,n}$ of $MSO(\Sigma)$ such that $\mathrm{Mod}^{m,n}(i,j)$ holds whenever $|w_i w_{i+1} \cdots w_j| \equiv m \pmod{n}$—that is, whenever $j - i + 1 \equiv m \pmod{n}$.

(c) Let $0 \leq m < n$. Give a sentence of $MSO(\Sigma)$ that defines $a^m(a^n)^*$.

(d) Give a sentence of $MSO(\{a, b\})$ that defines the language of words such that every two bs with no other b in between are separated by a block of as of odd length.

☆ ▣ **Exercise 131.** Consider a formula $\varphi(X)$ of $MSO(\Sigma)$ that does not contain any occurrence of predicates of the form $Q_a(x)$. Given two interpretations that assign the same set of positions to X, we have that either both interpretations satisfy $\varphi(X)$, or none of them does. Thus, we can speak of the sets of natural numbers satisfying $\varphi(X)$.

This observation can be used to automatically prove some (very) simple properties of the natural numbers. Consider, for instance, the following "conjecture": every finite set of natural numbers has a minimal element.[3] The conjecture holds iff the formula

$$\mathrm{Has\_min}(X) := \exists x \in X\; \forall y \in X\; (x \leq y)$$

is satisfied by every interpretation in which X is nonempty. Construct an automaton for Has_min(X), and check that it recognizes all nonempty sets.

★ ▣ **Exercise 132.** The encoding of a set is a word that can be seen as the encoding of a number. We can use this observation to express addition in monadic second-order logic. More precisely, give a formula Sum(X, Y, Z) that holds iff $n_X + n_Y = n_Z$, where n_X, n_Y, and n_Z are respectively the numbers encoded by the sets X, Y, and Z using the LSBF-encoding. For instance, the words

$$
\begin{array}{c}
X \\ Y \\ Z
\end{array}
\begin{bmatrix} 0 \\ 1 \\ 1 \end{bmatrix}
\begin{bmatrix} 1 \\ 1 \\ 0 \end{bmatrix}
\begin{bmatrix} 0 \\ 0 \\ 1 \end{bmatrix}
\quad \text{and} \quad
\begin{bmatrix} 1 \\ 1 \\ 0 \end{bmatrix}
\begin{bmatrix} 1 \\ 1 \\ 1 \end{bmatrix}
\begin{bmatrix} 1 \\ 1 \\ 1 \end{bmatrix}
\begin{bmatrix} 1 \\ 1 \\ 1 \end{bmatrix}
\begin{bmatrix} 1 \\ 0 \\ 0 \end{bmatrix}
\begin{bmatrix} 0 \\ 0 \\ 1 \end{bmatrix}
\begin{bmatrix} 0 \\ 0 \\ 0 \end{bmatrix}
\begin{bmatrix} 0 \\ 0 \\ 0 \end{bmatrix}
$$

should satisfy the formula since the first encodes $2 + 3 = 5$, and the second encodes $31 + 15 = 46$.

---

3. Of course, it also holds for all infinite set, but we cannot prove it using MSO over finite words.

9 Application III: Presburger Arithmetic

Presburger arithmetic is a logical language for expressing properties of numbers by means of addition and comparison. A typical example of such a property is "$x + 2y > 2z$ and $2x - 3z = 4y$." The property is satisfied by some triples (n_x, n_y, n_z) of natural numbers, like $(4, 2, 0)$ and $(8, 1, 4)$, but not by others, like $(6, 0, 4)$ or $(2, 2, 4)$. Valuations satisfying the property are called *solutions* or *models*.

We show how to construct, for a given formula φ of Presburger arithmetic, an NFA A_φ recognizing the solutions of φ. We proceed as follows. In section 9.1, we introduce the syntax and semantics of Presburger arithmetic; in section 9.2, we construct an NFA recognizing all solutions over the natural numbers; and in section 9.3, we construct an NFA recognizing all solutions over the integers.

9.1 Syntax and Semantics

Formulas of Presburger arithmetic are constructed out of an infinite set of *variables* $V = \{x, y, z, \ldots\}$ and the constants 0 and 1. The syntax of formulas is defined in three steps. First, the set of *terms* is inductively defined as follows:

- the symbols 0 and 1 are terms,
- every variable is a term, and
- if t and u are terms, then $t + u$ is a term.

An *atomic formula* is an expression $t \leq u$, where t and u are terms. The set of Presburger formulas is inductively defined as follows:

- every atomic formula is a formula, and
- if φ_1 and φ_2 are formulas, then so are $\neg\varphi_1$, $\varphi_1 \vee \varphi_2$, and $\exists x\, \varphi_1$.

As usual, variables within the scope of an existential quantifier are bounded and otherwise free. Besides standard abbreviations like $\forall$, $\wedge$, $\rightarrow$, we also introduce

$$\overbrace{n := 1 + 1 + \ldots + 1,}^{n \text{ times}} \qquad\qquad \overbrace{nx := x + x + \ldots + x,}^{n \text{ times}}$$

$$t \geq t' := t' \leq t, \qquad\qquad t < t' := t \leq t' \wedge \neg(t = t'),$$

$$t = t' := t \leq t' \wedge t \geq t', \qquad\qquad t > t' := t' < t.$$

An *interpretation* is a function $\mathcal{V} \colon V \to \mathbb{N}$. An interpretation $\mathcal{V}$ is extended to terms in the natural way: $\mathcal{V}(0) = 0$, $\mathcal{V}(1) = 1$, and $\mathcal{V}(t + u) = \mathcal{V}(t) + \mathcal{V}(u)$. The satisfaction relation $\mathcal{V} \models \varphi$ for an interpretation $\mathcal{V}$ and a formula φ is inductively defined as follows, where $\mathcal{V}[n/x]$ denotes the interpretation that assigns the number n to the variable x and the same numbers as $\mathcal{V}$ to all other variables:

$$\mathcal{V} \models t \leq u \quad \text{iff } \mathcal{V}(t) \leq \mathcal{V}(u),$$

$$\mathcal{V} \models \neg \varphi_1 \quad \text{iff } \mathcal{V} \not\models \varphi_1,$$

$$\mathcal{V} \models \varphi_1 \vee \varphi_2 \text{ iff } \mathcal{V} \models \varphi_1 \text{ or } \mathcal{V} \models \varphi_2,$$

$$\mathcal{V} \models \exists x\, \varphi \quad \text{iff there exists } n \geq 0 \text{ such that } \mathcal{V}[n/x] \models \varphi.$$

It is easy to see that whether $\mathcal{V}$ satisfies φ or not depends only on the values $\mathcal{V}$ assigns to the *free* variables of φ (i.e., if two interpretations assign the same values to the free variables, then either both satisfy the formula, or none does). The *solutions* of φ are the projection onto the free variables of φ of the interpretations that satisfy φ. If we fix a total order on the set V of variables and if a formula φ has k free variables, then its set of solutions can be represented as a subset of $\mathbb{N}^k$ or as a relation of arity k over the universe $\mathbb{N}$. We call this subset the *solution space* of φ and denote it by $Sol(\varphi)$.

Example 9.1   The solution space of the formula $x - 2 \geq 0$ is the set $\{2, 3, 4, \ldots\}$. The free variables of the formula $\exists x\, (2x = y \wedge 2y = z)$ are y and z. The solutions of the formula are the pairs $\{(2n, 4n) : n \geq 0\}$, where we assume that the first and second components correspond to the values of y and z, respectively.

Automata encoding natural numbers.   We use transducers to represent, compute, and manipulate solution spaces of formulas. As in section 5.1 of chapter 5, we encode natural numbers as strings over $\{0, 1\}$ using the least-significant-bit-first encoding LSBF. If a formula has free variables $x_1, \ldots, x_k$, then its solutions are encoded as words over $\{0, 1\}^k$. For instance, the word

$$\begin{array}{c} x_1 \\ x_2 \\ x_3 \end{array} \quad \begin{bmatrix} 1 \\ 0 \\ 0 \end{bmatrix} \begin{bmatrix} 0 \\ 1 \\ 0 \end{bmatrix} \begin{bmatrix} 1 \\ 0 \\ 0 \end{bmatrix} \begin{bmatrix} 0 \\ 1 \\ 0 \end{bmatrix}$$

encodes the solution $(5, 10, 0)$. The *language* of a formula φ is defined as

$$\mathcal{L}(\varphi) = \bigcup_{s \in Sol(\varphi)} \text{LSBF}(s),$$

where LSBF(s) denotes the set of all encodings of the tuple s of natural numbers. In other words, $\mathcal{L}(\varphi)$ is the encoding of the relation $Sol(\varphi)$.

9.2   An NFA for the Solutions over the Naturals

Given a Presburger formula φ, we construct a transducer A_φ such that $\mathcal{L}(A_\varphi) = \mathcal{L}(\varphi)$. Recall that $Sol(\varphi)$ is a relation over $\mathbb{N}$ whose arity is given by the number of free variables of φ. The last section of chapter 5 implements operations on relations of arbitrary arity. These operations can be used to compute the solution space of the negation of a formula, the disjunction of two formulas, and the existential quantification of two formulas:

- The solution space of the negation of a formula with k free variables is the complement of its solution space with respect to the universe U^k. In general, when computing the complement of a relation, we have to worry about ensuring that the NFAs we obtain only accept words that encode some tuple of elements (i.e., some cleanup may be necessary to ensure that automata do not accept words encoding nothing). For Presburger arithmetic, this is not necessary, because in the LSBF encoding, *every* word encodes some tuple of numbers.

- The solution space of a disjunction $\varphi_1 \vee \varphi_2$, where φ_1 and φ_2 have the same free variables, is clearly the union of their solution spaces and can be computed as **Union**$(Sol(\varphi_1), Sol(\varphi_2))$. If φ_1 and φ_2 have different sets V_1 and V_2 of free variables, then some preprocessing is necessary. Define $Sol_{V_1 \cup V_2}(\varphi_i)$ as the set of valuations of $V_1 \cup V_2$ whose projection onto V_i belongs to $Sol(\varphi_i)$. Transducers recognizing $Sol_{V_1 \cup V_2}(\varphi_i)$ for $i \in \{1, 2\}$ are easy to compute from transducers recognizing $Sol(\varphi_i)$, and the solution space is **Union**$(Sol_{V_1 \cup V_2}(\varphi_1), Sol_{V_1 \cup V_2}(\varphi_2))$.

- The solution space of a formula $\exists x \varphi$, where x is a free variable of φ, is **Projection_I**$(Sol(\varphi))$, where I contains the indices of all variables with the exception of the index of x.

It only remains to construct automata recognizing the solution space of atomic formulas. Consider an expression of the form

$$\varphi = a_1 x_1 + \ldots + a_n x_n \le b,$$

where $a_1, \ldots, a_n, b \in \mathbb{Z}$ (not $\mathbb{N}$!). Since we allow negative integers as coefficients, for every atomic formula, there is an equivalent expression in this form (i.e., an expression with the same solution space). For example, $x \ge y + 4$ is equivalent to $-x + y \le -4$. Letting $a = (a_1, \ldots, a_n)$, $x = (x_1, \ldots, x_n)$, and denoting the scalar product of a and x by $a \cdot x$, we write $\varphi = a \cdot x \le b$.

We construct a DFA for $Sol(\varphi)$. The states of the DFA are integers. We choose transitions and final states of the DFA so that the following property holds:

State $q \in \mathbb{Z}$ recognizes the encodings of the tuples $c \in \mathbb{N}^n$ such that $a \cdot c \le q$.   (9.1)

Given a state $q \in \mathbb{Z}$ and a letter $\zeta \in \{0, 1\}^n$, let us determine the target state q' of the transition $\delta(q, \zeta)$ of the DFA. A word $w \in (\{0, 1\}^n)^*$ is accepted from q' iff the word ζw is accepted from q. Since we use the LSBF encoding, if $c \in \mathbb{N}^n$ is the tuple of natural numbers encoded by w, then the tuple encoded by ζw is $2c + \zeta$. So $c \in \mathbb{N}^n$ is accepted from q' iff $2c + \zeta$ is accepted from q. Therefore, in order to satisfy property (9.1), we must choose q' so that $a \cdot c \leq q'$ iff $a \cdot (2c + \zeta) \leq q$. A little arithmetic yields

$$q' = \left\lfloor \frac{q - a \cdot \zeta}{2} \right\rfloor,$$

and hence we define the transition function of the DFA by

$$\delta(q, \zeta) = \left\lfloor \frac{q - a \cdot \zeta}{2} \right\rfloor.$$

For the final states, we observe that a state is final iff it accepts the empty word iff it accepts the tuple $(0, \ldots, 0) \in \mathbb{N}^n$. So, in order to satisfy (9.1), we must make state q final iff $q \geq 0$. As initial state, we choose the integer b. This leads to the algorithm $AFtoDFA(\varphi)$ of algorithm 42, where for clarity, the state corresponding to an integer $k \in \mathbb{Z}$ is denoted by s_k.

Algorithm 42   Conversion of an atomic formula into a DFA recognizing the LSBF encoding of its solutions.

$AFtoDFA(\varphi)$
Input: Atomic formula $\varphi = a \cdot x \leq b$
Output: DFA $A_\varphi = (Q, \Sigma, \delta, q_0, F)$ such that $\mathcal{L}(A_\varphi) = \mathcal{L}(\varphi)$

1   $Q, \delta, F \leftarrow \emptyset; q_0 \leftarrow s_b$
2   $W \leftarrow \{s_b\}$
3   **while** $W \neq \emptyset$ **do**
4   **pick** s_k **from** W
5   **add** s_k **to** Q
6   **if** $k \geq 0$ **then add** s_k **to** F
7   **for all** $\zeta \in \{0, 1\}^n$ **do**
8           $j \leftarrow \left\lfloor \dfrac{k - a \cdot \zeta}{2} \right\rfloor$
9   **if** $s_j \notin Q$ **then add** s_j **to** W
10   **add** (s_k, ζ, s_j) **to** δ

Example 9.2   Consider the atomic formula $2x - y \leq 2$. The DFA obtained by applying $AFtoDFA$ to it is shown in figure 9.1. The initial state is 2. Transitions leaving state 2 are given by

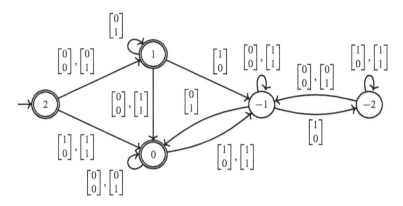

Figure 9.1
DFA for the formula $2x - y \leq 2$.

$$\delta(2, \zeta) = \left\lfloor \frac{2 - (2, -1) \cdot (\zeta_x, \zeta_y)}{2} \right\rfloor = \left\lfloor \frac{2 - 2\zeta_x + \zeta_y}{2} \right\rfloor,$$

and hence we have $2 \xrightarrow{[0,0]} 1$, $2 \xrightarrow{[0,1]} 1$, $2 \xrightarrow{[1,0]} 0$, and $2 \xrightarrow{[1,1]} 0$. States 2, 1, and 0 are final. The DFA accepts, for example, the word

$$\begin{bmatrix} 0 \\ 0 \end{bmatrix} \begin{bmatrix} 0 \\ 1 \end{bmatrix} \begin{bmatrix} 1 \\ 0 \end{bmatrix} \begin{bmatrix} 1 \\ 0 \end{bmatrix} \begin{bmatrix} 0 \\ 1 \end{bmatrix} \begin{bmatrix} 0 \\ 1 \end{bmatrix}$$

which encodes $x = 12$ and $y = 50$ and, indeed, $24 - 50 \leq 2$. If we remove the last letter, then the word encodes $x = 12$ and $y = 18$ and is not accepted, which indeed corresponds to $24 - 18 \not\leq 2$.

Now, consider the formula $x + y \geq 4$. We rewrite it as $-x - y \leq -4$ and apply the algorithm. The resulting DFA is shown in figure 9.2. The initial state is -4. Transitions leaving -4 are given by

$$\delta(-4, \zeta) = \left\lfloor \frac{-4 - (-1, -1) \cdot (\zeta_x, \zeta_y)}{2} \right\rfloor = \left\lfloor \frac{-4 + \zeta_x + \zeta_y}{2} \right\rfloor,$$

and hence we have

$$-4 \xrightarrow{[0,0]} -2, \ -4 \xrightarrow{[0,1]} -2, \ -4 \xrightarrow{[1,0]} -2 \text{ and } -4 \xrightarrow{[1,1]} -1.$$

Note that the DFA is not minimal, since states 0 and 1 can be merged.

Partial correctness of *AFtoDFA* is easily proved by showing that for every $q \in \mathbb{Z}$ and every word $w \in (\{0, 1\}^n)^*$, the state q accepts w iff w encodes $c \in \mathbb{N}^n$ satisfying $a \cdot c \leq q$. The proof proceeds by induction of $|w|$.

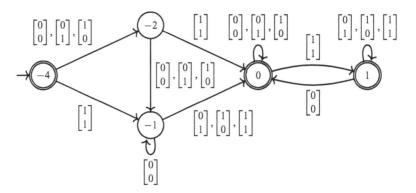

Figure 9.2
DFA for the formula $x + y \geq 4$.

For $|w| = 0$, the result follows immediately from the definition of the final states and, for $|w| > 0$, from the fact that δ satisfies (9.1) and from the induction hypothesis. Details are left to the reader. Termination of *AFtoDFA* also requires a proof: in principle, the algorithm could keep generating new states forever. We show that this is not the case.

Lemma 9.3   *Let* $\varphi = a \cdot x \leq b$ *and let* $s = \sum_{i=1}^{k} |a_i|$. *All states* s_j *added to the workset during the execution of AFtoDFA(φ) satisfy* $- |b| - s \leq j \leq |b| + s$.

Proof   The property holds for s_b, the first state added to the workset. We show that, at any point in time, if all the states added to the workset so far satisfy the property, then so does the next one. Let s_j be this next state. There exists a state s_k added to the workset in the past, and $\zeta \in \{0, 1\}^n$ such that $j = \lfloor \frac{1}{2}(k - a \cdot \zeta) \rfloor$. Since, by assumption, s_k satisfies the property, we have

$$- |b| - s \leq k \leq |b| + s$$

and hence

$$\left\lfloor \frac{- |b| - s - a \cdot \zeta}{2} \right\rfloor \leq j \leq \left\lfloor \frac{|b| + s - a \cdot \zeta}{2} \right\rfloor. \tag{9.2}$$

Now, we manipulate the right and left sides of (9.2). A little arithmetic yields

$$- |b| - s \leq \frac{- |b| - 2s}{2} \leq \left\lfloor \frac{- |b| - s - a \cdot \zeta}{2} \right\rfloor,$$

$$\left\lfloor \frac{|b| + s - a \cdot \zeta}{2} \right\rfloor \leq \frac{|b| + 2s}{2} \leq |b| + s,$$

which together with (9.2) leads to

$$- |b| - s \leq j \leq |b| + s. \qquad \square$$

Example 9.4 We compute all natural solutions of the system of linear inequations

$$2x - y \leq 2$$

$$x + y \geq 4,$$

such that both x and y are multiples of 4. This corresponds to computing a DFA for the Presburger formula

$$\exists z \, (x = 4z) \wedge \exists w \, (y = 4w) \wedge (2x - y \leq 2) \wedge (x + y \geq 4).$$

The minimal DFA for the first two conjuncts can be computed using projections and intersections, but the result is also easy to guess: it is the DFA of figure 9.3 (where a trap state has been omitted). The solutions are then represented by the intersection of the DFAs depicted in figure 9.1, figure 9.2 (after merging states 0 and 1), and figure 9.3. The result is shown in figure 9.4. (Some states from which no final state can be reached are omitted.)

9.2.1 Equations

A slight modification of *AFtoDFA* directly constructs a DFA for the solutions of $a \cdot x = b$, without having to intersect DFAs for $a \cdot x \leq b$ and $-a \cdot x \leq -b$. The states of the DFA are a

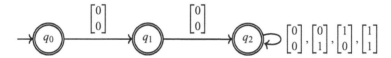

Figure 9.3
DFA for the formula $\exists z \, (x = 4z) \wedge \exists w \, (y = 4w)$.

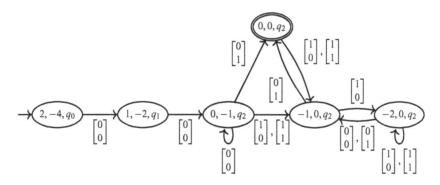

Figure 9.4
Intersection of the DFAs of figures 9.1–9.3. States from which no final state is reachable have been omitted.

trap state q_t accepting the empty language, plus integers satisfying:

State $q \in \mathbb{Z}$ recognizes the encodings of the tuples $c \in \mathbb{N}^n$ such that $a \cdot c = q$.   (9.3)

For the trap state q_t, we take $\delta(q_t, \zeta) = q_t$ for every $\zeta \in \{0, 1\}^n$. For a state $q \in \mathbb{Z}$ and a letter $\zeta \in \{0, 1\}^n$, we determine the target state q' of transition $\delta(q, \zeta)$. Given a tuple $c \in \mathbb{N}^n$, property (9.3) requires $c \in \mathcal{L}(q')$ iff $a \cdot c = q'$. As in the case of inequations, we have

$$c \in \mathcal{L}(q') \iff 2c + \zeta \in \mathcal{L}(q)$$
$$\iff a \cdot (2c + \zeta) = q \qquad \text{(by property [9.3] for } q)$$
$$\iff a \cdot c = \frac{q - a \cdot \zeta}{2}.$$

If $q - a \cdot \zeta$ is odd, then, since $a \cdot c$ is an integer, the equation $a \cdot c = (q - a \cdot \zeta)/2$ has no solution. So, in order to satisfy property (9.3), we must choose q' satisfying $\mathcal{L}(q') = \emptyset$, and so we take $q' = q_t$. If $q - a \cdot \zeta$ is even, then we must choose q' satisfying $a \cdot c = q'$, and hence we take $q' = (q - a \cdot \zeta)/2$. Therefore, the transition function of the DFA is given by

$$\delta(q, \zeta) = \begin{cases} q_t & \text{if } q = q_t \text{ or } q - a \cdot \zeta \text{ is odd,} \\ (q - a \cdot \zeta)/2 & \text{if } q - a \cdot \zeta \text{ is even.} \end{cases}$$

For the final states, recall that a state is final iff it accepts the tuple $(0, \dots, 0)$. So q_t is nonfinal and, by property (9.3), $q \in \mathbb{Z}$ is final iff $a \cdot (0 \dots, 0) = q$. Hence, the only final state is $q = 0$. The result is algorithm 43. The algorithm does not construct the trap state.

Example 9.5 Consider the formulas $x + y \leq 4$ and $x + y = 4$. The result of applying *AFtoDFA* to $x + y \leq 4$ is depicted at the top of figure 9.5. Observe the similarities and differences with the DFA for $x + y \geq 4$ illustrated in figure 9.2. The bottom of figure 9.5 shows the result of applying *EqtoDFA* to $x + y = 4$. Note that the transitions are a subset of the transitions of the DFA for $x + y \leq 4$. This example shows that the DFA is not necessarily minimal, since state -1 can be deleted.

Partial correctness and termination of *EqtoDFA* are easily proved following similar steps to the case of inequations.

9.3   An NFA for the Solutions over the Integers

We construct an NFA recognizing the encodings of the *integer solutions* (positive or negative) of a formula. In order to deal with negative numbers, we use *two's complements*. A *two's complement encoding* of an integer $x \in \mathbb{Z}$ is any word $a_0 a_1 \cdots a_n$ over the alphabet $\{0, 1\}$, where $n \geq 1$, satisfying

---

Algorithm 43 Conversion of an equation into a DFA recognizing the LSBF encodings of its solutions.

$EqtoDFA(\varphi)$
Input: Equation $\varphi = (a \cdot x = b)$
Output: DFA $A = (Q, \Sigma, \delta, q_0, F)$ such that $\mathcal{L}(A) = \mathcal{L}(\varphi)$
          (without trap state)

```
1   Q, δ, F ← ∅; q₀ ← s_b
2   W ← {s_b}
3   while W ≠ ∅ do
4       pick s_k from W
5       add s_k to Q
6       if k = 0 then add s_k to F
7       for all ζ ∈ {0, 1}ⁿ do
8           if (k − a · ζ) is even then
9               j ← (k − a · ζ)/2
10              if s_j ∉ Q then add s_j to W
11              add (s_k, ζ, s_j) to δ
```

$$x = \sum_{i=0}^{n-1} a_i \cdot 2^i - a_n \cdot 2^n. \tag{9.4}$$

We call a_n the *sign bit*. For example, 110 encodes $1 + 2 - 0 = 3$, and 111 encodes $1 + 2 - 4 = -1$. If the word has length 1, then its only bit is the sign bit; in particular, the word 0 encodes the number 0, and the word 1 encodes the number -1. The empty word encodes no number. Observe that all of $110, 1100, 11000, \ldots$ encode 3, and all of $1, 11, 111, \ldots$ encode -1. In general, it is easy to see that all words of the regular expression $a_0 \ldots a_{n-1} a_n a_n^*$ encode the same number: for $a_n = 0$, this is obvious, and for $a_n = 1$, both $a_0 \ldots a_{n-1} 1$ and $a_0 \ldots a_{n-1} 1 1^m$ encode the same number because

$$-2^{m+n} + 2^{m-1+n} + \ldots + 2^{n+1} = 2^n.$$

This property allows us to encode tuples of numbers using padding. Instead of padding with 0, we pad with the sign bit.

Example 9.6 The triple $(12, -3, -14)$ is encoded by all the words of the regular expression

$$\begin{bmatrix} 0 \\ 1 \\ 0 \end{bmatrix} \begin{bmatrix} 0 \\ 0 \\ 1 \end{bmatrix} \begin{bmatrix} 1 \\ 1 \\ 0 \end{bmatrix} \begin{bmatrix} 1 \\ 1 \\ 0 \end{bmatrix} \begin{bmatrix} 0 \\ 1 \\ 1 \end{bmatrix} \begin{bmatrix} 0 \\ 1 \\ 1 \end{bmatrix}^*$$

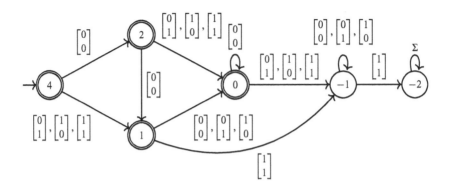

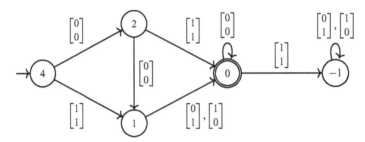

Figure 9.5
DFAs for the formulas $x+y \leq 4$ (top) and $x+y=4$ (bottom).

The words

$$\begin{bmatrix}0\\1\\0\end{bmatrix}\begin{bmatrix}0\\0\\1\end{bmatrix}\begin{bmatrix}1\\1\\0\end{bmatrix}\begin{bmatrix}1\\1\\0\end{bmatrix}\begin{bmatrix}0\\1\\1\end{bmatrix} \text{ and } \begin{bmatrix}0\\1\\0\end{bmatrix}\begin{bmatrix}0\\0\\1\end{bmatrix}\begin{bmatrix}1\\1\\0\end{bmatrix}\begin{bmatrix}1\\1\\0\end{bmatrix}\begin{bmatrix}0\\1\\1\end{bmatrix}\begin{bmatrix}0\\1\\1\end{bmatrix}\begin{bmatrix}0\\1\\1\end{bmatrix}$$

encode the triples (x, y, z) and (x', y', z') given by

$$x = 0+0+4+8-0 \;=\; 12,$$

$$y = 1+0+4+8-16 = -3,$$

$$z = 0+2+0+0-16 = -14,$$

$$x' = 0+0+4+8+0+0-0 \;=\; 12,$$

$$y' = 1+0+4+8+16+32-64 = -3,$$

$$z' = 0+2+0+0+16+32-64 = -14.$$

We construct an NFA (no longer a DFA!) recognizing the integer solutions of an atomic formula $a \cdot x \leq b$. As usual, we take integers for the states, and the NFA should satisfy:

State $q \in \mathbb{Z}$ recognizes the encodings of the tuples $c \in \mathbb{Z}^n$ such that $a \cdot c \leq q$.   (9.5)

However, integer states are no longer enough, because no state $q \in \mathbb{Z}$ can be final: in the two's complement encoding, the empty word encodes no number, and so, since q cannot accept the empty word by property (9.5), q must be nonfinal. But we need at least one final state, and so we add to the NFA a unique final state q_f without any outgoing transitions, accepting only the empty word.

Given a state $q \in \mathbb{Z}$ and a letter $\zeta \in \{0, 1\}^n$, we determine the targets q' of the transitions of the NFA of the form $q' \in \delta(q, \zeta)$, where $\zeta \in \{0, 1\}^n$. (There will be either one or two such transitions.) A word $w \in (\{0, 1\}^n)^*$ is accepted from some target state q iff ζw is accepted from q. In the two's complement encoding, there are two cases:

(1) If $w \neq \varepsilon$, then ζw encodes the tuple $2c + \zeta \in \mathbb{Z}^n$, where c is the tuple encoded by w. (This follows easily from the definition of two's complements.)

(2) If $w = \varepsilon$, then ζw encodes the tuple $-\zeta \in \mathbb{Z}^n$, because in this case, ζ is the sign bit.

In case (1), property (9.5) requires a target state q' such that $a \cdot c \leq q$ iff $a \cdot (2c + \zeta) \leq q'$. Thus, we take

$$q' = \left\lfloor \frac{q - a \cdot \zeta}{2} \right\rfloor.$$

In case (2), property (9.5) only requires a target state q' if $a \cdot (-\zeta) \leq q$, and if so, then it requires q' to be a *final* state. So, if $q + a \cdot \zeta \geq 0$, then we add

$$q \xrightarrow{\zeta} q_f$$

to the set of transitions; in this case, the automaton has two transitions leaving state q and labeled by ζ. Summarizing, we define the transition relation by

$$\delta(q, \zeta) = \begin{cases} \left\{ \lfloor (q - a \cdot \zeta)/2 \rfloor, q_f \right\} & \text{if } q + a \cdot \zeta \geq 0, \\ \{ \lfloor (q - a \cdot \zeta)/2 \rfloor \} & \text{otherwise.} \end{cases}$$

Observe that the NFA contains all the states and transitions of the DFA for the natural solutions of $a \cdot x \leq b$, plus possibly other transitions. All integer states are now nonfinal; the only final state is q_f.

Example 9.7   Figure 9.6 shows the NFA recognizing all integer solutions of $2x - y \leq 2$. It has all states and transitions of the DFA for the natural solutions, plus some more (compare with figure 9.1). The final state q_f and the transitions leading to it are colored. Consider, for instance, state -1. In order to determine the letters $\zeta \in \{0, 1\}^2$ for which $q_f \in \delta(-1, \zeta)$,

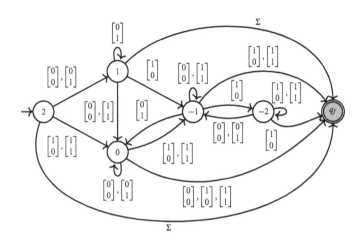

Figure 9.6
NFA for the integer solutions of $2x - y \leq 2$.

we compute $q + a \cdot \zeta = -1 + 2\zeta_x - \zeta_y$ for each $(\zeta_x, \zeta_y) \in \{0, 1\}^2$ and compare the result to 0. We obtain that the letters leading to q_f are $(1, 0)$ and $(1, 1)$.

9.3.1 Equations

In order to construct an NFA for the integer solutions of an equation $a \cdot x = b$, we can proceed as for inequations. The result is again an NFA containing all states and transitions of the DFA for the natural solutions computed in section 9.2.1, plus possibly some more. The automaton has an additional final state q_f and a transition

$$q \xrightarrow{\zeta} q_f \text{ iff } q + a \cdot \zeta = 0.$$

Graphically, we can also obtain the NFA by starting with the NFA for $a \cdot x \leq b$ and then removing all transitions

$$q \xrightarrow{\zeta} q' \text{ such that } q' \neq (q - a \cdot \zeta)/2,$$

$$q \xrightarrow{\zeta} q_f \text{ such that } q + a \cdot \zeta \neq 0.$$

Example 9.8 The NFA for the integer solutions of $2x - y = 2$ is depicted in figure 9.7. Its transitions are a subset of those of the NFA for $2x - y \leq 2$.

The NFA for the integer solutions of an equation has an interesting property. Since $q + a \cdot \zeta = 0$ holds iff $(q + a \cdot \zeta)/2 = 2q/2 = q$, the NFA has a transition

$$q \xrightarrow{\zeta} q_f \text{ iff it also has a self-loop } q \xrightarrow{\zeta} q.$$

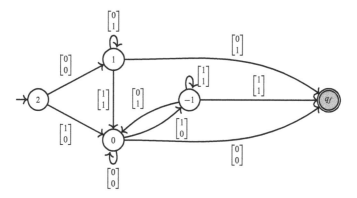

Figure 9.7
NFA for the integer solutions of $2x - y = 2$.

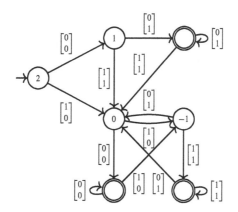

Figure 9.8
Minimal DFA for the integer solutions of $2x - y = 2$.

For instance, state 1 of the NFA of figure 9.7 has a colored transition labeled by $(0, 1)$ and a self-loop labeled by $(0, 1)$. Using this property, it is easy to see that the powerset construction does not cause a blowup in the number of states: it only adds one extra state for each predecessor of the final state.

Example 9.9 The DFA obtained by applying the powerset construction to the NFA for $2x - y = 2$ is shown in figure 9.8 (the trap state has been omitted). Each of the three predecessors of q_f gets "duplicated."

Moreover, the DFA obtained by means of the powerset construction is *minimal*. This can be proved by showing that any two states recognize different languages. If exactly one of the states is final, we are done. If both states are nonfinal, say, k and k', then they recognize the solutions of $a \cdot x = k$ and $a \cdot x = k'$, and so their languages are not only distinct but even disjoint. If both states are final, then they are the "duplicates" of two nonfinal states k and k', and their languages are those of k and k', plus the empty word. So, again, their languages are distinct.

9.3.2 Algorithms

The procedures for the construction of the NFAs are described in algorithm 44. Additions to the previous algorithms are shown in gray.

Algorithm 44 Converting equations and inequations into NFAs accepting the two's complement encoding of the solution space.

IneqZtoNFA(φ)
Input: $\varphi = (a \cdot x \leq b)$ over $\mathbb{Z}$
Output: NFA $A = (Q, \Sigma, \delta, Q_0, F)$
     such that $\mathcal{L}(A) = \mathcal{L}(\varphi)$

1   $Q, \delta, F \leftarrow \emptyset;\ Q_0 \leftarrow \{s_b\}$
2   $W \leftarrow \{s_b\}$
3   **while** $W \neq \emptyset$ **do**
4   **pick** s_k **from** W
5   **add** s_k **to** Q
6   **for all** $\zeta \in \{0,1\}^n$ **do**
7       $j \leftarrow \lfloor (k - a \cdot \zeta)/2 \rfloor$
8   **if** $s_j \notin Q$ **then add** s_j **to** W
9   **add** (s_k, ζ, s_j) **to** δ
10   **if** $k + a \cdot \zeta \geq 0$ **then**
11   **add** q_f **to** Q and F
12   **add** (s_k, ζ, q_f) **to** δ

EqZtoNFA(φ)
Input: $\varphi = (a \cdot x = b)$ over $\mathbb{Z}$
Output: NFA $A = (Q, \Sigma, \delta, Q_0, F)$
     such that $\mathcal{L}(A) = \mathcal{L}(\varphi)$

1   $Q, \delta, F \leftarrow \emptyset;\ Q_0 \leftarrow \{s_b\}$
2   $W \leftarrow \{s_b\}$
3   **while** $W \neq \emptyset$ **do**
4   **pick** s_k **from** W
5   **add** s_k **to** Q
6   **for all** $\zeta \in \{0,1\}^n$ **do**
7   **if** $k - a \cdot \zeta$ is even **then**
8   **if** $k + a \cdot \zeta = 0$ **then**
9   **add** s_k **to** F
10        $j \leftarrow (k - a \cdot \zeta)/2$
11   **if** $s_j \notin Q$ **then add** s_j **to** W
12   **add** (s_k, ζ, s_j) **to** δ
13   **if** $k + a \cdot \zeta \geq 0$ **then**
14   **add** q_f **to** Q and F
15   **add** (s_k, ζ, q_f) **to** δ

9.4 Exercises

☆ 🖳 **Exercise 133.** Express the following expressions in Presburger arithmetic:

(a) $x = 0$ and $y = 1$ (if 0 and 1 were not part of the syntax),

(b) $z = \max(x, y)$ and $z = \min(x, y)$.

☆ ✔ **Exercise 134.** How can one determine algorithmically whether two formulas from Presburger arithmetic have the same solutions?

★ 🔲 **Exercise 135.** Let $r \geq 0$ and $n \geq 1$. Give a Presburger formula φ such that $\mathcal{J} \models \varphi$ iff $\mathcal{J}(x) \geq \mathcal{J}(y)$ and $\mathcal{J}(x) - \mathcal{J}(y) \equiv r \pmod{n}$. Give an automaton that accepts the solutions of φ for $r = 0$ and $n = 2$.

☆ 🎛 **Exercise 136.** Construct an automaton for the Presburger formula $\exists y\, (x = 3y)$ using the algorithms of the chapter.

★ ✔ **Exercise 137.** Algorithm *AFtoDFA* yields a DFA that recognizes solutions of a linear inequation encoded using the LSBF encoding. We may also use the most-significant-bit-first encoding, for example,

$$\text{MSBF}\left(\begin{bmatrix} 2 \\ 3 \end{bmatrix}\right) = \begin{bmatrix} 0 \\ 0 \end{bmatrix}^* \begin{bmatrix} 1 \\ 1 \end{bmatrix} \begin{bmatrix} 0 \\ 1 \end{bmatrix}.$$

(a) Construct a DFA for $2x - y \leq 2$, w.r.t. MSBF encodings, by considering the reversal of the DFA given in figure 9.1 for LSBF encodings.

(b) Rename the states of the DFA obtained in (a) by their minimal state number, and explicitly introduce a trap state named 3. Compare values $2x - y$ and q for tuples $[x, y]$ that lead to a state q. What do you observe?

(c) Adapt algorithm *AFtoDFA* to the MSBF encoding.

Hint: Design an infinite automaton obtained from $a \cdot c = q$ and make it finite based on (b).

★ ✔ **Exercise 138.** Suppose it is late and you are craving for chicken nuggets. Since you are stuck in the subway, you have no idea how hungry you will be when reaching the restaurant. Since nuggets are only sold in boxes of 6, 9, and 20, you wonder if it will be possible to buy exactly the amount of nuggets you will be craving for when arriving. You also wonder whether it is always possible to buy an exact number of nuggets if one is hungry enough. Luckily, you can answer these questions since you are quite knowledgeable about Presburger arithmetic and automata theory.

For every finite set $S \subseteq \mathbb{N}$, we say that number $n \in \mathbb{N}$ is an *S-number* if n can be obtained as a linear combination of elements of S. For example, if $S = \{6, 9, 20\}$, then 67 is an S-number since $67 = 3 \cdot 6 + 1 \cdot 9 + 2 \cdot 20$, but 25 is not. For some sets S, there are only finitely many numbers that are not S-numbers. When this is the case, we say that the largest number that is not an S-number is the *Frobenius number* of S. For example, 7 is the Frobenius number of $\{3, 5\}$, and $S = \{2, 4\}$ has no Frobenius number.

To answer your questions, it suffices to come up with algorithms for Frobenius numbers and to instantiate them with $S = \{6, 9, 20\}$.

(a) Give an algorithm that decides, on input $n \in \mathbb{N}$ and a finite set $S \subseteq_{\text{finite}} \mathbb{N}$, whether n is an S-number.

(b) Give an algorithm that decides, on input $S \subseteq_{\text{finite}} \mathbb{N}$, whether S has a Frobenius number.

(c) Give an algorithm that computes, on input $S \subseteq_{\text{finite}} \mathbb{N}$, the Frobenius number of S (assuming it exists).

(d) Show that $S = \{6, 9, 20\}$ has a Frobenius number, and identify it.

☆ 🔲 **Exercise 139.** Automata are more expressive than Presburger arithmetic. They can represent

$$\varphi(x, y) = \text{``}x \text{ is the largest power of 2 that divides } y\text{,''} \text{ and}$$

$$\psi(x, y) = \text{``}x \text{ is the largest power of 2 smaller or equal to } y\text{,''}$$

while Presburger arithmetic can express neither φ nor ψ, since, informally, addition is not powerful enough to achieve exponentiation. Give automata representing φ and ψ, where numbers are over $\mathbb{N}$ and given by LSBF encodings.

★ 🕮 **Exercise 140.** Converting a Presburger formula over k variables into a DFA yields an alphabet of 2^k letters. In order to mitigate this combinatorial explosion, one can instead label transitions with boolean expressions. For example, $[0, 1]$ can be written as $\neg x \wedge y$, and the set $\{[1, 0], [1, 1]\}$ can be written as x. Such expressions can internally be represented, for example, as binary decision diagrams.

(a) Give DFAs for formulas $x < y$ and $y < z$, using boolean expressions rather than letters.

(b) Construct a DFA for $x < y < z$.

II AUTOMATA ON INFINITE WORDS

10 Classes of ω-Automata and Conversions

Automata on infinite words, called ω-automata in this book, were introduced in the 1960s as an auxiliary tool for proving the decidability of some problems in mathematical logic. As the name suggests, they are automata whose input is a word of infinite length. Therefore, the run of an automaton on a word does not terminate.

An ω-automaton makes little sense as a language acceptor that decides whether a word satisfies a property or not: not many people are willing to wait infinitely long to get an answer to a question! However, ω-automata still make perfect sense as a data structure, that is, as a finite representation of a (possibly infinite) set of infinite words.

There are objects that must be represented as infinite words. The example that first comes to mind are the real numbers. A second example, more relevant for applications, are program executions. Programs may have nonterminating executions, either because of programming errors or because they are designed this way. Indeed, many programs whose purpose is to keep a system running, like routines of operating systems, network infrastructures, communication protocols, and so on, are designed to be in constant operation. Automata on infinite words can be used to finitely represent the set of executions of such programs. They are an important tool for the theory and practice of program verification.

In the second part of this book, starting now, we develop the theory of ω-automata as a data structure for languages of infinite words. This first chapter introduces ω-regular expressions, a textual notation for defining languages of infinite words, and then proceeds to present different classes of automata on infinite words, most of them with the same expressive power as ω-regular expressions, and conversion algorithms between them.

10.1 ω-Languages and ω-Regular Expressions

Let Σ be an alphabet. An *infinite* word, also called an ω-*word*, is an infinite sequence $a_0 a_1 a_2 \cdots$ of letters from Σ. A set $L \subseteq \Sigma^\omega$ of ω-words is an *infinitary language* or ω-*language* over Σ. We denote by Σ^ω the set of all ω-words over Σ.

The concatenation of a finite word $u = a_0 \cdots a_n$ and an ω-word $v = b_0 b_1 \cdots$ is the ω-word $uv = a_0 \cdots a_n b_0 b_1 \cdots$, sometimes also denoted $u \cdot v$. (Observe that the concatenation of two ω-words is not defined.) We extend this definition to languages. The *concatenation* of a language L_1 and an ω-language L_2 is the ω-language $L_1 L_2 = \{w_1 w_2 \in \Sigma^\omega : w_1 \in L_1, w_2 \in L_2\}$, also denoted $L_1 \cdot L_2$.

The ω-*iteration* of a language $L \subseteq \Sigma^*$ is the ω-language obtained by concatenating infinitely many nonempty words of L. In other words, $L^\omega = \{w_1 w_2 \cdots : w_i \in L \setminus \{\varepsilon\}\}$.

Remark 10.1 Note that $\{\varepsilon\}^\omega = \emptyset^\omega = \emptyset$. Intuitively, it is impossible to construct an ω-word by concatenating words of length 0 or words taken out of the empty set.

We extend regular expressions to ω-regular expressions, a formalism to define ω-languages.

Definition 10.2 *The ω-regular expressions over an alphabet Σ are defined by the following grammar, where $r \in \mathcal{RE}(\Sigma)$ is an arbitrary regular expression:*

$$s ::= r^\omega \mid rs_1 \mid s_1 + s_2.$$

Sometimes we write $r \cdot s_1$ instead of rs_1. The set of all ω-regular expressions over Σ is denoted by $\mathcal{RE}_\omega(\Sigma)$.

The language $\mathcal{L}_\omega(s) \subseteq \Sigma^\omega$ *of an ω-regular expression $s \in \mathcal{RE}_\omega(\Sigma)$ is defined inductively as follows:*

- $\mathcal{L}_\omega(r^\omega) = (\mathcal{L}(r))^\omega$,
- $\mathcal{L}_\omega(rs_1) = \mathcal{L}(r) \cdot \mathcal{L}_\omega(s_1)$, *and*
- $\mathcal{L}_\omega(s_1 + s_2) = \mathcal{L}_\omega(s_1) \cup \mathcal{L}_\omega(s_2)$.

A language L is ω-regular if $L = \mathcal{L}_\omega(s)$ for some ω-regular expression s.

As for regular expressions, we often write s instead of $\mathcal{L}_\omega(s)$ if there is no risk of confusion.

Example 10.3 Here are some examples of ω-regular expressions and their languages.

- $(a + b)^\omega$ denotes the language of all ω-words over $\{a, b\}$.
- $(a + b)^* b^\omega$ denotes the language of all ω-words over $\{a, b\}$ containing only finitely many a's.
- $(a^* ab + b^* ba)^\omega$ denotes the language of all ω-words over $\{a, b\}$ containing infinitely many as and infinitely many bs; an even shorter expression for this language is $((a + b)^* ab)^\omega$.
- $((b + c)^* a(a + c)^* b(b + a)^* c)^\omega$ denotes the language of all ω-words over $\{a, b, c\}$ containing infinitely many as, infinitely many bs, and infinitely many cs. Indeed, this is the set of all ω-words w satisfying: w contains at least one a; after every occurrence of a, there is a later occurrence of b; after every occurrence of b, there is a later occurrence of c; and, after every occurrence of c, there is a later occurrence of a. This is precisely the language denoted by the ω-regular expression.

Remark 10.4

- Since any word $w \in \Sigma^*$ is also a regular expression, w^ω is an ω-regular expression. We have $\mathcal{L}_\omega(\varepsilon^\omega) = \emptyset$. If $w \neq \varepsilon$, then $\mathcal{L}_\omega(w^\omega) = \{www \cdots\}$, and so $\mathcal{L}_\omega(w^\omega)$ is a language containing a single ω-word. Abusing notation, this word is also denoted w^ω. Compare with $\mathcal{L}(a^*)$, which is a language containing not one but infinitely many words.

- Recall that the symbol $\emptyset$ is part of the syntax of regular expressions and denotes the language of finite words containing no elements. The symbol is necessary, because a regular expression r that does not contain any occurrence of $\emptyset$ satisfies $\mathcal{L}(r) \neq \emptyset$, and so without the symbol $\emptyset$, no regular expression would denote the empty language. This is no longer the case for ω-regular expressions. The symbol $\emptyset$ is not needed, because $\mathcal{L}_\omega(\varepsilon^\omega) = \emptyset$.

10.2   ω-Automata and the Quest for an ω-Trinity

In chapter 1, we introduced NFAs and DFAs, plus auxiliary automata classes. In the realm of ω-words, we need to introduce different *types* of ω-automata, each of which contains nondeterministic and deterministic automata. Let us introduce a precise definition of ω-automaton and the idea of an automata type.

Semi-automata and runs.   A *(nondeterministic) semi-automaton* is a tuple $S = (Q, \Sigma, \delta, Q_0)$, where Q, Σ, δ, and Q_0 are defined as for NFAs. A semi-automaton S is *deterministic* if Q_0 is a singleton set, and $\delta(q, a)$ is also a singleton set for every $q \in Q$ and $a \in \Sigma$. Abusing language, we denote a deterministic semi-automaton by $S = (Q, \Sigma, \delta, q_0)$ and write $\delta(q, a) = q'$ instead of $\delta(q, a) = \{q'\}$. A *run* of a semi-automaton S on an ω-word $a_0a_1a_2 \cdots \in \Sigma^\omega$ is an infinite sequence $\rho = q_0 \xrightarrow{a_0} q_1 \xrightarrow{a_1} \cdots$ such that $q_0 \in Q_0, q_i \in Q$ and $q_{i+1} \in \delta(q_i, a_i)$ for every $i \in \mathbb{N}$.

Acceptance conditions.   Intuitively, runs on ω-words never terminate, and so we cannot define whether a run is accepting in terms of the state it leads to. Instead, we define acceptance in terms of the states visited by the run *infinitely often*. An acceptance condition divides the subsets of Q into accepting and nonaccepting, and a run is accepting if the set of states it visits infinitely often is accepting. Formally, given a run $\rho = q_0 \xrightarrow{a_0} q_1 \xrightarrow{a_1} \cdots$, let

$$\mathrm{inf}(\rho) = \{q \in Q : q_i = q \text{ for infinitely many } i \in \mathbb{N}\}.$$

An *acceptance condition* is a mapping $\alpha : 2^Q \to \{0, 1\}$. A run ρ is *accepting* or *satisfies the acceptance condition* if $\alpha(\mathrm{inf}(\rho)) = 1$.

ω-automata.   A (nondeterministic) ω-automaton is a pair $A = (S, \alpha)$, where S is a semi-automaton, and α is an acceptance condition. We say that A is *deterministic* if S is deterministic. An ω-automaton *accepts* an ω-word $w \in \Sigma^\omega$ if it has an accepting run on w. The language *recognized* by an ω-automaton A is the set $\mathcal{L}_\omega(A) = \{w \in \Sigma^\omega : w \text{ is accepted by } A\}$. We sometimes write $A = (Q, \Sigma, \delta, Q_0, \alpha)$ instead of $A = (S, \alpha)$.

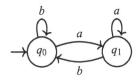

Figure 10.1
Example of a semi-automaton.

Example 10.5 Consider the deterministic semi-automaton S of figure 10.1 and the acceptance condition α defined by $\alpha(Q') = 1$ iff $q_1 \in Q'$. With this acceptance condition, a run ρ is accepting iff $q_1 \in \inf(\rho)$. In words, ρ is accepting iff it visits q_1 infinitely often. (Observe that there is no condition on q_0. If ρ visits q_1 infinitely often, then it is accepting, regardless of whether it visits q_0 finitely or infinitely often.)

The language recognized by the ω-automaton $A = (S, \alpha)$ is the set of all words over $\{a, b\}$ containing infinitely many occurrences of a. Indeed, since all transitions labeled by a lead to q_1, the run of A on an ω-word containing infinitely many as visits q_1 infinitely often, and so the word is accepted. Further, since every transition leading to q_1 is labeled by a, every accepting run reads infinitely many as.

Types of ω-automata. Types of ω-automata differ on the *types* of their acceptance conditions. For example, in the next sections, we will examine Büchi conditions. An acceptance condition α is a *Büchi condition* if there exists a set $F \subseteq Q$ of states such that $\alpha(Q') = 1$ iff $Q' \cap F \neq \emptyset$. In words, a run is accepting if it visits at least one state of F infinitely often.

Example 10.6 Consider again the semi-automaton of example 10.5. The acceptance condition α defined by $\alpha(Q') = 1$ iff $q_1 \in Q'$ is a Büchi condition with $F = \{q_1\}$. The acceptance condition β given by $\beta(Q') = 1$ iff $Q' = \{q_1\}$ is not a Büchi condition (i.e., there is no $F \subseteq \{q_0, q_1\}$ such that $\beta(Q') = 1$ iff $Q' \cap F \neq \emptyset$). In particular, the language of (S, β) consists of all words containing finitely many bs, but no Büchi condition recognizes the same language.

Representing acceptance conditions. Observe that a Büchi condition is completely determined by the set F. Abusing language, we speak of "*the Büchi condition F*" as an abbreviation of "*the Büchi condition induced by F*." We also call a tuple $A = (Q, \Sigma, \delta, Q_0, F)$ a *Büchi automaton*, meaning that A is the automaton (S, α) where $S = (Q, \Sigma, \delta, Q_0)$, and α is the Büchi condition induced by F. We proceed in the same way for the forthcoming automata types.

10.2.1 The Quest for an ω-Trinity

In chapter 1, we introduced a *trinity* of formalisms: regular expressions, DFAs, and NFAs. As depicted in figure 10.2, we proved that all three express exactly the regular languages, and we described conversion algorithms between them.

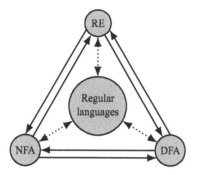

Figure 10.2
Trinity of regular languages. An arrow from X to Y means "for every X there is an equivalent Y."

In this section, we search for a corresponding *ω-trinity* for *ω*-regular languages. Sections 10.2.2 and 10.2.3 examine two simple types of *ω*-automata, called Büchi and co-Büchi automata, and show that they do not form an *ω*-trinity. Section 10.2.4 introduces a more sophisticated automata type, Rabin automata, which does.

10.2.2   Büchi Automata

Büchi automata were introduced by J. R. Büchi in the 1960s.

Definition 10.7   *Let* $S = (Q, \Sigma, \delta, Q_0)$ *be a semi-automaton. An acceptance condition* $\alpha : 2^Q \to \{0, 1\}$ *is a* Büchi condition *if there exists a set* $F \subseteq Q$ *of accepting states such that* $\alpha(Q') = 1$ *iff* $Q' \cap F \neq \emptyset$.
A nondeterministic Büchi automaton *(NBA) is a pair* $A = (S, F)$, *where* $F \subseteq Q$ *is a* Büchi condition. *We refer to a deterministic NBA as a* DBA.

Observe that we maintain the symbol F to denote the set of accepting states. We also maintain the same graphical representation: accepting states are drawn as double circles. Looking only at the graphical representation, one cannot tell whether an automaton is an NFA or an NBA, but the context will make it clear.

Example 10.8   The automaton of example 10.5 is a Büchi automaton with $\{q_1\}$ as set of accepting states. Figure 10.3 depicts four other Büchi automata over the alphabet $\{a, b, c\}$.
The top-left automaton, which is nondeterministic, recognizes the *ω*-words containing a finite number of *a*s. Intuitively, the automaton can always stay in the initial state until it reads the last *a*, guess (correctly) that it is the last one, and move to the state on the right immediately after.
The top-right automaton recognizes the *ω*-words in which, for each occurrence of *a*, there is a later occurrence of *b*. So, for instance, it accepts $(ab)^\omega$, c^ω, or $(bc)^\omega$ but not ac^ω or $ab(ac)^\omega$.

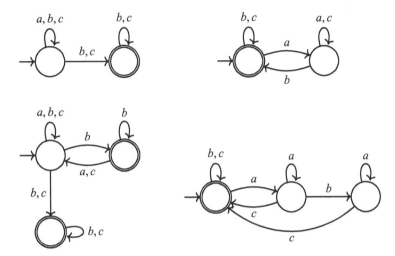

Figure 10.3
Four Büchi automata.

The bottom-left automaton recognizes the ω-words that contain finitely many occurrences of a (possibly zero) or infinitely many occurrences of a *and* infinitely many occurrences of b.

Finally, the bottom-right automaton recognizes the ω-words in which, between each occurrence of a and the next occurrence of c, there is *at most one* occurrence of b; more precisely, for any two numbers $i < j$, if the letter at position i is an a and the first occurrence of c after i is at position j, then there is at most one number $i < k < j$ such that the letter at position k is b.

10.2.2.1 Equivalence of NBAs and ω-Regular Expressions
We show that ω-regular expressions and nondeterministic Büchi automata have the same expressive power. We present algorithms for converting an ω-regular expression into an equivalent NBA and vice versa.

From ω-regular expressions to NBAs. We give a procedure that transforms an ω-regular expression s into an equivalent NBA. Using the results of chapter 1, we can transform a regular expression r into an NFA in three steps:

1. Transform r into an equivalent regular expression $\widehat{r}$ such that either $\widehat{r} = \emptyset$ or $\widehat{r}$ does not contain any occurrence of the symbol $\emptyset$. (See the first part of section 1.4.3.) If $\widehat{r} = \emptyset$, then output a one-state NFA with no final states and no transitions. Otherwise, move to the next step.

2. Transform $\widehat{r}$ into an equivalent NFA-ε. The resulting NFA-ε has a unique initial state; a unique final state, different from the initial state; no transition leading to the initial state; and no transition leaving the final state. (See the second part of section 1.4.3.)

3. Transform the NFA-ε into an equivalent NFA. (See algorithm 2 of section 1.4.2.)

The procedure for translating an ω-regular expression s into an NBA is very similar.

1. Transform s into an equivalent ω-regular expression $\hat{s}$ that does not contain any occurrence of the symbol $\emptyset$.

2. Transform $\hat{s}$ into an equivalent NBA-ε. An NBA-ε is a tuple $A = (Q, \Sigma, \delta, Q_0, F)$, where $\delta \colon Q \times (\Sigma \cup \{\varepsilon\}) \to \mathcal{P}(Q)$. A run $\rho = q_0 \xrightarrow{a_0} q_1 \xrightarrow{a_1} \cdots$ of A is accepting if $\inf(\rho) \cap F \neq \emptyset$ and $a_i \in \Sigma$ for infinitely many $i \in \mathbb{N}$ (this ensures that accepting runs only accept ω-words). In particular, any NBA-ε containing only ε-transitions recognizes the empty language.

3. Transform the NBA-ε into an equivalent NBA, using the same algorithm as for NFA-ε.

We describe steps 1 and 2.

Step 1. Given a regular expression r, let $\hat{r}$ denote the equivalent expression mentioned above, satisfying that either $\hat{r} = \emptyset$ or $\hat{r}$ does not contain any occurrence of $\emptyset$. We define $\hat{s}$ inductively as follows:

- Case $s = r^{\omega}$. If $\hat{r} = \emptyset$, then $\hat{s} = \varepsilon^{\omega}$; otherwise, $\hat{s} = (\hat{r})^{\omega}$.
- Case $s = rs_1$. If $\hat{r} = \emptyset$, then $\hat{s} = \varepsilon^{\omega}$; otherwise, $\hat{s} = \hat{r}\hat{s}_1$.
- Case $s = s_1 + s_2$. We take $\hat{s} = \hat{s}_1 + \hat{s}_2$.

Step 2. We translate $\hat{s}$ into an equivalent NBA-ε $A_{\hat{s}}$ with a single initial state and no transitions leading to it. Since $\hat{s}$ contains no occurrence of $\emptyset$, the algorithm of section 1.4.3 transforms every regular expression r appearing in $\hat{s}$ into an equivalent NFA-ε A_r with a unique initial state q_0; a unique final state q_f, different from q_0; no transition leading to q_0; and no transition leaving q_f. We proceed by induction on the structure of $\hat{s}$.

- If $\hat{s} = r^{\omega}$, then let $A_{\hat{s}}$ be the result of adding to A_r a transition (q_f, a, q) for every transition of the form (q_0, a, q) with $a \in \Sigma \cup \{\varepsilon\}$. (See the diagram at the top of figure 10.4.)
- If $\hat{s} = rs$, then let $A_{\hat{s}}$ be the result of merging the unique final state of A_r and the initial state of A_s (which is unique by induction hypothesis) and making q_f non-accepting. (See the diagram in the middle of figure 10.4.)
- If $\hat{s} = s_1 + s_2$, then let $A_{\hat{s}}$ be the result of "putting A_{s_1} and A_{s_2} side by side"—that is, taking the union of their states, transitions, and initial and accepting states, assuming without loss of generality that they are disjoint, and merging their initial states—which, by induction hypothesis, have no incoming transitions. (See the diagram at the bottom of figure 10.4.)

The complexity is the same as for regular expressions. Indeed, the number of states of the NBA-ε is linear in the length of the original ω-regular expression, and then the same algorithm as for NFAs is applied.

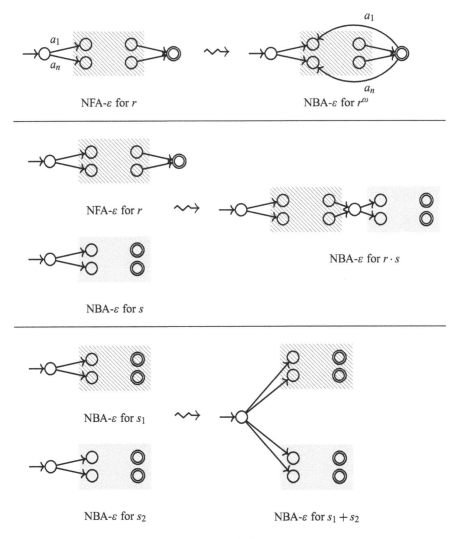

Figure 10.4
From ω-regular expressions to Büchi automata.

From NBAs to ω-regular expressions. Let $A = (Q, \Sigma, \delta, Q_0, F)$ be an NBA. We construct an ω-regular expression s_A such that $\mathcal{L}_\omega(s_A) = \mathcal{L}_\omega(A)$.

Given states $q, q' \in Q$, we are interested in a regular expression $r_{q,q'}$ for the finite words read by finite runs that start at state q and, after leaving q, visit q' *exactly once*; more precisely, a finite word $w = a_0\, a_1 \ldots a_{k-1}$ belongs to $\mathcal{L}\left(r_{q,q'}\right)$ if there is a run $q_0 \xrightarrow{a_0} q_1 \xrightarrow{a_1} q_2 \cdots q_{k-1} \xrightarrow{a_{k-1}} q_k$ such that $q_0 = q$, $q_k = q'$, and $q_i \neq q'$ for every $1 \leq i \leq$

$k-1$. We can easily compute $r_{q,q'}$ as follows: first, redirect all transitions of A leading to state q' to a new state q''; second, make q the unique initial state and q'' the unique final state; and third, apply *NFA-εtoRE* (algorithm 3 of chapter 1) to the resulting automaton, interpreting it as an NFA.

We use the regular expressions $r_{q,q'}$ to compute the ω-regular expression s_A. For each initial state $q_0 \in Q_0$ and each accepting state $q \in F$, let $L_{q_0,q} \subseteq \mathcal{L}_\omega(A)$ be the set of ω-words accepted by runs of A that start at q_0 and visit q infinitely often. We have $\mathcal{L}_\omega(A) = \bigcup_{q_0 \in Q_0, q \in F} L_{q_0,q}$. Every ω-word $w \in L_{q_0,q}$ can be split into an infinite sequence $w_0 w_1 w_2 \cdots$ of finite nonempty words, where w_0 is the word read by A until it visits q for the first time after leaving q_0, and, for every $i > 0$, w_i is the word read by the automaton between the ith and the $(i+1)$th visits to q. It follows that $w_0 \in \mathcal{L}\left(r_{q_0,q}\right)$, and $w_i \in \mathcal{L}\left(r_{q,q}\right)$ for every $i > 0$. Thus, we have $L_{q_0,q} = \mathcal{L}_\omega\left(r_{q_0,q}\left(r_{q,q}\right)^\omega\right)$, and hence we can take

$$s_A := \sum_{q_0 \in Q_0, q \in F} r_{q_0,q}\left(r_{q,q}\right)^\omega.$$

Example 10.9 Consider the NBA of figure 10.5.

We compute $s_A := r_{0,1}(r_{1,1})^\omega + r_{0,2}(r_{2,2})^\omega$. Let us abbreviate $(a+b+c)$ to Σ. Applying *NFAtoRE* and simplifying, we get

$$r_{0,1} = \Sigma^* b \qquad\qquad r_{0,2} = \left(\Sigma + bb^*(a+c)\right)^*(b+c)$$

$$r_{1,1} = b + (a+c)\Sigma^* b \qquad\qquad r_{2,2} = (b+c)$$

Substitution in the expression for s_A and simplification yields

$$s_A = \Sigma^* b(b+(a+c)\Sigma^* b)^\omega + \left(\Sigma + bb^*(a+c)\right)^*(b+c)(b+c)^\omega$$

$$\equiv (\Sigma^* b)^\omega + \Sigma^*(b+c)^\omega.$$

10.2.2.2   Nonequivalence of NBAs and DBAs

Unfortunately, deterministic Büchi automata do not recognize all ω-regular languages, and so they do not have the same expressive power as NBAs. We show that the language of

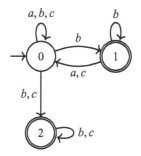

Figure 10.5
A Büchi automaton.

ω-words over $\{a, b\}$ containing finitely many occurrences of a, which is recognized by a two-state NBA that "guesses" the last occurrence of a, is not recognized by any DBA.

Proposition 10.10   *The language* $\mathcal{L}_\omega\left((a+b)^* b^\omega\right)$ *is not recognized by any DBA.*

Proof   Let $L = \mathcal{L}_\omega\left((a+b)^* b^\omega\right)$. We prove that every DBA accepting all words of L must also accept words that do not belong to L. Let $A = (Q, \{a, b\}, q_0, \delta, F)$ be an arbitrary DBA such that $L \subseteq \mathcal{L}_\omega(A)$. Define $\hat{\delta}: Q \times \{a, b\}^* \to Q$ by $\hat{\delta}(q, \varepsilon) = q$ and $\hat{\delta}(q, wa) = \delta(\hat{\delta}(q, w), a)$. That is, $\hat{\delta}(q, w)$ denotes the unique state reached in A by reading w from state q. Consider the ω-word $w_0 = b^\omega$. Since $w_0 \in L$ and $L \subseteq \mathcal{L}_\omega(A)$, the run of A on w_0 is accepting, and so $\hat{\delta}(q_0, u_0) \in F$ for some finite prefix u_0 of w_0. Let $w_1 = u_0 a b^\omega$. We have $w_1 \in L$, and so by $L \subseteq \mathcal{L}_\omega(A)$, the run of A on w_1 is accepting, which implies $\hat{\delta}(q_0, u_0 a u_1) \in F$ for some finite prefix $u_0 a u_1$ of w_1. In a similar fashion, we continue constructing finite words u_i such that $\hat{\delta}(q_0, u_0 a u_1 a \cdots a u_i) \in F$. Since Q is finite, there are indices $0 \leq i < j$ such that $\hat{\delta}(q_0, u_0 a \cdots u_i) = \hat{\delta}(q_0, u_0 a \cdots u_i a \cdots u_j)$. It follows that A has an accepting run on the ω-word

$$u_0 a \cdots u_i (a u_{i+1} \cdots a u_j)^\omega.$$

Since a occurs infinitely often in this ω-word, it does not belong to L. Thus, $L \neq \mathcal{L}_\omega(A)$, and we are done. $\square$

Since DBA are strictly less expressive than NBA, Büchi automata do not form an ω-trinity. Indeed, as depicted in figure 10.6, all arrows leading to DBA are missing. So, the quest for an ω-trinity goes on.

10.2.3   Co-Büchi automata

Recall that a run of a Büchi automaton is accepting if it visits a distinguished set F of states infinitely often. Intuitively, visiting a state of F is a good thing for you, like, say, going for a jog, and to be accepted you have to go for a jog again and again. We introduce co-Büchi

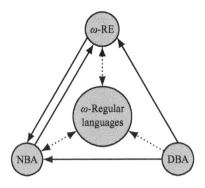

Figure 10.6
Relations between ω-regular expressions, NBAs, and DBAs. An arrow from X to Y means "for every X there is an equivalent Y."

automata, where a run is accepting if it visits the set F only *finitely* often. The intuition is now the opposite; visiting a state of F is a bad thing for you, like smoking a cigarette, and to be accepted, you must eventually quit.

Definition 10.11 *Let $S = (Q, \Sigma, \delta, Q_0)$ be a semi-automaton. An acceptance condition $\alpha: 2^Q \to \{0, 1\}$ is a* co-Büchi condition *if there exists a set $F \subseteq Q$ of states such that $\alpha(Q') = 1$ iff $Q' \cap F = \emptyset$. Abusing language, we speak of the co-Büchi condition F.*

A nondeterministic co-Büchi automaton *(NCA) is a pair $A = (S, F)$, where $F \subseteq Q$ is a co-Büchi acceptance condition. We refer to a deterministic NCA as a DCA.*

Observe that a run of an NCA is accepting iff it is not accepting as run of an NBA with the same set F. (This is the reason for the name "co-Büchi.") Intuitively, if new research would prove that jogging is actually bad for you, then the runs that were accepting before would become nonaccepting and vice versa. In particular, the language recognized by a DCA $A = (S, F)$ is the complement of the language recognized by the DBA $A = (S, F)$. (Notice that this holds only for *deterministic* automata!)

Example 10.12 Consider the automata on the top of figure 10.3, but this time as co-Büchi automata. A run of the NCA on the top left is accepting iff it stays in the left state forever. So, the NCA recognizes all ω-words.

A run of the DCA on the top right is accepting iff it eventually stays in the right state forever. So, the automaton recognizes the set of all ω-words in which there is an occurrence of a with no later occurrence of b. This is indeed the complement of its language as a DBA—as should be the case, because the automaton is deterministic.

10.2.3.1 Equivalence of NCAs and DCAs

We show that co-Büchi automata can be determinized, i.e., that for every NCA, there is an equivalent DCA. Recall that for NFAs, this is achieved by means of the powerset construction (i.e., algorithm 1 of chapter 1). The following example shows that this approach no longer works.

Example 10.13 Consider the NCA depicted on the left of figure 10.7. It recognizes the set of all words containing finitely many occurrences of a.

The powerset construction yields the deterministic semi-automaton shown on the right of figure 10.7. We claim that no accepting condition on this semi-automaton, of any type,

Figure 10.7
An NCA (left) and the DCA arising from the powerset construction (right).

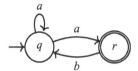

Figure 10.8
Running example for the determinization procedure.

recognizes the same language. Consider the ω-words $w = a^\omega$ and $w' = ab^\omega$, and let ρ, ρ' be the runs on w and w', respectively. Since $\inf(\rho)$ and $\inf(\rho')$ are equal (both are the singleton set containing only the state $\{q_0, q_1\}$), no acceptance condition can make ρ accepting and ρ' nonaccepting.

In the rest of the section, we show how to "enhance" the powerset construction. We fix an NCA $A = (Q, \Sigma, \delta, Q_0, F)$ with n states and construct an equivalent DCA B in three steps:

(a) We define a mapping dag that assigns to each $w \in \Sigma^\omega$ a directed acyclic graph (dag for short), which we denote $dag(w)$.

(b) We define the *breakpoints* of a dag and prove that an ω-word w is accepted by A iff $dag(w)$ contains only finitely many breakpoints.

(c) We construct a DCA B that accepts w iff $dag(w)$ contains finitely many breakpoints.

We use the NCA of figure 10.8 as running example.

The mapping *dag*. Intuitively, $dag(w)$ is the result of "bundling together" all runs of A on the ω-word w. Figure 10.9 shows the initial parts of $dag(aba^\omega)$ and $dag((ab)^\omega)$.

Formally, the directed acyclic graph $dag(w)$ for the ω-word $w = a_0 a_1 \cdots$ is a labeled directed graph whose nodes are elements of $Q \times \mathbb{N}$ and whose edges are labeled by letters of Σ. The graph is inductively defined as follows:

- $dag(w)$ contains a node $\langle q, 0 \rangle$ for every initial state $q \in Q_0$;
- if $dag(w)$ contains a node $\langle q, i \rangle$ and $q' \in \delta(q, a_i)$, then $dag(w)$ also contains a node $\langle q', i+1 \rangle$ and an edge $\langle q, i \rangle \xrightarrow{a_i} \langle q', i+1 \rangle$; and
- $dag(w)$ contains no other nodes or edges.

Clearly, $q_0 \xrightarrow{\sigma_1} q_1 \xrightarrow{\sigma_2} \cdots$ is a run of A iff $\langle q_0, 0 \rangle \xrightarrow{\sigma_1} \langle q_1, 1 \rangle \xrightarrow{\sigma_2} \cdots$ is an infinite path of $dag(w)$. So A accepts w iff some infinite path of $dag(w)$ visits states of F only finitely often.

We partition the nodes of $dag(w)$ into *levels*, with the ith level containing all nodes of $dag(w)$ of the form $\langle q, i \rangle$. One could be tempted to think that the acceptance condition "some infinite path of $dag(w)$ visits states of F only finitely often" is equivalent to "only finitely many levels of $dag(w)$ contain states of F," but $dag(aba^\omega)$ shows this is false: even

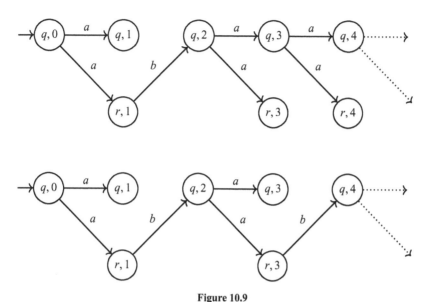

Figure 10.9
Fragments of $dag(aba^\omega)$ and $dag((ab)^\omega)$. For clarity, we write q, i instead of $\langle q, i \rangle$.

though all paths of $dag(aba^\omega)$ visit states of F only finitely often, infinitely many levels (in fact, all levels $i \geq 3$) contain states of F. For this reason, we introduce the set of *breakpoint levels* of the graph $dag(w)$, inductively defined as follows:

- The 0th level of $dag(w)$ is a breakpoint.
- If level ℓ is a breakpoint, then the next nonempty level $\ell' > \ell$ such that *every* path between nodes of ℓ and ℓ' visits a state of F at level $\ell + 1$, or at level $\ell + 2, \ldots,$ or at level ℓ' is also a breakpoint.

We claim that "some infinite path of $dag(w)$ visits states of F only finitely often" is equivalent to "the set of breakpoint levels of $dag(w)$ is finite." The argument uses a simple version of König's lemma:

Lemma 10.14 *Let v_0 be a node of a dag G, and let $Reach(v_0)$ be the set of nodes of G reachable from v_0. If $Reach(v_0)$ is infinite but every node of $Reach(v_0)$ has only finitely many successors, then G has an infinite path starting at v_0.*

Proof For every $i \geq 1$, let v_i be a successor of v_{i-1} such that $Reach(v_i)$ is infinite. The conditions of the lemma guarantee that v_i exists. Therefore, $v_0 v_1 v_2 \cdots$ is an infinite path.

□

Let us now prove the claim. If the set of breakpoints is infinite, then in particular, $dag(w)$ has infinitely many nodes and, by lemma 10.14, contains at least an infinite path. Moreover, by the definition of a breakpoint, this path visits states of F infinitely often. If the set of breakpoint levels is finite, let i be the last breakpoint. If $dag(w)$ is finite, then there are no infinite paths, and we are done. If $dag(w)$ is infinite, then for every $j > i$, there is a path π_j from level i to level j that does not visit any state of F. The paths $\{\pi_j\}_{j>i}$, put together, form an acyclic subgraph of $dag(w)$, in which every node has only finitely many successors. By lemma 10.14, this subgraph contains an infinite path that never visits any state of F, and the claim is proved.

If we were able to tell that a level is a breakpoint by just examining it, without inspecting the previous levels, we could construct a DCA as follows: take the set of all possible levels as states, the possible transitions between levels as transitions, and the breakpoints as accepting states. The run of this DCA on an ω-word w would be an encoding of $dag(w)$, and it would be accepting iff $dag(w)$ contains only finitely many breakpoints, as required by the co-Büchi acceptance condition. However, since levels are just sets of states, this corresponds to applying the powerset construction used in chapter 1 to determinize NFAs, just with a different acceptance condition, and we have already seen in example 10.13 that such an approach cannot work. Intuitively, whether a level is a breakpoint or not cannot be decided with only the information contained in the level.

The solution is to put additional information in the states. We take for the states of the DCA pairs $[P, O]$, where $O \subseteq P \subseteq Q$, with the following intended meaning: P is the set of states of a level, and $q \in O$ iff q is the endpoint of some path starting at the last breakpoint that has not yet visited any state of F. We call O the set of *owing* states—states for which some path "owes" a visit to F. The breakpoints correspond to the state $[P, O]$ such that $O = \emptyset$. To ensure that O has this intended meaning, we define the DCA $B = (\tilde{Q}, \Sigma, \tilde{\delta}, \tilde{q}_0, \tilde{F})$ as follows:

- The initial state $\tilde{q}_0$ is the pair $[Q_0, \emptyset]$. (Intuitively, there is no breakpoint before level 0, and so no paths from that breakpoint to level 0.)
- The transition relation is given by $\tilde{\delta}([P, O], a) = [P', O']$, where $P' = \delta(P, a)$, and
    - if $O \neq \emptyset$, then $O' = \delta(O, a) \setminus F$, and
    - if $O = \emptyset$ (i.e., if the current level is a breakpoint, and the automaton must start searching for the next one), then $O' = \delta(P, a) \setminus F$; in other words, all states of the next level that do not belong to F become owing.
- The states of $\tilde{F}$ are those at which a breakpoint is reached because there are no owing states, that is, $[P, O] \in \tilde{F}$ iff $O = \emptyset$.

With this definition, a run is accepting iff it contains finitely many breakpoints. The procedure for the construction is formalized in algorithm 45.

Figure 10.10 shows our running example at the top and the result of applying *NCAtoDCA* on the bottom left. The DCA on the bottom right is the result of applying the powerset construction, which is not equivalent to the NCA at the top. In particular, it accepts b^ω, which is rejected by the NCA, because it has no run on it, and it rejects a^ω, which is accepted by the NCA.

Algorithm 45 Algorithm to convert an NCA into a DCA.

NCAtoDCA(A)

Input: NCA $A = (Q, \Sigma, \delta, Q_0, F)$

Output: DCA $B = (\tilde{Q}, \Sigma, \tilde{\delta}, \tilde{q}_0, \tilde{F})$ with $\mathcal{L}_\omega(A) = \mathcal{L}_\omega(B)$

1   $\tilde{Q}, \tilde{\delta}, \tilde{F} \leftarrow \emptyset$; $\tilde{q}_0 \leftarrow [Q_0, \emptyset]$

2   $W \leftarrow \{\tilde{q}_0\}$

3   **while** $W \neq \emptyset$ **do**

4   **pick** $[P, O]$ **from** W; **add** $[P, O]$ **to** $\tilde{Q}$

5   **if** $O = \emptyset$ **then add** $[P, O]$ **to** $\tilde{F}$

6   **for all** $a \in \Sigma$ **do**

7         $P' = \delta(P, a)$

8   **if** $O \neq \emptyset$ **then** $O' \leftarrow \delta(O, a) \setminus F$ **else** $O' \leftarrow P' \setminus F$

9   **add** $([P, O], a, [P', O'])$ **to** $\tilde{\delta}$

10   **if** $[P', O'] \notin \tilde{Q}$ **then add** $[P', Q']$ **to** W

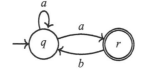

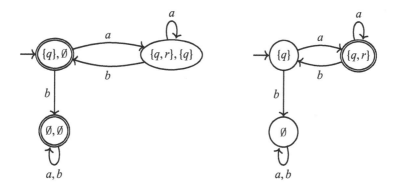

Figure 10.10
NCA of figure 10.8 (top), output of *NCAtoDCA* (bottom left), and result of applying the powerset construction (bottom right).

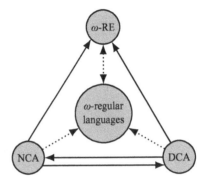

Figure 10.11
Relations between ω-regular expressions, NCAs, and DCAs. An arrow from X to Y means "for every X there is an equivalent Y."

For the complexity, observe that the number of states of the DCA is bounded by the number of pairs $[P, O]$ such that $O \subseteq P \subseteq Q$. For every state $q \in Q$, there are three mutually exclusive possibilities: $q \in O$, $q \in P \setminus O$, and $q \in Q \setminus P$. Thus, if A has n states, then B has at most 3^n states.

10.2.3.2   Nonequivalence of NCAs and ω-Regular Expressions

The following proposition shows that, unfortunately, co-Büchi automata do not recognize all ω-regular languages.[1]

Proposition 10.15   *The language denoted by $(b^*a)^\omega$ is not recognized by any NCA.*

Proof   Assume some NCA recognizes $L = \mathcal{L}_\omega((b^*a)^\omega)$. Since every NCA can be determinized, some DCA A recognizes L. Look at A as a DBA. The DBA A recognizes the complement of L: indeed, a word w is recognized by the DBA A iff the run of A on w visits states of F infinitely often iff w is not recognized by the DCA A. But the complement of L is $\mathcal{L}_\omega((a+b)^*b^\omega)$, and so by proposition 10.10, it is not recognized by any DBA. We have reached a contradiction, which proves the claim. $\square$

So, the trinity diagram for co-Büchi automata, depicted in figure 10.11, is missing the arrows from the ω-regular expressions and the ω-regular languages to NCAs and DCAs. The quest for an ω-trinity goes on.

10.2.4   Rabin Automata

The Büchi and co-Büchi conditions require that a distinguished set of states is visited infinitely and only finitely often, respectively. Rabin conditions generalize both.

---

1. Every language recognized by a co-Büchi automaton is ω-regular, a fact that will be proved in the next section for a more general type of ω-automata. Together with proposition 10.15, we obtain that NCAs are strictly less expressive than NBAs, a counterintuitive fact.

Definition 10.16   *Let $S = (Q, \Sigma, \delta, Q_0)$ be a semi-automaton. A* Rabin pair *is a pair $\langle F, G \rangle$ of sets of states (i.e., $F, G \subseteq Q$). An acceptance condition $\alpha : 2^Q \rightarrow \{0, 1\}$ is a* Rabin condi-*tion if there exists a set $\mathcal{R}$ of Rabin pairs such that $\alpha(Q') = 1$ iff $Q' \cap F \neq \emptyset$ and $Q' \cap G = \emptyset$ for some $\langle F, G \rangle \in \mathcal{R}$. Abusing language, we speak of the Rabin condition $\mathcal{R}$.*

A nondeterministic Rabin automaton *(NRA) is a pair $A = (S, \mathcal{R})$, where $\mathcal{R} \subseteq 2^Q \times 2^Q$ is a Rabin acceptance condition.*

In words, a run of a Rabin automaton with acceptance condition $\mathcal{R}$ is accepting if it visits F infinitely often and G finitely often for some Rabin pair $\langle F, G \rangle \in \mathcal{R}$. Given a semi-automaton with Q as set of states, the following holds:

- A Büchi condition F is equivalent to the Rabin acceptance condition $\mathcal{R} = \{\langle F, \emptyset \rangle\}$. Indeed, the condition requiring that states of the empty set are visited finitely often is vacuously true.

- A co-Büchi acceptance condition G is equivalent to the Rabin acceptance condition $\mathcal{R} = \{\langle Q, G \rangle\}$. Indeed, the condition that Q is visited infinitely often is vacuously true, since runs are infinite sequences of states of Q.

10.2.4.1   Equivalence of NRAs and ω-Regular Expressions
We show that for every NBA, there is an equivalent NRA and vice versa. Since NBAs are as expressive as ω-regular expressions, it follows that NRAs and ω-regular expressions have the same expressive power.

NBA → NRA.   As argued above, given an NBA $A = (Q, \Sigma, \delta, Q_0, F)$, then the NRA $B = (Q, \Sigma, \delta, Q_0, \{\langle F, \emptyset \rangle\})$ satisfies $\mathcal{L}_\omega(A) = \mathcal{L}_\omega(B)$.

NRA → NBA.   Let $A = (S, \mathcal{R})$ be an NRA. We consider first the case in which $\mathcal{R}$ contains a single Rabin pair $\langle F, G \rangle$ and construct an equivalent NBA B. Since an accepting run ρ of A satisfies $\inf(\rho) \cap G = \emptyset$, from some point on, ρ only visits states of $Q \setminus G$. So, ρ consists of an initial finite part, say ρ^0, that may visit all states, and an infinite part, say ρ^1, that only visits states of $Q \setminus G$. Further, since ρ visits F infinitely often, we can assume that the last state of ρ_0 belongs to $(Q \setminus G) \cap F$. Thus, we construct the NBA B as follows:

- Put two copies S^0 and S^1 of S "side by side." The first copy S^0 is a full copy, containing all states and transitions of A, and S^1 is a partial copy, containing only the states of $Q \setminus G$ and the transitions between them (see figure 10.12). Let q^0 denote the copy of state $q \in Q$ in S^0 and q^1 the copy of state $q \in Q \setminus G$ in S^1.
- Add transitions that "jump" from S^0 to S^1. For every transition $q^0 \overset{a}{\rightarrow} r^0$ of S^0 such that $q \in (Q \setminus G) \cap F$ and $r \in Q \setminus G$, add a transition $q^0 \overset{a}{\rightarrow} r^1$ that "jumps" to r^1, the "twin state" of r^0 in S^1 (dashed colored transitions in figure 10.12). Intuitively, B simulates ρ by executing the finite prefix ρ^0 in A^0, then jumping to S^1, and executing ρ^1 there.
- Choose the Büchi condition of B as $F_B = \{q^1 : q \in (Q \setminus G) \cap F\}$ (recall that F is the first component of the Rabin pair of A). This choice guarantees that an accepting run of B

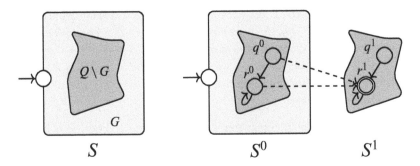

Figure 10.12
Sketch of the conversion NRA $\rightarrow$ NBA, where the given NRA has only one Rabin pair $\langle F, G \rangle$. Observe that q^0 and r^0 belong to F, but they are not accepting states of the resulting NBA.

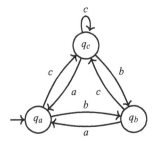

Figure 10.13
Semi-automaton of a Rabin automaton.

eventually "jumps" to S^1, leaving S^0 forever, and thus ensuring that states of G are visited only finitely often and that the run visits F infinitely often after the jump.

Now, consider the general case in which $\mathcal{R} = \{\langle F_1, G_1 \rangle, \ldots, \langle F_m, G_m \rangle\}$. We put $m + 1$ copies of S side by side. The first copy S^0 is a full copy, containing all states and transitions of A, and S^i for $1 \leq i \leq m$ is a partial copy, containing only the states of $Q \setminus G_i$ and the transitions between them. The set of accepting states is $F_B = \bigcup_{i=1}^m \{q^i : q \in F_i\}$. For each S^i, we define jump transitions from S^0 to S^i as before. Since the copies $S^1, \ldots, S^m$ are disjoint, a run of B is accepting iff it eventually jumps from S^0 to S^i for some $1 \leq i \leq m$ and then visits the states of F_i infinitely often. It follows that $\mathcal{L}_\omega(A) = \mathcal{L}_\omega(B)$.

Example 10.17   Consider the Rabin automaton $A = (S, \mathcal{R})$, where the semi-automaton S is depicted in figure 10.13, and $\mathcal{R} = \{\langle \boldsymbol{a}, \boldsymbol{b} \rangle, \langle \boldsymbol{b}, \boldsymbol{a} \rangle\}$, with $\boldsymbol{a} := \{q_a\}$ and $\boldsymbol{b} := \{q_b\}$.

The accepting runs are those visiting $\boldsymbol{a}$ infinitely often and $\boldsymbol{b}$ finitely often or vice versa. The procedure above converts A into the NBA of figure 10.14.

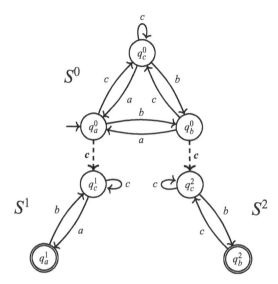

Figure 10.14
Conversion of A into an NBA.

The NBA consists of a full copy S^0 of S, plus two partial copies S^1 and S^2, having (copies of) $Q \setminus b = \{q_a, q_c\}$ and $Q \setminus a = \{q_b, q_c\}$ as sets of states, respectively. The "jumps," dashed and colored in figure 10.14, connect S^0 to S^1 and S^2. Jumps into S^1 must leave S^0 from a, the set of states that must be visited infinitely often in the first Rabin pair, so only the jump from q_a^0 to q_c^1 is possible. Similarly, the only jump to S^2 goes from q_b^0 to q_c^2.

Complexity. Given an NRA $A = (S, \mathcal{F})$, with n states and m Rabin pairs, each of the copies $S^0, S^1, \ldots, S^m$ has at most n states, and so the NBA B has at most $n(m+1)$ states.

10.2.4.2 Equivalence of NRAs and DRAs
Rabin automata can be determinized, and so deterministic Rabin automata recognize all ω-regular languages. The proof of this result goes beyond the scope of this book and is omitted (see the bibliographical remarks).

Theorem 10.18 *An NRA with n states can be effectively transformed into a DRA with $n^{\mathcal{O}(n)}$ states. Moreover, there exists a family $\{L_n\}_{n \geq 2}$ of languages recognizable by NRAs with $\mathcal{O}(n)$ states such that every equivalent DRA has at least n! states.*

In particular, the DRA with the semi-automaton shown in figure 10.15 and a Rabin condition with a single Rabin pair $\langle \{r\}, \{q\} \rangle$ recognizes the language $L = (a + b)^* b^{\omega}$, which, as shown in proposition 10.10, is not recognized by any DBA.

Theorem 10.18 also shows that determinization of NRAs is strictly more expensive than determinization of NFAs but only by a $\log n$-factor in the exponent. Indeed, in the

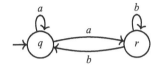

Figure 10.15
A semi-automaton.

conversion NFA → DFA, the number of states goes from n to $\mathcal{O}(2^n)$ and, in the conversion NRA → DRA, from n to $n^{\mathcal{O}(n)} = 2^{\mathcal{O}(n \log n)}$.

10.3   Beyond ω-Trinities

The results of section 10.2.4 show that ω-regular expressions, NRAs, and DRAs constitute an ω-trinity, as depicted in figure 10.16.

Moreover, the blowup induced by the conversions is in all cases comparable to the blowup for NFAs: the conversions from regular expressions to NFAs and from ω-regular expressions to NRA are polynomial, and the conversion from NRA to DRA has single exponential blowup, albeit with exponent $\mathcal{O}(n \log n)$ instead of n.

However, the finite word trinity also has further properties. In section 3.1 of chapter 3, we showed that all boolean operations can be easily implemented on DFAs. In particular:

- DFAs can be complemented in linear time without changing the semi-automaton; it suffices to take another acceptance condition of the same type (change the set of final states from F to $Q \setminus F$, maintaining that a run is accepting if its last state is final).

- Union and intersection can be implemented uniformly for DFAs using the pairing operation. More precisely, given two DFAs A_1, A_2, there exist two DFAs recognizing $\mathcal{L}(A_1) \cup \mathcal{L}(A_2)$ and $\mathcal{L}(A_1) \cap \mathcal{L}(A_2)$ whose semi-automata are identical and equal to the pairing $[A_1, A_2]$ (see definition 3.1 in chapter 3). The DFAs only differ on their sets of final states.

Is there an ω-trinity that also satisfies these properties? We examine this question. In section 10.3.1, we show that Rabin automata satisfy the property for union but not for intersection or complement. In sections 10.3.2 and 10.3.3, we introduce two further automata types, Streett and parity automata, that "restore the symmetry": Streett automata satisfy the property for intersection, but not for union or complement, and parity automata satisfy the property for complementation, but not for union or intersection. Finally, in section 10.3.4, we conclude our tour of automata types by introducing Muller automata; they satisfy all three properties but, as we shall see, at a high price.

Remark 10.19   In the rest of this section, we describe several constructions that do not necessarily produce automata in normal form, that is, automata such that every state is

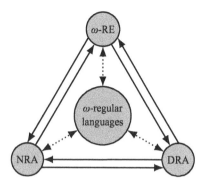

Figure 10.16
Trinity of ω-regular languages through Rabin automata. An arrow from X to Y means "for every X there is an equivalent Y."

reachable from some initial state. In all cases, this can be remedied by starting from the initial states, constructing iteratively only the successors of the states constructed so far.

10.3.1   Rabin Automata, Again

We analyze the complexity of union, intersection, and complementation for DRAs. We show that union can be implemented using pairing, but intersection cannot. Further, complementation cannot be implemented without changing the semi-automaton.

Union.   Given two DRAs $A_1 = (S_1, \mathcal{F}_1)$ and $A_2 = (S_2, \mathcal{F}_2)$, we construct a DRA $A_1 \cup A_2$ such that $\mathcal{L}_\omega(A_1 \cup A_2) = \mathcal{L}_\omega(A_1) \cup \mathcal{L}_\omega(A_2)$. The DRA has the pairing $[S_1, S_2]$ as semi-automaton (see definition 3.1 from chapter 3) and the following set of $\mathcal{F}$ of Rabin pairs as acceptance condition:

$$\mathcal{F} = \{\langle F_1 \times Q_2, G_1 \times Q_2 \rangle : \langle F_1, G_1 \rangle \in \mathcal{F}_1\} \cup$$

$$\{\langle Q_1 \times F_2, Q_1 \times G_2 \rangle : \langle F_2, G_2 \rangle \in \mathcal{F}_2\}.$$

To see why $\mathcal{L}_\omega(A_1 \cup A_2) = \mathcal{L}_\omega(A_1) \cup \mathcal{L}_\omega(A_2)$ holds, consider the case in which $\mathcal{F}_1 = \{\langle F_1, G_1 \rangle\}$ and $\mathcal{F}_2 = \{\langle F_2, G_2 \rangle\}$, and so $\mathcal{F} = \{\langle F_1 \times Q_2, G_1 \times Q_2 \rangle, \langle Q_1 \times F_2, Q_1 \times G_2 \rangle\}$ (the general case is analogous). Recall that if the runs of S_1 and S_2 on an ω-word $w = a_1 a_2 \cdots$ are

$$\rho_1 = q_{01} \xrightarrow{a_1} q_{11} \xrightarrow{a_2} \cdots \xrightarrow{a_i} q_{i1} \xrightarrow{a_{i+1}} \cdots$$

$$\rho_2 = q_{02} \xrightarrow{a_1} q_{12} \xrightarrow{a_2} \cdots \xrightarrow{a_i} q_{i2} \xrightarrow{a_{i+1}} \cdots$$

then the run of $[S_1, S_2]$ on w is

$$\rho = \begin{bmatrix} q_{01} \\ q_{02} \end{bmatrix} \xrightarrow{a_1} \begin{bmatrix} q_{11} \\ q_{12} \end{bmatrix} \xrightarrow{a_2} \cdots \xrightarrow{a_i} \begin{bmatrix} q_{i1} \\ q_{i2} \end{bmatrix} \xrightarrow{a_{i+1}} \cdots$$

and vice versa. Let $\inf(\rho)$ be the set of states of $[S_1, S_2]$ that appear infinitely often in ρ. We get:

$$w \in \mathcal{L}_\omega(A_1) \cup \mathcal{L}_\omega(A_2)$$

iff $\inf(\rho_1) \cap F_1 \neq \emptyset$ and $\inf(\rho_1) \cap G_1 = \emptyset$
or
$\inf(\rho_2) \cap F_2 \neq \emptyset$ and $\inf(\rho_2) \cap G_2 = \emptyset$

iff $\inf(\rho) \cap (F_1 \times Q_2) \neq \emptyset$ and $\inf(\rho) \cap (G_1 \times Q_2) = \emptyset$
or
$\inf(\rho) \cap (Q_1 \times F_2) \neq \emptyset$ and $\inf(\rho) \cap (Q_1 \times G_2) = \emptyset$

iff ρ satisfies the Rabin acceptance condition
$\{\langle F_1 \times Q_2, G_1 \times Q_2 \rangle, \langle Q_1 \times F_2, Q_1 \times G_2 \rangle\}$

iff $w \in \mathcal{L}_\omega(A_1 \cup A_2)$.

Observe that this last argument fails if we replace "or" by "and." Indeed, a run satisfies a Rabin condition $\{\langle F, G \rangle, \langle F', G' \rangle\}$ iff it satisfies $\{\langle F, G \rangle\}$ *or* $\{\langle F', G' \rangle\}$, not $\{\langle F, G \rangle\}$ *and* $\{\langle F', G' \rangle\}$.

Intersection and complement.   It is not difficult to find a DRA $A = (S, \mathcal{R})$ such that no Rabin condition over the semi-automaton S recognizes $\overline{\mathcal{L}_\omega(A)}$. For example, let S be the semi-automaton of figure 10.20 from example 10.26. It is easy to give a Rabin condition such that the resulting DRA recognizes the words containing finitely many as or finitely many bs, but, as shown in the example, no Rabin condition makes S recognize the words containing infinitely many as and infinitely many bs. Similarly, one can exhibit DRAs $A_1 = (S_1, \mathcal{R}_1)$ and $A_2 = (S_2, \mathcal{R}_2)$ such that no Rabin condition on the semi-automaton $[S_1, S_2]$ recognizes $\mathcal{L}_\omega(A_1) \cap \mathcal{L}_\omega(A_2)$. It is even the case that the smallest semi-automata for these languages may be exponentially larger than the original ones. We state these results without proof (see the bibliographical remarks).[2]

Proposition 10.20   *There exists a family $\{A_n, B_n\}_{n \geq 1}$ of pairs of DRAs with $\mathcal{O}(n)$ states and $\mathcal{O}(n)$ Rabin pairs such that every DRA recognizing $\mathcal{L}_\omega(A_n) \cap \mathcal{L}_\omega(B_n)$ has $\Theta(2^n)$ states.*

Proposition 10.21   *There exists a family $\{A_n\}_{n \geq 1}$ of DRAs with $\mathcal{O}(n)$ states and $\mathcal{O}(n)$ Rabin pairs such that every DRA recognizing $\overline{\mathcal{L}_\omega(A_n)}$ has at least $n!$ states.*

Thus, DRAs behave "asymmetrically" with respect to union and intersection. We introduce *Streett automata*, which also behave "asymmetrically" but exchanging the roles of union and intersection.

_____

2. Actually, the interested reader can find a proof of proposition 10.21 as proposition 11.10 of chapter 11.

10.3.2 Streett Automata

As for Rabin automata, the acceptance condition of Streett automata (NSA) consists of a collection $\mathcal{F} = \{\langle F_1, G_1 \rangle, \ldots, \langle F_m, G_m \rangle\}$ of *Streett pairs*.

Definition 10.22 *Let* $S = (Q, \Sigma, \delta, Q_0)$ *be a semi-automaton. A* Streett pair *is a pair* $\langle F, G \rangle$ *of sets of states, that is,* $F, G \subseteq Q$. *An acceptance condition* $\alpha \colon 2^Q \to \{0, 1\}$ *is a* Streett condition *if there exists a set* St *of Streett pairs such* $\alpha(Q') = 1$ *iff* $Q' \cap F = \emptyset$ *or* $Q' \cap G \neq \emptyset$ *holds for every* $\langle F, G \rangle \in St$.

A nondeterministic Streett automaton *(NSA) is a pair* $A = (S, St)$, *where* $St \subseteq 2^Q \times 2^Q$ *is a Streett acceptance condition.*

In words, a run of an NSA is accepting if it visits F finitely often or G infinitely often for every Streett pair $\langle F, G \rangle \in St$.

Streett automata could also be called co-Rabin automata. Let us see why. Recall that a run of a DBA A is accepting if it is a rejecting run of the DCA A (i.e., of the same automaton, but with a co-Büchi instead of a Büchi condition) and vice versa. The same holds for Rabin and Streett automata. Indeed, let $\mathcal{F}$ be a set of pairs of the form $\langle F, G \rangle$ for $F, G \subseteq Q$. We have:

$$\rho \text{ is a rejecting run of the DSA } A = (S, \mathcal{F})$$
$$\text{iff} \quad \neg \forall \langle F, G \rangle \in \mathcal{F} \colon \inf(\rho) \cap F = \emptyset \text{ or } \inf(\rho) \cap G \neq \emptyset$$
$$\text{iff} \quad \exists \langle F, G \rangle \in \mathcal{F} \colon \inf(\rho) \cap F \neq \emptyset \text{ and } \inf(\rho) \cap G = \emptyset$$
$$\text{iff} \quad \rho \text{ is an accepting run of the DRA } A = (S, \mathcal{F}).$$

In other words, if we let $\mathcal{L}^R_\omega(A)$ and $\mathcal{L}^S_\omega(A)$ be the languages of a deterministic automaton A when $\mathcal{F}$ is interpreted as a Rabin and as a Streett condition, respectively, then $\mathcal{L}^S_\omega(A) = \overline{\mathcal{L}^R_\omega(A)}$.

10.3.2.1 Equivalence of NSAs and ω-Regular Expressions

We show that for every NBA, there is an equivalent NSA and vice versa, which shows that NSAs are equivalent to ω-regular expressions.

NBA $\to$ NSA. Given an NBA $A = (S, F)$, the NSA $B = (S, \{\langle Q, F \rangle\})$, where Q is the set of states of S, satisfies $\mathcal{L}_\omega(A) = \mathcal{L}_\omega(B)$. Indeed, a run of B is accepting iff $\inf(\rho) \cap Q = \emptyset$ or $\inf(\rho) \cap F \neq \emptyset$. Since every run visits at least one state infinitely often, this is the case iff $\inf(\rho) \cap F \neq \emptyset$.

NSA $\to$ NBA. This conversion requires some more work and involves an exponential blowup. Let $A = (S, St)$ be an NSA. For every $I \subseteq St$, define $\bar{I} = St \setminus I$ and $F_I = \bigcup_{\langle F, G \rangle \in I} F$. Applying the definition of the Streett condition and standard rules of propositional logic, we obtain the following for every run ρ of A:

ρ is accepting

$$\Longleftrightarrow \bigwedge_{\langle F, G\rangle \subseteq St} (\inf(\rho) \cap F = \emptyset \vee \inf(\rho) \cap G \neq \emptyset)$$

$$\Longleftrightarrow \bigvee_{I \subseteq St} \left(\left(\bigwedge_{\langle F, G\rangle \in I} \inf(\rho) \cap F = \emptyset \right) \wedge \left(\bigwedge_{\langle F, G\rangle \in \bar{I}} \inf(\rho) \cap G \neq \emptyset \right) \right)$$

$$\Longleftrightarrow \bigvee_{I \subseteq St} \left(\inf(\rho) \cap \left(\bigcup_{\langle F, G\rangle \in I} F \right) = \emptyset \wedge \left(\bigwedge_{\langle F, G\rangle \in \bar{I}} \inf(\rho) \cap G \neq \emptyset \right) \right)$$

$$\Longleftrightarrow \bigvee_{I \subseteq St} \left(\inf(\rho) \cap F_I = \emptyset \wedge \left(\bigwedge_{\langle F, G\rangle \in \bar{I}} \inf(\rho) \cap G \neq \emptyset \right) \right) \tag{10.1}$$

We consider first the case in which the disjunction over the subsets of St consists of a single disjunct. (More precisely, the case in which all disjuncts, but the one for a certain subset I, are vacuously false, and so they can be removed from the condition.) We then consider the general case.

We assume that $\bar{I} = \{\langle F_0, G_0\rangle, \ldots, \langle F_k, G_k\rangle\}$ for some $k \geq 0$; in particular, $\bar{I}$ is nonempty. (This can be done without loss of generality: if $\bar{I} = \emptyset$, we can equivalently set $\bar{I} = \{\langle \emptyset, Q\rangle\}$, because every run ρ satisfies $\inf(\rho) \cap \emptyset = \emptyset \wedge \inf(\rho) \cap Q \neq \emptyset$.) Let L_I be the language of all words for which there is a run ρ of A satisfying (10.1) for I. We construct an NBA B recognizing L_I in two steps.

Construction of B, first step. The first step repeats a construction we already presented in the conversion NRA $\to$ NBA. Let us recall it. Every run ρ satisfying $\inf(\rho) \cap F_I = \emptyset$ and $\inf(\rho) \cap G \neq \emptyset$ for every $\langle F, G\rangle \in \bar{I}$ reaches a point after which the run only visits states of $Q \setminus F_I$. So, ρ consists of an initial finite part, say ρ^0, that may visit all states, followed by an infinite part, say ρ^1, that only visits states of $Q \setminus F_I$. Further, if $\bar{I} \neq \emptyset$, then we can assume that the last state visited by ρ^0 belongs to G_0. We construct a semi-automaton S_I as follows:

- Put two copies S^0 and S^1 of S "side by side" (figure 10.17 illustrates a case in which $\bar{I}$ contains three Streett pairs with second components G_0, G_1, and G_2). The copy S^0 is a full copy, containing all states and transitions of S, and S^1 is a partial copy, containing only the states of $Q \setminus F_I$ and the transitions between them. Let q^0 denote the copy of state $q \in Q$ in S^0 and q^1 the copy of state $q \in Q \setminus F_I$ in S^1.
- Add transitions that "jump" from S^0 to S^1. For every transition $q \xrightarrow{a} r$ of S^0 such that $q \in G_0$ and $r \in Q \setminus F_I$, add a transition $q^0 \xrightarrow{a} r^1$. Intuitively, B simulates ρ by executing the finite prefix ρ^0 in S^0, then jumping to S^1, and executing ρ^1 there.

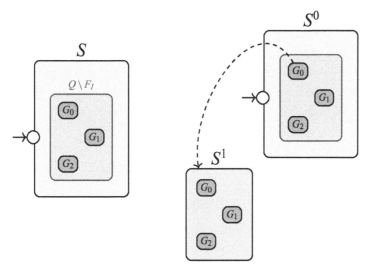

Figure 10.17
First step of the conversion NSA $\rightarrow$ NBA. The figure illustrates a special case in which G_0, G_1, and G_2 are pairwise disjoint and included in $Q \setminus F_I$.

Construction of B, second step. By definition of the semi-automaton S_I, the language L_I contains exactly the words on which S_I has a run $\rho^0 \rho^1$, where ρ^0 stays in S^0 and ρ^1 is a run of S^1 satisfying $\inf(\rho^1) \cap G \neq \emptyset$ for every $\langle F, G \rangle \in \bar{I}$. Thus, ρ^1 visits *all* of $G_0, \ldots, G_k$ infinitely often. The problem is that this condition is not of Büchi type. To solve this problem, we replace S^1 by another semi-automaton. Observe that a run ρ^1 visits each of $G_0, \ldots, G_k$ infinitely often iff the following two conditions hold:

(a) ρ^1 eventually visits G_0, and

(b) for all $0 \leq i < m$, every visit of ρ^1 to G_i is eventually followed by a later visit to $G_{i \oplus 1}$, where $\oplus$ denotes addition modulo k. (Between the visits to G_i and $G_{i \oplus 1}$, there can be arbitrarily many visits to other sets.)

This suggests replicating S^1 into k "copies" $S^1_0, \ldots, S^1_{k-1}$, but with a modification: the NBA "jumps" from the ith to the $(i \oplus 1)$th copy whenever it visits a state of G_i (see figure 10.18). More precisely, the transitions of the ith copy that leave a state of G_i are redirected to the $(i \oplus 1)$th copy. This way, visiting the accepting states of *each* copy infinitely often is equivalent to visiting the accepting states of the *first* copy infinitely often. The jumps from S to S^1 are adapted: instead of a jump $q^0 \xrightarrow{a} r^1$, we now have $q^0 \xrightarrow{a} r^1_0$. We take B as the NBA with this structure and G^0_1 as Büchi condition.

Formal definition of B. Formally, let $A = (Q, \Sigma, \delta, Q_0, \mathcal{S}t)$ be an NSA, let $I \subseteq \mathcal{S}t$, and let $F_I = \bigcup_{\langle F, G \rangle \in I} F$. Further, assume $\bar{I} = \{\langle F_0, G_0 \rangle, \ldots, \langle F_{k-1}, G_{k-1} \rangle\}$. The NBA B is defined

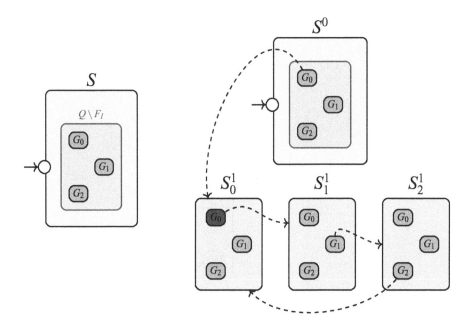

Figure 10.18
Second step of the conversion NSA → NBA, illustrating the replication of S^1.

as follows:

- *States:* $\{q^0 : q \in Q\} \cup \{q_0^1, \ldots, q_{k-1}^1 : q \in Q \setminus F_I\}$.
- *Transitions:* The set of transitions contains
  - (q^0, a, r^0) for all $(q, a, r) \in \delta$,
  - (q^0, a, r_0^1) for all $(q, a, r) \in \delta$ s.t. $q \in G_0$ and $r \in Q \setminus F_I$,
  - (q_i^1, a, r_i^1) for all $(q, a, r) \in \delta$ s.t. $q \in (Q \setminus F_I) \setminus G_i$ and $r \in Q \setminus F_I$, and
  - $(q_i^1, a, r_{i \oplus 1}^1)$ for all $(q, a, r) \in \delta$ s.t. $q \in (Q \setminus F_I) \cap G_i$ and $r \in Q \setminus F_I$.
- *Initial states:* $\{q^0 : q \in Q_0\}$.
- *Accepting states:* $\{q_0^1 : q \in G_0\}$.

This concludes the description of the construction when the disjunction (10.1) over the subsets of St only contains one disjunct. Now, consider the general case, with k such disjuncts for sets $I_1, \ldots, I_k \subseteq St$. We proceed again in two steps. In the first step, we take a full copy S^0 of S and partial copies $S^1, \ldots, S^k$, one for each of $I_1, \ldots, I_k$, constructed as in the previous case. For each I_j, we add jumps from S^0 to S^j, also as before. In the second step, each of the S^j is replicated, also as before. The forthcoming example 10.23 describes a case with two disjuncts.

Complexity. If A has n states and m Streett pairs, then the number of states of B_I is bounded by $n(m+1)$. Since there exist 2^m sets $I \subseteq \mathcal{F}$, the number of states of B is $\mathcal{O}(2^m nm)$.

Example 10.23 Consider again the automaton of example 10.17 with acceptance condition $\mathcal{S}t = \{\langle a, b \rangle, \langle b, a \rangle\}$, where $a = \{q_a\}$ and $b = \{q_b\}$, but this time interpreted as a Streett condition. The automaton accepts the ω-words containing finitely many as or infinitely many bs, and finitely many bs or infinitely many as, with no constraint on the number of cs. We construct an equivalent NBA. We have

ρ is accepting

iff $(\inf(\rho) \cap a = \emptyset \vee \inf(\rho) \cap b \neq \emptyset) \wedge (\inf(\rho) \cap b = \emptyset \vee \inf(\rho) \cap a \neq \emptyset)$

iff $(\inf(\rho) \cap a = \emptyset \wedge \inf(\rho) \cap b = \emptyset) \vee (\inf(\rho) \cap b \neq \emptyset \vee \inf(\rho) \cap a \neq \emptyset)$.

Note that we have removed "$(\inf(\rho) \cap a = \emptyset \wedge \inf(\rho) \cap a \neq \emptyset)$" and "$(\inf(\rho) \cap b = \emptyset \wedge \inf(\rho) \cap b \neq \emptyset)$" because they are equivalent to **false**.

Let S be the semi-automaton of the NSA. Intuitively, a run of the NBA stays in the full copy S^0 of S until it "decides" which of the two disjuncts it wants to satisfy, after which it "jumps" to another copy. Without loss of generality, we request that the run leaves S^0 from the set of states it must visit infinitely often according to the chosen disjunct; if there is more than one set, then we request it to leave from the first one. This yields the NBA of figure 10.19.

Consider the first disjunct: $(\inf(\rho) \cap a = \emptyset \wedge \inf(\rho) \cap b = \emptyset)$. A run satisfying it must eventually only visit q_c. So the copy S^1 of S only contains state q_c. Without loss of generality, we request that the run leaves S^0 from q_c, and so the only (colored dashed) jump leads from q_c^0 to q_c^1.

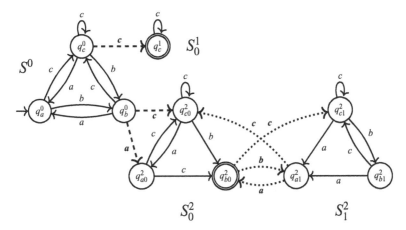

Figure 10.19
Büchi automaton obtained from a Streett automaton.

Consider now the second disjunct: $(\inf(\rho) \cap \boldsymbol{b} \neq \emptyset \wedge \inf(\rho) \cap \boldsymbol{a} \neq \emptyset)$. The disjunct does not require any state to be visited only finitely often, and so the NBA contains two full copies S_0^2 and S_1^2 of S. Intuitively, a run jumps from S^0 to S_1^1 when it "decides" to satisfy this disjunct and then stays in S_0^2 until it visits $\boldsymbol{b}$ and in S_1^2 until it visits $\boldsymbol{a}$. Jumps from S^0 to S_0^2 leave from $\boldsymbol{b}$; there are two of them, leading from q_b^0 to q_{a0}^2 and q_{c0}^2 (colored dashed transitions). Transitions of S_0^2 leaving from $\boldsymbol{b}$ "land" in S_1^2, and transitions of S_1^2 leaving from $\boldsymbol{a}$ "land" in S_0^2 (colored dotted transitions).

Intersection. As mentioned at the beginning of the section, a run of a DRA is accepting iff it is a rejecting run of the DSA with the same semi-automaton and acceptance condition, but of Streett type. It follows immediately that the construction shown in the previous section for union of DRAs is also a construction for intersection of DSAs. Let us see why. Given an automaton $A = (S, \mathcal{F})$, let $\mathcal{L}^R(A)$ and $\mathcal{L}^S(A)$ be its language as a Rabin and Streett automaton, respectively (i.e., interpreting the pairs of $\mathcal{F}$ as Rabin pairs, or as Streett pairs, respectively). Further, given two automata A_1, A_2, let $A_1 \cup A_2$ be the automaton defined in the previous section using the pairing construction. There, we proved $\mathcal{L}^R(A_1 \cup A_2) = \mathcal{L}^R(A_1) \cup \mathcal{L}^R(A_2)$. Now, we prove $\mathcal{L}^S(A_1 \cup A_2) = \mathcal{L}^S(A_1) \cap \mathcal{L}^S(A_2)$:

$$\mathcal{L}^S(A_1 \cup A_2) = \overline{\mathcal{L}^R(A_1 \cup A_2)} \qquad \text{(as } A_1 \text{ and } A_2 \text{ are deterministic)}$$

$$= \overline{\mathcal{L}^R(A_1) \cup \mathcal{L}^R(A_2)} \qquad \text{(by the previous section)}$$

$$= \overline{\mathcal{L}^R(A_1)} \cap \overline{\mathcal{L}^R(A_2)} \qquad \text{(by De Morgan's law)}$$

$$= \mathcal{L}^S(A_1) \cap \mathcal{L}^S(A_2) \qquad \text{(as } A_1 \text{ and } A_2 \text{ are deterministic).}$$

Union and complement. In the previous section, we saw that given two DRAs with $\mathcal{O}(n)$ states, the smallest DRA for the union of their languages can have $\Theta(2^n)$ states, and that given a DRA with $\mathcal{O}(n)$ states, the smallest DRA recognizing its complement language can have $n!$ states (proposition 10.20 and proposition 10.21). Using that a run of a DRA is accepting iff it is a rejecting run of the DSA with the same semi-automaton and acceptance condition, we obtain the same bounds for union and complementation of Streett automata.

10.3.3 Parity Automata

We now present an automata type for which complementation can be implemented without changing the semi-automaton, at the price of an exponential blowup for *both* union and intersection.

The acceptance condition of parity automata is a chain of sets of states.

Definition 10.24 *Let $S = (Q, \Sigma, \delta, Q_0)$ be a semi-automaton. An acceptance condition $\alpha: 2^Q \to \{0, 1\}$ is a parity condition if there exists a sequence $\mathcal{P} = (F_1, F_2, \ldots, F_{2m})$ of sets of states, where $F_1 \subseteq F_2 \subseteq \cdots \subseteq F_{2m} = Q$, such that $\alpha(Q') = 1$ iff the smallest index i*

satisfying $Q' \cap F_i \neq \emptyset$ is even. (Observe that i exists because $F_{2m} = Q$.) Abusing language, we speak of the parity condition $\mathcal{P}$.

A nondeterministic parity automaton *(NPA) is a pair $A = (S, \mathcal{P})$, where $\mathcal{P} \subseteq (2^Q)^*$ is a parity acceptance condition.*

At first sight, the parity condition looks very different from the Rabin or Streett conditions. We show that this is not the case. Note first that we can reformulate a parity condition $(F_1, F_2, \ldots, F_{2m})$ as follows: a run ρ is accepting iff

$$\inf(\rho) \cap F_1 = \emptyset \quad \text{and} \quad \inf(\rho) \cap F_2 \neq \emptyset,$$
$$\text{or} \quad \inf(\rho) \cap (F_1 \cup F_2 \cup F_3) = \emptyset \quad \text{and} \quad \inf(\rho) \cap F_4 \neq \emptyset,$$
$$\text{or} \qquad \qquad \cdots$$
$$\text{or} \quad \inf(\rho) \cap (F_1 \cup \cdots \cup F_{2m-1}) = \emptyset \quad \text{and} \quad \inf(\rho) \cap F_{2m} \neq \emptyset.$$

Since $F_1 \subseteq F_2 \subseteq \cdots F_{2m}$, the condition is equivalent to the following: a run ρ is accepting iff

$$\inf(\rho) \cap F_1 = \emptyset \quad \text{and} \quad \inf(\rho) \cap F_2 \neq \emptyset,$$
$$\text{or} \quad \inf(\rho) \cap F_3 = \emptyset \quad \text{and} \quad \inf(\rho) \cap F_4 \neq \emptyset,$$
$$\text{or} \qquad \qquad \cdots$$
$$\text{or} \quad \inf(\rho) \cap F_{2m-1} = \emptyset \quad \text{and} \quad \inf(\rho) \cap F_{2m} \neq \emptyset,$$

and so the parity condition $(F_1, F_2, \ldots, F_{2m})$ is equivalent to the Rabin condition

$$\{\langle F_{2m}, F_{2m-1} \rangle, \ldots, \langle F_3, F_2 \rangle, \langle F_2, F_1 \rangle\}.$$

Therefore, the parity condition is a *special case* of the Rabin condition in which the sets appearing in the Rabin pairs form a nonincreasing chain with respect to set inclusion, starting at the set Q. Interestingly, the parity condition is also a special case of the Streett condition. It is not difficult to prove (see exercise 154) that the parity condition $(F_1, F_2, \cdots, F_{2m})$ is also equivalent to the Streett condition

$$\{\langle \emptyset, F_1 \rangle, \langle F_2, F_3 \rangle, \ldots, \langle F_{2m-2}, F_{2m-1} \rangle\}.$$

10.3.3.1 Equivalence of NPAs and ω-Regular Expressions
It is very easy to give conversions NBA → NPA → NRA, which prove the equivalence of NPAs and ω-regular expressions.

NBA → NPA. An NBA with states Q and accepting states F recognizes the same language as the same semi-automaton with parity condition $(\emptyset, F, Q, Q)$. Indeed, for every run ρ of a semi-automaton:

ρ satisfies the parity condition $(\emptyset, F, Q, Q)$

$\Longleftrightarrow (\inf(\rho) \cap \emptyset = \emptyset \wedge \inf(\rho) \cap F \neq \emptyset) \vee (\inf(\rho) \cap Q = \emptyset \wedge \inf(\rho) \cap Q \neq \emptyset)$

$\Longleftrightarrow \inf(\rho) \cap F \neq \emptyset$

$\Longleftrightarrow \rho$ satisfies the Büchi condition F.

NPA → NRA. By the observation above on the relation between parity and Rabin conditions, an NPA with acceptance condition $(F_1, F_2, \ldots, F_{2m})$ recognizes the same language as the same automaton with Rabin condition $\{\langle F_{2m}, F_{2m-1}\rangle, \ldots, \langle F_3, F_2\rangle, \langle F_2, F_1\rangle\}$, and we are done.

Together, the two conversions NBA → NPA and NPA → NRA show that the languages recognizable by NPAs are exactly the ω-regular languages and that ω-regular expressions can be translated into NPAs and vice versa with polynomial blowup.

10.3.3.2　Equivalence of NPAs and DPAs
It is possible to modify the determinization of the theorem 10.18 procedure so that it yields a DPA instead of a DRA. Again, the proof is beyond the scope of the book.

Theorem 10.25　*An NPA with n states can be effectively transformed into a DPA with $n^{\mathcal{O}(n)}$ states and an acceptance condition with $\mathcal{O}(n)$ sets.*

10.3.3.3　Boolean Operations for DPAs
It can be shown that union and intersection of DPAs both involve an exponential blowup, that is, the smallest DPA for the union or the intersection of two DPAS with $\mathcal{O}(n)$ states may have $\Omega(2^n)$ states. However, complementation can be very elegantly implemented without changing the semi-automaton as follows. Let $A(S, \mathcal{P})$ be a DPA with $\mathcal{P} = (F_1, F_2, \ldots, F_{2m})$. Consider the DPA $\overline{A} = (S, \overline{\mathcal{P}})$, where

$$\overline{\mathcal{P}} = (G_1, G_2, \ldots, G_{2m+2}) := (\emptyset, F_1, F_2, \ldots, F_{2m}, F_{2m}).$$

(That is, $G_1 := \emptyset$, $G_2 := F_1$, and so on.) Let ρ be a run of A. We have

$$\rho \text{ is a rejecting run of } A$$
iff　the minimal index i such that $\inf(\rho) \cap F_i \neq \emptyset$ is not even
iff　the minimal index i such that $\inf(\rho) \cap F_i \neq \emptyset$ is odd
iff　the minimal index j such that $\inf(\rho) \cap G_j \neq \emptyset$ is even
iff　ρ is an accepting run of $\overline{A}$.

Therefore, $\mathcal{L}_\omega\left(\overline{A}\right) = \overline{\mathcal{L}_\omega(A)}$.

Example 10.26　Consider the semi-automaton S depicted in figure 10.20. We examine several languages over Σ and determine for each of them if there exist Rabin, Streett, or parity conditions that, added to S, yield Rabin, Streett, or parity automata recognizing the language. We use the following notation: $Q = \{q_a, q_b, q_c\}$, $a = \{q_a\}$, $b = \{q_b\}$, and $ab = \{q_a, q_b\}$.

Words containing infinitely many as. Semi-automaton S recognizes this language with the Rabin condition $\{\langle a, \emptyset\rangle\}$, the Streett condition $\{\langle Q, a\rangle\}$, and the parity condition $(\emptyset, a, Q, Q)$.

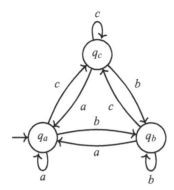

Figure 10.20
Example of a semi-automaton.

Words containing infinitely many *a*s *or* infinitely many *b*s. Semi-automaton S recognizes this language with the Rabin condition $\{\langle ab, \emptyset \rangle\}$, the Streett condition $\{\langle Q, ab \rangle\}$, and the parity condition $(\emptyset, ab, Q, Q)$.

Words containing infinitely many *a*s *and* infinitely many *b*s. Semi-automaton S recognizes this language with the Streett condition $\{\langle Q, a \rangle, \langle Q, b \rangle\}$. However, no Rabin condition allows S to recognize it. To see why, assume the contrary, and let ρ be an accepting run for $(ab)^{\omega}$. We have $\inf(\rho) = ab$. Since ρ is accepting, the Rabin condition contains at least one Rabin pair $\langle F, G \rangle$ such that $F \cap ab \neq \emptyset$ and $G \cap ab = \emptyset$. But then S accepts no word at all (case $F = \emptyset$) or it accepts a^{ω} (case $q_a \in F$) or it accepts b^{ω} (case $q_b \in F$), which in all cases leads to a contradiction. Finally, since the parity condition is a special case of the Rabin condition, no parity condition allows S to recognize the language.

Words containing finitely many *a*s *or* finitely many *b*s. This language is the complement of the previous one. Since S is deterministic, it recognizes a language with a Rabin (Streett) condition if it recognizes its complement with a Streett (Rabin) condition. So, S recognizes this language with the Rabin condition $\{\langle Q, a \rangle, \langle Q, b \rangle\}$, and there is no Streett condition recognizing it. Further, since the parity condition is a special case of the Streett condition, no parity condition allows S to recognize the language.

10.3.4 Muller Automata

We have found three different ω-trinities: the Rabin, Streett, and parity trinities. In each of them, one of the three fundamental boolean operations (union, intersection, and complement) can be implemented essentially as for DFAs, but the other two cannot and involve exponential blowups in the number of states. Is there an ω-automaton type in which all three boolean operations can be implemented as for DFAs, with polynomial blowups in the number of states?

The answer is "yes, but." Muller automata, the automata type presented below, allow us to implement complementation without changing the semi-automaton and to implement both union and intersection by means of pairing. However, this comes at the price of an exponential blowup, *not* in the number of states *but* in the size of the acceptance condition. Let us explain this.

In a DFA, the size of an automaton (i.e., the number of bits required to encode it) is determined by the cardinalities of the set of states and the alphabet. Indeed, a DFA with n states over an alphabet with m letters has exactly nm transitions and at most n final states. Therefore, the size of the DFA is $\Theta(nm)$. This is no longer the case for DRAs, DSAs, or DPAs. Indeed, the acceptance condition of a DRA with n states can contain up to 4^n Rabin pairs, and hence the size of the automaton can be dominated by the size of the acceptance condition. So, the question of whether all three boolean operations can be implemented "as for DFAs" can be given both a positive and a negative answer: yes, if we are only interested in the semi-automaton and the number of states of the resulting automata; no, if we also take into account the size of the acceptance condition.

To introduce Muller automata, consider again example 10.26. We showed there that no Rabin automaton with the semi-automaton of figure 10.20 recognizes the language of the words containing infinitely many as and infinitely many bs. The reason is that the condition "both q_a and q_b are visited infinitely often" cannot be expressed using Rabin pairs, although it can be expressed using Streett pairs. Muller automata solve this problem in a radical way, by allowing *all* possible acceptance conditions.

Definition 10.27 *Let $S = (Q, \Sigma, \delta, Q_0)$ be a semi-automaton. A nondeterministic Muller automaton (NMA) is a pair $A = (S, \alpha)$, where $\alpha : 2^Q \to \{0, 1\}$ is an acceptance condition.*

We represent an acceptance condition α by its associated Muller set, *defined as the set $\mathcal{M} := \{Q' \subseteq Q : \alpha(Q') = 1\}$. Abusing language, we speak of the Muller acceptance condition $\mathcal{M}$ and of the NMA $A = (S, \mathcal{M})$.*

Example 10.28 Consider the semi-automaton S of example 10.26 depicted in figure 10.20. Let us give Muller conditions recognizing all four languages of the example.

Words containing infinitely many as. Semi-automaton S recognizes this language with the Muller condition

$$\{ \{q_a\}, \{q_a, q_b\}, \{q_a, q_c\}, \{q_a, q_b, q_c\} \}.$$

(All sets containing q_a.)

Words containing infinitely many as *or* infinitely many bs. Semi-automaton S recognizes this language with the Muller condition

$$\{ \{q_a\}, \{q_b\}, \{q_a, q_c\}, \{q_b, q_c\}, \{q_a, q_b, q_c\} \}.$$

(All sets containing q_a or q_b.)

Words containing infinitely many *a*s *and* infinitely many *b*s. Semi-automaton S recognizes this language with the Muller condition

$$\{ \{q_a, q_b\}, \{q_a, q_b, q_c\} \}.$$

(All sets containing q_a and q_b.)

Words containing finitely many *a*s *or* finitely many *b*s. Semi-automaton S recognizes this language with the Muller condition

$$\{ \{q_a\}, \{q_b\}, \{q_c\}, \{q_a, q_c\}, \{q_b, q_c\} \}.$$

(All sets not containing q_a or not containing q_b.)

10.3.4.1 Equivalence of NMAs and ω-Regular Expressions

We give translations NBA $\rightarrow$ NMA $\rightarrow$ NBA, which shows that NMAs are as expressive as ω-regular expressions.

NBA $\rightarrow$ NMA. Given an NBA $A = (S, F)$ where $S = (Q, \Sigma, \delta, Q_0)$ and a set of states $R \subseteq Q$, let $B = (S, \mathcal{M})$ be the NMA such that $R \in \mathcal{M}$ iff $R \cap F \neq \emptyset$—that is, $\mathcal{M}$ contains all subsets of Q that intersect F. We show that, for every word $w \in \Sigma^{\omega}$, we have $w \in \mathcal{L}_{\omega}(A)$ iff $w \in \mathcal{L}_{\omega}(B)$:

$$w \in \mathcal{L}_{\omega}(A)$$
iff $\quad \inf(\rho) \cap F \neq \emptyset$ for some run ρ of A on w
iff $\quad \inf(\rho) \in \mathcal{M}$ for some run ρ of B on w $\qquad$ (by definition of $\mathcal{M}$)
$$w \in \mathcal{L}_{\omega}(B).$$

While B has the same number of states and transitions as A, the cardinality of $\mathcal{M}$ is $2^{|Q|} - 2^{|Q \setminus F|}$, which in the worst case is exponential in the number of states of A and B. For example, a Büchi automaton with states $Q = \{q_0, \ldots, q_n\}$ and Büchi condition $\{q_n\}$ is transformed into an NMA with a Muller set $\{F \subseteq Q : q_n \in F\}$ of cardinality 2^n.

NMA $\rightarrow$ NBA. We present a translation NMA $\rightarrow$ NSA $\rightarrow$ NBA. Since we already have a translation NSA $\rightarrow$ NBA, it suffices to present a translation NMA $\rightarrow$ NSA.

Let $A = (S, \mathcal{M})$ be an NMA with $\mathcal{M} = \{F_1, \ldots, F_m\}$. We construct an equivalent NSA B. By definition of the Muller condition, we have $\mathcal{L}_{\omega}(A) = \cup_{i=1}^{m} \mathcal{L}_{\omega}(A_i)$, where A_i is the NMA $A_i = (S, \{F_i\})$. So it suffices to translate each A_i into an equivalent NSA B_i and then define B as the result of putting all these NSAs "side by side." To construct B_i, it suffices to convert the Muller condition $\{F_i\}$ into an equivalent Streett condition St as follows:

$$\rho \text{ is an accepting run of } A_i = (S, \{F_i\}), \text{ where } S = (Q, \Sigma, \delta, Q_0)$$

$$\Longleftrightarrow \inf(\rho) = F_i$$

$$\Longleftrightarrow \inf(\rho) \cap Q \setminus F_i = \emptyset \wedge \bigwedge_{q \in F_i} \inf(\rho) \cap \{q\} \neq \emptyset$$

$$\Longleftrightarrow \left(\inf(\rho) \cap Q \setminus F_i = \emptyset \vee \inf(\rho) \cap \emptyset \neq \emptyset \right) \wedge$$

$$\bigwedge_{q \in F_i} \left(\inf(\rho) \cap Q = \emptyset \vee \inf(\rho) \cap \{q\} \neq \emptyset \right)$$

$$\Longleftrightarrow \rho \text{ is an accepting run of the NSA } B_i = (S, \mathcal{S}t), \text{ where}$$

$$\mathcal{S}t = \{ \langle Q \setminus F_i, \emptyset \rangle \} \cup \{ \langle Q, \{q\} \rangle : q \in F_i \}.$$

Complexity. Let $n = |Q|$ and $m = |\mathcal{M}|$. Each of the NSAs $B_1, \ldots, B_m$ has n states and an acceptance condition containing at most $n + 1$ Streett pairs. Each of the equivalent NBAs has $\mathcal{O}(2^n nm)$ states, and after putting them side by side, we finally obtain an NBA with $\mathcal{O}(2^n nm^2)$ states.

10.3.4.2 Equivalence of NMAs and DMAs

We can show that NMAs can be determinized by proving that for every DRA there is an equivalent DMA. Indeed, we can then combine the translations NMA $\rightarrow$ NBA $\rightarrow$ NRA $\rightarrow$ DRA $\rightarrow$ DMA, where NRA $\rightarrow$ DRA follows from theorem 10.18. There exist direct algorithms, but they are beyond the scope of this book.

DRA $\rightarrow$ DMA. The conversion is very similar to NBA $\rightarrow$ NMA. Given a DRA $A = (S, \mathcal{R})$, we construct the DMA $B = (S, \mathcal{M})$, where a set $R \subseteq Q$ belongs to $\mathcal{M}$ iff there exists $\langle F, G \rangle \in \mathcal{R}$ such that $R \cap F \neq \emptyset$ and $R \cap G = \emptyset$. We have

$$\rho \text{ is an accepting run of } A$$
$$\text{iff} \quad \inf(\rho) \cap F \neq \emptyset \text{ and } \inf(\rho) \cap G = \emptyset \text{ for some } \langle F, G \rangle \in \mathcal{R}$$
$$\text{iff} \quad \inf(\rho) \in \mathcal{M}$$
$$\text{iff} \quad \rho \text{ is an accepting run of } B.$$

10.3.4.3 Boolean Operations on DMAs

Complement. We can easily complement a DMA $A = (S, \mathcal{M})$ while preserving the type and the semi-automaton. Indeed, the DMA $\overline{A} = (S, 2^Q \setminus \mathcal{M})$ satisfies $\mathcal{L}_\omega(\overline{A}) = \overline{\mathcal{L}_\omega(A)}$: for every word w, we have $w \in \mathcal{L}_\omega(A)$ iff the run ρ of A on w is accepting iff $\inf(\rho) \in \mathcal{M}$ iff $\inf(\rho) \notin 2^Q \setminus \mathcal{M}$ iff ρ is not an accepting run of $\overline{A}$ iff $w \notin \mathcal{L}_\omega(\overline{A})$.

Union and intersection. Let $A_1 = (S_1, \mathcal{M}_1)$ and $A_2 = (S_2, \mathcal{M}_2)$ be DMAs with sets of states Q_1 and Q_2, respectively. Given $R \subseteq Q_1 \times Q_2$, let

$$R|_1 = \{ q_1 \in Q_1 : \exists q_2 \in Q_2 \, (q_1, q_2) \in R \},$$

$$R|_2 = \{ q_2 \in Q_2 : \exists q_1 \in Q_1 \, (q_1, q_2) \in R \},$$

be the projections of R onto Q_1 and Q_2, respectively. Let us see that the DMAs $A_1 \cup A_2$ and $A_1 \cap A_2$ having the pairing $[S_1, S_2]$ as semi-automaton and Muller conditions

$$\mathcal{M}_\cup = \{R \subseteq Q_1 \times Q_2 : R|_1 \in \mathcal{M}_1 \text{ or } R|_2 \in \mathcal{M}_2\},$$

$$\mathcal{M}_\cap = \{R \subseteq Q_1 \times Q_2 : R|_1 \in \mathcal{M}_1 \text{ and } R|_2 \in \mathcal{M}_2\},$$

recognize $\mathcal{L}_\omega(A_1) \cup \mathcal{L}_\omega(A_2)$ and $\mathcal{L}_\omega(A_1) \cap \mathcal{L}_\omega(A_2)$, respectively.

Let w be an arbitrary word, and let ρ_1, ρ_2, and ρ be the runs of S_1, S_2, and $[S_1, S_2]$ on w, respectively. We have $\inf(\rho)|_i = \inf(\rho_i)$ for both $i \in \{1, 2\}$. So, we obtain for $A_1 \cup A_2$:

$$w \in \mathcal{L}_\omega(A_1) \cup \mathcal{L}_\omega(A_2)$$

$\Longleftrightarrow \ \inf(\rho_1) \in \mathcal{M}_1 \text{ or } \inf(\rho_2) \in \mathcal{M}_2$ (by def. of the Muller condition)

$\Longleftrightarrow \ \inf(\rho)|_1 \in \mathcal{M}_1 \text{ or } \inf(\rho)|_2 \in \mathcal{M}_2$ (by $\inf(\rho)|_i = \inf(\rho_i)$)

$\Longleftrightarrow \ \inf(\rho) \in \mathcal{M}_\cup$ (by def. of $\mathcal{M}_\cup$)

$\Longleftrightarrow \ w \in \mathcal{L}_\omega(A_1 \cup A_2)$ (by def. of $A_1 \cup A_2$).

The result for $A_1 \cap A_2$ is analogous.

10.3.4.4 Size of the Acceptance Condition

Recall that the conversion NBA $\rightarrow$ NMA described in section 10.3.4.1 causes an exponential blowup in the size of the acceptance condition. A Büchi automaton with (by definition) one set of accepting states may be translated into a Muller automaton with exponentially many sets of accepting states.

We show that the exponential blowup is not a feature of the specific conversion we have presented; any other conversion will have the same problem. In fact, we prove this for any conversion from ω-regular expression to NMAs. (Observe that, since the conversion ω-regular expression $\rightarrow$ NBA only causes a polynomial blowup in size, any conversion NBA $\rightarrow$ NMA must then cause an exponential one.)

Consider, for every $n \geq 1$, the ω-regular expression $s_n = ((a(bb)^*)^n \#)^\omega$ over the alphabet $\{a, b, \#\}$. Words of $\mathcal{L}_\omega(s_n)$ are of the form $w_1 \# w_1 \# w_2 \# w_3 \# \cdots$, where every w_i contains exactly n occurrences of a separated by possibly different but even numbers of bs. The ω-language $\mathcal{L}_\omega(s_n)$ is recognized by the DMA shown in figure 10.21. It only has $2n + 1$ states but a very large acceptance condition, containing all 2^n sets of the form $\{q_0, \ldots, q_n\} \cup R$, where $R \subseteq \{\widehat{q}_1, \ldots, \widehat{q}_n\}$. The next proposition shows that *every* NMA recognizing this language has an acceptance condition of at least this size.

Proposition 10.29 *Let $\Sigma = \{a, b, \#\}$. For all $n \geq 1$, the acceptance condition of any NMA recognizing the language of the ω-regular expression $s_n = \big((a(bb)^*)^n \#\big)^\omega$ contains at least 2^n sets of states.*

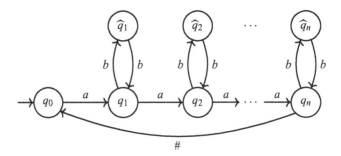

Figure 10.21
A DMA recognizing the language of the ω-regular expression $\big((a(bb)^*)^n\#\big)^\omega$. The acceptance condition consists
of all subsets of $\{q_0, \widehat{q}_1, \ldots, \widehat{q}_n\}$ that contain q_0.

Proof Fix an arbitrary $n \geq 1$, and let A be the DMA of figure 10.21, with set of states
Q. It is easy to see that A recognizes $\mathcal{L}(s_n)$, and so it suffices to show that the acceptance
condition of any NMA equivalent to A, contains at least 2^n sets of states. Before proceeding,
we make the following claim:

Claim 1. Let $\mathcal{L}_\omega(q)$ denote the language recognized by A with $q \in Q$ as initial state. For
every two distinct states q, q' of A, we have $\mathcal{L}_\omega(q) \cap \mathcal{L}_\omega(q') = \emptyset$.

Proof Let $u \in \mathcal{L}_\omega(q)$ and $u' \in \mathcal{L}_\omega(q')$. We prove $u \neq u'$. Since every accepting run visits
q_0 infinitely often, u and u' contain infinitely many occurrences of $\#$. Consider three cases:

- $q = q_0$ and $q' \neq q_0$. Then u contains exactly n occurrences of a before the first occurrence
of $\#$, but u' contains fewer.

- $q \in \{q_i, \widehat{q}_i\}$ and $q' \in \{q_j, \widehat{q}_j\}$ for $i \neq j$. Then u contains exactly $n - i$ occurrences of a before
the first occurrence of $\#$, and u' contains $n - j$.

- $\{q, q'\} = \{q_i, \widehat{q}_i\}$ for some i. Let k_u be the number of occurrences of b in u before the first
occurrence of $\#$. Define $k_{u'}$ analogously. Then k_u and $k_{u'}$ have different parity.   □

Let B be an NMA equivalent to A with set of states R; further, let $\mathcal{L}_\omega(r)$ denote the language recognized by B with $r \in R$ as initial state. Without loss of generality, we assume that
$\mathcal{L}_\omega(r) \neq \emptyset$ for every $r \in R$ (if $\mathcal{L}_\omega(r) = \emptyset$, then r can be removed). We make two claims:

Claim 2. For every $r \in R$, there is a unique state $q \in Q$ such that $\mathcal{L}_\omega(r) = \mathcal{L}_\omega(q)$.

Proof Let $r \in R$. Since A and B are equivalent, we have $\mathcal{L}_\omega(r) \subseteq \bigcup_{q \in Q} \mathcal{L}_\omega(q)$. So, by claim
1, it suffices to show that some state $q \in Q$ satisfies $\mathcal{L}_\omega(r) \subseteq \mathcal{L}_\omega(q)$. Let w be any finite
word leading from some initial state r_0 of B to r, and let q be the unique state of A such that
$q_0 \xrightarrow{w} q$. We prove $\mathcal{L}_\omega(r) \subseteq \mathcal{L}_\omega(q)$.

$\quad\quad u \in \mathcal{L}_\omega(r)$

$\Rightarrow \quad B$ has an accepting run $\rho_u = r \xrightarrow{u}$ from r

$\Rightarrow$ B has an accepting run $\rho = r_0 \xrightarrow{w} r \xrightarrow{u}$ from r_0 (because $\inf(\rho) = \inf(\rho_u)$)

$\Rightarrow$ $wu \in \mathcal{L}_\omega(B)$ (because r_0 is an initial state)

$\Rightarrow$ $wu \in \mathcal{L}_\omega(A)$ (because A and B are equivalent)

$\Rightarrow$ A has an accepting run $\rho' = q_0 \xrightarrow{w} q \xrightarrow{u} \cdots$

$\Rightarrow$ A has an accepting $\rho'_u = q \xrightarrow{u} \cdots$ from q (because $\inf(\rho'_u) = \inf(\rho')$)

$\Rightarrow$ $u \in \mathcal{L}_\omega(q)$.

Before stating the third claim, we need a definition. For every $1 \le i \le n$, let $R_i = \{r \in R : \mathcal{L}_\omega(r) = \mathcal{L}_\omega(\widehat{q}_i)\}$. Observe that, by claim 2, $R_i \neq \emptyset$ for every $1 \le i \le n$, and by claim 1, $R_i \cap R_j \neq \emptyset$ for every $i \neq j$.

Claim 3. Let $q_0 \xrightarrow{u} q \xrightarrow{v} \cdots$ and $r_0 \xrightarrow{u} r \xrightarrow{v} \cdots$ be accepting runs of A and B on a word uv. For every $1 \le i \le n$, we have $q = \widehat{q}_i$ iff $r \in R_i$.

Proof Since the suffixes $q \xrightarrow{v} \cdots$ and $r \xrightarrow{v} \cdots$ visit the same states infinitely often as the runs themselves, we have $v \in \mathcal{L}_\omega(q) \cap \mathcal{L}_\omega(r)$. Claim 1 and claim 2 yield $\mathcal{L}_\omega(q) = \mathcal{L}_\omega(r)$. If $q = \widehat{q}_i$, then $r \in R_i$ by the definition of R_i. If $r \in R_i$, then $q = \widehat{q}_i$ by the definition of R_i and claim 2. $\qquad\square$

Proof of the proposition. For every $H \subseteq \{1, \dots, n\}$, consider the word

$$w_H = \left(a(bb)^{k_1} a(bb)^{k_2} a \cdots (bb)^{k_n} \# \right)^\omega$$

where $k_i = 1$ if $i \in H$, and $k_i = 0$ otherwise. For example, if $n = 4$ and $H = \{1, 3\}$, then $w_H = (abbaabba\#)^\omega$. Let ρ_H^A and ρ_H^B be accepting runs of A and B on w_H. We have $\widehat{q}_i \in \inf(\rho_H^A)$ iff $i \in H$. By claim 3, ρ_H^B visits R_i infinitely often iff $i \in H$, and so $\inf(\rho_B^H) \cap R_i \neq \emptyset$ iff $i \in H$. It follows $\inf(\rho_B^H) \neq \inf(\rho_B^{H'})$ for every two distinct subsets $H, H' \subseteq \{1, \dots, n\}$, and thus $|\mathcal{M}| \ge 2^n$. $\qquad\square$

10.4   Summary

In chapter 1 and chapter 3, we have shown that automata on finite words and regular expressions form a trinity and that all boolean operations can be implemented in linear or quadratic time with *deterministic* automata as data structure. The fact that a single type of automata *simultaneously* enjoys all of these properties is often taken for granted. It should not be. It is a remarkable fact, which, as we have seen in this chapter, does not hold anymore for automata on infinite words.

Table 10.1 summarizes the contents of the chapter. The first column lists automata types. The next two columns indicate which of the properties of an ω-trinity hold, and the last three columns indicate which of the properties concerning boolean operations hold. More precisely, the meaning of each column is as follows:

Table 10.1
Summary of the results of this chapter. The first column lists automata types, and the other columns indicate which types satisfy each property. An underlined $\underline{Y}$ indicates that the type enjoys the property, and moreover, the underlying conversion or algorithm only requires polynomial time.

Automaton Type		Expr.	Det.	Union	Inters.	Comp.
NFA/DFA		$\underline{Y}$	Y	$\underline{Y}$	$\underline{Y}$	$\underline{Y}$
NBA/DBA	(Büchi)	$\underline{Y}$	N	$\underline{Y}$	N	N
NCA/DCA	(Co-Büchi)	N	Y	N	$\underline{Y}$	N
NRA/DRA	(Rabin)	$\underline{Y}$	Y	$\underline{Y}$	N	N
NSA/DSA	(Streett)	$\underline{Y}$	Y	N	$\underline{Y}$	N
NPA/DPA	(Parity)	$\underline{Y}$	Y	N	N	$\underline{Y}$
NMA/DMA	(Muller)	Y	Y	Y	Y	Y

- **Expr.** Every ω-regular expression (for the row NFA/DFA, every regular expression) can be converted into an automaton of this type.
- **Det.** For every nondeterministic automaton of this type, there is an equivalent deterministic automaton of the same type.
- **Union.** Union of deterministic automata of this type can be implemented using the pairing construction.
- **Inters.** Intersection of deterministic automata of this type can be implemented using the pairing construction.
- **Comp.** Complementation of deterministic automata of this type can be implemented without changing the semi-automaton or the type of the acceptance condition.

The entries of the table are as follows: N (the property does not hold), Y (the property holds, but the underlying conversion or algorithm requires exponential time), and $\underline{Y}$ (the property holds and the underlying conversion or algorithm only requires polynomial time). In particular, $\underline{Y}$ indicates that the resulting automaton has polynomial size in the input.

The consequence of these results is that for each application, one must choose the adequate type of ω-automaton. Our main application in this book is automatic verification, and for this purpose, in the next chapter, we choose *generalized Büchi automata*, a type of ω-automata whose acceptance condition lies between the Büchi and Streett conditions.

10.5   Exercises

★ 🖳 **Exercise 141.** Construct Büchi automata and ω-regular expressions, as small as possible, recognizing the following ω-languages over the alphabet $\{a, b, c\}$. Recall that $inf(w)$ is the set of letters of $\{a, b, c\}$ that occur infinitely often in w.

(a) $\{w \in \{a, b, c\}^\omega : \{a, b\} \supseteq inf(w)\}$,

(b) $\{w \in \{a, b, c\}^{\omega} : \{a, b\} = inf(w)\}$,

(c) $\{w \in \{a, b, c\}^{\omega} : \{a, b\} \subseteq inf(w)\}$.

★ 🔲 **Exercise 142.** Construct Büchi automata and ω-regular expressions, as small as possible, recognizing the following ω-languages over the alphabet $\{a, b, c\}$. Recall that $inf(w)$ is the set of letters of $\{a, b, c\}$ that occur infinitely often in w.

(a) $\{w \in \{a, b, c\}^{\omega} : \{a, b, c\} = inf(w)\}$,

(b) $\{w \in \{a, b, c\}^{\omega} : \text{if } a \in inf(w) \text{ then } \{b, c\} \subseteq inf(w)\}$.

☆ 🔲 **Exercise 143.** Give deterministic Büchi automata for the following ω-languages over $\Sigma = \{a, b, c\}$:

(a) $\{w \in \Sigma^{\omega} : w \text{ contains at least one } c\}$,

(b) $\{w \in \Sigma^{\omega} : \text{every } a \text{ in } w \text{ is immediately followed by a } b\}$,

(c) $\{w \in \Sigma^{\omega} : \text{between two successive } as \text{ in } w \text{ there are at least two } bs\}$.

☆ ■ **Exercise 144.** Prove or disprove the following statements:

(a) For every Büchi automaton A, there exists an NBA B with a single initial state and such that $\mathcal{L}_{\omega}(A) = \mathcal{L}_{\omega}(B)$.

(b) For every Büchi automaton A, there exists an NBA B with a single accepting state and such that $\mathcal{L}_{\omega}(A) = \mathcal{L}_{\omega}(B)$.

★ ■ **Exercise 145.** Recall that every finite set of finite words is a regular language. Prove that this does not hold for infinite words. More precisely:

(a) Prove that every nonempty ω-regular language contains an *ultimately periodic* ω-word (i.e., an ω-word of the form uv^{ω} for some finite words $u \in \Sigma^*$ and $v \in \Sigma^+$).

(b) Give an ω-word w such that $\{w\}$ is not an ω-regular language.   *Hint: Use (a).*

★ ■ **Exercise 146.** Consider the class of nondeterministic automata over ω-words with the following acceptance condition: an infinite run is accepting iff it visits an accepting state *at least once*. Show that no such automaton accepts the language of all words over $\{a, b\}$ containing infinitely many a and infinitely many b.

★ 🔲 **Exercise 147.** The *limit* of a language $L \subseteq \Sigma^*$ is the ω-language $lim(L)$, defined as follows: $w \in lim(L)$ iff infinitely many prefixes of w are words of L (e.g., the limit of $(ab)^*$ is $\{(ab)^{\omega}\}$).

(a) Determine the limit of the following regular languages over $\{a, b\}$:

(i) $(a + b)^* a$,

(ii) the set of words containing an even number of a,

(iii) $a^* b$.

(b) Prove the following: An ω-language is recognizable by a deterministic Büchi automaton iff it is the limit of a regular language.

(c) Exhibit a nonregular language whose limit is ω-regular.

(d) Exhibit a nonregular language whose limit is not ω-regular.

☆ ■ **Exercise 148.** Let $L_1 = (ab)^\omega$ and let L_2 be the ω-language of all ω-words over $\{a,b\}$ containing infinitely many a and infinitely many b.

(a) Exhibit three different DBAs with three states recognizing L_1.

(b) Exhibit six different DBAs with three states recognizing L_2.

(c) Show that no DBA with at most two states recognizes L_1 or L_2.

☆ ▣ **Exercise 149.** Find ω-regular expressions for the following languages:

(a) $\{w \in \{a,b\}^\omega : k \text{ is even for each subword } ba^k b \text{ of } w\}$,

(b) $\{w \in \{a,b\}^\omega : w \text{ has no occurrence of } bab\}$.

☆ ■ **Exercise 150.** In definition 2.20, we introduced the quotient A/P of an NFA A with respect to a partition P of its states. In lemma 2.22, we proved $\mathcal{L}(A) = \mathcal{L}(A/P_\ell)$ for the language partition P_ℓ that puts two states q_1, q_2 in same the block iff $\mathcal{L}_A(q_1) = \mathcal{L}_A(q_2)$. Let $B = (Q, \Sigma, \delta, Q_0, F)$ be an NBA. Given a partition P of Q, define the quotient B/P of B with respect to P as for an NFA.

(a) Let P_ℓ be the partition of Q that puts two states q_1, q_2 of B in same block iff $L_{\omega,B}(q_1) = L_{\omega,B}(q_2)$, where $L_{\omega,B}(q)$ denotes the ω-language containing the words accepted by B with q has initial state. Does $\mathcal{L}_\omega(B) = \mathcal{L}_\omega(B/P_\ell)$ always hold?

(b) Let CSR be the coarsest stable refinement of the equivalence relation with equivalence classes $\{F, Q \setminus F\}$. Does $\mathcal{L}_\omega(A) = \mathcal{L}_\omega(A/CSR)$ always hold?

☆ ■ **Exercise 151.** Let L be an ω-language over alphabet Σ, and let $w \in \Sigma^*$. The w-*residual* of L is the ω-language $L^w = \{w' \in \Sigma^\omega : ww' \in L\}$. An ω-language L' is a *residual* of L if $L' = L^w$ for some word $w \in \Sigma^*$. We show that the theorem stating that a language of finite words is regular iff it has finitely many residuals does not extend to ω-regular languages.

(a) Prove this statement: If L is an ω-regular language, then it has finitely many residuals.

(b) Disprove this statement: Every ω-language with finitely many residuals is ω-regular.

Hint: Consider a nonultimately periodic ω-word w and its language $Tail_w$ of infinite tails.

☆ ✔ **Exercise 152.** The solution to exercise 150(2) shows that the reduction algorithm for NFAs that computes the partition CSR of a given NFA A and constructs the quotient A/CSR can also be applied to NBAs. Generalize the algorithm so that it works for NGAs.

⋆ 🔲 **Exercise 153.** Let $L = \{w \in \{a, b\}^{\omega} : w$ contains finitely many $a\}$.

(a) Give a deterministic Rabin automaton for L.

(b) Give an NBA for L and try to "determinize" it by using the NFA to DFA powerset construction. What is the language accepted by the resulting DBA?

(c) What ω-language is accepted by the following Muller automaton with acceptance condition $\{\{q_0\}, \{q_1\}, \{q_2\}\}$? And with acceptance condition $\{\{q_0, q_1\}, \{q_1, q_2\}, \{q_2, q_0\}\}$?

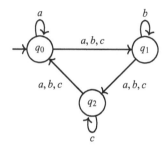

(d) Show that any Büchi automaton that accepts the ω-language of (c), under the first acceptance condition, has more than three states.

(e) For every $m, n \in \mathbb{N}_{>0}$, let $L_{m,n}$ be the ω-language over alphabet $\{a, b\}$ described by the ω-regular expression $(a + b)^*((a^m bb)^{\omega} + (a^n bb)^{\omega})$.

(i) Describe a family of Büchi automata accepting the family of ω-languages $\{L_{m,n}\}_{m,n \in \mathbb{N}_{>0}}$.

(ii) Show that there exists $c \in \mathbb{N}$ such that for all $m, n \in \mathbb{N}_{>0}$, the language $L_{m,n}$ is accepted by a Rabin automaton with at most $\max(m, n) + c$ states.

(iii) Modify your construction in (ii) to obtain Muller automata instead of Rabin automata.

(iv) Convert the Rabin automaton for $L_{m,n}$ obtained in (ii) into a Büchi automaton.

☆ ■ **Exercise 154.** Show that a parity condition $(F_1, F_2, \ldots, F_{2m})$ is equivalent to the Streett condition $\{\langle \emptyset, F_1 \rangle, \langle F_2, F_3 \rangle, \ldots, \langle F_{2m-2}, F_{2m-1} \rangle\}$.

11 Boolean Operations: Implementations

In chapters 3 and 5 of part I of the book, we implemented the list of operations on sets of objects and relations between objects shown in table 0.1 of chapter 0. The implementation assumes that objects are encoded as finite words and uses automata on finite words as data structure. In this chapter and in chapter 12, we undertake the same task, but assuming that objects are encoded as ω-words and using automata on infinite words as data structure.

The list of table 0.1 is split into three parts: operations on sets, tests on sets, and operations on relations. In this chapter, we deal with the operations on sets: union, intersection, and complement. Chapter 12 will deal with the tests on sets. There is no chapter devoted to the operations on relations, because their implementation, at least in a first approximation, does not require new ideas beyond those of chapter 5.

In chapter 10, we have already implemented union, intersection, and complement using deterministic Muller automata (DMA) as data structure. However, all three operations have worst-case exponential blow up (see table 10.1). The conversions of the chapter also allow us to use deterministic Rabin, Streett, or parity automata as data structure, but in each case, two out of the three operations still have exponential blow up.

We can do better by going from deterministic to nondeterministic automata. We present an implementation based on nondeterministic *generalized Büchi automata* (NGA), an automata type whose acceptance condition can be seen as a generalization of the Büchi condition—hence the name—or as a special case of the Streett condition. In particular, the implementation directly constructs a complement NGA without determinizing the original NGA first.

The chapter is divided into four sections. In section 11.1, we introduce NGAs and give a simple NGA $\rightarrow$ NBA conversion. In section 11.2, we show that union and intersection can be elegantly implemented on NGAs, as in the case of finite words. More precisely, given two NGAs with n_1 and n_2 states, we can construct union and intersection NGAs with $O(n_1 + n_2)$ and $O(n_1 n_2)$ states, respectively. In section 11.3, we undertake the much harder task of implementing complementation. The complementation procedure is indirect, in the sense that we present a direct complementation procedure for NBAs and use the NGA $\rightarrow$ NBA conversion to lift it to a procedure for NGAs.

11.1   Generalized Büchi Automata

Recall that Büchi automata have one set of accepting states, which accepting runs must visit infinitely often. Generalized Büchi automata have a *collection* of sets of accepting states, and accepting runs must visit each set in the collection infinitely often.

Definition 11.1   *Let $S = (Q, \Sigma, \delta, Q_0)$ be a semi-automaton. An acceptance condition on S is a* generalized Büchi condition *if there exists a set $\mathcal{G} \subseteq 2^Q$ of sets of states such that a run ρ is accepting iff it visits every set of $\mathcal{G}$ infinitely often (i.e., iff $\inf(\rho) \cap F \neq \emptyset$ for every $F \in \mathcal{G}$).*

A nondeterministic generalized Büchi automaton (NGA) *is a tuple $A = (Q, \Sigma, \delta, Q_0, F)$, where $F \subseteq Q$ is a generalized Büchi condition.*

Example 11.2   Consider the structure S from example 10.26, which is recalled in figure 11.1.

With the generalized Büchi condition $\{\{q_a\}, \{q_b\}\}$, the language of S is the set of words containing infinitely many *a*s *and* infinitely many *b*s. With the generalized Büchi condition $\{\{q_a, q_b\}\}$, which is also a standard Büchi condition, S recognizes the set of words containing infinitely many *a*s *or* infinitely many *b*s.

Observe that Büchi automata correspond to generalized Büchi automata whose acceptance condition contains a single set of accepting states. However, we can also see NGAs as a special class of nondeterministic Streett automata. Recall that a Streett acceptance condition is a set S of Streett pairs $\langle F, G \rangle$ such that a run ρ is accepting iff for every $\langle F, G \rangle \in S$, the run visits F finitely often or G infinitely often, that is, if $\inf(\rho) \cap F = \emptyset$ or $\inf(\rho) \cap G \neq \emptyset$ holds for every $\langle F, G \rangle \in S$. It follows that a generalized Büchi condition $\mathcal{G} = \{F_0, \ldots, F_{m-1}\}$ is equivalent to the Streett condition $S = \{\langle Q, F_0 \rangle, \ldots, \langle Q, F_{m-1} \rangle\}$. Indeed, since no run can visit Q finitely often, because runs are infinite by definition, the condition that a run visits

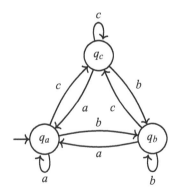

Figure 11.1
Example of a semi-automaton.

Q finitely often or F_i infinitely often, corresponding to the Streett pair $\langle Q, F_i \rangle$, is equivalent to requiring only that the run visits F_i infinitely often.

In section 10.3.2.1, we described a conversion NSA $\rightarrow$ NBA. Since NGAs are a special case of Streett automata, the conversion can also be applied to them. However, in this special case, the conversion becomes much simpler. Let $A = (S, \mathcal{G})$ be a NGA with $\mathcal{G} = \{F_0, \ldots, F_{m-1}\}$. As observed in section 10.3.2.1, a run ρ of S visits each set of $\mathcal{G}$ infinitely often iff it eventually visits F_0, and for every $0 \leq i \leq m-1$, every visit of ρ to F_i is eventually followed by a later visit to $F_{i\oplus 1}$, where $\oplus$ denotes addition modulo m. So, the NBA contains replicas $S_0, \ldots, S_{m-1}$ of S, with the modification that transitions of S_i leaving the replica q^i of a state $q \in F_i$ are redirected to $S_{i\oplus 1}$. The Büchi acceptance condition is $\{q^0 : q \in F_0\}$, that is, a state is accepting if it is the replica in S_0 of one of the states of F_0. Algorithm 46 describes the procedure in detail.

Algorithm 46 Conversion from NGA to NBA.

NGAtoNBA(A)
Input: NGA $A = (Q, \Sigma, Q_0, \delta, \mathcal{G})$, where $\mathcal{G} = \{F_0, \ldots, F_{m-1}\}$
Output: NBA $A' = (Q', \Sigma, \delta', Q'_0, F')$

```
 1   Q', δ', F' ← ∅; Q'₀ ← {q⁰ : q ∈ Q₀}
 2   W ← Q'₀
 3   while W ≠ ∅ do
 4       pick qⁱ from W
 5       add qⁱ to Q'
 6       if q ∈ F₀ and i = 0 then add q⁰ to F'
 7       for all a ∈ Σ, r ∈ δ(q, a) do
 8           if q ∉ Fᵢ then
 9               if rⁱ ∉ Q' then add rⁱ to W
10               add (qⁱ, a, rⁱ) to δ'
11           else /* q ∈ Fᵢ */
12               if r^{i⊕1} ∉ Q' then add r^{i⊕1} to W
13               add (qⁱ, a, r^{i⊕1}) to δ'
14   return (Q', Σ, δ', Q'₀, F')
```

11.2 Union and Intersection

Let $A_1 = (S_1, \mathcal{G}_1)$ and $A_2 = (S_2, \mathcal{G}_2)$ be two NGAs, where $S_1 = (Q_1, \Sigma, \delta_1, Q_{01})$, $S_2 = (Q_2, \Sigma, \delta_2, Q_{02})$, $\mathcal{G}_1 = \{F_1^1, \ldots, F_1^{m_1}\}$, and $\mathcal{G}_2 = \{F_2^1, \ldots, F_2^{m_2}\}$. Assume without loss of generality that Q_1 and Q_2 are disjoint sets.

Union. Let $S_1 \cup S_2$ be the result of putting S_1 and S_2 side by side, that is, $S_1 \cup S_2 = (Q_1 \cup Q_2, \Sigma, \delta_1 \cup \delta_2, Q_{01} \cup Q_{02})$. Let $m = \max\{m_1, m_2\}$, and assume without loss of generality that $m = m_1$. For every $1 \le i \le m$, let

$$F^i = \begin{cases} F_1^i \cup F_2^i & \text{if } i \le m_2, \\ F_1^i \cup Q_2 & \text{otherwise}, \end{cases}$$

and define $\mathcal{G} = \{F^1, \ldots, F^m\}$. We show that the NGA $A_1 \cup A_2 = (S_1 \cup S_2, \mathcal{G})$ satisfies $\mathcal{L}_\omega(A_1 \cup A_2) = \mathcal{L}_\omega(A_1) \cup \mathcal{L}_\omega(A_2)$.

Note that, since Q_1 and Q_2 are disjoint, a run of $S_1 \cup S_2$ is either a run of S_1 or a run of S_2. If ρ is a run of S_1, then it never visits any state of Q_2, and so

ρ is an accepting run of $A_1 \cup A_2$

$$\iff \quad \bigwedge_{i=1}^m \inf(\rho) \cap F^i \ne \emptyset \qquad \text{(by def. of } \mathcal{G})$$

$$\iff \quad \bigwedge_{i=1}^m \inf(\rho) \cap F_1^i \ne \emptyset \qquad \text{(as } \rho \text{ does not visit } Q_2)$$

$$\iff \quad \rho \text{ is an accepting run of } A_1 \qquad \text{(by def. of } \mathcal{G}_1).$$

Similarly, if ρ is a run of A_2, then it never visits any state of Q_1, and so ρ is an accepting run of $A_1 \cup A_2$ iff it is an accepting run of A_2. It follows that ρ is an accepting run of $A_1 \cup A_2$ iff it is an accepting run of A_1 or an accepting run of A_2, and we are done.

Intersection. Let $[S_1, S_2]$ be the pairing of S_1 and S_2—that is, the semi-automaton $[S_1, S_2] = (Q_1 \times Q_2, \Sigma, \delta, Q_{01} \times Q_{02})$, where $\delta([q_1, q_2], a) = \delta(q_1, a) \times \delta(q_2, a)$. Define

$$\mathcal{G} = \{F_1^1 \times Q_2, \ldots, F_1^{m_1} \times Q_2\} \cup \{Q_1 \times F_2^1, \ldots, Q_1 \times F_2^{m_2}\}.$$

Note that $\mathcal{G}$ contains $m_1 + m_2$ sets. We show that the NGA $A_1 \cap A_2 = ([S_1, S_2], \mathcal{G})$ satisfies $\mathcal{L}_\omega(A_1 \cap A_2) = \mathcal{L}_\omega(A_1) \cap \mathcal{L}_\omega(A_2)$.

If ρ is a run of $[S_1, S_2]$, then its projections ρ_1 and ρ_2 onto Q_1 and Q_2 are runs of S_1 and S_2 satisfying $\inf(\rho)|_1 = \inf(\rho_1)$ and $\inf(\rho)|_2 = \inf(\rho_2)$, where $\inf(\rho)|_i$ is the projection of $\inf(\rho)$ onto Q_i. Thus, we have

ρ is an accepting run of $A_1 \cap A_2$

$$\iff \quad \bigwedge_{i=1}^{m_1} \inf(\rho) \cap (F_1^i \times Q_2) \ne \emptyset \text{ and } \bigwedge_{i=1}^{m_2} \inf(\rho) \cap (Q_1 \times F_2^i) \ne \emptyset$$

(by definition of $\mathcal{G}$)

$$\Longleftrightarrow \quad \bigwedge_{i=1}^{m_1} \inf(\rho)|_1 \cap F_1^i \neq \emptyset \text{ and } \bigwedge_{i=1}^{m_2} \inf(\rho)|_2 \cap F_2^i \neq \emptyset$$

(by definition of projection)

$$\Longleftrightarrow \quad \bigwedge_{i=1}^{m_1} \inf(\rho_1) \cap F_1^i \neq \emptyset \text{ and } \bigwedge_{i=1}^{m_2} \inf(\rho_2) \cap F_2^i \neq \emptyset$$

(since $\inf(\rho)|_1 = \inf(\rho_1)$ and $\inf(\rho)|_2 = \inf(\rho_2)$)

$$\Longleftrightarrow \quad \rho_1 \text{ is an accepting run of } A_1 \text{ and } \rho_2 \text{ is an accepting run of } A_2.$$

Algorithm 47 describes the algorithmic implementation that only constructs the states of the pairing reachable from the initial states.

Algorithm 47 NGA intersection.

$IntersNGA(A_1, A_2)$

Input: NGAs $A_1 = (Q_1, \Sigma, \delta_1, Q_{01}, \mathcal{G}_1)$, $A_2 = (Q_2, \Sigma, \delta_2, Q_{02}, \mathcal{G}_2)$, where
$\mathcal{G}_1 = \{F_1^1, \dots, F_1^{m_1}\}$, $\mathcal{G}_2 = \{F_2^1, \dots, F_2^{m_2}\}$

Output: NGA $A_1 \cap A_2 = (Q, \Sigma, \delta, Q_0, \mathcal{G})$, where $\mathcal{G} = \{F^1, \dots, F^{m_1+m_2}\}$,
satisfying $\mathcal{L}_\omega(A_1 \cap A_2) = \mathcal{L}_\omega(A_1) \cap \mathcal{L}_\omega(A_2)$

1   $Q, \delta, F \leftarrow \emptyset$; $Q_0 \leftarrow Q_{01} \times Q_{02}$
2   $W \leftarrow Q_0$
3   **while** $W \neq \emptyset$ **do**
4   pick $[q_1, q_2]$ from W
5   add $[q_1, q_2]$ to Q
6   **for all** $i = 1$ to m_1 **do**
7   **if** $q_1 \in F_1^i$ **then** add $[q_1, q_2]$ to F^i
8   **for all** $i = 1$ to m_2 **do**
9   **if** $q_2 \in F_2^i$ **then** add $[q_1, q_2]$ to F^{m_1+i}
10   **for all** $a \in \Sigma$ **do**
11   **for all** $q_1' \in \delta_1(q_1, a)$, $q_2' \in \delta_2(q_2, a)$ **do**
12   **if** $[q_1', q_2'] \notin Q$ **then** add $[q_1', q_2']$ to W
13   add $([q_1, q_2], a, [q_1', q_2'])$ to δ

Figure 11.2
Two NGAs.

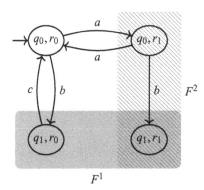

Figure 11.3
Intersection of the two NGAs from figure 11.2.

Example 11.3 Consider again the first two Büchi automata of example 10.8 as depicted in figure 11.2, but this time as NGAs with one set of accepting states: $F_1^1 = \{q_1\}$ for the automaton on the left and $F_2^1 = \{r_1\}$ for the one on the right.

For union, the construction yields an NGA whose semi-automaton is the result of putting the two semi-automata above "side by side," with acceptance condition $\{F_1^1 \cup F_2^1\} = \{\{q_1, r_1\}\}$. For intersection, we obtain the NGA of figure 11.3, with acceptance condition $\{F^1, F^2\}$, where $F^1 = F_1^1 \times Q_2 = \{[q_1, r_0], [q_1, r_1]\}$ and $F^2 = Q_1 \times F_2^1 = \{[q_0, r_1], [q_1, r_1]\}$. The result is no longer an NBA.

Since accepting runs must visit both F^1 and F^2 infinitely often, they are the runs that travel back an forth infinitely between $[q_0, r_1]$ and $[q_1, r_0]$ (no infinite run ever visits $[q_1, r_1]$). In particular, state $[q_1, r_1]$ can be removed without changing the language. Compare with the result we would obtain if the two automata were NFAs. In that case, the resulting NFA would have the same semi-automaton, but the only accepting state would be $[q_1, r_1]$.

A special case. Note that $A_1 \cap A_2$ is not necessarily an NBA, even when A_1 and A_2 are NBAs. We do obtain an NBA if, additionally, $\mathcal{G}_1 = \{F_1^1\} = \{Q_1\}$—that is, when A_1 is an

NBA in which every state is accepting. Indeed, according to the definition above, in this case, we get

$$\mathcal{G} = \{F_1^1 \times Q_2\} \cup \{Q_1 \times F_2^1\} = \{Q_1 \times Q_2, Q_1 \times F_2^1\},$$

and since every run of $A_1 \cap A_2$ visits states of $Q_1 \times Q_2$ infinitely often, we can replace $\mathcal{G}$ by the Büchi condition $Q_1 \times F_2^1$. Observe that this is exactly the result we obtain when we consider A_1 and A_2 as NFAs. In other words, in this special case, we can compute an automaton for the intersection by means of the same algorithm we used for automata on finite words. While this case seems to be very special, it will be relevant in the application to verification in chapter 13.

11.3   Complement

Recall that an NFA is complemented by first converting it into an equivalent DFA and then exchanging the final and nonfinal states of the DFA. For NGAs, this approach cannot work, because not every NGA has an equivalent DGA. To see why, observe that the conversion NGA → NBA shown in section 11.1 preserves determinism—that is, it is also a conversion DGA → DBA. Therefore, if for every NGA there is an equivalent DGA, then we can produce the chain of conversions NBA → NGA → DGA → DBA, contradicting the fact that not every NBA has an equivalent DBA (proposition 10.10).

We can complement NGAs using the results of chapter 10 for Muller automata. Indeed, we can use a chain of conversions NGA → NMA → DMA to transform an NGA A into an equivalent DMA B, which can be converted into a DMA $\overline{B}$ recognizing $\overline{\mathcal{L}_\omega(A)}$, which can be converted into an equivalent NGA $\overline{A}$ using the conversion DMA → NBA. However, this requires to use determinization procedures for ω-automata, like those announced, but not presented, in theorem 10.18 or theorem 10.25. These constructions are more involved than the ones presented so far in this book. More important, they are difficult to handle algorithmically; in particular they often produce many redundant states that can be removed without changing the language. Naive implementations spend much time exploring and constructing such states, which makes them very inefficient. Therefore, efficient implementations must design heuristics to detect and remove redundant states as early as possible, and this is difficult to do.

In this chapter, we follow a different approach. We describe a construction for the direct complementation of NBAs, bypassing the determinization step.[1] In order to complement an NGA, we first transform it into an NBA using the conversion of section 11.1 and then apply the complementation procedure for NBAs.

The complementation procedure for NBAs builds upon section 10.2.3, in which we presented a determinization procedure for NCAs. We assume that the reader is familiar with

---

1. Which, since not every NBA has an equivalent DBA, does not even exist!

it. Given an NCA A, the procedure introduced a mapping *dag* that assigns to each word w a directed acyclic graph *dag*(w) "bundling" all runs of A on w, in the sense that the runs of A on w correspond to the paths of the dag. The procedure then constructed a DCA B satisfying for every word w

> A accepts w
> iff   some path of *dag*(w) visits accepting states of A finitely often
> iff   the run of w in B visits accepting states of B finitely often
> iff B accepts w.

We present the complementation procedure for NBA in a similar way. Fix an NBA $A = (S, F)$, where $S = (Q, \Sigma, \delta, Q_0)$ is a semi-automaton with n states. Our goal is to build another NBA $\overline{A}$ such that for every word w

> A rejects w
> iff   no path of *dag*(w) visits accepting states of A infinitely often
> iff   some run of w in $\overline{A}$ visits accepting states of $\overline{A}$ infinitely often
> iff $\overline{A}$ accepts w.

In a first step, we introduce the notion of *odd ranking* of an ω-word. For the moment, it suffices to say that a ranking of w is the result of decorating the nodes of *dag*(w) with numbers, that w may have multiple rankings, and that an odd ranking is a ranking in which certain nodes have odd rank. The definition of ranking will ensure that

> A rejects w
> iff   no path of *dag*(w) visits accepting states of A infinitely often
> iff   *dag*(w) has an odd ranking.

In the second step, we reuse the construction we applied to determinize NCAs, but this time to construct an NBA $\overline{A}$. Intuitively, the runs of $\overline{A}$ on a word w correspond to the rankings of *dag*(w), and the odd rankings correspond to the accepting runs. This yields

> *dag*(w) has an odd ranking
> iff $\overline{A}$ has an accepting run on w
> iff $\overline{A}$ accepts w.

11.3.1   Rankings and Level Rankings

In the rest of the chapter, we use the NBA of figure 11.4 as running example.

Recall that the directly acyclic graph *dag*(w) of $w \in \Sigma^\omega$ is the result of bundling together the runs of A on w (see section 10.2.3). Figure 11.5 depicts the initial fragments of *dag*(aba^ω) and *dag*($(ab)^\omega$) (ignore the numbers on top of the states for the moment).

A *ranking* of *dag*(w) is a mapping R_w that associates to each node of *dag*(w) a natural number in the range $[0, 2n]$, called a *rank*, satisfying two properties:

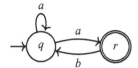

Figure 11.4
Running example for the complementation procedure.

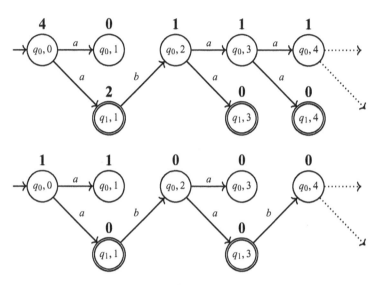

Figure 11.5
Two rankings of the running example.

(a) the rank of a node is greater than or equal to the rank of its children, and

(b) the ranks of accepting nodes are even.

By (a), the ranks of the nodes along an infinite path form a nonincreasing sequence, and so there is a node such that all its infinitely many successors in the path have the same rank; we call this number the *stable rank* of the path.

Example 11.4 Figure 11.5 shows two possible rankings for the dags $dag(aba^\omega)$ and $dag((ab)^\omega)$ of our running example. For each node $\langle q, i \rangle$, the rank $R_w(\langle q, i \rangle)$ is the number on top of the node. Both dags have a single infinite path, with stable ranks 1 and 0, respectively.

Recall that the *i*th level of $dag(w)$ is the set of nodes of the form $\langle q, i \rangle$. A ranking R_w of $dag(w)$ can be decomposed into an infinite sequence $lr_1, lr_2, \ldots$ of *level rankings*, where the level ranking lr_i is defined as follows: $lr_i(q) = R_w(\langle q, i \rangle)$ if $\langle q, i \rangle$ is a node of $dag(w)$, and

$lr_i(q) = \bot$ otherwise. Further, for two level rankings lr and lr' and a letter $a \in \Sigma$, we write $lr \overset{a}{\mapsto} lr'$ to denote, intuitively, that lr' can be the a-successor of lr in a ranking. Formally, we have $lr \overset{a}{\mapsto} lr'$ if the following holds for every state q':

- $lr'(q') \neq \bot$ iff $lr(q) \neq \bot$ for some q such that $q \overset{a}{\rightarrow} q'$.

(Informally: the states of lr' are the a-successors of the states of lr.)

- $lr(q) \geq lr'(q')$ for every q such that $lr(q) \neq \bot$ and $q \overset{a}{\rightarrow} q'$.

(Informally: the rank of a state of lr is at least as large as the rank of its a-successors in lr'.)

Example 11.5 If we represent a level ranking lr of our running example by the vector

$$\begin{bmatrix} lr(q_0) \\ lr(q_1) \end{bmatrix},$$

then the rankings of example 11.4 correspond to the sequences

$$\begin{bmatrix} 4 \\ \bot \end{bmatrix} \begin{bmatrix} 0 \\ 2 \end{bmatrix} \begin{bmatrix} 1 \\ \bot \end{bmatrix} \begin{bmatrix} 1 \\ 0 \end{bmatrix}^{\omega}$$

$$\begin{bmatrix} 1 \\ \bot \end{bmatrix} \begin{bmatrix} 1 \\ 0 \end{bmatrix} \left(\begin{bmatrix} 0 \\ \bot \end{bmatrix} \begin{bmatrix} 0 \\ 0 \end{bmatrix} \right)^{\omega}$$

and we have

$$\begin{bmatrix} 4 \\ \bot \end{bmatrix} \overset{a}{\mapsto} \begin{bmatrix} 0 \\ 2 \end{bmatrix} \overset{b}{\mapsto} \begin{bmatrix} 1 \\ \bot \end{bmatrix} \left(\overset{a}{\mapsto} \begin{bmatrix} 1 \\ 0 \end{bmatrix} \right)^{\omega}$$

$$\begin{bmatrix} 0 \\ \bot \end{bmatrix} \overset{a}{\mapsto} \begin{bmatrix} 1 \\ 0 \end{bmatrix} \left(\overset{b}{\mapsto} \begin{bmatrix} 0 \\ \bot \end{bmatrix} \overset{a}{\mapsto} \begin{bmatrix} 0 \\ 0 \end{bmatrix} \right)^{\omega}.$$

We prove the following fundamental property of rankings, which requires to introduce *odd rankings*.

Definition 11.6 *For every word w, a ranking of dag(w) is* odd *if*

1. *every infinite path of dag(w) visits nodes of odd rank infinitely often, and*

2. *the initial nodes $\langle q_0, 0 \rangle$ for $q_0 \in Q_0$ have rank 2n.*

For example, the top ranking of figure 11.5 is an odd ranking, because its only infinite path visits infinitely often nodes of rank 1. The ranking at the bottom is not odd, because only the first node of its unique infinite path has an odd ranking, and the rank of the initial node is not 4. The following proposition characterizes the words rejected by A as those whose dag admits an odd ranking.

Proposition 11.7 *Let n be the number of states of A. For every word $w \in \Sigma^\omega$, w is rejected by A iff dag(w) has an odd ranking.*

Proof $\Leftarrow$) Assume that $dag(w)$ has an odd ranking. Then every infinite path of $dag(w)$ has odd stable rank, and so it only contains finitely many nodes with even rank. Since all accepting nodes have even ranks, no path of $dag(w)$ visits accepting nodes infinitely often. So w is rejected by A.

$\Rightarrow$) Assume that w is rejected by A. We construct a ranking that is almost odd, defined as a ranking that satisfies property 1 of definition 11.6, and such that every initial node $\langle q_0, 0 \rangle$ has rank at most $2n$. This suffices, because we can then increase the ranks of the initial nodes to $2n$, if necessary, since this change preserves all properties of a ranking.

Given two directed acyclic graphs (dags) D and D', let $D' \subseteq D$ denote that D' can be obtained from D through deletion of some nodes and all their adjacent edges. We proceed in two steps. First we assign ranks to nodes, and then we prove that the assignment satisfies all properties of an odd ranking.

Assigning ranks to nodes. We define a function f that assigns to each node $\langle q, l \rangle$ of $dag(w)$ a natural number $f(q, l)$. We first inductively define an infinite chain $D_0 \supseteq D_1 \supseteq D_2 \supseteq \cdots$ of dags and define $f(q, l)$ as the number i such that $\langle q, l \rangle$ belongs to D_i but not to D_{i+1}.

We say that a node of a (possibly finite) dag $D \subseteq dag(w)$ is

- *crosshatched* iff it has only finitely many descendants;

- *hatched* iff it has infinitely many descendants, but none of them (including the node itself) is accepting; and

- *solid* otherwise.

In particular, hatched nodes are not accepting. Observe also that the children of a crosshatched node are crosshatched, and the children of a hatched node are crosshatched or hatched. Now we define the following (see figure 11.6 for an example):

- $D_0 = dag(w)$,

- D_{2i+1} is the result of deleting all the crosshatched nodes of D_{2i}, and

- D_{2i+2} is the result of deleting all the hatched nodes of D_{2i+1}.

Proving that f is an odd ranking. As mentioned above, it suffices to prove that f is almost an odd ranking. The proof is divided into four parts:

(1) f assigns all nodes a number in the range $[0, 2n]$.

(2) If $\langle q', l' \rangle$ is a child of $\langle q, l \rangle$, then $f(q', l') \leq f(q, l)$.

(3) If $\langle q, l \rangle$ is an accepting node, then $f(q, l)$ is even.

(4) Every infinite path of $dag(w)$ visits nodes $\langle q, l \rangle$ such that $f(q, l)$ is odd infinitely often.

D_0:

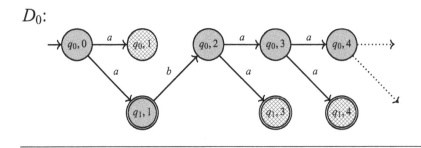

D_1:

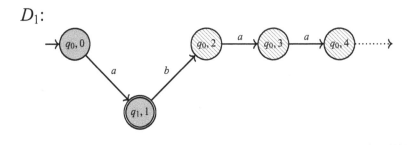

D_2:

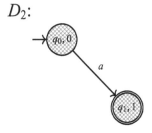

Figure 11.6
Initial fragments of the dags D_0, D_1, and D_2 for $dag(aba^\omega)$. The map f assigns to $dag(aba^\omega)$ the ranking shown at the top of example 11.4, with the exception that f assigns rank 2 to $\langle q_0, 0 \rangle$. However, increasing the rank of $\langle q_0, 2 \rangle$ to 4 preserves all properties of an odd ranking.

Part 1 f assigns all nodes a number in the range $[0, 2n]$.

We prove that the dag D_{2n+1} is empty, which implies that f assigns all nodes of $dag(w)$ a number in the range $[0, 2n]$ by the definition of f. By the definition of D_{2n+1}, it suffices to show that D_{2n} is finite. For this we proceed as follows: we prove by induction on i that for every $i \geq 0$, the levels of D_{2i} eventually have at most $(n - i)$ nodes; formally, there exists $\ell_i \geq 0$ such that for every $\ell \geq \ell_i$, the ℓth level of D_{2i} contains at most $(n - i)$ nodes. Taking $i = n$, we obtain that the levels of D_{2n} eventually contain 0 nodes, and so that D_{2n} is finite.

Base case i = 0. Since for every state q, a level contains at most one node of the form $\langle q, \ell \rangle$, every level of $dag(w) = D_0$ contains at most n nodes.

Induction step i > 0. Assume now that the hypothesis holds for i; we prove it for $i + 1$. Consider the dag D_{2i}. If D_{2i} is finite, then D_{2i+1} is empty. Thus, D_{2i+2} is empty as well, and we are done. So, assume that D_{2i} is infinite. We make the following claim:

Claim 1: D_{2i+1} contains some hatched node.

Proof of claim 1: Assume that no node in D_{2i+1} is hatched. We show that $dag(w)$ contains a path that visits accepting nodes infinitely often, contradicting the assumption that A rejects w. It suffices to prove that every node of D_{2i+1} has a descendant, different from itself, that is accepting. Let $\langle q, \ell \rangle$ be an arbitrary node of D_{2i+1}. Since D_{2i+1} is obtained by removing all crosshatched nodes from D_{2i}, the node has at least one child. Since, by assumption, the child is not hatched, the child has an accepting descendant, and we are done.

Let $\langle q, \ell \rangle$ be a hatched node in D_{2i+1}, which exists by claim 1. We prove that the levels of D_{2i+2} eventually contain at most $n - (i + 1)$ nodes. By induction hypothesis, we know that the levels of D_{2i} eventually contain at most $n - i$ nodes. Therefore, it suffices to show that the levels of D_{2i+2} eventually contain at least one node less than the same level of D_{2i}. We do this. Since $\langle q, \ell \rangle$ is a node of D_{2i+1}, it is not crosshatched in D_{2i}. Thus, $\langle q, l \rangle$ has infinitely many descendants in D_{2i}. By König's lemma (lemma 10.14), D_{2i} contains an infinite path $\pi = \langle q, \ell \rangle \langle q_1, \ell + 1 \rangle \langle q_2, \ell + 2 \rangle \ldots$. We claim the following:

Claim 2: No node of π is in D_{2i+2}.

Proof of claim 2: Since all nodes of π have infinitely many descendants, none of them is crosshatched in D_{2i}, and so π also exists in D_{2i+1}. Since $\langle q, \ell \rangle$ is hatched and, by definition, the children of a hatched node are crosshatched or hatched, π is a hatched path. So every node of π is deleted from D_{2i+1} to obtain D_{2i+2}, and the claim is proved.

By the claim, every level after the ℓth level has at least one node less in D_{2i+2} than in D_{2i}, and we are done.

Part 2 If $\langle q', l' \rangle$ is a child of $\langle q, l \rangle$, then $f(q', l') \leq f(q, l)$.

This follows from the definition of f and from the fact that the children of a crosshatched node in D_{2i} are crosshatched, and the children of a hatched node in D_{2i+1} are hatched.

Part 3 If $\langle q, l \rangle$ is an accepting node, then $f(q, l)$ is even.

If $f(q, l)$ is odd, then $\langle q, l \rangle$ is hatched at D_{2i+1} for some i, and so q is not accepting.

Part 4 Every infinite path of $dag(w)$ visits nodes $\langle q, l \rangle$ such that $f(q, l)$ is odd infinitely often.

It suffices to prove that the stable rank of every infinite path of $dag(w)$ is odd. Since w is rejected by A, every infinite path of A visits the accepting states of A finitely often. Take an arbitrary infinite path of $dag(w)$, and let $\langle q, l \rangle$ be the first node of the path that is assigned the stable rank. Since $\langle q, l \rangle$ has infinitely many descendants (it belongs to an infinite path), it cannot have received its rank because it was a crosshatched node of a dag D_{2i}. So, it received its rank because it was a hatched node of a dag D_{2i+1}. Thus, $\langle q, l \rangle$ is assigned rank $2i + 1$, which is odd. $\square$

11.3.2   The Complement NBA $\overline{A}$

Given an NBA $A = (Q, \Sigma, \delta, Q_0, F)$, we construct an NBA $\overline{A}$ such that for every word w:

(a) A run of $\overline{A}$ on w is a ranking of $dag(w)$ with ranks in the range $[0, 2n]$ and vice versa.

(b) An accepting run of $\overline{A}$ on w is an odd ranking of $dag(w)$ and vice versa.

Such an automaton satisfies for every word w:

$$A \text{ rejects } w$$

$$\Longleftrightarrow dag(w) \text{ has an odd ranking (by proposition 11.7)}$$

$$\Longleftrightarrow \overline{A} \text{ has an accepting run on } w$$

$$\Longleftrightarrow \overline{A} \text{ accepts } w.$$

Thus, it recognizes the complement of the language of A.

Using the representation of a ranking as an infinite sequence of level rankings, it is easy to construct a semi-automaton satisfying (a):

• The states are the level rankings with ranks in the range $[0, 2n]$, that is, the mappings $lr \colon Q \to [0, 2n] \cup \{\bot\}$ such that $lr(q)$ is even for every accepting state q.

• The (unique) initial state is the level ranking lr_0 given by $lr_0(q) = 2n$ if $q \in Q_0$, and $lr(q) = \bot$ otherwise.

• The transitions are the triples (lr, a, lr'), where lr and lr' are level rankings, $a \in \Sigma$, and $lr \overset{a}{\mapsto} lr'$ holds.

If we could define a Büchi acceptance condition on this semi-automaton such that the resulting NBA also satisfies condition (b), we would be done. However, we cannot decide if a ranking is odd or not if the only information we have is which level rankings are visited infinitely often. Fortunately, we already solved a very similar problem in section 10.2.3.1 of chapter 10, when we used the breakpoint construction to determinize NCAs. Let us briefly recall what we did.

Breakpoint construction. In section 10.2.3.1, we introduced the set of breakpoint levels—or just breakpoints—of a dag $dag(w)$:

- The 0th level of $dag(w)$ is a breakpoint.
- If level ℓ of $dag(w)$ is a breakpoint, then the next level $\ell' > \ell$ such that *every* path between nodes of ℓ and ℓ' (excluding nodes of ℓ and including nodes of ℓ') visits an accepting state is also a breakpoint.

We then proved the following:

> some path of $dag(w)$ visits accepting states finitely often
> iff   the set of breakpoints of $dag(w)$ is finite,

which is logically equivalent to

> every path of $dag(w)$ visits accepting states infinitely often
> iff   the set of breakpoints of $dag(w)$ is infinite.

Finally, we defined the states of the DCA as the pairs $[P, O]$, where P is the set of states of a level, and O contains the states of P that owe a visit to the accepting states (see section 10.2.3.1 for the formal definition); further, the accepting states are the breakpoints, defined as the pairs where $O = \emptyset$.

Adapting the breakpoint construction for NCA $\rightarrow$ DCA. We redefine the set of breakpoints of $dag(w)$:

- The 0th level of $dag(w)$ is a breakpoint.
- If level ℓ is a breakpoint, then the next level $\ell' > \ell$ such that *every* path between nodes of ℓ and ℓ' (excluding nodes of ℓ and including nodes of ℓ') visits *a node of odd rank* is also a breakpoint.

That is, we replace the visits to accepting nodes in the previous definition by visits to the nodes of odd rank. The same proof as in section 10.2.3.1 now yields the following:

> every path of $dag(w)$ visits nodes of odd rank infinitely often
> iff   the set of breakpoints of $dag(w)$ is infinite.

Finally, we define the states of $\overline{A}$ as the pairs $[lr, O]$, where lr is a level ranking, and O is the set of nodes of the ranking that owe a visit *to a node of odd rank*. The accepting states are the breakpoints (i.e., the pairs $[lr, O]$ with $O = \emptyset$). Let us give a precise definition and summarize the correctness proof.

Formal definition of $\overline{A}$. Let $A = (Q, \Sigma, \delta, Q_0, F)$ be an NBA. The NBA $\overline{A}$ is defined as follows:

States: The states are pairs $[lr, O]$, where lr is a level ranking with ranks in the range $[0;$ $2n]$, and $O \subseteq Q$ is a set of owing states.

Transitions: The transitions are triples $[lr, O] \xrightarrow{a} [lr', O']$ such that $lr \xmapsto{a} lr'$ and

$$O' = \begin{cases} \{q \in \delta(O, a) : lr'(q) \text{ is even}\} & \text{if } O \neq \emptyset, \\ \{q \in Q : lr'(q) \text{ is even}\} & \text{if } O = \emptyset. \end{cases}$$

Initial states: The only initial state is the pair $[lr_0, \emptyset]$.

Accepting states: A state $[lr, O]$ is accepting if $O = \emptyset$.

The proof that $\overline{A}$ recognizes $\overline{\mathcal{L}_\omega(A)}$ follows from chaining these three facts:

- A run of $\overline{A}$ on w is accepting iff the ranking of $dag(w)$ encoded by the run contains infinitely many breakpoints.
  This follows immediately from the fact that the accepting states of $\overline{A}$ are the breakpoints.
- A ranking of $dag(w)$ contains infinitely many breakpoints iff it is odd.
  In section 10.2.3, we proved that the set of breakpoints of $dag(w)$ is infinite iff every path of $dag(w)$ visits accepting states infinitely often. Exactly the same proof yields now: the set of breakpoints of a ranking of $dag(w)$ is infinite iff every path of the ranking visits accepting states of $\overline{A}$ infinitely often (i.e., iff the ranking is odd).
- $dag(w)$ has an odd ranking iff A rejects w.
  This is the fundamental property of rankings.

The pseudocode for the complementation algorithm, constructing only the reachable states, is described in algorithm 48. In the pseudocode, we let lr_0 denote the level ranking given by $lr(q) = 2|Q|$ if $q \in Q_0$ and $lr(q) = \bot$ otherwise. Further, $lr \xmapsto{a} lr'$ denotes that for every $q' \in Q$, (1) $lr'(q') \neq \bot$ iff $lr(q) \neq \bot$ for some q such that $q \xrightarrow{a} q'$, and (2) if $lr'(q') \neq \bot$, then $lr(q) \geq lr'(q')$ for every q such that $lr(q) \neq \bot$ and $q \xrightarrow{a} q'$.

Complexity. Let n be the number of states of A. Recall that level rankings are mappings $lr \colon Q \to \{\bot\} \cup [0, 2n]$. So there at most $(2n + 2)^n$ level rankings, and so $\overline{A}$ has at most $(2n + 2)^n \cdot 2^n \in n^{\mathcal{O}(n)}$ states. In order to compare this with the complexity of complementation for NFAs, observe that $n^{\mathcal{O}(n)} = 2^{\mathcal{O}(n \log n)}$ and that, given an NFA with n states, the complementation algorithm yields an automaton with at most 2^n states. Thus, for NBAs, we get an extra $\log n$ factor in the exponent.

Example 11.8 We construct the complements $\overline{A}_1$ and $\overline{A}_2$ of the only two NBAs over alphabet $\{a\}$ having one state and one transition (depicted in figure 11.7).
We have $\mathcal{L}_\omega(A_1) = \{a^\omega\}$ and $\mathcal{L}_\omega(A_2) = \emptyset$. The construction yields the automata of figure 11.8.

Algorithm 48 Algorithm to complement an NBA.

$CompNBA(A)$
Input: NBA $A = (Q, \Sigma, \delta, Q_0, F)$
Output: NBA $\overline{A} = (\overline{Q}, \Sigma, \overline{\delta}, \overline{q}_0, \overline{F})$ with $\mathcal{L}_\omega(\overline{A}) = \overline{\mathcal{L}_\omega(A)}$

```
1   Q̄, δ̄, F̄ ← ∅
2   q̄₀ ← [lr₀, ∅]
3   W ← {[lr₀, ∅]}
4   while W ≠ ∅ do
5       pick [lr, O] from W; add [lr, O] to Q̄
6       if O = ∅ then add [lr, O] to F̄
7       for all a ∈ Σ, lr' s.t. lr ↦ᵃ lr' do
8           if O ≠ ∅ then O' ← {q ∈ δ(O, a) : lr'(q) is even}
9           else O' ← {q ∈ Q : lr'(q) is even }
10          add ([lr, O], a, [lr', O']) to δ̄
11          if [lr', O'] ∉ Q̄ then add [lr', O'] to W
12  return (Q̄, Σ, δ̄, q̄₀, F̄)
```

We explain why, beginning with $\overline{A}_1$. A state of $\overline{A}_1$ is a pair $\langle lr, O \rangle$, where lr is the rank of the state q (since there is only one state, we can identify lr and $lr(q)$). The initial state is $\langle 2, \emptyset \rangle$. Let us compute the successors of $\langle 2, \emptyset \rangle$ under the letter a. Let $\langle lr', O' \rangle$ be a successor. Since $\delta(q, a) = \{q\}$, we have $lr' \neq \bot$, and since q is accepting, we have $lr' \neq 1$. So, either $lr' = 0$ or $lr' = 2$. In both cases, the visit to a node of odd rank is still "owed," which implies $O' = \{q\}$. So, the successors of $\langle 2, \emptyset \rangle$ are $\langle 2, \{q\} \rangle$ and $\langle 0, \{q\} \rangle$. Let us now compute the successors of $\langle 0, \{q\} \rangle$. Let $\langle lr', O' \rangle$ be a successor. We have $lr' \neq \bot$ and $lr' \neq 1$ as before, but now, since ranks cannot increase along a path, we also have $lr' \neq 2$. Thus, $lr' = 0$, and since the visit to the node of odd rank is still "owed," the only successor of $\langle 0, \{q\} \rangle$ is $\langle 0, \{q\} \rangle$. Similarly, the successors of $\langle 2, \{q\} \rangle$ are $\langle 2, \{q\} \rangle$ and $\langle 0, \{q\} \rangle$. Since $\langle 2, \emptyset \rangle$ is the only accepting state, $\overline{A}_1$ recognizes the empty ω-language.

Let us now construct $\overline{A}_2$. The difference with $\overline{A}_1$ is that, since q is no longer accepting, it can also have odd rank 1. So, $\langle 2, \emptyset \rangle$ has three successors: $\langle 2, \{q\} \rangle$, $\langle 1, \emptyset \rangle$, and $\langle 0, \{q\} \rangle$. The

Figure 11.7
Two NBAs with a single state and transition.

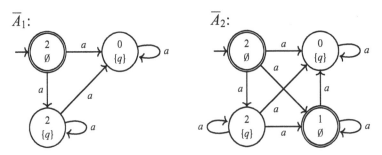

Figure 11.8
Complement of the NBAs from figure 11.7.

successors of $\langle 1, \emptyset \rangle$ are $\langle 1, \emptyset \rangle$ and $\langle 0, \{q\} \rangle$. The accepting states are $\langle 2, \emptyset \rangle$ and $\langle 1, \emptyset \rangle$, and $\overline{A}_2$ recognizes a^{ω}.

11.3.3　A Lower Bound on the Size of $\overline{A}$

We exhibit a family $\{L_n\}_{n \geq 1}$ of ω-languages such that L_n is accepted by a Büchi automaton A_n with $n+1$ states and any Büchi automaton accepting the complement of L_n has at least $n! \in 2^{\Theta(n \log n)}$ states.

Let $\Sigma_n = \{1, \ldots, n, \#\}$. We associate to a word $w \in \Sigma_n^{\omega}$ a directed graph G_w. The nodes of G_w are the numbers $\{1, \ldots, n\}$, and there is an edge from node i to node j iff the finite word ij occurs infinitely often in w.

Example 11.9　Consider the words $w = (12\#1\#2)^{\omega}$ and $v = (12\#)^{\omega}$ over $\Sigma_2 = \{1, 2, \#\}$.

- G_w contains two nodes, 1 and 2, and two edges, $1 \to 2$ and $2 \to 1$.
- G_v has the same nodes but only one edge, $1 \to 2$.

Let L_n be the language of words $w \in \Sigma_n^{\omega}$ such that G_w has at least one cycle. For example, for the words of example 11.9, we have $w \in L_2$ and $v \notin L_2$. Let $\overline{L}_n$ denote the complement of L_n (i.e., the set of words w such that G_w is acyclic).

In the rest of the section, we prove the following proposition:

Proposition 11.10　For all $n \geq 1$, the language L_n is recognized by an NBA with $n+1$ states, and every NBA recognizing $\overline{L}_n$ has at least $n!$ states.

An NBA for L_n.　Let A_n be the NBA with states $\{1, 2, \ldots, n, \mathbf{ch}\}$, initial states $\{1, \ldots, n\}$, accepting state $\mathbf{ch}$, and the following transitions:

- $\mathbf{i} \xrightarrow{\sigma} \mathbf{i}$ for every $1 \leq i \leq n$ and every $\sigma \in \Sigma_n$, and
- $\mathbf{i} \xrightarrow{i} \mathbf{ch}$ and $\mathbf{ch} \xrightarrow{j} \mathbf{j}$ for every $1 \leq i, j \leq n$. (Intuitively, $\mathbf{ch}$ is an "interchange station" that allows one to move from $\mathbf{i}$ to $\mathbf{j}$ by reading ij.)

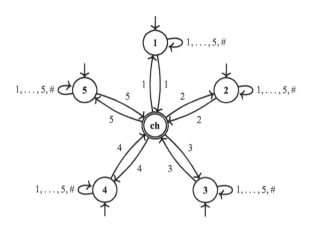

Figure 11.9
The Büchi automaton A_5.

Figure 11.9 depicts A_5. We prove that A_n recognizes L_n in two steps.

(1) If $w \in L_n$, then A_n accepts w.

Choose a cycle $i_0 i_2 \cdots i_{k-1} i_0$ of G_w. We construct an accepting run of A_n by picking $\mathbf{i_0}$ as the initial state and iteratively applying the following rule, where $j \oplus 1$ is an abbreviation for $(j + 1) \bmod k$:

If the current state is $\mathbf{i_j}$, stay in $\mathbf{i_j}$ until the next occurrence of $i_j\, i_{j\oplus 1}$ in w, and then take

$$\mathbf{i_j} \xrightarrow{i_j} \mathbf{ch} \xrightarrow{i_{j\oplus 1}} \mathbf{i_{j\oplus 1}}$$

to move from $\mathbf{i_j}$ to $\mathbf{i_{j\oplus 1}}$.

By definition of G_w, state $\mathbf{ch}$ is visited infinitely often, and so w is accepted.

Example 11.11   Consider again the word $w = (12\#1\#2)^\omega$ of example 11.9. The graph G_w has the cycle $\mathbf{1} \to \mathbf{2} \to \mathbf{1}$. The accepting run of A_2 on w is

$$\mathbf{1} \xrightarrow{1} \mathbf{ch} \xrightarrow{2} \mathbf{2} \xrightarrow{\#} \mathbf{2} \xrightarrow{1} \mathbf{2} \xrightarrow{\#} \mathbf{2} \xrightarrow{2} \mathbf{ch} \xrightarrow{1} \mathbf{1} \xrightarrow{1} \mathbf{ch} \xrightarrow{2} \mathbf{2} \cdots .$$

(2) If A_n accepts w, then $w \in L_n$.

We show that every node i of G_w has at least one outgoing edge $i \to j$, which proves that G_w contains a cycle. Let ρ be an accepting run of A_n on w. Since ρ is accepting, it cannot stay in any of the states $\mathbf{1}, \dots, \mathbf{n}$ forever, and hence for each $\mathbf{i} \in \inf(\rho)$, there is $\mathbf{j} \in \inf(\rho)$ such that the sequence $\mathbf{i}\ \mathbf{ch}\ \mathbf{j}$ of states occurs infinitely often in ρ. Since the only path of A_n

matching this sequence of states is

$$\mathbf{i} \xrightarrow{i} \mathbf{ch} \xrightarrow{j} \mathbf{j},$$

the finite word ij occurs infinitely often in w, and so $i \to j$ is an edge of G_w.   □

Every NBA recognizing $\overline{L_n}$ has at least $n!$ states.   We need some preliminaries. Let $\tau = \langle \tau_1, \ldots, \tau_n \rangle$ denote a permutation of $\langle 1, \ldots, n \rangle$. We make two observations:

(a) $(\tau \#)^\omega \in \overline{L}_n$ for every permutation τ.
Indeed, the graph $G((\tau \#)^\omega)$ is just the path $\tau_1 \to \tau_2 \to \cdots \to \tau_n$, which is acyclic.

(b) If a word w contains infinitely many occurrences of two different permutations τ and τ' of $\langle 1, \ldots, n \rangle$, then $w \in L_n$.

   Since τ and τ' are different, there are $i, j \in \{1, \ldots, n\}$ such that i precedes j in τ and j precedes i in τ'. Since w contains infinitely many occurrences of τ, the graph G_w has a path from i to j. Since it also contains infinitely many occurrences of τ', the graph also has a path from j to i. Hence, G_w contains a cycle, which implies $w \in L_n$.

   Now, let A be a Büchi automaton recognizing $\overline{L}_n$, and let τ, τ' be two arbitrary permutations of $1, \ldots, n$. By (a), there exist runs ρ and ρ' of A accepting $(\tau \#)^\omega$ and $(\tau' \#)^\omega$, respectively. We prove that the intersection of $\inf(\rho)$ and $\inf(\rho')$ is empty. This implies that A has at least as many accepting states as there are permutations of $1, \ldots, n$, which proves the proposition. We proceed by contradiction. Assume $q \in \inf(\rho) \cap \inf(\rho')$. We construct an accepting run ρ'' by concatenating finite paths ρ and ρ' as follows:

(0) Starting from the initial state of ρ, follow ρ until it reaches q.

(1) Starting from q, follow ρ' until it returns to q for the first time, after having visited some accepting state and having read the word τ' at least once in between.

(2) Starting from q, follow ρ until it returns to q for the first time, after having visited some accepting state and having read the word τ at least once in between.

(3) Go to (1).

The word accepted by ρ'' contains infinitely many occurrences of both τ and τ'. By (b), this word belongs to L_n, contradicting $\mathcal{L}_\omega(A) = \overline{L}_n$.   □

11.4   Exercises

☆ ✿ **Exercise 155.** Consider the two Büchi automata (NBAs) below. Interpret them as generalized Büchi automata (NGAs), construct their intersection, and convert the resulting NGA into an NBA.

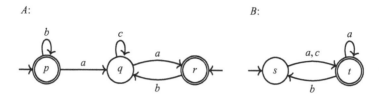

☆ ⚙ **Exercise 156.** Let $L_\sigma = \{w \in \{a, b, c\}^\omega : w$ contains infinitely many σ's$\}$. Give deterministic Büchi automata for languages L_a, L_b, and L_c; construct the intersection of these automata interpreted as NGAs; and convert the resulting NGA as a Büchi automaton.

☆ ⚙ **Exercise 157.** Give Büchi automata for the following ω-languages:

(i) $L_1 = \{w \in \{a, b\}^\omega : w$ contains infinitely many $as\}$,

(ii) $L_2 = \{w \in \{a, b\}^\omega : w$ contains finitely many $bs\}$, and

(iii) $L_3 = \{w \in \{a, b\}^\omega :$ each occurrence of a in w is followed by a $b\}$.

Construct the intersection of these automata interpreted as NGAs, and convert the resulting NGA as a Büchi automaton.

☆ 🖳 **Exercise 158.** An ω-automaton has acceptance on transitions if the acceptance condition specifies which transitions must appear infinitely often in a run. All classes of ω-automata (Büchi, Rabin, etc.) can be defined with acceptance on transitions rather than states.

Give minimal deterministic automata, for the language of words over $\{a, b\}$ containing infinitely many a and infinitely many b, of the following kinds: (a) Büchi (with state-based accepting condition), (b) generalized Büchi (with state-based accepting condition), (c) Büchi with acceptance on transitions, and (d) generalized Büchi with acceptance on transitions.

★ ⚙ **Exercise 159.** Consider the following Büchi automaton over $\Sigma = \{a, b\}$:

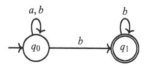

(a) Sketch dag($abab^\omega$) and dag($(ab)^\omega$).

(b) Let r_w be the ranking of dag(w) defined by

$$r_w(q, i) = \begin{cases} 1 & \text{if } q = q_0 \text{ and } \langle q_0, i \rangle \text{ appears in dag}(w), \\ 0 & \text{if } q = q_1 \text{ and } \langle q_1, i \rangle \text{ appears in dag}(w), \\ \bot & \text{otherwise.} \end{cases}$$

Are r_{abab^ω} and $r_{(ab)^\omega}$ odd rankings?

(c) Show that r_w is an odd ranking if and only if $w \notin \mathcal{L}_\omega(B)$.

(d) Build a Büchi automaton accepting $\overline{\mathcal{L}_\omega(B)}$ using the construction seen in the chapter.

Hint: By (c), it is sufficient to use $\{0, 1\}$ as ranks.

☆ ✦ **Exercise 160.** Design algorithms for the following decision problems:

(a) Given finite words $u, v, x, y \in \Sigma^*$, decide whether the ω-words uv^ω and xy^ω are equal.

(b) Given a Büchi automaton A and finite words u, v, decide whether A accepts the ω-word uv^ω.

Assume that you can algorithmically test whether the language of a given Büchi automaton is empty or not (we will cover such procedures in chapter 12).

☆ ■ **Exercise 161.** Show that, for every DBA A with n states, there is an NBA B with $2n$ states such that $\mathcal{L}_\omega(B) = \overline{\mathcal{L}_\omega(A)}$. Explain why your construction does not work for NBAs.

★ ☞ **Exercise 162.** A Büchi automaton $A = (Q, \Sigma, \delta, Q_0, F)$ is *weak* if no strongly connected component (SCC) of A contains both accepting and nonaccepting states—that is, every SCC $C \subseteq Q$ satisfies either $C \subseteq F$ or $C \subseteq Q \setminus F$.

(a) Prove that a Büchi automaton A is *weak* iff for every run ρ either $inf(\rho) \subseteq F$ or $inf(\rho) \subseteq Q \setminus F$.

(b) Prove that the algorithms for union, intersection, and complementation of DFAs are correct for weak DBAs. More precisely, show that the algorithms return weak DBAs recognizing respectively the union, intersection, and complement of the languages of the input automata.

☆ ✦ **Exercise 163.** Give algorithms that directly complement deterministic Muller and parity automata, without going through Büchi automata.

☆ ■ **Exercise 164.** Let $A = (Q, \Sigma, q_0, \delta, \{\langle F_0, G_0 \rangle, \ldots, \langle F_{m-1}, G_{m-1} \rangle\})$ be a deterministic automaton. What is the relation between the languages recognized by A seen as a deterministic Rabin automaton and seen as a deterministic Streett automaton?

★ ☞ **Exercise 165.** Consider Büchi automata with universal accepting condition (UBA): an ω-word w is accepted if *every* run of the automaton on w is accepting, that is, if *every* run of the automaton on w visits accepting states infinitely often.

Recall that automata on finite words with existential and universal accepting conditions recognize the same languages (see exercise 21). Prove that this does not hold for automata on ω-words by showing that, for every UBA, there is a DBA that recognizes the same language. This implies that the ω-languages recognized by UBAs are a proper subset of ω-regular languages.

Hint: On input w, the DBA checks that every path of $dag(w)$ visits some final state infinitely often. The states of the DBA are pairs (Q', O) of sets of the UBA where $O \subseteq Q'$ is a set of "owing" states. Loosely speaking, the transition relation is defined to satisfy the following property: after reading a prefix w' of w, the DBA is at the state (Q', O) given by

- *Q' is the set of states reached by the runs of the UBA on w';*
- *O is the subset of states of Q' that "owe" a visit to a final state of the UBA (see the construction for the complement of a Büchi automaton).*

12 Emptiness Check: Implementations

After implementing boolean operations on NGAs in chapter 11, we present an implementation of the tests on sets of objects shown in table 0.1 of chapter 0. The list contains four sets: membership, emptiness, containment, and equivalence. We only consider emptiness, as all other tests can be reduced to it:

- The membership test **Member**(x, X) takes as input an object x and a set of objects X, encoded, respectively, as an ω-word and an ω-regular language over some alphabet Σ. However, the test is only well defined after we fix a finite representation for ω-words, which for cardinality reasons only can represent a countable subset of Σ^ω. We can limit the test to ω-words w for which there exists an ω-regular expression s such that $\mathcal{L}_\omega(s) = \{w\}$. In this case, the membership test can be reduced to the emptiness set by converting s into an ω-automaton, computing its intersection with the ω-automaton for the ω-regular language encoding X, and conducting an emptiness test on the result.

- As seen in chapter 3, testing the inclusion $L_1 \subseteq L_2$ reduces to testing the emptiness of $L_1 \cap \overline{L}_2$, and testing the equivalence $L_1 = L_2$ reduces to testing the inclusions $L_1 \subseteq L_2$ and $L_2 \subseteq L_1$.

We present efficient algorithms for checking whether a given NGA $A = (Q, \Sigma, \delta, Q_0, \mathcal{G})$ recognizes the empty language. Since transition labels are irrelevant for checking emptiness, in this chapter, we redefine δ as a set of pairs of states:

$$\delta := \{(q, q') \in Q \times Q : (q, a, q') \in \delta \text{ for some } a \in \Sigma\}$$

We assume that initially, the algorithms only know the set Q_0 of initial states of A. Further, the algorithms can query δ—that is, they can submit a state q to an oracle that returns $\delta(q)$ and the collection of sets $F \in \mathcal{G}$ such that $q \in F$. So, the algorithms must determine if A recognizes the empty language while exploring it, and only "forward" exploration is possible. In particular, the algorithms can contain loops of the form "**for** $q' \in \delta(q)$ **do** $\cdots$" but no loops of the form "**for** $q' \in \delta^{-1}(q)$ **do** $\cdots$"; computing the predecessors of a state is not a primitive operation. We say that these algorithms operate *on-the-fly*.

Example 12.1   To illustrate the notion of an on-the-fly algorithm, consider the problem of deciding whether an NFA, not necessarily in normal form, recognizes the empty language. An NFA recognizes a nonempty language iff some final state is reachable from some initial state. In principle, this can be checked by means of a *forward search* that explores the NFA from the initial states, looking for final states, or by a *backward search* that explores the NFA backward from the final states, looking for initial states. The first algorithm works on-the-fly: it can be implemented even if initially only Q_0 is known and δ can be queried. The second one does not work on-the-fly.

To understand the advantage of on-the-fly algorithms, consider the problem of deciding whether the intersection of the languages of two NGAs, say A_1 and A_2, is empty. We can first use *IntersNGA* (algorithm 47) to construct an NGA A recognizing $\mathcal{L}_\omega(A_1) \cap \mathcal{L}_\omega(A_2)$ and then apply the emptiness algorithm to it, but this requires to construct the complete automaton A. We can do better by observing that *IntersNGA* constructs A in a "forward manner" too, starting at the initial states and iteratively constructing the successors of the states $[q_1, q_2]$ constructed so far. This allows us to link the intersection and emptiness algorithms: a query $\delta([q_1, q_2])$ to the oracle of the on-the-fly emptiness algorithm is answered by the intersection algorithm, which computes the successors of $[q_1, q_2]$ in A according to *IntersNGA*. The composite algorithm may be able to determine that A has a nonempty language after having constructed only a small part of it.

On-the-fly emptiness algorithms are needed for the on-the-fly approach to automatic verification described in section 7.4.2 of chapter 7, where the reader can find a more detailed discussion.

We need a few graph-theoretical notions. If $(q, r) \in \delta$, then r is a *successor* of q and q is a *predecessor* of r. A *path* is a sequence $q_0, q_1, \ldots, q_n$ of states such that q_{i+1} is a successor of q_i for every $i \in \{0, \ldots, n-1\}$; we say that the path *leads* from q_0 to q_n. Note that a path may consist of only one state; in this case, the path is *empty* and leads from a state to itself. A *cycle* is a nonempty path that leads from a state to itself. We write $q \rightsquigarrow r$ to denote that there is a path from q to r.

Clearly, A is nonempty iff it has an *accepting lasso*—that is, a path $q_0 q_1 \ldots q_{n-1} q_n$ such that $q_n = q_i$ for some $i \in \{0, \ldots, n-1\}$ and $\{q_i, q_{i+1}, \ldots, q_{n-1}\} \cap F \neq \emptyset$ for every $F \in \mathcal{G}$. The lasso consists of a path $q_0 \ldots q_i$, followed by a cycle $q_i q_{i+1} \ldots q_{n-1} q_i$. We are interested in emptiness checks that on input A report EMPTY or NONEMPTY (sometimes abbreviated to EMP and NEMP) and in the latter case return an accepting lasso as a *witness* of nonemptiness.

The chapter is divided into two sections, which present algorithms based on depth-first search (DFS) and breadth-first search (BFS) of the NGA, respectively. In all algorithms, we first consider the special case in which the automaton is an NBA. Emptiness of GAs can then be checked by applying the conversion NGA $\rightarrow$ NBA, but for all algorithms except one, we present a more efficient alternative that sidesteps the conversion.

12.1   Emptiness Algorithms Based on Depth-First Search

We present two emptiness algorithms that explore A using depth-first search (DFS). We start with a brief description of DFS and some of its properties.

A DFS of A is the result of conducting DFSs from each initial state of A. Assume one of these DFSs starts at an initial state q_0. If the current state q still has unexplored outgoing transitions, then one of them is selected. If the transition leads to a not yet discovered state r, then r becomes the current state. If all of q's outgoing transitions have been explored, then the search "backtracks" to the state from which q was discovered (i.e., this state becomes the current state). The process continues until q_0 becomes the current state again and all its outgoing transitions have been explored. Algorithm 49 provides a pseudocode implementation (ignore algorithm *DFS_Tree* for the moment).

Observe that *DFS* is nondeterministic, since we do not fix the order in which the states of $\delta(q)$ are examined by the **for** loop. Since, by hypothesis, every state of an automaton is reachable from the initial state, we always have $S = Q$ after termination. Moreover, after termination, every state $q \neq q_0$ has a distinguished input transition—the one that led to the discovery of q during the search. It is well known that the graph with states as nodes and these distinguished transitions as edges is a tree with root q_0, called a *DFS-tree*. If some path of the DFS-tree leads from q to r, then we say that q is an *ascendant* of r, and r is a *descendant* of q (in the tree).

It is easy to modify *DFS* so that it returns a DFS-tree, together with *timestamps* for the states. The algorithm, which we call *DFS_Tree*, is shown below, on the right of *DFS*. While

---

Algorithm 49   Depth-first search algorithm.

DFS(A)	*DFS_Tree(A)*
Input: NGA $A = (Q, \Sigma, \delta, Q_0, F)$	**Input:** NGA $A = (Q, \Sigma, \delta, Q_0, F)$
	Output: Time-stamped tree (S, T, d, f)
1 $S \leftarrow \emptyset$	1 $S \leftarrow \emptyset$
2 **for all** $q_0 \in Q_0$ **do** $dfs(q_0)$	2 $T \leftarrow \emptyset; t \leftarrow 0$
	3 $dfs(q_0)$
3 proc $dfs(q)$	
4 **add** q to S	4 proc $dfs(q)$
5 **for all** $r \in \delta(q)$ **do**	5 $t \leftarrow t + 1; d[q] \leftarrow t$
6 **if** $r \notin S$ **then** $dfs(r)$	6 **add** q to S
7 **return**	7 **for all** $r \in \delta(q)$ **do**
	8 **if** $r \notin S$ **then**
	9 **add** (q, r) to T; $dfs(r)$
	10 $t \leftarrow t + 1; f[q] \leftarrow t$
	11 **return** (S, T, d, f)

---

timestamps are not necessary for conducting a search, many algorithms based on depth-first search use them for other purposes.[1] Each state q is assigned two timestamps. The first one, $d[q]$, records the time at which q is first discovered, and the second, $f[q]$, the time at which the search finishes examining the outgoing transitions of q. Since we are only interested in the relative order in which states are discovered and finished, we assume that the timestamps are integers ranging between 1 and $2|Q|$, that is, we assume that the clock only ticks when a state is discovered or when the search from a state finishes.

In our analyses, we also assume that at every time point, a state is *white*, *gray*, or *black*. A state q is white during the interval $[0, d[q])$, gray during the interval $[d[q], f[q])$, and black during the interval $[f[q], 2|Q|]$. So, loosely speaking, q is white if it has not been yet discovered, gray if it has already been discovered but still has unexplored outgoing edges, and black if all its outgoing edges have been explored. Timestamp 0 refers to the initial moment where the whole graph is white, that is, no state has been discovered yet. It is easy to see that at all times, the gray states form a path (the *gray path*) starting at q_0 and ending at the state being currently explored, that is, at the state q such that $dfs(q)$ is being currently executed; moreover, this path is always part of the DFS-tree.

Example 12.2   The following picture shows the DFS-tree and the discovery and finishing times of two possible runs of *DFS_Tree* on a NBA. Thick colored transitions belong to the DFS-tree. The interval $[d, f)$ on top of a state gives the discovery time d and finishing time f. The interval corresponds to the time during which the state is gray. At time 0, all states are white, and at time $2|Q| = 12$, they are all black.

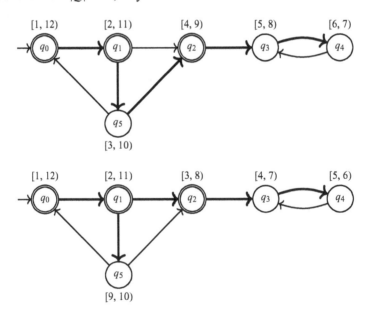

---

1. In the rest of the chapter, and in order to present the algorithms in a more compact form, we omit the instructions for computing the timestamps and just assume they are there.

Observe that in the first run, the DFS-tree is just a path. Notice also that the discovery and finishing times do not completely determine a run. For example, in the first run, we do not know whether the DFS explored the transition $q_5 \rightarrow q_0$ before $q_5 \rightarrow q_2$ or the other way round. In the second run, the gray path is q_0 at time 1, $q_0q_1q_2q_3$ at time 4, and $q_0q_1q_5$ at time 9.

We recall without proof two important properties of depth-first searches. Both follow easily from the fact that a procedure call suspends the execution of the caller, which is only resumed after the execution of the callee terminates.

Theorem 12.3: parenthesis theorem. *Let $I(q)$ denote the interval $[d[q], f[q]]$, and let $I(q) \prec I(r)$ denote that $f[q] < d[r]$ holds. In a DFS-tree, for any two states q and r, one of the following four conditions holds:*

- *$I(q) \subseteq I(r)$ and q is a descendant of r;*
- *$I(r) \subseteq I(q)$ and r is a descendant of q;*
- *$I(q) \prec I(r)$, and neither q is a descendant of r, nor r is a descendant of q; and*
- *$I(r) \prec I(q)$, and neither r is a descendant of q, nor q is a descendant of r.*

Theorem 12.4: white-path theorem. *In a DFS-tree, r is a descendant of q (and so $I(r) \subseteq I(q)$) if and only if, at time $d[q] - 1$, state r can be reached from q along a path of white states.*

Example 12.5 In the first run of example 12.2 for every two states q_i and q_j, we have $I(q_i) \subseteq I(q_j)$ or $I(q_j) \subseteq I(q_i)$. By the parenthesis theorem, either q_i is a descendant of q_j or vice versa, which implies that the DFS-tree is a path, as is indeed the case.

Now, compare the discovery times of q_2 and q_5 in the first and second runs. In the first run, we have $d[q_2] = 4$ and $d[q_5] = 3$. So at time 2, the path $q_5 \rightarrow q_2$ is white. By the white-path theorem, q_2 is a descendant of q_5 in the DFS-tree, and so, by the parenthesis theorem, $I(q_2) \subseteq I(q_5)$. In the second run, we have $d[q_2] = 3$ and $d[q_5] = 9$. So at time 8 no path from q_5 to q_2 is white. By the white-path theorem and the parenthesis theorem, $I(q_2) \prec I(q_5)$.

12.1.1 The Nested-DFS Algorithm

Let A be an NBA. To determine if A is empty, we can search for the accepting states of A and check if at least one of them belongs to a cycle. A naive implementation proceeds in two phases, searching for accepting states in the first and for cycles in the second. The runtime is quadratic: since an automaton with n states and m transitions has $\mathcal{O}(n)$ accepting states, and since searching for a cycle containing a given state takes time $\mathcal{O}(n + m)$, we obtain a bound of $\mathcal{O}(n^2 + nm)$.

We introduce the nested-DFS algorithm, which runs in time $\mathcal{O}(n + m)$. It uses the first phase not only to discover the reachable accepting states but also to *sort* them. The searches of the second phase are conducted according to the order determined by the sorting. As we shall see, conducting the search in this order avoids repeated visits to the same state.

The first phase is carried out by a DFS, and the accepting states are sorted by increasing *finishing* (not discovery!) time. This is known as the *postorder* induced by the DFS. Assume that in the second phase, we have already performed a search starting from the state q and the search has failed (i.e., no cycle of A contains q). Suppose we proceed with a search from another state r (which implies $f[q] < f[r]$), and this search discovers some state s that had already been discovered by the search starting at q. We claim that *it is not necessary to explore the successors of s again*. More precisely, we claim that $s \not\rightsquigarrow r$, and so it is useless to explore the successors of s, because the exploration cannot return any cycle containing r. The proof of the claim is based on the following lemma:

Lemma 12.6 *If $q \rightsquigarrow r$ and $f[q] < f[r]$ in some DFS-tree, then some cycle of A contains q.*

Proof Let π be a path leading from q to r, and let s be the first node of π that is discovered by the DFS. By definition, we have $d[s] \le d[q]$. We prove that $q \ne s$, $q \rightsquigarrow s$ and $s \rightsquigarrow q$ hold, which implies that some cycle of A contains q.

- $q \ne s$. If $s = q$, then at time $d[q] - 1$, the path π is white, and so $I(r) \subseteq I(q)$ by the white-path theorem. This contradicts $f[q] < f[r]$.

- $q \rightsquigarrow s$. Obvious, because s belongs to π.

- $s \rightsquigarrow q$. Since $d[s] \le d[q]$ and $s \ne q$, we have $d[s] < d[q]$. By the parenthesis theorem, we either have $I(q) \subseteq I(s)$ or $I(s) \prec I(q)$. We show that the latter is impossible. By minimality of s, at time $d[s] - 1$, the subpath of π leading from s to r is white. Hence, by the white-path theorem, we have $I(r) \subseteq I(s)$. But $I(r) \subseteq I(s)$ and $I(s) \prec I(q)$ contradict $f[q] < f[r]$, and so $I(s) \prec I(q)$ does not hold. It follows $I(q) \subseteq I(s)$, and hence q is a descendant of s, by the parenthesis theorem. This implies $s \rightsquigarrow q$.   □

Example 12.7 The NBA of example 12.2 contains a path from q_1 to q_0. Moreover, the depicted DFS-trees satisfy $f[q_1] = 11 < 12 = f[q_0]$. As guaranteed by lemma 12.6, some cycle contains q_1, namely, the cycle $q_1 q_5 q_0$.

To prove our previous claim, we assume that $s \rightsquigarrow r$ holds, and derive a contradiction. Since s was previously discovered by the search starting at q, we have $q \rightsquigarrow s$, and so $q \rightsquigarrow r$. Since $f[q] < f[r]$, by lemma 12.6, some cycle of A contains q, contradicting the assumption that the search from q failed.

Hence, during the second phase, we only need to explore a transition at most once—namely, when its source state is discovered for the first time. This guarantees the correctness of this algorithm:

- Perform a DFS from each initial state of A, and output the accepting states in postorder.[2] Let $q_1, \ldots, q_k$ be the output of the search, that is, $f[q_1] < \cdots < f[q_k]$.

---

2. Notice that this does not require to apply any sorting algorithm; it suffices to output an accepting state immediately after blackening it.

- For $i = 1$ to k, perform a DFS from the state q_i, with the following changes:
  - if the search visits a state q that was already discovered by any of the searches starting at $q_1, \ldots, q_{i-1}$, then the search backtracks;
  - if the search visits q_i, it stops and returns NONEMPTY.
- If none of the searches from $q_1, \ldots, q_k$ returns NONEMPTY, return EMPTY.

Example 12.8 We apply the algorithm to the NBA of example 12.1. Assume that the first DFS proceeds as depicted in the first run. The search outputs the accepting states in postorder, that is, in the order q_2, q_1, q_0. Figure 12.1 shows the transitions explored during the searches of the second phase. Transitions explored during the search starting at accepting state q_i have a label of the form "$i.j$."

The search from q_2 explores the transitions labeled by 2.1, 2.2, and 2.3. The search from q_1 explores the transitions 1.1, $\ldots$, 1.5. Notice that the search backtracks after exploring 1.1, because the state q_2 was already visited by the previous search. Moreover, this search is successful, because transition 1.5 reaches state q_1, and so a cycle containing q_1 has been found.

The running time of the algorithm can be easily determined. The first DFS runs in $\mathcal{O}(|Q| + |\delta|)$ time. During the searches of the second phase, each transition is explored at most once, and so they can be executed together in time $\mathcal{O}(|Q| + |\delta|)$.

12.1.1.1 Nesting the two searches

Recall that we are looking for algorithms that return an accepting lasso when A is nonempty. The algorithm we have described is not good for this purpose. Define the *DFS-path* of a state as the unique path of the DFS-tree leading from the initial state to it. When the second phase answers NONEMPTY, the DFS-path of the state being currently explored, say q, is an accepting cycle but usually not an accepting lasso. For an accepting lasso, we can prefix this path with the DFS-path of q obtained during the first phase. However, since the first phase cannot foresee the future, it does not know which accepting state, if any, will be identified by the second phase as belonging to an accepting lasso. So either the first search must store the DFS-paths of *all* the accepting states it discovers, or a third phase is necessary, in which a new DFS-path is recomputed.

This problem can be solved by *nesting* the first and the second phases: whenever the first DFS blackens an accepting state q, we immediately launch a second DFS to check if q

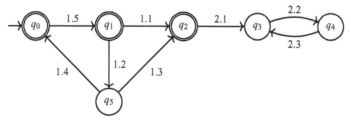

Figure 12.1
An execution of the nested-DFS algorithm.

is reachable from itself. We obtain the nested-DFS algorithm, due to Courcoubetis, Vardi, Wolper, and Yannakakis:

- Perform a DFS from each initial state.
- Whenever the search blackens an accepting state q, launch a new DFS from q. If this second DFS visits q again (i.e., if it explores some transition leading to q), stop with NONEMPTY. Otherwise, when the second DFS terminates, continue with the first DFS.
- If the first DFS terminates for every initial state, output EMPTY.

An implementation is shown in algorithm 50. For clarity, the program on the left does not include the instructions for returning an accepting lasso. A variable *seed* is used to store

---

Algorithm 50 Nested depth-first search algorithm.

NestedDFS(A)
Input: NBA $A = (Q, \Sigma, \delta, Q_0, F)$
Output: EMP if $\mathcal{L}_\omega (A) = \emptyset$
              NEMP otherwise

1 $S \leftarrow \emptyset$
2 **for all** $q_0 \in Q_0$ **do** $dfs1(q_0)$
3 **report** EMP

4 proc $dfs1(q)$
5   **add** $[q, 1]$ **to** S
6   **for all** $r \in \delta(q)$ **do**
7   **if** $[r, 1] \notin S$ **then** $dfs1(r)$
8   **if** $q \in F$ **then** *seed* $\leftarrow q$; $dfs2(q)$
9   **return**

10 proc $dfs2(q)$
11   **add** $[q, 2]$ **to** S
12   **for all** $r \in \delta(q)$ **do**
13   **if** $r = seed$ **then report** NEMP
14   **if** $[r, 2] \notin S$ **then** $dfs2(r)$
15   **return**

NestedDFSwithWitness(A)
Input: NBA $A = (Q, \Sigma, \delta, Q_0, F)$
Output: EMP if $\mathcal{L}_\omega (A) = \emptyset$
              NEMP otherwise

1 $S \leftarrow \emptyset$; *succ* $\leftarrow$ **false**
2 **for all** $q_0 \in Q_0$ **do** $dfs1(q_0)$
3 **report** EMP

4 proc $dfs1(q)$
5   **add** $[q, 1]$ **to** S
6   **for all** $r \in \delta(q)$ **do**
7   **if** $[r, 1] \notin S$ **then** $dfs1(r)$
8   **if** *succ* **then return** $[q, 1]$
9   **if** $q \in F$ **then**
10   *seed* $\leftarrow q$; $dfs2(q)$
11   **if** *succ* **then return** $[q, 1]$
12   **return**

13 proc $dfs2(q)$
14   **add** $[q, 2]$ **to** S
15   **for all** $r \in \delta(q)$ **do**
16   **if** $[r, 2] \notin S$ **then** $dfs2(r)$
17   **if** $r = seed$ **then**
18   *succ* $\leftarrow$ **true**
19   **if** *succ* **then return** $[q, 2]$
20   **return**

---

the state from which the second DFS is launched. The instruction **report** X produces the output X and stops the execution. The set S is usually implemented by means of a hash table. Notice that it is not necessary to store states $[q, 1]$ and $[q, 2]$ separately. Instead, when a state q is discovered, either during the first or the second search, it is stored at the hash address, and two extra bits are used to store which of the following three possibilities hold: only $[q, 1]$ has been discovered so far, only $[q, 2]$, or both. So, if a state is encoded by a bitstring of length c, then the algorithm needs $c + 2$ bits of memory per state.

The algorithm on the right is a modification of *NestedDFS* that returns either EMP or an accepting lasso. It uses a global boolean variable *succ* (for success), initially set to false. If *dfs2(q)* observes that $r = seed$ holds, it sets *succ* to true. This causes procedure calls in *dfs1(q)* and *dfs2(q)* to be replaced by **return** $[q, 1]$ and **return** $[q, 2]$, respectively. The lasso is produced in reverse order (i.e., with the initial state at the end).

12.1.1.2 A small improvement

We show that *dfs2* can already return NONEMPTY if it discovers a state that belongs to the DFS-path of *dfs1*. Let q_k be an accepting state. Assume that *dfs1* discovers q_k and that the DFS-path of q_k in *dfs1* is $q_0 q_1 \cdots q_{k-1} q_k$. Assume further that *dfs2(q_k)* discovers q_i for some $0 \le i \le k - 1$ and that the DFS-path of *dfs2* is $q_k q_{k+1} \cdots q_{k+l} q_i$. The path $q_0 q_1 \cdots q_{k-1} q_k \cdots q_{k+l} q_i$ is a lasso, and, since q_k is accepting, it is an accepting lasso. So, stopping with NONEMPTY is correct. Implementing this modification requires to keep track during *dfs1* of the states that belong to the DFS-path of the state being currently explored. Notice, however, that we do not need information about their order. So we can use a set P to store the states of the path and implement P as, for example, a hash table. We do not need the variable *seed* anymore, because the case $r = seed$ is subsumed by the more general $r \in P$. A pseudocode implementation is given in algorithm 51.

Algorithm 51 Improved nested depth-first search algorithm.

ImprovedNestedDFS(A)
Input: NBA $A = (Q, \Sigma, \delta, Q_0, F)$
Output: EMP if $\mathcal{L}_\omega (A) = \emptyset$, NEMP otherwise

```
1   S ← ∅; P ← ∅
2   for all q₀ ∈ Q₀ do dfs1(q₀)
3   report EMP
```

4 **proc** *dfs1(q)*	11 **proc** *dfs2(q)*
5 **add** $[q, 1]$ **to** S; **add** q **to** P	12 **add** $[q, 2]$ **to** S
6 **for all** $r \in \delta(q)$ **do**	13 **for all** $r \in \delta(q)$ **do**
7 **if** $[r, 1] \notin S$ **then** *dfs1(r)*	14 **if** $r \in P$ **then report** NEMP
8 **if** $q \in F$ **then** *dfs2(q)*	15 **if** $[r, 2] \notin S$ **then** *dfs2(r)*
9 **remove** q **from** P	16 **return**
10 **return**	

12.1.1.3 Extension to NGAs

Contrary to the other algorithms studied in the coming sections, the nested-DFS algorithm cannot be generalized to emptiness of NGAs by conducting some minor changes in the pseudocode. The simplest way to extend it to NGAs is by applying the conversion NGA $\rightarrow$ NBA. Given an NGA with accepting condition $\{F_0, \ldots, F_{m-1}\}$, the conversion "replicates" each state m times. Since the nested-DFS algorithm visits each state at most twice, this gives at most $2m$ calls to dfs for each state q of the NGA. Let us now (informally) argue that any generalization of the nested-DFS algorithm requires at least m calls in the worst case. For this, observe that, while any NBA accepting a nonempty language has an accepting lasso $q_0 \ldots q_i q_{i+1} \ldots q_n = q_i$ such that the states $q_0, q_1 \ldots, q_{n-1}$ are distinct, this is no longer true for NGAs. For example, every lasso of the NGA having the same semi-automaton as the NBA of figure 11.9 and accepting condition $\{\{1\}, \ldots, \{5\}\}$ visits the state **ch** at least five times. If we assume that a generalization of the nested-DFS algorithm starts a new DFS-search whenever the current search hits a state of a set F_i of accepting states that has not been visited before, then, when applied to this NGA, the algorithm will call $dfs(\mathbf{ch})$ at least five times.

12.1.1.4 Evaluation

The strong point of the nested-DFS algorithm is its very modest space requirements. Apart from the space needed to store the stack of calls to the recursive procedures, the algorithm just needs two extra bits for each state of the automaton. However, in many practical applications, the automaton can easily have millions or tens of millions of states, and each state may require many bytes of storage. In these cases, the two extra bits per state are negligible.

The algorithm has two weak points. First, as explained above, it cannot be easily generalized to NGAs. Moreover, it is not optimal, in the following sense. A search-based algorithm explores an NBA A starting from the initial states. At each point t in time, the algorithm has explored a subset of the states and the transitions of the algorithm, which form a sub-NBA $A_t = (Q_t, \Sigma, \delta_t, Q_{0t}, F_t)$ of A. Clearly, a search-based algorithm can only report NONEMPTY at time t if A_t contains an accepting lasso. A search-based algorithm is *optimal* if the converse holds, that is, if it reports NONEMPTY at the earliest time t such that A_t contains an accepting lasso. It is easy to see that *NestedDFS* is not optimal. Consider the automaton on the left of figure 12.2. Initially, the algorithm chooses between the transitions (q_0, q_1) and (q_0, q_2). Assume it chooses (q_0, q_1) (the algorithm does not know that there is a long tail behind q_2). The algorithm explores (q_0, q_1) and then (q_1, q_0) at some time t. The automaton A_t already contains an accepting lasso, but since q_0 has not been blackened yet, $dfs1$ continues its execution with (q_0, q_2) and explores *all* transitions of A before $dfs2$ is called for the first time and reports NONEMPTY. So the time elapsed between the first moment at which the algorithm has enough information to report NONEMPTY and the moment at which the report occurs can be arbitrarily long.

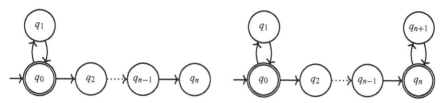

Figure 12.2
Two bad examples for *NestedDFS*.

The automaton on the right of figure 12.2 shows another problem of algorithm *NestedDFS* related to nonoptimality. If it selects (q_0, q_1) first, then, since q_n precedes q_0 in postorder, $dfs2(q_n)$ is executed before $dfs2(q_0)$, and it succeeds, reporting $q_0 q_2 \cdots q_n q_{n+1} q_n$, instead of the much shorter lasso $q_0 q_1 q_0$.

In the next section, we describe an algorithm that, while also based on DFS, calls $dfs(q)$ at most once for every state q, can be easily extended to NGAs, and is optimal.

12.1.2 An Algorithm Based on Strongly Connected Components

Recall that the nested-DFS algorithm searches for accepting states of A and then checks if they belong to some cycle. We design another algorithm that, loosely speaking, proceeds the other way round: it searches for states that belong to some cycle of A and checks if they are accepting.

12.1.2.1 Strongly connected components, roots, and the active graph

A *strongly connected component* (*SCC*) of A is a maximal set of states $S \subseteq Q$ such that $q \rightsquigarrow r$ for every $q, r \in S$.[3] Observe that every state belongs to exactly one SCC. The first state of an SCC that is discovered by a DFS is called the *root* of the SCC (with respect to this DFS).

Let us fix a time t, and let A_t be the subgraph of A containing the states and transitions of A explored by the DFS up to time t. We call A_t the *explored graph*. An SCC of A_t (not of A!) is *active* if it is currently visited by the gray path (i.e., if at least one of its states appears in the gray path), and *inactive* otherwise. A state is *active* if its SCC in A_t is active. (Observe that an active state may not belong to the gray path, as long as some other state of the SCC does.) The *active graph* at time t is the subgraph of A_t containing the active states and the discovered transitions between them.

Example 12.9 Figure 12.3 shows a DFS on a graph with six states A, B, ..., F. Each state is labeled with the interval given by its discovery and finishing times. At state D, the search explores the curved edge first and, at states E and F, the straight edge first. The right part of the picture shows three snapshots of the DFS, taken at three different times. Unexplored

---

3. Note that a path consisting of just a state q and no transitions is a path leading from q to q.

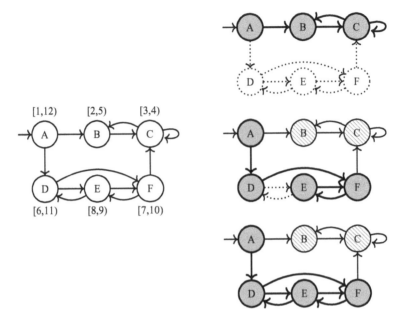

Figure 12.3
A DFS (left) and the explored and active graphs at three different snapshots (right). Bold solid colored nodes and edges are active; hatched colored nodes are inactive.

states and edges are dotted. The explored graph contains all solid states and edges. The active graph contains the bold colored states and edges.

- First snapshot: Before backtracking from B. The gray path is A, B. The active SCCs are {A} and {B, C}, with roots A and B, respectively. The explored graph and the active graph coincide.
- Second snapshot: After exploring the edge E → F. The gray path is A, D, F, E. The active SCCs are {A}, {D}, and {E, F}. States B and C are now explored but inactive.
- Third snapshot: Before backtracking from D. The gray path is A, D. The active SCCs are {A} and {D, E, F}.

We analyze the structure of the active graph with the help of several observations:

(1) If r is the root of an SCC, then $d[r] \leq d[q]$ for every state q of the SCC; in other words, the root is the first state of an SCC discovered by the DFS.

This follows from the definition of a root.

(2) If r is the root of an SCC, then $f[r] \geq f[q]$ for every state q of the SCC; in other words, the root is also the last state of the SCC blackened by the DFS.

At time $d[r] - 1$, there are white paths from r to all states of the SCC. By the white-path theorem, all states of the SCC are discovered before backtracking from r. By the parenthesis theorem, the DFS backtracks from all states of the SCC before it backtracks from r.

(3) An SCC becomes inactive when the DFS backtracks from its root (i.e., when it is blackened).

This follows immediately from (2).

(4) An inactive SCC of A_t is also an SCC of A.

This follows from (2) and (3).

(5) At every moment, the roots of all currently active SCCs occur in the gray path.

This follows from (3) and the fact that the root of an active SCC must be on the gray path.

(6) Let q be an active state of A_t, and let r be the root of its SCC. No state s such that $d[r] < d[s] < d[q]$ is an active root.

Assume s is an active root such that $d[r] < d[s] < d[q]$. We show that r and s belong to the same SCC, contradicting that s is a root. It suffices to show that both $r \rightsquigarrow s$ and $s \rightsquigarrow r$ hold. For $r \rightsquigarrow s$, observe that, by (5), both r and s are on the gray path, and r precedes s in the path because $d[r] < d[s]$. For $s \rightsquigarrow r$, observe that, since s is active and $d[s] < d[q]$, state q is discovered during the execution of $dfs(s)$, and so $s \rightsquigarrow q$; moreover, since r is the root of the SCC of q, we have $q \rightsquigarrow r$, and so $s \rightsquigarrow r$.

(7) If q and r are active states of A_t and $d[q] \leq d[r]$, then $q \rightsquigarrow r$.

Let q' and r' be the roots of the SCCs of q and r. Then, $q \rightsquigarrow q'$ and $r' \rightsquigarrow r$, and so it suffices to prove $q' \rightsquigarrow r'$. Since q' and r' are roots, they belong to the gray path by (5), and so at least one of $q' \rightsquigarrow r'$ and $r' \rightsquigarrow q'$ holds. By (6), we have $d[q'] \leq d[r']$, and so $q' \rightsquigarrow r'$ holds.

From (1) to (7), we get that the active graph has a *necklace structure* sketched in figure 12.4. The chain of the necklace is the gray path, and the beads of the necklace are the active SCCs. All roots of the active SCCs belong to the gray path, but the gray path may also contain other nodes. Given two consecutive roots q and r in the gray path such that $d[q] < d[r]$, the SCC of q contains exactly the active nodes s discovered between q (inclusive) and r (exclusive). Formally, the SCC of q contains all nodes s such that $d[q] \leq d[s] < d[r]$.

12.1.2.2   The Algorithm

The algorithm maintains the explored graph and the necklace structure of the active graph while the DFS is conducted. More precisely, the algorithm maintains the following data:

- The set S of states visited by the DFS so far.

- The mapping $rank \colon S \rightarrow \mathbb{N}$ that assigns to each state a number in the order they are discovered, called the *discovery rank* of the state. Formally, the discovery rank of q is the number of states of S immediately after q is visited.

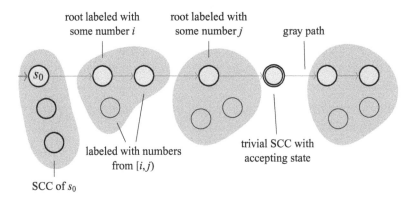

Figure 12.4
Structure of the active graph.

- The mapping $act\colon S \to \{\textbf{true}, \textbf{false}\}$ that assigns **true** to a state iff it is currently active.
- The *necklace stack* N. The elements of N are of the form (r, C), where C is the set of states of an active SCC, and r is its root. We call the pair (r, C) a *bead*. The oldest bead (i.e., the one with the oldest root) is at the bottom of the stack, and the newest is at the top.

After the initialization step, the DFS is always either exploring a new edge (which may lead to a new state or to a state already visited) or backtracking along an edge explored earlier. We show how to update S, *rank*, *act*, and N after an initialization, exploration, or backtracking step, so that, assuming they satisfy their definitions before the step, they continue to satisfy them after it. Further, we show how to check after each step whether the explored graph contains an accepting lasso.

Initialization.   Initially, both the explored and active graphs consist only of the initial state q_0 and no edges. The necklace has only one bead—namely, $(q_0, \{q_0\})$. Thus, we initialize S to q_0; set *rank*(q_0) and *act*(q_0) to 1 and **true**, respectively; and push $(q_0, \{q_0\})$ onto N.

Exploration of new edges.   Assume the algorithm explores a new edge from state q to state r. Assume further that S, *rank*, *act*, and N match the current explored and active graphs and that the explored graph does not contain an accepting lasso. We distinguish six cases.

(i) r is a new state (i.e., $r \notin S$).

Then the explored graph is extended with state r, which is active. So, we add r to S, and set *rank*(r) and *act*(r) to $|S|$ and **true**, respectively. Since r forms a trivial SCC, we push a new bead $(r, \{r\})$ to N. Finally, we recursively call *dfs*(r).

The following figure shows the explored and active graphs before and after the DFS explores the edge $B \to C$, discovering C. The value of N is updated from $(A, \{A\})(B, \{B\})$ (with the bottom of the stack on the left) to $(A, \{A\})(B, \{B\})(C, \{C\})$.

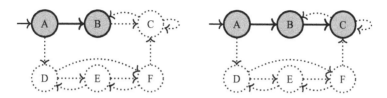

(ii) r has been visited by the DFS before and is inactive. Formally, $r \in S$ and $act(r) = \textbf{false}$.

Since r is inactive, its SCC has already been completely explored by the DFS (by (2) and (3)). So, q and r belong to different SCCs, and in particular, $r \not\leadsto q$. It follows that the new edge from q to r cannot create an accepting lasso, if there was none before. So in this case, no data structure needs to be updated, and no recursive DFS call is started.

The following figure shows the explored and active graphs before and after the DFS explores the edge $F \to C$, which is currently inactive.

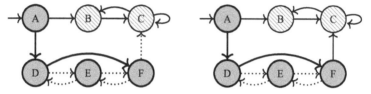

(iii) r has been visited by the DFS before, is active, and was discovered strictly after q. Formally, $r \in S$, $act(r) = \textbf{true}$, and $rank(r) > rank(q)$.

In this case, both q and r are active and already belong to the necklace. Since $rank(r) > rank(q)$, either q and r belong to the same SCC, or the SCC of q is before the SCC of r in the necklace. In both cases, the new edge does not change the structure of the necklace. It cannot create an accepting lasso either, if no accepting lasso existed before. No state changes its active/nonactive status. So, again, there is nothing to do, and no recursive DFS call is started.

The following figure shows the explored and active graphs before and after the DFS explores the edge $D \to E$. Observe that E was discovered after D.

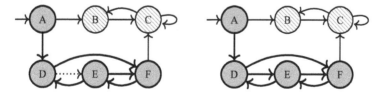

(iv) r has been visited by the DFS before, is active, and was not discovered strictly after q. Formally, $r \in S$, $act(r) = \textbf{true}$, and $rank(r) \leq rank(q)$.

Observe that $rank(r) \leq rank(q)$ implies $d[r] \leq d[q]$ and so, because of (7), we have $r \leadsto q$. So, q and r belong to the same SCC of the automaton. Let r' be the root of the SCC of r in the necklace. Since the DFS explores an edge from q to r, state q is the last state of the gray path, that is, the end of the necklace. So, all SCCs of the necklace from r' upward must be merged into one SCC. For example, if in figure 12.4, the search would now discover an edge leading from the last gray state to the state labeled by i, then the last four SCCs would have to be merged. The merge is achieved as follows. We pop beads (s, C) from N and keep merging the sets C, stopping when the bead satisfies $rank(s) \leq rank(r)$, which implies $r' = s$. Then, we push a new bead (s, D), where D is the result of the merge.

The edge from q to r can create a first accepting lasso only if one of the merged SCCs was hitherto consisting of just an accepting state and no edges. Therefore, while popping beads from N, we simply check whether any of the roots is an accepting state.

The following figure shows the explored and active graphs before and after the DFS explores the edge $E \to D$. Before exploring the edge the value of N is $(A, \{A\})$, $(D, \{D\})$, $(F, \{E, F\})$. We pop the last two beads, merging the SCCs $\{D\}$ and $\{E, F\}$, and push the new bead $(D, \{D, E, F\})$. If D is a final state, the algorithm returns NEMP.

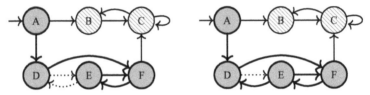

The following figure gives another example where $rank(r) = rank(q)$ and hence $r = q$. It shows the explored and active graphs before and after the DFS explores the edge $C \to C$. We pop $(C, \{C\})$ and push it back. If C is a final state, then the algorithm reports NEMP.

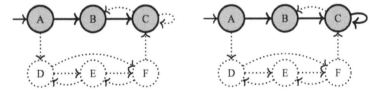

Backtracking. Assume that the algorithm has already explored all the edges leaving a state q and now proceeds to backtrack from q. Notice that q is active. We consider two cases:

(v) q is a root of the active graph.

Then, before backtracking from q, the top element of N is of the form (q, C). After backtracking, q and its entire SCC become inactive by (3), and they do not belong to the active graph anymore. So we pop (q, C) from N and set $act(r)$ to **false** for every $r \in C$.

The following figure shows the explored and active graphs before and after the DFS backtracks from D. The SCC $\{D, E, F\}$ becomes inactive, and the bead $(D, \{D, E, F\})$ is popped from N.

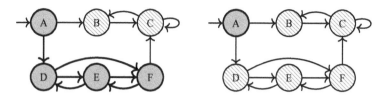

(vi) q is not a root of the active graph.

Then, by (2) and (3), the root of the SCC of q is active and remains active after backtracking. The active graph does not change, and there is nothing to do.

The following figure shows the explored and active graphs before and after the DFS backtracks from E. At that moment, the SCC of E is $\{D, E, F\}$, with root D. Neither the explored nor the active graph change.

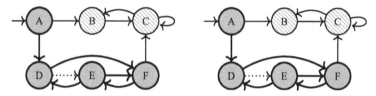

The pseudocode for the algorithm, which we call *SCCsearch*, is described in algorithm 52. The initialization is carried out in lines 1–2. Case (i) corresponds to $r \notin S$ in line 8. Case (ii) does not require to do anything, which is indeed what happens when the conditions at lines 8 and 9 do not hold. Cases (iii) and (iv) are dealt with uniformly in the **repeat-until** loop. Indeed, if $d[r] > d[q]$ (case (iii)), then the loop is executed exactly once, with the result that the top stack element is popped from the stack in line 12 and pushed again in line 15. If $d[r] \leq d[q]$ (case (iv)), then the loop performs the necessary merge of SCCs. Finally, the two backtracking cases correspond to lines 16–18.

12.1.2.3 Runtime

We show that *SCCsearch*(A) runs in time $\mathcal{O}(n + m)$, where n and m are the numbers of states and transitions of A, respectively. For the sake of simplicity, we consider set unions to be atomic. A finer implementation and analysis, left as an exercise, yields the same complexity if such unions are not atomic. The total number of steps of type (i) to (vi) is $2m$, because the DFS traverses each transition twice, once in the direction of the transition and once in the opposite direction, when it backtracks from the destination state. Steps of types (i) to (iii) and (vi) only require to perform a constant number of operations on the data structures and take time $\mathcal{O}(m)$ together. Now, consider the steps of type (iv) and (v).

• Type (iv). The beads that enter the necklace N during a run of *SCCsearch*(A) are either beads of the form $(q, \{q\})$ pushed into N at line 6 or beads obtained by removing two or more beads from N, merging them, and adding the result back to N in line 15. Since there

---

Algorithm 52 SCC-based search algorithm.

SCCsearch(*A*)

Input: NBA $A = (Q, \Sigma, \delta, Q_0, F)$

Output: EMP if $\mathcal{L}_\omega (A) = \emptyset$, NEMP otherwise

1 $S, N \leftarrow \emptyset; n \leftarrow 0$

2 *dfs*(q_0)

3 **report** EMP

4 proc *dfs*(*q*)

5      $n \leftarrow n + 1; rank(q) \leftarrow n$

6   **add** *q* **to** *S*; $act(q) \leftarrow$ **true**; **push** $(q, \{q\})$ **onto** *N*

7   **for all** $r \in \delta(q)$ **do**

8   **if** $r \notin S$ **then** *dfs*(*r*)

9   **else if** $act(r)$ **then**

10             $D \leftarrow \emptyset$

11   **repeat**

12   **pop** (s, C) **from** *N*; **if** $s \in F$ **then report** NEMP

13                 $D \leftarrow D \cup C$

14   **until** $rank(s) \leq rank(r)$

15   **push** (s, D) **onto** *N*

16   **if** *q* **is the top root in** *N* **then**

17   **pop** (q, C) **from** *N*

18   **for all** $r \in C$ **do** $act(r) \leftarrow$ **false**

---

are *n* of the former, and each merge decreases the number of beads by 1 or more, at most *n* of the latter are pushed onto *N*. So line 13 is executed $\mathcal{O}(n)$ times.

• Type (v). Steps of type (v) pop a bead (q, C) from *N* at line 17 and then set the active bits of all states of *C* to **false** at line 18; for this, they traverse the list representing *C*. Since all transitions from *q* have already been explored, *q* is black. By (2), all states of *C* are also black, and so none of them is ever active again. So every state is deactivated exactly once at line 18, and the algorithm spends time $\mathcal{O}(n)$ executing it.

12.1.2.4 Extension to NGAs

We show that *SCCsearch* can be easily extended to an emptiness check for NGAs, without using the conversion NGA → NBA. We have the following characterization of nonemptiness:

Fact 12.10 Let A be an NGA with accepting condition $\mathcal{G}$. It is the case that $\mathcal{L}_\omega(A) \neq \emptyset$ iff some SCC S of A satisfies $S \cap F \neq \emptyset$ for every $F \in \mathcal{G}$.

Assume $\mathcal{G} = \{F_0, F_1, \ldots, F_{m-1}\}$. Let $[m] = \{0, \ldots, m-1\}$. Let us label each state q with the indices $I_q \subseteq [m]$ of the acceptance sets it belongs to. For example, $I_q = \{1, 3\}$ if q belongs to F_1 and F_3. We extend beads with a third component; a bead is now a triple (q, C, I), where q is a state, C is a set of states, and I is an index set. We modify *SCCsearch* so that $I = \cup_{q \in C} I_q$ holds for every bead (q, C, I) that enters the necklace, and let it report nonemptiness if $I = [m]$. It suffices to adjust the pseudocode as follows:

line	*SCCsearch* for NBA	*SCCsearch* for NGA
6	**push**$(q, \{q\})$	**push**$(q, \{q\}, I_q)$
10	$D \leftarrow \emptyset$	$D \leftarrow \emptyset; J \leftarrow \emptyset$
12	**pop**(s, C); **if** $s \in F$ ...	**pop**(s, C, I)
13	$D \leftarrow D \cup C$	$D \leftarrow D \cup C; J \leftarrow J \cup I$
15	**push**(s, D)	**push**(s, D, J); **if** $J = [m]$ **then report** NEMP
17	**pop**(q, C)	**pop**(q, C, I)

12.1.2.5 Evaluation

Recall that the weak points of the nested-DFS algorithm were that it cannot be directly extended to NGAs, and it is not optimal. In comparison, the SCC-based algorithm extends to NGAs and is optimal. Indeed, an accepting lasso can only appear after a step of type (iv), and if it appears then the algorithm returns NEMP before exploring any other transition.

The strong point of the nested-DFS algorithm was its very modest space requirements: just two extra bits for each state of A. Let us examine the space needed by the SCC-based algorithm. It is convenient to compute it for automata recognizing the empty language, because in this case, both the nested-DFS and the SCC-based algorithms must visit all states.

Because of the check $rank[s] \leq rank[r]$, the algorithm needs to store the rank of each state. This is done by extending the hash table S. In principle, we need $\log n$ bits to store a rank; however, in practice, a rank is stored using a word of memory, because if the number of states of A exceeds 2^w, where w is the number of bits of a word, then A cannot be stored in main memory anyway. So the hash table S requires $c + w + 1$ bits per state, where c is the number of bits required to store a state (the extra bit is the active bit).

The stack N does not need to store the states themselves but the memory addresses at which they are stored. Ignoring hashing collisions, this requires w additional bits per state. For generalized Büchi automata, we must also add the k bits needed to store the set of indices. So the algorithm uses a total of $c + 3w + 1$ bits per state ($c + 3w + k + 1$ in the version for NGA), compared to the $c + 2$ bits required by the nested-DFS algorithm. In most cases, w is much smaller than c, and so the influence of the additional memory requirements on the performance is small.

12.2 Algorithms Based on Breadth-First Search

In this section, we describe algorithms for checking emptiness based on breadth-first search (BFS). As in the previous section, we first present an algorithm for NBAs and then extend it to one for NGAs.

No linear-time BFS-based emptiness check is known, so this section may appear superfluous at first. However, BFS-based algorithms can be suitably described using operations and checks on sets of states, which allows us to implement them using automata as data structures. In many cases, the gain obtained by the use of the data structure more than compensates for the quadratic worst-case behavior, making the algorithms competitive.

Breadth-first search maintains the set of states that have been discovered but not yet explored, often called the *frontier* or *boundary*. A BFS from a set Q' of states (in this section, we consider searches from an arbitrary set of states of A) initializes both the set of discovered states and its frontier to Q' and then proceeds in rounds. In a *forward* search, a round explores the *outgoing* transitions of the states in the current frontier; the new states found during the round are added to the set of discovered states, and they become the next frontier. A *backward* BFS proceeds similarly but explores *incoming* transitions rather than outgoing ones. The pseudocode implementations of both BFS variants, shown in algorithm 53, use two variables S and B to store the set of discovered states and the boundary, respectively. We assume the existence of oracles that, given the current boundary B, return either $\delta(B) = \cup_{q \in B} \delta(q)$ or $\delta^{-1}(B) = \cup_{q \in B} \delta^{-1}(q)$.

Algorithm 53   Forward and backward BFS algorithms.

$ForwardBFS(A, Q')$		$BackwardBFS(A, Q')$	
Input: NBA $A = (Q, \Sigma, \delta, Q_0, F)$, $\quad Q' \subseteq Q$		**Input:** NBA $A = (Q, \Sigma, \delta, Q_0, F)$, $\quad Q' \subseteq Q$	
1	$S, B \leftarrow Q'$	1	$S, B \leftarrow Q'$
2	**repeat**	2	**repeat**
3	$\quad B \leftarrow \delta(B) \setminus S$	3	$\quad B \leftarrow \delta^{-1}(B) \setminus S$
4	$\quad S \leftarrow S \cup B$	4	$\quad S \leftarrow S \cup B$
5	**until** $B = \emptyset$	5	**until** $B = \emptyset$

Both BFS variants compute the successors or predecessors of a state exactly once, that is, if in the course of the algorithm, the oracle is called twice with arguments B_i and B_j, respectively, then $B_i \cap B_j = \emptyset$. To prove this in the forward case (the backward case is analogous), observe that $B \subseteq S$ is an invariant of the repeat loop and that the value of S never decreases. Now, let $B_1, S_1, B_2, S_2, \ldots$ be the sequence of values of the variables B and S right before the ith execution of line 3. We have $B_i \subseteq S_i$ by the invariant, $S_i \subseteq S_j$ for every $j \geq i$, and $B_{j+1} \cap S_j = \emptyset$ by line 3. So $B_j \cap B_i = \emptyset$ for every $j > i$.

As data structures for the sets S and B, we can use a hash table and a queue, respectively. But we can also take the set Q of states of A as a finite universe and use automata for fixed-length languages to represent both S and B. Moreover, we can represent $\delta \subseteq Q \times Q$ by a finite transducer T_δ and reduce the computation of $\delta(B)$ and $\delta^{-1}(B)$ in line 3 to computing **Post**(B, δ) and **Pre**(B, δ), respectively.

12.2.1 Emerson–Lei's Algorithm

Let A be an NBA. A state q of A is *live* if some infinite path starting at q visits accepting states infinitely often. Clearly, A is nonempty if and only if at least one initial state is live. We describe an algorithm due to Emerson and Lei for computing the set of live states. For every $n \geq 0$, the *n-live* states of A are inductively defined as follows:

- every state is 0-live, and
- a state q is $(n+1)$-live if some path containing at least one transition leads from q to an accepting n-live state.

Loosely speaking, a state q is n-live if starting from q, it is possible to visit accepting states n times. Let $L[n]$ denote the set of n-live states of A. We have the following:

Lemma 12.11 *The following holds:*

(a) $L[n] \supseteq L[n+1]$ *for every $n \geq 0$.*
(b) *The sequence $L[0] \supseteq L[1] \supseteq L[2] \supseteq \cdots$ reaches a fixpoint $L[i]$ (i.e., there is a least index $i \geq 0$ such that $L[i+1] = L[i]$), and $L[i]$ is the set of live states.*

Proof We prove (a) by induction on n. The case where $n = 0$ is trivial. Assume $n > 0$, and let $q \in L[n+1]$. There is a path containing at least one transition that leads from q to an accepting state $r \in L[n]$. By induction hypothesis, $r \in L[n-1]$, and so $q \in L[n]$.

To prove (b), first notice that, since Q is finite, the fixpoint $L[i]$ exists. Let L be the set of live states. Clearly, $L \subseteq L[i]$ for every $i \geq 0$. Moreover, since $L[i] = L[i+1]$, every state of $L[i]$ has a proper descendant that is accepting and belongs to $L[i]$. So $L[i] \subseteq L$. □

Emerson–Lei's algorithm computes the fixpoint $L[i]$ of the sequence $L[0] \supseteq L[1] \supseteq L[2] \supseteq \cdots$. To compute $L[n+1]$ given $L[n]$, we observe that a state is $(n+1)$-live if some nonempty path leads from it to an n-live accepting state, and so

$$L[n+1] = BackwardBFS(\mathbf{Pre}(L[n] \cap F, \delta)).$$

The pseudocode for the algorithm is shown on the left-hand side of algorithm 54; the variable L is used to store the elements of the sequence $L[0], L[1], L[2], \ldots$.

The repeat loop is executed at most $|Q| + 1$-times, because each iteration but the last one removes at least one state from L. Since each iteration takes time $\mathcal{O}(|Q| + |\delta|)$, the algorithm runs in time $\mathcal{O}(|Q| \cdot (|Q| + |\delta|))$.

Algorithm 54   Emerson–Lei's algorithm.

EmersonLei(A)	*EmersonLei2(A)*
Input: NBA $A = (Q, \Sigma, \delta, Q_0, F)$	**Input:** NBA $A = (Q, \Sigma, \delta, Q_0, F)$
Output: EMP if $\mathcal{L}_\omega(A) = \emptyset$,	**Output:** EMP if $\mathcal{L}_\omega(A) = \emptyset$,
NEMP otherwise	NEMP otherwise

1	$L \leftarrow Q$	1	$L \leftarrow Q$
2	**repeat**	2	**repeat**
3	$OldL \leftarrow L$	3	$OldL \leftarrow L$
4	$L \leftarrow \mathbf{Pre}(L \cap F, \delta)$	4	$L \leftarrow \mathbf{Pre}(L \cap F, \delta)$
5	$L \leftarrow BackwardBFS(L)$	5	$L \leftarrow BackwardBFS(L \setminus (OldL \cap F))$
6	**until** $L = OldL$	6	**until** $L = OldL$
7	**if** $Q_0 \cap L \neq \emptyset$ **then report** NEMP	7	**if** $Q_0 \cap L \neq \emptyset$ **then report** NEMP
8	**else report** NEMP	8	**else report** NEMP

The algorithm may compute the predecessors of a state twice. For instance, if $q \in F$ and there is a transition (q, q), then after line 4 is executed, the state still belongs to L. The version on the right of algorithm 54 avoids this.

12.2.1.1   Generalization to NGAs

Emerson–Lei's algorithm can be easily generalized to NGAs. The generalization of the first version is described in algorithm 55.

Proposition 12.12   *GenEmersonLei(A) reports NEMP iff $\mathcal{L}_\omega(A) \neq \emptyset$.*

Proof   For every $k \geq 0$, redefine the n-live states of A as follows: every state is 0-live, and q is $(n + 1)$-live if some path having at least one transition leads from q to a n-live state of $F_{(n \bmod m)}$. Let $L[n]$ denote the set of n-live states. Proceeding as in lemma 12.11, we can easily show that $L[(n + 1) \cdot m] \supseteq L[n \cdot m]$ holds for every $n \geq 0$.

We claim that the sequence $L[0] \supseteq L[m] \supseteq L[2 \cdot m] \supseteq \cdots$ reaches a fixpoint $L[i \cdot m]$ (i.e., there is a least index $i \geq 0$ such that $L[(i + 1) \cdot m] = L[i \cdot m]$), and $L[i \cdot m]$ is the set of live states. Since Q is finite, the fixpoint $L[i \cdot m]$ exists. Let q be a live state. There is a path starting at q that visits F_j infinitely often for every $j \in \{0, \dots, m - 1\}$. In this path, every occurrence of a state of F_j is always followed by some later occurrence of a state of $F_{(j+1) \bmod m}$, for every $j \in \{0, \dots, m - 1\}$. So, $q \in L[i \cdot m]$. We now show that every state of $L[i \cdot m]$ is live. For every state $q \in L[(i + 1) \cdot m]$, there is a path $\pi = \pi_{m-1}\pi_{m-2} \cdots \pi_0$ such that for every $j \in \{0, \dots, m - 1\}$, the segment π_j contains at least one transition and leads to a state of $L[i \cdot m + j] \cap F_j$. In particular, π visits states of $F_0, \dots, F_{m-1}$, and

---

Algorithm 55 Generalized Emerson–Lei's algorithm.

GenEmersonLei(A)
Input: NGA $A = (Q, \Sigma, \delta, q_0, \{F_0, \ldots, F_{m-1}\})$
Output: EMP if $\mathcal{L}_\omega(A) = \emptyset$, NEMP otherwise

```
1   L ← Q
2   repeat
3     OldL ← L
4     for i = 0 to m − 1
5       L ← Pre(L ∩ Fᵢ, δ)
6       L ← BackwardBFS(L)
7   until L = OldL
8   if Q₀ ∩ L ≠ ∅ then report NEMP
9   else report NEMP
```

---

since $L[(i+1) \cdot m] = L[i \cdot m]$, it leads from a state of $L[(i+1) \cdot m]$ to another state of $L[(i+1) \cdot m]$. So every state of $L[(i+1) \cdot m] = L[i \cdot m]$ is live, which proves the claim.

Since *GenEmersonLei(A)* computes the sequence $L[0] \supseteq L[m] \supseteq L[2 \cdot m] \supseteq \cdots$, after termination, L contains the set of live states. $\qquad\square$

12.2.2 A Modified Emerson–Lei's Algorithm

There exist many variants of Emerson–Lei's algorithm that have the same worst-case complexity but try to improve the efficiency, at least in some cases, by means of heuristics. We present here one of these variants, which we call the modified Emerson–Lei's algorithm (*MEL*). We only present a version for checking emptiness of NBAs.

Given a set $S \subseteq Q$ of states, let *inf(S)* denote the states $q \in S$ such that some infinite path starting at q contains only states of S. Instead of computing $\mathbf{Pre}(OldL \cap F, \delta)$ at each iteration step, *MEL* computes $\mathbf{Pre}(inf(OldL) \cap F, \delta)$.

In the following, we show that *MEL*, shown in algorithm 56, is correct and then compare it with Emerson–Lei's algorithm. As we shall see, while *MEL* introduces the overhead of repeatedly computing *inf*-operations, it still makes sense in many cases because it reduces the number of executions of the repeat loop.

To prove correctness, we claim that, after termination, L contains the set of live states. Recall that the set of live states is the fixpoint $L[i]$ of the sequence $L[0] \supseteq L[1] \supseteq L[2] \supseteq \cdots$. By definition of liveness, we have $inf(L[i]) = L[i]$. Let us define $L'[0] = Q$, and $L'[n+1] = \mathbf{Pre}^+(inf(L'[n]) \cap F, \delta)$. Clearly, *MEL* computes the sequence $L'[0] \supseteq L'[1] \supseteq L'[2] \supseteq \cdots$. Since $L[n] \supseteq L'[n] \supseteq L[i]$ for every $n > 0$, we have that $L[i]$ is also the fixpoint of the sequence $L'[0] \supseteq L'[1] \supseteq L'[2] \supseteq \cdots$, and so *MEL* computes $L[i]$.

Algorithm 56   Modified Emerson–Lei's algorithm.

$MEL(A)$
Input: NBA $A = (Q, \Sigma, \delta, q_0, F)$
Output: EMP if $\mathcal{L}_\omega (A) = \emptyset$, NEMP otherwise

```
 1   L ← Q
 2   repeat
 3       OldL ← L
 4       L ← inf(OldL)
 5       L ← Pre(L ∩ F, δ)
 6       L ← BackwardBFS(L)
 7   until L = OldL
 8   if Q₀ ∩ L ≠ ∅ then report NEMP
 9   else report NEMP

10   function inf(S)
11       repeat
12           OldS ← S
13           S ← S ∩ Pre(S, δ)
14       until S = OldS
15       return S
```

Since $inf(S)$ can be computed in time $\mathcal{O}(|Q| + |\delta|)$ for any set S, MEL runs in time $\mathcal{O}(|Q| \cdot (|Q| + |\delta|))$.

Interestingly, we have already met Emerson–Lei's algorithm in chapter 11. In the proof of proposition 11.7, we defined a sequence $D_0 \supseteq D_1 \supseteq D_2 \supseteq \cdots$ of infinite acyclic graphs. In the terminology of this chapter, D_{2i+1} was obtained from D_{2i} by removing all nodes having only finitely many descendants, and D_{2i+2} was obtained from D_{2i+1} by removing all nodes having only nonaccepting descendants. This corresponds to $D_{2i+1} = inf(D_{2i})$ and $D_{2i+2} = \mathbf{Pre}^+(D_{2i+1} \cap F, \delta)$. So, in fact, we can look at this procedure as the computation of the live states of D_0 using MEL.

12.2.3   Comparing the Algorithms

We give two families of examples showing that MEL may outperform Emerson-Lei's algorithm but not always.

A case where *MEL* is better.   Consider the automaton of figure 12.5. The ith iteration of Emerson–Lei's algorithm removes q_{n-i+1}. The number of calls to $BackwardBFS$ is $(n + 1)$, although a simple modification allowing the algorithm to stop if $L = \emptyset$ spares the $(n + 1)$th operation. On the other hand, the first inf-operation of MEL already sets the variable L to

Figure 12.5
An example in which the *MEL*-algorithm outperforms the Emerson–Lei algorithm.

Figure 12.6
An example in which Emerson–Lei's algorithm outperforms the *MEL*-algorithm.

the empty set of states, and so, with the same simple modification, the algorithm stops after one iteration.

A case where *MEL* is not better.   Consider the automaton from figure 12.6. The ith iteration of Emerson–Lei's algorithm removes $q_{(n-i+1),1}$ and $q_{(n-i+1),2}$, and so the algorithm calls *BackwardBFS* $(n+1)$ times. The ith iteration of the *MEL*-algorithm removes no state as a result of the *inf*-operation, and states $q_{(n-i+1),1}$ and $q_{(n-i+1),2}$ as a result of the call to *BackwardBFS*. So, in this case all *inf* operations are redundant.

12.3   Exercises

☆ ⚙ **Exercise 166.** Let B be the following Büchi automaton:

(a) Execute the emptiness algorithm *NestedDFS* on B. Assume that states are picked in ascending order with respect to their indices.

(b) Recall that *NestedDFS* is a nondeterministic algorithm, and different choices of runs may return different lassos. Which lassos of B can be found by *NestedDFS*?

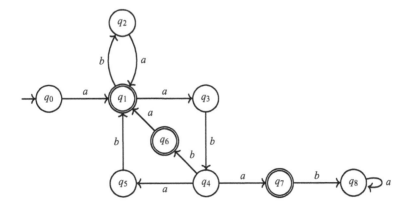

(c) Show that *NestedDFS* is not optimal by exhibiting some search sequence on *B*.

(d) Execute the SCC-based emptiness algorithm on *B*. Assume that states are picked in ascending order with respect to their indices.

(e) Execute the SCC-based emptiness algorithm on *B*. Assume that transitions labeled by *a* are picked before those labeled by *b*.

(f) Which lassos of *B* can be found by the SCC-based algorithm?

Exercise 167. Let A be an NBA, and let A_t be the sub-NBA of A containing the states and transitions discovered by a DFS up to (and including) time t. Show that if a state q belongs to some cycle of A, then it already belongs to some cycle of $A_{f[q]}$.

Exercise 168. Recall from exercise 162 that a Büchi automaton is *weak* if none of its strongly connected components contains both accepting and nonaccepting states. Give an emptiness algorithm for weak Büchi automata. What is the complexity of your algorithm?

Exercise 169. Execute *SCCsearch* on the Büchi automaton below. When a state has many outgoing transitions, pick letters in this order: $a < b < c$.

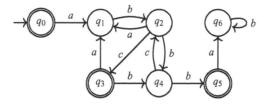

Exercise 170. Recall that *SCCsearch* runs in time $\mathcal{O}(|Q| + |\delta|)$ if we consider set unions as atomic. However, set unions are generally not constant-time operations. Explain how beads can be implemented so that *SCCsearch* truly runs in linear time.

Hint: Can two beads share a state?

Exercise 171. Recall that exercise 170 gives an implementation of *SCCsearch* that truly works in linear time. Let us now take the memory usage into account. Let a_t and b_t denote, respectively, the number of active states and the number of beads at time t. Let $f(t)$ be the number of bits used at time t to store the current beads. Let w be the size of an address.

The solution of exercise 170 satisfies $f(t) = 2(a_t + b_t)w$. Indeed, it uses two addresses per active state (one pointing to the state itself and one to its successor), plus two extra addresses per bead (for the head and tail). Give an implementation of *SCCsearch* that halves the memory usage—namely, one that runs in linear time and satisfies $f(t) = (a_t + b_t)w$.

Hint: Use two stacks, one for roots and one for active states.

★ 🖌 **Exercise 172.** Consider Muller automata with accepting condition $\{F\}$, that is, ρ is accepting iff $inf(\rho) = F$. Give an efficient algorithm for checking emptiness of these automata.   *Hint: Adapt SCCsearch.*

☆ ⚙ **Exercise 173.** Execute Emerson–Lei's algorithm and *MEL* on this NBA:

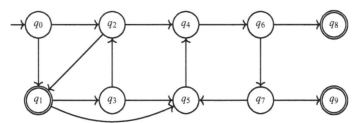

☆ ⚙ **Exercise 174.** Execute *GenEmersonLei* on the following generalized Büchi automata, with accepting condition $\mathcal{F} = \{\{q_1, q_8\}, \{q_2, q_6\}, \{q_4, q_9\}\}$:

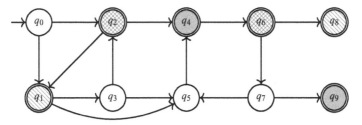

★ 🖌 **Exercise 175.** This exercise deals with a variation of Emerson–Lei's algorithm.

(a) For every $R, S \subseteq Q$, let $pre^+(R, S)$ be the set of states q such that there is a nonempty path π from q to some state of R where π only contains states from S. Give an algorithm to compute $pre^+(R, S)$.

(b) Execute the algorithm from (a) on the following automaton, where states from R and S are respectively solid and hatched:

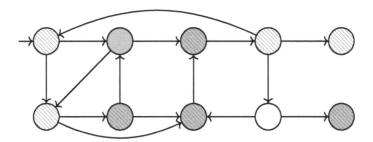

(c) Show that the following modification of Emerson–Lei's algorithm is correct:

MEL2(A)
Input: NBA $A = (Q, \Sigma, \delta, Q_0, F)$
Output: EMP if $\mathcal{L}_\omega(A) = \emptyset$, NEMP otherwise

```
1   L ← Q
2   repeat
3      OldL ← L
4      L ← pre⁺(L ∩ F, L)
5   until L = OldL
6   if q₀ ∈ L then report NEMP
7   else report NEMP
```

(d) What is the difference between the sequences of sets computed by *MEL* and *MEL2*?

13 Application I: Verification and Temporal Logic

Recall that, intuitively, liveness properties are those stating that the system will eventually do something good. More formally, they are properties that are only violated by infinite executions of the system. In other words, by examining only a finite prefix of an infinite execution, it is not possible to determine whether the infinite execution satisfies the property. In this chapter, we apply the theory of ω-automata to the problem of automatically verifying liveness properties.

13.1 Automata-Based Verification of Liveness Properties

In chapter 7, we introduced some basic concepts about systems: configurations, possible executions, and executions. We extend these notions to the infinite case. An ω-execution of a system is an infinite sequence $c_0 c_1 c_2 \ldots$ of configurations where c_0 is some initial configuration, and for every $i \geq 1$, configuration c_i is a legal successor—according to the semantics of the system—of configuration c_{i-1}. Note that according to this definition, if a configuration has no legal successors, then it does not belong to any ω-execution. Usually, this is undesirable, and it is more convenient to assume that such a configuration c has exactly one legal successor—namely, c itself. In this way, every reachable configuration of the system belongs to some ω-execution. The terminating executions are then the ω-executions of the form $c_0 \cdots c_{n-1} c_n^\omega$ for some terminating configuration c_n. The set of terminating configurations can usually be identified syntactically. For instance, in a program, the terminating configurations are usually those in which control is at some particular program line.

In chapter 7, we showed how to construct a system NFA recognizing all the executions of a given system. The same construction can be used to define a *system NBA* recognizing all the ω-executions.

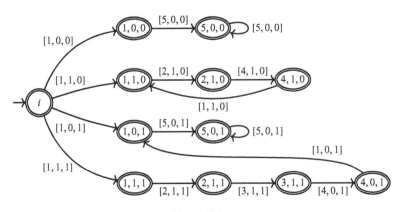

Figure 13.1
System NBA of the simple program.

Example 13.1   Let us reconsider the simple program of chapter 7:

```
1   while x = 1 do
2      if y = 1 then
3         x ← 0
4      y ← 1 − x
5   end
```

Its system NFA is depicted in the middle of figure 7.1. The system NBA is the result of adding self-loops to the states [5, 0, 0] and [5, 0, 1] as depicted in figure 13.1.

13.1.1   Checking Liveness Properties

In section 7.5 of chapter 7, we introduced safety and liveness properties. Intuitively, safety properties state that "nothing bad ever happens" and liveness properties that "something good eventually happens." In order to check if a system satisfies a safety property, we construct a system NFA recognizing the set E of executions of the system and a regular expression for the set V of potential executions of the system that violate a given safety property. Checking that the safety property holds amounts to checking that $E \cap V = \emptyset$ holds. This can be done automatically by converting the regular expression into a property NFA, computing its intersection with the system NFA, and checking that the resulting NFA recognizes the empty language.

We explained in section 7.5 that extending this approach to liveness properties required to develop a theory of automata on ω-words. Indeed, consider a liveness property like "eventually every execution of the program terminates" (in example 13.1, this is the property "eventually every execution of the program reaches a configuration of the form $[5, x, y]$"). No finite execution of the program witnesses that the property is violated, because the execution might be extended to a longer one ending at such a configuration. The violations are ω-words that do not contain any configuration of the form $[5, x, y]$, and expressing and manipulating sets of ω-words require a theory of ω-automata.

We now have such a theory in place. We can replace regular expressions with ω-regular expressions and NFAs with NGAs (which include NBAs as special case). In section 10.2.2.1 of chapter 10, we have seen how to convert ω-regular expressions into NBAs. In section 11.2 of chapter 11, we have given an algorithm to intersect NGAs. Finally, in chapter 12, we have presented algorithms to check emptiness of NGAs. Let us apply these constructions to an example.

Example 13.2   We check two liveness properties of the program from example 13.1.

First property.   We wish to know whether all full executions of the program starting at configurations satisfying $x = y$ terminate. Let Σ be the set of all configurations, and let At_5 be the set of all configurations $[\ell, x, y]$ such that $\ell = 5$. An ω-regular expression for the set of violations is

$$([1, 0, 0] + [1, 1, 1]) \, (\Sigma \setminus At_5)^\omega.$$

Indeed, the language of this expression is the set of potential executions that start at a configuration satisfying $x = y$ and never terminate.

Translating the expression into a property NBA yields the automaton of figure 13.2, where we use colors as identifiers of the states.

We now apply *IntersNGA* to the system NBA of figure 13.1 and the NBA of figure 13.2. Note that we are in the special case discussed at the end of section 11.2: in one of the NBAs, all states are accepting.

In this case, *IntersNGA* and *IntersNFA* coincide, and we obtain the NBA of figure 13.3, whose states are graphically represented by coloring a state of the system NBA with the color of a state of the property NBA. Since this NBA does not contain any accepting lasso, it recognizes the empty language, and so the system satisfies the property.

Second property.   We wish to know whether all full executions that visit line 4 terminate. Let Σ be the set of all configurations, and let At_4 and At_5 be the sets of configurations where the program is at line 4 and at line 5, respectively. An ω-regular expression for the set of

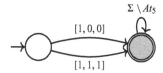

Figure 13.2
NBA for the first property.

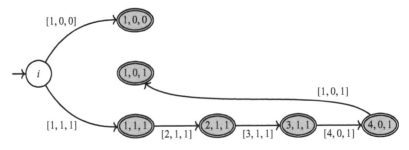

Figure 13.3
NBA obtained from *IntersNGA* (first property).

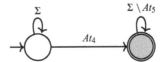

Figure 13.4
NBA for the second property.

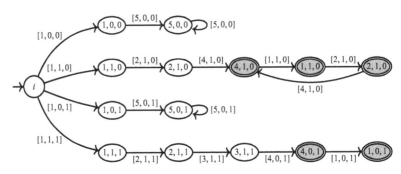

Figure 13.5
NBA obtained from *IntersNGA* (second property).

violations is

$$\Sigma^* At_4(\Sigma \setminus At_5)^\omega.$$

The translation of this property into an NBA is depicted in figure 13.4. Applying *IntersNGA*, we obtain the automaton depicted in figure 13.5. The emptiness algorithm returns that this NBA accepts the word

$$([1, 1, 0]\ [2, 1, 0]\ [4, 1, 0])^\omega$$

which corresponds to a full execution that violates the property.

13.1.2   Networks of Automata and Fairness

In chapter 7, we used Lamport-Burns' mutual exclusion algorithm to illustrate how to check safety properties of concurrent programs modeled using networks of automata. The program text and the network of automata are shown in algorithm 39 and figure 7.5 of chapter 7. We apply the theory of ω-automata to check the most important liveness property of a mutual exclusion algorithm: if a process tries to access its critical section, it eventually will. We call it the *finite waiting* property.

Figure 13.6 shows the asynchronous product arising from the network of automata modeling the algorithm. From the asynchronous product, we easily obtain a system NBA: as in example 13.1, it suffices to add the initial state i, connecting it to the initial state of the asynchronous product; relabel every transition with its target configuration; and make all stats accepting. Observe that in this case, every configuration has at least a successor, and so no self-loops need to be added.

Recall that a configuration of the system is a fourtuple $[b_0, b_1, \ell_0, \ell_1]$, where $b_0, b_1 \in \{0, 1\}$, $\ell_0 \in \{nc_0, t_0, c_0\}$, and $\ell_1 \in \{nc_1, t_1, q_1, q'_1, c_1\}$. The set of all configurations, which we

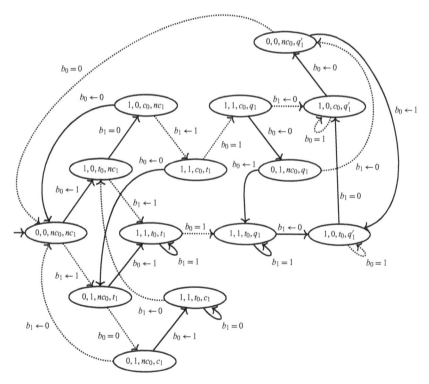

Figure 13.6
Asynchronous product of the Lamport–Burns algorithm. Solid (respectively, dotted) transitions correspond to moves by process 0 (respectively, process 1).

denote by Σ, contains sixty elements, of which, as shown in figure 13.6, only fourteen are reachable.

For $i \in \{0, 1\}$, let NC_i, T_i, C_i be the sets of configurations in which process i is in the noncritical section, is trying to access the critical section, and is in the critical section, respectively. The possible ω-executions that violate the finite waiting property for process i are represented by the ω-regular expression

$$s_i = \Sigma^* \, T_i \, (\Sigma \setminus C_i)^{\omega}.$$

We can check this property using the same procedure as in example 13.2. The property NBA has again two states. The result of the check for process 0 yields that the property fails. One of the possible counterexamples is the ω-execution

$$[0, 0, nc_0, nc_1] \, [1, 0, t_0, nc_1] \, [1, 1, t_0, t_1]^{\omega}.$$

In this execution, both processes request access to the critical section, but, from then on, process 1 never makes any further step. Only process 0 continues operating, but all it does is repeatedly check that the current value of b_1 is 1. Intuitively, this corresponds to process 1 crashing after requesting access. But we do not expect the finite waiting property to hold even if processes may crash while waiting. So, in fact, our *definition* of the finite waiting property was wrong. We can repair the definition by reformulating the property as follows: in any ω-execution *in which both processes execute infinitely many steps*, if process 0 tries to access its critical section, then it eventually will. The condition that both processes must move infinitely often is called a *fairness assumption*.

The task now is to give an ω-regular expression formalizing the property. We face the problem that the label of a transition of the system NBA does not currently contain information about which process is making a move. We solve this problem by enriching the alphabet of the system NBA. Instead of labeling a transition only with the name of the target configuration, we also label it with the number of the process responsible for the move leading to that configuration: 0 if the transition is solid and 1 if it is dotted. For instance, the transition

$$[0, 0, nc_0, nc_1] \xrightarrow{[1,0,t_0,nc_1]} [1, 0, t_0, nc_1]$$

becomes

$$[0, 0, nc_0, nc_1] \xrightarrow{([1,0,t_0,nc_1],0)} [1, 0, t_0, nc_1]$$

to reflect the fact that $[1, 0, t_0, nc_1]$ is reached by a move of process 0. The new alphabet of the NBA is $\Sigma \times \{0, 1\}$. If we let $M_0 := \Sigma \times \{0\}$ and $M_1 := \Sigma \times \{1\}$ denote the "moves" of process 0 and process 1, respectively, then the ω-regular expression

$$\mathit{inf} = \big((M_0 + M_1)^* M_0 M_1\big)^{\omega}$$

represents all ω-executions in which both processes move infinitely often. Further, $\mathcal{L}_{\omega}$ (s_i) $\cap$ $\mathcal{L}_{\omega}$ (*inf*) (where s_i is suitably rewritten to account for the larger alphabet) is the set of violations of the reformulated finite waiting property.

To check if some ω-execution is a violation, we can construct NGAs for s_i and *inf* and compute their intersection with the system NBA. For process 0, the check yields that the property indeed holds. For process 1, the property still fails because of, for instance, the full execution

$$([0,0,nc_0,nc_1]\,[0,1,nc_0,t_1]\,[1,1,t_0,t_1]\,[1,1,t_0,q_1]$$

$$[1,0,t_0,q_1']\,[1,0,c_0,q_1']\,[0,0,nc_0,q_1'])^{\omega}$$

in which process 1 repeatedly tries to access its critical section but always lets process 0 access first.

13.2 Linear Temporal Logic

In the previous section, we have formalized properties of systems using ω-regular expressions or NGAs. This becomes rather difficult for all but the easiest properties. For instance, the NGA or the ω-regular expression for the modified finite waiting property is already quite involved, and it is difficult to be convinced that they have the intended meaning. In this section, we introduce a new language for specifying safety and liveness properties, called *linear temporal logic (LTL)*. LTL is closer to natural language than ω-regular expressions but still has a formal semantics.

Formulas of LTL are constructed from a set *AP* of *atomic propositions*. Intuitively, atomic propositions are abstract names for basic properties of configurations, whose meaning is fixed only after a concrete system is considered. Formally, given a system with a set C of configurations, the meaning of the atomic propositions is fixed by a *valuation function* $\mathcal{V} \colon AP \to 2^C$ that assigns to each abstract name the set of configurations at which it holds.

Example 13.3 Consider the program of example 13.1. Let C be the set of configurations of the program. We choose

$$AP = \{\texttt{at\_1}, \texttt{at\_2}, \dots, \texttt{at\_5}, \texttt{x=0}, \texttt{x=1}, \texttt{y=0}, \texttt{y=1}\}$$

and define the valuation function $\mathcal{V} \colon AP \to 2^C$ as follows:

- $\mathcal{V}(\texttt{at\_i}) = \{[\ell,x,y] \in C : \ell = i\}$ for every $i \in \{1,\dots,5\}$,
- $\mathcal{V}(\texttt{x=0}) = \{[\ell,x,y] \in C : x = 0\}$, and similarly for the other cases.

Under this valuation, $\texttt{at\_i}$ expresses that the program is at line i, and $\texttt{x=j}$ expresses that the current value of x is j.

Atomic propositions are combined by means of the usual boolean operators and the temporal operators **X** ("next") and **U** ("until"). Intuitively, as a first approximation, $\mathbf{X}\varphi$ means "φ holds at the next configuration" (the configuration reached after one step of the program), and $\varphi\,\mathbf{U}\,\psi$ means "φ holds until a configuration is reached satisfying ψ." The set of LTL formulas over AP is defined as follows.

Definition 13.4 *Let AP be a finite set of atomic propositions. The set $LTL(AP)$ of LTL formulas over AP is the set of expressions generated by the grammar*

$$\varphi ::= \textbf{\textit{true}} \mid p \mid \neg\varphi_1 \mid \varphi_1 \wedge \varphi_2 \mid \mathbf{X}\varphi_1 \mid \varphi_1\,\mathbf{U}\,\varphi_2 \,.$$

Formulas are interpreted on infinite sequences $\sigma = \sigma_0\sigma_1\sigma_2\cdots$, where $\sigma_i \subseteq AP$ for every $i \geq 0$. We call these sequences *computations*. The *executable computations* of a system are the computations σ for which there exists an ω-execution $c_0c_1c_2\cdots$ such that for every $i \geq 0$, the set of atomic propositions satisfied by c_i is exactly σ_i. We formally define when a computation satisfies a formula.

Definition 13.5 *For every computation σ over AP, let σ^j denote the suffix $\sigma_j\sigma_{j+1}\cdots$ of σ; in particular, $\sigma^0 = \sigma$. The satisfaction relation $\sigma \models \varphi$ (read "σ satisfies φ") is inductively defined by*

- $\sigma \models \textbf{\textit{true}}$,
- $\sigma \models p$ *iff* $p \in \sigma_0$,
- $\sigma \models \neg\varphi$ *iff* $\sigma \not\models \varphi$,
- $\sigma \models \varphi_1 \wedge \varphi_2$ *iff* $\sigma \models \varphi_1$ *and* $\sigma \models \varphi_2$,
- $\sigma \models \mathbf{X}\varphi$ *iff* $\sigma^1 \models \varphi$, *and*
- $\sigma \models \varphi_1\,\mathbf{U}\,\varphi_2$ *iff* $\exists k \geq 0$ *s.t.* $\sigma^k \models \varphi_2$ *and* $\sigma^i \models \varphi_1$ *for all* $0 \leq i < k$.

Observe that, in the last line above, if $k = 0$, then the condition $\sigma^i \models \varphi_1$ for all $0 \leq i < 0$ is true for every φ_1, because the set of indices i satisfying $0 \leq i < 0$ is empty. Intuitively, if φ_2 already holds initially, then it is not necessary for φ_1 to hold at any position. We use the following abbreviations:

- *false*, $\vee$, $\rightarrow$ and $\leftrightarrow$, defined in the usual way.
- $\mathbf{F}\varphi = \textbf{\textit{true}}\,\mathbf{U}\,\varphi$ ("eventually φ," or "now or sometime in the future φ"). According to the semantics above, $\sigma \models \mathbf{F}\varphi$ holds iff there exists $k \geq 0$ such that $\sigma^k \models \varphi$. Observe that if $\sigma \models \varphi$, then $\sigma^0 \models \varphi$, and so $\sigma \models \mathbf{F}\varphi$.
- $\mathbf{G}\varphi = \neg\mathbf{F}\neg\varphi$ ("always φ" or "globally φ"). According to the semantics above, $\sigma \models \mathbf{G}\varphi$ holds iff $\sigma^k \models \varphi$ for every $k \geq 0$.

The set of computations that satisfy a formula φ is denoted by $\mathcal{L}_\omega(\varphi)$. A system *satisfies* φ if *all* its executable computations satisfy φ.

Example 13.6 The system NBA of example 13.1 has exactly four ω-executions:

$$e_1 = [1,0,0]\,[5,0,0]^{\omega},$$

$$e_2 = ([1,1,0]\,[2,1,0]\,[4,1,0])^{\omega},$$

$$e_3 = [1,0,1]\,[5,0,1]^{\omega},$$

$$e_4 = [1,1,1]\,[2,1,1]\,[3,1,1]\,[4,0,1]\,[1,0,1]\,[5,0,1]^{\omega}.$$

The corresponding executable computations for the set AP of example 13.3 are

$$\sigma_1 = \{\texttt{at\_1}, \texttt{x=0}, \texttt{y=0}\}\,\{\texttt{at\_5}, \texttt{x=0}, \texttt{y=0}\}^{\omega},$$

$$\sigma_2 = (\{\texttt{at\_1}, \texttt{x=1}, \texttt{y=0}\}\,\{\texttt{at\_2}, \texttt{x=1}, \texttt{y=0}\}\,\{\texttt{at\_4}, \texttt{x=1}, \texttt{y=0}\})^{\omega},$$

$$\sigma_3 = \{\texttt{at\_1}, \texttt{x=0}, \texttt{y=1}\}\,\{\texttt{at\_5}, \texttt{x=0}, \texttt{y=1}\}^{\omega},$$

$$\sigma_4 = \{\texttt{at\_1}, \texttt{x=1}, \texttt{y=1}\}\,\{\texttt{at\_2}, \texttt{x=1}, \texttt{y=1}\}\,\{\texttt{at\_3}, \texttt{x=1}, \texttt{y=1}\}\,\{\texttt{at\_4}, \texttt{x=0}, \texttt{y=1}\}$$

$$\{\texttt{at\_1}, \texttt{x=0}, \texttt{y=1}\}\,\{\texttt{at\_5}, \texttt{x=0}, \texttt{y=1}\}^{\omega}.$$

We give some examples of LTL properties:

• $\varphi_0 = \texttt{x=1} \wedge \mathbf{X}\,\texttt{y=0} \wedge \mathbf{XX}\,\texttt{at\_4}$. In natural language: the value of x in the first configuration of the execution is 1, the value of y in the second configuration is 0, and in the third configuration, the program is at location 4. We have $\sigma_2 \models \varphi_0$, and $\sigma_1, \sigma_3, \sigma_4 \not\models \varphi_0$.

• $\varphi_1 = \mathbf{F}\,\texttt{at\_5}$. In natural language: the execution eventually reaches a configuration in which the program is at line 5. Since this is the line corresponding to the termination of the execution, program satisfies this property if all its executions terminate. We have $\sigma_1, \sigma_3, \sigma_4 \models \varphi_1$, but $\sigma_2 \not\models \varphi_1$, and so the program does not satisfy the property. Observe that $\sigma_1, \sigma_2, \sigma_3, \sigma_4 \models \mathbf{F}\,\texttt{at\_1}$, because $\sigma_1^0, \sigma_2^0, \sigma_3^0, \sigma_4^0 \models \texttt{at\_1}$.

• $\varphi_2 = \texttt{x=0}\ \mathbf{U}\ \texttt{at\_5}$. In natural language: x stays equal to 0 until the execution reaches location 5. However, this description is ambiguous: Do executions that never reach location 5 satisfy the property? Do executions that set x to 1 immediately before reaching location 5 satisfy the property? The formal definition removes the ambiguities: the answer to the first question is "no"; to the second, "yes." We have $\sigma_1, \sigma_3 \models \varphi_2$ and $\sigma_2, \sigma_4 \not\models \varphi_2$.

• $\varphi_3 = \texttt{at\_5}\ \mathbf{U}\ \texttt{x=0}$. In natural language: the execution stays at location 5 until x takes the value 0. But, again, the description is ambiguous. We certainly have $\sigma_2, \sigma_4 \not\models \varphi_3$, but do σ_1 and σ_3, for which x is initially 0, satisfy the property? The formal definition says "yes." As mentioned before, if $\sigma^0 \models \varphi$, then $\sigma \models \psi\ \mathbf{U}\ \varphi$ for any ψ.

• $\varphi_4 = \texttt{y=1} \wedge \mathbf{F}(\texttt{y=0} \wedge \texttt{at\_5}) \wedge \neg(\mathbf{F}(\texttt{y=0} \wedge \mathbf{X}\,\texttt{y=1}))$. In natural language: the initial configuration satisfies $y = 1$, the execution terminates in a configuration with $y = 0$, and y never increases during the execution. This is one of the properties we analyzed in chapter 7, and it is not satisfied by any ω-execution.

Example 13.7   We express properties of Lamport-Burns' algorithm (see chapter 7) using LTL formulas. As system NBA, we use the one in which transitions are labeled with the name of the target configuration and with the number of the process responsible for the move leading to that configuration. We take $AP = \{NC_0, T_0, C_0, NC_1, T_1, C_1, M_0, M_1\}$, with the obvious valuation.

- The mutual exclusion property is expressed by the formula

$$\mathbf{G}(\neg C_0 \vee \neg C_1).$$

The algorithm satisfies the formula.

- The property that process i cannot access the critical section without having requested it first is expressed by

$$\neg(\neg T_i \mathbf{U} C_i).$$

Both processes satisfy this property.

- The naive finite waiting property for process i is expressed by

$$\mathbf{G}(T_i \rightarrow \mathbf{F} C_i).$$

The modified version in which both processes must execute infinitely many moves is expressed by

$$(\mathbf{GF}M_0 \wedge \mathbf{GF}M_1) \rightarrow \mathbf{G}(T_i \rightarrow \mathbf{F} C_i).$$

Observe how fairness assumptions can be very elegantly expressed in LTL. The assumption itself is expressed as a formula ψ, and the property that ω-executions satisfying the fairness assumption also satisfy φ is expressed by $\psi \rightarrow \varphi$.

   None of the processes satisfies the naive version of the finite waiting property. Process 0 satisfies the modified version but not process 1.

- The bounded overtaking property for process 0 is expressed by

$$\mathbf{G}(T_0 \rightarrow (\neg C_1 \mathbf{U} (C_1 \mathbf{U} (\neg C_1 \mathbf{U} C_0)))).$$

The formula states that whenever T_0 holds, the computation continues with a (possibly empty) interval at which $\neg C_1$ holds, followed by a (possibly empty) interval at which C_1 holds, followed by a (possibly empty) interval at which $\neg C_1$ holds, followed by a point at which C_0 holds. The property holds.

Example 13.8   Formally speaking, it is not correct to say "$\varphi \mathbf{U} \psi$ means that some future configuration satisfies φ, and until then, all configurations satisfy ψ." The reason is that formulas do not hold at configurations but at computations. The correct phrasing is: "the suffix of the computation starting at the next configuration satisfies φ, and some suffix of the computation satisfies ψ."

To illustrate this point, let $AP = \{p, q\}$, and consider the formula $\varphi = (\mathbf{F}p) \mathbf{U} q$ and the computation $\tau = \emptyset \, \emptyset \, \{q\} \, \emptyset \, \{p\} \, \emptyset^\omega$. One might think that τ does not satisfy φ, because no configuration before the one satisfying q satisfies p. But that is not the case; we have $\tau \models \varphi$. Indeed, the suffix $\tau^2 = \{q\} \, \emptyset \, \{p\} \, \emptyset^\omega$ satisfies q, and the suffixes $\tau^0 = \tau$ and $\tau^1 = \emptyset \, \{q\} \, \emptyset \, \{p\} \, \emptyset^\omega$ satisfy $\mathbf{F}p$; the fact that p only holds after q holds is irrelevant.

13.3   From LTL Formulas to Generalized Büchi Automata

We present an algorithm that, given a formula $\varphi \in LTL(AP)$, returns an NGA A_φ over the alphabet 2^{AP} recognizing $\mathcal{L}_\omega(\varphi)$. Then we derive a fully automatic procedure that, given a system and an LTL formula, decides whether all executable computations of the system satisfy the formula.

13.3.1   Satisfaction Sequences and Hintikka Sequences

We define the satisfaction sequence and the Hintikka sequence of a computation σ and a formula φ. We first need to introduce the notions of *closure* of a formula and *atom* of the closure.

Definition 13.9   *Given a formula φ, the* negation *of φ is the formula ψ if $\varphi = \neg\psi$ and the formula $\neg\varphi$ otherwise. The* closure *$cl(\varphi)$ of a formula φ is the set containing all subformulas of φ and their negations. A nonempty set $\alpha \subseteq cl(\varphi)$ is an* atom *of $cl(\varphi)$ if it satisfies the following properties:*

(a0) If $\mathbf{true} \in cl(\varphi)$, then $\mathbf{true} \in \alpha$.

(a1) For every $\varphi_1 \wedge \varphi_2 \in cl(\varphi)$: $\varphi_1 \wedge \varphi_2 \in \alpha$ if and only if $\varphi_1 \in \alpha$ and $\varphi_2 \in \alpha$.

(a2) For every $\neg\varphi_1 \in cl(\varphi)$: $\neg\varphi_1 \in \alpha$ if and only if $\varphi_1 \notin \alpha$.

The set of all atoms of $cl(\varphi)$ is denoted by $at(\varphi)$.

Observe that if α is the set of all formulas of $cl(\varphi)$ satisfied by a computation, then α is necessarily an atom. Indeed, every computation satisfies $\mathbf{true}$; if a computation satisfies the conjunction of two formulas, then it satisfies each of the conjuncts; and finally, if a computation satisfies a formula, then it does not satisfy its negation and vice versa. Notice as well that, because of (a2), if $cl(\varphi)$ contains k formulas, then every atom of $cl(\varphi)$ contains exactly $k/2$ formulas.

Example 13.10   The closure of the formula $p \wedge (p \mathbf{U} q)$ is

$$\{p, \ \neg p, \ q, \ \neg q, \ p \mathbf{U} q, \ \neg(p \mathbf{U} q), \ p \wedge (p \mathbf{U} q), \ \neg(p \wedge (p \mathbf{U} q))\}.$$

We claim that the only two atoms containing $p \wedge (p \mathbf{U} q)$ are

$$\{p, \ q, \ p \mathbf{U} q, \ p \wedge (p \mathbf{U} q)\} \text{ and } \{p, \ \neg q, \ p \mathbf{U} q, \ p \wedge (p \mathbf{U} q)\}.$$

Let us see why. By (a2), an atom always contains either a subformula or its negation but not both. So in principle, there are sixteen possibilities for atoms, since we have to choose exactly one of p and $\neg p$, q and $\neg q$, $p \, \mathbf{U} \, q$ and $\neg (p \, \mathbf{U} \, q)$, and $p \wedge (p \, \mathbf{U} \, q)$ and $\neg \, (p \wedge (p \, \mathbf{U} \, q))$. Since we look for atoms containing $p \wedge (p \, \mathbf{U} \, q)$, we are left with eight possibilities. But, by (a1), every atom α containing $p \wedge (p \, \mathbf{U} \, q)$ must contain both p and $p \, \mathbf{U} \, q$. Thus, the only freedom left is the possibility to choose q or $\neg q$. None of these choices violates any of the conditions, and so exactly two atoms contain $p \wedge (p \, \mathbf{U} \, q)$.

Definition 13.11   *The satisfaction sequence for a computation σ and a formula φ is the infinite sequence of atoms*

$$sats(\sigma, \varphi) = sats(\sigma, \varphi, 0) \; sats(\sigma, \varphi, 1) \; sats(\sigma, \varphi, 2) \; \cdots$$

where $sats(\sigma, \varphi, i)$ is the atom containing the formulas of $cl(\varphi)$ satisfied by σ^i.

Intuitively, the satisfaction sequence of a computation σ is obtained by "completing" the computation: while σ only indicates which atomic propositions hold at each point in time, the satisfaction sequence also indicates which atoms hold.

Example 13.12   Let $\varphi = p \, \mathbf{U} \, q$, and consider $\sigma_1 = \{p\}^\omega$ and $\sigma_2 = (\{p\} \, \{q\})^\omega$. We have

$$sats(\sigma_1, \varphi) = \{p, \; \neg q, \; \neg (p \, \mathbf{U} \, q)\}^\omega,$$

$$sats(\sigma_2, \varphi) = (\{p, \; \neg q, \; p \, \mathbf{U} \, q\} \, \{\neg p, \; q, \; p \, \mathbf{U} \, q\})^\omega.$$

Observe that σ satisfies φ if and only if $\varphi \in sats(\sigma, \varphi, 0)$ (i.e., if and only if φ belongs to the first atom of σ).

Satisfaction sequences have a *semantic* definition: in order to know which atom holds at a point, one must know the semantics of LTL. Hintikka sequences provide a *syntactic* characterization of satisfaction sequences. The definition of a Hintikka sequence does not involve the semantics of LTL, that is, someone who ignores the semantics can still determine whether a given sequence is a Hintikka sequence or not. We prove that a sequence is a satisfaction sequence if and only if it is a Hintikka sequence.

Definition 13.13   *A pre-Hintikka sequence for φ is an infinite sequence $\alpha_0 \alpha_1 \alpha_2 \cdots$ of atoms satisfying the following conditions for every $i \geq 0$:*

($\ell 1$) For every $\mathbf{X}\varphi_1 \in cl(\varphi)$:
$$\mathbf{X}\varphi_1 \in \alpha_i \; \textit{iff} \; \varphi_1 \in \alpha_{i+1}.$$

($\ell 2$) For every $\varphi_1 \, \mathbf{U} \, \varphi_2 \in cl(\varphi)$:
$$\varphi_1 \, \mathbf{U} \, \varphi_2 \in \alpha_i \; \textit{iff} \; \varphi_2 \in \alpha_i, \; \textit{or} \; \varphi_1 \in \alpha_i \; \textit{and} \; \varphi_1 \, \mathbf{U} \, \varphi_2 \in \alpha_{i+1}.$$

A pre-Hintikka sequence is a Hintikka sequence *if it also satisfies*

(g) For every $\varphi_1 \mathbf{U} \varphi_2 \in \alpha_i$, there exists $j \geq i$ such that $\varphi_2 \in \alpha_j$.

A pre-Hintikka or Hintikka sequence α matches a computation σ if $\sigma_i \subseteq \alpha_i$ for every $i \geq 0$.

Note that conditions ($\ell 1$) and ($\ell 2$) are *local*: in order to determine if α satisfies them, we only need to inspect every pair α_i, α_{i+1} of consecutive atoms. On the contrary, condition (g) is *global*, since the distance between the indices i and j can be arbitrarily large.

Example 13.14   Let $\varphi = \neg(p \wedge q) \mathbf{U} (r \wedge s)$. We consider several sequences and examine whether they are Hintikka sequences.

- Let $\alpha_1 = \{p, \neg q, r, s, \varphi\}$. The sequence α_1^{ω} is not a Hintikka sequence for φ, because α_1 is not an atom; indeed, by (a1), every atom containing r and s must contain $r \wedge s$.

- Let $\alpha_2 = \{\neg p, r, \neg \varphi\}$. The sequence α_2^{ω} is not a Hintikka sequence for φ, because α_2 is not an atom; indeed, by (a2), every atom must contain either q or $\neg q$ and either s or $\neg s$.

- Let $\alpha_3 = \{\neg p, q, \neg r, s, r \wedge s, \varphi\}$. The sequence α_3^{ω} is not a Hintikka sequence for φ, because α_3 is not an atom; indeed, by (a2), every atom must contain either $(p \wedge q)$ or $\neg(p \wedge q)$.

- Let $\alpha_4 = \{p, q, (p \wedge q), r, s, r \wedge s, \neg \varphi\}$. The set α_4 is an atom, but the sequence α_4^{ω} is not a Hintikka sequence for φ, because it violates condition ($\ell 2$): since α_4 contains $(r \wedge s)$, it must also contain φ.

- Let $\alpha_5 = \{p, \neg q, \neg(p \wedge q), \neg r, s, \neg(r \wedge s), \varphi\}$. The set α_5 is an atom, and the sequence α_5^{ω} is a pre-Hintikka sequence. However, it is not a Hintikka sequence because it violates condition (g): since α_5 contains φ, some atom in the sequence must contain $(r \wedge s)$, which is not the case.

- Let $\alpha_6 = \{p, q, (p \wedge q), r, s, (r \wedge s), \varphi\}$. The sequences $(\alpha_6)^{\omega}$ and $(\alpha_5 \alpha_6)^{\omega}$ are two examples of Hintikka sequences for φ.

It follows immediately from the definition of Hintikka sequences that if $\alpha = \alpha_0 \alpha_1 \alpha_2 \cdots$ is a satisfaction sequence, then every pair α_i, α_{i+1} satisfies ($\ell 1$) and ($\ell 2$), and the sequence α itself satisfies (g). So, every satisfaction sequence is a Hintikka sequence. The following theorem shows that the converse also holds: every Hintikka sequence is a satisfaction sequence.

Theorem 13.15   *Let σ be a computation and let φ be a formula. The unique Hintikka sequence for φ matching σ is the satisfaction sequence $sats(\sigma, \varphi)$.*

Proof   As observed above, it follows from the definitions that $sats(\sigma, \varphi)$ is a Hintikka sequence for φ matching σ. To show that no other Hintikka sequence matches $sats(\sigma, \varphi)$, let $\alpha = \alpha_0 \alpha_1 \alpha_2 \cdots$ be a Hintikka sequence for φ matching σ, and let ψ be an arbitrary formula of $cl(\varphi)$. We prove that for all $i \geq 0$: $\psi \in \alpha_i$ if and only if $\psi \in sats(\sigma, \varphi, i)$. The proof is by induction on the structure of ψ.

- $\psi = \mathbf{true}$. We have $\mathbf{true} \in sats(\sigma, \varphi, i)$ and, since α_i is an atom, $\mathbf{true} \in \alpha_i$.

- $\psi = p$ for an atomic proposition p. Since α matches σ, we have $p \in \alpha_i$ if and only if $p \in \sigma_i$. By definition of satisfaction sequences, $p \in \sigma_i$ if and only if $p \in sats(\sigma, \varphi, i)$. Thus, $p \in \alpha_i$ if and only if $p \in sats(\sigma, \varphi, i)$.

- $\psi = \varphi_1 \wedge \varphi_2$. We have

$$\varphi_1 \wedge \varphi_2 \in \alpha_i$$

$$\Longleftrightarrow \varphi_1 \in \alpha_i \text{ and } \varphi_2 \in \alpha_i \qquad\qquad \text{(by condition (a1))}$$

$$\Longleftrightarrow \varphi_1 \in sats(\sigma, \varphi, i) \text{ and } \varphi_2 \in sats(\sigma, \varphi, i) \text{ (by. ind. hypothesis)}$$

$$\Longleftrightarrow \varphi_1 \wedge \varphi_2 \in sats(\sigma, \varphi, i) \qquad\qquad \text{(by def. of } sats(\sigma, \varphi)).$$

- $\psi = \neg\varphi_1$ or $\psi = \mathbf{X}\varphi_1$. The proofs are very similar to the last one.

- $\psi = \varphi_1 \mathbf{U} \varphi_2$.

(a) If $\varphi_1 \mathbf{U} \varphi_2 \in \alpha_i$, then $\varphi_1 \mathbf{U} \varphi_2 \in sats(\sigma, \varphi, i)$.

By condition ($\ell 2$) of the definition of a Hintikka sequence, we have to consider two cases:

- $\varphi_2 \in \alpha_i$. By induction hypothesis, $\varphi_2 \in sats(\sigma, \varphi)$, and hence $\varphi_1 \mathbf{U} \varphi_2 \in sats(\sigma, \varphi, i)$.

- $\varphi_1 \in \alpha_i$ and $\varphi_1 \mathbf{U} \varphi_2 \in \alpha_{i+1}$. By condition (g), there is at least one index $j \geq i$ such that $\varphi_2 \in \alpha_j$. Let j_m be the smallest of these indices. We prove the result by induction on $j_m - i$. If $i = j_m$, then $\varphi_2 \in \alpha_{j_m}$, and we proceed as in the case $\varphi_2 \in \alpha_i$. If $i < j_m$, then since $\varphi_1 \in \alpha_i$, we have $\varphi_1 \in sats(\sigma, \varphi, i)$ (by induction on ψ). Since $\varphi_1 \mathbf{U} \varphi_2 \in \alpha_{i+1}$, we have either $\varphi_2 \in \alpha_{i+1}$ or $\varphi_1 \in \alpha_{i+1}$. In the first case, we have $\varphi_2 \in sats(\sigma, \varphi, i+1)$, and so $\varphi_1 \mathbf{U} \varphi_2 \in sats(\sigma, \varphi, i)$. In the second case, by induction hypothesis (on $j_m - i$), we have $\varphi_1 \mathbf{U} \varphi_2 \in sats(\sigma, \varphi, i+1)$, and so $\varphi_1 \mathbf{U} \varphi_2 \in sats(\sigma, \varphi, i)$.

(b) If $\varphi_1 \mathbf{U} \varphi_2 \in sats(\sigma, \varphi, i)$, then $\varphi_1 \mathbf{U} \varphi_2 \in \alpha_i$.

We consider again two cases.

- $\varphi_2 \in sats(\sigma, \varphi, i)$. By induction hypothesis, $\varphi_2 \in \alpha_i$, and hence $\varphi_1 \mathbf{U} \varphi_2 \in \alpha_i$.

- $\varphi_1 \in sats(\sigma, \varphi, i)$ and $\varphi_1 \mathbf{U} \varphi_2 \in sats(\sigma, \varphi, i+1)$. By the definition of a satisfaction sequence, there is at least one index $j \geq i$ such that $\varphi_2 \in sats(\sigma, \varphi, j)$. Proceed now as in case (a). $\qquad\qquad\qquad\qquad\qquad\qquad\qquad\qquad\qquad\qquad\qquad\qquad\qquad \square$

13.3.2   Constructing the NGA for an LTL Formula

Given a formula φ, we construct an NGA A_φ recognizing $\mathcal{L}_\omega(\varphi)$. By the definition of a satisfaction sequence, a computation σ satisfies φ if and only if $\varphi \in sats(\sigma, \varphi, 0)$. Moreover, by theorem 13.15, $sats(\sigma, \varphi)$ is the (unique) Hintikka sequence for φ matching σ. Thus, A_φ recognizes the computations σ satisfying: the first atom of the unique Hintikka sequence for φ matching σ contains φ.

To achieve this, we apply the following strategy:

(a) Define the states and transitions of the automaton so that the runs of the NGA A_φ are all the sequences

$$\alpha_0 \xrightarrow{\sigma_0} \alpha_1 \xrightarrow{\sigma_1} \alpha_2 \xrightarrow{\sigma_2} \cdots$$

such that $\sigma = \sigma_0 \sigma_1 \cdots$ is a computation, and $\alpha = \alpha_0 \alpha_1 \cdots$ is a pre-Hintikka sequence of φ matching σ.

(b) Define the sets of accepting states so that a run is accepting if and only if its corresponding pre-Hintikka sequence is also a Hintikka sequence.

Condition (a) determines all but the accepting states of A_φ:

- the alphabet of A_φ is 2^{AP};
- the states of A_φ are atoms of φ;
- the initial states are the atoms α such that $\varphi \in \alpha$; and
- the output transitions of a state α, where α is an atom, are the triples $\alpha \xrightarrow{\sigma} \beta$ such that σ matches α, and the pair α, β satisfies conditions $(\ell 1)$ and $(\ell 2)$ (where α and β play the roles of α_i and α_{i+1}).

The sets of accepting states of A_φ are determined by condition (g). By definition of Hintikka sequences, we must guarantee that in every run $\alpha_0 \xrightarrow{\sigma_0} \alpha_1 \xrightarrow{\sigma_1} \cdots$, if any α_i contains a subformula $\varphi_1 \mathbf{U} \varphi_2$, then there is $j \geq i$ such that $\varphi_2 \in \alpha_j$. By condition $(\ell 2)$, this amounts to ensuring that every run contains infinitely many indices i such that $\varphi_2 \in \alpha_i$, or infinitely many indices j such that $\neg(\varphi_1 \mathbf{U} \varphi_2) \in \alpha_j$. Thus, we choose the sets of accepting states as follows:

- The accepting condition contains a set $F_{\varphi_1 \mathbf{U} \varphi_2}$ of accepting states for each subformula $\varphi_1 \mathbf{U} \varphi_2$ of φ. An atom belongs to $F_{\varphi_1 \mathbf{U} \varphi_2}$ if it does not contain $\varphi_1 \mathbf{U} \varphi_2$ or if it contains φ_2.

The pseudocode for the translation is described in algorithm 57.

Example 13.16 We construct the automaton A_φ for the formula $\varphi = p \mathbf{U} q$. The closure $cl(\varphi)$ has eight atoms, corresponding to all the possible ways of choosing between p and $\neg p$, q and $\neg q$, and $p \mathbf{U} q$ and $\neg(p \mathbf{U} q)$. However, we can easily see that the atoms $\{p, q, \neg(p \mathbf{U} q)\}$, $\{\neg p, q, \neg(p \mathbf{U} q)\}$, and $\{\neg p, \neg q, p \mathbf{U} q\}$ have no output transitions, because those transitions would violate condition $(\ell 2)$. Since states without output transitions cannot appear in any run, they can be removed, and we are left with the five atoms shown in figure 13.7.

The three atoms on the left contain $p \mathbf{U} q$, and so they become the initial states. Figure 13.7 uses some conventions to simplify the graphical representation. Observe that every transition of A_φ leaving an atom α is labeled by $\alpha \cap AP$. For instance, all transitions leaving the state $\{\neg p, q, p \mathbf{U} q\}$ are labeled with $\{q\}$, and all transitions leaving $\{\neg p, \neg q, \neg(p \mathbf{U} q)\}$ are labeled with $\emptyset$. Therefore, since the label of a transition can be deduced from its source state, we omit transition labels in the figure.

Algorithm 57   Algorithm to convert an LTL formula into an NGA.

LTLtoNGA(φ)
Input: formula φ over AP
Output: NGA $A_\varphi = (Q, 2^{AP}, Q_0, \delta, \mathcal{F})$ with $\mathcal{L}_\omega(A_\varphi) = \mathcal{L}_\omega(\varphi)$

```
1   Q₀ ← {α ∈ at(φ) : φ ∈ α}; Q ← ∅; δ ← ∅
2   W ← Q₀
3   while W ≠ ∅ do
4      pick α from W
5      add α to Q
6      for all φ₁ U φ₂ ∈ cl(φ) do
7         if φ₁ U φ₂ ∉ α or  φ₂ ∈ α then add α to F_{φ₁ U φ₂}
8      for all β ∈ at(φ) do
9         if α, β satisfies (ℓ1) and (ℓ2) then
10            add (α, α ∩ AP, β) to δ
11            if β ∉ Q then add β to W
12   F ← ∅
13   for all φ₁ U φ₂ ∈ cl(φ) do F ← F ∪ {F_{φ₁ U φ₂}}
14   return (Q, 2^{AP}, Q₀, δ, F)
```

Moreover, since φ only has one subformula of the form $\varphi_1 \mathbf{U} \varphi_2$, the NGA is in fact an NBA, and we can represent the accepting states as for NBAs. The accepting states of $F_{p\,\mathbf{U}\,q}$ are the atoms that do not contain $p\,\mathbf{U}\,q$—the two atoms on the right—and the atoms containing q—the leftmost atom and the atom at the top.

Consider, for example, the atoms

$$\alpha = \{\neg p, \neg q, \neg(p\,\mathbf{U}\,q)\} \text{ and } \beta = \{p, \neg q, p\,\mathbf{U}\,q\}.$$

Automaton A_φ contains a transition $\alpha \xrightarrow{\{p\}} \beta$ because $\{p\}$ matches β, and α, β satisfy conditions $(\ell 1)$ and $(\ell 2)$. Condition $(\ell 1)$ holds vacuously, since φ contains no subformulas of the form $\mathbf{X}\psi$, while condition $(\ell 2)$ holds as $p\,\mathbf{U}\,q \notin \alpha$ and $q \notin \beta$ and $p \notin \alpha$. On the other hand, there is no transition from β to α as it would violate condition $(\ell 2)$: $p\,\mathbf{U}\,q \in \beta$, but neither $q \in \beta$ nor $p\,\mathbf{U}\,q \in \alpha$.

NGAs obtained from LTL formulas by means of *LTLtoNGA* have a very particular structure:

- As observed above, all transitions leaving a state carry the same label.
- Every computation accepted by the NGA has a single accepting run.

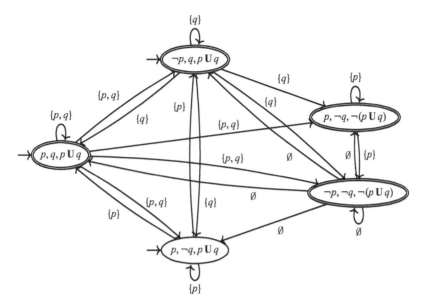

Figure 13.7
An NGA (NBA) for the formula $p \, \mathbf{U} \, q$, with three initial states and four accepting states.

By definition of the NGA, if $\alpha_0 \xrightarrow{\sigma_0} \alpha_1 \xrightarrow{\sigma_1} \cdots$ is an accepting run, then $\alpha_0 \, \alpha_1 \cdots$ is the satisfaction sequence of $\sigma_0 \, \sigma_1 \cdots$. Since the satisfaction sequence of a given computation is by definition unique, there can be only one accepting run.

- The sets of computations recognized by any two distinct states of the NGA are disjoint.

Let σ be a computation, and let $sats(\sigma, \varphi) = sats(\sigma, \varphi, 0) \, sats(\sigma, \varphi, 1) \ldots$ be its satisfaction sequence. Then σ is only accepted from the state $sats(\sigma, \varphi, 0)$.

13.3.3 Size of the NGA

Let n be the length of the formula φ. It is easy to see that the set $cl(\varphi)$ has size $\mathcal{O}(n)$. Thus, the NGA A_φ has at most $\mathcal{O}(2^n)$ states. Since φ contains at most n subformulas of the form $\varphi_1 \, \mathbf{U} \, \varphi_2$, the automaton A_φ has at most n sets of accepting states.

We now prove a matching lower bound on the number of states. We exhibit a family of formulas $\{\varphi_n\}_{n \geq 1}$ such that φ_n has length $\mathcal{O}(n)$, and every NGA recognizing $\mathcal{L}_\omega(\varphi_n)$ has at least 2^n states. For this, we exhibit a family $\{D_n\}_{n \geq 1}$ of ω-languages over an alphabet Σ such that for every $n \geq 0$:

(a) every NGA recognizing D_n has at least 2^n states, and
(b) there is a formula $\varphi_n \in LTL(\Sigma)$ of length $\mathcal{O}(n)$ such that $\mathcal{L}_\omega(\varphi_n) = D_n$.

Note that in (2), we are abusing language, because if $\varphi_n \in LTL(\Sigma)$, then $\mathcal{L}_\omega(\varphi_n)$ contains words over the alphabet 2^Σ, and so $\mathcal{L}_\omega(\varphi_n)$ and D_n are languages over different alphabets. With $\mathcal{L}_\omega(\varphi_n) = D_n$, we mean that for every computation $\sigma \in (2^\Sigma)^\omega$, we have $\sigma \in \mathcal{L}_\omega(\varphi_n)$ iff $\sigma = \{a_1\}\{a_2\}\{a_3\} \cdots$ for some ω-word $a_1 a_2 a_3 \cdots \in D_n$.

We let $\Sigma = \{0, 1, \#\}$ and choose the language D_n as follows:

$$D_n = \{ww\#^\omega : w \in \{0, 1\}^n\}.$$

(a) Every NGA recognizing D_n has at least 2^n states.

Assume that an NGA $A = (Q, \{0, 1, \#\}, \delta, q_0, \{F_1, \ldots, F_k\})$ with $|Q| < 2^n$ recognizes D_n. For every word $w \in \{0, 1\}^n$, there is a state q_w such that A accepts $w\#^\omega$ from q_w. By the pigeonhole principle, we have $q_{w_1} = q_{w_2}$ for two distinct words $w_1, w_2 \in \{0, 1\}^n$. But then A accepts $w_1 w_2 \#^\omega$, which does not belong to D_n, contradicting the hypothesis.

(b) There is a formula $\varphi_n \in LTL(\Sigma)$ of length $\mathcal{O}(n)$ such that $\mathcal{L}_\omega(\varphi_n) = D_n$.

We need three auxiliary formulas. The first one expresses that at every position, exactly one atomic proposition holds:

$$\varphi_{n1} = \mathbf{G}[(0 \vee 1 \vee \#) \wedge \neg(0 \wedge 1) \wedge \neg(0 \wedge \#) \wedge \neg(1 \wedge \#)].$$

The second expresses that $\#$ does not hold at any of the first $2n$ positions, and it holds at all later positions:

$$\varphi_{n2} = \neg \# \wedge \left(\bigwedge_{i=1}^{2n-1} \mathbf{X}^i \neg \# \right) \wedge \mathbf{X}^{2n} \mathbf{G} \#.$$

The third formula expresses that if the atomic proposition holding at a position is 0 or 1, then n positions later the atomic proposition holding is the same one, or $\#$:

$$\varphi_{n3} = \mathbf{G}[(0 \to \mathbf{X}^n(0 \vee \#)) \wedge (1 \to \mathbf{X}^n(1 \vee \#))].$$

Clearly, $\varphi_n = \varphi_{n1} \wedge \varphi_{n2} \wedge \varphi_{n3}$ is the formula we are looking for. Observe that φ_n contains $\mathcal{O}(n)$ characters.

13.4 Automatic Verification of LTL Formulas

We sketch a procedure for the automatic verification of properties expressed by LTL formulas. The input to the procedure is

• a system NBA A_s obtained either directly from the system or by computing the asynchronous product of a network of automata,

• a formula φ of LTL over a set of atomic propositions AP, and

- a valuation $\nu : AP \rightarrow 2^C$, where C is the set of configurations of A_s, describing for each atomic proposition the set of configurations at which the proposition holds.

The procedure follows these steps:

(1) Compute an NGA A_ν for the *negation* of the formula φ. Automaton A_ν recognizes all the computations that *violate* φ.

(2) Compute an NGA $A_{\nu s}$ recognizing the executable computations of the system that violate the formula.

(3) Check emptiness of $A_{\nu s}$.

Step (1) can be carried out by applying *LTLtoNGA* and step (3) by any of the algorithms of chapter 12. For step (2), observe first that the alphabets of A_ν and A_s are different: the alphabet of A_ν is 2^{AP}, while the alphabet of A_s is the set C of configurations of the system. So, we first apply the valuation $\mathcal{V}$ to transform A_ν into an automaton, say A'_ν, with C as alphabet. For example, if $q \xrightarrow{\{p_1,p_2\}} q'$ is a transition of A_ν, where p_1 and p_2 are two atomic propositions, then A'_ν contains a transition $q \xrightarrow{c} q'$ for every configuration c such that $c \in \mathcal{V}(p_1) \cap \mathcal{V}(p_2)$. The NGA $A_{\nu s}$ can then be computed as the result of applying *IntersNGA* to A'_ν and A_s (algorithm 47 in chapter 11).

Example 13.17 In example 13.2, we proved the following property of the program of example 13.1: all full executions starting at configurations satisfying $x = y$ terminate (first property of the example). For this, we represented the property by an ω-regular expression. Let us now examine the same property, but this time expressing it as an LTL formula.

We choose the set of atomic propositions $AP = \{\texttt{at\_5}, \texttt{x=y}\}$. The valuation assigns to $\texttt{at\_5}$ all configurations where the program is at line 5 and to $\texttt{x=y}$ all configurations where the values of variables x and y coincide. The LTL property we wish to verify is $\varphi = \texttt{x=y} \rightarrow \mathbf{F}\,\texttt{at\_5}$. The smallest NGA A_ν for $\neg\varphi = \texttt{x=y} \wedge \mathbf{G}\neg\texttt{at\_5}$ is depicted in figure 13.8.

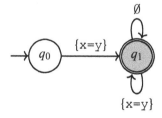

Figure 13.8
An NGA for $\neg\varphi = \texttt{x=y} \wedge \mathbf{G}\neg\texttt{at\_5}$.

Applying the valuation, we obtain that the sets $C_\emptyset$ and $C_{\{x=y\}}$ of configurations satisfying the corresponding sets of atomic propositions are

$$C_\emptyset = \{[\ell, x, y] : \ell \neq 5 \text{ and } x \neq y\} = \{[\ell, 0, 1], [\ell, 1, 0] : \ell \neq 5\},$$

$$C_{\{x=y\}} = \{[\ell, x, y] : \ell \neq 5 \text{ and } x = y\} = \{[\ell, 0, 0], [\ell, 1, 1] : \ell \neq 5\}.$$

Both sets contain eight configurations. The automaton A'_v is the result of replacing in A_v the transition $(q_0, \{x=y\}, q_1)$ by eight transitions of the form (q_0, c, q_0), one for each configuration $c \in C_{x=y}$, and proceeding similarly with the other two transitions. From this moment on, we proceed as in example 13.2. The NGA A_{vs} is exactly the one shown in example 13.2 for the first property. Since it contains no accepting lasso, the program satisfies the property.

Observe that steps (1) to (3) can be carried out simultaneously. The states of A_{vs} are pairs $[\alpha, c]$, where α is an atom of φ, and c is a configuration of the system. Let us see in detail how to compute their successors. Algorithm 58 takes a pair $[\alpha, c]$ as input and returns its successors in the NGA A_{vs}. The algorithm first computes the successors of c in A_s. Then, for each successor c' of c, it computes the set P of atomic propositions satisfied by c' according to the valuation. Finally, the algorithm computes the set of atoms β such that β matches P and the pair α, β satisfies conditions $(\ell 1)$ and $(\ell 2)$ of definition 13.13. The successors of $[\alpha, c]$ are all the pairs $[\beta, c']$.

Algorithm 58 Computation of successors.

$Succ([\alpha, c])$

1    $S \leftarrow \emptyset$
2   **for all** $c' \in \delta_s(c)$ **do**
3        $P \leftarrow \emptyset$
4   **for all** $p \in AP$ **do**
5   **if** $c' \in v(p)$ **then add** p **to** P
6   **for all** $\beta \in at(\varphi)$ matching P **do**
7   **if** α, β satisfies $(\ell 1)$ and $(\ell 2)$ **then add** c' **to** S
8   **return** S

This algorithm can be inserted in the algorithm for the emptiness check. For instance, if we use *SCCsearch*, then we just replace

6   **for all** $r \in \delta(q)$ **do**

by a call to *Succ*:

6   **for all** $[\beta, c'] \in Succ([\alpha, c])$ **do**

13.5 Exercises

☆ ■ **Exercise 176.** Prove formally the following equivalences:

(a) $\neg \mathbf{X}\varphi \equiv \mathbf{X}\neg\varphi$

(b) $\neg \mathbf{F}\varphi \equiv \mathbf{G}\neg\varphi$

(c) $\neg \mathbf{G}\varphi \equiv \mathbf{F}\neg\varphi$

(d) $\mathbf{XF}\varphi \equiv \mathbf{FX}\varphi$

(e) $\mathbf{XG}\varphi \equiv \mathbf{GX}\varphi$

☆ ■ **Exercise 177.** The *weak until* operator $\mathbf{W}$ has the following semantics:

$$\sigma \models \varphi_1 \mathbf{W} \varphi_2 \iff \exists k \geq 0 : (\sigma^k \models \varphi_2 \text{ and } \forall 0 \leq i < k \ \sigma^i \models \varphi_1), \text{ or } \forall k \geq 0 \ (\sigma^k \models \varphi_1).$$

Prove the following equivalences:

$$p \mathbf{W} q \equiv \mathbf{G}p \vee (p \mathbf{U} q) \equiv \mathbf{F}\neg p \to (p \mathbf{U} q) \equiv p \mathbf{U} (q \vee \mathbf{G}p).$$

☆ ▣ **Exercise 178.** Let $AP = \{p, q\}$ and $\Sigma = 2^{AP}$. Give LTL formulas defining the following languages:

(a) $\{p, q\} \, \varnothing \, \Sigma^\omega$

(b) $\Sigma^* \, (\{p\} + \{p, q\}) \, \Sigma^* \, \{q\} \, \Sigma^\omega$

(c) $\Sigma^* \, \{q\}^\omega$

(d) $\{p\}^* \, \{q\}^* \, \varnothing^\omega$

★ ▣ **Exercise 179.** Let $AP = \{p, q, r\}$. Give LTL formulas that hold for the computations satisfying the following properties. If you are unsure of the exact meaning of the property, then choose an interpretation. Here are two solved examples:

- p is false before q: $\mathbf{F}q \to (\neg p \mathbf{U} q)$.
- p becomes true before q: $\neg q \mathbf{W} (p \wedge \neg q)$.

Now it is your turn:

(a) p is true between q and r.

(b) p precedes q before r.

(c) p precedes q after r.

(d) after p and q eventually r.

(e) p alternates between true and false.

(f) p, and only p, holds at even positions, and q, and only q, holds at odd positions.

☆ ▣ **Exercise 180.** Let $AP = \{p, q\}$ and let $\Sigma = 2^{AP}$. Give Büchi automata for the ω-languages over Σ defined by the following LTL formulas:

(a) $\mathbf{XG}\neg p$

(b) $(\mathbf{GF}p) \to (\mathbf{F}q)$

(c) $p \wedge \neg(\mathbf{XF}p)$

(d) $\mathbf{G}(p \mathbf{U} (p \to q))$

(e) $\mathbf{F}q \to (\neg q \mathbf{U} (\neg q \wedge p))$

🔒   ☆ ■ **Exercise 181.** Say which of the following equivalences hold. For every equivalence that does not hold, give an instantiation of φ and ψ together with a computation
that disproves the equivalence.

(a) $\mathbf{X}(\varphi \vee \psi) \equiv \mathbf{X}\varphi \vee \mathbf{X}\psi$

(b) $\mathbf{X}(\varphi \wedge \psi) \equiv \mathbf{X}\varphi \wedge \mathbf{X}\psi$

(c) $\mathbf{X}(\varphi \mathbf{U} \psi) \equiv (\mathbf{X}\varphi \mathbf{U} \mathbf{X}\psi)$

(d) $\mathbf{F}(\varphi \vee \psi) \equiv \mathbf{F}\varphi \vee \mathbf{F}\psi$

(e) $\mathbf{F}(\varphi \wedge \psi) \equiv \mathbf{F}\varphi \wedge \mathbf{F}\psi$

(f) $\mathbf{G}(\varphi \vee \psi) \equiv \mathbf{G}\varphi \vee \mathbf{G}\psi$

(g) $\mathbf{G}(\varphi \wedge \psi) \equiv \mathbf{G}\varphi \wedge \mathbf{G}\psi$

(h) $\mathbf{GF}(\varphi \vee \psi) \equiv \mathbf{GF}\varphi \vee \mathbf{GF}\psi$

(i) $\mathbf{GF}(\varphi \wedge \psi) \equiv \mathbf{GF}\varphi \wedge \mathbf{GF}\psi$

(j) $\rho \mathbf{U} (\varphi \vee \psi) \equiv (\rho \mathbf{U} \varphi) \vee (\rho \mathbf{U} \psi)$

(k) $(\varphi \vee \psi) \mathbf{U} \rho \equiv (\varphi \mathbf{U} \rho) \vee (\psi \mathbf{U} \rho)$

(l) $\rho \mathbf{U} (\varphi \wedge \psi) \equiv (\varphi \mathbf{U} \rho) \wedge (\psi \mathbf{U} \rho)$

(m) $(\varphi \wedge \psi) \mathbf{U} \rho \equiv (\varphi \mathbf{U} \rho) \wedge (\psi \mathbf{U} \rho)$

🔓   ☆ ■ **Exercise 182.** Let $\mathcal{V} \in \{\mathbf{F}, \mathbf{G}\}^*$ be a sequence made of the temporal operators $\mathbf{F}$ and
$\mathbf{G}$. Show that $\mathbf{FG}p \equiv \mathcal{V} \mathbf{FG}p$ and $\mathbf{GF}p \equiv \mathcal{V} \mathbf{GF}p$.

🔓   ☆ ■ **Exercise 183.** Recall that a formula is a tautology if all computations satisfy it. Which
of the following formulas of LTL are tautologies? If the formula is not a tautology, then give
a computation that does not satisfy it.

(a) $\mathbf{G}p \to \mathbf{F}p$

(b) $\mathbf{G}(p \to q) \to (\mathbf{G}p \to \mathbf{G}q)$

(c) $\mathbf{F}(p \wedge q) \leftrightarrow (\mathbf{F}p \wedge \mathbf{F}q)$

(d) $\neg \mathbf{F}p \to \mathbf{F}\neg \mathbf{F}p$

(e) $(\mathbf{G}p \to \mathbf{F}q) \leftrightarrow (p \mathbf{U} (\neg p \vee q))$

(f) $(\mathbf{FG}p \to \mathbf{GF}q) \leftrightarrow \mathbf{G}(p \mathbf{U} (\neg p \vee q))$

(g) $\mathbf{G}(p \to \mathbf{X}p) \to (p \to \mathbf{G}p)$

🔓   ★ ☞ **Exercise 184.** We say that an LTL formula is *negation-free* if negations only occur
in front of atomic formulas (that is, $\neg\mathbf{true}$ or $\neg a$ where a is an atomic proposition). In this
exercise, we show how to construct a deterministic Büchi automaton for negation-free LTL
formulas. In the remainder, we assume that φ denotes such a formula over a set of atomic
propositions AP. We inductively define the formula $af(\varphi, \nu)$, read "φ after ν" where $\nu \in 2^{AP}$,
as follows:

$$af(\mathbf{true}, \nu) = \mathbf{true}, \qquad af(\varphi \wedge \psi, \nu) = af(\varphi, \nu) \wedge af(\psi, \nu),$$

$$af(\mathit{false}, \nu) = \mathit{false}, \qquad af(\varphi \vee \psi, \nu) = af(\varphi, \nu) \vee af(\psi, \nu),$$

$$af(a, \nu) = af(a \in \nu, \nu), \qquad af(\mathbf{X}\varphi, \nu) = \varphi,$$

$$af(\neg a, \nu) = af(a \notin \nu, \nu), \qquad af(\varphi \mathbf{U} \psi, \nu) = af(\psi, \nu) \vee (af(\varphi, \nu) \wedge \varphi \mathbf{U} \psi).$$

We extend it to finite words: $af(\varphi, \epsilon) = \varphi$ and $af(\varphi, \nu w) = af(af(\varphi, \nu), w)$ for every $\nu \in 2^{AP}$
and every finite word w. Prove the following statements:

(a) For every formula φ, finite word $w \in \left(2^{AP}\right)^*$ and ω-word $w' \in \left(2^{AP}\right)^{\omega}$:

$$ww' \models \varphi \iff w' \models af(\varphi, w).$$

So, intuitively, $af(\varphi, w)$ holds "after reading w" iff φ holds "at the beginning" of ww'.

(b) For every negation-free formula φ: $w \models \varphi$ iff $af(\varphi, w') \equiv \mathbf{true}$ for some finite prefix w' of w.

(c) For every formula φ and ω-word $w \in \left(2^{AP}\right)^{\omega}$: $af(\varphi, w)$ is a positive boolean combination of subformulas of φ.

(d) For every formula φ of length n: the set of formulas $\{af(\varphi, w) : w \in \left(2^{AP}\right)^*\}$ has at most 2^{2^n} equivalence classes up to LTL-equivalence.

(e) There exists a deterministic Büchi automaton recognizing $\mathcal{L}_{\omega}(\varphi)$ with at most 2^{2^n} states, where n is the length of φ.   *Hint: Use (b)–(d).*

★✎ **Exercise 185.** In this exercise, we show that the reduction algorithm of exercise 150(2) does not reduce the Büchi automata generated from LTL formulas, as well as show that a little modification to the algorithm *LTLtoNGA* (algorithm 57) can alleviate this problem.

Let φ be a formula of LTL(AP), and let $A_{\varphi} = LTLtoNGA(\varphi)$.

(a) Prove that the reduction algorithm of exercise 150(2) does not reduce A, that is, show that $A = A/CSR$.

(b) Prove that $\mathcal{L}_{\omega}\left(B_{\varphi}\right) = \mathcal{L}_{\omega}\left(A_{\varphi}\right)$, where B_{φ} is the result of modifying A_{φ} as follows:

• add a new state q_0 and make it the unique initial state.

• for every initial state q of A_{φ}, add a transition $q_0 \xrightarrow{q \cap AP} q$ to B_{φ} (recall that q is an atom of $cl(\varphi)$, and so $q \cap AP$ is well defined).

• replace every transition $q_1 \xrightarrow{q_1 \cap AP} q_2$ of A_{φ} by $q_1 \xrightarrow{q_2 \cap AP} q_2$.

(c) Construct the automaton B_{φ} for the automaton of figure 13.7.

(d) Apply the reduction algorithm of exercise 150(2) to B_{φ}. Is the resulting automaton minimal?

☆▦ **Exercise 186.** Let $A = (Q, \Sigma, \delta, q_0, F)$ be an automaton such that $Q = P \times [1..n]$ for some finite set P and $n \geq 1$. Automaton A models a system made of n processes. A state $(p, i) \in Q$ represents the current global state p of the system, and the last process i that was executed.

We define two predicates exec_j and enab_j over Q indicating whether process j is respectively executed and enabled. More formally, for every $q = (p, i) \in Q$ and $j \in [1..n]$, let

$$\text{exec}_j(q) \iff i = j,$$

$$\text{enab}_j(q) \iff (p, i) \to (p', j) \text{ for some } p' \in P.$$

(a) Give LTL formulas over Q^ω for the following statements:

(i) All processes are executed infinitely often.

(ii) If a process is enabled infinitely often, then it is executed infinitely often.

(iii) If a process is eventually permanently enabled, then it is executed infinitely often.

(b) The three above properties are known respectively as *unconditional*, *strong*, and *weak* fairness. Show the following implications, and show that the reverse implications do not hold:

$$\text{unconditional fairness} \implies \text{strong fairness} \implies \text{weak fairness}.$$

★ ■ **Exercise 187.** In this exercise, we prove that, in the worst case, the number of states of the smallest deterministic Rabin automaton for an LTL formula can be doubly exponential in the size of the formula. Let $\Sigma_0 = \{a, b\}$, $\Sigma_1 = \{a, b, \#\}$ and $\Sigma = \{a, b, \#, \$\}$. For every $n \geq 0$, let us define the ω-language $L_n \subseteq \Sigma^\omega$ as follows:

$$L_n = \sum_{w \in \Sigma_0^n} \Sigma_1^* \, \# \, w \, \# \, \Sigma_1^* \, \$ \, w \, \#^\omega.$$

Informally, an ω-word belongs to L_n iff

- it contains a single occurrence of $\$$,
- the word to the left of $\$$ is of the form $w_0 \# w_1 \# \cdots \# w_k$ for some $k \geq 1$ and (possibly empty) words $w_0, \ldots, w_k \in \Sigma_0^*$,
- the ω-word to the right of $\$$ consists of a word $w \in \Sigma_0^n$ followed by an infinite tail $\#^\omega$, and
- w is equal to at least one of $w_0, \ldots, w_n$.

Show the following statements:

(a) There is an infinite family $\{\varphi_n\}_{n \geq 0}$ of formulas of LTL(Σ) such that φ_n has size $\mathcal{O}(n^2)$ and $\mathcal{L}_\omega(\varphi_n) = L_n$. Here, "$\mathcal{L}_\omega(\varphi_n) = L_n$" stands for $\sigma \in \mathcal{L}_\omega(\varphi_n)$ iff $\sigma = \{a_1\}\{a_2\}\{a_3\} \cdots$ for some ω-word $a_1 a_2 a_3 \cdots \in L_n$.

(b) The smallest deterministic Rabin automaton recognizing L_n has at least 2^{2^n} states.

14 Application II: Logics on ω-Words and Linear Arithmetic

In chapter 8, we showed that the languages expressible in monadic second-order logic on finite words are exactly the regular languages, and we derived an algorithm that, given a formula, constructs an NFA accepting exactly the set of interpretations of the formula. This result can be easily extended to the case of infinite words: in the forthcoming section 14.1, we show that the languages expressible in monadic second-order logic on ω-words are exactly the ω-regular languages.

In chapter 9, we introduced Presburger arithmetic, a logical language for expressing properties of the integers, and showed how to construct, for a given formula φ of Presburger arithmetic, an NFA A_φ recognizing the solutions of φ. In the forthcoming section 14.2, we extend this result to linear arithmetic, a language for describing properties of real numbers with the same syntax as Presburger arithmetic.

14.1 Monadic Second-Order Logic on ω-Words

Monadic second-order logic on ω-words has the same syntax as its counterpart on finite words and a very similar semantics as well.

Definition 14.1 *Let $X_1 = \{x, y, z, \ldots\}$ and $X_2 = \{X, Y, Z, \ldots\}$ be two infinite sets of* first-order *and* second-order variables. *Let $\Sigma = \{a, b, c, \ldots\}$ be a finite alphabet. The set $MSO(\Sigma)$ of monadic second-order formulas over Σ is the set of expressions generated by the grammar*

$$\varphi ::= Q_a(x) \mid x < y \mid x \in X \mid \neg\varphi \mid \varphi \vee \varphi \mid \exists x\, \varphi \mid \exists X\, \varphi$$

An interpretation of a formula φ is a pair $(w, \mathcal{V})$ where $w \in \Sigma^\omega$, and $\mathcal{V}$ is a mapping that assigns every free first-order variable x a position $\mathcal{V}(x) \in \mathbb{N}$ and every free second-order variable X a set of positions $\mathcal{V}(X) \subseteq \mathbb{N}$.[1] (The mapping may also assign positions to other variables.)

---

1. In chapter 8 it was convenient to split $\mathcal{V}$ into two mappings $\mathcal{V}_1$ and $\mathcal{V}_2$ for first and second-order variables, respectively. This is no longer necessary, and so now we write just $\mathcal{V}$.

The satisfaction relation $(w, \mathcal{V}) \models \varphi$ *between a formula* φ *of* $MSO(\Sigma)$ *and an interpreta-tion* $(w, \mathcal{V})$ *of* φ *is defined as follows:*

$$(w, \mathcal{V}) \models Q_a(x) \quad \textit{iff} \quad w[\mathcal{V}(x)] = a,$$
$$(w, \mathcal{V}) \models x < y \quad \textit{iff} \quad \mathcal{V}(x) < \mathcal{V}(y),$$

$$(w, \mathcal{V}) \models \neg\varphi \qquad \textit{iff} \quad (w, \mathcal{V}) \not\models \varphi,$$
$$(w, \mathcal{V}) \models \varphi_1 \vee \varphi_2 \quad \textit{iff} \quad (w, \mathcal{V}) \models \varphi_1 \text{ or } (w, \mathcal{V}) \models \varphi_2,$$
$$(w, \mathcal{V}) \models \exists x\, \varphi \qquad \textit{iff} \quad \text{some } i \in \mathbb{N} \text{ satisfies } (w, \mathcal{V}[i/x]) \models \varphi,$$
$$(w, \mathcal{V}) \models x \in X \qquad \textit{iff} \quad \mathcal{V}(x) \in \mathcal{V}(X),$$
$$(w, \mathcal{V}) \models \exists X\, \varphi \qquad \textit{iff} \quad \text{some } S \subseteq \mathbb{N} \text{ satisfies } (w, \mathcal{V}[S/X]) \models \varphi,$$

where $w[i]$ *is the letter of* w *at position* i, $\mathcal{V}[i/x]$ *is the interpretation that assigns* i *to* x *and otherwise coincides with* $\mathcal{V}$, *and* $\mathcal{V}[S/X]$ *is the interpretation that assigns* S *to* X *and otherwise coincides with* $\mathcal{V}$ — *whether* $\mathcal{V}$ *is defined for* x *and* X *or not.*

If $(w, \mathcal{V}) \models \varphi$, *then we say that* $(w, \mathcal{V})$ *is a* model *of* φ. *Two formulas are* equivalent *if they have the same models. The language* $\mathcal{L}(\varphi)$ *of a sentence* $\varphi \in MSO(\Sigma)$ *is the set* $\mathcal{L}(\varphi) = \{w \in \Sigma^\omega : w \models \phi\}$, *where* $w \models \phi$ *iff* w *is a model of* ϕ *w.r.t. the empty mapping. An* ω-*language* $L \subseteq \Sigma^\omega$ *is* MSO-definable *if* $L = \mathcal{L}(\varphi)$ *for some formula* $\varphi \in MSO(\Sigma)$.

Example 14.2   The language $a^* b^\omega$ over alphabet $\{a, b\}$ can be expressed by the formula

$$\exists x\, \forall y\, [(y < x) \leftrightarrow Q_a(y)].$$

Variable x refers to the position of the first b.

14.1.1   Expressive Power of $MSO(\Sigma)$ on ω-Words

We show that the ω-languages expressible in monadic second-order logic are exactly the ω-regular languages. The proof is very similar to its counterpart for languages of finite words (proposition 8.26) and actually even a bit simpler.

Proposition 14.3   *If* $L \subseteq \Sigma^\omega$ *is* ω-*regular, then* L *is definable in* $MSO(\Sigma)$.

Proof   Let $A = (Q, \Sigma, \delta, Q_0, F)$ be an NBA with $Q = \{q_0, \ldots, q_n\}$ and $\mathcal{L}_\omega(A) = L$. We construct a formula φ_A such that for all $w \in \Sigma^\omega$, $w \models \varphi_A$ iff $w \in \mathcal{L}_\omega(A)$.

We start with some notations. Let $w = a_1 a_2 \cdots \in \Sigma^\omega$, and let

$$P_q = \left\{ i \in \mathbb{N} : q \in \hat{\delta}(q_0, a_1 \cdots a_i) \right\}.$$

In words, $i \in P_q$ iff A can be in state q immediately *after* reading letter a_i.

We can construct a formula $\text{VisitRecord}(X_0, \ldots, X_n)$ with free second-order variables $X_0, \ldots, X_n$ exactly as in proposition 8.26. This formula has the property that $\mathcal{V}(X_i) = P_{q_i}$ holds for *every* model $(w, \mathcal{V})$ and for every $0 \le i \le n$. In words, $\text{VisitRecord}(X_0, \ldots X_n)$ is only true when X_i takes the value P_{q_i} for every $0 \le i \le n$. Thus, we can take the following formula, which further states that accepting states are visited infinitely often:

$$\varphi_A := \exists X_0 \cdots \exists X_n \text{ VisitRecord}(X_0, \ldots, X_n) \wedge \forall x\, \exists y \left(x < y \wedge \bigvee_{q_i \in F} y \in X_i \right). \qquad \Box$$

It remains to prove that *MSO*-definable ω-languages are ω-regular. Given a sentence $\varphi \in MSO(\Sigma)$, we encode an interpretation $(w, \mathcal{V})$ as an ω-word. We proceed as for finite words. Consider, for instance, a formula with first-order variables x, y and second-order variables X, Y. Consider the interpretation

$$\left(a(ab)^\omega, \begin{array}{l} x \mapsto 2 \\ y \mapsto 6 \\ X \mapsto \text{set of prime numbers} \\ Y \mapsto \text{set of even numbers} \end{array} \right)$$

We encode it as

	a	a	b	a	b	a	b	a	$\cdots$
x	0	1	0	0	0	0	0	0	$\cdots$
y	0	0	0	0	0	1	0	0	$\cdots$
X	0	1	1	0	1	0	1	0	$\cdots$
Y	0	1	0	1	0	1	0	1	$\cdots$

corresponding to the ω-word

$$\begin{bmatrix} a \\ 0 \\ 0 \\ 0 \\ 0 \end{bmatrix} \begin{bmatrix} a \\ 1 \\ 0 \\ 1 \\ 1 \end{bmatrix} \begin{bmatrix} b \\ 0 \\ 0 \\ 1 \\ 0 \end{bmatrix} \begin{bmatrix} a \\ 0 \\ 0 \\ 0 \\ 1 \end{bmatrix} \begin{bmatrix} b \\ 0 \\ 0 \\ 1 \\ 0 \end{bmatrix} \begin{bmatrix} a \\ 0 \\ 1 \\ 0 \\ 1 \end{bmatrix} \begin{bmatrix} b \\ 0 \\ 0 \\ 1 \\ 0 \end{bmatrix} \begin{bmatrix} a \\ 0 \\ 0 \\ 0 \\ 1 \end{bmatrix} \begin{array}{c} \cdots \\ \\ \cdots \\ \\ \cdots \end{array} \qquad \text{over alphabet } \Sigma \times \{0, 1\}^4.$$

Definition 14.4 *Let φ be a formula with n free variables, and let $(w, \mathcal{V})$ be an interpretation of φ. We denote by $\text{enc}(w, \mathcal{V})$ the word over the alphabet $\Sigma \times \{0, 1\}^n$ described above. The ω-language of φ is $\mathcal{L}_\omega(\varphi) = \{\text{enc}(w, \mathcal{V}) : (w, \mathcal{V}) \models \varphi\}$.*

A proof by induction on the structure of φ shows that $\mathcal{L}_\omega(\varphi)$ is ω-regular. The proof is a straightforward modification of the proof for the case of finite words; it constructs a NGA A_φ such that $\mathcal{L}_\omega(A_\varphi) = \mathcal{L}_\omega(\varphi)$. Operations on NFAs are replaced by their corresponding operations on NGAs.

14.2 Linear Arithmetic

Linear arithmetic is a language for describing properties of real numbers. It has the same syntax as Presburger arithmetic (see chapter 9), but formulas are interpreted over the reals, instead of the natural numbers or the integers. Given a formula φ of linear arithmetic, we show how to construct an NGA A_φ recognizing the solutions of φ. Section 14.2.1 discusses how to encode real numbers as ω-words, and section 14.2.2 constructs the NGA.

14.2.1 Encoding Real Numbers

We encode real numbers as infinite words in two steps. First, we encode reals as pairs of numbers and then these pairs as words.

We encode each real number $x \in \mathbb{R}$ as a pair (x_I, x_F), where $x_I \in \mathbb{Z}$, $x_F \in [0, 1]$ and $x = x_I + x_F$. We call x_I and x_F the *integer* and *fractional parts* of x. So, for instance, $(1, 1/3)$ encodes $4/3$, and $(-1, 2/3)$ encodes $-1/3$ (*not* $-5/3$). Every integer is encoded by two different pairs, for example, 2 is encoded by $(1, 1)$ and $(2, 0)$. We are not bothered by this; note that in the standard decimal representation of real numbers, integers also have two representations; for example, 2 is represented by both 2.0 and $1.\overline{9}$.

We encode each pair (x_I, x_F) as an infinite word $w_I \star w_F$. The word w_I is a two's complement encoding of x_I (see chapter 9). However, unlike in chapter 9, we use the MSBF encoding instead of the LSBF encoding. This is not essential, but it leads to a more elegant construction. Thus, w_I is any word $w_I = a_n a_{n-1} \cdots a_0 \in \{0, 1\}^+$ satisfying

$$x_I = -a_n \cdot 2^n + \sum_{i=0}^{n-1} a_i \cdot 2^i. \tag{14.1}$$

The ω-word w_F is any infinite sequence $b_1 b_2 b_3 \cdots \in \{0, 1\}^\omega$ satisfying

$$x_F = \sum_{i=1}^{\infty} b_i \cdot 2^{-i}. \tag{14.2}$$

The only ω-word $b_1 b_2 b_3 \cdots$ for which we have $x_F = 1$ is 1^ω. So, in particular, the encodings of the integer 1 are the ω-words of $0^* 1 \star 0^\omega$ and $0^* 0 \star 1^\omega$. Equation (14.2) also has two solutions for some fractions, for example, the encodings of $1/2$ are the ω-words of $0^* 0 \star 10^\omega$ and $0^* 0 \star 01^\omega$. Other fractions have a unique form, for example, $0^* 0 \star (01)^\omega$ for $1/3$.

Example 14.5 Numbers $3.\overline{3}$, 3, and -3.75 are encoded by

$$3.\overline{3} \mapsto 0^* 011 \star (01)^\omega,$$

$$3 \mapsto 0^* 011 \star 0^\omega \text{ and } 0^* 010 \star 1^\omega,$$

$$-3.75 \mapsto 1^* 100 \star 010^\omega \text{ and } 1^* 100 \star 001^\omega.$$

When encoding tuples of reals, we use padding to make the symbols $\star$ fall on the same column. For instance, a possible encoding of the triple $(-6.75, 12.\overline{3}, 3)$ is

$$\begin{bmatrix}1\\0\\0\end{bmatrix}\begin{bmatrix}1\\1\\0\end{bmatrix}\begin{bmatrix}0\\1\\0\end{bmatrix}\begin{bmatrix}0\\0\\1\end{bmatrix}\begin{bmatrix}1\\0\\1\end{bmatrix}\begin{bmatrix}\star\\\star\\\star\end{bmatrix}\begin{bmatrix}0\\0\\0\end{bmatrix}\begin{bmatrix}1\\1\\0\end{bmatrix}\left(\begin{bmatrix}0\\0\\0\end{bmatrix}\begin{bmatrix}0\\1\\0\end{bmatrix}\right)^{\omega}.$$

14.2.2 Constructing an NGA for the Real Solutions

Given a linear arithmetic formula φ, we construct an NGA A_φ accepting the encodings of the solutions of φ. If φ is a negation, disjunction, or existential quantification, then we proceed as in chapter 9, replacing the operations on NFAs and transducers by operations on NGAs.

Let us now consider an atomic formula of the form $\varphi = a \cdot x \leq b$. The NGA A_φ (which will actually be an NBA) must accept the encodings of all tuples $c \in \mathbb{R}^n$ satisfying $a \cdot c \leq b$. We decompose the problem into two subproblems for integer and fractional parts. Given $c \in \mathbb{R}^n$, let c_I and c_F be the integer and fractional part of c for some encoding of c. For instance, if $c = (2.\overline{3}, -2.75, 1)$, then we can have $c_I = (2, -3, 1)$ and $c_F = (0.\overline{3}, 0.25, 0)$, corresponding to the encoding

$$[010 \star (01)^{\omega}, 101 \star 010^{\omega}, 001 \star 0^{\omega}],$$

or $c_I = (2, -3, 0)$ and $c_F = (0.\overline{3}, 0.25, 1)$, corresponding to

$$[00010 \star (01)^{\omega}, 11101 \star 001^{\omega}, 00000 \star 1^{\omega}].$$

Let α^+ and α^- be respectively the sum of the positive and negative components of a; for instance, if $a = (1, -2, 0, 3, -1)$, then $\alpha^+ = 4$ and $\alpha^- = -3$. We show the following:

Proposition 14.6 *It is the case that $c \in \mathbb{R}^n$ is a solution of $\varphi = a \cdot x \leq b$ iff:*

- $a \cdot c_I \leq b - \alpha^+$, *or*
- $a \cdot c_I = \beta$ *for some integer* $\beta \in [b - \alpha^+ + 1, b - \alpha^-]$ *and* $a \cdot c_F \leq b - \beta$.

Proof First note that, since $c_F \in [0, 1]^n$, we have $a \cdot c_F \in [\alpha^-, \alpha^+]$.

$\Rightarrow$) Let us assume that $a \cdot c_I > b - \alpha^+$, as we are otherwise done. Since c is a solution of φ, we have $a \cdot c_I + a \cdot c_F = a \cdot (c_I + c_F) = a \cdot c \leq b$. In particular, this means that $a \cdot c_I \leq b - a \cdot c_F$ and hence that $a \cdot c_I \leq b - \alpha^-$. By assumption, this implies that $a \cdot c_I = \beta$, where $\beta \in [b - \alpha^+ + 1, b - \alpha^-]$. Furthermore, $a \cdot c_F \leq b - a \cdot c_I = b - \beta$.

$\Leftarrow$) If $a \cdot c_I \leq b - \alpha^+$, then we are done since

$$a \cdot c = a \cdot c_I + a \cdot c_F \leq (b - \alpha^+) + a \cdot c_F \leq (b - \alpha^+) + \alpha^+ = b.$$

Thus, let us assume that $a \cdot c_I = \beta$ for some integer $\beta \in [b - \alpha^+ + 1, b - \alpha^-]$ such that $a \cdot c_F \leq b - \beta$. We are done since $a \cdot c = a \cdot c_I + a \cdot c_F = \beta + a \cdot c_F \leq \beta + (b - \beta) = b$. $\qquad\square$

To simplify the notation, let $\beta^- = b - \alpha^+ + 1$ and $\beta^+ = b - \alpha^-$. By proposition 14.6, we can decompose the solution space of φ as follows:

$$Sol(\varphi) = \{c_I + c_F : a \cdot c_I < \beta^-\} \cup \bigcup_{\beta^- \leq \beta \leq \beta^+} \{c_I + c_F : a \cdot c_I = \beta \text{ and } a \cdot c_F \leq b - \beta\}.$$

Example 14.7   We use $\varphi = 2x - y \leq 0$ as a running example. We have $[\alpha^-, \alpha^+] = [1, 2]$, $b = 0$ and $[\beta^-, \beta^+] = [-1, 1]$. Thus, $(x, y) \in \mathbb{R}^2$ is a solution of φ iff one of the following conditions holds:

- $2x_I - y_I \leq -2$,
- $2x_I - y_I = -1 \wedge 2x_F - y_F \leq 1$,

- $2x_I - y_I = 0 \wedge 2x_F - y_F \leq 0$,
- $2x_I - y_I = 1 \wedge 2x_F - y_F \leq -1$.

Observe that solutions of $a \cdot c_I < \beta^-$ and $a \cdot c_I = \beta$ can be computed using algorithms *IneqZtoNFA* and *EqZtoNFA* of section 9.3. Recall that both algorithms use the LSBF encoding, but it is easy to transform their output into NFAs for the MSBF encoding: since the algorithms deliver NFAs with exactly one final state, it suffices to *reverse* the transitions of the NFA and exchange the initial and accepting states. This way, the new automaton recognizes a word w iff the old one recognizes its reverse w^R, and so it recognizes exactly the MSBF encodings.

Example 14.8   Figure 14.1 shows NFAs for the solutions of $2x_I - y_I \leq -2$ in LSBF (left) and MSBF encodings (right). The NFA on the right is obtained by reversing the transitions

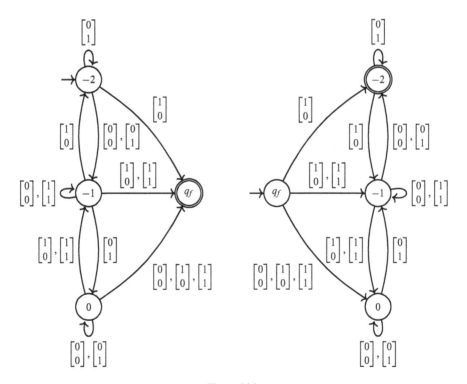

Figure 14.1
NFAs for the solutions of $2x - y \leq -2$ over $\mathbb{Z}$ with LBSF (left) and MSBF (right) encodings.

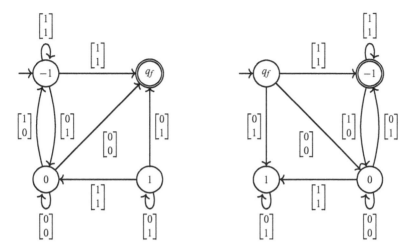

Figure 14.2
NFAs for the solutions of $2x - y = -1$ over $\mathbb{Z}$ with LBSF (left) and MSBF (right) encodings.

and exchanging the initial and final states. Similarly, figure 14.2 shows NFAs for the solutions of $2x_I - y_I = -1$.

It remains to show how to compute an automaton for the solutions of an inequation of the form $a \cdot x_F \leq \beta - b$. This is done in the next section.

14.2.2.1 A DBA for the Solutions of $a \cdot x_F \leq \beta - b$

We construct a DBA recognizing the solutions of formulas of the form $a \cdot x_F \leq d$ such that $0 \leq x_F \leq 1$. The algorithm is similar to *AFtoNFA* from section 9.2. The states of the DBA are integers. We choose transitions and accepting states so that the following property holds:

$$q \in \mathbb{Z} \text{ recognizes the encodings of the tuples } c_F \in [0, 1]^n \text{ s.t. } a \cdot c_F \leq q. \qquad (14.3)$$

However, recall that $a \cdot c_F \in [\alpha^-, \alpha^+]$ for every $c_F \in [0, 1]^n$, and therefore:

- all states $q \geq \alpha^+$ accept all tuples of reals in $[0, 1]^n$ and can be merged with state α^+, and
- all states $q < \alpha^-$ accept no tuples in $[0, 1]^n$ and can be merged with state $(\alpha^- - 1)$.

Calling these two merged states "*all*" and "*none*," respectively, the states of the DBA (not all of them may be reachable from the initial state) are

$$all, \ none \text{ and } \{q \in \mathbb{Z} : \alpha^- \leq q < \alpha^+\}.$$

All of these states but *none* are accepting, and the initial state is β. Let us now define the set of transitions. Given a state q and a letter $\zeta \in \{0, 1\}^n$, let us determine the target state q' of the unique transition labeled by ζ from q. Clearly, if $q = all$, then $q' = all$, and if $q = none$, then $q' = none$. If $q \in \mathbb{Z}$, then we compute the value v that q' must have in order to satisfy property 14.3, and then we set

$$
q' = \begin{cases} q & \text{if } v \in [\alpha^-, \alpha^+), \\ none & \text{if } v < \alpha^-, \\ all & \text{if } v \geq \alpha^+. \end{cases}
$$

To compute v, observe that a word $w \in (\{0,1\}^n)^\omega$ is accepted from q' iff the word ζw is accepted from q. Thus, the tuple $c' \in \mathbb{R}^n$ encoded by w and the tuple $c \in \mathbb{R}^n$ encoded by ζw are related by the following equation:

$$
c = \frac{1}{2}\zeta + \frac{1}{2}c'. \tag{14.4}
$$

Since c' is accepted from q' iff c is accepted by q, to fulfill property 14.3, we must choose v so that $a \cdot (\frac{1}{2}\zeta + \frac{1}{2}c') \leq q$ holds iff $a \cdot c' \leq v$ holds. We get $v = 2q - a \cdot \zeta$, and so we define the transition function of the DBA as follows:

$$
\delta(q, \zeta) = \begin{cases} q & \text{if } q \in \{none, all\}, \\ 2q - a \cdot \zeta & \text{if } 2q - a \cdot \zeta \in [\alpha^-, \alpha^+), \\ none & \text{if } 2q - a \cdot \zeta < \alpha^-, \\ all & \text{if } 2q - a \cdot \zeta \geq \alpha^+. \end{cases}
$$

Example 14.9 Figure 14.3 depicts the DBA for $2x_F - y_F \leq 1$, where the trap state *none* has been omitted for the sake of readability. Since $\alpha^+ = 2$ and $\alpha^- = -1$, the possible states are $\{all, none, -1, 0, 1\}$. The initial state is 1. Let us determine the target state of the transitions leaving state 1. We instantiate the definition of $\delta(q, \zeta)$ with $q = 1$, $\alpha^+ = 2$ and $\alpha^- = -1$, and get

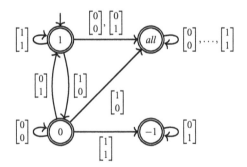

Figure 14.3
DBA for the solutions of $2x - y \leq 1$ over $\{0,1\}^2$.

$$\delta(1, \zeta) = \begin{cases} 2 - 2\zeta_x + \zeta_y & \text{if } 2 - 2\zeta_x + \zeta_y \in \{-1, 0, 1\}, \\ none & \text{if } 2 - 2\zeta_x + \zeta_y < -1, \\ all & \text{if } 2 - 2\zeta_x + \zeta_y \geq 2, \end{cases}$$

which can be simplified to

$$\delta(1, \zeta) = \begin{cases} all & \text{if } \zeta_x = 0, \\ \zeta_y & \text{otherwise.} \end{cases}$$

Recall that, by property 14.3, a state $q \in \mathbb{Z}$ accepts the encodings of the pairs (x_F, y_F) such that $2x_F - y_F \leq q$. This allows us to immediately derive the DBAs for $2x_F - y_F \leq 0$ and $2x_F - y_F \leq -1$: they are the DBA of figure 14.3 with 0 as initial state, and the same DBA with -1 as initial state, respectively.

The procedure to construct the DBA for $a \cdot x_F \leq d$ is summarized in algorithm 59.

Algorithm 59 Converting an inequality into a DBA recognizing the MSBF encodings of its solutions.

IneqtoDBA(φ)
Input: Inequation $\varphi = a \cdot x_F \leq d$
Output: DBA $A = (Q, \Sigma, \delta, q_0, F)$ such that $\mathcal{L}_\omega(A) = \mathcal{L}(\varphi)$
          (without trap state)

1    $Q, \delta, F \leftarrow \emptyset$; $q_0 \leftarrow d$
2    $W \leftarrow \{d\}$
3    $\alpha^- \leftarrow \sum_{i:a_i < 0} a_i$; $\alpha^+ \leftarrow \sum_{i:a_i \geq 0} a_i$
4   **while** $W \neq \emptyset$ **do**
5   **pick** q **from** W
6   **add** q **to** Q
7   **add** q **to** F
8   **for all** $\zeta \in \{0, 1\}^n$ **do**
9          $q' \leftarrow 2q - a \cdot \zeta$
10   **if** $q' \geq \alpha^-$ **then**
11   **if** $q = all$ **or** $q' \geq \alpha^+$ **then** $q' \leftarrow all$
12   **if** $q' \notin Q$ **then add** q' **to** W
13   **add** (q, ζ, q') **to** δ

Example 14.10 Let $\varphi = 2x - y \leq 0$. We construct the full NBA A_φ by putting all the pieces together. Recall that $(x, y) \in \mathbb{R}^2$ is a solution of φ iff (at least) one of the following conditions holds:

(i) $2x_I - y_I \leq -2$,

(iii) $2x_I - y_I = 0 \wedge 2x_F - y_F \leq 0$,

(ii) $2x_I - y_I = -1 \wedge 2x_F - y_F \leq 1$,

(iv) $2x_I - y_I = 1 \wedge 2x_F - y_F \leq -1$.

The top of figure 14.4 depicts an NBA for (i). This NBA is easily obtained from the NFA for the solutions of $2x_I - y_I \leq -2$ depicted on the right of figure 14.1.

The NBA at the bottom of figure 14.4 recognizes pairs $(x, y) \in \mathbb{R}^2$ satisfying (ii), (iii), or (iv). To construct it, we "concatenate" the NFA on the right of figure 14.2 and the DBA of figure 14.3. The resulting NBA recognizes the solutions of $2x_I - y_I = -1$ and $2x_F - y_F \leq 1$, which is adequate for (ii). For (iii) and (iv), we respectively connect state 0 to 0 and 1 to -1 (with $\star$).

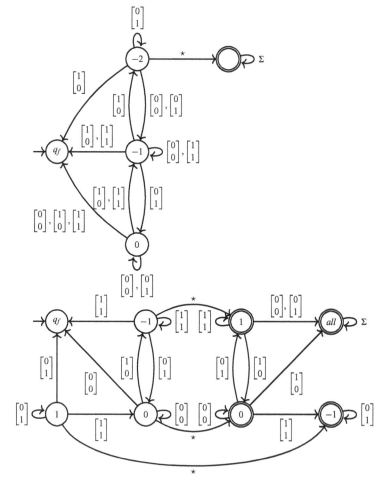

Figure 14.4
NBA for the real solutions of $2x - y \leq 0$ satisfying (i) (top) and (ii), (iii), or (iv) (bottom).

14.3 Exercises

☆ 🔳 **Exercise 188.** Give an $MSO(\{a, b\})$ sentence for each of the following ω-regular languages:

(a) Finitely many as: $(a + b)^* b^\omega$
(b) Infinitely many bs: $((a + b)^* b)^\omega$
(c) as at each even position: $(a(a + b))^\omega$

What regular languages would you obtain if your sentences were interpreted over finite words?

☆ 🔳 **Exercise 189.** Let us revisit exercise 131 over infinite words rather than finite ones. Consider a formula $\phi(X)$ of $MSO(\Sigma)$ that does not contain any occurrence of predicates of the form $Q_a(x)$. Given two interpretations that assign the same set of positions to X, we have that either both interpretations satisfy $\phi(X)$, or none of them does. Thus, we can speak of the sets of natural numbers satisfying $\phi(X)$. This observation can be used to automatically prove some (very) simple properties of the natural numbers. Consider, for instance, the following "conjecture": every set of natural numbers has a minimal element.[2] The conjecture holds iff the formula

$$\text{Has\_min}(X) := \exists x \in X \; \forall y \in X \; (x \leq y)$$

is satisfied by every interpretation in which X is nonempty. Construct an automaton for Has_min(X), and check that it recognizes all nonempty sets.

☆ ⚙ **Exercise 190.** Construct a DBA for $x_F + 3 \cdot y_F \leq 2$ using *IneqtoDBA*.

☆ 🔳 **Exercise 191.** Let φ be a formula from linear arithmetic s.t. $\mathcal{V} \models \varphi$ iff $\mathcal{V}(x) \geq \mathcal{V}(y) \geq 0$. Give an NBA that accepts the solutions of φ (over $\mathbb{R}$), without necessarily following the construction presented in the chapter.

★ 🔳 **Exercise 192.** Reconsider Exercise 191 with a strict inequality, i.e. $\mathcal{V}(x) > \mathcal{V}(y) \geq 0$.

★ 🔳 **Exercise 193.** Linear arithmetic cannot express the operations $y = \lceil x \rceil$ (ceiling) and $y = \lfloor x \rfloor$ (floor). Explain how they can be implemented with Büchi automata.

★ ■ **Exercise 194.** Let c be an irrational number such as π, e, or $\sqrt{2}$. Show that *no* formula from linear arithmetic is such that $\mathcal{V} \models \varphi$ iff $\mathcal{V}(x) = c$.

---

2. We only proved the case of *finite* sets in exercise 131. Here, we handle finite and infinite sets.

Solutions

Solutions for Chapter 1

☆ 🔲 **Exercise 1.** Give a regular expression for the language of all words over $\Sigma = \{a, b\}$

(a) beginning and ending with the same letter.
(b) having two occurrences of a at distance 3.
(c) with no occurrence of the subword aa.

Solution: Let us write Σ^* for $(a+b)^*$. The expressions are as follows:

(a) $a + b + a\Sigma^*a + b\Sigma^*b$
(b) $\Sigma^*a\Sigma\Sigma a\Sigma^*$
(c) $(a+\varepsilon)(b^* + ba)^*$ or equivalently $(b^* + ab)^*(\varepsilon + a)$

☆ ■ **Exercise 3.** Show that the language of the regular expression $r = (a+\varepsilon)(b^* + ba)^*$ is the language A of all words over $\{a, b\}$ that do not contain any occurrence of aa.

Solution:

- $\mathcal{L}(r) \subseteq A$. Let $w \in \mathcal{L}(r)$. By definition of r, we have $w = u_1 u_2 \cdots u_n$ for some $n \geq 1$ and some words $u_1 \in \{\varepsilon, a\}$ and $u_2, \ldots, u_n \in \mathcal{L}(b^* + ba)$. For the sake of contradiction, assume that w contains an occurrence of aa. Since none of the u_i contains aa, there must exist some $i \in \{1, \ldots, n-1\}$ such that u_i ends with a and u_{i+1} starts with a. The only possible case for u_{i+1} is $u_{i+1} = u_1 = a$, which means that $i = 0$. This is a contradiction.
- $A \subseteq \mathcal{L}(r)$. Let $w \in A$. There exist $n \geq 0$ and $i, j_1, j_2, \ldots j_n, k \geq 0$ such that
  - $w = b^i a b^{j_1} a b^{j_2} \cdots a b^{j_n} a b^k$, and
  - $j_1, j_2, \ldots, j_n > 0$.
  If $i = 0$, then $w \in \mathcal{L}(r)$ since

$$w = a\, b^{j_1 - 1}\, ba\, \cdots\, b^{j_n - 1}\, ba\, b^k \in \mathcal{L}\left(a\, b^*\, ba\, \cdots\, b^*\, ba\, b^*\right) \subseteq \mathcal{L}(r).$$

  If $i > 0$, then $w \in \mathcal{L}(r)$ since

$$w = b^{i-1}\, ba\, b^{j_1 - 1}\, ba\, \cdots\, b^{j_n - 1}\, ba\, b^k \in \mathcal{L}\left(\varepsilon\, b^*\, ba\, b^*\, ba\, \cdots\, b^*\, ba\, b^*\right) \subseteq \mathcal{L}(r). \qquad \square$$

☆ ■ **Exercise 5.**

(a) Prove that for all languages A and B, the following holds: $A \subseteq B \implies A^* \subseteq B^*$.
(b) Prove that the regular expressions $((a+ab)^* + b^*)^*$ and Σ^* represent the same language, where $\Sigma = \{a, b\}$ and where Σ^* stands for $(a+b)^*$.

Solution:

(a) Let us assume that $A \subseteq B$. Let $w \in A^*$. We must show that $w \in B^*$. If $w = \varepsilon$, then w is trivially in B^*. Otherwise, there exist $n > 0$ and words $v_1, \ldots, v_n \in A$ such that $w = v_1 \cdots v_n$. Since $A \subseteq B$, we know that $v_i \in B$ for every $i \in \{1, \ldots, n\}$, and so $w = v_1 \ldots v_n \in B^*$. ☐
(b) The language Σ^* contains all words over alphabet Σ, so in particular, it contains all words from $\mathcal{L}(((a+ab)^* + b^*)^*)$. For the other direction, let $A = \Sigma$ and $B = \mathcal{L}((a+ab)^* + b^*)$. We have $A \subseteq B$. Thus, by (a), we have $A^* \subseteq B^*$, which means that $\Sigma^* \subseteq \mathcal{L}(((a+ab)^* + b^*)^*)$. ☐

★ ▣ **Exercise 7.** For each of the following properties, provide a syntax that describes the regular expressions r satisfying the property.

(a) $\mathcal{L}(r) = \emptyset$,
(b) $\mathcal{L}(r) = \{\varepsilon\}$,
(c) $\varepsilon \in \mathcal{L}(r)$,
(d) $(\mathcal{L}(r) = \mathcal{L}(rr)) \implies (\mathcal{L}(r) = \mathcal{L}(r^*))$.

Solution:

(a) They are the regular expressions generated by the "two-level" syntax

$$r ::= \emptyset \mid rs \mid sr \mid r+r$$

where s denotes an arbitrary regular expression. A simple proof by induction shows that if r is generated by this syntax, then $\mathcal{L}(r) = \emptyset$. For the converse, let t be an arbitrary regular expression such that $\mathcal{L}(t) = \emptyset$. If $t = \emptyset$, then we are done because t is generated by the syntax. The cases $t = \varepsilon$ and $t = a$ are impossible. If $t = t_1 t_2$, then we have $\mathcal{L}(t_1) = \emptyset$ or $\mathcal{L}(t_2) = \emptyset$; by induction hypothesis, either t_1 or t_2 is generated by the syntax, and thus so is t. If $t = t_1 + t_2$, then we have $\mathcal{L}(t_1) = \emptyset$ and $\mathcal{L}(t_2) = \emptyset$; by induction hypothesis, both t_1 and t_2 are generated by the syntax, and thus so is t.
(b) They are the regular expressions generated by the syntax

$$r ::= \varepsilon \mid s^* \mid rr \mid s+r \mid r+s \mid r+r \mid r^*$$

where s denotes an arbitrary regular expression from (a).
(c) They are the regular expressions generated by the syntax

$$r ::= \varepsilon \mid rr \mid r+s \mid s+r \mid s^*$$

where s denotes an arbitrary regular expression.
(d) Suppose that $\mathcal{L}(r) = \mathcal{L}(rr)$. We have

$$\mathcal{L}(rrr) = \mathcal{L}(rr)\,\mathcal{L}(r) = \mathcal{L}(r)\,\mathcal{L}(r) = \mathcal{L}(rr) = \mathcal{L}(r).$$

Hence, by repeated application of this argument, we obtain $\mathcal{L}\left(r^i\right) = \mathcal{L}\left(r\right)$ for every $i \geq 1$. In particular, this means that $\mathcal{L}\left(r\right) = \mathcal{L}\left(rr\right)$ implies $\mathcal{L}\left(r^*\right) = \{\varepsilon\} \cup \mathcal{L}\left(r\right)$. We use this observation to prove that the implication holds iff $\mathcal{L}\left(r\right) \neq \emptyset$.

$\Rightarrow$): Assume $\mathcal{L}\left(r\right) = \emptyset$. We have $\mathcal{L}\left(rr\right) = \emptyset = \mathcal{L}\left(r\right)$, but $\mathcal{L}\left(r\right) = \emptyset \neq \{\varepsilon\} = \mathcal{L}\left(r^*\right)$, and so the implication does not hold.

$\Leftarrow$): Assume $\mathcal{L}\left(r\right) \neq \emptyset$. We consider two cases.

• Case $\varepsilon \in \mathcal{L}\left(r\right)$. If $\mathcal{L}\left(r\right) = \mathcal{L}\left(rr\right)$ then $\mathcal{L}\left(r^*\right) = \{\varepsilon\} \cup \mathcal{L}\left(r\right)$ by the above observation. Since $\varepsilon \in \mathcal{L}\left(r\right)$, we get $\mathcal{L}\left(r^*\right) = \{\varepsilon\} \cup \mathcal{L}\left(r\right) = \mathcal{L}\left(r\right)$, and so the implication holds.

• Case $\varepsilon \notin \mathcal{L}\left(r\right)$. Let k be the length of a shortest word in $\mathcal{L}\left(r\right)$. The shortest word in $\mathcal{L}\left(rr\right)$ has length $2k$. Since $\varepsilon \notin \mathcal{L}\left(r\right)$, we have $k > 0$ and so $2k \neq k$. Thus, $\mathcal{L}\left(rr\right) \neq \mathcal{L}\left(r\right)$, and the implication holds vacuously.

Consequently, the regular expressions satisfying the implication are exactly those whose language is nonempty. These are the regular expressions generated by the syntax

$$r ::= \varepsilon \mid a \mid rr \mid s + r \mid r + s \mid s^*$$

where s denotes an arbitrary regular expression.

☆ ▣ **Exercise 8.** Use the solution to exercise 7 to define inductively the predicates $IsEmpty(r)$, $IsEpsilon(r)$, and $HasEpsilon(r)$ over regular expressions given by

• $IsEmpty(r) \Leftrightarrow (\mathcal{L}\left(r\right) = \emptyset)$,
• $IsEpsilon(r) \Leftrightarrow (\mathcal{L}\left(r\right) = \{\varepsilon\})$,
• $HasEpsilon(r) \Leftrightarrow (\varepsilon \in \mathcal{L}\left(r\right))$.

Solution:

• $IsEmpty(r)$ is defined by

$$IsEmpty(\emptyset) = \textbf{true},$$

$$IsEmpty(\varepsilon) = IsEmpty(a) = IsEmpty(r^*) = \textbf{false},$$

$$IsEmpty(r_1 + r_2) = IsEmpty(r_1) \wedge IsEmpty(r_2),$$

$$IsEmpty(r_1 r_2) = IsEmpty(r_1) \vee IsEmpty(r_2).$$

• $IsEpsilon(r)$ is defined by

$$IsEpsilon(\varepsilon) = \textbf{true},$$

$$IsEpsilon(\emptyset) = IsEpsilon(a) = \textbf{false},$$

$$IsEpsilon(r_1 + r_2) = (IsEpsilon(r_1) \wedge IsEmpty(r_2)) \vee$$
$$(IsEmpty(r_1) \wedge IsEpsilon(r_2)) \vee$$
$$(IsEpsilon(r_1) \wedge IsEpsilon(r_2)),$$

$$IsEpsilon(r_1 r_2) = IsEpsilon(r_1) \wedge IsEpsilon(r_2),$$

$$IsEpsilon(r^*) = IsEpsilon(r) \vee IsEmpty(r).$$

- *HasEpsilon*(*r*) is defined by

$$HasEpsilon(\varepsilon) = HasEpsilon(r^*) = \textbf{true},$$

$$HasEpsilon(\emptyset) = HasEpsilon(a) = \textbf{false},$$

$$HasEpsilon(r_1 + r_2) = HasEpsilon(r_1) \vee HasEpsilon(r_2),$$

$$HasEpsilon(r_1 r_2) = HasEpsilon(r_1) \wedge HasEpsilon(r_2).$$

☆ 🔲 **Exercise 10.** Let $L \subseteq \{a,b\}^*$ be the language described by the regular expression $a^* b^* a^* a$.

(a) Give an NFA-ε that accepts L.
(b) Give an NFA that accepts L.
(c) Give a DFA that accepts L.

Solution:

(a)

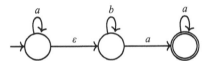

(b)

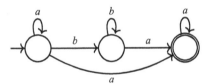

(c)

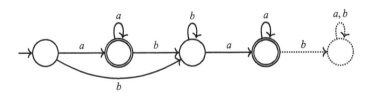

⭐ ■ **Exercise 11.** Let $|w|_\sigma$ denote the number of occurrences of letter σ in word w. For every $k \geq 2$, let $L_{k,\sigma} = \{w \in \{a,b\}^* : |w|_\sigma \bmod k = 0\}$.

(a) Give a DFA with k states that accepts $L_{k,\sigma}$.
(b) Show that any NFA accepting $L_{m,a} \cap L_{n,b}$ has at least $m \cdot n$ states.

Hint: Consider using the pigeonhole principle.

Solution:

(a) Graphically, the automaton A is as follows:

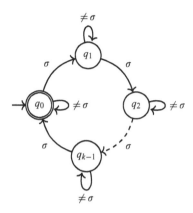

Formally, we define $A = (\{q_0, q_1, \ldots, q_{k-1}\}, \{a, b\}, \delta, \{q_0\}, \{q_0\})$ where

$$\delta(q_i, x) = \begin{cases} q_{(i+1 \bmod k)} & \text{if } x = \sigma, \\ q_i & \text{if } x \neq \sigma. \end{cases}$$

(b) Let $A = (Q, \{a, b\}, \delta, Q_0, F)$ be a minimal NFA that accepts $L_{m,a} \cap L_{n,b}$. For the sake of contradiction, suppose that $|Q| < m \cdot n$. Let $w_{i,j} = a^i b^j$. Since $w_{i,j} a^{(m-1)i} b^{(n-1)j} \in \mathcal{L}(A)$, the word $w_{i,j}$ can be read in A—that is, there exist $p_{i,j} \in Q_0$ and $q_{i,j} \in Q$ such that

$$p_{i,j} \xrightarrow{w_{i,j}} q_{i,j}.$$

By the pigeonhole principle, there exist $0 \leq i, i' < m$ and $0 \leq j, j' < n$ such that $(i,j) \neq (i',j')$ and $q_{i,j} = q_{i'\!,j'}$. Moreover, since A is minimal, $q_{i,j}$ can reach some final state $q_f \in F$ through some $v \in \Sigma^*$, as otherwise, $q_{i,j}$ could be removed. Therefore, we have

$$p_{i,j} \xrightarrow{w_{i,j} v} q_f \text{ and } p_{i'\!,j'} \xrightarrow{w_{i'\!,j'} v} q_f.$$

This means that $w_{i,j} v \in \mathcal{L}(A)$ and $w_{i'\!,j'} v \in \mathcal{L}(A)$. Thus, we have

$$(i + |v|_a) \bmod m = 0 = (i' + |v|_a) \bmod m,$$

$$(j + |v|_b) \bmod n = 0 = (j' + |v|_b) \bmod n.$$

This implies $i = i'$ and $j = j'$, which is a contradiction. Hence, $|Q| \geq m \cdot n$ as claimed. $\qquad \square$

☆ ■ **Exercise 15.** Prove or disprove: Every regular language is recognized by an NFA

(a) having one single initial state,

(b) having one single final state,

(c) whose initial states have no incoming transitions,

(d) whose final states have no outgoing transitions,

(e) all of the above,

(f) whose states are all initial,

(g) whose states are all final.

Which of the above hold for DFAs? Which ones for NFA-ε?

Solution: For NFAs:

(a) Yes. We can add a single initial state q_0, make all former initial states $q \in Q_0$ noninitial, and add transitions $\delta(q_0, a) = \delta(q, a)$. Moreover, we make q_0 final iff some $q \in Q_0$ was final.

(b) Yes. The argument is symmetric to (a).

(c) Yes. This follows from (a).

(d) Yes. This follows from (b).

(e) No. There is no such NFA accepting a^*.

(f) No. There is no such NFA accepting $\{a\}$, as it would otherwise also accept ε.

(g) No. There is no such NFA accepting $\{a\}$, as it would otherwise also accept ε.

   For NFA-ε, the same holds except for (e), which is true. Indeed, we can add a single initial and final state respectively connected to the former initial and final states with ε-transitions. For DFAs:

(a) Yes. We do the same as for NFAs.

(b) No. There is no such DFA accepting $\{\varepsilon, a\}$.

(c) Yes. This follows from (a).

(d) No. There is no such DFA accepting $\{\varepsilon, a\}$.

(e) No. It is already false for NFAs.

(f) No. It is already false for NFAs.

(g) No. It is already false for NFAs.

⭐ 🖳 **Exercise 16.** Given a regular expression r, construct an NFA A that satisfies $\mathcal{L}(A) = \mathcal{L}(r)$ and the following properties:

- initial states have no incoming transitions,
- accepting states have no outgoing transitions,
- all input transitions of a state (if any) carry the same label,
- all output transitions of a state (if any) carry the same label.

Apply your construction on $r = (a(b + c))^*$.

Solution: Let $A = (Q, \Sigma, \delta, Q_0, F)$ be an NFA such that $\mathcal{L}(A) = \mathcal{L}(r)$. We define $A' = (Q', \Sigma', \delta', Q'_0, F')$ as

$$Q' = Q \times \Sigma^2,$$

$$Q'_0 = Q_0 \times \Sigma^2,$$

$$F' = F \times \Sigma^2,$$

$$\delta' = \{((q,x,y),y,(r,y,z)) : (q,y,r) \in \delta, x,y \in \Sigma\}.$$

Clearly, every state (q,x,y) only has incoming transitions labeled with x and only has outgoing transitions labeled with y. To deal with the initial and final states, we modify A' by copying every initial and final state and deleting all incoming or outgoing transitions, respectively.

Alternatively, it is possible to construct an NFA inductively from r. If r is $\emptyset$, ε, or a, then we can take A as one of these three automata:

If $r = r_1 + r_2$ or $r = r_1 r_2$, then by induction hypothesis, there exist NFAs $A_1 = (Q_1, \Sigma, \delta_1, Q_{01}, F_1)$ and $A_2 = (Q_2, \Sigma, \delta_2, Q_{02}, F_2)$ that satisfy the above properties for r_1 and r_2. In the former case, it suffices to put A_1 and A_2 side by side. In the latter case, we would like to "glue A_2 to the end of A_1." However, since transitions with different letters cannot enter a common state, we make $|\Sigma|$ copies of A_1. More formally, we construct $A = (Q, \Sigma, \delta, Q_0, F)$, where

$$Q = \{q_a : q \in Q_1, a \in \Sigma\} \cup Q_2,$$

$$\delta = \{(p_a, b, q_a) : q \in \delta_1(p,b), a \in \Sigma\} \cup$$

$$\{(p_a, a, q) : p \in F_1, a \in \Sigma, q \in \delta_2(Q_{02}, a)\} \cup \delta_2,$$

$$Q_0 = \{q_a : q \in Q_{01}\},$$

$$F = F_2.$$

It remains to handle the case of $r = s^*$. By induction hypothesis, there exists an NFA $A = (Q, \Sigma, \delta, Q_0, F)$ that satisfies the above properties for s. Let us construct an NFA $A' = (Q', \Sigma, \delta', Q'_0, F')$ that satisfies the claim. Note that s^* is equivalent to $\varepsilon + s^+$. So it suffices to deal with s^+ and add a disjoint singleton NFA for ε. Informally, we wish to connect F' to Q'_0 with ε-transitions. However, we cannot use ε-transitions. Moreover, we must respect the constraints. Hence, we make $1 + |\Sigma|$ copies of each accepting state of A. The purpose of the first copy is to satisfy the fact that accepting states cannot have outgoing transitions. Each other copy is associated to the letter that may leave an accepting state. Formally, we define

$$Q' = Q \cup \{q_a : q \in F, a \in \Sigma\},$$

$$\delta' = \delta \cup \{(p, b, q_a) : q \in F \cap \delta_2(p,b), a \in \Sigma\} \cup$$

$$\{(p_a, a, q) : p \in F, a \in \Sigma, q \in \delta(Q_0, a)\},$$

$$Q'_0 = Q_0,$$

$$F' = F.$$

Let us apply the construction on $r = (a(b + c))^*$. We obtain the following NFAs for a and $b + c$:

By applying the construction for concatenation, we obtain

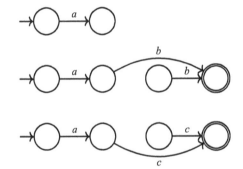

By cleaning the NFA, we obtain

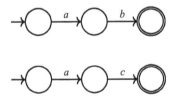

By applying the construction for the Kleene star, we obtain

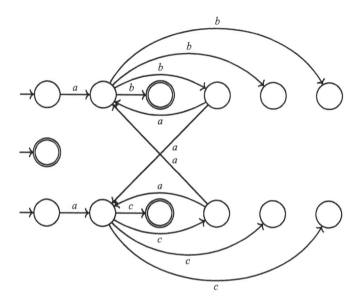

By cleaning the NFA, we obtain an NFA for $(a(b+c))^*$ that satisfies all of the constraints:

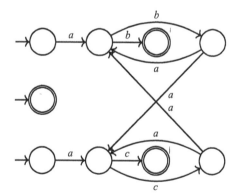

☆ ⚙ **Exercise 17.** Convert this NFA-ε to an NFA using the algorithm *NFAεtoNFA*:

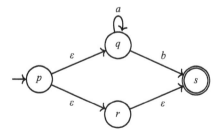

Solution: We obtain the resulting NFA B in seven steps:

Iter.	$B = (Q', \Sigma, \delta', Q'_0, F')$	δ'' (ε-transitions)	Workset W
0			$\{(p, \varepsilon, q), (p, \varepsilon, r)\}$
1			$\{(p, \varepsilon, r), (p, a, q),$ $(p, b, s)\}$
2			$\{(p, a, q), (p, b, s),$ $(p, \varepsilon, s)\}$
3			$\{(p, b, s), (p, \varepsilon, s),$ $(q, a, q), (q, b, s)\}$
4			$\{(p, \varepsilon, s), (q, a, q),$ $(q, b, s)\}$
5			$\{(q, a, q), (q, b, s)\}$
6			$\{(q, b, s)\}$
7			$\emptyset$

★ ▣ **Exercise 19.** Let $\Sigma_n = \{1, 2, \ldots, n\}$, and let L_n be the set of all words $w \in \Sigma_n$ such that at least one letter of Σ_n does not appear in w. So, for instance, $1221, 32, 1111 \in L_3$ and $123, 2231 \notin L_3$.

(a) Give an NFA for L_n with $\mathcal{O}(n)$ states and transitions.

(b) Give a DFA for L_n with 2^n states.

(c) Show that any DFA for L_n has at least 2^n states.

(d) Do the bounds of (a), (b), and (c) also hold for $\overline{L_n}$?

Solution:

(a)

$\Sigma_n \setminus \{1\}$ $\Sigma_n \setminus \{n\}$

(b) We construct a DFA $A = (Q, \Sigma_n \delta, q_0, F)$ whose states are subsets of the alphabet:

$$Q = \mathcal{P}(\Sigma_n),$$

$$\delta(S, a) = S \cup \{a\} \text{ for every } S \in Q, a \in \Sigma_n,$$

$$q_0 = \emptyset,$$

$$F = Q \setminus \{\Sigma_n\}.$$

(c) For every word $w \in \Sigma_n^*$, let $\alpha(w)$ denote the subset of letters of Σ_n that appear in w. Let $A_n = (Q, \Sigma_n, \delta, q_0, F)$ be a DFA recognizing L_n. Let w_1, w_2 be two words such that $\alpha(w_1) \neq \alpha(w_2)$, and let $q_1, q_2 \in Q$ be the states such that

$$q_0 \xrightarrow{w_1} q_1 \text{ and } q_0 \xrightarrow{w_2} q_2.$$

We claim that $q_1 \neq q_2$. Since $\alpha(w_1) \neq \alpha(w_2)$, we may assume w.l.o.g. that $\alpha(w_1) \nsubseteq \alpha(w_2)$. Thus, there is a word v such that $w_1 v$ contains all letters of Σ_n, but $w_2 v$ does not. By definition of L_n, we have $w_1 v \notin L_n$ and $w_2 v \in L_n$, which implies $q_1 \neq q_2$, and we are done.

By the claim, the number of states of A_n is larger than or equal to the number of subsets of Σ_n, and hence A_n has at least 2^n states. □

(d) Clearly, (b) holds as we can simply complement the DFA for L_n. Moreover, (c) holds because the minimal DFAs for a language and for its complement have the same number of states. We prove that (a) does not hold, that is, that every NFA for $\overline{L_n}$ has 2^n states.

Let Σ_1, Σ_2 be two different subsets of Σ_n, and let $w_1 \in \Sigma_1^*$ and $w_2 \in \Sigma_2^*$. Let A be an NFA that recognizes $\overline{L_n}$. We show that A has runs ρ_1 on w_1 and ρ_2 on w_2, leading to different states q_1 and q_2. Since $\Sigma_1 \neq \Sigma_2$, w.l.o.g. there are words v_1 and v_2 such that $w_1 v_1, w_2 v_2 \in \overline{L_n}$, but $w_2 v_1 \notin \overline{L_n}$. Let ρ_1, ρ_2 be accepting runs for $w_1 v_1$ and $w_2 v_2$. Let q_1 and q_2 be the states reached by the runs after reading w_1 and w_2. If $q_1 = q_2$, then $w_2 v_1 \in \overline{L_n}$, which is a contradiction. Thus, $q_1 \neq q_2$. □

☆ 🔲 **Exercise 20.** Let M_n be the language of the following regular expression:

$$(0+1)^*0(0+1)^{n-1}0(0+1)^*.$$

These are the words containing at least one pair of 0s at distance n. For example, $101101, 001001, 000000 \in M_3$ and $101010, 000111, 011110 \notin M_3$.

(a) Give an NFA for M_n with $\mathcal{O}(n)$ states and transitions.
(b) Give a DFA for M_n with $\Omega(2^n)$ states.
(c) Show that any DFA for M_n has at least 2^n states.

Solution:

(a) We give an NFA for M_3; the generalization to M_n is straightforward:

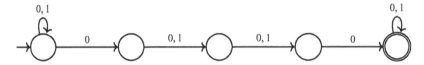

(b) The DFA has $2^n + 1$ states: one for each word from $\{0, 1\}^n$ and one final state q_f. Intuitively, the DFA is at state $b_1 \cdots b_n \in \{0, 1\}^n$ if these are the last n letters that were read. Accordingly, for every $b_2 \cdots b_n \in \{0, 1\}^{n-1}$, the DFA has four transitions of the form

$$0b_2 \cdots b_n \xrightarrow{0} q_f,$$

$$0b_2 \cdots b_n \xrightarrow{1} b_2 \cdots b_n 1,$$

$$1b_2 \cdots b_n \xrightarrow{0} b_2 \cdots b_n 0,$$

$$1b_2 \cdots b_n \xrightarrow{1} b_2 \cdots b_n 1.$$

Initially, the DFA has not yet read anything, but this is equivalent to having read only 1s so far: in both cases, there can be no pair of 0s at distance n before n steps. Thus, we take 1^n as the initial state.

(c) The proof is very similar to the one of exercise 19(c): one may show that the states reached by the DFA after reading any two distinct words $w_1, w_2 \in \{0, 1\}^n$ must be different.

★ 🕮 **Exercise 21.** Recall that an NFA A accepts a word w if at least one of the runs of A on w is accepting. This is sometimes called the *existential* accepting condition. Consider the variant where A accepts word w if *all* runs of A on w are accepting (in particular, if A has no run on w, then it trivially accepts w). This is called the *universal* accepting condition. Note that a DFA accepts the same language with both the existential and the universal accepting conditions.

Intuitively, we can imagine an automaton with universal accepting condition as executing all runs in parallel. After reading a word w, the automaton is simultaneously in all states reached by all runs labeled by w and accepts if all those states are accepting.

Consider the language $L_n = \{ww : w \in \{0, 1\}^n\}$.

(a) Give an automaton of size $\mathcal{O}(n)$ with universal accepting condition that recognizes L_n.

(b) Prove that every NFA (and so in particular every DFA) recognizing L_n has at least 2^n states.

(c) Give an algorithm that transforms an automaton with universal accepting condition into a DFA recognizing the same language. This shows that automata with universal accepting condition recognize the regular languages.

Solution:

(a) Note that $v \in L_n$ iff for every $1 \leq i \leq n$ the ith and $i + n$th letters of v coincide. This is a conjunction of conditions. We construct a universal automaton that has a run on v for each of these conditions, and the run accepts iff the condition holds.

The automaton has a spine of states $q_0, \ldots, q_n$, with transitions $q_i \xrightarrow{0,1} q_{i+1}$ for every $0 \leq i \leq n - 1$. At every state q_i, the automaton can leave the spine remembering the $(i + 1)$th letter by means of transitions

$$q_i \xrightarrow{0} r_1 \text{ and } q_i \xrightarrow{1} r_1'.$$

The automaton then reads the next $n - 1$ letters by transitions $r_i \xrightarrow{0,1} r_{i+1}$ and $r_i' \xrightarrow{0,1} r_{i+1}'$ for every $1 \leq i \leq n - 1$ and checks whether the $(i+n)$th letter matches the $(i+1)$th letter by transitions

$$r_n \xrightarrow{0} q_f \text{ and } r_n' \xrightarrow{1} q_f,$$

where q_f is the unique final state.

(b) We use the same technique as in exercise 19. Let A be an NFA recognizing L_n. For every word $ww \in \{0, 1\}^{2n}$, the automaton A has at least one accepting run on ww. Let q_w be the state reached by one such run after reading the first w. We claim that for any two different words $w, w' \in \{0, 1\}^n$, the states $q_w, q_{w'}$ are different. For the sake of contradiction, suppose that $q_w = q_{w'}$. Automaton A has an accepting run on ww', obtained by concatenating the first half of the accepting run on ww and the second half of the accepting run on ww'. Since $ww' \notin L_n$, this is a contradiction. Consequently, A has a different state q_w for each word $ww \in \{0, 1\}^{2n}$, and hence it has at least 2^n states. $\qquad\square$

(c) It suffices to replace line 6 of *NFAtoDFA* by **if** $Q' \subseteq F$ **then add** Q' to $\mathcal{F}$. In other words, all states of Q' must be accepting rather than at least one.

★ ☞ **Exercise 22.** The existential and universal accepting conditions can be combined, yielding *alternating automata*. The states of an alternating automaton are partitioned into *existential* and *universal* states. An existential state q accepts a word w, denoted $w \in \mathcal{L}(q)$, if either $w = \varepsilon$ and $q \in F$ or $w = aw'$ and *there exists* a transition (q, a, q') such that $w' \in \mathcal{L}(q')$. A universal state q accepts a word w if either $w = \varepsilon$ and $q \in F$ or $w = aw'$ and $w' \in \mathcal{L}(q')$ *for every* transition (q, a, q'). The language recognized by an alternating automaton is the set of words accepted by its initial state.

Give an algorithm that transforms an alternating automaton into a DFA recognizing the same language.

Solution: As an example, let us consider this alternating automaton A:

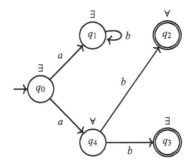

After reading the letter a, the automaton is in either state q_1 or q_4, which we can write as $q_1 \vee q_4$. If the automaton reads b from q_1, then it is in q_1. If it reads b from q_4, then it is "in both" q_2 and q_3, which we write as $q_2 \wedge q_3$. Altogether, reading the word ab in A leads to $q_1 \vee (q_2 \wedge q_3)$. If we substitute each state q_i by **true** iff q_i is accepting, then the resulting boolean value indicates whether the word is accepted. In our example, ab is accepted since **false** $\vee$ (**true** $\wedge$ **true**) = **true**.

Now, consider an arbitrary alternating automaton A. Let $Q = \{q_1, \ldots, q_n\}$ be its set of states. The above example suggests to define the states of the DFA as the set of all positive boolean formulas over variables Q. However, since there are infinitely many such formulas, we define the states as the equivalence classes of formulas (where, as usual, two formulas are equivalent if they are true for the same valuations of the variables).

The initial state is the (equivalence class of) the formula q_0. The final states are the formulas that are true when all accepting states are set to **true** and all nonaccepting states to **false**. Given a formula f, the unique formula f' such that (f, a, f') belongs to the transition relation is defined as follows. For each state q:

- If q is existential and $(q, a, q_1), \ldots, (q, a, q_n)$ are the output transitions of q, then replace every occurrence of q in f by $(q_1 \vee \cdots \vee q_n)$. If $n = 0$, then replace it by **false**.
- If q is universal and $(q, a, q_1), \ldots, (q, a, q_n)$ are the output transitions of q, then replace every occurrence of q in f by $(q_1 \wedge \cdots \wedge q_n)$. If $n = 0$, then replace it by **true**.

For example, the resulting DFA for the alternating automaton above is

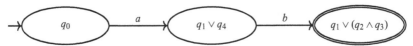

☆ ⚙ **Exercise 24.** Execute algorithm *NFAεtoNFA* on the following NFA-ε over $\Sigma = \{a_1, \ldots, a_n\}$ to show that the algorithm may increase the number of transitions quadratically:

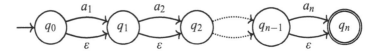

Solution: Let us execute the algorithm by prioritizing ε-transitions. The contents of the workset W evolve as follows during the first few iterations:

Iter.	W
0	$\{(q_0, a_1, q_1), (q_0, \varepsilon, q_1)\}$
1	$\{(q_0, a_1, q_1), (q_0, a_2, q_2), (q_0, \varepsilon, q_2)\}$
2	$\{(q_0, a_1, q_1), (q_0, a_2, q_2), (q_0, a_3, q_3), (q_0, \varepsilon, q_3)\}$
$\vdots$	$\vdots$
$n-1$	$\{(q_0, a_1, q_1), (q_0, a_2, q_2), (q_0, a_3, q_3), \ldots, (q_0, a_n, q_n), (q_0, \varepsilon, q_n)\}$
n	$\{(q_0, a_1, q_1), (q_0, a_2, q_2), (q_0, a_3, q_3), \ldots, (q_0, a_n, q_n)\}$
$n+1$	$\{(q_0, a_2, q_2), (q_0, a_3, q_3), \ldots, (q_0, a_n, q_n), (q_1, a_2, q_2), (q_1, \varepsilon, q_2)\}$
$n+2$	$\{(q_0, a_2, q_2), (q_0, a_3, q_3), \ldots, (q_0, a_n, q_n), (q_1, a_2, q_2), (q_1, a_3, q_3), (q_1, \varepsilon, q_3)\}$
$\vdots$	$\vdots$
$2n-1$	$\{(q_0, a_2, q_2), (q_0, a_3, q_3), \ldots, (q_0, a_n, q_n), (q_1, a_2, q_2), (q_1, a_3, q_3), \ldots, (q_1, a_n, q_n), (q_1, \varepsilon, q_n)\}$
$2n$	$\{(q_0, a_2, q_2), (q_0, a_3, q_3), \ldots, (q_0, a_n, q_n), (q_1, a_2, q_2), (q_1, a_3, q_3), \ldots, (q_1, a_n, q_n)\}$

Thus, after these iterations, we have discovered transitions

$$\{(q_0, a_j, q_j) : 0 < j \le n\} \cup \{(q_1, a_j, q_j) \mid 1 < j \le n\},$$

which will all be part of the resulting NFA. By continuing the execution, we will discover the set of transitions $\{(q_i, a_j, q_j) : 0 \le i < j < n\}$, which has size $(n-1) + \ldots + 1 = n(n-1)/2$. Thus, the resulting NFA has a quadratic number of transitions:

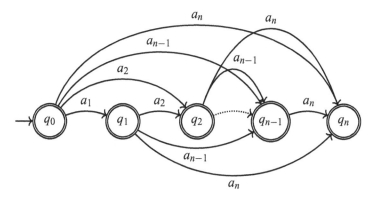

★ 回 **Exercise 27.** Let L be a regular language over Σ. Show that the following languages are also regular by constructing automata:

(a) $\sqrt{L} = \{w \in \Sigma^* : ww \in L\}$,

(b) $\mathrm{Cyc}(L) = \{vu \in \Sigma^* : uv \in L\}$.

Solution: Let $A = (Q, \Sigma, \delta, Q_0, F)$ be an NFA that accepts L.

(a) Intuitively, we construct an automaton B that guesses an intermediate state p and then reads w simultaneously from an initial state q_0 and from p. The automaton accepts if it simultaneously reaches p and some $q_F \in F$. Formally, let $B = (Q', \Sigma, \delta', Q_0', F')$ be such that

$$Q' = Q \times Q \times Q,$$

$$Q_0' = \{(p, q, p) : p \in Q, q \in Q_0\},$$

$$F' = \{(p, p, q) : p \in Q, q \in F\},$$

and, for every $p, q, r \in Q$ and $a \in \Sigma$,

$$\delta'((p, q, r), a) = \{(p, q', r') : q' \in \delta(q, a), r' \in \delta(r, a)\}.$$

(b) Intuitively, we construct an automaton B that guesses a state p and reads a prefix v of the input word until it reaches a final state. Then, automaton B moves nondeterministically to an initial state from which it reads the remainder u of the input word, and it accepts if it reaches p. More formally, let $B = (Q', \Sigma, \delta', Q_0', F')$ be such that

$$Q' = Q \times \{0, 1\} \times Q,$$

$$Q_0' = \{(p, 0, p) : p \in Q\},$$

$$F' = \{(p, 1, p) : p \in Q\},$$

and, for every $p, q \in Q$ and $a \in \Sigma \cup \{\varepsilon\}$,

$$\delta'((p, b, q), a) = \begin{cases} \{(p, b, q') : q' \in \delta(q, a)\} & \text{if } a \in \Sigma, \\ \{(p, 1, q') : q' \in Q_0\} & \text{if } a = \varepsilon, b = 0 \text{ and } q \in F, \\ \emptyset & \text{otherwise.} \end{cases}$$

★ 🖳 **Exercise 28.** For every $n \in \mathbb{N}$, let $\mathrm{MSBF}(n)$ be the set of *most-significant-bit-first* encodings of n (i.e., the words that start with an arbitrary number of leading zeros, followed by n written in binary). For example, $\mathrm{MSBF}(3) = \mathcal{L}(0^*11)$, $\mathrm{MSBF}(9) = \mathcal{L}(0^*1001)$, and $\mathrm{MSBF}(0) = \mathcal{L}(0^*)$. Similarly, let $\mathrm{LSBF}(n)$ denote the set of *least-significant-bit-first* encodings of n (i.e., the set containing for each word $w \in \mathrm{MSBF}(n)$ its reverse). For example, $\mathrm{LSBF}(6) = \mathcal{L}(0110^*)$ and $\mathrm{LSBF}(0) = \mathcal{L}(0^*)$.

(a) Construct and compare DFAs recognizing the set of even numbers w.r.t. the unary encoding (where n is encoded by the word 1^n), the MSBF-encoding, and the LSBF-encoding.

(b) Do the same for the set of numbers divisible by 3.

(c) Give regular expressions corresponding to the languages of (b).

Solution:

(a) Here are the three DFAs:

- Unary encoding:

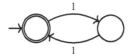

- MSBF encoding:

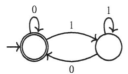

- LSBF encoding:

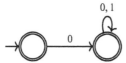

(b) The DFA for the unary encoding is, loosely speaking, a cycle of length 3. We now give a DFA for the MSBF encoding. The idea is that the state reached after reading a word w corresponds to the remainder of the number represented by w when dividing by 3. We therefore take as states $Q = \{0, 1, 2\}$ with 0 as both initial and final state. If a word w encodes a number k, then wa encodes the number $2k + a$. Thus, for every state $q \in \{0, 1, 2\}$, we define

$$\delta(q, a) = (2q + a) \bmod 3.$$

This yields the automaton:

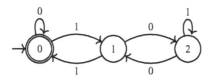

To obtain a DFA for the LSBF encoding, we "reverse" the DFA as follows: exchange initial and final states, and reverse the transitions. In general, this yields an NFA, but in this case the result of this operation is the same automaton! Thus, we have shown that a binary number $b_1 b_2 \cdots b_n$ is divisible by 3 iff the number $b_n b_{n-1} \cdots b_1$ is also divisible by 3.

(c) For the unary encoding, we can take $(111)^*$. For the two other encodings, we can take the regular expression $(0 + 1(01^*0)^*1)^*$.

★ ■ **Exercise 29.** Consider this DFA over alphabet $\{[0,0],[0,1],[1,0],[1,1]\}$:

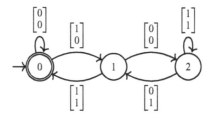

A word w encodes a pair of natural numbers $(X(w), Y(w))$, where $X(w)$ and $Y(w)$ are obtained by reading the top and bottom rows in MSBF encoding. For instance, the following word encodes $(44, 19)$:

$$w = \begin{bmatrix} 1 \\ 0 \end{bmatrix} \begin{bmatrix} 0 \\ 1 \end{bmatrix} \begin{bmatrix} 1 \\ 0 \end{bmatrix} \begin{bmatrix} 1 \\ 0 \end{bmatrix} \begin{bmatrix} 0 \\ 1 \end{bmatrix} \begin{bmatrix} 0 \\ 1 \end{bmatrix}.$$

Show that the above DFA recognizes the set of words w such that $X(w) = 3 \cdot Y(w)$ (i.e., the solutions of the equation $x - 3y = 0$).

Solution: We write $\emptyset$ to denote the implicit trap state. Let $f \colon \Sigma^* \to \mathbb{Z}$ be defined as $f(w) = X(w) - 3 \cdot Y(w)$. Note that $-3 \le f(c) \le 1$ for all $c \in \Sigma$. Further, by the definition of the MSBF-encoding, $f(wc) = 2f(w) + f(c)$ for every $w \in \Sigma^*$ and $c \in \Sigma$. We will show, for all $w \in \Sigma^*$, that $\delta(q_0, w) = f(w)$ if $f(w) \in \{0, 1, 2\}$, and $\delta(q_0, w) = \emptyset$ otherwise. As the only final state is 0, this shows that w is accepted iff $f(w) = 0$. The proof proceeds by induction on the length of w. Clearly, $f(\varepsilon) = 0 = \delta(q_0, \varepsilon)$. For the induction step, let $w \in \Sigma^*$ and $c \in \Sigma$. We consider the following two cases:

- If $f(w) \in \{0, 1, 2\}$, then $f(wc) = 2f(w) + f(c)$ (as above). It is easy to check for all $q \in Q$ that $\delta(q, c) = 2q + f(c)$ holds if $2q + f(c) \in \{0, 1, 2\}$, and $\delta(q, c) = \emptyset$ otherwise. Using the induction hypothesis, we have $\delta(q_0, wc) = \delta(\delta(q_0, w), c) = \delta(f(w), c)$, and the statement follows.
- If $\delta(q_0, w) = \emptyset$, then by induction hypothesis, we have either $f(w) \ge 3$ or $f(w) \le -1$. For the former, we have $f(wc) = 2f(w) + f(c) \ge 6 - 3 = 3$, and for the latter, $2f(w) + f(c) \le -2 + 1 \le -1$. (Recall $-3 \le f(c) \le 1$.) In both cases, we have shown $f(wc) \notin \{0, 1, 2\}$; correspondingly, $\delta(\emptyset, c) = \emptyset$ (due to $\emptyset$ being the trap state) implies the statement.   □

★ 🎓 **Exercise 30.** Algorithm *NFAtoRE* transforms a finite automaton into a regular expression representing the same language by iteratively eliminating states of the automaton. In this exercise, we present an algebraic reformulation of the algorithm. We represent an NFA as a system of *language equations* with as many variables as states and solve the system by eliminating variables. A language equation over an alphabet Σ and a set V of variables is an equation of the form $r_1 = r_2$, where r_1 and r_2 are regular expressions over $\Sigma \cup V$. For instance, $X = aX + b$ is a language equation. A solution of a system of equations is a mapping that assigns to each variable X a regular expression over Σ, such that the languages of the left- and right-hand sides of each equation are equal. For instance, a^*b is a solution of $X = aX + b$ because $\mathcal{L}(a^*b) = \mathcal{L}(aa^*b + b)$.

(a) Arden's lemma states that, given two languages $A, B \subseteq \Sigma^*$, the smallest language $X \subseteq \Sigma^*$ satisfying $X = AX + B$ is the language A^*B. Moreover, if $\varepsilon \notin A$, then the solution is unique. Prove Arden's lemma.

(b) Consider the following system of equations, where variables X and Y represent languages (regular expressions) over the alphabet $\Sigma = \{a, b, c, d, e, f\}$:

$$X = aX + bY + c$$

$$Y = dX + eY + f.$$

Find the unique solution with the help of Arden's lemma.

Hint: As a first step, consider X not as a variable but as a constant language, and solve the equation for Y using Arden's lemma.

(c) We can associate to any NFA $A = (Q, \Sigma, \delta, \{q_0\}, F)$ a system of linear equations as follows. We take Q as variables, which we call here $X, Y, Z, \ldots$, with X as initial state. The system has the following equation for each state Y:

$$
Y = \begin{cases}
\displaystyle\sum_{(Y,a,Z) \in \delta} aZ & \text{if } Y \notin F, \\[2em]
\left(\displaystyle\sum_{(Y,a,Z) \in \delta} aZ \right) + \varepsilon & \text{if } Y \in F.
\end{cases}
$$

Consider the DFA (1)(a) from the Tour of Conversions on page 35.

Let X, Y, Z, W be the states of the automaton, read from top to bottom and from left to right. The associated system of linear equations is

$$X = aY + bZ + \varepsilon \qquad\qquad Y = aX + bW$$

$$Z = bX + aW \qquad\qquad W = bY + aZ.$$

Compute the solution of this system by iteratively eliminating variables. Start with Y, then eliminate Z, and finally W. Compare with the elimination procedure depicted in step (1) of the Tour of Conversions on page 35.

Solution:

(a) We first show that A^*B is a solution of $X = AX + B$:

$$A^*B = \left(\bigcup_{k \geq 0} A^k \right) B$$

$$= \bigcup_{k \geq 0} A^k B \qquad\qquad \text{(by distributivity)}$$

$$= B \cup \bigcup_{k \geq 1} A^k B$$

$$= B \cup A \left(\bigcup_{k \geq 0} A^k \right) B \qquad \text{(by distributivity)}$$

$$= A(A^*B) \cup B.$$

Now, let L be an arbitrary solution of $X = AX + B$. We must show that $A^*B \subseteq L$. Since $L = AL + B$, we have

$$L = AL + B$$

$$L = A(AL + B) + B \qquad = B + AB + A^2 L$$

$$L = A(A(AL + B) + B) + B = B + AB + A^2 B + A^3 L$$

$$\vdots$$

and so, by induction, we get for all $k \geq 0$

$$L = A^{k+1} L \cup \bigcup_{\ell=0}^{k} A^\ell B.$$

In particular, this implies $A^\ell B \subseteq L$ for every $\ell \geq 0$, and hence $A^*B \subseteq L$.

To conclude, let us consider the case where $\varepsilon \notin A$. Let $w \in L$ and $k = |w|$. We have $w \notin A^{k+1} L$ and hence $w \in \bigcup_{0 \leq \ell \leq k} A^\ell B \subseteq A^*B$. Thus, $L \subseteq A^*B$, which implies $L = A^*B$.

(b) By Arden's lemma, the unique solution of the equation

$$Y = dX + eY + f = eY + (dX + f)$$

is the language $e^*(dX + f)$ independently of the value of X. Substituting into the equation for X, we obtain

$$X = aX + be^*(dX + f) + c$$

$$= (a + be^*d)X + be^*f + c,$$

which by Arden's lemma yields

$$X = (a + be^*d)^*(be^*f + c)$$

$$Y = e^*(d(a + be^*d)^*(be^*f + c) + f).$$

(c) In order to eliminate Y, we simply substitute the equation $Y = aX + bW$ into the remaining equations, yielding

$$X = aaX + abW + bZ + \varepsilon$$

$$Z = bX + aW$$

$$W = aZ + baX + bbW.$$

Similarly, we may eliminate Z:

$$X = aaX + abW + bbX + baW + \varepsilon = (aa + bb)X + (ab + ba)W + \varepsilon$$

$$W = abX + aaW + baX + bbW \qquad = (aa + bb)W + (ab + ba)X.$$

By Arden's lemma, the parametrized unique solution for W is $(aa + bb)^*(ab + ba)X$. So, we obtain the single equation

$$X = (aa + bb)X + (ab + ba)(aa + bb)^*(ab + ba)X + \varepsilon$$

$$= \big(aa + bb + (ab + ba)(aa + bb)^*(ab + ba)\big)X + \varepsilon,$$

whose unique solution is

$$X = \big(aa + bb + (ab + ba)(aa + bb)^*(ab + ba)\big)^*.$$

This is the same regular expression as obtained in the chapter. In fact, the elimination of states corresponds to the elimination of the corresponding variables in the underlying system of linear equations.

★ 🔲 **Exercise 31.** Consider a deck of cards (with arbitrary many cards) in which black and colored cards alternate, the top card is black, and the bottom card is colored. The set of possible decks is given by the regular expression $(BR)^*$. Cut the deck at any point into two piles, and then perform a perfect riffle shuffle to yield a new deck (where cards strictly alternate). For example, we can cut a deck with six cards 123456 (with 1 as the top card) into two piles 12 and 3456, and the riffle yields 345162 (we start the riffle with the first pile). Give a regular expression over the alphabet $\{B, R\}$ describing the possible configurations of the decks after the riffle.

Hint: After the cut, the last card of the first pile can be black or colored. In the first case, the two piles belong to $(BR)^*B$ and $R(BR)^*$ and in the second case to $(BR)^*$ and $(BR)^*$. Let $Rif(r_1, r_2)$ be the language of all decks obtained by performing a riffle on decks taken from $\mathcal{L}(r_1)$ and $\mathcal{L}(r_2)$. We are looking for a regular expression for

$$Rif\big((BR)^*B, R(BR)^*\big) + Rif\big((BR)^*, (BR)^*\big).$$

Use exercise 30 to set up a system of equations over the variables $X = Rif((BR)^*B, R(BR)^*)$ and $Y = Rif((BR)^*, (BR)^*)$, and solve it.

Solution: By definition of a riffle, for every regular expressions r, r_1, r_2 and letters $a, b \in \Sigma$:

$$Rif(r, \varepsilon) = r,$$

$$Rif(\varepsilon, r) = r,$$

$$Rif(r_1 + r_2, r) = Rif(r_1, r) + Rif(r_2, r),$$

$$Rif(r, r_1 + r_2) = Rif(r, r_1) + Rif(r, r_2),$$

$$Rif(r_1 a, r_2 b) = Rif(r_1, r_2)ba.$$

Applying these identities, we get

$$Rif\big((BR)^*B, R(BR)^*\big) = Rif\big((BR)^*B, (RB)^*R\big)$$

$$= Rif\big((BR)^*, (RB)^*\big)\, RB,$$

$$Rif\big((BR)^*, (RB)^*\big) = Rif\big(\varepsilon + (BR)^*BR, \varepsilon + (RB)^*RB\big)$$

$$= (BR)^* + (RB)^* + Rif\big((BR)^*B, (RB)^*R\big)\, BR.$$

By introducing variables X and Y for $Rif((BR)^*B, R(BR)^*)$ and $Rif((BR)^*, (RB)^*)$, we obtain the following system of equations:

$$X = YRB$$

$$Y = (BR)^* + (RB)^* + XBR.$$

Substituting Y in the equation for X yields

$$X = \big((BR)^* + (RB)^* + XBR\big)\, RB = \big((BR)^* + (RB)^*\big)\, RB + XBR$$

whose unique solution is

$$X = \big((BR)^* + (RB)^*\big)\, RB(BR)^*.$$

Substituting in the equation for Y yields

$$Y = \big((BR)^* + (RB)^*\big)\, \big(\varepsilon + RB(BR)^*BR\big).$$

★ ■ **Exercise 32.** Let L be an arbitrary language over a one-letter alphabet. Prove that L^* is regular.

Solution: We assume that $L \neq \emptyset$ and $L \neq \{\varepsilon\}$, as the claim is otherwise trivial. Let $w \in L$ be the shortest nonempty word of L. Let $v_0 = \varepsilon$. Note that $v_0\{w\}^* \subseteq L^*$. If $L^* = v_0\{w\}^*$, then we are done. Otherwise, let $v_1 \in L^*$ be the shortest word such that $v_1 \in L^* \setminus v_0\{w\}^*$. We have $(v_0 + v_1)\{w\}^* \subseteq L^*$. If $L^* = (v_0 + v_1)\{w\}^*$, then we are done. Otherwise, we can continue this process by picking the shortest word $v_i \in L^* \setminus (v_0 + v_1 + \ldots + v_{i-1})\{w\}^*$ and checking whether $L^* = (v_0 + v_1 + \ldots + v_i)\{w\}^*$. Let $p = |w|$. This process is guaranteed to terminate in $n < p$ steps, which means that $L = (v_0 + v_1 + \ldots + v_n)\{w\}^*$, which is regular. Indeed, for the sake of contradiction, suppose it does not terminate in less than p steps. By the pigeonhole principle, there exists $0 \leq i < p$ such that $|v_p| \equiv |v_i| \pmod{p}$. Since $|v_i| < |v_p|$, we have $v_p \in v_i\{w\}^*$, which contradicts the way v_p was picked.   □

★ ■ **Exercise 34.** Let $K_n = (V_n, E_n)$ be the complete directed graph of n nodes, that is, with nodes $V_n = \{1, \ldots, n\}$ and edges $E_n = \{(i,j) : 1 \leq i,j \leq n\}$. A path of K_n is a sequence of nodes, and a circuit is a path that begins and ends in the same node. Let $A_n = (Q_n, \Sigma_n, \delta_n, q_{0n}, F_n)$ be the DFA defined by $Q_n = \{1, \ldots, n\} \cup \{\bot\}$, $\Sigma_n = \{a_{ij} : 1 \leq i,j \leq n\}$, $q_{0n} = 1$, $F_n = \{1\}$ and

$$\delta_n(q, a_{ij}) = \begin{cases} \bot & \text{if } q = \bot \text{ or } q \neq i, \\ j & \text{otherwise (if } q = i). \end{cases}$$

The language accepted by A_n consists of all words encoding circuits of K_n from node 1 to itself. For example, the following DFA A_3 accepts $a_{1,3}a_{3,2}a_{2,1}$, which encodes the circuit 1321 of K_3.

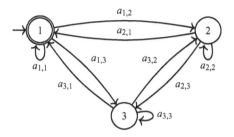

The *size* of a regular expression r, denoted $|r|$, is defined recursively as 1 if $r \in \{\varepsilon, \emptyset\} \cup \Sigma_n$; $|r_1| + |r_2|$ if $r = r_1 + r_2$ or $r = r_1 r_2$; and $|s|$ if $r = s^*$. Similarly, we define the *length* of r, denoted $\text{len}(r)$, as 1 if $r \in \{\varepsilon, \emptyset\} \cup \Sigma_n$; $\max(\text{len}(r_1), \text{len}(r_2))$ if $r = r_1 + r_2$; $\text{len}(r_1) + \text{len}(r_2)$ if $r = r_1 r_2$; and $\text{len}(s)$ if $r = s^*$. Note that $|r| \geq \text{len}(r)$.

A *path expression* r is a regular expression over Σ_n that encodes paths of K_n. We seek to show that any path expression for $\mathcal{L}(A_n)$, and hence any regular expression, must have length $\Omega(2^n)$. As a consequence, this means that DFAs can be exponentially more succinct than regular expressions.

(a) Let π be a circuit of K_n and let r be a path expression. We say that r *covers* π if $\mathcal{L}(r)$ contains a word uwv such that w encodes π. Furthermore, we say that r *covers* π^* if $\mathcal{L}(r)$ covers π^k for every $k \geq 0$. It can be shown that if r covers $\pi^{2 \cdot \text{len}(r)}$, then it covers π^*.

From this, show that if r covers π^* and no proper subexpression of r does, then $r = s^*$ for some expression s, and every word of $\mathcal{L}(s)$ encodes a circuit starting at a node of π.

(b) For every $1 \leq k \leq n+1$, let $[k]$ denote the permutation of $\{1, 2, \ldots, n+1\}$ that cyclically shifts every index k positions to the right. More formally, node i is renamed to $i + k$ if $i + k \leq n+1$ and to $i + k - (n+1)$ otherwise. Let $\pi[k]$ be the result of applying the permutation to π. For example, if $n = 4$ and $\pi = 24142$, we obtain

$$\pi[1] = 35253, \quad \pi[2] = 41314, \quad \pi[3] = 52425, \quad \pi[4] = 13531, \quad \pi[5] = 24142 = \pi.$$

Let π be a circuit of K_n. Show that $\pi[k]$ is a circuit of K_{n+1} that does not pass through node k.

(c) Let us define a circuit g_n of K_n inductively:

$$g_1 = 11,$$

$$g_{n+1} = 1 \, (g_n[1])^{2^n} \, (g_n[2])^{2^n} \, \cdots \, (g_n[n+1])^{2^n} \qquad \text{for every } n \geq 1.$$

In particular, we have

$$g_1 = 11,$$

$$g_2 = 1 \, (22)^2 \, (11)^2,$$

$$g_3 = 1 \, (2 \, (33)^2 \, (22)^2)^4 \, (3 \, (11)^2 \, (33)^2 \, 3)^4 \, (1 \, (22)^2 \, (11)^2)^4.$$

Prove, using (a)–(b), that every path expression r covering g_n is such that $|r| \geq 2^{n-1}$.

(d) Show that any regular expression r_n such that $\mathcal{L}(r_n) = \mathcal{L}(A_n)$ is such that $|r_n| \geq 2^{n-1}$.

Solution:

(a) Let r be a path expression that covers π^* and with no proper subexpression of r covering π^*. For the sake of contradiction, suppose r is not of the form s^*. If $r = r_1 + r_2$, then, since r covers $\pi^{2 \cdot \mathrm{len}(r)}$, either r_1 or r_2 covers $\pi^{2 \cdot \mathrm{len}(r)}$. This means that either r_1 or r_2 covers π^*, which contradicts the minimality of r. Similarly, if $r = r_1 r_2$, then, since r covers $\pi^{4 \cdot \mathrm{len}(r)+1}$, either r_1 or r_2 covers $\pi^{2 \cdot \mathrm{len}(r)}$, which is a contradiction.

Thus, we have $r = s^*$ for some s. Let us consider two words of $\mathcal{L}(s)$:

$$w_1 = a_{i_1,i_2} a_{i_2,i_3} \cdots a_{i_{k-1},i_k} \text{ and } w_2 = a_{j_1,j_2} a_{j_2,j_3} \cdots a_{j_{\ell-1},j_\ell}.$$

Since r is a path expression and $r = s^*$, the words $w_1 w_1$, $w_1 w_2$, $w_2 w_1$, and $w_2 w_2$ encode paths. Consequently, we have $i_1 = i_k = j_1 = i_k = j_\ell$. Thus, all words of $\mathcal{L}(s)$ encode circuits starting and ending at the same node, say i. It remains to prove that i is a node of π. For the sake of contradiction, suppose it is not the case. For every $k \geq 1$, any shortest word of $\mathcal{L}(s^*)$ that covers π^k must also be a word of s, because the first and last letters of a word of $\mathcal{L}(s)$ cannot be used to encode π. It follows that s covers π^*, contradicting the assumption that no proper subexpression of r covers π^*. $\qquad\square$

(b) Since π is a path of K_n, it does not pass through node $n+1$. The node permuted to node k by the permutation $[k]$ is $n+1$. Thus, the circuit $\pi[k]$ does not pass through node k. $\quad\square$

(c) We proceed by induction. The claim is obvious for $n = 1$ since $|r| \geq 1 = 2^{1-1}$. Now, let r be a path expression covering g_{n+1} such that no proper subexpression of r covers g_{n+1}. By definition, r covers $(g_n[i])^{2^n}$ for every $1 \leq i \leq n+1$. Thus, by (a), either r covers $(g_n[i])^*$ for every $1 \leq i \leq n+1$, or $\mathrm{len}(r) \geq 2^{n-1}$. Let us assume the former, as we are done in the latter case since $|r| \geq \mathrm{len}(r)$. Expression r contains, for every $1 \leq i \leq n+1$, a minimal subexpression r_i covering $(g_n[i])^*$. By (a), $r_i = s_i^*$ for some expression s_i. Let s be of minimal size among $s_1, \ldots, s_{n+1}$. By (a), there is a node j such that every word of $\mathcal{L}(s)$ encodes a circuit starting at j. Consider s^* and s_j^*. By induction hypothesis, each of them has size at least 2^{n-2}. By minimality of s^*, we have that s_j^* cannot be a proper subexpression of s^*. Thus, there are two possible cases: (1) neither s^* is a subexpression of s_j^*, nor s_j^* is a subexpression of s^*, or (2) s^* is a subexpression of s_j^*. Let us handle both cases.

(1) We have $|r| \geq |s^*| + |s_j^*| \geq 2^{n-2} + 2^{n-2} = 2^{n-1}$.

(2) Recall that s_j covers $g_n[j]$, which by (b) does not pass through node j. By (a), no word of $\mathcal{L}(s_j)$ can encode a circuit starting at j. Recall that every word of $\mathcal{L}(s)$ encodes a circuit starting at j. This implies $s \neq s_j$, and hence s^* is a proper subexpression of s_j. It follows that $s_j[s^*/\varepsilon]$ (i.e., the result of substituting s^* by ε in s_j), still covers $(g_n[j])^*$, since the substitution only loses circuits containing j, which $(g_n[j])^*$ does not visit. By induction hypothesis, $|s_j[s^*/\varepsilon]| \geq 2^{n-2}$. Since $|s^*| \geq 2^{n-2}$, we obtain $|s_j| \geq 2^{n-1}$. Since s_j^* is a subexpression of r, we finally conclude that $|r| \geq 2^{n-1}$. $\qquad\square$

(d) Let r_n be a regular expression such that $\mathcal{L}(r_n) = \mathcal{L}(A_n)$. Note that $\mathcal{L}(r_n)$ encodes all circuits from node 1 to itself. Thus, in particular, it covers circuit g_n. By (d), we have $|r_n| \geq 2^{n-1}$. □

★ ■ **Exercise 35.** Let us introduce weakly acyclic DFAs, NFAs, and regular expressions:

- A DFA $A = (Q, \Sigma, \delta, q_0, F)$ is *weakly acyclic* if $\delta(q, w) = q$ implies $\delta(q, a) = q$ for every letter a occurring in w.
- An NFA $A = (Q, \Sigma, \delta, Q_0, F)$ is *weakly acyclic* if $q \in \delta(q, w)$ implies $\delta(q, a) = \{q\}$ for every letter a occurring in w.
- *Weakly acyclic* regular expressions over an alphabet Σ are regular expressions generated by

$$r ::= \emptyset \mid \Gamma^* \mid \Lambda^* a r \mid r + r \qquad \text{where } \Gamma, \Lambda \subseteq \Sigma \text{ and } a \in \Sigma \setminus \Lambda.$$

Finally, a regular language is *weakly acyclic* if it is recognized by some weakly acyclic DFA. Show the following statements:

(a) An NFA $A = (Q, \Sigma, \delta, q_0, F)$ is weakly acyclic iff it satisfies any of the following three conditions:

(i) the binary relation $\preceq \subseteq Q \times Q$, given by $q \preceq q'$ iff $\delta(q, w) = \{q'\}$ for some word w, is a partial order;

(ii) each strongly connected component of the underlying directed graph of A contains a single state; and

(iii) the underlying directed graph of A does not contain any simple cycle beyond self-loops.

(b) If A is a weakly acyclic NFA, then $B = NFAtoDFA(A)$ is a weakly acyclic DFA.

(c) For every weakly acyclic regular expression r, there is a weakly acyclic DFA that accepts $\mathcal{L}(r)$.

(d) For every weakly acyclic NFA A, there is a weakly acyclic regular expression for $\mathcal{L}(A)$.

Since every weakly acyclic DFA is also a weakly acyclic NFA by definition, we conclude that a language is *weakly acyclic* iff it is recognized by a weakly acyclic DFA iff it is recognized by a weakly acyclic NFA iff it is the language of a weakly acyclic regular expression.

Solution:

(a) We only prove (i), because (ii) and (iii) follow immediately from (i) and the definitions of strongly connected components and simple cycle.

⇒) Assume $q \in \delta(q, w)$ implies $\delta(q, a) = \{q\}$ for every letter a occurring in w. We prove that the relation $\preceq$ is a partial order. For every state q, we have $\delta(q, \varepsilon) = \{q\}$ and so $q \preceq q$, which proves that $\preceq$ is reflexive. Since $q' \in \delta(q, w)$ and $q'' \in \delta(q', w')$ implies $q'' \in \delta(q, ww')$, we conclude that $q \preceq q'$ and $q' \preceq q''$ implies $q \preceq q''$, which proves that $\preceq$ is transitive. It remains to show that $\preceq$ is antisymmetric. For this, we assume that $q \preceq q'$ and $q' \preceq q$ hold and show that $q = q'$. By definition of $\preceq$, there exist words $w, w' \in \Sigma^*$ and a state q' such that $q' \in \delta(q, w)$ and $q \in \delta(q', w') = \{q\}$. It follows that $q \in \delta(q, ww')$ and so, by definition of weakly acyclic NFAs, we have $\delta(q, a) = \{q\}$ for every letter a occurring in either w or w'. This implies $\delta(q, w) = \{q\}$. Since $q' \in \delta(q, w)$ by assumption, we get $q = q'$.

$\Leftarrow$) Assume that $\preceq$ is a partial order and that $\delta(q, w) = \{q\}$ holds for some state q and word w. For every letter a occurring in w, there are words $w', w'' \in \Sigma^*$ such that $w = w'aw''$. Letting q', q'' be the states such that $\delta(q, w') = \{q'\}$ and $\delta(q', a) = \{q''\}$, we have $\delta(q'', w'') = \{q\}$, and from the definition of $\preceq$, we get $q \preceq q' \preceq q'' \preceq q$. Since $\preceq$ is a partial order by assumption, this implies $q = q' = q''$, and so $\delta(q, a) = q$. $\square$

(b) Let $A = (Q, \Sigma, \delta, Q_0, F)$. Recall that the states of B are sets of states from A and that $Q_1 \xrightarrow{a} Q_2$ is a transition of B iff $\delta(Q_1, a) = Q_2$. Hence, by (a), applied to B, it suffices to show that the relation $\preceq \subseteq 2^Q \times 2^Q$ defined by $Q_1 \preceq Q_2$ iff $\delta(Q_1, w) = Q_2$ for some word w is a partial order. It was shown in (a) that the relation is reflexive and transitive for any DFA, and so it suffices to show that $\preceq$ is antisymmetric (i.e., that $\delta(Q_1, w_1) = Q_2$ and $\delta(Q_2, w_2) = Q_1$ implies $Q_1 = Q_2$).

Assume $\delta(Q_1, w_1) = Q_2$ and $\delta(Q_2, w_2) = Q_1$. We say that a state $q \in Q_1$ is *cyclic* if there is some $n \geq 1$ such that $q \in \delta(q, (w_1 w_2)^n)$. We prove that every state of Q_1 is cyclic, which shows $Q_1 = Q_2$. For the sake of contradiction, suppose Q_1 contains some acyclic state q. We can pick q minimal w.r.t. $\preceq$. Since $\delta(Q_1, w_1 w_2) = Q_1$ by assumption, there is some $q' \in Q_1$ such that $q \in \delta(q', w_1 w_2)$, and so $q \succeq q'$. Since q is acyclic, we have $q' \neq q$, and so $q \succ q'$. By minimality of q, the state q' is cyclic. Since A is weakly acyclic, we have $\delta(q', a) = \{q'\}$ for every letter a that occurs in $w_1 w_2$, and so, in particular, $\delta(q', w_1 w_2) = \{q'\}$. This contradicts $q \neq q'$. $\square$

(c) We proceed by structural induction on expression r. The claim is obvious for both $r = \emptyset$ and $r = \Gamma^*$. Assume $r = \Lambda^* ar$ for some $\Lambda \subseteq \Sigma$ and $a \notin \Lambda$. By induction, there exists a weakly acyclic DFA $A = (Q, \Sigma, \delta, q_0, F)$ such that $\mathcal{L}(A) = \mathcal{L}(r)$. The following weakly acyclic DFA accepts $\Lambda^* a \mathcal{L}(r)$:

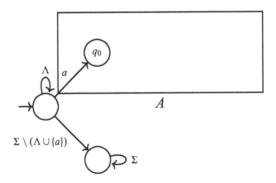

Assume r is of the form $r_1 + r_2$. By induction, there exist weakly acyclic DFAs $A_1 = (Q_1, \Sigma, \delta_1, q_{01}, F_1)$ and $A_2 = (Q_2, \Sigma, \delta_2, q_{02}, F_2)$ such that $\mathcal{L}(A_i) = \mathcal{L}(r_i)$ for both $i \in \{1, 2\}$.

The NFA $A = (Q_1 \cup Q_2, \Sigma, \delta_1 \cup \delta_2, \{q_{01}, q_{02}\}, F_1 \cup F_2)$ accepts $\mathcal{L}(r)$. Moreover, by (b), $B = NFAtoDFA(A)$ is a weakly acyclic DFA that accepts $\mathcal{L}(A)$. Thus, we are done.   □

(d) Let $A = (Q, \Sigma, \delta, Q_0, F)$ be a weakly acyclic NFA. If we omit the self-loops of A, then we obtain a directed acyclic graph and hence finitely many paths. Therefore, $\mathcal{L}(A)$ is a finite union of languages of the form $\Lambda_1^* a_1 \cdots \Lambda_n^* a_n \Gamma^*$ where $\Lambda_1, \ldots, \Lambda_n, \Gamma \subseteq \Sigma$ and each $a_i \notin \Lambda_i$.   □

Solutions for Chapter 2

☆ ▣ **Exercise 36.** For each language $L \subseteq \{a, b, c\}^*$ below, say whether L has finitely many residuals, and, if so, describe the residuals.

(a) $(ab + ba)^*$,

(b) $(aa)^*$,

(c) $\{a^n b^n c^n : n \geq 0\}$.

Solution:

(a) We have $L^\varepsilon = \mathcal{L}((ab + ba)^*)$, $L^a = \mathcal{L}(b(ab + ba)^*)$, $L^b = \mathcal{L}(a(ab + ba)^*)$, and $L^c = \emptyset$. All other residuals are equal to one of these four.

(b) We have $L^\varepsilon = \mathcal{L}((aa)^*)$, $L^a = \mathcal{L}(a(aa)^*)$, and $L^b = \emptyset$. All other residuals are equal to one of these three.

(c) Every prefix of a word of the form $a^n b^n c^n$ has a different residual. For all other words, the residual is the empty set. Thus, there are infinitely many residuals.

☆ ▣ **Exercise 37.** Consider the most-significant-bit-first (MSBF) encoding of natural numbers over alphabet $\Sigma = \{0, 1\}$. Recall that every number has infinitely many encodings, because all the words of $0^* w$ encode the same number as w. Construct the minimal DFAs accepting the following languages, where Σ^4 denotes all words of length 4:

(a) $\{w : \text{MSBF}^{-1}(w) \bmod 3 = 0\} \cap \Sigma^4$.

(b) $\{w : \text{MSBF}^{-1}(w) \text{ is a prime}\} \cap \Sigma^4$.

Solution:

(a) The DFA must recognize the encodings of $\{0, 3, 6, 9, 12, 15\}$—that is, the language

$$\{0000, 0011, 0110, 1001, 1100, 1111\}.$$

Thus, we obtain

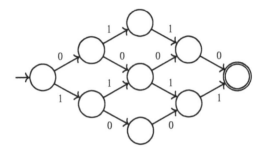

(b) The DFA must recognize the encodings of $\{2, 3, 5, 7, 11, 13\}$—that is, the language

$$\{0010, 0011, 0101, 0111, 1011, 1101\}.$$

Thus, we obtain

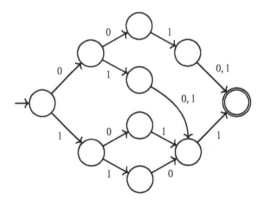

☆ ■ **Exercise 38.** Prove or disprove the following statements:

(a) A subset of a regular language is regular.
(b) A superset of a regular language is regular.
(c) If L_1 and $L_1 L_2$ are regular languages, then L_2 is regular.
(d) If L_2 and $L_1 L_2$ are regular languages, then L_1 is regular.

Solution: All statements are false. Since $\emptyset$ and Σ^* are both regular, any of (a) or (b) would imply that every language is regular, which is certainly not the case (e.g. $A = \{a^{n^2} : n \geq 0\}$ is not regular). For (c), let $L_1 = \mathcal{L}(a^*)$ and let $L_2 = A$. We have $L_1 L_2 = \mathcal{L}(a^*)$, which is regular, but L_2 is not. Similarly, (d) is disproved with $L_1 = A$ and $L_2 = \mathcal{L}(a^*)$. $\qquad\square$

☆ ⚙ **Exercise 39.** Consider the following DFA A:

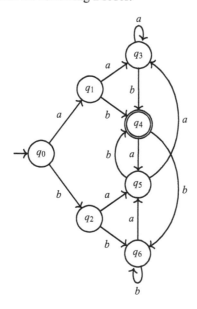

(a) Compute the language partition of A.
(b) Construct the quotient of A with respect to its language partition.
(c) Give a regular expression for $\mathcal{L}(A)$.

Solution:

(a)

Iter.	Block to split	Splitter	New partition
0	—	—	$\{q_0, q_1, q_2, q_3, q_5, q_6\}, \{q_4\}$
1	$\{q_0, q_1, q_2, q_3, q_5, q_6\}$	$(b, \{q_4\})$	$\{q_0, q_2, q_6\}, \{q_1, q_3, q_5\}, \{q_4\}$
2	none, partition is stable	—	—

The language partition is $P_\ell = \{\{q_0, q_2, q_6\}, \{q_1, q_3, q_5\}, \{q_4\}\}$.

(b)

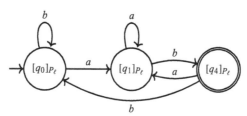

(c) $(a+b)^*ab$.

★ ■ **Exercise 43.** Let A_1 and A_2 be DFAs with n_1 and n_2 states such that $\mathcal{L}(A_1) \neq \mathcal{L}(A_2)$. Show that there exists a word w of length at most $n_1 + n_2 - 2$ such that $w \in (\mathcal{L}(A_1) \setminus \mathcal{L}(A_2)) \cup (\mathcal{L}(A_2) \setminus \mathcal{L}(A_1))$.
Hint: Consider the NFA obtained by putting A_1 and A_2 "side by side" and CSR(A).

Solution: Let A be the NFA obtained by taking the disjoint union of A_1 and A_2. Since $\mathcal{L}(A_1) \neq \mathcal{L}(A_2)$, automaton A has at least one final and one nonfinal state. Thus, the procedure that computes CSR(A) initially has a partition of two blocks. Since every split increases the number of blocks by 1, and the maximal possible number of blocks is $n_1 + n_2$, the algorithm performs at most $n_1 + n_2 - 2$ splits. Hence, it suffices to show that if two states q_1 and q_2 are put in different blocks at the kth split, then the language $(\mathcal{L}(q_1) \setminus \mathcal{L}(q_2)) \cup (\mathcal{L}(q_2) \setminus \mathcal{L}(q_1))$ contains a word w of length at most k. We prove this by induction on k. If $k = 0$, then exactly one of q_1 or q_2 is a final state, and we can take $w = \varepsilon$. If $k > 0$, then right before q_1 and q_2 are put in different blocks, there is a letter a and transitions

$$q_1 \xrightarrow{a} q_1' \text{ and } q_2 \xrightarrow{a} q_2',$$

such that q_1' and q_2' already belong to different blocks. By induction hypothesis, the language

$$\left(\mathcal{L}(q_1') \setminus \mathcal{L}(q_2') \right) \cup \left(\mathcal{L}(q_2') \setminus \mathcal{L}(q_1') \right)$$

contains a word w' of length $k - 1$. Thus, we can take $w = aw'$.   □

★ ▣ **Exercise 44.** Let $\Sigma = \{a, b\}$. Let A_k be the minimal DFA such that $\mathcal{L}(A_k) = \{ww : w \in \Sigma^k\}$.

(a) Construct A_2.
(b) Construct a DFA that accepts $\mathcal{L}(A_k)$.
(c) How many states does A_k contain for $k > 2$?

Solution:

(a) The trap state is omitted for the sake of readability:

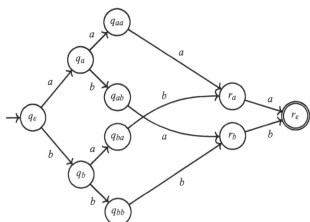

(b) We generalize the construction given in (a) for $k = 2$: state q_w indicates that word w has been read so far, and state r_w indicates that w must be read in order to accept. More formally, let $A_k = (Q, \Sigma, \delta, q_0, F)$ be the following automaton, which we complete with a trap state:

$$Q = \{q_w : w \in \Sigma^*, |w| \leq k\} \cup \{r_w : w \in \Sigma^*, |w| < k\},$$

$$\delta = \{(q_u, a, q_{ua}) : |u| < k\} \cup$$

$$\{(q_{av}, a, r_v) : a \in \Sigma, |v| = k - 1\} \cup$$

$$\{(r_{av}, a, r_v) : a \in \Sigma, |v| < k - 1\},$$

$$q_0 = q_\varepsilon,$$

$$F = \{r_\varepsilon\}.$$

(c) Note that A_k defined in (b) has $f(k) = (2^{k+1} - 1) + (2^k - 1) + 1 = 3 \cdot 2^k - 1$ states. We show that A_k is minimal. To prove it, we show that $\mathcal{L}(A_k)$ has $f(k)$ residuals. To simplify the notation, let $L = \mathcal{L}(A_k)$.

- We have $L^v = \emptyset$ for every $v \in \Sigma^*$ such that $|v| > 2k$. Hence, $\emptyset$ is our first residual.
- For every word v of length at most $k - 1$, we have $L^v = \{uvu : u \in \Sigma^*, |vu| = k\}$. Note that all of these sets contain at least two words, and they are all distinct. There are as many of them as words of length at most k, and so we get $\sum_{i=0}^{k-1} 2^i = 2^k - 1$ new residuals.
- For every word v such that $k \leq |v| \leq 2k$, we have $v = v_1 v_2 v_3$, where $|v_1 v_2| = k$ and $|v_1| = |v_3|$. If $v_1 \neq v_3$, then $L^v = \emptyset$, which is not a new residual. If $v_1 = v_3$, then $L^v = \{v_2\}$ is a new residual as all other residuals we have seen so far had either zero or at least two words. Thus, we get a new residual for every word v_2 of length $0 \leq |v_2| \leq k$, and hence $\sum_{i=0}^{k} 2^i = 2^{k+1} - 1$ residuals.

In total, we have at least $1 + (2^k - 1) + (2^{k+1} - 1) = 3 \cdot 2^k - 1$ residuals, which matches the upper bound given by the number of states of A_k.

⭐■ **Exercise 45.** For every language $L \subseteq \Sigma^*$ and word $w \in \Sigma^*$, let $^wL = \{u \in \Sigma^* : uw \in L\}$. A language $L' \subseteq \Sigma^*$ is an *inverse residual* of L if $L' = {}^wL$ for some $w \in \Sigma^*$.

(a) Determine the inverse residuals of the first two languages of exercise 36: $(ab + ba)^*$ and $(aa)^*$.

(b) Show that a language is regular iff it has finitely many inverse residuals.

(c) Does a language always have as many residuals as inverse residuals?

Solution:

(a) • We give the inverse residuals of $L = \mathcal{L}((ab + ba)^*)$ as regular expressions:

$$^\varepsilon L = (ab + ba)^*, \qquad\qquad\qquad {}^a L = (ab + ba)^* b,$$

$$^b L = (ab + ba)^* a, \qquad\qquad\qquad {}^{aa} L = \emptyset.$$

All other inverse residuals are equal to one of these four. The language has the same number of residuals and inverse residuals, but they are not same languages.

- We give the inverse residuals of $(aa)^*$ as regular expressions:

$$^\varepsilon L = (aa)^*, \qquad\qquad ^a L = (aa)^* a, \qquad\qquad ^b L = \emptyset.$$

All other inverse residuals are equal to one of these three. In this case, the residuals and the inverse residuals of the language coincide.

(b) Let L be a language and let L^R be the reverse of L (see exercise 14). We have $u \in {}^w L$ iff $uw \in L$ iff $w^R u^R \in L^R$ iff $u^R \in (L^R)^{w^R}$. Thus, K is an inverse residual of L iff K^R is a residual of L^R. In particular, the number of inverse residuals of L is equal to the number of residuals of L^R. Consequently:

$$
\begin{aligned}
&L \text{ is regular} \\
\text{iff}\quad &L^R \text{ is regular} &&\text{(by exercise 14)} \\
\text{iff}\quad &L^R \text{ has finitely many residuals} \\
\text{iff}\quad &L \text{ has finitely many residuals.}
\end{aligned}
$$

(c) No. Consider the language L over $\{a, b\}$ containing all words ending with a (i.e., $(a + b)^* a$). The language has two residuals:

$$L^w = \begin{cases} (a+b)^* a + \varepsilon & \text{if } w \text{ ends with } a, \\ (a+b)^* a & \text{if } w \text{ ends with } b \text{ or } w = \varepsilon. \end{cases}$$

but three inverse residuals:

$$^w L = \begin{cases} (a+b)^* a & \text{if } w = \varepsilon, \\ (a+b)^* & \text{if } w \text{ ends with } a, \\ \emptyset & \text{if } w \text{ ends with } b. \end{cases}$$

★ ☞ **Exercise 48.** A DFA with *negative transitions* (DFA-n) is a DFA whose transitions are partitioned into *positive* and *negative* transitions. A run of a DFA-n is accepting if

- it ends in a final state *and* the number of occurrences of negative transitions is even, *or*
- it ends in a nonfinal state *and* the number of occurrences of negative transitions is odd.

The intuition is that taking a negative transition "inverts the polarity" of the acceptance condition.

(a) Show that the language accepted by a DFA-n is regular.

(b) Give a DFA-n for a regular language L, which has fewer states than the minimal DFA for L.

(c) Show that the minimal DFA-n for a language is not necessarily unique.

Solution:

(a) Let $A = (Q, \Sigma, \delta, q_0, F)$ be a DFA-n. We construct a DFA B that behaves as A but that also remembers the parity of the number of occurrences of negative transitions. This allows the automaton to determine whether the current state should be accepting or not. More formally, let $B = (Q', \Sigma, \delta', q_0', F')$ be the DFA such that

$$Q' = Q \times \{0, 1\},$$

$$\delta'((q,x),a) = \begin{cases} (\delta(q,a), 1-x) & \text{if } (q,a) \text{ is negative,} \\ (\delta(q,a), x) & \text{otherwise,} \end{cases}$$

$$q_0' = (q_0, 0),$$

$$F' = \{(q,0) : q \in F\} \cup \{(q,1) : q \notin F\}.$$

A simple induction shows that $\mathcal{L}(B) = \mathcal{L}(A)$.

(b) Let $L = \{w \in \{a\}^* : |w|_a \text{ is even}\}$. The minimal DFA that accepts L has two states. The following DFA-n, with a single negative transition, accepts L:

(c) Let $L = \{w \in \{a,b\}^* : w \text{ ends with } a \iff |w|_b \mod 2 = 1\}$. The minimal DFA that accepts L has four states. The following DFA-n, whose negative transitions are colored and dashed, both accept L:

Let us show that these automata are indeed minimal. Suppose they are not. This means that there exists a DFA-n A with a single state q that accepts L. It must necessarily loop upon reading a and b. Moreover, q is initial and also final since $\varepsilon \in \mathcal{L}(A)$. The a-transition must be negative, as otherwise $a \in \mathcal{L}(A)$. Similarly, the b-transition must be negative, as otherwise $b \in \mathcal{L}(A)$. This implies that $ab \in \mathcal{L}(A)$, which is a contradiction since $ab \notin L$.

★ ■ **Exercise 49.** We say that a residual of a regular language L is *composite* if it is the union of other residuals of L and that it is *prime* otherwise. Show that every regular language L is recognized by an NFA whose number of states is equal to the number of prime residuals of L.

Solution: We define an NFA $A_L = (Q_L \cup \{q_0\}, \Sigma, \delta_L, Q_0, F_L)$ where

- Q_L is the set of prime residuals of L;
- for every $K \in Q_L$ and every $a \in \Sigma$, we define $\delta(K, a)$ as the set $\mathcal{K}$ of prime residuals of L such that $\bigcup_{K' \in \mathcal{K}} K' = K^a$;
- Q_0 is the set of prime residuals of L such that $\bigcup_{K \in Q_0} K = L$; and
- F_L is the set of prime residuals of L that contain the empty word.

We claim that a word $w \in \Sigma^*$ is accepted from state K iff $w \in K$. This implies $\mathcal{L}(A_L) = L$ as desired.

We proceed by induction on $|w|$. If $w = \varepsilon$, then w is accepted from state K iff $K \in F_L$ iff $\varepsilon \in K$. Assume that $w = av$ for some letter a and word v. If w is accepted from K, then there exists $K' \in \delta(K, a)$ such that v is accepted from K'. By induction hypothesis, we have $v \in K'$. Since $K' \subseteq K^a$, we have $v \in K^a$ and hence $w = av \in K$. Conversely, if $w \in K$, then we have $v \in K^a$. By definition of δ, we have $v \in K'$ for some $K' \in \delta(K, a)$. By induction hypothesis, v is accepted from K', which implies that w is accepted from K. $\square$

★ ■ **Exercise 53.** Let $Rev(A)$ be the algorithm of exercise 14 that, given an NFA A as input, returns a trimmed NFA A^R such that $\mathcal{L}(A^R) = \mathcal{L}(A)^R$, where L^R denotes the reverse of L. Recall that an NFA is trimmed if every state accepts at least one word (see exercise 52). Prove that, for every NFA A, the following DFA is the unique minimal DFA that accepts $\mathcal{L}(A)$:

$$NFAtoDFA(Rev(NFAtoDFA(Rev(A)))).$$

Solution: Let $B = NFAtoDFA(Rev(A))$ and $C = Rev(B)$. The following holds:

$$\mathcal{L}(B) = \mathcal{L}(A)^R \text{ and } \mathcal{L}(C) = \mathcal{L}(B)^R = \left(\mathcal{L}(A)^R\right)^R = \mathcal{L}(A).$$

Since B is deterministic, NFA C is reverse-deterministic. Moreover, since B has one single initial state, C has a single final state. Finally, by definition of Rev, C is trimmed. Thus, by exercise 52, $D = NFAtoDFA(C)$ is a minimal DFA recognizing the same language as C, which is $\mathcal{L}(A)$. $\square$

★ 回 **Exercise 54.**

(a) Let $\Sigma = \{a, b\}$. Find a language $L \subseteq \Sigma^*$ that has infinitely many residuals and that satisfies $|L^w| > 0$ for all $w \in \Sigma^*$.

(b) Let $\Sigma = \{a\}$. Find a language $L \subseteq \Sigma^*$, such that $L^w = L^{w'} \implies w = w'$ for all words $w, w' \in \Sigma^*$.

Solution:

(a) $L = \{ww : w \in \Sigma^*\}$. First we prove that L has infinitely many residuals by showing that for each pair of words of the infinite set $\{a^i b : i \geq 0\}$, the corresponding residuals are not equal. Let $u = a^i b$ and $v = a^j b$ be such that $i < j$. We have $L^u \neq L^v$ since $u \in L^u$, but $u \notin L^v$. For the second half of the statement, observe that $w \in L^w$ for any word $w \in \Sigma^*$.

(b) Let $L = \{a^{2^n} : n \geq 0\}$. Let $i < j$. We show that $L^{a^i} \neq L^{a^j}$. Let d_i and d_j denote respectively the distance from i and j to the closest larger power of 2 (e.g., if $i = 13$, then $d_i = 16 - i = 3$). If $d_i < d_j$, then we are done since $a^{d_i} \in L^{a^i}$ and $a^{d_i} \notin L^{a^j}$. Similarly, if $d_i > d_k$, then $a^{d_i} \notin L^{a^i}$ and $a^{d_i} \in L^{a^j}$. Thus, assume $d_i = d_j$. Let d_i' and d_j' denote the distance from i and j to the second closest larger power of 2 (e.g., if $i = 13$, then $d_i' = 32 - i = 19$). These two numbers must be unequal since the gaps between powers of 2 are strictly increasing. Thus, we are done by repeating the above argument.

★■ **Exercise 55.** Recall the master automaton M defined in section 2.1.1. Does M have...

(a) other states than $\emptyset$ and Σ^* that can only reach themselves?
(b) states that cannot be reached from any other state?
(c) states that can reach all other states?
(d) states with infinitely many immediate predecessors?
(I.e., states L such that $L' \xrightarrow{a} L$ for infinitely many states L'?)
(e) two states having the same successor for every letter of Σ?
(f) bottom strongly connected components with infinitely many states?
(A bottom strongly connected component is a maximal set of states S such that for every state $s \in S$, the set of states reachable from S is exactly S.)
(g) bottom strongly connected components with arbitrarily many states?

Solution: Let L, L' denote both a language and a regular expression for it.

(a) No. The only two such states are $\emptyset$ and Σ^*. If a state L can only reach itself, then the canonical DFA for L has one state. There are two DFAs with one state, differing in whether this state is final or not. They recognize the languages Σ^* and $\emptyset$, and so these are the only two states of M.

(b) No. For every language L, consider the language $L' = a \cdot L$. We have $L' \neq L$, because the shortest words of L are strictly shorter than the shortest words of L'. The master automaton has a transition $L' \xrightarrow{a} L$. For example, in figure 2.4, we have $a\Sigma + b(\varepsilon + \Sigma^2\Sigma) \xrightarrow{a} \Sigma$.

(c) No. The states reachable from a state L are the states of the canonical DFA for L, and there are only finitely many of them.

(d) It depends. If Σ has at least two elements, then every language of the form $a \cdot L + b \cdot L''$, where $a \neq b$ and L'' is arbitrary, has a transition $a \cdot L + b \cdot L'' \xrightarrow{a} L$, and so every language L has infinitely many predecessors. If the alphabet contains only one letter, say a, then L has exactly two predecessors—namely, the languages aL and $aL + \varepsilon$.

(e) Yes. Let L be any regular language such that $\varepsilon \in L$. Languages L and $L \setminus \{\varepsilon\}$ have the same successors for every letter in the alphabet. In figure 2.4, we have $\Sigma \xrightarrow{a} \varepsilon$, and $\Sigma + \varepsilon \xrightarrow{a} \varepsilon$, which is not depicted.

(f) No. If there were, then there would be states that can reach infinitely many other states.

(g) Yes. Fix $n \geq 0$ and $a \in \Sigma$. For every $0 \leq m < n$, let L_m be the language of all words $w \in \Sigma^*$ such that the number of as in w is congruent to m modulo n. The set of languages $\{L_0, \ldots, L_m\}$ is a bottom strongly connected component of the master automaton. For example, over $\Sigma = \{a, b\}$, there is a bottom strongly connected component consisting of words with an odd number of as and words with an even number of as:

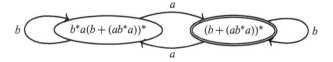

✩ ■ **Exercise 56.** Recall the master automaton M defined in section 2.1.1. A *symmetry* is a bijection f on the states of the master automaton such that $L \xrightarrow{a} L'$ iff $f(L) \xrightarrow{a} f(L')$. Loosely speaking, after applying f, we still obtain the same graph. Show that the bijection given by $f(L) = \overline{L}$ is a symmetry.

Solution: We have $\overline{L^a} = (\overline{L})^a$ since

$$w \in \overline{L^a} \text{ iff } w \notin L^a \text{ iff } aw \notin L \text{ iff } aw \in \overline{L} \text{ iff } w \in (\overline{L})^a.$$

Let us show $L \xrightarrow{a} L'$ iff $\overline{L} \xrightarrow{a} \overline{L'}$. Assume $L \xrightarrow{a} L'$. We have $L' = L^a$. Further, $\overline{L} \xrightarrow{a} (\overline{L})^a$ holds by definition of the master automaton. Since $(\overline{L})^a = \overline{L^a} = f(L^a)$, we get $\overline{L} \xrightarrow{a} \overline{L'}$. Now, assume $\overline{L} \xrightarrow{a} \overline{L'}$. By the result we have just proved, we have $\overline{\overline{L}} \xrightarrow{a} \overline{\overline{L'}}$, and so $L \xrightarrow{a} L'$. Observe, however, that the symmetry exchanges final and nonfinal states. Indeed, we have $\varepsilon \in L$ iff $\varepsilon \notin \overline{L}$. In figure 2.4, this symmetry is graphically represented as a reflection on the horizontal axis.   □

★ ■ **Exercise 57.** Recall that weakly acyclic DFAs were introduced in exercise 35. Show that weakly acyclic DFAs are closed under minimization (i.e., prove that the unique minimal DFA equivalent to a given weakly acyclic DFA is also weakly acyclic).

Solution: Let $A = (Q, \Sigma, \delta, q_0, F)$ be a weakly acyclic DFA. Given two states $p, q \in Q$, we write $p \preceq q$ if $p \xrightarrow{w} q$ for some word $w \in \Sigma^*$. As shown in exercise 35(a), the relation $\preceq$ is a partial order.

Let B be the minimal DFA equivalent to A. For the sake of contradiction, suppose that B is not weakly acyclic. By exercise 35(a), B has a cycle of length at least 2. Since the states of B are equivalence classes of the language partition of A, this cycle contains two distinct states $Q_1, Q_2 \subseteq Q$. Since B is minimal, we have $\mathcal{L}(Q_1) \neq \mathcal{L}(Q_2)$, and $\mathcal{L}(Q_1) \neq \emptyset \neq \mathcal{L}(Q_2)$. By definition of B, $q \xrightarrow{w_1} r \xrightarrow{w_2} s$ holds in A for some $q, s \in Q_1$, $r \in Q_2$, and words $w_1, w_2 \in \Sigma^*$. By definition of $\preceq$, we have $q \preceq r \preceq s$. Moreover, we have $q \neq s$ because otherwise, A would not be weakly acyclic. Since $q, s \in Q_1$ and $r \in Q_2$, we have $\mathcal{L}(q) = \mathcal{L}(s)$ and $\mathcal{L}(q) \neq \mathcal{L}(r) \neq \mathcal{L}(s)$. We show that this leads to a contradiction.

Let $w = w_1 w_2$, and let $\Gamma \subseteq \Sigma$ be the set of letters that occur in w. Let s_{max} be the maximal state of A w.r.t. $\preceq$ such that $q \xrightarrow{w^n} s_{max}$ for some $n \geq 1$. We have $\mathcal{L}(q)^w = \mathcal{L}(s) = \mathcal{L}(q)$. Therefore, by repeating this identity n times, we obtain $\mathcal{L}(q) = \mathcal{L}(q)^{w^n} = \mathcal{L}(s_{max})$. Further, since s_{max} is maximal, we have $s_{max} \xrightarrow{w} s_{max}$. Finally, since A is weakly acyclic, $s_{max} \xrightarrow{a} s_{max}$ for every letter $a \in \Gamma$. So $\mathcal{L}(q) = \mathcal{L}(s_{max}) = \Gamma^* L$ for some nonempty language L. Since $\mathcal{L}(r) = \mathcal{L}(q)^{w_1}$ and $w_1 \in \Gamma^*$, we have $\mathcal{L}(r) = \Gamma^* L$. Thus, $\mathcal{L}(q) = \mathcal{L}(r)$, which is a contradiction.   □

Solutions for Chapter 3

✩ ▣ **Exercise 60.** Give a regular expression for the words over $\{0, 1\}$ that do not contain 010 as subword.

Solution: Different solutions are possible (e.g., $(1 + 00^*11)^*(0^* + 00^*1))$ which we can obtain as follows. First, we construct an NFA for the words containing 010 as a subword:

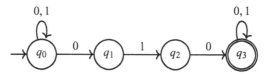

Determinization and complementation yield

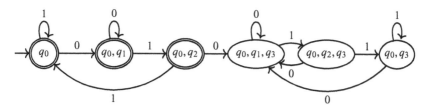

We safely remove the three rightmost states as they cannot reach final states:

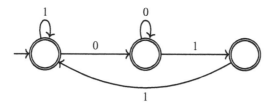

We further turn the automaton into an NFA-ε, which can then be converted into a regular expression:

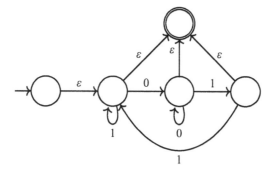

We may now convert the automaton into a regular expression. After removing one state, we obtain

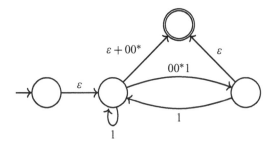

After removing a second state, we obtain

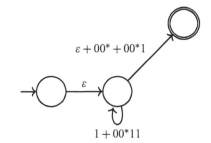

After removing the last state, we obtain the final expression $(1 + 00^*11)^*(\varepsilon + 00^* + 00^*1)$, which can be simplified to $(1 + 00^*11)^*(0^* + 00^*1)$:

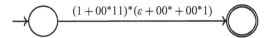

✦ ⚙ **Exercise 61.** In example 1.9, we presented an automaton that recognizes words over alphabet $\Sigma = \{-, \cdot, 0, 1, \ldots, 9\}$ that encode real numbers with a finite decimal part (e.g., 37, 10.503, and -0.234 are accepted, but 002, -0, and 3.10000000 are not). This language is described by these four properties:

(a) a word encoding a number consists of an integer part, followed by a possibly empty fractional part; the integer part consists of an optional minus sign, followed by a nonempty sequence of digits;

(b) if the first digit of the integer part is 0, then it is the only digit of the integer part;

(c) if the fractional part is nonempty, then it starts with "." followed by a nonempty sequence of digits that does not end with 0; and

(d) if the integer part is -0, then the fractional part is nonempty.

We seek to obtain the automaton presented in example 1.9 in a more modular and algorithmic way. More precisely, give an automaton for each of the above properties, construct the pairing of these automata, and minimize the resulting automaton.

Solution: Let $D = \{0, 1, \ldots 9\}$ and let $D_+ = D \setminus \{0\}$. We represent properties (a) to (d), respectively, by the following automata:

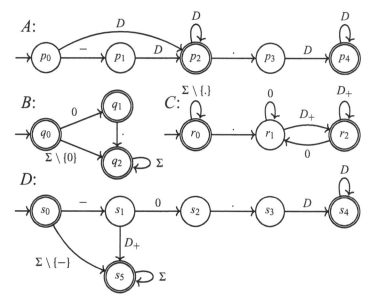

By pairing all four automata, we obtain the following automaton:

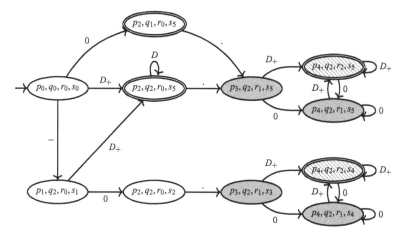

The hatched and solid states above respectively have the same residuals. Hence, they can be merged. This leads to the following minimal automaton, which is exactly the one of example 1.9:

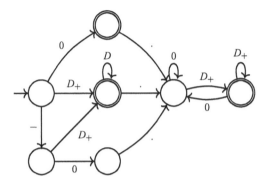

★ 🖳 **Exercise 63.** Find a family of NFAs $\{A_n\}_{n\geq1}$ with $\mathcal{O}(n)$ states such that *every* NFA recognizing the complement of $\mathcal{L}(A_n)$ has at least 2^n states.

Hint: See exercise 21.

Solution: Let $L_n = \{ww : w \in \{0,1\}^n\}$. The language $\overline{L}_n$ is made of the set X_n of all words of length different from $2n$, plus the set Y_n of all words w such that the ith and $(i+n)$th letter of w differ for some $1 \leq i \leq n$. Note that X_n and Y_n are not disjoint. We give NFAs for these two languages for the case $n = 3$, from which the general construction can be easily deduced. Here is a NFA recognizing X_3:

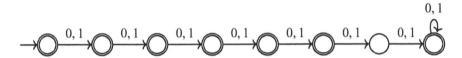

Let us construct an NFA for Y_3. The NFA nondeterministically chooses a position $1 \leq i \leq 3$ and the letter at that position: if the letter is 0, it moves up, otherwise down. The NFA then reads two more letters and checks that the next letter is the opposite of the one it chose:

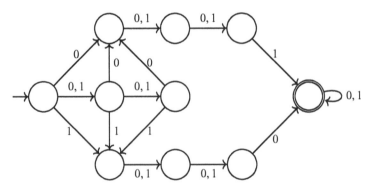

☆ ■ **Exercise 65.** Consider the variant of *IntersNFA* in which line 7

if $(q_1 \in F_1)$ **and** $(q_2 \in F_2)$ **then add** $[q_1, q_2]$ **to** F

is replaced by

if $(q_1 \in F_1)$ **or** $(q_2 \in F_2)$ **then add** $[q_1, q_2]$ to F.

Let $A_1 \otimes A_2$ be the result of applying this variant to two NFAs A_1 and A_2. An NFA $A = (Q, \Sigma, \delta, Q_0, F)$ is *complete* if $\delta(q, a) \neq \emptyset$ for all $q \in Q$ and all $a \in \Sigma$.

- Prove the following: If A_1 and A_2 are complete NFAs, then $\mathcal{L}(A_1 \otimes A_2) = \mathcal{L}(A_1) \cup \mathcal{L}(L_2)$.
- Give NFAs A_1 and A_2, which are *not complete* and such that $\mathcal{L}(A_1 \otimes A_2) = \mathcal{L}(A_1) \cup \mathcal{L}(A_2)$.

Solution:

- Let $A_1 = (Q_1, \Sigma, \delta_1, Q_{01}, F_1)$ and $A_2 = (Q_2, \Sigma, \delta_2, Q_{02}, F_2)$ be complete NFAs. Note that any word can be read in both automata by completeness. Hence, if A_1 accepts a word w, then A_2 can read it (regardless of whether it is accepted or not) and vice versa. Thus, we have

$$w \in \mathcal{L}(A_1) \cup \mathcal{L}(A_2)$$

$$\iff \exists q_{01} \xrightarrow{w} q_1, q_{02} \xrightarrow{w} q_2, q_{01} \in Q_{01}, q_{02} \in Q_{02}, (q_1 \in F_1 \vee q_2 \in F_2)$$

$$\iff \exists [q_{01}, q_{02}] \xrightarrow{w} [q_1, q_2] \text{ and } [q_1, q_2] \in F.$$

- The two first NFAs below accept $(a+b)^*a$ and $(a+b)^*b$, respectively, and the resulting third NFA correctly accepts $(a+b)^*(a+b)$:

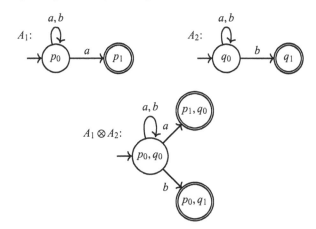

★ 🔲 **Exercise 66.** The *even part* of a word $w = a_1 a_2 \cdots a_n$ over alphabet Σ is the word $a_2 a_4 \cdots a_{2 \cdot \lfloor n/2 \rfloor}$. Given an NFA A, construct an NFA A' such that $\mathcal{L}(A')$ is the even parts of the words of $\mathcal{L}(A)$.

Solution: Let $A = (Q, \Sigma, \delta, Q_0, F)$. We define the NFA $A' = (Q, \Sigma, \delta', Q_0, F')$ as follows. For every, $q \in Q$ and $a, b \in \Sigma$, we let $\delta'(q, b) = \hat{\delta}(q, ab)$. By taking $F' = F$, we would obtain an automaton A' that accepts the even parts of the even-length words of $\mathcal{L}(A)$. To deal with odd-length words, we instead set $F' = F \cup \{q \in Q : \delta(q, a) \cap F \neq \emptyset$ for some $a \in \Sigma\}$. For example:

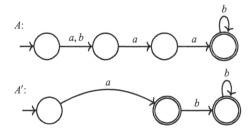

☆ 🖳 **Exercise 67.** Let $L_i = \{w \in \{a\}^* : \text{the length of } w \text{ is divisible by } i\}$.

(a) Construct an NFA for $L = L_4 \cup L_6$ with a single initial state and at most eleven states.
(b) Construct the minimal DFA for L.

Solution: The NFA is as follows:

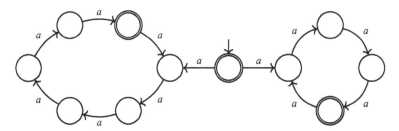

We construct DFAs for L_4 (four states) and L_6 (six states), construct the union by taking the pairing (twenty-four states), and minimize. The resulting minimal DFA has states $Q = \{0, 1, \ldots, 11\}$ organized in a circle (i.e., where $\delta(i, a) = (i + 1) \bmod 12$). Its final states are $F = \{0, 4, 6, 8\}$.

☆ ✦ **Exercise 68.** Modify algorithm *Empty* so that it returns a witness when the automaton is nonempty (i.e., a word accepted by the automaton). Explain how could you further return a *shortest* witness. What is the complexity of your procedure?

Solution: We can perform a breadth-first search of the automaton from the set of initial states. If the search terminates without finding any final state, then we return "empty." Otherwise, we halt the search as soon as some final state q_f is found.

During the search, each time a state q is discovered via a transition $p \xrightarrow{a} q$, we store $\text{pred}[q] = (p, a)$. This allows to reconstruct a shortest path (labeled by some word) backward from q_f to some initial state q_0. The procedure runs in linear time w.r.t. the number of states and transitions. Note that if there is a total order on the letters (e.g., $a < b < c < \cdots < z$), then prioritizing them in that order will further yield a shortest certificate with respect to the lexicographical order.

★ 🔲 **Exercise 72.** Let Σ_1, Σ_2 be two alphabets. A *homomorphism* is a map $h\colon \Sigma_1^* \to \Sigma_2^*$ such that $h(\varepsilon) = \varepsilon$ and $h(uv) = h(u)h(v)$ for every $u, v \in \Sigma_1^*$. Observe that if $\Sigma_1 = \{a_1, \ldots, a_n\}$, then h is completely determined by the values $h(a_1), \ldots, h(a_n)$. Let $h\colon \Sigma_1^* \to \Sigma_2^*$ be a homomorphism.

(a) Construct an NFA for the language $h(\mathcal{L}(A)) = \{h(w) : w \in \mathcal{L}(A)\}$ where A is an NFA over Σ_1.

(b) Construct an NFA for $h^{-1}(\mathcal{L}(A)) = \{w \in \Sigma_1^* : h(w) \in \mathcal{L}(A)\}$ where A is an NFA over Σ_2.

(c) Recall that the language $\{0^n 1^n : n \in \mathbb{N}\}$ is not regular. Use the preceding results to show that $\{(01^k 2)^n 3^n : k, n \in \mathbb{N}\}$ is also not regular.

Solution:

(a) We consider $A = (Q, \Sigma_1, \delta, q_0, F)$ to be a DFA as we could otherwise determinize it. We construct a finite automaton $A' = (Q, \Sigma_2, \delta', q_0, F)$ whose transitions are labeled by words over Σ_2, more precisely by the words $h(\Sigma_1) = \{h(a) : a \in \Sigma_1\}$. Note that this set is finite as Σ_1 is finite. We set $\delta'(q, h(a)) = \delta(q, a)$ for all $a \in \Sigma_1$. In other words, we apply h to the edge labels of the graph underlying A (i.e., if $q \xrightarrow{a} q'$ in A, then $q \xrightarrow{h(a)} q'$ in A').

Let us show that $\mathcal{L}(A') = h(\mathcal{L}(A))$.

⊇) Consider some word $w = a_1 a_2 \cdots a_n \in \mathcal{L}(A)$. There is an accepting run of A on w, that is,

$$q_0 \xrightarrow{a_1} q_1 \xrightarrow{a_2} \cdots \xrightarrow{a_n} q_n \text{ with } q_n \in F.$$

By definition of δ', we have $q_i \xrightarrow{h(a_i)} q_{i+1}$ in A' for all transitions along this run. So $w' = h(w)$ is accepted by A', and so $h(\mathcal{L}(A)) \subseteq \mathcal{L}(A')$.

⊆) Let $w' \in \mathcal{L}(A')$. There is some accepting run of A'

$$q_0 \xrightarrow{u_1} q_1 \xrightarrow{u_2} \cdots \xrightarrow{u_n} q_n \text{ with } q_n \in F \text{ and } u_i \in h(\Sigma_1).$$

By definition of δ', for every transition $q_i \xrightarrow{u_i} q_{i+1}$ of A', there is some letter $a_i \in \Sigma_1$ with $h(a_i) = u_i$ such that $q_i \xrightarrow{a_i} q_{i+1}$ in A. By construction, the following is an accepting run of A:

$$q_0 \xrightarrow{a_1} q_1 \xrightarrow{a_2} \cdots \xrightarrow{a_l} q_n \text{ with } q_n \in F.$$

Therefore, $a_1 a_2 \cdots a_n \in \mathcal{L}(A)$ and $h(a_1 a_2 \ldots a_n) = w'$. So, $\mathcal{L}(A') \subseteq h(\mathcal{L}(A))$. □

(b) We consider $A' = (Q, \Sigma_2, \delta, q_0, F)$ to be a DFA as we could otherwise determinize it. We construct a finite automaton A accepting $h^{-1}(\mathcal{L}(A'))$. Intuitively, a transition of A labeled by $a \in \Sigma_1$ summarizes the behavior of A' when reading the word $h(a)$. Let

$$\delta(q, a) = \hat{\delta}'(q, h(a)) \text{ for all } a \in \Sigma_1.$$

Let $A = (Q, \Sigma_1, \delta, q_0, F)$. We claim that $\hat{\delta}(q_0, w) = \hat{\delta}'(q_0, h(w))$ for every $w \in \Sigma_1^*$. Its validity shows that $\mathcal{L}(A) = h^{-1}(\mathcal{L}(A'))$ as desired. Let us prove the claim by induction on $|w|$. If $|w| = 0$, then $w = \varepsilon$ and the claim is obvious. If $|w| > 0$, then $w = ua$ for some $u \in \Sigma_1^*$ and

$a \in \Sigma_1$. We have

$$\hat{\delta}(q_0, w) = \delta(\hat{\delta}(q_0, u), a)$$

$$= \delta(\hat{\delta}'(q_0, h(u)), a) \qquad \text{(by induction hypothesis)}$$

$$= \hat{\delta}'(\hat{\delta}'(q_0, h(u)), h(a)) \qquad \text{(by def. of } \delta\text{)}$$

$$= \hat{\delta}'(q_0, h(u)h(a))$$

$$= \hat{\delta}'(q_0, h(ua)) \qquad \text{(since } h \text{ is a homomorphism)}$$

$$= \hat{\delta}'(q_0, h(w)). \qquad\qquad\qquad\qquad\qquad\qquad\qquad\qquad \square$$

(c) Let $L = \{(01^k 2)^n 3^n : k, n \geq 0\}$. For the sake of contradiction, suppose that L is regular (i.e., that there exists some finite automaton A with $L = \mathcal{L}(A)$). Let $h \colon \{0, 1, 2, 3\}^* \to \{0, 1\}^*$ be the homomorphism uniquely determined by

$$h(0) = 0, h(1) = \varepsilon, h(2) = \varepsilon \text{ and } h(3) = 1.$$

We have $h(L) = \{0^n 1^n : n \geq 0\}$. By the preceding results, there is a finite automaton A' with $\mathcal{L}(A') = \{0^n 1^n : n \geq 0\}$, which is a contradiction. $\qquad\qquad\qquad\qquad\qquad \square$

☆ ✔ **Exercise 74.** Given alphabets Σ and Δ, a *substitution* is a map $f \colon \Sigma \to 2^{\Delta^*}$ assigning to each letter $a \in \Sigma$ a language $L_a \subseteq \Delta^*$. A substitution f can be canonically extended to a map $2^{\Sigma^*} \to 2^{\Delta^*}$ by defining $f(\varepsilon) = \varepsilon$, $f(wa) = f(w)f(a)$, and $f(L) = \bigcup_{w \in L} f(w)$. Note that a homomorphism can be seen as the special case of a substitution in which all L_as are singletons.

Let $\Sigma = \{\text{Name}, \text{Tel}, :, \#\}$, let $\Delta = \{A, \ldots, Z, 0, 1, \ldots, 9, :, \#\}$, and let f be the substitution:

$$f(\text{Name}) = (A + \cdots + Z)^*$$
$$f(:) = \{:\}$$
$$f(\text{Tel}) = 0049(1 + \ldots + 9)(0 + 1 + \ldots + 9)^{10} +$$
$$\qquad\qquad 00420(1 + \ldots + 9)(0 + 1 + \ldots + 9)^8$$
$$f(\#) = \{\#\}$$

(a) Draw a DFA recognizing $L = \text{Name} : \text{Tel}(\#\text{Tel})^*$.

(b) Sketch an NFA recognizing $f(L)$.

(c) Give an algorithm that takes as input an NFA A, a substitution f, and for every $a \in \Sigma$ an NFA recognizing $f(a)$ and returns an NFA recognizing $f(\mathcal{L}(A))$.

Solution:

(a)

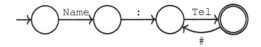

(b)

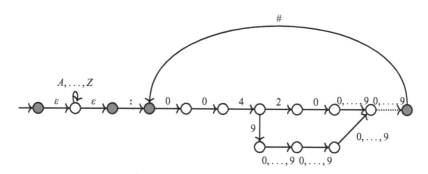

(c) As suggested by the above example, to replace each transition $p \xrightarrow{a} q$, we remove the transition, make a copy of the NFA for $f(a)$, add ε-transitions from p to its initial states, and add ε-transitions from its final states to q. Once this is done, we can remove the ε-transitions.

★ ■ **Exercise 75.** Let A_1 and A_2 be two NFAs with n_1 and n_2 states. Let

$$B = NFAtoDFA(IntersNFA(A_1, A_2)),$$

$$C = IntersDFA(NFAtoDFA(A_1), NFAtoDFA(A_2)).$$

A superficial analysis shows that B and C have $\mathcal{O}(2^{n_1 \cdot n_2})$ and $\mathcal{O}(2^{n_1 + n_2})$ states, respectively, wrongly suggesting that C might be more compact than B. Show that, in fact, B and C are isomorphic and hence have the same number of states.

Solution: The following claims follow easily from the definitions of *NFAtoDFA* and *IntersNFA*:

• Let $A = (Q, \Sigma, \delta, Q_0, F)$ be an NFA. A set $Q' \subseteq Q$ is a state of *NFAtoDFA(A)* iff there is a word $w \in \Sigma^*$ such that $Q' = \delta(Q_0, w)$.

• Let $A_1 = (Q_1, \Sigma, \delta_1, Q_{01}, F_1)$ and $A_2 = (Q_2, \Sigma, \delta_2, Q_{02}, F_2)$ be two NFAs. A pair $[q_1, q_2] \in Q_1 \times Q_2$ is a state of *IntersNFA(A_1, A_2)* iff there is a word $w \in \Sigma^*$ such that $q_1 \in \delta_1(Q_{01}, w)$ and $q_2 \in \delta_2(Q_{02}, w)$.

Combining the claims, we obtain the following:

(a) A pair $[Q_1', Q_2'] \in \mathcal{P}(Q_1) \times \mathcal{P}(Q_2)$ is a state of C iff there is $w \in \Sigma^*$ such that

$$[Q_1', Q_2'] = [\delta_1(Q_{01}, w), \delta_2(Q_{02}, w)].$$

(b) A set $Q' \in \mathcal{P}(Q_1 \times Q_2)$ is a state of B iff there is $w \in \Sigma^*$ such that

$$Q' = \delta_1(Q_{01}, w) \times \delta_2(Q_{02}, w).$$

By (a) and (b), the map $\mathcal{P}(Q_1) \times \mathcal{P}(Q_2) \to \mathcal{P}(Q_1 \times Q_2)$ defined by $[Q_1', Q_2'] \mapsto Q_1' \times Q_2'$ is a bijection between the states of B and C. Moreover, the map preserves transitions; indeed, by definitions of *NFAtoDFA* and *IntersNFA*, we have

- $[Q_1', Q_2'] \xrightarrow{a} (Q_1'', Q_2'')$ in C iff there is $w \in \Sigma^*$ such that

$$[Q_1', Q_2'] = [\delta_1(Q_{01}, w), \delta_2(Q_{02}, w)] \text{ and } [Q_1'', Q_2''] = [\delta_1(Q_{01}, wa), \delta_2(Q_{02}, wa)].$$

- $Q' \xrightarrow{a} Q''$ in B iff there is $w \in \Sigma^*$ such that

$$Q' = \delta_1(Q_{01}, w) \times \delta_2(Q_{02}, w) \text{ and } Q'' = \delta_1(Q_{01}, wa) \times \delta_2(Q_{02}, wa).$$

The mapping also preserves initial and final states, and so it is an isomorphism between B and C.

★ 🎓 **Exercise 76.** Let $A = (Q, \Sigma, \delta, q_0, F)$ be a DFA. A word $w \in \Sigma^*$ is a *synchronizing word* of A if reading w from any state of A leads to a common state (i.e., if there exists $q \in Q$ such that for every $p \in Q$, $p \xrightarrow{w} q$). A DFA is *synchronizing* if it has a synchronizing word.

(a) Show that the following DFA is synchronizing:

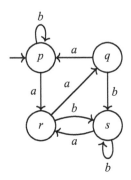

(b) Give a DFA that is not synchronizing.

(c) Give an exponential time algorithm to decide whether a DFA is synchronizing.

Hint: Use the powerset construction.

(d) Show that a DFA $A = (Q, \Sigma, \delta, q_0, F)$ is synchronizing iff for every $p, q \in Q$, there exist $w \in \Sigma^*$ and $r \in Q$ such that $p \xrightarrow{w} r$ and $q \xrightarrow{w} r$.

(e) Give a polynomial time algorithm to test whether a DFA is synchronizing.

Hint: Use d.

(f) Show that (d) implies that every synchronizing DFA with n states has a synchronizing word of length at most $(n^2 - 1)(n - 1)$.

Hint: You might need to reason in terms of pairing.

(g) Show that the upper bound obtained in (f) is not tight by finding a synchronizing word of length $(4-1)^2$ for the following DFA:

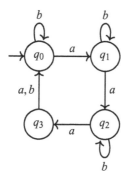

Solution:

(a) ba is a synchronizing word:

$$p \xrightarrow{b} p \xrightarrow{a} r \,,$$

$$q \xrightarrow{b} s \xrightarrow{a} r \,,$$

$$r \xrightarrow{b} s \xrightarrow{a} r \,,$$

$$s \xrightarrow{b} s \xrightarrow{a} r \,.$$

(b) The following DFA is not synchronizing:

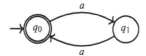

(c) Let $A = (Q, \Sigma, \delta, q_0, F)$ be a DFA, and let $A_q = (Q, \Sigma, \delta, q, F)$ for every $q \in Q$. A word w is synchronizing for A iff reading w from each automaton A_q leads to the same state. Therefore, we build a DFA B that simulates every automaton A_q simultaneously and tests whether a common state can be reached. More formally, let $B = (\mathcal{P}(Q), \Sigma, \delta', \{Q\}, F')$, where

- $\delta'(Q', a) = \{\delta(q, a) : q \in Q'\}$, and
- $F' = \{\{q\} : q \in Q\}$.

Automaton A is synchronizing iff $\mathcal{L}(B) \neq \emptyset$. It is possible to construct B and test $\mathcal{L}(B) \neq \emptyset$ simultaneously by adapting *NFAtoDFA*:

IsSynchronizing(A)
Input: DFA $A = (Q, \Sigma, \delta, q_0, F)$
Output: A is synchronizing?

```
 1   if |Q| = 1 then return true
 2   Q, ← ∅; W ← {Q}
 3   while W ≠ ∅ do
 4      pick Q′ from W
 5      add Q′ to Q
 6      for all a ∈ Σ do
 7         Q″ ← {δ(q, a) : q ∈ Q′}
 8         if |Q″| = 1 then return true
 9         if Q″ ∉ Q then add Q″ to W
10   return false
```

(d)
$\Rightarrow$) Immediate.
$\Leftarrow$) Let $Q = \{q_0, q_1, \ldots, q_n\}$. For every $1 \le i, j \le n$, let $w(i,j) \in \Sigma^*$ be such that $\hat{\delta}(q_i, w(i,j)) = \hat{\delta}(q_j, w(i,j))$. Let us define the following sequence of words:

$$u_1 = w(q_0, q_1)$$

$$u_\ell = w(\hat{\delta}(q_\ell, u_1 u_2 \cdots u_{\ell-1}), \hat{\delta}(q_{\ell-1}, u_1 u_2 \cdots u_{\ell-1})) \qquad \text{for every } 2 \le \ell \le n.$$

We claim that $u_1 u_2 \cdots u_n$ is a synchronizing word. To see that, let us prove by induction on ℓ that for every $1 \le i, j \le \ell$,

$$\hat{\delta}(q_i, u_1 u_2 \cdots u_\ell) = \hat{\delta}(q_j, u_1 u_2 \cdots u_\ell).$$

For $\ell = 1$, the claim holds by definition of u_1. Let $2 \le \ell \le n$. Assume that the claim holds for $\ell - 1$. Let $1 \le i, j \le \ell$. If $i, j < \ell$, then

$$\hat{\delta}(q_i, u_1 u_2 \cdots u_\ell) = \hat{\delta}(\hat{\delta}(q_i, u_1 u_2 \cdots u_{\ell-1}), u_\ell)$$

$$= \hat{\delta}(\hat{\delta}(q_j, u_1 u_2 \cdots u_{\ell-1}), u_\ell) \qquad \text{(by induction hypothesis)}$$

$$= \hat{\delta}(q_j, u_1 u_2 \cdots u_\ell).$$

If $i = \ell$ and $j < \ell$, then

$$\hat{\delta}(q_i, u_1 u_2 \cdots u_\ell) = \hat{\delta}(\hat{\delta}(q_i, u_1 u_2 \cdots u_{\ell-1}), u_\ell)$$

$$= \hat{\delta}(\hat{\delta}(q_{i-1}, u_1 u_2 \cdots u_{\ell-1}), u_\ell) \qquad \text{(by definition of } u_\ell)$$

$$= \hat{\delta}(\hat{\delta}(q_j, u_1 u_2 \cdots u_{\ell-1}), u_\ell) \qquad \text{(by induction hypothesis)}$$

$$= \hat{\delta}(q_j, u_1 u_2 \cdots u_\ell).$$

The case where $i < \ell$ and $i = \ell$ is symmetric, and the case where $i = j = \ell$ is trivial. □

(e) We use the approach used in (c), but instead of simulating every automaton A_q at once, we simulate all pairs A_p and A_q. From (d), this is sufficient. The adapted algorithm is as follows:

IsSynchronizing(A)
Input: DFA $A = (Q, \Sigma, \delta, q_0, F)$
Output: A is synchronizing?

```
1    for all p, q ∈ Q s.t. p ≠ q do
2        if ¬PairSynchronizable(p, q) then return false
3    return true

4    PairSynchronizable(p, q)

5        Q, ← ∅; W ← {{p, q}}
6        while W ≠ ∅ do
7            pick Q' from W
8            add Q' to Q
9            for all a ∈ Σ do
10               Q'' ← {δ(q, a) : q ∈ Q'}
11               if |Q''| = 1 then return true
12               if Q'' ∉ Q then add Q'' to W
13       return false
```

The **for** loop at line 1 is iterated at most $|Q|^2$ times. The **while** loop of the subprocedure is iterated at most $|Q|^2$, and the **for** loop within it is iterated at most $|\Sigma|$ times. Hence, the total running time of the algorithm is in $\mathcal{O}(|Q|^4 \cdot |\Sigma|)$.

Note that our algorithm runs in time $\mathcal{O}(|Q|^4 \cdot |\Sigma|)$ and computes a synchronizing word of length $\mathcal{O}(|Q|^3)$, if there exists one. It is possible to do better. An algorithm presented in [Epp90] computes a synchronizing word of length $\mathcal{O}(|Q|^3)$, if there exists one, in time $\mathcal{O}(|Q|^3 + |Q|^2 \cdot |\Sigma|)$.

(f) We say that a word w is (p, q)-synchronizing if $\hat{\delta}(p, w) = \hat{\delta}(q, w)$. In the proof of (d), we have built a synchronizing word $w = u_1 u_2 \cdots u_{|Q|-1}$ where each u_i is a (p, q)-synchronizing word for some $p, q \in Q$. We claim that if there exists a (p, q)-synchronizing word, then there exists one of length at most $|Q|^2 - 1$. This leads to the overall $(|Q| - 1)(|Q|^2 - 1)$ upper bound. To see that the claim holds, assume for the sake of contradiction that every (p, q)-synchronizing word has length at least $|Q|^2$. Let w be such a minimal word. Let $r = \hat{\delta}(p, w)$. We have

$$p \xrightarrow{w} r,$$

$$q \xrightarrow{w} r.$$

This yields the following run in the pairing of A and itself:

$$\begin{bmatrix} p \\ q \end{bmatrix} \xrightarrow{w} \begin{bmatrix} r \\ r \end{bmatrix}.$$

Since $|w(p, q)| \geq |Q|^2$, by the pigeonhole principle, there exist $s, t \in Q, x, z \in \Sigma^*$, and $y \in \Sigma^+$ such that $w = xyz$ and

$$\begin{bmatrix} p \\ q \end{bmatrix} \xrightarrow{x} \begin{bmatrix} s \\ t \end{bmatrix} \xrightarrow{y} \begin{bmatrix} s \\ t \end{bmatrix} \xrightarrow{z} \begin{bmatrix} r \\ r \end{bmatrix}.$$

Hence, xz is a smaller (p, q)-synchronizing word, which is a contradiction. $\qquad \square$

Note that is possible to get a slightly better upper bound. If there exist $s, t \in Q$, $x, z \in \Sigma^*$, and $y \in \Sigma^+$ such that $w = xyz$ and

$$\begin{bmatrix} p \\ q \end{bmatrix} \xrightarrow{x} \begin{bmatrix} s \\ t \end{bmatrix} \xrightarrow{y} \begin{bmatrix} t \\ s \end{bmatrix} \xrightarrow{z} \begin{bmatrix} r \\ r \end{bmatrix},$$

then xz is a also a shorter (p, q)-synchronizing word. Moreover, if there exist $s \in Q$, $x \in \Sigma^*$, and $y \in \Sigma^+$ such that $w = xy$ and

$$\begin{bmatrix} p \\ q \end{bmatrix} \xrightarrow{x} \begin{bmatrix} s \\ s \end{bmatrix} \xrightarrow{z} \begin{bmatrix} r \\ r \end{bmatrix},$$

then x is a shorter (p, q)-synchronizing word. Thus, at most $\binom{n}{2}$ states of the form $[s \, t]$ appear along the path of a minimal (p, q)-synchronizing word, followed by a state of the form $[r \, r]$. Therefore, a minimal (p, q)-synchronizing word is of size at most $\binom{n}{2} = (n^2 - n)/2$. Overall, this yields a synchronizing word of length at most $(n - 1)((n^2 - n)/2) = n^3/2 - n^2 + n/2$.

(g) ba^3ba^3b is such a word. It can be obtained, for example, from the algorithm designed in c:

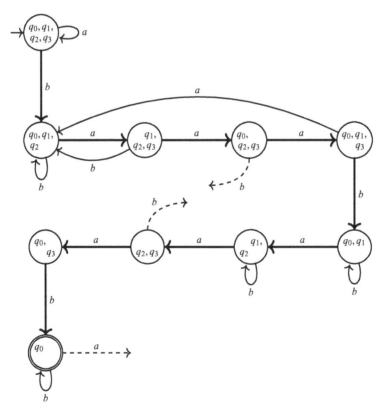

For the interested reader, note that the *Černý conjecture* states that every synchronizing DFA has a synchronizing word of length at most $(|Q| - 1)^2$. Since 1964, no one has been able to prove or disprove this conjecture. To this day, the best upper bound on the length of minimal synchronizing words is $((|Q|^3 - |Q|)/6) - 1$ (see [Pin83]).

★ 🖅 **Exercise 77.**

(a) Prove that the following problem is PSPACE-complete:

Given: DFAs $A_1, \ldots, A_n$ over the same alphabet Σ;
Decide: whether $\bigcap_{i=1}^{n} \mathcal{L}(A_i) = \emptyset$.

Hint: Reduce from the acceptance problem for deterministic linearly bounded automata.

(b) Prove that if the DFAs are acyclic, but the alphabet is arbitrary, then the problem is coNP-complete. Here, acyclic means that the graph induced by transitions has no cycle, apart from a self-loop on a trap state.   *Hint: Reduce from 3-SAT.*

(c) Prove that if Σ is a one-letter alphabet, then the problem is coNP-complete.

Solution: (a) Recall that a linearly bounded automaton is a deterministic Turing machine whose head never leaves the part of the tape containing the input (plus possibly two cells to the left and to the right of the input, so that the machine can recognize when it has reached the "border"). The automaton accepts an input w if its run on w visits some final state.

Given a linearly bounded automaton M and an input $w = a_1 \cdots a_n$, we construct DFAs $A_1, \ldots, A_n$ such that M accepts w iff $\bigcap_{i=1}^{n} \mathcal{L}(A_i) = \emptyset$. Let Q be the set of states of M, and let Σ_M be its alphabet. The transition function of M is of the form $\delta \colon Q \times \Sigma_M \to Q \times \Sigma_M \times \{L, R\}$, where L and R stand for "move left" and "move right." The common alphabet Σ of the DFAs $A_1, \ldots, A_n$ contains all tuples (x, q, a, q', a', L) such that $0 < x \leq n$ and $\delta(q, a) = (q', a', L)$, and all tuples (x, q, a, q', a', R) such that $0 \leq x < n$ and $\delta(q, a) = (q', a', R)$. Intuitively, a letter of Σ contains all the information about a "move" of M: x, q, and a are respectively the current position of the head, the current state, and the letter being currently read; q' and a' are the new state and the new letter; and R or L gives the direction of the move.

The states of the DFA A_i are the tuples (x, q, a) where $0 \leq x \leq n + 1$, $q \in Q$, and $a \in \Sigma_M$, plus a trap state t. Intuitively, A_i is in state (x, q, a) if the head currently reads the xth cell, the current state of M is q, and the current letter on the ith cell is a. The initial state of A_i is $(1, q_0, a_i)$, where q_0 is the initial state of M, and a_i is the ith letter of the input word w. The final states of A_i are the tuples (x, q, a) such that q is a final state of M.

The transition function δ_i of A_i is defined as follows. First, we define $\delta_i(t, \alpha) = t$ for every letter $\alpha \in \Sigma$ (trap state). Let $\sigma = (x, q, a)$ be a state of A_i, and let $\alpha = (y, q_1, a_1, q_2, a_2, D)$ be a letter of Σ. We only consider the case where $D = R$; the case $D = L$ is analogous. We say that σ and α *match* if $x = y$, $q = q_1$ and either $x \neq i$ or $x = i$ and $a = a_1$. We define $\delta_i(\sigma, \alpha)$ as follows:

• If σ and α match and $x \neq i$, then $\delta_i(\sigma, \alpha) = (x + 1, q_2, a)$.
Intuitively, as the head is not on the ith cell, after the move, the ith cell still contains an a.
• If σ and α match and $x = i$, $a = a_1$, then $\delta_i(\sigma, \alpha) = (i + 1, q_2, a_2)$.
Intuitively, since the head writes on the ith cell, we update its contents to a_2.

- If σ and α do not match, then $\delta_i(\sigma, \alpha) = t$ (the trap state).

Intuitively, this corresponds to a "malfunction": M executes a "wrong" letter.

By construction, M can execute a sequence of moves leading to a configuration with the head on cell x, state q, and tape contents $b_1 \cdots b_n$ iff the run of each A_i on the word corresponding to this sequence of moves leads to the state (x, q, b_i). If M accepts x, then, after accepting the sequence of moves, each A_i has reached a final state, and so $\bigcap_{i=1}^{n} \mathcal{L}(A_i) \neq \emptyset$. If M does not accept x, then for every word of Σ^*, one of two cases holds: either the word does not correspond to a legal sequence of moves, in which case after reading it, at least one A_i is in its trap state, or it corresponds to a legal sequence of moves, in which case after reading it, none of the A_i is in a final state. So we have $\bigcap_{i=1}^{n} \mathcal{L}(A_i) = \emptyset$.

(b) For the membership in coNP, observe that an acyclic DFA with m states can only accept words of length at most $m - 1$. Therefore, the set $\bigcap_{i=1}^{n} \mathcal{L}(A_i)$ is nonempty iff it contains a word of length at most $m - 1$, where m is the maximal number of states of $A_1, \ldots, A_n$. Consider the nondeterministic algorithm that guesses a word of length at most $m - 1$ and checks whether it is accepted by all of $A_1, \ldots, A_n$. Since the algorithm runs in polynomial time, the emptiness problem is in coNP.

To prove coNP-hardness, we reduce 3-SAT to the *non*emptiness problem. Let $\varphi = C_1 \wedge \cdots \wedge C_m$ be a boolean formula in CNF over the variables $X = \{x_1, \ldots, x_n\}$, where each clause C_i contains exactly three literals. For every clause C_i, let $L_i \subseteq \{0, 1\}^n$ be the language of truth assignments to the variables of X that satisfy C_i. For example, if $n = 5$ and $C_i = (x_1 \vee x_3 \vee \neg x_4)$, then L_i is the language of the following regular expression:

$$1(0 + 1)^4 + (0 + 1)^2 1(0 + 1)^2 + (0 + 1)^3 0(0 + 1).$$

It is easy to construct a DFA A_i with $\mathcal{O}(n)$ states recognizing L_i. Therefore, the words of $\bigcap_{i=1}^{n} \mathcal{L}(A_i)$ are the truth assignments that satisfy all clauses of φ, and so $\bigcap_{i=1}^{n} \mathcal{L}(A_i) \neq \emptyset$ iff φ is satisfiable.

(c) Let φ be a formula as in (b), and let $p_1, \ldots, p_n$ be the first n prime numbers. We encode a truth assignment $B = b_1 \cdots b_n \in \{0, 1\}^n$ as the number $\widehat{B} = \sum_{i=1}^{n} p_i^{b_i}$. Observe that different assignments are encoded as different numbers because each number has a unique prime decomposition.

For every clause C_i, let N_i be the numbers that are divisible by the prime number corresponding to some positive literal of C_i or nondivisible by the prime number of some negative literal of C_i. For example, let us reconsider $n = 5$ and $C_i = (x_1 \vee x_3 \vee \neg x_4)$. Since the first, third, and fourth prime numbers are 2, 5, and 7, the set N_i contains the numbers that are divisible by 2, or divisible by 5, or not divisible by 7. It follows that a number belongs to N_i iff it is a multiple of the encoding of some assignment satisfying C_i.

Let $L_i = \{a^k : k \in N_i\}$. We sketch how to construct a DFA A_i recognizing L_i by means of the above example. First, we construct three DFAs with 2, 5, and 7 states, recognizing the languages of words whose length is divisible by 2 and 5 and not divisible by 7. Then, we construct a DFA with $2 \cdot 5 \cdot 7 = 70$ states recognizing the union of these languages. In general, if the literals of C_i are $p_{i_1}, p_{i_2}, p_{i_3}$, then the resulting DFA has $p_{i_1} \cdot p_{i_2} \cdot p_{i_3}$ states.

It follows from this construction that $\bigcap_{i=1}^{n} \mathcal{L}(A_i) \neq \emptyset$ iff φ is satisfiable. Indeed, we have $a^k \in \bigcap_{i=1}^{n} \mathcal{L}(A_i)$, iff the truth assignment that sets x_i to **true** iff p_i divides k is a satisfying assignment of φ. It remains to show that the DFAs have polynomially many states. For this, we use a well-known bound on the size of the nth prime number (see the prime number theorem): $p_n < n(\log n + \log \log n) \leq 2n \log n$. Consequently, A_i has at most $\mathcal{O}(n^3 \log n^3)$ states, and we are done.

☆ ■ **Exercise 78.** Let $A = (Q, \Sigma, \delta, Q_0, F)$ be an NFA. Show that, with the universal accepting condition of exercise 21, automaton $A' = (Q, \Sigma, \delta, q_0, Q \setminus F)$ recognizes the complement of $\mathcal{L}(A)$.

Solution: Note that A and A' have exactly the same runs on a given word w. Thus:

A accepts w

$\Longleftrightarrow$ some run of A on w leads to a state of F

$\Longleftrightarrow$ it is not the case that all runs of A' lead to a state of $Q \setminus F$

$\Longleftrightarrow A'$ does not accept w. $\square$

★ ☞ **Exercise 79.** Recall the model of alternating automata introduced in exercise 22.

(a) Show that alternating automata can be complemented by exchanging existential and universal states, as well as final and nonfinal states. More precisely, let $A = (Q_1, Q_2, \Sigma, \delta, q_0, F)$ be an alternating automaton, where Q_1 and Q_2 are respectively the sets of existential and universal states and where $\delta \colon (Q_1 \cup Q_2) \times \Sigma \to \mathcal{P}(Q_1 \cup Q_2)$. Show that the alternating automaton $\overline{A} = (Q_2, Q_1, \Sigma, \delta, q_0, Q \setminus F)$ recognizes the complement of the language recognized by A.

(b) Give linear time algorithms that take two alternating automata recognizing languages L_1 and L_2 and that deliver a third alternating automaton recognizing $L_1 \cup L_2$ and $L_1 \cap L_2$.
Hint: The algorithms are very similar to UnionNFA.

(c) Show that testing emptiness for alternating automata is PSPACE-complete.
Hint: Use exercise 77.

Solution:

(a) For every state q and each automaton B, let $L_B(q)$ be the set of words accepted by the automaton with the same structure as B but having q as initial state. We prove that for every state q and word w, the following holds: $w \in L_A(q)$ iff $w \notin L_{\overline{A}}(q)$. We proceed by induction on $|w|$.

If $|w| = 0$, then $w = \varepsilon$. We have $\varepsilon \in L_A(q)$ iff q is a final state of A iff q is not a final state of $\overline{A}$ iff $\varepsilon \notin L_A(q)$. If $|w| > 0$, then $w = aw'$ for some letter a and word w'. Assume that q is an existential state of A and so a universal state of $\overline{A}$ (the other case is analogous). We have

$$aw' \in L_A(q) \Longleftrightarrow \bigvee_{q' \in \delta(q,a)} w' \in L_A(q') \qquad \text{(as } q \text{ is an exist. state of } A\text{)}$$

$$\Longleftrightarrow \bigvee_{q' \in \delta(q,a)} w' \notin L_{\overline{A}}(q') \qquad \text{(by induction hypothesis)}$$

$$\Longleftrightarrow \neg \bigwedge_{q' \in \delta(q,a)} w' \in L_{\overline{A}}(q') \qquad \text{(by De Morgan's law)}$$

$$\Longleftrightarrow aw' \notin L_{\overline{A}}(q) \qquad \text{(as } q \text{ is a univ. state of } \overline{A}). \qquad \square$$

(b) Let q_{01} and q_{02} be the initial states of the two alternating automata, and let δ_1, δ_2 be their transition functions. For union, we put the two automata side by side; add a fresh initial *existential* state q_0, and add transitions from q_0 to all states in $\delta_1(q_{01}, a) \cup \delta_2(q_{02}, a)$ for every letter a. For intersection, we proceed in the same way but making q_0 *universal* instead of existential.

(c) We reduce from the following problem, which is shown PSPACE-complete in exercise 77:

Given: DFAs $A_1, \ldots, A_n$ over the same alphabet Σ;
Decide: whether $\bigcap_{i=1}^n \mathcal{L}(A_i) = \emptyset$.

   More precisely, given DFAs $A_1, \ldots, A_n$, we consider them as alternating automata made of existential states. We then construct an alternating automaton for their intersection using repeatedly the construction of (b). The resulting automaton has an empty language iff $\bigcap_{i=1}^n \mathcal{L}(A_i) = \emptyset$.

☆ ■ **Exercise 80.** Recall that weakly acyclic DFAs were introduced in exercise 35. Show that if A is a weakly acyclic DFA, then *CompDFA(A)* is also weakly acyclic, and that for all binary boolean operator $\odot$, if A_1 and A_2 are weakly acyclic DFAs, then *BinOp*$[\odot](A_1, A_2)$ is also weakly acyclic.

Solution: The first part follows immediately from the fact that the graphs of A and *CompDFA(A)* coincide. For the second part, assume that A_1 and A_2 are weakly acyclic, but $B = BinOp[\odot](A_1, A_2)$ is not. By exercise 35(a), B has a cycle of length at least 2. Let $[q_1, q_2]$ and $[r_1, r_2]$ be distinct states of the cycle, and let w, v be words such that $[q_1, q_2] \xrightarrow{w} [r_1, r_2] \xrightarrow{v} [q_1, q_2]$. Assume without loss of generality that $q_1 \neq r_1$. By definition of B, we have $q_1 \xrightarrow{w_1} r_1 \xrightarrow{w_1} q_1$ in A_1. Thus, A_1 has a cycle containing at least two distinct states, contradicting that A_1 is weakly acyclic. $\qquad \square$

Solutions for Chapter 4

★ ✔ **Exercise 81.** Use ideas from the main text to design an algorithm for the pattern matching problem that *identifies* a matched $[i,j]$-factor of the text, where position j is minimal and where position i is as close to j as possible (i.e., maximal w.r.t. j). Run your algorithm on text $t = caabac$ and pattern $p = a^+(b+c)a^+ + bac$. What is the complexity of your algorithm?

Solution: Let $A = (Q, \Sigma, \delta, Q_0, F)$ be an NFA for p. Let us assume that $\varepsilon \notin \mathcal{L}(A)$ and $\mathcal{L}(A) \neq \emptyset$ as we can otherwise simply report $(0, 0)$ or $\bot$. Let A' be the NFA obtained by adding a fresh initial state q_{wait} to A, by making Q_0 noninitial, and by allowing q_{wait} to either self-loop on a letter or move to where this letter would lead from Q_0. More formally, let

$A' = (Q \cup \{q_{\text{wait}}\}, \Sigma, \delta', \{q_{\text{wait}}\}, F)$, where δ' extends δ with $\delta'(q_{\text{wait}}, a) = \{q_{\text{wait}}\} \cup \delta(Q_0, a)$ for each $a \in \Sigma$. Note that $\mathcal{L}(A') = \mathcal{L}(\Sigma^* p)$.

We give an algorithm that constructs A' from p and reads the text until a final state q is reached. The moment at which q is reached determines the minimal position j. In order to find the position i, we could store the predecessor of each discovered state and go back from q to an ancestor $p \in Q$ whose predecessor is q_{wait}. This corresponds to the moment where we moved to NFA A and started matching the pattern. There may exist many such moments due to nondeterminism. Since we want the maximal i w.r.t. j, we more carefully store the maximal moments we moved from q_{wait} to A:

FindFactorNFA(t, p)
Input: text $t = a_1 \cdots a_n \in \Sigma^+$, pattern p
Output: indices (i, j) s.t. the $[i, j]$-factor of t matches p, j is minimal and i is maximal w.r.t. j; or $\perp$ if no such factor exists.

```
 1   A ← RegtoNFA(p)
 2   construct A' from A
 3   initialize start[q] ← −∞ for each state q of A'
 4
 5   S ← {q_wait}
 6   for all k = 0 to n − 1 do
 7      S' ← ∅
 8      for all p ∈ S do
 9         for all q ∈ δ'(p, a_{k+1}) do
10            add q to S'
11            if p = q_wait and q ≠ q_wait then start[q] ← k
12            else if p ≠ q_wait then start[q] ← max(start[q], start[p])
13
14         for all q ∈ S' do
15            if q ∈ F then return (start[q], k + 1)
16      S ← S'
17   return ⊥
```

The algorithm takes the same time as solution 1 from the main text (i.e., $\mathcal{O}(k(k+m)^2 + nm^2)$). Indeed, the construction of A' from A and the initialization of "start" can be done in linear time. The rest is as in solution 1 but with the extra constant time checks and bookkeeping operations.

Let us illustrate the algorithm on text $t = caabac$ and pattern $p = a^+(b+c)a^+ + bac$. The automaton A' is as follows, where the original NFA A is depicted in a darker shade (with states q_0 and q_4 formerly initial):

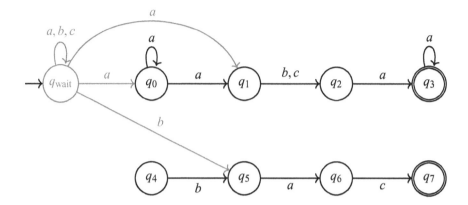

Schematically, reading the five first letters of $t = caabac$ in A' yields this trace:

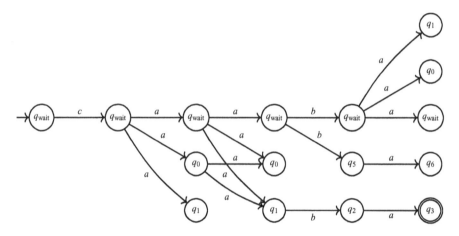

In other words, we can see column k of the above graph as the contents of S at iteration k, and each arc (p, σ, q) indicates the discovery of state q from state p via letter σ. We stop as soon as we discover a final state, here q_3. Paths from q_{wait} to q_3, with no intermediate occurrence of q_{wait}, correspond to factors that match the pattern. In our case, they are $aaba$ (factor $[1, 5]$) and aba (factor $[2, 5]$). We would like to return the latter as $2 > 1$. Hence, the algorithm memorizes the latest "start moment" of each state. Schematically, these numbers would evolve as follows:

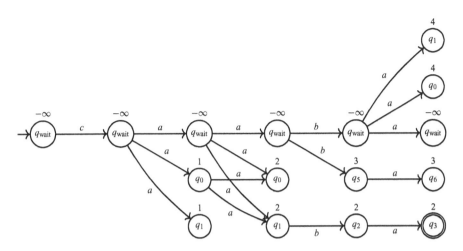

Observe that suffix bac of the text (factor $[3, 6]$) is also a match. It is not detected as we stop as soon as possible. It would be discovered if we were to read the last letter c and discover state q_7.

☆ ✎ **Exercise 83.** Suppose we have an algorithm that solves the pattern matching problem—that is, that finds the first $[i,j]$-factor (w.r.t. j) of a text t that matches a pattern p. How can we use it as a black box to find the *last* $[i,j]$-factor w.r.t. i?

Solution: We first construct the reverse of p inductively using these rules:

$$\emptyset^R = \emptyset \qquad\qquad\qquad (r_1 r_2)^R = r_2^R r_1^R$$

$$\varepsilon^R = \varepsilon \qquad\qquad\qquad (r_1 + r_2)^R = r_1^R + r_2^R$$

$$a^R = a \qquad\qquad\qquad (r^*)^R = (r^R)^*.$$

We then solve the pattern matching problem for text t^R and pattern p^R. If the procedure (as a black box) reports $[i,j]$, then we report $[|t| - j, |t| - i]$.

☆ ✎ **Exercise 84.** Use the ideas of exercises 81 and 83 to obtain an algorithm that solves the pattern matching problem, but this time by finding the first $[i,j]$-factor w.r.t. i (instead of j).

Solution: The algorithm of exercise 81 stops as soon as it finds a final state. We can easily adapt it to stop at the last encountered final state. This would yield a factor $[i,j]$ that matches the pattern and where j is maximal and i is as close to j as possible. Using the idea of exercise 83, we can run our new procedure on t^R and p^R. This will yield a factor $[i,j]$ that matches the pattern and where i is minimal and j is as close to i as possible.

☆ ■ **Exercise 86.** We have shown that lazy DFAs for a word pattern may need more than n steps to read a text of length n but not more than $2n + m$, where m is the length of the pattern. Find a text t and a word pattern p such that the run of B_p on t takes at most n steps and the run of C_p takes at least $2n - 1$ steps.

Hint: A simple pattern of the form a^k is sufficient.

Solution: Let $t = a^{n-1}b$ and $p = a^n$. The automata B_p and C_p are as follows:

B_p:

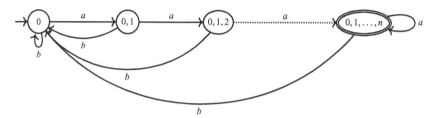

C_p:

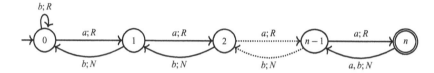

The runs over t on B_p and C_p are, respectively,

$$\{0\} \xrightarrow{a} \{0,1\} \xrightarrow{a} \{0,1,2\} \xrightarrow{a} \cdots \xrightarrow{a} \{0,1,\ldots,n-1\} \xrightarrow{b} \{0\},$$

and

$$0 \xrightarrow{a} 1 \xrightarrow{a} 2 \xrightarrow{a} \cdots \xrightarrow{a} (n-1) \xrightarrow{b} (n-2) \xrightarrow{b} (n-3) \xrightarrow{b} \cdots \xrightarrow{b} 0.$$

⭐ ✎ **Exercise 87.** Give an algorithm that, given a text t and a word pattern p, counts the number of occurrences of p in t. Try to obtain a complexity of $\mathcal{O}(|t| + |p|)$.

Solution: We could "slide a window" and count the number of occurrences of p. However, this would not run in linear time. Instead, we construct a lazy DFA C_p for p and read t in C. We increment a counter each time the final state is reached.

Note that we technically have to count the number of times the final state is reached with R (right move), not from N (no move). However, there is no transition to the final state with N. Indeed, "no moves" occur when a state delegates to its tail. Moreover, the final state contains n, while a tail cannot contain n since it is the largest number.

⭐ ☞ **Exercise 88.** Two-way DFAs are an extension of lazy automata where the reading head is also allowed to move left. Formally, a *two-way DFA (2DFA)* is a tuple $A = (Q, \Sigma, \delta, q_0, F)$ where $\delta : Q \times (\Sigma \cup \{\vdash, \dashv\}) \to Q \times \{L, N, R\}$. Given a word $w \in \Sigma^*$, A starts in q_0 with its reading tape initialized with $\vdash w \dashv$ and its reading head pointing on $\vdash$. When reading a letter, A moves the head according to δ (Left, No move, Right). Moving left on $\vdash$ or right on $\dashv$ does not move the reading head. A accepts w if, and only if, it reaches $\dashv$ in a state of F.

(a) Let $n \in \mathbb{N}$. Give a 2DFA that accepts $(a+b)^*a(a+b)^n$.

(b) Give a 2DFA that does not terminate on any input.

(c) Describe an algorithm to test whether a given 2DFA A accepts a given word w.

(d) Let $A_1, A_2, \ldots, A_n$ be DFAs over a common alphabet. Give a 2DFA B such that

$$\mathcal{L}(B) = \mathcal{L}(A_1) \cap \mathcal{L}(A_2) \cap \cdots \cap \mathcal{L}(A_n).$$

Solution:

(a) The following 2DFA accepts $(a+b)^*a(a+b)^n$. Transitions not drawn lead to a trap state without moving the head.

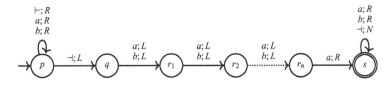

(b)

(c) From (b), we know that simply reading an input word is not sufficient since the automaton could loop forever. Instead, we keep track of all configurations that are encountered when reading the input word w. A configuration is a pair (q, i) where q is a state and $0 \leq i \leq |w| + 1$ is a position of the reading head. If $(q_f, |w| + 1)$ with $q_f \in F$ is encountered, then the automaton accepts w. If a configuration is seen twice, then the automaton loops forever.

We obtain the following algorithm:

Input: 2DFA $A = (Q, \Sigma, \delta, q_0, F)$ and $w \in \Sigma^*$
Output: $w \in \mathcal{L}(A)$?

```
 1   W ← ∅; q ← q₀; i ← 0
 2   while (q, i) ∉ W do
 3       if q ∈ F and i = |w| + 1 then return true
 4
 5       if i = 0 then q, d ← δ(q, ⊢)
 6       else if i = |w| + 1 then q, d ← δ(q, ⊣)
 7       else  q, d ← δ(q, wᵢ)
 8
 9       if d = L and i > 0 then i ← i − 1
10       else if d = R and i ≤ |w| then i ← i + 1
11   return false
```

(d) We build a 2DFA B that first simulates A_1 on w. If a final state of A_1 is reached in $\dashv$, then B rewinds the tape. Automaton B then repeats this process on $A_2, \ldots, A_n$. If every A_i accepts w, then B finally moves the reading head to $\dashv$ in a final state. The construction looks as follows:

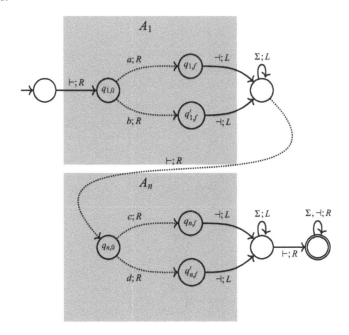

Let $A_i = (Q_i, \Sigma, \delta_i, q_{i,0}, F_i)$. Formally, B is defined as $B = (Q, \Sigma, \delta, \{p\}, \{r\})$, where

- $Q = \{p, s\} \cup Q_1 \cup Q_2 \cup \cdots \cup Q_n \cup \{r_i : 1 \leq i \leq n\}$,

- $\delta(q, a) = \begin{cases} (q_{1,0}, R) & \text{if } q = p \text{ and } a = \vdash, \\ (\delta_i(q, a), R) & \text{if } q \in Q_i \text{ and } a \in \Sigma, \\ (r_i, L) & \text{if } q \in F_i \text{ and } a = \dashv, \\ (r_i, L) & \text{if } q = r_i \text{ and } a \in \Sigma, \\ (q_{i+1,0}, R) & \text{if } q = r_i, a = \vdash \text{ and } 1 \leq i < n, \\ (s, R) & \text{if } q = r_n, a = \vdash, \\ (s, R) & \text{if } q = s, a \in \Sigma \cup \{\dashv\}. \end{cases}$

It is known that the *intersection problem*, which is defined as follows, is PSPACE-complete [Koz77]:

Given: DFAs $A_1, A_2, \ldots, A_n$;
Decide: whether $\mathcal{L}(A_1) \cap \mathcal{L}(A_2) \cap \cdots \cap \mathcal{L}(A_n)$.

We have seen how to build, in polynomial time, a 2DFA B such that $\mathcal{L}(B) = \mathcal{L}(A_1) \cap \mathcal{L}(A_2) \cap \cdots \cap \mathcal{L}(A_n)$. Thus, testing emptiness for 2DFAs is "at least as hard" as the intersection problem (i.e., it is PSPACE-hard). In fact, the emptiness problem for 2DFAs is PSPACE-complete [GJ79, Hun73].

Solutions for Chapter 5

☆ ✔ **Exercise 90.** In phone dials, letters are mapped into digits as follows:

$$\begin{array}{llll} \text{ABC} \mapsto 2 & \text{DEF} \mapsto 3 & \text{GHI} \mapsto 4 & \text{JKL} \mapsto 5 \\ \text{MNO} \mapsto 6 & \text{PQRS} \mapsto 7 & \text{TUV} \mapsto 8 & \text{WXYZ} \mapsto 9 \end{array}$$

This map can be used to assign a telephone number to a given word. For instance, the number for AUTOMATON is 288662866.

Consider the problem of, given a telephone number (for simplicity, we assume that it contains neither 1 nor 0), finding the set of English words that are mapped into it. For instance, the set of words mapping to 233 contains at least ADD, BED, and BEE. Let N be a given DFA over alphabet $\{A, \ldots, Z\}$ that recognizes the set of all English words. Given a number n, explain how to construct an NFA recognizing the set of all words mapped to n.

Solution: Let R be the set of all pairs (m, w) where m is a number, and w is a word mapped to m, and let E be the set of English words. We are looking for an NFA recognizing $\textbf{Post}(\{n\}, R) \cap E$.

Let A_n be the obvious DFA over $\{2, \ldots 9\}$ recognizing the number n. The relation R is recognized by the transducer T_R with one state q_0, both initial and final, and transitions

$$(q_0, [2, A], q_0), (q_0, [2, B], q_0), \ldots, (q_0, [9, Y], q_0), (q_0, [9, Z], q_0).$$

Thus, the NFA we are looking for can be computed as $InterNFA(Post(A_n, T_R), N)$.

☆ ✔ **Exercise 91.** As we have seen, the application of the **Post** and **Pre** operations to transducers requires to compute the padding closure in order to guarantee that the resulting automaton accepts either all or none of the encodings of an object. The padding closure has been defined for encodings where padding occurs *on the right* (i.e., w belongs to the padding closure of an NFA A iff $w\#^k \in \mathcal{L}(A)$ for some $k \in \mathbb{N}$). However, in some natural encodings, like the *most-significant-bit-first* encoding of natural numbers, padding occurs *on the left*. Give an algorithm for computing the padding closure of an NFA when padding occurs on the left (i.e., where we consider $\#^k w$).

Solution: Instead of enlarging the set of final states as done by *PadClosure*, we symmetrically enlarge the set of initial states Q_0 to the set

$$Q_0' = \{q : q_0 \xrightarrow{0^n} q \text{ for some } q_0 \in Q_0, n \in \mathbb{N}\}.$$

This modification yields the following algorithm:

PadClosure'(A, #)
Input: NFA $A = (\Sigma, Q, \delta, Q_0, F)$
Output: new set Q_0' of initial states

```
1   W ← Q₀; Q'₀ ← ∅;
2   while W ≠ ∅ do
3      pick q from W
4      add q to Q'₀
5      for all (q, #, q') ∈ δ do
6         if q' ∉ Q'₀ then add q' to W
7   return Q'₀
```

For example, the NFA depicted below on the left recognizes the set of numbers $\{1, 3\}$ under MSBF encodings ($\# = 0$). Its padding closure, which recognizes the same set, is depicted on the right:

★ ▣ **Exercise 93.** Let $U = \mathbb{N}$ be the universe of natural numbers, and consider MSBF encodings. Give transducers for the sets of pairs $(n, m) \in \mathbb{N}^2$ such that

(a) $m = n + 1$,
(b) $m = \lfloor n/2 \rfloor$,
(c) $n \le 2m$.

Solution:

(a) Two words w_n and w_{n+1} are MSBF encodings of n and $n + 1$ of the same length iff there is a (possibly empty) word w and some $k \ge 0$ such that $w_n = w01^k$ and $w_{n+1} = w10^k$. Thus, the transducer is as follows:

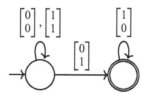

(b) The transducer has to recognize all pairs of words of the form $[0^k wb, 0^k 0w]$, where $w \in \{0, 1\}^*$ and $b \in \{0, 1\}$ since dividing by 2 shifts the bits to the right.

The transducer is shown as follows. It reads $[0, 0]$s until it finds the first 1 of s_n (if any). From this moment on, it moves between the two states labeled by 0 and 1. The intuitive meaning of state 0 is "the last bit of n I have read was a 0" and similarly for state 1. The transitions are then given by the requirement that the next bit of m must be equal to the last bit of n. So, for instance, $\delta(1, [0, 1]) = 0$ because the next bit of m must be a 1, and after reading a 0, the last bit of n read by the transducer is a 0. Note that state 0 could be merged with the initial state.

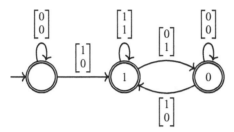

(c) We first construct the two transducers T_1 and T_2, respectively, as follows for relations $\{(n, k) : n \le k\}$ and $\{(k, m) : k = 2m\}$:

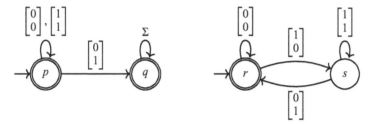

Then, we compute the transducer $T_1 \circ T_2$ as follows for relation $\{(n, m) : n \le 2m\}$:

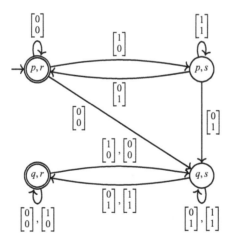

☆ ■ **Exercise 94.** Let U be some universe of objects, and let us fix an encoding of U over Σ^*. Prove or disprove: If a relation $R \subseteq U \times U$ is regular, then the following language is regular:

$$L_R = \{w_x w_y : (w_x, w_y) \text{ encodes a pair } (x, y) \in R\}.$$

Solution: False. Let $U = \{a, b\}^*$, and consider the identity encoding (i.e., a word $w \in \{a, b\}^*$ is encoded by itself and its paddings). The identity relation $R = \{[w, w] : w \in \{a, b\}^*\}$ is regular. Indeed, it is recognized by a transducer with a single state q, both initial and final. However, we have $L_R = \{ww : w \in \{a, b\}^*\}$, which is not regular.

☆ ✔ **Exercise 96.** We have defined transducers as NFAs whose transitions are labeled by pairs of symbols $(a, b) \in \Sigma \times \Sigma$. With this definition, transducers can only accept pairs of words $(a_1 \cdots a_n, b_1 \cdots b_n)$ of the same length, which is not suitable for many applications.

An ε-*transducer* is an NFA whose transitions are labeled by elements of $(\Sigma \cup \{\varepsilon\}) \times (\Sigma \cup \{\varepsilon\})$. An ε-transducer accepts a pair (w, w') of words if it has a run

$$q_0 \xrightarrow{(a_1, b_1)} q_1 \xrightarrow{(a_2, b_2)} \cdots \xrightarrow{(a_n, b_n)} q_n \text{ with } a_i, b_i \in \Sigma \cup \{\varepsilon\}$$

such that $w = a_1 \cdots a_n$ and $w' = b_1 \cdots b_n$. Note that $|w| \leq n$ and $|w'| \leq n$. The relation accepted by the ε-transducer T is denoted by $\mathcal{L}(T)$. The following figure depicts an ε-transducer over alphabet $\{a, b\}$ that, intuitively, duplicates the letters of a word (e.g., on input *aba*, it outputs *aabbaa*).

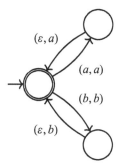

Give an algorithm $Post^\varepsilon(A, T)$ that, given an NFA A and an ε-transducer T, both over a common alphabet Σ, returns an NFA recognizing the language

$$post_{T_\varepsilon}(A) = \{w : \exists\, w' \in \mathcal{L}(A) \text{ such that } (w', w) \in \mathcal{L}(T)\}.$$

Hint: View ε as an additional letter.

Solution: Given an alphabet Σ, let $\Sigma_\varepsilon = \Sigma \cup \{\varepsilon\}$, where we consider ε as a symbol, not as the representation of the empty word. Let T_ε be the *standard* transducer over Σ_ε obtained from T by considering ε as another alphabet letter. So, for instance, if T is the ε-transducer above, then T_ε accepts, for instance, the pair $(a\varepsilon b\varepsilon, aabb)$. Further, let A_ε be NFA over Σ_ε obtained from A by adding to each state q of A a loop (q, ε, q). Clearly, we have

$$\mathcal{L}(A_\varepsilon) = \bigcup_{a_1 \cdots a_n \in \mathcal{L}(A)} \varepsilon^* a_1 \varepsilon^* \cdots \varepsilon^* a_n \varepsilon^*$$

and therefore

$$post_{T_\varepsilon}(A) = proj_\Sigma(post_{T_\varepsilon}(A_\varepsilon)).$$

This equation leads to the following algorithm: first we construct A_ε; then we construct the NFA $B_\varepsilon = Post(A_\varepsilon, T_\varepsilon)$, where $Post$ is the algorithm defined in the chapter; and finally, we construct an NFA B recognizing the projection of $\mathcal{L}(B_\varepsilon)$ onto Σ. Since computing the projection is equivalent to considering ε as the empty word, we can take $B = NFA\varepsilon toNFA(B_\varepsilon)$, where we consider B_ε as an NFA-ε. Thus, more compactly:

$$Post^\varepsilon(A, T) = NFA\varepsilon toNFA(Post(A_\varepsilon, T_\varepsilon)).$$

★ ■ **Exercise 97.** In exercise 96, we have shown how to compute preimages and postimages of relations described by ε-transducers. In this exercise, we show that, unfortunately, and unlike standard transducers, ε-transducers are not closed under intersection.

(a) Construct ε-transducers T_1 and T_2 recognizing the relations

$$R_1 = \{(a^n b^m, c^{2n}) : n, m \ge 0\} \text{ and } R_2 = \{(a^n b^m, c^{2m}) : n, m \ge 0\}.$$

(b) Show that no ε-transducer recognizes $R_1 \cap R_2$.

Solution:

(a)

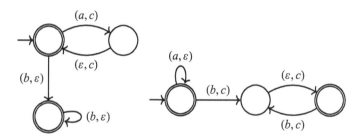

(b) We have $R_1 \cap R_2 = \{(a^n b^n, c^{2n}) : n \ge 0\}$. For the sake of contradiction, suppose there exists an ε-transducer T recognizing $R_1 \cap R_2$. Let us replace each transition of the form

$$q \xrightarrow{(x,y)} q' \text{ by } q \xrightarrow{x} q', \text{ where } x, y \in \Sigma \cup \{\varepsilon\}.$$

We obtain an NFA recognizing the language $\{a^n b^n : n \ge 0\}$, which is not regular. Thus, we derive a contradiction, and hence no ε-transducer recognizes $R_1 \cup R_2$. □

★ ▣ **Exercise 98.** Consider transducers whose transitions are labeled by elements of $(\Sigma \cup \{\varepsilon\}) \times \Sigma^*$. Intuitively, at each transition, these transducers read one letter or no letter and write a string of arbitrary length. These transducers can be used to perform operations on strings like, for instance, capitalizing all the words in the string: if the transducer reads, say, "singing in the rain", it writes "Singing In The Rain". Sketch ε-transducers for the following operations, each of which is informally defined by means of two or three examples. In each example, when the transducer reads the string on the left, it writes the string on the right.

`Company\Code\index.html`	`Company\Code`
`Company\Docs\Spec\specs.doc`	`Company\Docs\Spec`
`International Business Machines`	`IBM`
`Principles Of Programming Languages`	`POPL`
`Oege De    Moor`	`Oege De Moor`
`Kathleen  Fisher   AT&T Labs`	`Kathleen Fisher AT&T Labs`
`Eran Yahav`	`Yahav, E.`
`Bill Gates`	`Gates, B.`
`004989273452`	`+49 89 273452`
`(00)4989273452`	`+49 89 273452`
`273452`	`+49 89 273452`

Solution: We give informal descriptions of the behavior of the ε-transducers.

(a) Here, x ranges over all symbols and y over all symbols but the backslash:

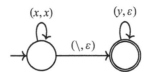

(b) Here, X ranges over uppercase letters and x is either a lowercase letter or a space:

(c) Here, x ranges over all symbols but the space symbol. In order to prevent trailing spaces, we remember seeing a space and output it before the next letter:

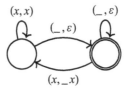

(d) We assume that the string is always of the form `Firstname Lastname`. Here, x ranges over all letters:

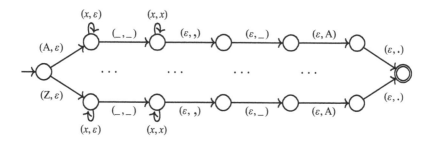

(e)

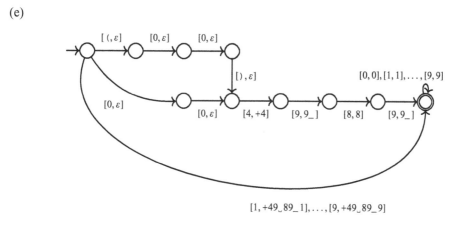

$$[1, +49\_89\_1], \ldots, [9, +49\_89\_9]$$

★ ☞ **Exercise 100.** Transducers can be used to capture the behavior of simple programs. For example, consider this program P and its control-flow diagram:

bool x, y **init** 0
$x \leftarrow ?$
write x
while *true* **do**
    read y **until** $y = x \wedge y$
    if $x = y$ **then write** y **end**
    $x \leftarrow x - 1$ **or** $y \leftarrow x + y$
    if $x \neq y$ **then write** x **end**

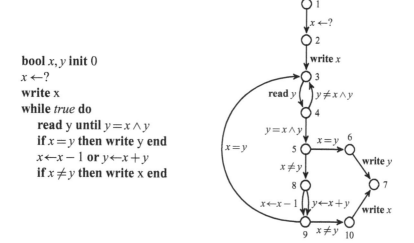

Program P communicates with the environment through its two boolean variables, both initialized to 0. The instruction **end** finishes the execution of P. The I/O-relation of P is the set of pairs $(w_I, w_O) \in \{0, 1\}^* \times \{0, 1\}^*$ such that there is an execution of P, during which P reads the sequence w_I of values and writes the sequence w_O.

Let $[i, x, y]$ denote the configuration of P in which P is at node i of the control-flow diagram, and the values of its two boolean variables are x and y, respectively. The initial configuration of P is $[1, 0, 0]$. By executing the first instruction, P moves nondeterministically to one of the configurations $[2, 0, 0]$ and $[2, 1, 0]$; no input symbol is read and no output symbol is written. Similarly, by executing its second instruction, the program P moves from $[2, 1, 0]$ to $[3, 1, 0]$ while reading nothing and writing 1.

(a) Give an ε-transducer recognizing the I/O-relation of P.

(b) Can an overflow error occur? That is, can a configuration be reached in which the value of x or y is not 0 or 1?

(c) Can node 10 of the control-flow graph be reached?

(d) What are the possible values of x upon termination, that is, upon reaching **end**?

(e) Is there an execution during which P reads 101 and writes 01?

(f) Let I and O be regular sets of inputs and outputs, respectively. Think of O as a set of dangerous outputs that we want to avoid. We wish to prove that the inputs from I are safe, that is, when P is fed inputs from I, none of the dangerous outputs can occur. Describe an algorithm that decides, given I and O, whether there are $i \in I$ and $o \in O$ such that (i, o) belongs to the I/O-relation of P.

Solution:

(a) The states of the transducer are the reachable configurations of P:

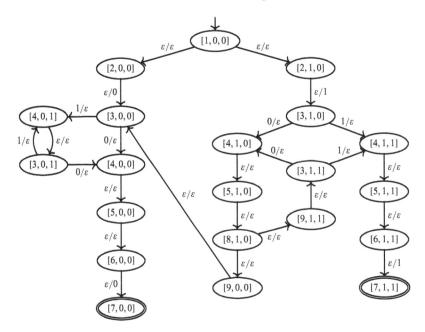

(b) No.

(c) No. The node is redundant. In fact, the last line of P can be removed without changing the behavior.

(d) 0 and 1, because the reachable final configurations are $[7, 0, 0]$ and $[7, 1, 1]$.

(e) Let T be transducer for P, and let A_I and A_O be NFAs recognizing I and O, respectively. A possible algorithm for the task is

$$EmptyNFA(IntersNFA(Post^\varepsilon(A_I, T), A_0)).$$

Solutions for Chapter 6

☆ ✔ **Exercise 102.** Give an *efficient* algorithm that receives as input the minimal DFA of a fixed-length language and returns the number of words it contains.

Solution: The algorithm recursively computes the number of words accepted by each state q of the DFA. If $q = q_\emptyset$, then the number is 0, and if $q = q_\varepsilon$, then it is 1. Otherwise, let $\Sigma = \{a_1, \ldots, a_n\}$ be the alphabet of the DFA; the number of words accepted by q is the sum of the number of words accepted by the a_i-successor of q. In pseudocode, we obtain

number(q)
Input: state q
Output: number of words recognized from q
1   **if** $G(q)$ is not empty **then return** $G(q)$
2   **if** $q = q_\emptyset$ **then return** 0
3   **else if** $q = q_\varepsilon$ **then return** 1
4   **else**
5      $G(q) \leftarrow number(q^{a_1}) + \cdots + number(q^{a_n})$
6   **return** $G(q)$

☆ ✔ **Exercise 103.** The algorithm for fixed-length universality given in table 28 has a best-case runtime equal to the length of the input state q. Give an improved algorithm that only needs $\mathcal{O}(|\Sigma|)$ time for inputs q such that $\mathcal{L}(q)$ is not fixed-size universal.

Solution: Let q be the input to the algorithm, and consider the set of states $\{q^a : a \in \Sigma\}$. If the set contains two distinct states q^a and q^b, then, since every state recognizes a different language, either q^a or q^b is not fixed-length universal, and we can conclude that q is not fixed-length universal. So the algorithm computes q^a for every $a \in \Sigma$ in time $\mathcal{O}(|\Sigma|)$. If at least two states are different, then the algorithm returns **false**. If all states are equal to the same state, say q', then the algorithm calls itself recursively with input q'. In pseudocode, we obtain:

univ′(*q*)
Input: state *q*
Output: **true** if $\mathcal{L}(q)$ is fixed-length universal,
          false otherwise
  1   **if** $q = q_\emptyset$ **then return false**
  2   **else if** $q = q_\varepsilon$ **then return true**
  3   **else**
  4      $q' \leftarrow q^{a_1}$
  5   **for all** $i = 2, \ldots, m$ **do**
  6   **if** $q^{a_i} \neq q'$ **then return false**
  7   **return** *univ′*(*q′*)

★ ✎ **Exercise 106.**

(a) Give an algorithm to compute $\mathcal{L}(p) \cdot \mathcal{L}(q)$ given states *p* and *q* of the fixed-length master automaton.

(b) Give an algorithm to compute both the length and size of $\mathcal{L}(q)$ given a state *q* of the fixed-length master automaton.

(c) The length and size of $\mathcal{L}(q)$ could be obtained in constant time if they were simply stored in the fixed-length master automaton table. Give a new implementation of *make* for this representation.

Solution:

(a) Let *L* and *L′* be fixed-length languages. We have

$$
L \cdot L' = \begin{cases} \emptyset & \text{if } L = \emptyset, \\ L' & \text{if } L = \{\varepsilon\}, \\ \displaystyle\bigcup_{a \in \Sigma} a \cdot L^a \cdot L' & \text{otherwise.} \end{cases}
$$

These identities give rise to the following algorithm:

concat(*p, q*)
Input: states *p* and *q*
Output: state *r* such that $\mathcal{L}(r) = \mathcal{L}(p) \cdot \mathcal{L}(q)$
  1   **if** $G(p, q)$ is not empty **then return** $G(p, q)$
  2   **if** $p = q_\emptyset$ **then return** $q_\emptyset$
  3   **else if** $p = q_\varepsilon$ **then return** q
  4   **else**
  5   **for all** $a \in \Sigma$ **do**
  6         $s_a \leftarrow concat(p^a, q)$
  7      $G(p, q) \leftarrow make(s)$
  8   **return** $G(p, q)$

(b) Let *L* be a fixed-length language. We have

$$length(L) = \begin{cases} \infty & \text{if } L = \emptyset, \\ 0 & \text{if } L = \{\varepsilon\}, \\ length(L^a) + 1 \text{ for any } a \in \Sigma \text{ s.t. } L^a \neq \emptyset & \text{otherwise.} \end{cases}$$

and

$$|L| = \begin{cases} 0 & \text{if } L = \emptyset, \\ 1 & \text{if } L = \{\varepsilon\}, \\ \sum_{a \in \Sigma} |L^a| & \text{otherwise.} \end{cases}$$

These identities give rise to the following algorithm:

len-size(q)
Input: states q
Output: length and size of $\mathcal{L}(q)$
1   **if** $G(q)$ is not empty **then return** $G(q)$
2   **if** $p = q_\emptyset$ **then return** $(\infty, 0)$
3   **else if** $p = q_\varepsilon$ **then return** $(0, 1)$
4   **else**
5      $k \leftarrow \infty$
6      $n \leftarrow 0$
7   **for all** $a \in \Sigma$ **do**
8         $k', n' \leftarrow len\text{-}size(q^a)$
9   **if** $k' \neq \infty$ **then** $k \leftarrow k' + 1$
10        $n \leftarrow n + n'$
11     $G(q) \leftarrow (k, n)$
12   **return** $G(q)$

(c) Let q be a state of the fixed-length master automaton. We denote the length and the size of q, respectively, by $len(q)$ and $|q|$. These values are encoded in two new columns of the table. We set

$$len(q_\emptyset) = \infty, \quad |q_\emptyset| = 0,$$

$$len(q_\varepsilon) = 0, \quad |q_\varepsilon| = 1.$$

From the observations made in (b), we obtain the following algorithm:

make'(q)
Input: mapping s from Σ to the fixed-length master automaton states
Output: state q s.t. $\mathcal{L}(q)^a = s_a$ for each $a \in \Sigma$
1   **if** Table contains s **then return** associated state
2   $r \leftarrow$ new state number
3   $k \leftarrow \infty$
4   $n \leftarrow 0$
5   **for all** $a \in \Sigma$ **do**
6   **if** $s_a \neq q_\emptyset$ **then** $k \leftarrow |s_a| + 1$
7      $n \leftarrow n + len(s_a)$
8   $Table(r) \leftarrow (s, k, n)$
9   **return** r

★ 🔲 **Exercise 107.** Let $k \in \mathbb{N}_{>0}$. Let flip: $\{0, 1\}^k \to \{0, 1\}^k$ be the function that inverts the bits of its input (e.g., flip(010) = 101). Let val: $\{0, 1\}^k \to \mathbb{N}$ be such that val(w) is the number represented by w with the "least-significant-bit-first" encoding.

(a) Describe the minimal transducer that accepts

$$L_k = \left\{ [x, y] \in (\{0, 1\} \times \{0, 1\})^k : \mathrm{val}(y) = \mathrm{val}(\mathrm{flip}(x)) + 1 \bmod 2^k \right\}.$$

(b) Build the state r of the fixed-length master transducer for L_3 and the state q of the fixed-length master automaton for $\{010, 110\}$.

(c) Adapt the algorithm *pre* seen in the chapter to compute *post*(r, q).

Solution:

(a) Let $[x, y] \in L_k$. We flip the bits of x while adding 1. If $x_1 = 1$, then $\neg x = 0$, and so adding 1 to val(flip(x)) results in $y_1 = 1$. Thus, for every $1 < i \le k$, we have $y_i = \neg x_i$. If $x_1 = 0$, then $\neg x_1 = 1$. Adding 1 yields $y_1 = 0$ with a carry. This carry is propagated as long as $\neg x_i = 1$ and thus as long as $x_i = 0$. When some position j with $x_j = 1$ is encountered, the carry is "consumed," and we flip the remaining bits of x. These observations give rise to the following minimal transducer for L_k:

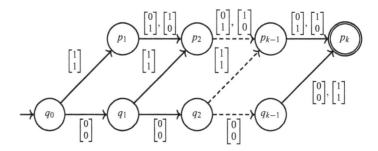

(b) The minimal transducer accepting L_3 is

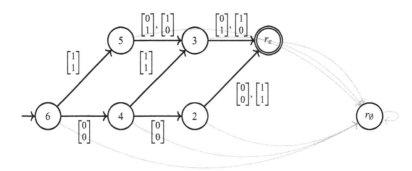

State 4 of the following fragment of the fixed-length master automaton accepts $\{010, 110\}$:

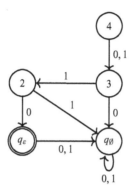

(c) We can establish the following identities similar to those obtained for *pre*:

$$
post_R(L) =
\begin{cases}
\emptyset & \text{if } R = \emptyset \text{ or } L = \emptyset, \\
\{\varepsilon\} & \text{if } R = \{[\varepsilon, \varepsilon]\} \text{ and } L = \{\varepsilon\}, \\
\displaystyle\bigcup_{a,b \in \Sigma} b \cdot post_{R^{[a,b]}}(L^a) & \text{otherwise.}
\end{cases}
$$

To see that these identities hold, let $b \in \Sigma$ and $v \in \Sigma^k$ for some $k \in \mathbb{N}$. We have

$$bv \in post_R(L) \iff \exists a \in \Sigma, u \in \Sigma^k \text{ s.t. } au \in L \text{ and } [au, bv] \in R$$

$$\iff \exists a \in \Sigma, u \in L^a \text{ s.t. } [au, bv] \in R$$

$$\iff \exists a \in \Sigma, u \in L^a \text{ s.t. } [u\,v] \in R^{[a,b]}$$

$$\iff \exists a \in \Sigma \text{ s.t. } v \in Post_{R^{[a,b]}}(L^a)$$

$$\iff v \in \bigcup_{a \in \Sigma} Post_{R^{[a,b]}}(L^a)$$

$$\iff bv \in \bigcup_{a \in \Sigma} b \cdot Post_{R^{[a,b]}}(L^a).$$

We obtain the following algorithm:

post(*r*, *q*)
Input: states *r* and *q* of the fixed-length master transducer and automaton
Output: $Post_R(\mathcal{L}(q))$ where $R = \mathcal{L}(r)$

```
1    if G(r, q) is not empty then return G(r, q)
2    else if r = r∅ or q = q∅ then return q∅
3    else if r = rε and q = qε then return qε
4    else
5        for all b ∈ Σ do
6            p ← q∅
7            for all a ∈ Σ do
8                p ← union(p, post(r^[a,b], q^a))
9            s_b ← p
10       G(r, q) ← make(s)
11   return G(r, q)
```

Note that the transducer for L_3 has a "strong" deterministic property. Indeed, for each state *r* and $b \in \{0, 1\}$, if $r^{[a,b]} \neq r_\emptyset$, then $r^{[\neg a, b]} = r_\emptyset$. Hence, for a fixed $b \in \{0, 1\}$, at most one $post(r^{[a,b]}, q^a)$ can differ from $q_\emptyset$ at line 8 of the algorithm. Thus, unions made on this transducer are trivial, and executing $post(6, 4)$ yields the following computation tree:

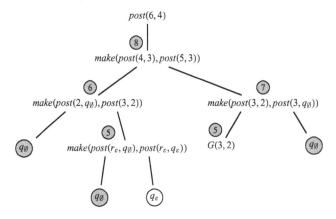

Calling *post*(6, 4) adds the following rows to the fixed-length master automaton table and returns 8:

Ident.	0-succ	1-succ
5	$q_\emptyset$	q_ε
6	$q_\emptyset$	5
7	5	$q_\emptyset$
8	6	7

The new fixed-length master automaton fragment:

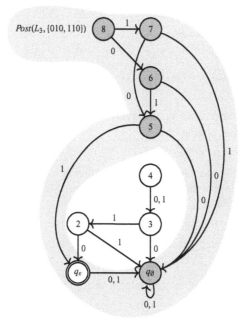

$Post(L_3, \{010, 110\})$

★ ✔ **Exercise 109.** Given $X \subseteq \{0, 1, \ldots, 2^k - 1\}$, where $k \geq 1$, let A_X be the minimal DFA recognizing the "least-significant-bit-first" encodings of length k of the elements of X.

(a) Let $X + 1 = \{x + 1 \bmod 2^k : x \in X\}$. Give an algorithm that on input A_X produces A_{X+1}.

(b) Let $A_X = (Q, \{0, 1\}, \delta, q_0, F)$. What is the set of numbers recognized by the automaton $A' = (Q, \{0, 1\}, \delta', q_0, F)$, where $\delta'(q, b) = \delta(q, 1 - b)$?

Solution:

(a) The following recursive algorithm takes as input the initial state of A_X (from the fixed-length master automaton) and returns the state for A_{X+1}:

$Add1(q)$
Input: state q recognizing a set X of numbers
Output: state of the same length as q recognizing $X + 1$
  1   **if** $G(q)$ is not empty **then return** $G(q)$
  2   **if** $q = q_\emptyset$ or $q = q_\varepsilon$ **then return** q
  3   **else**
  4       $r_0 \leftarrow Add1(q^1)$
  5       $r_1 \leftarrow q^0$
  6       $G(q) \leftarrow make(r_0, r_1)$
  7   **return** $G(q)$

(b) Automaton A' recognizes a word $b_1 \cdots b_k$ iff A_X recognizes $(1 - b_1) \cdots (1 - b_k)$. Thus, the set of numbers Y recognized by A' is $Y = \{(2^k - 1) - x : x \in X\}$.

★ ■ **Exercise 110.** Recall that weakly acyclic languages and DFAs have been introduced in exercise 35. Recall that the relation $\preceq$ on the states of a weakly acyclic DFA, defined by $q \preceq q'$ iff $\delta(q, w) = q'$ for some word w, is a partial order. Show that:

(a) Every fixed-length language is weakly acyclic.

(b) If L is weakly acyclic, then L^w is also weakly acyclic for every $w \in \Sigma^*$.

Given weakly acyclic languages L and L', let $L \preceq_{\mathcal{L}} L'$ denote that $L = (L')^w$ for some word w. Show that:

(c) $\preceq_{\mathcal{L}}$ is a partial order on the set of all weakly acyclic languages.

(d) $\preceq_{\mathcal{L}}$ has no infinite descending chains.

(e) The only two minimal languages w.r.t. $\preceq_{\mathcal{L}}$ are $\emptyset$ and Σ^*.

Recall that, by exercise 57, the minimal DFA recognizing a given weakly acyclic language is weakly acyclic. We define the *weakly acyclic master automaton* over alphabet Σ as $M = (Q_M, \Sigma, \delta_M, F_M)$, where

- Q_M is the set of all weakly acyclic languages over Σ;
- $\delta: Q_M \times \Sigma \to Q_M$ is given by $\delta(L, a) = L^a$ for every $q \in Q_M$ and $a \in \Sigma$; and
- $L \in F_M$ iff $\varepsilon \in L$.

Prove the following result, which generalizes the corresponding one for fixed-length languages:

(f) For every weakly acyclic language L, the language recognized from the state L of the weakly acyclic master automaton M is L.

Solution:

(a) Let L be a fixed-length language of length n. We prove that L is weakly acyclic by induction on n. If $n = 0$, then $L = \emptyset$ or $L = \{\varepsilon\}$, which is clearly weakly acyclic. If $n > 0$, then L^a has length $n - 1$ for every $a \in \Sigma$, and by induction hypothesis, it is weakly acyclic. So there is a weakly acyclic DFA A^a recognizing L^a. Let q_0^a be the initial state of A^a, and let A be the DFA obtained by putting the DFAs A^a side by side, adding a new initial state q_0, and adding transitions $q_0 \xrightarrow{a} q_0^a$ for every $a \in \Sigma$. We have $\mathcal{L}(A) = L$. Further, since all of the A^a are weakly acyclic, so is A, and therefore L is weakly acyclic. □

(b) Let $A = (Q, \Sigma, \delta, q_0, F)$ be a weakly acyclic DFA recognizing L, and let q be the state such that $\delta(q_0, w) = q$. We have $\mathcal{L}(q) = L^w$. Let A_q be the DFA obtained by removing from A all states not reachable from q and making q the initial state. Clearly, we have $\mathcal{L}(A_q) = L^w$. Since removing states from a weakly acyclic DFA cannot destroy weak acyclicity, A_q is also weakly acyclic. □

(c) The relation $\preceq_{\mathcal{L}}$ is clearly reflexive and transitive. We show that it is also antisymmetric. Let $L, L' \subseteq \Sigma^*$ be weakly acyclic languages, and let $w, w' \in \Sigma^*$ be words such that $L' = L^w$ and $L = (L')^{w'}$. We prove that $L = L'$. Let $A = (Q, \Sigma, \delta, q_0, F)$ be the minimal weakly acyclic DFA recognizing L. Let q be the state such that $\delta(q_0, w) = q$. Since A is minimal, q_0 and q are the unique states of A such that $\mathcal{L}(q_0) = L$ and $\mathcal{L}(q) = L'$. So we have $\delta(q, w) = q_0$, which implies $q_0 \preceq q \preceq q_0$. Since $\preceq$ is a partial order, $q_0 = q$ follows, and so $L = L'$. □

(d) This follows from (c) and the fact that a regular language has finitely many residuals.
□

(e) By definition of $\preceq_{\mathcal{L}}$, a language L is minimal w.r.t. $\preceq_{\mathcal{L}}$ iff $L = L^a$ for every $a \in \Sigma$. Thus, either $L = \emptyset$ or $L = \Sigma^*$.
□

(f) By (d) and (e), it suffices to show that the property holds for $L = \emptyset$ and $L = \Sigma^*$, and that if L^a satisfies the property for every $a \in \Sigma$ such that $L^a \neq L$, then L satisfies it too. For $L = \emptyset$, observe that $L = L^a$, and so every transition leaving L is a self-loop. Further, L is not final. Thus, the language accepted from L is $\emptyset$. The proof for $L = \Sigma^*$ is similar. Finally, assume that the language recognized from every state L^a such that $L^a \neq L$ is L^a. Let E_L be defined as $\{\varepsilon\}$ if $\varepsilon \in L$ and $\emptyset$ otherwise. The language recognized from L is

$$E_L \cup \left(\bigcup_{a \in \Sigma, L^a \neq L} a L^a \right) \cup \left(\bigcup_{a \in \Sigma, L^a = L} a L \right)$$

$$= E_L \cup \left(\bigcup_{a \in \Sigma, L^a \neq L} a L^a \right) \cup \left(\bigcup_{a \in \Sigma, L^a = L} a L^a \right)$$

$$= E_L \cup \bigcup_{a \in \Sigma} a L^a$$

$$= L.$$
□

★ ✔ **Exercise 111.** Recall that exercise 110 establishes that weakly acyclic languages can be represented by a weakly acyclic master automaton. A state q of the weakly acyclic master automaton can be represented by a table as follows. A *node* is a triple $\langle q, s, b \rangle$, where

- q is a *state identifier*;
- $s = (\alpha_1, \ldots, \alpha_m)$ is the *successor tuple* of the node, where for every $1 \leq i \leq m$, the component α_i is either a state identifier or the special symbol SELF; and
- $b \in \{0, 1\}$ indicates whether the state is accepting ($b = 1$) or not ($b = 0$).

For example, if $\Sigma = \{a, b\}$ and q is an accepting state satisfying $\delta(q, a) = q'$ and $\delta(q, b) = q$, then q is represented by the triple $\langle q, s, b \rangle$, where $s = (q', \text{SELF})$ and $b = 1$. The state identifiers of the states for the languages $\emptyset$ and Σ^* are denoted, respectively, by $q_\emptyset$ and q_{Σ^*}.

Given a table T that represents a fragment of the weakly acyclic master automaton, the procedure *make*(s, b) returns the state identifier of the unique state of T having s as successor tuple and b as boolean flag, if such a state exists; otherwise, it adds a new node $\langle q, s, b \rangle$ to T, where q is a fresh identifier, and it returns q.

(a) Give an algorithm to compute $\mathcal{L}(q_1) \cap \mathcal{L}(q_2)$ given states q_1 and q_2 of the weakly acyclic master automaton.

(b) Give an algorithm to compute $\mathcal{L}(q_1) \cup \mathcal{L}(q_2)$ given states q_1 and q_2 of the weakly acyclic master automaton.

(c) Give an algorithm to compute $\overline{\mathcal{L}(q)}$ given a state q of the weakly acyclic master automaton.

Solution:

(a) The following properties lead to the recursive algorithm $inter(q_1, q_2)$ shown as below:

- if $L_1 = \emptyset$ or $L_2 = \emptyset$, then $L_1 \cap L_2 = \emptyset$;
- if $L_1 = \Sigma^*$ and $L_2 = \Sigma^*$, then $L_1 \cap L_2 = \Sigma^*$; and
- if $L_1, L_2 \notin \{\emptyset, \Sigma^*\}$, then $L_1 \cap L_2 = (L_1 \cap L_2 \cap \{\varepsilon\}) \cup \bigcup_{a \in \Sigma} a \cdot (L_1 \cap L_2)^a$.

$inter(q_1, q_2)$
Input: states q_1, q_2 of the weakly acyclic master automaton
Output: state recognizing $\mathcal{L}(q_1) \cap \mathcal{L}(q_2)$

```
 1   if G(q₁, q₂) is not empty then return G(q₁, q₂)
 2   if q₁ = q∅ or q₂ = q∅ then return q∅
 3   else if q₁ = qΣ* and q₂ = qΣ* then return qΣ*
 4   else /* q₁, q₂ ∉ {q∅, qΣ*} */
 5       for all i = 1, ..., m do
 6           if q₁ᵃⁱ = q₂ᵃⁱ = SELF then rᵢ ← SELF
 7           else if q₁ᵃⁱ = SELF then rᵢ ← inter(q₁, q₂ᵃⁱ)
 8           else if q₂ᵃⁱ = SELF then rᵢ ← inter(q₁ᵃⁱ, q₂)
 9           else rᵢ ← inter(q₁ᵃⁱ, q₂ᵃⁱ)
10       b ← q₁ᵇ ∧ q₂ᵇ
11       G(q₁, q₂) ← make(r₁, ..., rₘ, b)
12       return G(q₁, q₂)
```

(b) The following properties lead to the recursive algorithm $union(q_1, q_2)$ shown as follows:

- if $L_1 = \emptyset$ and $L_2 = \emptyset$, then $L_1 \cup L_2 = \emptyset$;
- if $L_1 = \Sigma^*$ or $L_2 = \Sigma^*$, then $L_1 \cup L_2 = \Sigma^*$; and
- if $L_1, L_2 \notin \{\emptyset, \Sigma^*\}$, then $L_1 \cup L_2 = ((L_1 \cap \{\varepsilon\}) \cup (L_2 \cap \{\varepsilon\})) \cup \bigcup_{a \in \Sigma} a \cdot (L_1 \cup L_2)^a$.

$union(q_1, q_2)$
Input: states q_1, q_2 of the weakly acyclic master automaton
Output: state recognizing $\mathcal{L}(q_1) \cup \mathcal{L}(q_2)$

```
 1   if G(q₁, q₂) is not empty then return G(q₁, q₂)
 2   if q₁ = q∅ and q₂ = q∅ then return q∅
 3   else if q₁ = qΣ* or q₂ = qΣ* then return qΣ*
 4   else /* q₁, q₂ ∉ {q∅, qΣ*} */
 5       for all i = 1, ..., m do
 6           if q₁ᵃⁱ = q₂ᵃⁱ = SELF then rᵢ ← SELF
 7           else if q₁ᵃⁱ = SELF then rᵢ ← union(q₁, q₂ᵃⁱ)
 8           else if q₂ᵃⁱ = SELF then rᵢ ← union(q₁ᵃⁱ, q₂)
 9           else rᵢ ← union(q₁ᵃⁱ, q₂ᵃⁱ)
10       b ← q₁ᵇ ∨ q₂ᵇ
11       G(q₁, q₂) ← make(r₁, ..., rₘ, b)
12       return G(q₁, q₂)
```

(c) The following properties lead to the recursive algorithm $comp(q)$ shown as follows:

- if $L = \emptyset$, then $\overline{L} = \Sigma^*$;
- if $L = \Sigma^*$, then $\overline{L} = \emptyset$; and
- if $L \notin \{\emptyset, \Sigma^*\}$, then $\overline{L} = (\overline{L} \cap \{\varepsilon\}) \cup \bigcup_{a \in \Sigma} a\,(\overline{L})^a$.

$comp(q)$
Input: state q of the weakly acyclic master automaton
Output: state recognizing $\overline{\mathcal{L}(q)}$

```
1    if G(q) is not empty then return G(q)
2    if q = q∅ then return qΣ*
3    if q = qΣ* then return q∅
4    else /* q ∉ {q∅, qΣ*} */
5       for all i = 1, . . . , m do
6          if q^ai = SELF then ri ← SELF
7          else ri ← comp(q^ai)
8       b ← ¬q^b
9       G(q) ← make(r1, . . . , rm, b)
10      return G(q1, q2)
```

☆ ☞ **Exercise 112.** Recall that we can associate a language to a boolean formula as done in exercise 108. Show that the following problem is NP-hard:

Given: a boolean formula φ,

Decide: whether the minimal DFA for $\mathcal{L}(\varphi)$ has more than one state.

Solution: We give a reduction from the NP-complete problem SAT. Recall that this problem asks whether a given boolean formula ψ is satisfiable. Let $x_1, \ldots, x_n$ be the variables that occur within ψ, and let y be a new variable. Let $\varphi = \psi \wedge y$. We claim that ψ is satisfiable iff the minimal DFA for $\mathcal{L}(\varphi)$ has more than one state.

$\Rightarrow$) If ψ is satisfiable, then there exists $w \in \{0, 1\}^n$ such that $\psi(w) = \textbf{true}$. Thus, $w1 \in \mathcal{L}(\varphi)$. Note that $w0 \notin \mathcal{L}(\varphi)$ as φ requires y to be true. Consequently, $\mathcal{L}(\varphi)$ is neither empty nor universal, which means that its minimal DFA has more than one state.

$\Leftarrow$) If the minimal DFA for φ has more than one state, then $\mathcal{L}(\varphi) \neq \emptyset$. This means there exists $w \in \{0, 1\}^n$ such that $\varphi(w, 1) = \textbf{true}$. In particular, this implies that $\psi(w) = \textbf{true}$. $\square$

Solutions for Chapter 7

☆ 🔲 **Exercise 113.** Exhibit a family $\{P_n\}_{n \geq 1}$ of sequential programs (like program 1) satisfying the following conditions:

- P_n has $\mathcal{O}(n)$ boolean variables, $\mathcal{O}(n)$ lines, and exactly one initial configuration;
- P_n has at least 2^n reachable configurations.

Solution: If nondeterminism is allowed, then we can simply define P_n as a program that nondeterministically sets variables $x_1, \ldots, x_n$ to 0 or 1 and terminates:

```
1   for all 1 ≤ i ≤ n do
2       xᵢ ← 0 or xᵢ ← 1
3   end
```

If we require the program to be deterministic, then we can take P_n as a program that repeatedly increases an n-bit counter, where x_i contains the value of the ith least significant bit. For instance, if $n = 3$, then the program visits the sequence of variable valuations $000, 001, 010, \ldots, 110, 111$. To increase a valuation, the program goes over all bits with value 1, setting them to 0, and then sets the first bit with value 0 (if any) to 1:

```
1   for all 0 ≤ i < n do xᵢ ← 0
2   while true do
3       for all 0 ≤ i < n do
4           xᵢ ← 1 − xᵢ
5           if xᵢ = 1 then break
6   end
```

These two programs have a constant number of lines, but the iterator of the loop is not a boolean variable. If we want to strictly adhere to the specification of the exercise (only boolean variables), then we can just replace the loop by a chain of if-then-else instructions.

☆ ✐ **Exercise 114.** When applied to program 1, algorithm *SysAut* outputs the system automaton shown in the middle of figure 7.1. Give an algorithm *SysAut'* that outputs the automaton depicted at the bottom.

Solution: First we modify line 14 of *SysAut* so that it adds transition

$$[q_1, \ldots, q_n] \xrightarrow{[q_1, \ldots, q_n]} [q'_1, \ldots, q'_n] \text{ rather than } [q_1, \ldots, q_n] \xrightarrow{[q'_1, \ldots, q'_n]} [q'_1, \ldots, q'_n].$$

We must further drop the initial state i. However, every reachable configuration c without any successor must now have an outgoing transition, labeled with c, leading to a final state f. We introduce a flag *no_successor* to determine if a configuration has some successor or not. The resulting algorithm is depicted as follows. The flag is set to **false** right after adding the first successor at line 15. If the configuration has no successors, then we add the new transition at line 17:

$SysAut'(A_1, \ldots, A_n)$
Input: a network of automata $\langle A_1, \ldots A_n \rangle$, where
$$A_1 = (Q_1, \Sigma_1, \delta_1, Q_{01}, Q_1), \ldots, A_n = (Q_n, \Sigma_n, \delta_n, Q_{0n}, Q_n)$$
Output: a system automaton $S = (Q, \Sigma, \delta, Q_0, F)$

```
1    Q, δ, F ← ∅
2    Q_0 ← Q_01 × ··· × Q_0n
3    W ← Q_0
4    while W ≠ ∅ do
5        pick [q_1, ..., q_n] from W
6        add [q_1, ..., q_n] to Q
7        add [q_1, ..., q_n] to F
8        no_successors ← true
9        for all a ∈ Σ_1 ∪ ... ∪ Σ_n do
10           for all i ∈ [1..n] do
11               if a ∈ Σ_i then Q'_i ← δ_i(q_i, a) else Q'_i = {q_i}
12           for all [q'_1, ..., q'_n] ∈ Q'_1 × ... × Q'_n do
13               if [q'_1, ..., q'_n] ∉ Q then add [q'_1, ..., q'_n] to W
14               add ([q_1, ..., q_n], [q_1, ..., q_n], [q'_1, ..., q'_n]) to δ
15               no_successors ← false
16           if no_successors = true then
17               add f to Q; add f to F; add ([q_1, ..., q_n], [q_1, ..., q_n], f) to δ
18   return (Q, Σ, δ, Q_0, F)
```

★ ▣ **Exercise 117.** Consider two processes (process 0 and process 1) being executed through the following generic mutual exclusion algorithm:

```
1    while true do
2        enter(process_id)
3        critical section
4        leave(process_id)
5        for arbitrarily many iterations do
6            noncritical section
7    end
```

(a) Consider the following implementations of enter and leave:

```
1    x ← 0
2    proc enter(i)
3        while x = 1 − i do
4            pass
5    proc leave(i)
6        x ← 1 − i
```

(i) Design a network of automata capturing the executions of the two processes.
(ii) Build the asynchronous product of the network.
(iii) Show that both processes cannot reach their critical sections at the same time.

(iv) If a process wants to enter its critical section, is it always the case that it can eventually enter it?   *Hint: Reason in terms of infinite executions.*

(b) Consider the following alternative implementations of enter and leave:

```
1   x_0 ← false
2   x_1 ← false
3   proc enter(i)
4       x_i ← true
5       while x_{1-i} do
6           pass
7   proc leave(i)
8       x_i ← false
```

(i) Design a network of automata capturing the executions of the two processes.

(ii) Say whether a deadlock can occur—that is, can both processes get stuck trying to enter their critical sections?

Solution:

(a)
(i)

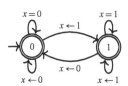

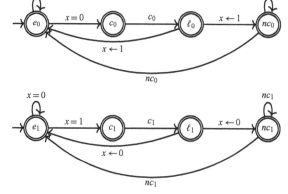

Note that the above network forces the processes to read the contents of x simultaneously. To avoid this, we can add new disjoint actions $x = 0'$ and $x = 1'$ as follows:

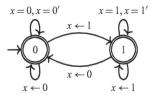

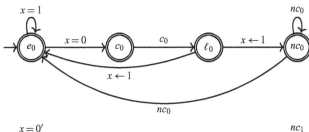

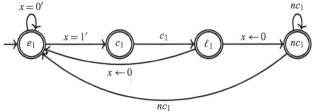

(ii)

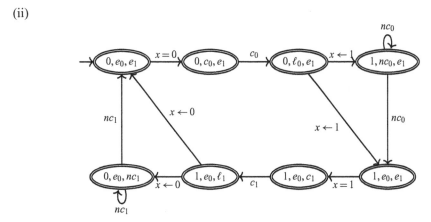

For the second solution where asynchronous reads are allowed, we obtain the following automaton:

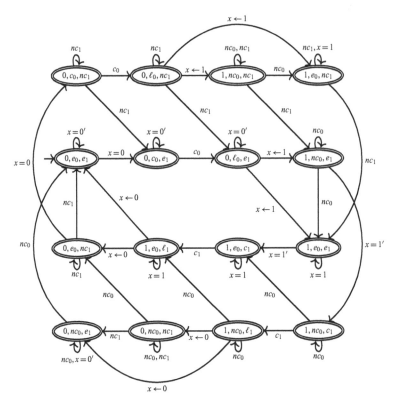

(iii) Both processes can reach their critical section at the same time iff the asynchronous product contains a state of the form (x, c_0, c_1). Since it contains none, this behavior cannot occur. It also cannot occur in our second modeling.

(iv) No. Consider the following infinite run:

$$(0, e_0, e_1) \xrightarrow{x=0} (0, c_0, e_1) \xrightarrow{c_0} (0, \ell_0, e_1) \xrightarrow{x \leftarrow 1} (1, nc_0, e_1) \xrightarrow{nc_0} (1, nc_0, e_1) \xrightarrow{nc_0} \cdots$$

illustrated as follows:

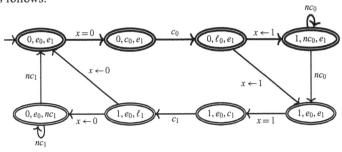

The second process remains in e_1 throughout this infinite run, so it never enters its critical section. Since we have restricted x to be read at the same time, a process can stay in its noncritical section as long as it wants while the other one cannot do anything.

In our second modeling, this infinite run still occurs as illustrated below. However, here the second process is not stuck since it could take transition $(1, nc_0, e_1) \xrightarrow{x=1'} (1, nc_0, c_1)$ to reach its critical section. Therefore, the colored infinite run only occurs if the process scheduler can let a process i run forever even though process $1 - i$ could make progress.

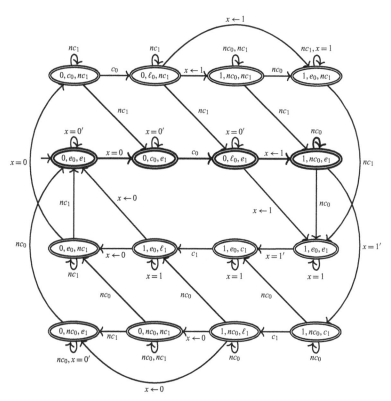

(b)
(i)

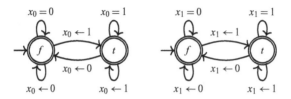

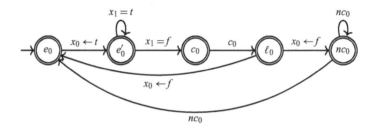

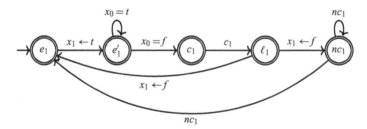

(ii) Yes, consider this fragment of the asynchronous product of the network:

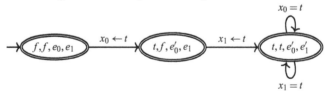

When (t, t, e'_0, e'_1) is reached, both processes are still trying to enter their critical section, and it is impossible to move to a new state.

⭐ 🖳 **Exercise 118.** Consider a circular railway divided into eight tracks: $0 \to 1 \to \ldots \to 7 \to 0$. Three trains, modeled by three automata T_1, T_2, and T_3, circulate on the railway. Each automaton T_i is defined as follows:

- states: $\{q_{i,0}, \ldots, q_{i,7}\}$;
- alphabet: $\{enter[i,j] : 0 \leq j \leq 7\}$, where $enter[i,j]$ models that train i enters track j;

- transition relation: $\{(q_{i,j}, enter[i, j \oplus 1], q_{i,j\oplus 1}) : 0 \le j \le 7\}$, where $\oplus$ denotes addition mod 8; and
- initial state: $q_{i,2i}$ (i.e., initially the trains occupy tracks 2, 4, and 6).

Describe automata $C_0, \ldots, C_7$, called *local controllers*, that ensure that two trains can never be on the same track or adjacent tracks (i.e., there must always be at least one empty track between two trains). Each controller C_j can only have knowledge of the state of tracks $j \ominus 1, j$, and $j \oplus 1$; there must be no deadlocks; and every train must eventually visit every track. More formally, the network of automata $\mathcal{A} = \langle C_0, \ldots, C_7, T_1, T_2, T_3 \rangle$ must satisfy the following specification:

(a) C_j only knows the state of local tracks: C_j has alphabet $\{enter[i, j \ominus 1], enter[i, j], enter[i, j \oplus 1] : 1 \le i \le 3\}$;

(b) no deadlock and each train eventually visits every segment: $\mathcal{L}(\mathcal{A})|_{\Sigma_i} = (enter[i, 2i] \ enter[i, 2i \oplus 1] \cdots enter[i, 2i \oplus 7])^*$ for each $i \in \{1, 2, 3\}$; and

(c) no two trains on the same or adjacent tracks: for every word $w \in \mathcal{L}(\mathcal{A})$, it is the case that $w = u \ enter[i, j] \ enter[i', j'] \ v$ and $i' \ne i$ implies $|j - j'| \notin \{0, 1, 7\}$.

Solution: Let us write $x \ne_? y$ as a shorthand for $\neg(x = y \wedge x \ne ?)$ (i.e., $x \ne y$ or $x = ? = y$). We define the states of C_j as triples assigning a track number from $\{j \ominus 1, j, j \oplus 1, ?\}$ to each train, where ? stands for an unknown track number w.r.t. the knowledge of the local controller:

$$Q_j = \{x \in \{j \ominus 1, j, j \oplus 1, ?\}^3 : x_1 \ne_? x_2, x_1 \ne_? x_3, x_2 \ne_? x_3,$$

$$\{x_1, x_2, x_3\} \setminus \{?\} \in \{\emptyset, \{j \ominus 1\}, \{j\}, \{j \oplus 1\}, \{j \ominus 1, j \oplus 1\}\}\}.$$

The constraints ensure that no two trains are either on the same track or on adjacent tracks w.r.t. $\{j \ominus 1, j, j \oplus 1\}$. The sole initial state of C_j is defined as $(f_j(1), f_j(2), f_j(3))$, where

$$f_j(i) = \begin{cases} 2i & \text{if } 2i \in \{j \ominus 1, j, j \oplus 1\}, \\ ? & \text{otherwise.} \end{cases}$$

The transition relation of C_j is defined as $\delta(x, enter[i, k]) = y$, where $y_i = k$ and $y_\ell = x_\ell$ for $\ell \ne i$. Note that an invalid move (e.g., train 1 moving to track j while train 2 is on track $j \oplus 1$), leads to an implicit trap state as no such state belongs to Q_j.

The definition of C_j takes care of (a) and (c). Item (b) follows by definition of T_1, T_2, and T_3.

Solutions for Chapter 8

☆ 🔲 **Exercise 119.** Give formulations in plain English of the languages described by the following formulas of FO($\{a, b\}$), and give a corresponding regular expression:

(a) $\exists x \ first(x)$

(b) $\forall x \ x < x$

(c) $[\neg \exists x \exists y \ (x < y \wedge Q_a(x) \wedge Q_b(y))] \wedge [\forall x \ (Q_b(x) \rightarrow \exists y \ x < y \wedge Q_a(y))] \wedge [\exists x \ \neg \exists y \ x < y]$

Solution:

(a) All nonempty words: $(a+b)(a+b)^*$.

(b) The empty word: ε.

(c) The first conjunct expresses that no a precedes an occurrence of b. The corresponding regular expression is b^*a^*. The second conjunct states that every b is followed (immediately or not) by an a; this excludes the words of b^+. Finally, the third conjunct expresses that there is a last letter (which, by the second conjunct, must be an a). So, the overall expression is b^*a^+.

★ ▣ **Exercise 120.** Let $\Sigma = \{a, b\}$.

(a) Give a formula $\varphi_n(x,y)$ from $\mathrm{FO}(\Sigma)$, of size $\mathcal{O}(n)$, that holds iff $y = x + 2^n$. Note that the abbreviation $y = x + k$ on page 202 has length $\mathcal{O}(k)$ and hence cannot be directly used.

(b) Give a sentence from $\mathrm{FO}(\Sigma)$, of size $\mathcal{O}(n)$, for the language $L_n = \{ww : w \in \Sigma^* \text{ and } |w| = 2^n\}$.

(c) Show that the minimal DFA accepting L_n has at least 2^{2^n} states.

Hint: Consider residuals.

Solution:

(a) To simplify the notation, let us write "$y = x + 2^n$" for "$\varphi_n(x,y)$." We can define $y = x + 2^n$ inductively as follows:

$$(y = x + 2^n) := \exists t \left(t = x + 2^{n-1} \wedge y = t + 2^{n-1} \right).$$

However, since the formula for n is roughly twice as long as the formula for $n-1$, this yields a formula of exponential size. It can be made linear by rewriting it in the following way:

$(y = x + 2^n)$

$= \exists t \, \forall x' \, \forall y' \left((x' = x \wedge y' = t) \rightarrow y' = x' + 2^{n-1} \right) \wedge \left((x' = t \wedge y' = y) \rightarrow y' = x' + 2^{n-1} \right)$

$= \exists t \, \forall x' \, \forall y' \left(\neg(x' = x \wedge y' = t) \vee y' = x' + 2^{n-1} \right) \wedge \left(\neg(x' = t \wedge y' = y) \vee y' = x' + 2^{n-1} \right)$

$= \exists t \, \forall x' \, \forall y' \left(\neg(x' = x \wedge y' = t) \wedge \neg(x' = t \wedge y' = y) \right) \vee y' = x' + 2^{n-1}$

$= \exists t \, \forall x' \, \forall y' \left((x' = x \wedge y' = t) \vee (x' = t \wedge y' = y) \right) \rightarrow y' = x' + 2^{n-1}$.

(b)

$$\overbrace{\left(\exists x,y,y',z \text{ first}(x) \land y = x + 2^n \land y' = y + 1 \land z = y' + 2^n \land \text{last}(z)\right)}^{\text{word has length } 2^n + 2^n}$$

$$\underbrace{\land \left(\forall x \, \forall y \bigwedge_{\sigma \in \{a,b\}} (Q_\sigma(x) \land y = x + 2^n) \to Q_\sigma(y)\right)}_{\text{word is of the form } ww}.$$

(c) Let $u, v \in \{a,b\}^*$ be distinct words such that $|u| = |v| = 2^n$. We have $uu \in L_n$ and $vu \notin L_n$. Thus, all words of length 2^n belong to distinct residuals. There are 2^{2^n} such words; hence, L_n has at least 2^{2^n} residuals. $\qquad\square$

★■ **Exercise 121.** The *nesting depth* $d(\varphi)$ of a formula φ of $\mathrm{FO}(\{a\})$ is defined inductively as follows:

- $d(Q_a(x)) = d(x < y) = 0$,
- $d(\neg \psi) = d(\psi)$,
- $d(\varphi_1 \lor \varphi_2) = \max\{d(\varphi_1), d(\varphi_2)\}$, and
- $d(\exists x \, \psi) = 1 + d(\psi)$.

Prove that every formula φ from $\mathrm{FO}(\{a\})$ of nesting depth n is equivalent to a formula f of QF having the same free variables as φ and such that every constant k appearing in f satisfies $k \leq 2^n$.   *Hint: Modify suitably the proof of theorem 8.17.*

Solution: We prove the claim by induction on the structure of formula φ. If it is of the form $Q_a(x)$, then the claim trivially holds as $Q_a(x)$ is a tautology over $\{a\}$, and no constant is involved. If $\varphi(x,y) = x < y$, then $d(\varphi) = 0$ and $\varphi \equiv x < y + 0$. If $\varphi = \neg \psi$, then, by induction hypothesis, ψ to a formula f of QF with constants of at most 2^d, where d is the depth of ψ and hence of φ. By De Morgan's rule, we can remove the negation (e.g., $\neg(x < k)$ becomes $x \geq k$). If $\varphi = \varphi_1 \lor \varphi_2$, then the claim follows immediately by induction hypothesis.

   Let us now consider the case where $\varphi = \exists x \, \psi$. Let d and $d + 1$ be the nesting depth of ψ and φ, respectively. By induction hypothesis, ψ is equivalent to a formula f of QF whose constants are at most 2^d, and we can further assume that f is in disjunctive normal form, say $f = f_1 \lor \ldots \lor f_n$. Thus, $\varphi \equiv \exists x f_1 \lor \exists x f_2 \lor \ldots \lor \exists x f_n$, and so it suffices to find a formula g_i of QF equivalent to $\exists x f_i$ and whose constants are of size at most 2^{d+1}. The formula g_i is a conjunction defined as follows. All conjuncts of f_i not containing x are also conjuncts of g_i; for every conjunct of f_i of the form $x \geq k$ or $x \geq y + k$, the formula g_i contains a conjunct $last \geq k$; for every two conjuncts of f_i containing x, the formula g_i contains a conjunct obtained by "quantifying x away." We only explain this by means of an example: if the conjuncts are $x \geq k_1$ and $y \geq x + k_2$, then g_i has the conjunct $y \geq k_1 + k_2$. It is easy to see that $g_i \equiv \exists x f_i$. Moreover, since the constants in the new conjuncts are the sum of the two old constants, the new constants are bounded by $2 \cdot 2^d = 2^{d+1}$. $\square$

☆ 🔲 **Exercise 124.** Give a formula Odd_card(X) from MSO(Σ) expressing that the set of positions X has odd cardinality.   *Hint: Follow the pattern of* Even(X).

Solution: We first give formulas First(x, X) and Last(x, X) expressing that x is the first and last position among those of X. We also give a formula Next(x, y, X) expressing that y is the successor of x in X. It is then easy to give a formula Odd(Y, X) expressing that Y is the set of odd positions of X. More precisely, Y contains the first position among those of X, the third, the fifth, and so on. Finally, formula Odd_card(X) expresses that the last position of X belongs to the set of odd positions of X.

$$\text{First}(x, X) := (x \in X) \land \forall y \, (y < x) \rightarrow (y \notin X),$$

$$\text{Last}(x, X) := (x \in X) \land \forall y \, (y > x) \rightarrow (y \notin X),$$

$$\text{Next}(x, y, X) := (x \in X) \land (y \in X) \land (x < y) \land \neg \exists z \, (x < z) \land (z < y) \land (z \in X),$$

$$\text{Odd}(Y, X) := \forall x \, (x \in Y \leftrightarrow (\text{First}(x, X) \lor \exists z \, \exists u \, (z \in Y) \land \text{Next}(z, u, X) \land \text{Next}(u, x, X)),$$

$$\text{Odd\_card}(X) := \exists Y \, (\text{Odd}(Y, X) \land \forall x \, \text{Last}(x, X) \rightarrow (x \in Y)).$$

☆ 🔲 **Exercise 125.** Give formulas of MSO($\{a, b\}$) that define the following languages:

(a) aa^*b^*,
(b) the set of words with an odd number of occurrences of a, and
(c) the set of words such that every two b with no other b in between are separated by a block of a of odd length.

Solution: We use the macros defined in the chapter and the solution of exercise 124:

(a) $\exists x \, Q_a(x) \land [\forall x \forall y \, (Q_a(x) \land Q_b(y)) \rightarrow (x < y)]$,
(b) $\exists X \, [\forall x \, (x \in X) \leftrightarrow Q_a(x)] \land \text{Odd\_card}(X)$,
(c) $\forall X \, [\text{Block}(X) \land \forall x \, Q_b(x) \leftrightarrow (\text{First}(x, X) \lor \text{Last}(x, X))] \rightarrow \text{Odd\_card}(X)$.

★ 🔲 **Exercise 126.** Given a formula φ from MSO(Σ) and a second order variable X not occurring in φ, show how to construct a formula φ^X with X as a free variable expressing "the projection of the word onto the positions of X satisfies φ." Formally, φ^X must satisfy the following property: for every interpretation $\mathcal{V}$ of φ^X, we have $(w, \mathcal{V}) \models \varphi^X$ iff $(w|_{\mathcal{V}(X)}, \mathcal{V}) \models \varphi$, where $w|_{\mathcal{V}(X)}$ denotes the result of deleting from w the letters at all positions that do not belong to $\mathcal{V}(X)$.

Solution: We first define two macros:

$$\exists x \in X \, \psi := \exists x \, (x \in X \land \psi),$$

$$\exists Y \subseteq X \, \psi := \exists Y \, (\forall x \, (x \in Y) \rightarrow (x \in X \land \psi)).$$

Now we define φ^X inductively as follows:

- if φ is of the form $Q_a(x)$, $x < y$, $x \in X$, $\neg \psi$ or $\varphi_1 \lor \varphi_2$, then $\varphi^X = \varphi$;
- if $\varphi = \exists x \, \psi$, then $\varphi^X = \exists x \in X \, \psi^X$; and
- if $\varphi = \exists Y \, \psi$, then $\varphi^X = \exists Y \subseteq X \, \psi^X$.

☆ ■ **Exercise 128.** Consider the logic PureMSO(Σ) with syntax

$$\varphi ::= X \subseteq Q_a \mid X < Y \mid X \subseteq Y \mid \neg \varphi \mid \varphi \vee \varphi \mid \exists X \; \varphi$$

Note that formulas of PureMSO(Σ) do not contain first-order variables. The satisfaction relation of PureMSO(Σ) is given by

$$
\begin{array}{llll}
(w, \mathcal{V}) & \models & X \subseteq Q_a & \text{iff} \quad w[p] = a \text{ for every } p \in \mathcal{V}(X), \\
(w, \mathcal{V}) & \models & X < Y & \text{iff} \quad p < p' \text{ for every } p \in \mathcal{V}(X), p' \in \mathcal{V}(Y), \\
(w, \mathcal{V}) & \models & X \subseteq Y & \text{iff} \quad \mathcal{V}(X) \subseteq \mathcal{V}(Y),
\end{array}
$$

with the rest as for MSO(Σ).

Prove that MSO(Σ) and PureMSO(Σ) have the same expressive power for sentences—that is, show that for all sentence ϕ of MSO(Σ), there is an equivalent sentence ψ of PureMSO(Σ) and vice versa.

Solution: $\Leftarrow$) Let ψ be a sentence of PureMSO(Σ). Let ϕ be the sentence of MSO(Σ) obtained by replacing every subformula of ψ of the form

$$
\begin{array}{lll}
X \subseteq Y & \text{by} & \forall x \; (x \in X \to x \in Y), \\
X \subseteq Q_a & \text{by} & \forall x \; (x \in X \to Q_a(x)), \\
X < Y & \text{by} & \forall x \forall y \; (x \in X \wedge y \in Y) \to (x < y).
\end{array}
$$

Clearly, ϕ and ψ are equivalent.

$\Rightarrow$) Let $\mathrm{Sing}(X) := \exists x \in X \; \forall y \in X \; (x = y)$ express that X is a singleton. Let ϕ be a sentence of MSO(Σ). Assume without loss of generality that for every first-order variable x, the second-order variable X does not appear in ϕ (otherwise, rename second-order variables appropriately). Let ψ be the sentence of PureMSO(Σ) obtained by replacing every subformula of ϕ of the form

$$
\begin{array}{lll}
Q_a(x) & \text{by} & X \subseteq Q_a, \\
x < y & \text{by} & X < Y, \\
x \in Y & \text{by} & X \subseteq Y, \\
\exists x \; \psi' & \text{by} & \exists X \; (\mathrm{Sing}(X) \wedge \psi'[x/X]), \\
& & \text{where } \psi'[x/X] \text{ is the result of substituting } X \text{ for } x \text{ in } \psi'.
\end{array}
$$

Clearly, ϕ and ψ are equivalent.   □

★ ■ **Exercise 129.** Recall the syntax of MSO(Σ):

$$\varphi := Q_a(x) \mid x < y \mid x \in X \mid \neg \varphi \mid \varphi \vee \varphi \mid \exists x \; \varphi \mid \exists X \; \varphi$$

We have introduced $y = x + 1$ ("y is the successor position of x") as an abbreviation:

$$(y = x + 1) := (x < y) \wedge \neg \exists z \; (x < z \wedge z < y).$$

Consider now the variant MSO$'$(Σ) in which, instead of an abbreviation, $y = x + 1$ is part of the syntax and replaces $x < y$. In other words, the syntax of MSO$'$(Σ) is

$$\varphi := Q_a(x) \mid y = x + 1 \mid x \in X \mid \neg \varphi \mid \varphi \vee \varphi \mid \exists x \; \varphi \mid \exists X \; \varphi$$

Prove that MSO$'$(Σ) has the same expressive power as MSO(Σ).

Solution: It suffices to give a formula of $\mathrm{MSO}'(\Sigma)$ with the same meaning as $x < y$. Observe that $x < y$ holds iff there is a set Y of positions containing y and satisfying the following property: every $z \in Y$ is either the successor of x or the successor of another element of Y. Formally:

$$(x < y) := \exists Y \, [y \in Y] \land [\forall z \in Y \, ((z = x + 1) \lor \exists u \in Y \, (z = u + 1))]. \qquad \square$$

☆ 🔲 **Exercise 131.** Consider a formula $\phi(X)$ of $\mathrm{MSO}(\Sigma)$ that does not contain any occurrence of predicates of the form $Q_a(x)$. Given two interpretations that assign the same set of positions to X, we have that either both interpretations satisfy $\phi(X)$, or none of them does. Thus, we can speak of the sets of natural numbers satisfying $\phi(X)$.

This observation can be used to automatically prove some (very) simple properties of the natural numbers. Consider, for instance, the following "conjecture": every finite set of natural numbers has a minimal element.[1] The conjecture holds iff the formula

$$\mathrm{Has\_min}(X) := \exists x \in X \; \forall y \in X \; (x \le y)$$

is satisfied by every interpretation in which X is nonempty. Construct an automaton for $\mathrm{Has\_min}(X)$, and check that it recognizes all nonempty sets.

Solution: After replacing abbreviations, we obtain the equivalent formula

$$\exists x \, [x \in X \land (\neg \exists y \, (y \in X \land y < x))].$$

The DFA for formula $\neg \exists y \, (y \in X \land y < x)$, where the encoding of x is at the top and the encoding for X is at the bottom, is as follows:

In words, this DFA checks that the 1 marking position x comes before or at the same time as the ones encoding the elements of X. Intersecting this DFA with one for formula $x \in X$ yields

---

1. Of course, it also holds for all infinite sets, but we cannot prove it using MSO over finite words.

After projection onto X (second row), we get a DFA for $Has\_min(X)$:

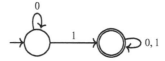

In words, this DFA recognizes all words with at least one 1, which corresponds to nonempty sets.

Solutions for Chapter 9

☆ 🔲 **Exercise 133.** Express the following expressions in Presburger arithmetic:

(a) $x = 0$ and $y = 1$ (if 0 and 1 were not part of the syntax),
(b) $z = \max(x, y)$ and $z = \min(x, y)$.

Solution:

(a) $x = x + x$ and $(x \leq y) \wedge \neg[\exists z \, \neg(z \leq x) \wedge \neg(y \leq z)]$,
(b) $[(y \leq x) \rightarrow (z = x) \wedge (x \leq y) \rightarrow (z = y)]$ and $[(y \leq x) \rightarrow (z = y) \wedge (x \leq y) \rightarrow (z = x)]$.

☆ ✒ **Exercise 134.** How can one determine algorithmically whether two formulas from Presburger arithmetic have the same solutions?

Solution: Given two formulas φ_1 and φ_2 over the same free variables, we can construct automata A_1 and A_2, respectively, for φ_1 and φ_2. It then suffices to check whether $\mathcal{L}(A_1) = \mathcal{L}(A_2)$, which can be done, for example, by testing $\mathcal{L}(A_1) \cap \overline{\mathcal{L}(A_2)} = \emptyset$ and $\overline{\mathcal{L}(A_1)} \cap A_2 = \emptyset$ using the pairing of A_1 and A_2.

☆ ⚙ **Exercise 136.** Construct an automaton for the Presburger formula $\exists y \, (x = 3y)$ using the algorithms of the chapter.

Solution: Let us rewrite the formula as $\exists y \, (x - 3y = 0)$. We first use algorithm *EqtoDFA* to obtain an automaton for the expression $x - 3y = 0$:

Iter.	Current automaton	W
0	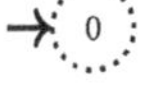	$\{0\}$
1	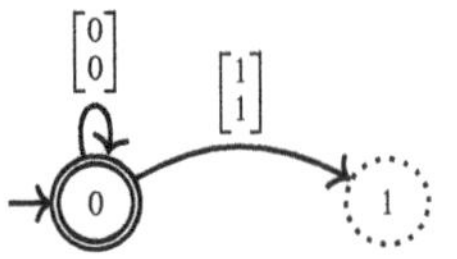	$\{1\}$
2	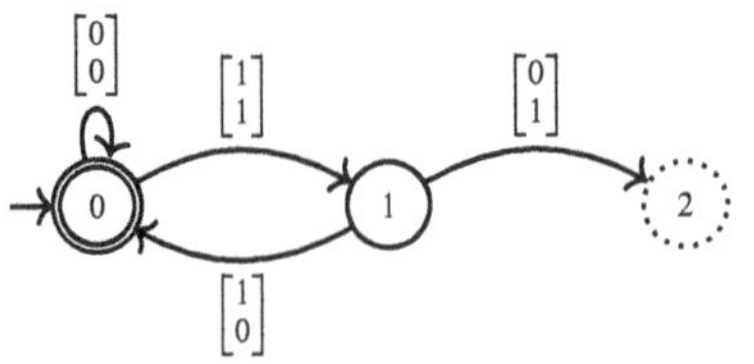	$\{2\}$
3	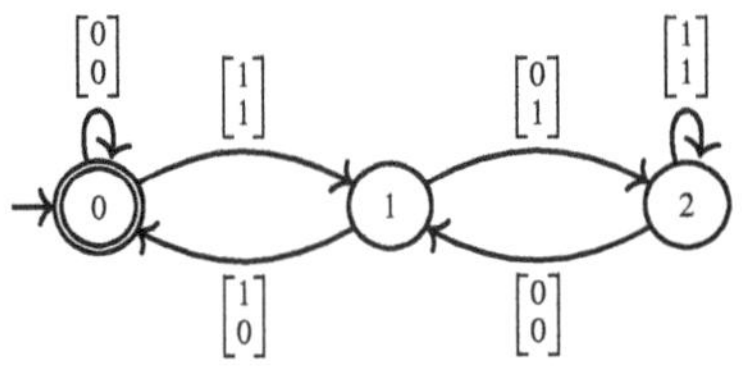	$\emptyset$

It remains to project the automaton on x (i.e., on the first component of the letters). We obtain

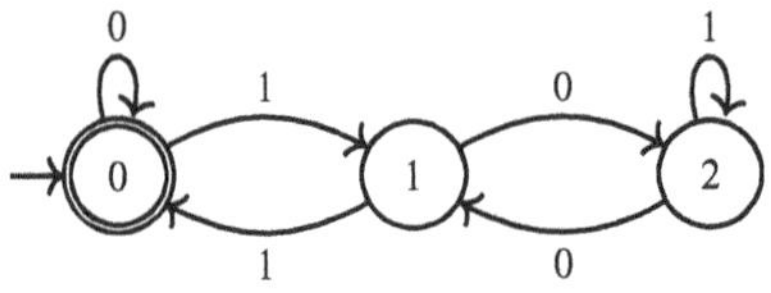

★✓ **Exercise 137.** Algorithm *AFtoDFA* yields a DFA that recognizes solutions of a linear inequation encoded using the LSBF encoding. We may also use the most-significant-bit-first encoding—for example,

$$\text{MSBF}\left(\begin{bmatrix}2\\3\end{bmatrix}\right) = \begin{bmatrix}0\\0\end{bmatrix}^* \begin{bmatrix}1\\1\end{bmatrix} \begin{bmatrix}0\\1\end{bmatrix}.$$

(a) Construct a DFA for $2x - y \leq 2$, w.r.t. MSBF encodings, by considering the reversal of the DFA given in figure 9.1 for LSBF encodings.

(b) Rename the states of the DFA obtained in (a) by their minimal state number, and explicitly introduce a trap state named 3. Compare values $2x - y$ and q for tuples $[x, y]$ that lead to a state q. What do you observe?

(c) Adapt algorithm *AFtoDFA* to the MSBF encoding.
Hint: Design an infinite automaton obtained from $a \cdot c = q$ and make it finite based on (b).

Solution:

(a) Let us consider the DFA from figure 9.1. By reversing its transitions, making its accepting states initial, and making its initial states accepting, we obtain this NFA:

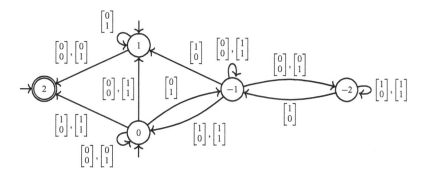

By determinizing the above NFA, we obtain this DFA:

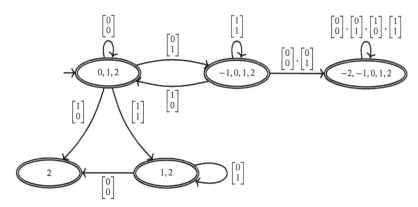

(b) By renaming the states of the DFA obtained in (a) by their minimal number, and by adding a trap state 3, we obtain this DFA:

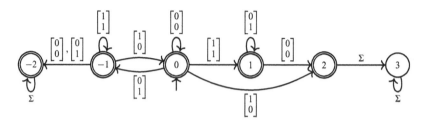

By inspection, we observe that the tuples $[x, y]$ that lead to state $q \in \{-1, 0, 1, 2\}$ are those that satisfy $2x - y = q$. For example, the word $[001001, 010011]$ leads to state -1, and it encodes $[9, 19]$, which yields $2 \cdot 9 - 19 = 18 - 19 = -1$. Furthermore, the tuples that lead to states $q = -2$ and $q = 3$ are those that respectively satisfy $2x - y \leq -2$ and $2x - y \geq 3$.

(c) We consider the language recognized by some state q of an automaton A to be the language recognized by A when making q its unique accepting state. The hint and the observation of (b) suggest to construct an automaton for $a \cdot c \leq b$ that satisfies the following property:

$$q \in \mathbb{Z} \text{ recognizes the encodings of the tuples } c \in \mathbb{N}^n \text{ s.t. } a \cdot c = q. \qquad (0.1)$$

Let $\Sigma = \{0, 1\}^n$. Given a state $q \in \mathbb{Z}$ and a letter $\zeta \in \Sigma$, let us determine the target state q' of the transition (q, ζ, q') of the automaton. A word $w \in \Sigma^*$ is recognized by q iff the word $w\zeta$ is recognized by q'. Since we use the MSBF encoding, if $c \in \mathbb{N}^n$ is the tuple of natural numbers encoded by w, then the tuple encoded by $w\zeta$ is $2c + \zeta$. Thus, $c \in \mathbb{N}^n$ is recognized by q iff $2c + \zeta$ is recognized by q'. Therefore, in order to satisfy property (0.1), we must choose q' so that $a \cdot c = q$ iff $a \cdot (2c + \zeta) = q'$. Consequently, $q' = 2(a \cdot c) + a \cdot \zeta = 2q + a \cdot \zeta$, and so we define the transition function of the automaton by $\delta(q, \zeta) = 2q + a \cdot \zeta$. We observe that a state is final iff it recognizes tuples c such that $a \cdot c = q$ for $q \leq b$; hence, we make all states $q \leq b$ final. We choose 0 as the initial state since $a \cdot (0, \ldots, 0) = 0$.

The resulting automaton is infinite. For example, let us reconsider $2x - y \leq 2$. We have

$$0 \xrightarrow{[1,0]} 2 \xrightarrow{[0,0]} 4 \xrightarrow{[0,0]} 8 \xrightarrow{[0,0]} \cdots, \text{ and}$$

$$0 \xrightarrow{[0,1]} -1 \xrightarrow{[0,0]} -2 \xrightarrow{[0,0]} -4 \xrightarrow{[0,0]} \cdots.$$

Nonetheless, once we reach -2 or 3, the next states are irrelevant: either we accept or reject forever. Indeed, from -2 and 3, only numbers respectively from $(-\infty, 2]$ and $[3, +\infty)$ can be generated. More generally, let

$$\Delta_- = \underbrace{\sum_{1 \leq i \leq n} \min(a_i, 0)}_{\text{sum of negative coefficients}} \text{ and } \Delta_+ = \underbrace{\sum_{1 \leq i \leq n} \max(a_i, 0)}_{\text{sum of positive coefficients}}.$$

It can be shown that states from $[\max(b + 1, -\Delta_-), +\infty)$ can only reach states from this set and that states from $(-\infty, \min(b, -\Delta_+)]$ can only reach states from this set. For example, for $2x - y \le 2$, we obtain the previously identified numbers:

$$\max(b+1, -\Delta_-) = \max(2+1, -(-1)) = \quad 3,$$
$$\min(b, -\Delta_+) = \min(2, -2) \qquad = -2.$$

This leads to the algorithm $AFtoDFA'(\varphi)$ below, where for clarity, the state corresponding to $k \in \mathbb{Z}$ is denoted by s_k:

$AFtoDFA'(\varphi)$
Input: Atomic formula $\varphi = a \cdot x \le b$
Output: DFA $A_\varphi = (Q, \Sigma, \delta, q_0, F)$ such that $\mathcal{L}(A_\varphi) = \mathcal{L}(\varphi)$

```
1    Q, δ, F ← ∅; q₀ ← s₀
2    W ← {s₀}
3    hi ← max(b + 1, − Σ₁≤ᵢ≤ₙ min(aᵢ, 0))
4    lo ← min(b, − Σ₁≤ᵢ≤ₙ max(aᵢ, 0))
5    while W ≠ ∅ do
6       pick sₖ from W
7       add sₖ to Q
8       if k ≤ b then add sₖ to F
9       for all ζ ∈ {0, 1}ⁿ do
10          j ← 2k + a · ζ
11          if j ≥ hi then j ← hi
12          if j ≤ lo then j ← lo
13          if sⱼ ∉ Q then add sⱼ to W
14          add (sₖ, ζ, sⱼ) to δ
```

Let us now prove that it is indeed correct to "finitize" the states as we did. Let $w \in \Sigma^*$ and $\zeta \in \Sigma$. Assume that $a \cdot \text{val}(w) \ge \max(b+1, -\Delta_-)$. First, note that w is rejected since $\text{val}(w) > b$. Moreover, we have $a \cdot \text{val}(w\zeta) \ge \max(b+1, -\Delta_-)$ since

$$a \cdot \text{val}(w\zeta) = 2 \cdot a \cdot \text{val}(w) + a \cdot \text{val}(\zeta)$$
$$\ge 2 \cdot \max(b+1, -\Delta_-) + a \cdot \text{val}(\zeta)$$
$$\ge 2 \cdot \max(b+1, -\Delta_-) + \sum_{1 \le i \le n} \min(a_i, 0)$$
$$= 2 \cdot \max(b+1, -\Delta_-) + \Delta_-$$
$$= \max(2(b+1), -\Delta_-)$$
$$\ge \max(b+1, -\Delta_-) \qquad \text{(by } -\Delta_- \ge 0\text{)}.$$

Thus, it is correct to "merge" all states from $[\max(b+1, -\Delta_-), +\infty)$ into a rejecting trap state.

Now, assume that $a \cdot \mathrm{val}(w) \leq \min(b, -\Delta_+)$. First, note that w is accepted since $\mathrm{val}(w) \leq b$. Moreover, we have $a \cdot \mathrm{val}(w\zeta) \leq \min(b, -\Delta_+)$ since

$$a \cdot \mathrm{val}(w\zeta) = 2 \cdot a \cdot \mathrm{val}(w) + a \cdot \mathrm{val}(\zeta)$$

$$\leq 2 \cdot \min(b, -\Delta_+) + a \cdot \mathrm{val}(\zeta)$$

$$\leq 2 \cdot \min(b, -\Delta_+) + \sum_{1 \leq i \leq n} \max(a_i, 0)$$

$$= 2 \cdot \min(b, -\Delta_+) + \Delta_+$$

$$= \min(2b, -\Delta_+)$$

$$\geq \min(b, -\Delta_+) \hspace{4cm} (\text{by } -\Delta_+ \leq 0).$$

So, it is correct to "merge" all states from $(-\infty, \min(b, -\Delta_+)]$ into a self-accepting state. $\hspace{1cm}\square$

★ ✔ **Exercise 138.** Suppose it is late and you are craving for chicken nuggets. Since you are stuck in the subway, you have no idea how hungry you will be when reaching the restaurant. Since nuggets are only sold in boxes of 6, 9, and 20, you wonder if it will be possible to buy exactly the amount of nuggets you will be craving for when arriving. You also wonder whether it is always possible to buy an exact number of nuggets if one is hungry enough. Luckily, you can answer these questions since you are quite knowledgeable about Presburger arithmetic and automata theory.

For every finite set $S \subseteq \mathbb{N}$, we say that number $n \in \mathbb{N}$ is an *S-number* if n can be obtained as a linear combination of elements of S. For example, if $S = \{6, 9, 20\}$, then 67 is an S-number since $67 = 3 \cdot 6 + 1 \cdot 9 + 2 \cdot 20$, but 25 is not. For some sets S, there are only finitely many numbers that are not S-numbers. When this is the case, we say that the largest number that is not an S-number is the *Frobenius number* of S. For example, 7 is the Frobenius number of $\{3, 5\}$, and $S = \{2, 4\}$ has no Frobenius number.

To answer your questions, it suffices to come up with algorithms for Frobenius numbers and to instantiate them with $S = \{6, 9, 20\}$.

(a) Give an algorithm that decides, on input $n \in \mathbb{N}$ and a finite set $S \subseteq_{\text{finite}} \mathbb{N}$, whether n is an S-number.

(b) Give an algorithm that decides, on input $S \subseteq_{\text{finite}} \mathbb{N}$, whether S has a Frobenius number.

(c) Give an algorithm that computes, on input $S \subseteq_{\text{finite}} \mathbb{N}$, the Frobenius number of S (assuming it exists).

(d) Show that $S = \{6, 9, 20\}$ has a Frobenius number, and identify it.

Solution:

(a) Let $S = \{a_1, a_2, \ldots, a_k\}$. A number $n \in \mathbb{N}$ is an S-number iff there exist $x_1, x_2, \ldots, x_k \in \mathbb{N}$ such that $n = a_1 x_1 + a_2 x_2 + \ldots + a_k x_k$ which is equivalent to $n - a_1 x_1 - a_2 x_2 - \ldots - a_k x_k = 0$. Therefore, given S, we do the following:

(i) construct a transducer A that accepts the solutions of $y - a_1 x_1 - a_2 x_2 - \ldots - a_k x_k = 0$ using algorithm *EqtoDFA*,

(ii) construct an automaton B obtained by projecting A onto y,

(iii) test whether LSBF(n) is accepted by B, and

(iv) return *true* iff LSBF(n) is accepted.

Note that A is a DFA, but B might be an NFA due to the projection.

(b) Let B be the automaton constructed in (a). Observe that S has a Frobenius number iff $\{n \in \mathbb{N} : \text{LSBF}(n) \notin \mathcal{L}(B)\}$ is finite. This suggests to complement B. Since B is an NFA, we first convert it to a DFA B' and then complement B'. Let C be the resulting DFA.

To test whether S has a Frobenius number, it is now tempting to test whether $\mathcal{L}(C)$ is finite. This is, however, incorrect. Indeed, every natural number has infinitely many LSBF encodings (e.g., 2 is encoded by 010*). Thus, $\mathcal{L}(C)$ will be infinite even if C accepts finitely many numbers. To address this issue, we prune $\mathcal{L}(C)$ by keeping only the minimal encoding of each number accepted by C. Note that an LSBF encoding is minimal iff it does not contain any trailing 0. Thus, we can construct a DFA M that accepts the set of minimal LSBF encodings:

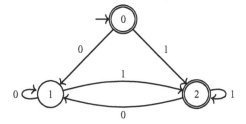

To prune $\mathcal{L}(C)$ of the redundant LSBF encodings, we construct a new DFA D obtained by intersecting C with M.

It remains to test whether $\mathcal{L}(D)$ is finite. By construction, every state of D is reachable from the initial state. However, due to our transformations, it may be the case that some states of D cannot reach a final state. We may remove these states in linear time. This can be done by (implicitly) reversing the arcs of D (seen as graph) and then performing a depth-first search from the final states. The states that are not explored by the search are removed from D. Let D' be the resulting DFA. Testing whether $\mathcal{L}(D')$ is finite amounts to testing whether D' contains no cycle. This can be done in linear time using a depth-first search.

The overall algorithm is as follows:

(i) convert B to a DFA B',

(ii) obtain a new DFA C by complementing B',

(iii) obtain a new DFA D by intersecting C with M,

(iv) obtain a new DFA D' by removing every state of D that cannot reach some final state,

(v) test whether D' contains a cycle, and

(vi) return *true* iff D' contains no cycle.

Let us show that it is indeed the case that $\mathcal{L}(D')$ is finite iff D' has no cycle or, equivalently, that $\mathcal{L}(D')$ is infinite iff D' contains a cycle. Let $D' = (Q, \{0, 1\}, \delta, q_0, F)$.

$\Rightarrow$) Assume $\mathcal{L}(D')$ is infinite. By assumption, D' accepts a word w such that $|w| = m$ for some $m > |Q|$. Let $q_0, q_1, \ldots, q_m \in Q$ be such that $q_0 \xrightarrow{w_1} q_1 \xrightarrow{w_2} q_2 \cdots \xrightarrow{w_m} q_m$. By the pigeonhole principle, there exist $0 \leq i < j \leq m$ such that $q_i = q_j$. Thus, D' contains the cycle

$$q_i \xrightarrow{w_{i+1}} q_{i+1} \xrightarrow{w_{i+2}} \cdots \xrightarrow{w_j} q_i.$$

$\Leftarrow$) Assume D' contains a cycle $q \xrightarrow{v} q$ for some $q \in Q$ and $v \in \{0, 1\}^+$. By construction of D', state q is reachable from q_0, and q can reach some final state $q_f \in F$. Therefore, there exist $u, w \in \{0, 1\}^*$ such that

$$q_0 \xrightarrow{u} q \xrightarrow{v} q \xrightarrow{w} q_f.$$

Since $q \xrightarrow{v} q$ can be iterated arbitrarily many times, every word of uv^*w is accepted by D', which implies that $\mathcal{L}(D')$ is infinite. $\qquad\square$

(c) Assume S has a Frobenius number. Let D' be the DFA obtained in (b). The Frobenius number of S is the largest natural number n accepted by D'. By assumption, $\mathcal{L}(D')$ is finite. Thus, we could find n by using a brute-force approach where we go through all words accepted by D'. It is, however, possible to find n much more efficiently with dynamic programming.

Observe that D' is acyclic. Therefore, we may compute a topological ordering $q_0, q_1, \ldots, q_m$ of Q. For every $0 \leq i \leq m$, let

$$\ell_i = \operatorname{argmax}_{w \in L_i} \operatorname{value}(w),$$

where $L_i = \{w \in \{0, 1\}^* : q_0 \xrightarrow{w} q_i\}$. Due to the topological ordering, each ℓ_i can be computed as follows:

$$\ell_i = \begin{cases} \varepsilon & \text{if } i = 0, \\ \operatorname{argmax}_{w \in W} \operatorname{value}(w), \text{ where} & \\ \quad W = \{\ell_j \cdot a : 0 \leq j < i, a \in \{0, 1\}, \delta(q_j, a) = q_i\} & \text{if } i > 0. \end{cases}$$

Once each ℓ_i is computed, we can easily derive n since $n = \max\{\operatorname{value}(\ell_i) : q_i \in F\}$.

Note that to test whether $\operatorname{value}(u) \geq \operatorname{value}(v)$, it is not necessary to convert u and v to their numerical values. Instead, the test can be carried by testing whether u is greater than or equal to v under the colexicographic ordering (i.e., $u^R \succeq_{\text{lex}} v^R$).

(d) By executing our procedure for $S = \{6, 9, 20\}$, we obtain a DFA D' with thirty states and no cycle. Thus, S has a Frobenius number. By executing the procedure described in (c), we obtain 43 as the Frobenius number of S.

★☞ **Exercise 140.** Converting a Presburger formula over k variables into a DFA yields an alphabet of 2^k letters. In order to mitigate this combinatorial explosion, one can instead label transitions with boolean expressions. For example, $[0, 1]$ can be written as $\neg x \wedge y$, and the set $\{[1, 0], [1, 1]\}$ can be written as x. Such expressions can internally be represented (e.g., as binary decision diagrams).

(a) Give DFAs for formulas $x < y$ and $y < z$, using boolean expressions rather than letters.
(b) Construct a DFA for $x < y < z$.

Solution:

(a)

(b) We intersect the two above DFAs by taking the conjunction of expressions. For example,

$$p_0 \xrightarrow{x \vee \neg y} p_0 \text{ and } q_0 \xrightarrow{\neg y \wedge z} q_1 \text{ yields } (p_0, q_0) \xrightarrow{(x \vee \neg y) \wedge (\neg y \wedge z)} (p_0, q_1).$$

The expression $(x \vee \neg y) \wedge (\neg y \wedge z)$ can be simplified to $\neg y \wedge z$. By proceeding this way and simplifying boolean expressions, we obtain the following DFA whose trap state is omitted for the sake of readability:

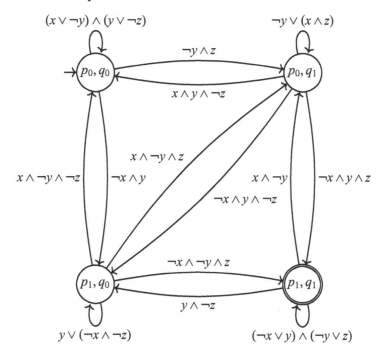

Note that the above DFA has fourteen explicit transitions plus three implicit transitions for the omitted trap states. The DFA we would obtain by using letters rather than boolean expressions would have twenty-eight explicit transitions plus twelve implicit transitions for the omitted trap states.

Solutions for Chapter 10

★ 🔲 **Exercise 141.** Construct Büchi automata and ω-regular expressions, as small as possible, recognizing the following ω-languages over the alphabet $\{a, b, c\}$. Recall that $inf(w)$ is the set of letters of $\{a, b, c\}$ that occur infinitely often in w.

(a) $\{w \in \{a, b, c\}^{\omega} : \{a, b\} \supseteq inf(w)\}$,
(b) $\{w \in \{a, b, c\}^{\omega} : \{a, b\} = inf(w)\}$,
(c) $\{w \in \{a, b, c\}^{\omega} : \{a, b\} \subseteq inf(w)\}$.

Solution: Let us first provide ω-regular expressions for the three languages:

(a) $[(b+c)^* a (a+c)^* b]^{\omega}$,
(b) $(a+b+c)^* (a+b)^{\omega}$,
(c) $(a+b+c)^* (aa^* bb^*)^{\omega}$.

We now provide Büchi automata for the three languages.

(a) The automaton must recognize the set of ω-words containing only finitely many c. We claim that the following Büchi automaton achieves this task. Indeed, every word with finitely many occurrences of c is accepted: the automaton just moves to q_1 after the last c. Conversely, every accepting run must eventually move to q_1, and so the word accepted contains only finitely many c.

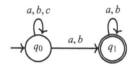

(b) The automaton must recognize the ω-words containing infinitely many a, infinitely many b, but only finitely many c. Every such ω-word is accepted by the following automaton: the automaton moves to q_1 after the last c. The rest of the word contains only a and b, both infinitely many times, and hence infinitely many occurrences of ab. At each of them, the automaton takes the loop through q_2. Conversely, every accepted word contains only finitely many c, because after moving to q_1, no further c can be read, and both infinitely many occurrences of a and b, because every accepting run must visit q_2 infinitely often, and each visit contributes an a and a b.

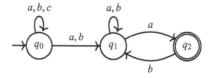

(c) The following automaton recognizes all ω-words containing infinitely many a and infinitely many b and either finitely or infinitely many c. To show that every such word is accepted by the automaton, we have to modify the argument of (b): now every word in the language contains infinitely many subwords of ac^*b, and the automaton accepts the word by moving to q_1 at each of these subwords. For the converse, it is clear that every visit to q_1 requires to read an a and a b, and so every accepted word contains both letters infinitely often. Note that we cannot remove q_2 and add a self-loop labeled by c to q_1, because then the automaton would accept, for instance, ac^ω.

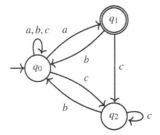

★ ■ **Exercise 145.** Recall that every finite set of finite words is a regular language. Prove that this does not hold for infinite words. More precisely:

(a) Prove that every nonempty ω-regular language contains an *ultimately periodic* ω-word (i.e., an ω-word of the form uv^ω for some finite words $u \in \Sigma^*$ and $v \in \Sigma^+$).

(b) Give an ω-word w such that $\{w\}$ is not an ω-regular language.   *Hint: Use (a).*

Solution:

(a) Let L be a nonempty ω-regular language and let $B = (Q, \{0, 1\}, \delta, Q_0, F)$ be an NBA that recognizes L. Since Q is finite, there exist $u \in \Sigma^*$, $v \in \Sigma^+$, $q_0 \in Q_0$, and $q \in F$ such that

$$q_0 \xrightarrow{u} q \xrightarrow{v} q.$$

Consequently, we have $uv^\omega \in L$ by iterating v from state q.   □

(b) Let $w \in \{0, 1\}^\omega$ be the word given by

$$w_i = \begin{cases} 1 & \text{if } i \text{ is a square,} \\ 0 & \text{otherwise.} \end{cases}$$

We prove that w is not ultimately periodic, which, by (a), implies that $\{w\}$ is not ω-regular. For the sake of contradiction, suppose $w = uv^\omega$ for some $u \in \{0, 1\}^*$ and $v \in \{0, 1\}^+$. If $v \in 0^*$, then we obtain a contradiction. Thus, there exists $1 \le i \le |v|$ such that $v_i = 1$. Let $m = |u| + i$ and $n = |v|$. By definition of w, $m + j \cdot n$ is a square for every $j \ge 0$. In particular, there exist $0 < a < b$ such that

$$m + n \cdot n = a^2 \text{ and } m + n \cdot n + n = b^2.$$

Note that $a \ge n$. Moreover,

$$b^2 = a^2 + n \le a^2 + a < a^2 + 2a + 1 = (a + 1)^2.$$

Therefore, $a^2 < b^2 < (a + 1)^2$, which is a contradiction.   □

★ ■ **Exercise 146.** Consider the class of nondeterministic automata over ω-words with the following acceptance condition: an infinite run is accepting iff it visits an accepting state *at least once*. Show that no such automaton accepts the language of all words over $\{a, b\}$ containing infinitely many a and infinitely many b.

Solution: For the sake of contradiction, suppose there exists such an automaton $B = (Q, \{a, b\}, \delta, Q_0, F)$ recognizing L. Let $n = |Q|$. Since $w = (ab^n)^{\omega}$ belongs to L, there exist $u, v \in \{a, b\}^*$, $q_0 \in Q_0$, $q_{acc} \in F$, and $r_0, r_1, \ldots, r_n \in Q$ such that

$$q_0 \xrightarrow{u} q_{acc} \xrightarrow{v} r_0 \xrightarrow{b} r_1 \xrightarrow{b} \cdots \xrightarrow{b} r_n.$$

By the pigeonhole principle, there exist $0 \le i < j \le n$ such that $r_i = r_j$. Therefore,

$$q_0 \xrightarrow{u} q_{acc} \xrightarrow{vb^i} r_i \xrightarrow{b^{j-i}} r_j \xrightarrow{b^{j-i}} r_j \xrightarrow{b^{j-i}} \cdots.$$

We conclude that $uvb^i(b^{j-i})^{\omega}$ is accepted by B, which is a contradiction as it contains finitely many occurrences of a.   □

★ ▣ **Exercise 147.** The *limit* of a language $L \subseteq \Sigma^*$ is the ω-language $lim(L)$ defined as $w \in lim(L)$ iff infinitely many prefixes of w are words of L (e.g., the limit of $(ab)^*$ is $\{(ab)^{\omega}\}$).

(a) Determine the limit of the following regular languages over $\{a, b\}$:

(i) $(a + b)^*a$,

(ii) the set of words containing an even number of a,

(iii) a^*b.

(b) Prove the following: An ω-language is recognizable by a deterministic Büchi automaton iff it is the limit of a regular language.

(c) Exhibit a nonregular language whose limit is ω-regular.

(d) Exhibit a nonregular language whose limit is not ω-regular.

Solution:

(a)

(i) The set of ω-words containing infinitely many a.

(ii) The set of ω-words containing infinitely many a, plus the set of ω-words containing a finite even number of a.

(iii) The empty ω-language.

(b) Let B be a deterministic Büchi automaton recognizing an ω-language L. Consider B as a DFA, and let L' be the regular language recognized by B. We show that $L = lim(L')$. If $w \in lim(L')$, then B (as a DFA) accepts infinitely many prefixes of w. Since B is deterministic, the runs of B on these prefixes are prefixes of the unique infinite run of B (as a DBA) on w. So the infinite run visits accepting states infinitely often, and so $w \in L$. If $w \in L$, then the unique run of B on w (as a DBA) visits accepting states infinitely often, and so infinitely many prefixes of w are accepted by B (as a DFA). Thus, $w \in lim(L')$.   □

(c) Let $L = \{a^{n^2} : n \geq 0\}$. We have $lim(L) = \{a^{\omega}\}$, which is ω-regular, although L is not regular. Alternatively, if $L = \{a^n b^n : n \geq 0\}$, then $lim(L) = \emptyset$, which is also ω-regular.

(d) Let $L = \{a^n b^n c^m : n, m \geq 0\}$. We have $lim(L) = \{a^n b^n c^{\omega} : n \geq 0\}$. Suppose this language is ω-regular and hence recognized by a Büchi automaton B. By the pigeonhole principle, there are distinct $n_1, n_2 \in \mathbb{N}$ and accepting runs ρ_1, ρ_2 of B on $a^{n_1} b^{n_1} c^{\omega}$ and $a^{n_2} b^{n_2} c^{\omega}$ such that the state reached in ρ_1 after reading a^{n_1} and the state reached in ρ_2 after reading a^{n_2} coincide. This means that B accepts $a^{n_1} b^{n_2} c^{\omega}$, which contradicts the assumption that B recognizes L.

☆■ **Exercise 148.** Let $L_1 = (ab)^{\omega}$ and let L_2 be the ω-language of all ω-words over $\{a, b\}$ containing infinitely many a and infinitely many b.

(a) Exhibit three different DBAs with three states recognizing L_1.

(b) Exhibit six different DBAs with three states recognizing L_2.

(c) Show that no DBA with at most two states recognizes L_1 or L_2.

Solution:

(a) We obtain three DBAs for L_1 from the one below by making q_0, q_1, or both accepting

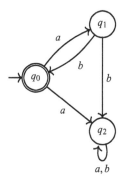

(b) Here are two different DBAs for L_2. We obtain two further DBAs from each of these automata by making either q_1 or q_2 the initial state.

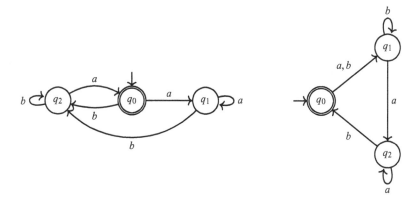

(c) Assume there is a DBA B with at most two states recognizing L_1. Since L_1 is nonempty, B has at least one (reachable) accepting state q. Consider the transitions leaving q labeled by a and b. If any of them leads to q again, then B accepts an ω-word of the form wa^ω or wb^ω for some finite word w. Since no word of this form belongs to L_1, we reach a contradiction. Thus, B must have two states q and q', and transitions

$$t_a = q \xrightarrow{a} q' \text{ and } t_b = q \xrightarrow{b} q'.$$

Consider any accepting run ρ of B. If the word accepted by the run does not belong to L_1, we are done. So assume it belongs to L_1. Since ρ is accepting, it contains some occurrence of t_a or t_b. Consider the run ρ' obtained by exchanging the first occurrence of one of them by the other (i.e., if t_a occurs first, then replace it by t_b and vice versa). Then, ρ' is an accepting run, and the word it accepts is the result of turning an a into a b or vice versa. In both cases, the resulting word does not belong to L_1, so we reach again a contradiction, and we are done.

The proof for L_2 is similar.   □

★ ■ **Exercise 150.** In definition 2.20, we introduced the quotient A/P of an NFA A with respect to a partition P of its states. In lemma 2.22, we proved $\mathcal{L}(A) = \mathcal{L}(A/P_\ell)$ for the language partition P_ℓ that puts two states q_1, q_2 in the same block iff $\mathcal{L}_A(q_1) = \mathcal{L}_A(q_2)$. Let $B = (Q, \Sigma, \delta, Q_0, F)$ be an NBA. Given a partition P of Q, define the quotient B/P of B with respect to P as for an NFA.

(a) Let P_ℓ be the partition of Q that puts two states q_1, q_2 of B in the same block iff $L_{\omega,B}(q_1) = L_{\omega,B}(q_2)$, where $L_{\omega,B}(q)$ denotes the ω-language containing the words accepted by B with q as initial state. Does $\mathcal{L}_\omega(B) = \mathcal{L}_\omega(B/P_\ell)$ always hold?

(b) Let CSR be the coarsest stable refinement of the equivalence relation with equivalence classes $\{F, Q \setminus F\}$. Does $\mathcal{L}_\omega(A) = \mathcal{L}_\omega(A/CSR)$ always hold?

Solution:

(a) No. The following Büchi automaton, which is even deterministic, is a counterexample. All states accept the same language: the words containing infinitely many a and infinitely many b. The quotient is an automaton with a single state, both initial and accepting, that recognizes the set of all words.   □

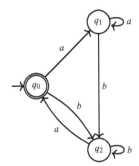

(b) Yes. The relation CSR partitions the set of states into blocks such that the states of a block are either all accepting or all nonaccepting (because every equivalence class of CSR is included in F or $Q \setminus F$). Moreover, since CSR is stable, for every two states q, r of a block of CSR and for every $(q, a, q') \in \delta$, there is a transition (r, a, r') such that q', r' belong to the same block. This implies $\mathcal{L}(q) = \mathcal{L}(r)$, because every run

$$q \xrightarrow{a_1} q_1 \xrightarrow{a_2} q_2 \cdots \xrightarrow{a_n} q_n$$

can be "matched" by a run

$$r \xrightarrow{a_1} r_1 \xrightarrow{a_2} r_2 \cdots \xrightarrow{a_n} r_n$$

in such a way that, for every $i \geq 1$, states q_i, r_i belong to the same block, and so, in particular, q_n is accepting iff r_n is accepting, which implies $a_1 \cdots a_n \in \mathcal{L}(q)$ iff $a_1 \cdots a_n \in \mathcal{L}(r)$.

Observe that we not only have that q_n and r_n are both accepting or nonaccepting: the same holds for every pair q_i, r_i. Moreover, the property also holds for ω-words: every infinite run

$$q \xrightarrow{a_1} q_1 \xrightarrow{a_2} q_2 \xrightarrow{a_3} q_3 \cdots$$

is "matched" by an infinite run

$$r \xrightarrow{a_1} r_1 \xrightarrow{a_2} r_2 \xrightarrow{a_3} r_3 \cdots$$

so that, for every $i \geq 1$, states q_i, r_i are both accepting or nonaccepting. This immediately proves $\mathcal{L}_\omega(A) = \mathcal{L}_\omega(A/CSR)$. $\qquad\square$

⭐ ■ **Exercise 151.** Let L be an ω-language over alphabet Σ, and let $w \in \Sigma^*$. The w-*residual* of L is the ω-language $L^w = \{w' \in \Sigma^\omega : ww' \in L\}$. An ω-language L' is a *residual* of L if $L' = L^w$ for some word $w \in \Sigma^*$. We show that the theorem stating that a language of finite words is regular iff it has finitely many residuals does not extend to ω-regular languages.

(a) Prove this statement: If L is an ω-regular language, then it has finitely many residuals.

(b) Disprove this statement: Every ω-language with finitely many residuals is ω-regular.

Hint: Consider a nonultimately periodic ω-word w and its language $Tail_w$ of infinite tails.

Solution:

(a) Let $B = (Q, \Sigma, \delta, Q_0, F)$ be an NBA that recognizes L. For every $Q' \subseteq Q$, let $\mathcal{L}_\omega(Q')$ be the language recognized by B with Q' as the set of initial states. For every $w \in \Sigma^*$, let

$$Q_w = \{q \in Q : q_0 \xrightarrow{w} q \text{ for some } q_0 \in Q_0\}.$$

Clearly, we have $L^w = \mathcal{L}_\omega(Q_w)$. Therefore, L has at most $2^{|Q|}$ residuals. $\qquad\square$

(b) Let w be some nonultimately periodic ω-word (e.g., the one from the solution of exercise 145 or the digits of π). Let $Tail_w$ be the set of all infinite suffixes of w, and define $L = \Sigma^* Tail_w$, where Σ is the alphabet of letters that appear in w. We show the following:

• L has only one residual.

Let $w_1, w_2 \in \Sigma^*$. We prove $L^{w_1} = L^{w_2}$. Let $w' \in L^{w_1}$. By the definition of residual and of L, we have $w_1 w' \in \Sigma^* Tail_w$. Note that $Tail_w$ is closed under suffix (i.e., if an ω-word belongs to $Tail_w$, then so do all their suffixes). Thus, we have $w' = uv$ for some $v \in Tail_w$. Consequently, $w_2 uv \in \Sigma^* Tail_w$, which implies $w_2 w' \in L$, and so $w' \in L^{w_2}$.

- L is not ω-regular.

Assume L is ω-regular. By exercise 145, L contains an ultimately periodic word uv^ω. This means that some tail of w is of the form $u'v^\omega$, and hence $w = u''v^\omega$ for some word u'', contradicting the fact that w is not ultimately periodic. $\square$

★ ✔ **Exercise 152.** The solution to exercise 150(2) shows that the reduction algorithm for NFAs that computes the partition CSR of a given NFA A and constructs the quotient A/CSR can also be applied to NBAs. Generalize the algorithm so that it works for NGAs.

Solution: Let $B = (Q, \Sigma, \delta, q_0, \{F_1, \ldots, F_n\})$ be an NGA. Let us consider the following partition of Q. Two states $q, r \in Q$ belong to the same block if

$$\text{for every } i \in \{1, \ldots, n\} \text{ either } \{q, r\} \subseteq F_i \text{ or } \{q, r\} \cap F_i = \emptyset.$$

Let CSR' be defined as the coarsest stable refinement of this partition. For every two states $q, r \in Q$ belonging to the same block of CSR', we now have that every infinite run

$$q \xrightarrow{a_1} q_1 \xrightarrow{a_2} q_2 \xrightarrow{a_3} q_3 \cdots$$

is "matched" by a run

$$r \xrightarrow{a_1} r_1 \xrightarrow{a_2} r_2 \xrightarrow{a_3} r_3 \cdots$$

so that for every $i \geq 1$ and for every $j \in \{1, \ldots, n\}$, either $\{q_i, r_i\} \subseteq F_j$ or $\{q_i, r_i\} \cap F_j = \emptyset$. Thus, we get $\mathcal{L}_\omega(B) = \mathcal{L}_\omega(B/CSR')$.

☆ ■ **Exercise 154.** Show that a parity condition $(F_1, F_2, \ldots, F_{2m})$ is equivalent to the Streett condition $\{\langle \emptyset, F_1 \rangle, \langle F_2, F_3 \rangle, \ldots, \langle F_{2m-2}, F_{2m-1} \rangle\}$.

Solution: With the parity condition $(F_1, F_2, \ldots, F_{2m})$, a run ρ is accepting iff the smallest index i satisfying $\inf \rho \cap F_i \neq \emptyset$ is even. This is equivalent to: A run ρ is accepting iff it is not the case that the minimal index i such that $\inf(\rho) \cap F_i \neq \emptyset$ is odd. In other words, ρ is accepting iff

$$\text{not} \left(\begin{array}{l} \quad \inf(\rho) \cap F_1 \neq \emptyset \\ \text{or} \quad \inf(\rho) \cap F_2 = \emptyset \quad \text{and} \quad \inf(\rho) \cap F_3 \neq \emptyset, \\ \text{or} \quad \cdots \\ \text{or} \quad \inf(\rho) \cap F_{2m-2} = \emptyset \quad \text{and} \quad \inf(\rho) \cap F_{2m-1} \neq \emptyset \end{array} \right)$$

which can be rewritten as

$$\begin{array}{l} \qquad \quad \inf(\rho) \cap \emptyset \neq \emptyset \quad \text{or} \quad \inf(\rho) \cap F_1 = \emptyset, \\ \text{and} \quad \inf(\rho) \cap F_2 \neq \emptyset \quad \text{or} \quad \inf(\rho) \cap F_3 = \emptyset, \\ \text{and} \quad \cdots \\ \text{and} \quad \inf(\rho) \cap F_{2m-2} \neq \emptyset \quad \text{or} \quad \inf(\rho) \cap F_{2m-1} = \emptyset. \end{array}$$

This is exactly the Streett condition $\{\langle \emptyset, F_1 \rangle, \langle F_2, F_3 \rangle, \ldots, \langle F_{2m-2}, F_{2m-1} \rangle\}$. $\square$

Solutions for Chapter 11

☆ ⚙ **Exercise 155.** Consider the following two Büchi automata (NBAs). Interpret them as generalized Büchi automata (NGAs), construct their intersection, and convert the resulting NGA into an NBA.

A:

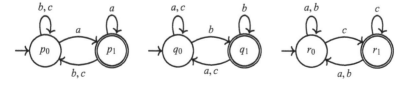

B:

Solution: We first obtain the following NGA with acceptance condition $\mathcal{G} = \{F_0, F_1\}$ depicted respectively as hatched and filled states:

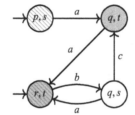

By making two copies, we obtain the following equivalent NBA:

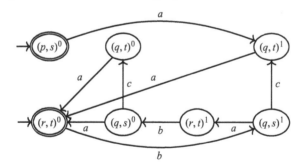

☆ ⚙ **Exercise 156.** Let $L_\sigma = \{w \in \{a, b, c\}^\omega : w \text{ contains infinitely many } \sigma s\}$. Give deterministic Büchi automata for languages L_a, L_b, and L_c; construct the intersection of these automata interpreted as NGAs; and convert the resulting NGA as a Büchi automaton.

Solution: The following Büchi automata respectively accept L_a, L_b, and L_c:

By applying the intersection and conversion procedures, we obtain the following deterministic Büchi automaton:

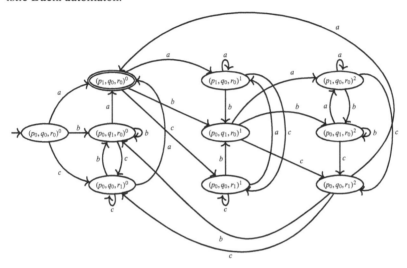

Note that $L_a \cap L_b \cap L_b$ is accepted by a smaller DBA:

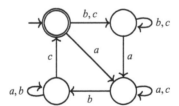

☆ 🖾 **Exercise 158.** An ω-automaton has acceptance on transitions if the acceptance
condition specifies which transitions must appear infinitely often in a run. All classes of
ω-automata (Büchi, Rabin, etc.) can be defined with acceptance on transitions rather than
states.

Give minimal deterministic automata, for the language of words over $\{a, b\}$ containing
infinitely many a and infinitely many b, of the following kinds: (a) Büchi (with state-
based accepting condition), (b) generalized Büchi (with state-based accepting condition),
(c) Büchi with acceptance on transitions, and (d) generalized Büchi with acceptance on
transitions.

Solution: Automata (a), (b), (c), and (d) are respectively as follows, where colored
patterns indicate the sets of accepting states or transitions:

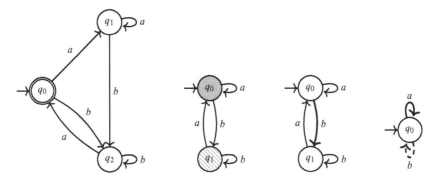

⭐ ⚙ **Exercise 159.** Consider the following Büchi automaton over $\Sigma = \{a, b\}$:

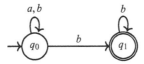

(a) Sketch dag($abab^\omega$) and dag($(ab)^\omega$).

(b) Let r_w be the ranking of dag(w) defined by

$$r_w(q, i) = \begin{cases} 1 & \text{if } q = q_0 \text{ and } \langle q_0, i \rangle \text{ appears in dag}(w), \\ 0 & \text{if } q = q_1 \text{ and } \langle q_1, i \rangle \text{ appears in dag}(w), \\ \perp & \text{otherwise.} \end{cases}$$

Are r_{abab^ω} and $r_{(ab)^\omega}$ odd rankings?

(c) Show that r_w is an odd ranking if and only if $w \notin \mathcal{L}_\omega(B)$.

(d) Build a Büchi automaton accepting $\overline{\mathcal{L}_\omega(B)}$ using the construction seen in the chapter.
Hint: By (c), it is sufficient to use $\{0, 1\}$ as ranks.

Solution:

(a) dag($abab^\omega$):

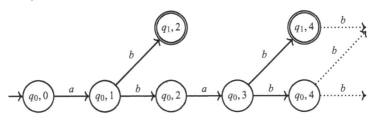

dag($(ab)^\omega$):

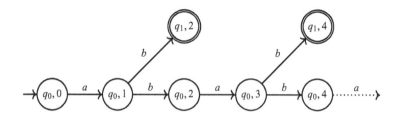

(b)

• r_{abab^ω} *is not* an odd ranking since

$$\langle q_0, 0\rangle \xrightarrow{a} \langle q_0, 1\rangle \xrightarrow{b} \langle q_0, 2\rangle \xrightarrow{a} \langle q_0, 3\rangle \xrightarrow{b} \langle q_1, 4\rangle \xrightarrow{b} \langle q_1, 5\rangle \xrightarrow{b} \cdots$$

is an infinite path of $\mathrm{dag}(abab^\omega)$ not visiting odd nodes i.o.

• $r_{(ab)^\omega}$ *is* an odd ranking since it has a single infinite path:

$$\langle q_0, 0\rangle \xrightarrow{a} \langle q_0, 1\rangle \xrightarrow{b} \langle q_0, 2\rangle \xrightarrow{a} \langle q_0, 3\rangle \xrightarrow{b} \langle q_0, 4\rangle \xrightarrow{a} \langle q_0, 5\rangle \xrightarrow{b} \cdots$$

which only visits odd nodes.

(c) $\Rightarrow$) Let $w \in \mathcal{L}_\omega(B)$. We have $w = ub^\omega$ for some $u \in \{a, b\}^*$. This implies that

$$\langle q_0, 0\rangle \xrightarrow{u} \langle q_0, |u|\rangle \xrightarrow{b} \langle q_1, |u| + 1\rangle \xrightarrow{b} \langle q_1, |u| + 2\rangle \xrightarrow{b} \cdots$$

is an infinite path of $\mathrm{dag}(w)$. Since this path does not visit odd nodes infinitely often, r is not odd for $\mathrm{dag}(w)$.

$\Leftarrow$) Let $w \notin \mathcal{L}_\omega(B)$. Suppose there exists an infinite path of $\mathrm{dag}(w)$ that does not visit odd nodes infinitely often. At some point, this path must only visit nodes of the form $\langle q_1, i\rangle$. Thus, there exists $u \in \{a, b\}^*$ such that

$$\langle q_0, 0\rangle \xrightarrow{u} \langle q_1, |u|\rangle \xrightarrow{b} \langle q_1, |u| + 1\rangle \xrightarrow{b} \langle q_1, |u| + 2\rangle \xrightarrow{b} \cdots .$$

This implies that $w = ub^\omega \in \mathcal{L}_\omega(B)$, which is a contradiction.   □

(d) By (c), for every $w \in \{a, b\}^\omega$, if $\mathrm{dag}(w)$ has an odd ranking, then it has one ranging over 0 and 1. Therefore, it suffices to execute *CompNBA* with rankings ranging over 0 and 1. We obtain the following Büchi automaton:

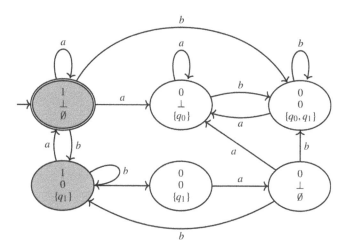

Actually, by (c), it is sufficient to only explore the colored states as they correspond to the family of rankings $\{r_w : w \in \Sigma^\omega\}$.

★ ☞ **Exercise 162.** A Büchi automaton $A = (Q, \Sigma, \delta, Q_0, F)$ is *weak* if no strongly connected component (SCC) of A contains both accepting and nonaccepting states—that is, every SCC $C \subseteq Q$ satisfies either $C \subseteq F$ or $C \subseteq Q \setminus F$.

(a) Prove that a Büchi automaton A is *weak* iff for every run ρ, either $\mathit{inf}(\rho) \subseteq F$ or $\mathit{inf}(\rho) \subseteq Q \setminus F$.

(b) Prove that the algorithms for union, intersection, and complementation of DFAs are correct for weak DBAs. More precisely, show that the algorithms return weak DBAs recognizing respectively the union, intersection, and complement of the languages of the input automata.

Solution:

(a) For every run ρ, any two states of $\mathit{inf}(\rho)$ are necessarily reachable from each other, and hence $\mathit{inf}(\rho)$ is contained in a SCC of A. Let C_ρ be this SCC.

$\Rightarrow$) If A is weak, then either $C_\rho \subseteq F$ or $C_\rho \subseteq Q \setminus F$, and so $\mathit{inf}(\rho) \subseteq F$ or $\mathit{inf}(\rho) \subseteq Q \setminus F$.

$\Leftarrow$) Assume that for every run ρ, either $\mathit{inf}(\rho) \subseteq F$ or $\mathit{inf}(\rho) \subseteq Q \setminus F$. Let C be an SCC of A. There is a word w such that the run ρ of A on w satisfies $\mathit{inf}(\rho) = C$. Therefore, we have $C \subseteq F$ or $C \subseteq Q \setminus F$. $\square$

(b) We first consider the complementation algorithm *CompDFA* (section 3.1.2). Recall that the algorithm simply exchanges accepting and nonaccepting states. Let $A = (Q, \Sigma, \delta, q_0, F)$ be a weak DBA, and let $\overline{A} = CompDFA(A)$. Since the SCCs of A and $\overline{A}$ coincide, $\overline{A}$ is also a weak DBA. Moreover, for every ω-word w, both A and $\overline{A}$ have the same run ρ on w. If A accepts w, then by (a), we have $\mathit{inf}(\rho) \subseteq F$, and so $\overline{A}$ does not accept w. If A does not accept w, then by (a), we have $\mathit{inf}(\rho) \subseteq Q \setminus F$, and so $\overline{A}$ accepts w.

We now consider the algorithm for intersection (the union is similar). Let $A_1 = (Q_1, \Sigma, \delta_1, q_{01}, F_1)$ and $A_2 = (Q_2, \Sigma, \delta_2, q_{02}, F_2)$ be weak DBAs. Let us recall the algorithm for intersection—that is, the result of instantiating algorithm *BinOp* (section 3.1.3) with the boolean operator "and." It constructs a deterministic automaton A with set of states $Q_1 \times Q_2$, initial state $[q_{01}, q_{02}]$, and set of final states $F_1 \times F_2$. Given an ω-word w, we have that

$$\rho_1 = q_{01} \xrightarrow{a_1} q_{11} \xrightarrow{a_2} q_{21} \cdots \xrightarrow{a_n} q_{n1} \cdots$$

$$\rho_2 = q_{02} \xrightarrow{a_1} q_{12} \xrightarrow{a_2} q_{22} \cdots \xrightarrow{a_n} q_{n2} \cdots$$

are the (unique) runs of A_1 and A_2 on w if and only if

$$\rho = \begin{bmatrix} q_{01} \\ q_{02} \end{bmatrix} \xrightarrow{a_1} \begin{bmatrix} q_{11} \\ q_{12} \end{bmatrix} \xrightarrow{a_2} \begin{bmatrix} q_{21} \\ q_{22} \end{bmatrix} \cdots \xrightarrow{a_n} \begin{bmatrix} q_{n1} \\ q_{n2} \end{bmatrix} \cdots$$

is the (unique) run of A on w.

We first show that A is weak. By (a), it suffices to show that for every run ρ, either $inf(\rho) \subseteq F$ or $inf(\rho) \subseteq Q \setminus F$. Consider two cases:

- ρ only visits states of F finitely often. We immediately have $inf(\rho) \subseteq Q \setminus F$.
- ρ visits states of F infinitely often. Since $F = F_1 \times F_2$, both ρ_1 and ρ_2 visit states of F_1 and F_2 infinitely often. Since A_1 and A_2 are weak, we have $inf(\rho_1) \subseteq F_1$ and $inf(\rho_2) \subseteq F_2$. Thus, there are indices i_1 and i_2 such that $q_{j1} \in F_1$ for every $j \geq i_1$, and $q_{j2} \in F_2$ for every $j \geq i_2$. Taking $i = \max\{i_1, i_2\}$, we get $[q_{j1}, q_{j2}] \in F$ for every $j \geq i$, and hence $inf(\rho) \subseteq F$.

It remains to show that $\mathcal{L}_\omega(A) = \mathcal{L}_\omega(A_1) \cap \mathcal{L}_\omega(A_2)$ holds. Let $w \in \Sigma^\omega$. Let ρ_1, ρ_2, and ρ be respectively the runs of A_1, A_2, and A on a word w.

$\subseteq$) Assume $w \in \mathcal{L}_\omega(A)$. Since ρ is accepting, it visits $F_1 \times F_2$ infinitely often, and hence ρ_1 and ρ_2 visit F_1 and F_2 infinitely often.

$\supseteq$) Assume $w \in \mathcal{L}_\omega(A_1) \cap \mathcal{L}_\omega(A_2)$. Since ρ_1 and ρ_2 are accepting, by (a), we have $inf(\rho_1) \subseteq F_1$ and $inf(\rho_2) \subseteq F_2$. Thus, there are indices i_1 and i_2 such that $q_{1j} \in F_1$ for every $j \geq i_1$, and $q_{2j} \in F_2$ for every $j \geq i_2$. Taking $i = \max\{i_1, i_2\}$, we get $[q_{1j}, q_{2j}] \in F$ for every $j \geq i$, and hence ρ is an accepting run of A. Thus, $w \in \mathcal{L}_\omega(A)$. $\qquad \square$

☆ ✒ **Exercise 163.** Give algorithms that directly complement deterministic Muller and parity automata, without going through Büchi automata.

Solution: Let us consider the case of a deterministic Muller automaton A with acceptance condition $\mathcal{F} = \{F_0, \ldots, F_{m-1}\} \subseteq 2^Q$. Since every ω-word w has a single run ρ_w in A, we have $w \notin \mathcal{L}_\omega(A)$ iff $inf(\rho_w) \in 2^Q \setminus \mathcal{F}$. Thus, to complement A, we change its acceptance condition to $\mathcal{F}' = 2^Q \setminus \mathcal{F}$.

Let us consider the case of a deterministic parity automaton A with acceptance condition $F_1 \subseteq \cdots \subseteq F_{2n}$. Since every ω-word w has a single run ρ_w in A, we have

$$w \in \mathcal{L}_\omega(A) \iff \min\{i : inf(\rho_w) \cap F_i \neq \emptyset\} \text{ is even.}$$

Thus, to complement A, it suffices to "swap the parity" of states. This can be achieved by adding a new dummy state $q_\perp$ to A and changing its acceptance condition to $\{q_\perp\} \subseteq (F_1 \cup \{q_\perp\}) \subseteq \cdots \subseteq (F_{2n} \cup \{q_\perp\})$, where the purpose of $q_\perp$ is to keep the chain of inclusion required by the definition.

☆ ■ **Exercise 164.** Let $A = (Q, \Sigma, q_0, \delta, \{\langle F_0, G_0 \rangle, \ldots, \langle F_{m-1}, G_{m-1} \rangle\})$ be a deterministic automaton. What is the relation between the languages recognized by A seen as a deterministic Rabin automaton and seen as a deterministic Streett automaton?

Solution: They accept the complement of their respective languages. Indeed, their runs are unique due to determinism. Moreover, the acceptance condition of a Streett automaton is the negation of the acceptance condition of a Rabin automaton.

★ ☞ **Exercise 165.** Consider Büchi automata with universal accepting condition (UBA): an ω-word w is accepted if *every* run of the automaton on w is accepting, that is, if *every* run of the automaton on w visits accepting states infinitely often.

Recall that automata on finite words with existential and universal accepting conditions recognize the same languages (see exercise 21). Prove that this does not hold for automata on ω-words by showing that, for every UBA, there is a DBA that recognizes the same language. This implies that the ω-languages recognized by UBAs are a proper subset of ω-regular languages.

Hint: On input w, the DBA checks that every path of dag(w) visits some final state infinitely often. The states of the DBA are pairs (Q', O) of sets of the UBA where $O \subseteq Q'$ is a set of "owing" states. Loosely speaking, the transition relation is defined to satisfy the following property: after reading a prefix w' of w, the DBA is at the state (Q', O) given by:

• *Q' is the set of states reached by the runs of the UBA on w';*
• *O is the subset of states of Q' that "owe" a visit to a final state of the UBA (see the construction for the complement of a Büchi automaton).*

Solution: This algorithm constructs a DBA from a given UBA by using the hint:

UBAtoDBA(A)
Input: Büchi automaton $A = (Q, \Sigma, \delta, Q_0, F)$ with univ. accepting condition
Output: DBA $B = (\mathcal{Q}, \Sigma, \Delta, \mathcal{Q}_0, \mathcal{F})$ with $\mathcal{L}(B) = \mathcal{L}(A)$

```
1    Q, Δ, F ← ∅
2    if q₀ ∈ F then Q₀ ← ({q₀}, ∅)
3    else Q₀ ← ({q₀}, {q₀})
4    W = {Q₀}
5    while W ≠ ∅ do
6        pick (Q', O) from W
7        add (Q', O) to Q
8        if O = ∅ then add (Q', O) to F
9        for all a ∈ Σ do
10           Q'' ← δ(Q', a)
11           if O = ∅ then
12               if (Q'', Q'' \ F) ∉ Q then add (Q'', Q'' \ F) to W
13           else
14               O' ← δ(O, a)
15               if (Q'', O') ∉ Q then add (Q'', O') to W
```

Solutions for Chapter 12

☆ ⚙ **Exercise 166.** Let B be the following Büchi automaton:

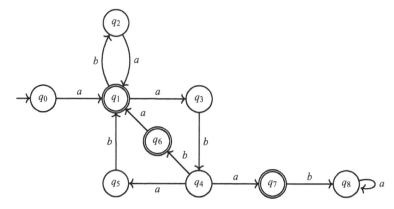

(a) Execute the emptiness algorithm *NestedDFS* on B. Assume that states are picked in ascending order with respect to their indices.

(b) Recall that *NestedDFS* is a nondeterministic algorithm and different choices of runs may return different lassos. Which lassos of B can be found by *NestedDFS*?

(c) Show that *NestedDFS* is not optimal by exhibiting some search sequence on B.

(d) Execute the SCC-based emptiness algorithm on B. Assume that states are picked in ascending order with respect to their indices.

(e) Execute the SCC-based emptiness algorithm on B. Assume that transitions labeled by a are picked before those labeled by b.

(f) Which lassos of B can be found by the SCC-based algorithm?

Solution:

(a) Procedure *dfs1* visits $q_0, q_1, q_2, q_3, q_4, q_5, q_6$, then calls *dfs2*, which visits $q_6, q_1, q_2, q_3, q_4, q_5, q_6$ and reports "nonempty."

(b) Since q_7 does not belong to any lasso, only lassos that contain state q_1 or q_6 can be found. In every run of the algorithm, *dfs1* blackens q_6 before q_1. The only lasso that contains q_6 is $q_0, q_1, q_3, q_4, q_6, q_1$. Therefore, this is the only lasso that can be found by the algorithm.

(c) The execution given in (a) shows that *NestedDFS* is not optimal since it returns the lasso $q_0, q_1, q_3, q_4, q_6, q_1$ even though the lasso q_0, q_1, q_2, q_1 was already appearing in the explored subgraph.

(d) The algorithm reports "nonempty" after the following execution:

Step	Active states, visited states and ranks	Stack

1

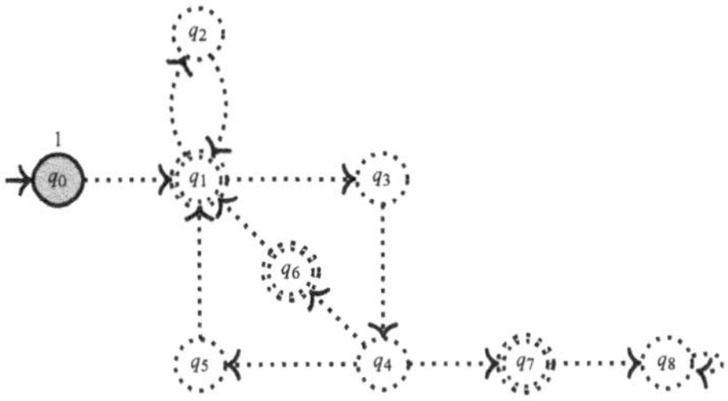

$(q_0, \{q_0\})$

2

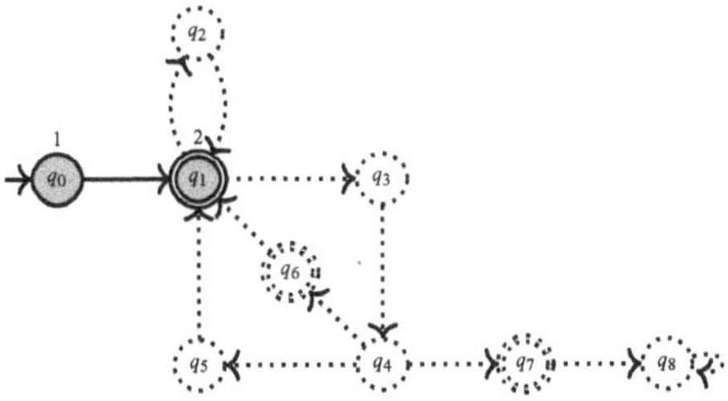

$(q_1, \{q_1\})$
$(q_0, \{q_0\})$

3

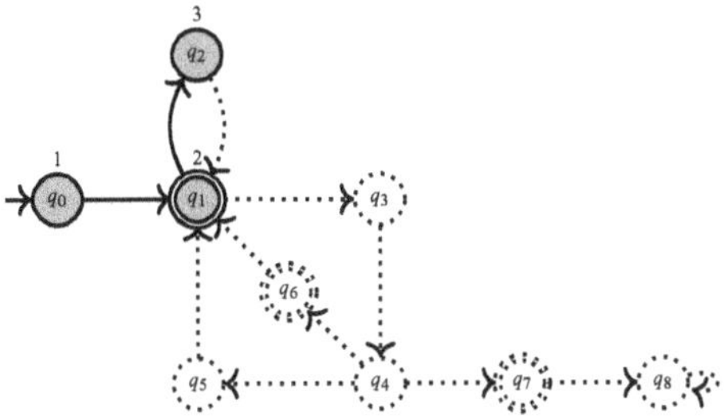

$(q_2, \{q_2\})$
$(q_1, \{q_1\})$
$(q_0, \{q_0\})$

4

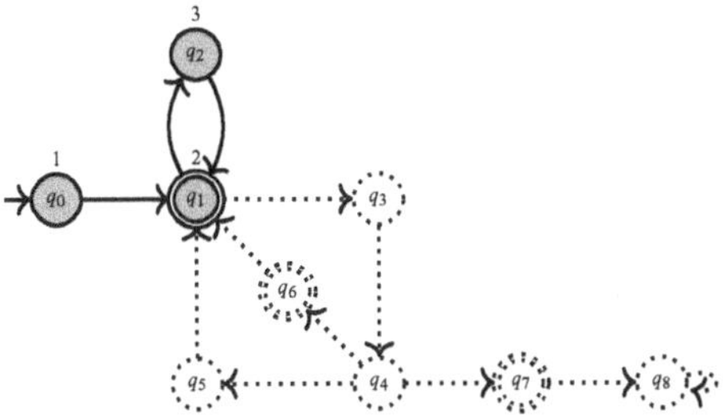

$(q_1, \{q_1, q_2\})$
$(q_0, \{q_0\})$

(e) The algorithm reports "nonempty" after the following execution:

Step	Active states, visited states and ranks	Stack
1		$(q_0, \{q_0\})$
2		$(q_1, \{q_1\})$ $(q_0, \{q_0\})$
3		$(q_3, \{q_3\})$ $(q_1, \{q_1\})$ $(q_0, \{q_0\})$
4		$(q_4, \{q_4\})$ $(q_3, \{q_3\})$ $(q_1, \{q_1\})$ $(q_0, \{q_0\})$

5

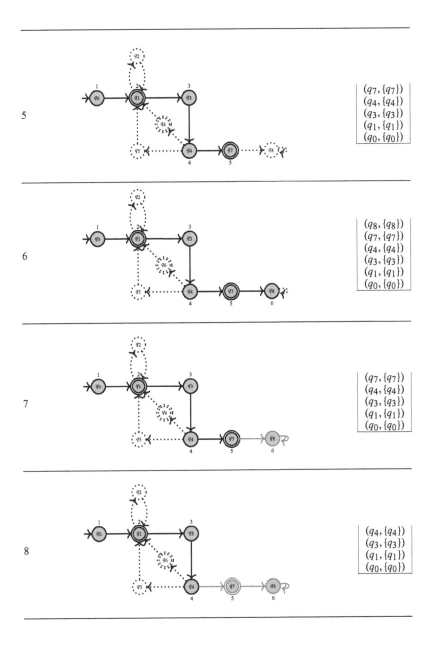

$\begin{vmatrix} (q_7, \{q_7\}) \\ (q_4, \{q_4\}) \\ (q_3, \{q_3\}) \\ (q_1, \{q_1\}) \\ (q_0, \{q_0\}) \end{vmatrix}$

6

$\begin{vmatrix} (q_8, \{q_8\}) \\ (q_7, \{q_7\}) \\ (q_4, \{q_4\}) \\ (q_3, \{q_3\}) \\ (q_1, \{q_1\}) \\ (q_0, \{q_0\}) \end{vmatrix}$

7

$\begin{vmatrix} (q_7, \{q_7\}) \\ (q_4, \{q_4\}) \\ (q_3, \{q_3\}) \\ (q_1, \{q_1\}) \\ (q_0, \{q_0\}) \end{vmatrix}$

8

$\begin{vmatrix} (q_4, \{q_4\}) \\ (q_3, \{q_3\}) \\ (q_1, \{q_1\}) \\ (q_0, \{q_0\}) \end{vmatrix}$

9

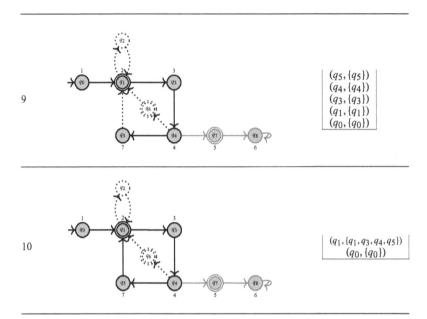

$(q_5, \{q_5\})$
$(q_4, \{q_4\})$
$(q_3, \{q_3\})$
$(q_1, \{q_1\})$
$(q_0, \{q_0\})$

10

$(q_1, \{q_1, q_3, q_4, q_5\})$
$(q_0, \{q_0\})$

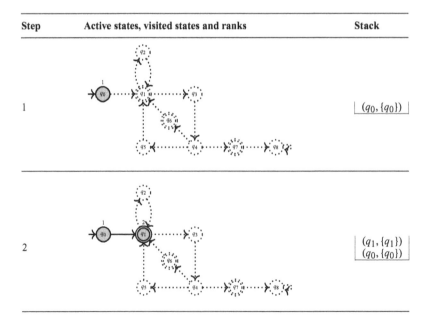

(f) All of them. The lasso q_0, q_1, q_2, q_1 was found by the execution of (d). The lasso $q_0, q_1, q_3, q_4, q_5, q_1$ was found by the execution of (e). The lasso $q_0, q_1, q_3, q_4, q_6, q_1$ was found by the following execution:

Step	Active states, visited states and ranks	Stack
1		$(q_0, \{q_0\})$
2		$(q_1, \{q_1\})$ $(q_0, \{q_0\})$

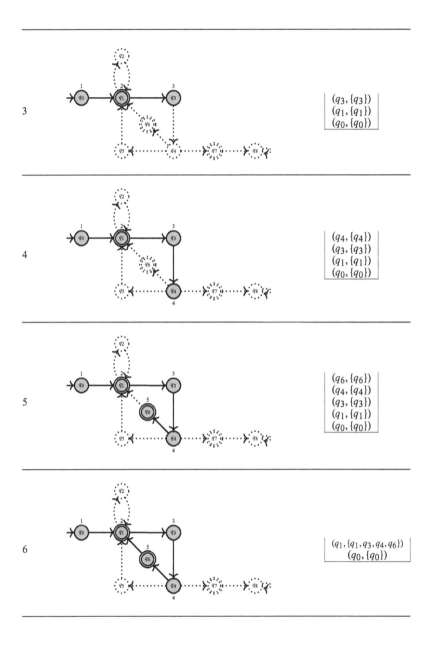

3

$$(q_3, \{q_3\})$$
$$(q_1, \{q_1\})$$
$$(q_0, \{q_0\})$$

4

$$(q_4, \{q_4\})$$
$$(q_3, \{q_3\})$$
$$(q_1, \{q_1\})$$
$$(q_0, \{q_0\})$$

5

$$(q_6, \{q_6\})$$
$$(q_4, \{q_4\})$$
$$(q_3, \{q_3\})$$
$$(q_1, \{q_1\})$$
$$(q_0, \{q_0\})$$

6

$$(q_1, \{q_1, q_3, q_4, q_6\})$$
$$(q_0, \{q_0\})$$

★ ■ **Exercise 167.** Let A be an NBA, and let A_t be the sub-NBA of A containing the states and transitions discovered by a DFS up to (and including) time t. Show that if a state q belongs to some cycle of A, then it already belongs to some cycle of $A_{f[q]}$.

Solution: Let π be a cycle containing q, and consider the snapshot of the DFS at time $f[q]$. If π is entirely black, then π is a cycle of $A_{f[q]}$, and we are done. Thus, assume that it contains at least one nonblack state. Let r be the last state of π such that all states on the subpath from q to r are black. Such a node exists since q is black. Let s be the successor of r in π, as depicted as follows:

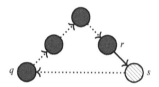

Since r is black and s is not black, we have $f[r] \le f[q] < f[s]$. Moreover, since all successors of r have been discovered at time $f[r]$, we have $d[s] < f[r]$. Altogether, we obtain $d[s] < f[r] \le f[q] < f[s]$. By the parenthesis theorem, intervals $[d[q], f[q]]$ and $[d[s], f[s]]$ are either disjoint, or one is a subinterval of the other one. Consequently, since $d[s] < f[q] < f[s]$, we must have $d[s] < d[q] < f[q] < f[s]$. By the parenthesis theorem, q is a DFS-descendant of s.

Let π' be the DFS-path from s to q. By the parenthesis theorem, each state p along π' is such that $d[p] < d[q] < f[q] < f[p]$. In particular, $d[p] < f[q]$ means that all states of π' have been discovered at time $f[q]$. Let σ be the cycle obtained by concatenating the prefix of π from q to r, transition (r, s), and π', as depicted in bold and color as follows:

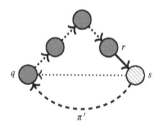

Recall that: the prefix of π is entirely black, the transition from r to s has been explored, and all states of π' have been discovered by time $d[q]$ via π'. Thus, cycle π' belongs to $A_{f[q]}$.   □

★ ⚙ **Exercise 169.** Execute *SCCsearch* on the Büchi automaton as follows. When a state has many outgoing transitions, pick letters in this order: $a < b < c$.

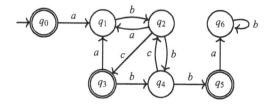

Solution:

Active graph	N

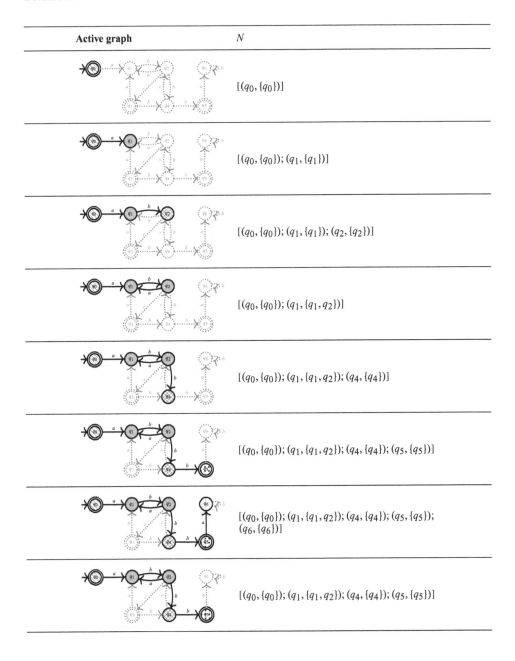

$[(q_0, \{q_0\})]$

$[(q_0, \{q_0\}); (q_1, \{q_1\})]$

$[(q_0, \{q_0\}); (q_1, \{q_1\}); (q_2, \{q_2\})]$

$[(q_0, \{q_0\}); (q_1, \{q_1, q_2\})]$

$[(q_0, \{q_0\}); (q_1, \{q_1, q_2\}); (q_4, \{q_4\})]$

$[(q_0, \{q_0\}); (q_1, \{q_1, q_2\}); (q_4, \{q_4\}); (q_5, \{q_5\})]$

$[(q_0, \{q_0\}); (q_1, \{q_1, q_2\}); (q_4, \{q_4\}); (q_5, \{q_5\});$
$(q_6, \{q_6\})]$

$[(q_0, \{q_0\}); (q_1, \{q_1, q_2\}); (q_4, \{q_4\}); (q_5, \{q_5\})]$

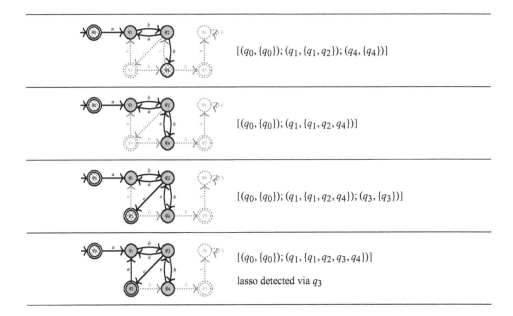

$[(q_0, \{q_0\}); (q_1, \{q_1, q_2\}); (q_4, \{q_4\})]$

$[(q_0, \{q_0\}); (q_1, \{q_1, q_2, q_4\})]$

$[(q_0, \{q_0\}); (q_1, \{q_1, q_2, q_4\}); (q_3, \{q_3\})]$

$[(q_0, \{q_0\}); (q_1, \{q_1, q_2, q_3, q_4\})]$

lasso detected via q_3

☆ ✎ **Exercise 170.** Recall that *SCCsearch* runs in time $\mathcal{O}(|Q| + |\delta|)$ if we consider set unions as atomic. However, set unions are generally not constant-time operations. Explain how beads can be implemented so that *SCCsearch* truly runs in linear time.
Hint: Can two beads share a state?

Solution: First note that the beads of *SCCsearch* are disjoint sets, that is, two beads share no state in common. Moreover, we need to support these operations: (1) initializing a trivial bead, (2) merging a bead into another one, (3) obtaining the root of a bead, and (4) iterating over the states of a bead. We have already taken into account that operation (4) works in time $\mathcal{O}(|Q|)$ when analyzing case (vi) of *SCCsearch*. Thus, we must implement operations (1) to (3) so that they operate in constant time.

We implement a bead (r, C) as a linked list whose head is r and whose elements are those of C stored in an arbitrary order. We further keep a pointer to the last state of the list, which we call the *tail*. The operations are respectively implemented as follows:

(1) We set r as both the head and tail, and we set the successor of r as "null."
(2) To merge $B' = (r', C')$ into $B = (r, C)$, we proceed as follows: the new head is r, the new tail is the tail of B', and the successor of the tail of B becomes the head of B' (i.e., r').
(3) We simply return the head.
(4) We iterate over the linked list from the head to the tail.

Operations (1) to (3) work in constant time as the head and tails are known.

Readers familiar with disjoint sets (also known as *union-find*) may have been tempted to use this data structure instead. However, it yields *quasilinear* time, typically $\mathcal{O}(n \log n)$ or

$\mathcal{O}(\alpha(n) \cdot n)$, where α is the (very slow-growing) inverse Ackermann function. Disjoint sets turn out to be an overkill since we do not need the "find" operation, that is, we never query whether a given state belongs to a given bead. This explains why we are able to obtain a better complexity.

★ ✔ **Exercise 171.** Recall that exercise 170 gives an implementation of *SCCsearch* that truly works in linear time. Let us now take the memory usage into account. Let a_t and b_t denote respectively the number of active states and the number of beads at time t. Let $f(t)$ be the number of bits used at time t to store the current beads. Let w be the size of an address.

The solution of exercise 170 satisfies $f(t) = 2(a_t + b_t)w$. Indeed, it uses two addresses per active state (one pointing to the state itself and one to its successor), plus two extra addresses per bead (for the head and tail). Give an implementation of *SCCsearch* that halves the memory usage—namely, one that runs in linear time and satisfies $f(t) = (a_t + b_t)w$.

Hint: Use two stacks, one for roots and one for active states.

Solution: Recall that the original implementation of *SCCsearch* uses stack N to store the beads. We get rid of N. Instead, we use a stack R to store the roots and a stack V to store the active states. We implement the algorithm in such a way that if q is the top of R and $r_1 r_2 \cdots r_k q$ is on the top of V, then $(q, \{r_1, r_2, \ldots, r_k, q\})$ is the current bead, that is, it would be the top of N in the original implementation. We call this a *proper encoding* of N. Such an encoding stores all beads together in V, and the top element of R gives enough information to pop the current bead from V, that is, it suffices to pop until we find the current root. This can be achieved with the following pseudocode:

```
1   S, R, V ← ∅; n ← 0
2   dfs(q₀)
3   report EMP

4   proc dfs(q)
5     n ← n + 1; rank(q) ← n
6     add q to S; act(q) ← true; push q onto R; push q onto V
7     for all r ∈ δ(q) do
8       if r ∉ S then dfs(r)
9       else if act(r) then
10          repeat
11            pop s from R; if s ∈ F then report NEMP
12          until rank(s) ≤ rank(r)
13          push s onto R
14      if top(R) = q then
15        pop q from R
16        repeat
17          pop r from V; act(r) ← false
18        until r = q
```

Let us explain why this implementation is correct. We do so by arguing that (R, V) remains a proper encoding of the original stack N throughout the execution:

- Line 6: Clearly, "**push** q **onto** R; **push** q **onto** V" properly implements "**push** $(q, \{q\})$ **onto** N."
- Lines 10–13: The difference with the original implementation is that there is no explicit union of the beads. Let s be the state found after the **repeat** loop. Suppose that prior to the loop, $q_\ell = s$, $R = q_1 \cdots q_\ell \cdots$, and $V = r_{1,1} \cdots r_{1,k_1} q_1 \cdots r_{\ell,1} \cdots r_{\ell,k_\ell} q_\ell \cdots$. After executing the loop and pushing s, we obtain $R = q_\ell \cdots$ and V has not changed. Thus, the top element of R correctly represents the bead obtained by merging beads $(q_1, \{q_{1,1}, \ldots, q_{1,k_1}\})$, $\ldots, (q_\ell, \{q_{\ell,1}, \ldots, q_{\ell,k_\ell}\})$. Note that this cleverly avoids any explicit union since V has not changed at all!
- Line 14: Since (R, V) is a proper encoding, we have "**top**$(R) = q$" iff q is the top root in N.
- Lines 15–18: Since (R, V) is a proper encoding, all states from the top of V down to state q correspond to the bead of q. Hence, the pop from R and the **repeat** loop properly implement "**pop** (q, C) **from** N."

It remains to consider the running time and memory usage for the beads. The algorithm runs in linear time. Indeed, the original analysis still applies but now without any set union to consider at all. Moreover, at time t, we have $|V| + |R| = a_t + b_t$. Thus, by storing addresses on the stack (pointing to the states), we use $f(t) = (a_t + b_t)w$ bits at time t.

☆ ⚙ **Exercise 173.** Execute Emerson–Lei's algorithm and *MEL* on this NBA:

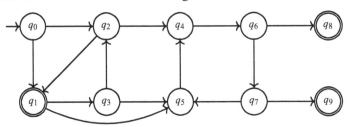

Solution: Let us first execute Emerson–Lei's algorithm:

Iter.	L
1	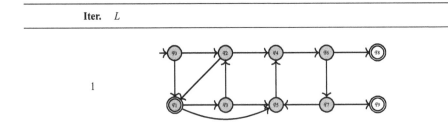

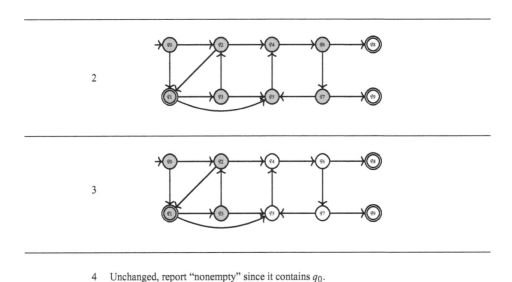

| 4 | Unchanged, report "nonempty" since it contains q_0. |

The very first iteration of *MEL* filters $\{q_8, q_9\}$ via line 4 and $\{q_4, q_5, q_6, q_7\}$ via lines 5 and 6:

| **Iter.** | *L* |

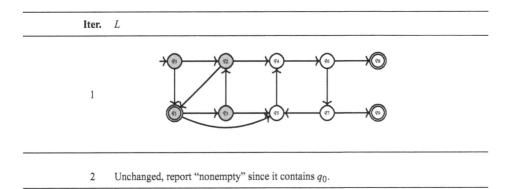

| 2 | Unchanged, report "nonempty" since it contains q_0. |

★ ✔ **Exercise 175.** This exercise deals with a variation of Emerson–Lei's algorithm.

(a) For every $R, S \subseteq Q$, let $pre^+(R, S)$ be the set of states q such that there is a nonempty path π from q to some state of R where π only contains states from S. Give an algorithm to compute $pre^+(R, S)$.

(b) Execute the algorithm from (a) on the following automaton, where states from R and S are respectively solid and hatched:

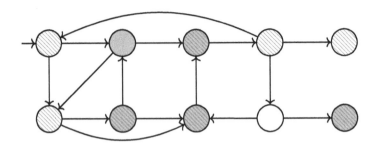

(c) Show that the following modification of Emerson–Lei's algorithm is correct:

$MEL2(A)$
Input: NBA $A = (Q, \Sigma, \delta, Q_0, F)$
Output: EMP if $\mathcal{L}_\omega(A) = \emptyset$, NEMP otherwise
  1 $L \leftarrow Q$
  2 **repeat**
  3    $OldL \leftarrow L$
  4    $L \leftarrow pre^+(L \cap F, L)$
  5 **until** $L = OldL$
  6 **if** $q_0 \in L$ **then report** NEMP
  7 **else report** NEMP

(d) What is the difference between the sequences of sets computed by MEL and $MEL2$?

Solution:

(a)

Input: NBA $A = (Q, \Sigma, \delta, Q_0, F)$ and sets $R, S \subseteq Q$
Output: $pre^+(R, S)$
  1 $L \leftarrow R \cap S$
  2 **repeat**
  3    $OldL \leftarrow L$
  4    $L \leftarrow pre(L) \cap S$
  5 **until** $L = OldL$
  6 **return** L

(b)

Iter.	*L*
0	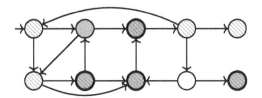
1	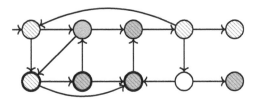
2	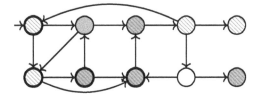
3	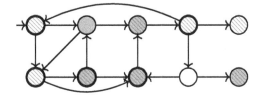

4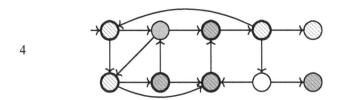

(c) Let $L[0] = L[0]'' = Q$, $L[n+1] = pre^+(L[n] \cap F)$, and $L[n+1]'' = pre^+(L[n]'' \cap F, L[n]'')$. Emerson–Lei's algorithm computes the fixpoint of the sequence $\{L[n]\}_{n \geq 0}$, while $MEL2$ computes the fixpoint of the sequence $\{L[n]''\}_{n \geq 0}$. Let $L[i]$ be the fixpoint of the first sequence. We claim that $L[i] \subseteq L[n]'' \subseteq L[n]$ holds for every $n \geq 0$. This claim implies that $MEL2$ is correct. Indeed, let $L[j]''$ be the fixpoint of the second sequence. Let $\ell = \max(i, j)$. We have $L[i] \subseteq L[\ell]'' \subseteq L[\ell] = L[i]$. Thus, $L[i] = L[\ell]'' = L[j]''$ and hence the two sequences have the same fixpoint.

It remains to show the claim. We proceed by induction. For $n = 0$, we trivially have $L[i] \subseteq Q = L[0]'' = L[0]$. Let $n \geq 0$. By induction hypothesis, we have $L[i] \subseteq L[n]'' \subseteq L[n]$. Since $L[i]$ is the fixpoint of the first sequence, we have $pre^+(L[i] \cap F) = L[i]$. This implies $pre^+(L[i] \cap F, L[i]) = L[i]$. Thus, the following holds:

$$L[i] = pre^+(L[i] \cap F, L[i]) \subseteq pre^+(L[n]'' \cap F, L[n]'') = L[n+1]''.$$

Moreover, we have

$$L[n+1]'' = pre^+(L[n]'' \cap F, L[n]'') \subseteq pre^+(L[n]'' \cap F)$$

$$\subseteq pre^+(L[n] \cap F) = L[n+1]. \qquad \square$$

(d) At each iteration, $MEL2$ computes set $f(L) = pre^+(L \cap F, L)$, and MEL computes set $g(L) = pre^+(inf(L) \cap F)$. Set $f(L)$ contains states that can reach an accepting state from L via a nonempty path within L. Set $g(L)$ contains states that can reach an accepting state from L, from which there exists a lasso within L. Therefore, $f(L)$ and $g(L)$ are incomparable.

Solutions for Chapter 13

☆ ■ **Exercise 176.** Prove formally the following equivalences:

(a) $\neg \mathbf{X}\varphi \equiv \mathbf{X}\neg\varphi$

(b) $\neg \mathbf{F}\varphi \equiv \mathbf{G}\neg\varphi$

(c) $\neg \mathbf{G}\varphi \equiv \mathbf{F}\neg\varphi$

(d) $\mathbf{XF}\varphi \equiv \mathbf{FX}\varphi$

(e) $\mathbf{XG}\varphi \equiv \mathbf{GX}\varphi$

Solution:

(a)

$$\sigma \models \neg \mathbf{X} \varphi \iff \sigma \not\models \mathbf{X} \varphi$$
$$\iff \sigma^1 \not\models \varphi$$
$$\iff \sigma^1 \models \neg \varphi$$
$$\iff \sigma \models \mathbf{X} \neg \varphi.$$

$\square$

(b)

$$\sigma \models \neg \mathbf{F} \varphi \iff \neg(\sigma \models \mathbf{F} \varphi)$$
$$\iff \neg(\exists k \geq 0 : \sigma^k \models \varphi)$$
$$\iff \forall k \geq 0 \; \neg(\sigma^k \models \varphi)$$
$$\iff \forall k \geq 0 \; (\sigma^k \models \neg \varphi)$$
$$\iff \mathbf{G} \neg \varphi.$$

$\square$

(c)

$$\sigma \models \neg \mathbf{G} \varphi \iff \neg(\sigma \models \mathbf{G} \varphi)$$
$$\iff \neg(\forall k \geq 0 \; (\sigma^k \models \varphi))$$
$$\iff \exists k \geq 0 : \neg(\sigma^k \models \varphi)$$
$$\iff \exists k \geq 0 : (\sigma^k \models \neg \varphi)$$
$$\iff \mathbf{F} \neg \varphi.$$

$\square$

(d)

$$\sigma \models \mathbf{XF} \varphi \iff \sigma^1 \models \mathbf{F} \varphi$$
$$\iff \exists k \geq 0 : (\sigma^1)^k \models \varphi$$
$$\iff \exists k \geq 0 : (\sigma^k)^1 \models \varphi$$
$$\iff \exists k \geq 0 : \sigma^k \models \mathbf{X} \varphi$$
$$\iff \sigma \models \mathbf{FX} \varphi.$$

$\square$

(e)

$$\sigma \models \mathbf{X}\mathbf{G}\varphi \iff \sigma^1 \models \mathbf{G}\varphi$$

$$\iff \forall k \geq 0 \, ((\sigma^1)^k \models \varphi)$$

$$\iff \forall k \geq 0 \, (\sigma^k \models \mathbf{X}\varphi)$$

$$\iff \sigma \models \mathbf{G}\mathbf{X}\varphi. \qquad \qquad \square$$

☆ 🔲 **Exercise 178.** Let $AP = \{p, q\}$ and $\Sigma = 2^{AP}$. Give LTL formulas defining the following languages:

(a) $\{p, q\} \, \emptyset \, \Sigma^\omega$

(b) $\Sigma^* \, (\{p\} + \{p, q\}) \, \Sigma^* \, \{q\} \, \Sigma^\omega$

(c) $\Sigma^* \, \{q\}^\omega$

(d) $\{p\}^* \, \{q\}^* \, \emptyset^\omega$

Solution:

(a) $(p \wedge q) \wedge \mathbf{X}(\neg p \wedge \neg q)$.

(b) $\mathbf{F}(p \wedge \mathbf{X}\mathbf{F}(\neg p \wedge q))$.

(c) $\mathbf{F}\mathbf{G}(\neg p \wedge q)$.

(d) $(p \wedge \neg q) \, \mathbf{U} \, [(\neg p \wedge q) \, \mathbf{U} \, \mathbf{G}(\neg p \wedge \neg q)]$.

☆ 🔲 **Exercise 180.** Let $AP = \{p, q\}$ and let $\Sigma = 2^{AP}$. Give Büchi automata for the ω-languages over Σ defined by the following LTL formulas:

(a) $\mathbf{X}\mathbf{G}\neg p$

(b) $(\mathbf{G}\mathbf{F}p) \to (\mathbf{F}q)$

(c) $p \wedge \neg(\mathbf{X}\mathbf{F}p)$

(d) $\mathbf{G}(p \, \mathbf{U} \, (p \to q))$

(e) $\mathbf{F}q \to (\neg q \, \mathbf{U} \, (\neg q \wedge p))$

Solution:

(a)

(b) Note that $\mathbf{G}\mathbf{F}p \to \mathbf{F}q \equiv \neg(\mathbf{G}\mathbf{F}p) \vee \mathbf{F}q \equiv \mathbf{F}\mathbf{G}\neg p \vee \mathbf{F}q$. We build Büchi automata for $\mathbf{F}\mathbf{G}\neg p$ and $\mathbf{F}q$ and take their union:

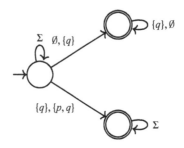

(c) Note that $p \wedge \neg(\mathbf{XF}p) \equiv p \wedge \mathbf{XG}\neg p$. We build a Büchi automaton for $p \wedge \mathbf{XG}\neg p$:

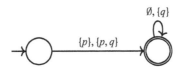

(d)

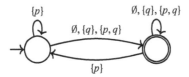

(e) Note that $\mathbf{F}q \rightarrow (\neg q \, \mathbf{U} \, (\neg q \wedge p)) \equiv \mathbf{G}\neg q \vee (\neg q \, \mathbf{U} \, (\neg q \wedge p))$. Computations that satisfy the latter formula either have no occurrence of p, and hence of q, or a first occurrence of p with no q before or at the same time:

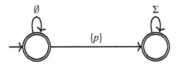

⭐ ■ **Exercise 182.** Let $\mathcal{V} \in \{\mathbf{F}, \mathbf{G}\}^*$ be a sequence made of the temporal operators $\mathbf{F}$ and $\mathbf{G}$. Show that $\mathbf{FG}p \equiv \mathcal{V} \, \mathbf{FG}p$ and $\mathbf{GF}p \equiv \mathcal{V} \, \mathbf{GF}p$.

Solution: Given LTL formulas φ and ψ, we denote by $\varphi \models \psi$ that every computation satisfying φ satisfies ψ. Note that $\varphi \equiv \sigma$ iff $\varphi \models \psi$ and $\psi \models \varphi$. It is readily seen that the following holds:

$$\mathbf{FF}\varphi \equiv \mathbf{F}\varphi, \tag{14.6}$$

$$\mathbf{GG}\varphi \equiv \mathbf{G}\varphi, \tag{14.7}$$

$$\mathbf{G}\varphi \models \varphi \text{ and } \varphi \models \mathbf{F}\varphi. \tag{14.8}$$

Let us show that (a) $\mathbf{FG}\varphi \equiv \mathbf{GFG}\varphi$ and (b) $\mathbf{GF}\varphi \equiv \mathbf{FGF}\varphi$.

(a) We have $\mathbf{GFG}\varphi \models \mathbf{FG}\varphi$ by (14.8). Let $\sigma \models \mathbf{FG}\varphi$. There exists $i \geq 0$ such that $\sigma^j \models \varphi$ for every $j \geq i$. Thus, for every $k \geq 0$ there is some $\ell \geq 0$ such that $(\sigma^k)^\ell \models \varphi$. Indeed, if $k \geq i$, then take $\ell = 0$, and if $k < i$, then take $\ell = i - k$. Therefore, we have $\sigma^k \models \mathbf{FG}\varphi$ for every $k \geq 0$, and hence $\sigma \models \mathbf{GFG}\varphi$. This means that $\mathbf{FG}\varphi \models \mathbf{GFG}\varphi$.

(b) We have $\mathbf{GF}\varphi \models \mathbf{FGF}\varphi$ by (14.8). It is the case that $\mathbf{FGF}\varphi \models \mathbf{GF}\varphi$. Indeed, if there exists $i \geq 0$ such that $\sigma^j \models \varphi$ holds for infinitely many $j \geq i$, then, in particular, $\sigma^j \models \varphi$ holds for infinitely many $j \geq 0$.

We prove $\mathbf{FG}\varphi \equiv \mathcal{V} \, \mathbf{FG}\varphi$ by induction on the length of $\mathcal{V}$. If $\mathcal{V} = \varepsilon$, then we are done. If $\mathcal{V} = \mathcal{U}\mathbf{F}$, then we have $\mathcal{V} \, \mathbf{FG}\varphi \equiv \mathcal{U} \, \mathbf{FG}\varphi$ by (14.6). If $\mathcal{V} = \mathcal{U}\mathbf{G}$, then we have the same equivalence by (a). By induction hypothesis, we get $\mathcal{U} \, \mathbf{FG}\varphi \equiv \mathbf{FG}\varphi$. The other equivalence is proved similarly using (14.7) and (b). $\qquad \square$

✩ ■ **Exercise 183.** Recall that a formula is a tautology if all computations satisfy it. Which of the following formulas of LTL are tautologies? If the formula is not a tautology, then give a computation that does not satisfy it.

(a) $\mathbf{G}p \to \mathbf{F}p$

(b) $\mathbf{G}(p \to q) \to (\mathbf{G}p \to \mathbf{G}q)$

(c) $\mathbf{F}(p \wedge q) \leftrightarrow (\mathbf{F}p \wedge \mathbf{F}q)$

(d) $\neg\mathbf{F}p \to \mathbf{F}\neg\mathbf{F}p$

(e) $(\mathbf{G}p \to \mathbf{F}q) \leftrightarrow (p\,\mathbf{U}\,(\neg p \vee q))$

(f) $(\mathbf{FG}p \to \mathbf{GF}q) \leftrightarrow \mathbf{G}(p\,\mathbf{U}\,(\neg p \vee q))$

(g) $\mathbf{G}(p \to \mathbf{X}p) \to (p \to \mathbf{G}p)$

Solution:

(a) $\mathbf{G}p \to \mathbf{F}p$ is readily seen to be a tautology from the definitions of $\mathbf{F}$ and $\mathbf{G}$.

(b) $\mathbf{G}(p \to q) \to (\mathbf{G}p \to \mathbf{G}q)$ is a tautology. The left-hand side states that any point of the computation that satisfies p also satisfies q. Thus, if every point satisfies p, then every point satisfies q.

(c) $\mathbf{F}(p \wedge q) \leftrightarrow (\mathbf{F}p \wedge \mathbf{F}q)$ is not a tautology. The computation $\{p\}\{q\}\emptyset^\omega$ satisfies $\mathbf{F}p \wedge \mathbf{F}q$ but not $\mathbf{F}(p \wedge q)$.

(d) $\neg\mathbf{F}p \to \mathbf{F}\neg\mathbf{F}p$ is a tautology. The formula $\varphi \to \mathbf{F}\varphi$ is clearly a tautology for every formula φ and hence in particular with $\varphi = \neg\mathbf{F}p$.

(e) $(\mathbf{G}p \to \mathbf{F}q) \leftrightarrow (p\,\mathbf{U}\,(\neg p \vee q))$ is a tautology. The left-hand side is equivalent to $\mathbf{F}\neg p \vee \mathbf{F}q \equiv \mathbf{F}(\neg p \vee q)$. If the right-hand side holds, then some point of the computation satisfies $\neg p \vee q$, and hence the left-hand side holds. If the left-hand side holds, then there exists a first point at which $\neg p \vee q$ holds, and, since it is the first, all points before it satisfy $p \wedge \neg q$, and so in particular, they all satisfy p. Thus, the right-hand side holds as well.

(f) $(\mathbf{FG}p \to \mathbf{GF}q) \leftrightarrow \mathbf{G}(p\,\mathbf{U}\,(\neg p \vee q))$ is a tautology. The left-hand side is equivalent to formulas $\mathbf{GF}\neg p \vee \mathbf{GF}q \equiv \mathbf{GF}(\neg p \vee q)$. If a computation $\sigma = \sigma_0\sigma_1 \cdots$ satisfies the right-hand side, then every suffix of σ satisfies $p\,\mathbf{U}\,(\neg p \vee q)$. So for every point of σ, some future point satisfies $\neg p \vee q$, which implies that the left-hand side holds. If a computation σ satisfies the left-hand side, then its points can be partitioned into the infinite set of points satisfying $\neg p \vee q$, and the rest, which satisfy $p \wedge q$, and so, in particular, p. Therefore, every suffix of σ satisfies $p\,\mathbf{U}\,(\neg p \vee q)$, which implies that σ satisfies $\mathbf{G}(p\,\mathbf{U}\,(\neg p \vee q))$.

(g) $\mathbf{G}(p \to \mathbf{X}p) \to (p \to \mathbf{G}p)$ is a tautology. We have

$$\mathbf{G}(p \to \mathbf{X}p) \to (p \to \mathbf{G}p) \equiv \neg\mathbf{G}(\neg p \vee \mathbf{X}p) \vee (\neg p \vee \mathbf{G}p)$$

$$\equiv \mathbf{F}(p \wedge \neg\mathbf{X}p) \vee \neg p \vee \mathbf{G}p$$

$$\equiv \mathbf{F}\neg p \vee \mathbf{G}p,$$

which is clearly a tautology.

★ ☞ **Exercise 184.** We say that an LTL formula is *negation-free* if negations only occur in front of atomic formulas (that is, $\neg\mathbf{true}$ or $\neg a$ where a is an atomic proposition). In this exercise, we show how to construct a deterministic Büchi automaton for negation-free LTL formulas. In the remainder, we assume that φ denotes such a formula over a set of atomic propositions AP. We inductively define the formula $af(\varphi, \nu)$, read "φ after ν" where $\nu \in 2^{AP}$, as follows:

$$af(\textbf{true}, v) = \textbf{true}, \qquad\qquad af(\varphi \wedge \psi, v) = af(\varphi, v) \wedge af(\psi, v),$$

$$af(\textbf{false}, v) = \textbf{false}, \qquad\qquad af(\varphi \vee \psi, v) = af(\varphi, v) \vee af(\psi, v),$$

$$af(a, v) = af(a \in v, v), \qquad\qquad af(\textbf{X}\varphi, v) = \varphi,$$

$$af(\neg a, v) = af(a \notin v, v), \qquad af(\varphi \textbf{ U } \psi, v) = af(\psi, v) \vee (af(\varphi, v) \wedge \varphi \textbf{ U } \psi).$$

We extend it to finite words: $af(\varphi, \epsilon) = \varphi$ and $af(\varphi, vw) = af(af(\varphi, v), w)$ for every $v \in 2^{AP}$ and every finite word w. Prove the following statements:

(a) For every formula φ, finite word $w \in \left(2^{AP}\right)^*$ and ω-word $w' \in \left(2^{AP}\right)^\omega$:

$$ww' \models \varphi \iff w' \models af(\varphi, w).$$

So, intuitively, $af(\varphi, w)$ holds "after reading w" iff φ holds "at the beginning" of ww'.

(b) For every negation-free formula φ: $w \models \varphi$ iff $af(\varphi, w') \equiv \textbf{true}$ for some finite prefix w' of w.

(c) For every formula φ and ω-word $w \in \left(2^{AP}\right)^\omega$: $af(\varphi, w)$ is a positive boolean combination of subformulas of φ.

(d) For every formula φ of length n: the set of formulas $\{af(\varphi, w) : w \in \left(2^{AP}\right)^*\}$ has at most 2^{2^n} equivalence classes up to LTL-equivalence.

(e) There exists a deterministic Büchi automaton recognizing $\mathcal{L}_\omega(\varphi)$ with at most 2^{2^n} states, where n is the length of φ.   *Hint: Use (b)–(d).*

Solution:

(a) First we prove the property for the case where w is a single letter $v \subseteq AP$—that is, we prove

$$vw' \models \varphi \iff w' \models af(\varphi, v) \tag{14.9}$$

by structural induction on φ. We only consider two representative cases.
- Case $\varphi = a$. We have

$$vw' \models a \iff a \in v$$

$$\iff af(a, v) = \textbf{true}$$

$$\iff w' \models af(a, v).$$

- Case $\varphi = \varphi' \textbf{ U } \varphi''$. We have

$$vw' \models \varphi' \textbf{ U } \varphi''$$

$$\iff vw' \models \varphi'' \vee (\varphi' \wedge \textbf{X}(\varphi' \textbf{ U } \varphi''))$$

$$\iff (vw' \models \varphi'') \vee [(vw' \models \varphi') \wedge (w' \models \varphi' \textbf{ U } \varphi'')]$$

$$\iff [w' \models af(\varphi'', v)] \vee [(w' \models af(\varphi', v)) \wedge (w' \models \varphi' \textbf{ U } \varphi'')]$$

$$\iff w' \models af(\varphi'', v) \vee (af(\varphi', v) \wedge \varphi' \, \mathbf{U} \, \varphi'')$$

$$\iff w' \models af(\varphi' \, \mathbf{U} \, \varphi'', v).$$

Now, let us prove the property for every word w by induction on the length of w. If $w = \varepsilon$, then $af(\varphi, w) = \varphi$, and hence

$$ww' \models \varphi \iff w' \models \varphi \iff w' \models af(\varphi, w).$$

If $w = vw''$ for some $v \in 2^{AP}$, then we have

$$w' \models af(\varphi, w) \iff w' \models af(\varphi, vw'')$$

$$\iff w' \models af(af(\varphi, v), w'') \qquad \text{(by def. of } af\text{)}$$

$$\iff w''w' \models af(\varphi, v) \qquad \text{(by induction hypothesis)}$$

$$\iff vw''w' \models \varphi \qquad \text{(by (14.9))}$$

$$\iff ww' \models \varphi.$$

(b) If $af(\varphi, w') \equiv \mathbf{true}$, then, by (a), we have $w'w'' \models \varphi$ for every w'', and so in particular, $w \models \varphi$. For the other direction, assume that $w \models \varphi$. The proof is by structural induction on φ. We only consider two representative cases as in (a).

• Case $\varphi = a$. Since $w \models \varphi$, we have $w = vw'$ for some word w' and some $v \in AP$ such that $a \in v$. By definition of af, we have $af(a, v) \equiv \mathbf{true}$.

• Case $\varphi = \varphi' \, \mathbf{U} \, \varphi''$. By the semantics of LTL, there exists $k \in \mathbb{N}$ such that $w^k \models \varphi''$ and $w^\ell \models \varphi'$ for every $0 \leq \ell < k$. By induction hypothesis, for every $0 \leq \ell < k$, there exists $i_\ell \geq \ell$ such that $af(\varphi', w[\ell..i_\ell]) \equiv \mathbf{true}$. Furthermore, there exists $i_k \geq k$ such that $af(\varphi'', w[k..i_k]) \equiv \mathbf{true}$. Let $m = \max\{i_j : 0 \leq j \leq k\}$. We show that $af(\varphi' \, \mathbf{U} \, \varphi'', w[0..m]) \equiv \mathbf{true}$ by induction on k.

• Case $k = 0$. We have

$$af(\varphi' \, \mathbf{U} \, \varphi'', w[0..m])$$

$$= af(\varphi'', w[0..m]) \vee (af(\varphi', w[0..m]) \wedge af(\varphi' \, \mathbf{U} \, \varphi'', w[1..m]))$$

$$= af(af(\varphi'', w[k..i_k]), w[i_k + 1..m]) \vee$$

$$\quad (af(\varphi', w[0..m]) \wedge af(\varphi' \, \mathbf{U} \, \varphi'', w[1..m]))$$

$$= af(\mathbf{true}, w[i_k + 1..m]) \vee$$

$$\quad (af(\varphi', w[0..m]) \wedge af(\varphi' \, \mathbf{U} \, \varphi'', w[1..m]))$$

$$\equiv \mathbf{true} \vee (af(\varphi_1, w[0..m]) \wedge af(\varphi' \, \mathbf{U} \, \varphi'', w[1..m]))$$

$$\equiv \mathbf{true}.$$

• Case $k > 0$. We have

$$af(\varphi' \, \mathbf{U} \, \varphi'', w[0..m])$$

$$= af(\varphi'', w[0..m]) \vee (af(\varphi', w[0..m]) \wedge af(\varphi' \mathbf{U} \varphi'', w[1..m]))$$

$$= af(\varphi'', w[0..m]) \vee$$

$$(af(af(\varphi', w[0..i_0]), w[i_0 + 1..m]) \wedge af(\varphi' \mathbf{U} \varphi'', w[1..m]))$$

$$= af(\varphi'', w[0..m]) \vee$$

$$(af(\mathbf{true}, w[i_0 + 1..m]) \wedge af(\varphi' \mathbf{U} \varphi'', w[1..m]))$$

$$\equiv af(\varphi'', w[0..m]) \vee (\mathbf{true} \wedge af(\varphi' \mathbf{U} \varphi'', w[1..m]))$$

$$\equiv af(\varphi'', w[0..m]) \vee (\mathbf{true} \wedge \mathbf{true})$$

$$\equiv \mathbf{true},$$

where $af(\varphi' \mathbf{U} \varphi'', w[1..m]) \equiv \mathbf{true}$ by induction hypothesis.

(c) This follows by a straightforward structural induction on φ since all definitions only involve **true**, *false*, $\wedge$, $\vee$, and subformulas of φ.

(d) We assign a boolean variable b_ψ to each subformula ψ of φ. Let

$$B_\varphi = \{b_\psi : \psi \text{ is a subformula of } \varphi\}.$$

Since φ has length n, the set B_φ contains at most n variables. By (c), we can assign to each formula $af(\varphi, w)$ a boolean function f_w over B_φ. Clearly, if f_w and $f_{w'}$ are equal, then $af(\varphi, w) \equiv af(\varphi, w')$. The result follows because there are 2^{2^n} boolean functions over n variables.

(e) The set of states are the equivalence classes of the formulas:

$$\left\{ af(\varphi, w) : w \in \left(2^{AP} \right)^* \right\}.$$

By (d), there are at most 2^{2^n} states. The only initial and final states are respectively the equivalence class of φ and **true**. The transition relation is given by $[\psi_1] \xrightarrow{v} [\psi_2]$ iff $af(\psi_1, v) \equiv \psi_2$. $\qquad\square$

★ ✔ **Exercise 185.** In this exercise, we show that the reduction algorithm of exercise 150(2) does not reduce the Büchi automata generated from LTL formulas, as well as show that a little modification to the algorithm *LTLtoNGA* (algorithm 57) can alleviate this problem.

Let φ be a formula of LTL(AP), and let $A_\varphi = LTLtoNGA(\varphi)$.

(a) Prove that the reduction algorithm of exercise 150(2) does not reduce A, that is, show that $A = A/CSR$.

(b) Prove that $\mathcal{L}_\omega (B_\varphi) = \mathcal{L}_\omega (A_\varphi)$, where B_φ is the result of modifying A_φ as follows:
• add a new state q_0 and make it the unique initial state.

• for every initial state q of A_φ, add a transition $q_0 \xrightarrow{q \cap AP} q$ to B_φ (recall that q is an atom of $cl(\varphi)$, and so $q \cap AP$ is well defined).

• replace every transition $q_1 \xrightarrow{q_1 \cap AP} q_2$ of A_φ by $q_1 \xrightarrow{q_2 \cap AP} q_2$.

(c) Construct the automaton B_φ for the automaton of figure 13.7.

(d) Apply the reduction algorithm of exercise 150(2) to B_φ. Is the resulting automaton minimal?

Solution:

(a) If the reduction algorithm merges two states q_1 and q_2, then we have $\mathcal{L}_\omega(q_1) = \mathcal{L}_\omega(q_2)$. Since the automata for LTL formulas satisfy $\mathcal{L}_\omega(q_1) \cap \mathcal{L}_\omega(q_2) = \emptyset$ for every two distinct states, no states are merged.   □

(b) Recall that, for every computation $\sigma = \sigma_0\sigma_1\sigma_2\cdots$, the unique run of A_φ on σ is

$$\alpha_0 \xrightarrow{\sigma_0} \alpha_1 \xrightarrow{\sigma_1} \alpha_2 \xrightarrow{\sigma_2} \ldots$$

where $\alpha = \alpha_0\alpha_1\alpha_2\cdots$ is the unique satisfaction sequence for φ matching σ. By definition of B_φ, the unique run of B_φ on σ is

$$q_0 \xrightarrow{\sigma_0} \alpha_0 \xrightarrow{\sigma_1} \alpha_1 \xrightarrow{\sigma_2} \alpha_2 \xrightarrow{\sigma_3} \ldots$$

□

(c) Automata A_φ and B_φ are respectively as follows:

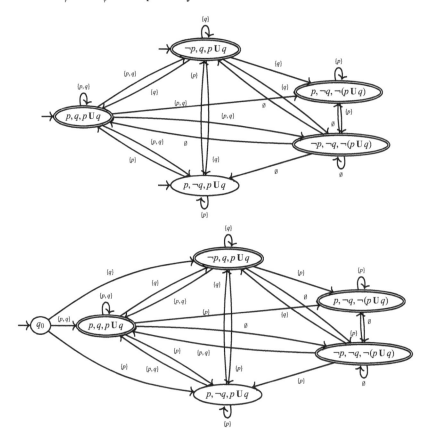

(d) The relation CSR' has three equivalence classes:

$$Q_0 = \Big\{q_0, \{p, \neg q, p \,\mathbf{U}\, q\}\Big\},$$

$$Q_1 = \Big\{\{p, q, p \,\mathbf{U}\, q\}, \{\neg p, q, p \,\mathbf{U}\, q\}, \{\neg p, \neg q, \neg(p \,\mathbf{U}\, q)\}\Big\},$$

$$Q_2 = \Big\{\{p, \neg q, \neg(p \,\mathbf{U}\, q)\}\Big\}.$$

This leads to the following reduced NBA:

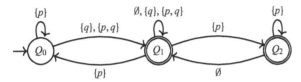

Note that the above reduced NBA is not minimal since it could be simplified to

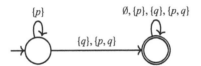

★ ■ **Exercise 187.** In this exercise, we prove that, in the worst case, the number of states of the smallest deterministic Rabin automaton for an LTL formula can be doubly exponential in the size of the formula. Let $\Sigma_0 = \{a, b\}$, $\Sigma_1 = \{a, b, \#\}$ and $\Sigma = \{a, b, \#, \$\}$. For every $n \geq 0$, let us define the ω-language $L_n \subseteq \Sigma^\omega$ as follows:

$$L_n = \sum_{w \in \Sigma_0^n} \Sigma_1^* \# w \# \Sigma_1^* \$ \, w \, \#^\omega.$$

Informally, an ω-word belongs to L_n iff

- it contains a single occurrence of $\$$,
- the word to the left of $\$$ is of the form $w_0 \# w_1 \# \cdots \# w_k$ for some $k \geq 1$ and (possibly empty) words $w_0, \ldots, w_k \in \Sigma_0^*$,
- the ω-word to the right of $\$$ consists of a word $w \in \Sigma_0^n$ followed by an infinite tail $\#^\omega$, and
- w is equal to at least one of $w_0, \ldots, w_n$.

Show the following statements:

(a) There is an infinite family $\{\varphi_n\}_{n \geq 0}$ of formulas of LTL(Σ) such that φ_n has size $\mathcal{O}(n^2)$ and $\mathcal{L}_\omega(\varphi_n) = L_n$. Here, "$\mathcal{L}_\omega(\varphi_n) = L_n$" stands for $\sigma \in \mathcal{L}_\omega(\varphi_n)$ iff $\sigma = \{a_1\}\{a_2\}\{a_3\} \cdots$ for some ω-word $a_1 a_2 a_3 \cdots \in L_n$.

(b) The smallest deterministic Rabin automaton recognizing L_n has at least 2^{2^n} states.

Solution:

(a) We first define some auxiliary formulas.

(i) Let

$$\text{Sing} := \mathbf{G}\left(\bigvee_{\alpha \in \Sigma} \alpha \wedge \bigwedge_{\alpha,\beta \in \Sigma} (\neg\alpha \vee \neg\beta)\right).$$

This formula expresses that at every position, exactly one proposition of Σ holds (i.e., the set of atomic propositions that hold is a singleton set). Therefore, for every computation satisfying Sing and for every position n, we can speak of "the" letter of Σ at position n.

(ii) Let

$$\text{One\_\$} := \neg\$ \, \mathbf{U} \, (\$ \wedge \mathbf{X}\mathbf{G}\neg\$).$$

Together with (i), this formula expresses that $\$$ occurs exactly once.

(iii) Let

$$\text{Match}_i := \# \wedge \bigwedge_{j=1}^{i} \left(\mathbf{X}^j a \wedge \mathbf{G}(\$ \to \mathbf{X}^j a)\right) \vee \left((\mathbf{X}^j b \wedge \mathbf{G}(\$ \to \mathbf{X}^j b))\right) \wedge \mathbf{X}^{i+1}\#.$$

Together with (i) and (ii), this formula expresses that the current letter and the next $i+1$ letters constitute a block of the form $\# w \#$ for some word $w \in \Sigma_0^*$, and moreover, w also occurs immediately after the only occurrence of $\$$.

(iv) For every $i \geq 0$, we define the formula After_$\$_i$ inductively as follows:

$$\text{After\_}\$_0 := \mathbf{G}\#,$$

$$\text{After\_}\$_{i+1} := (a \vee b) \wedge \mathbf{X}\,\text{After\_}\$_i.$$

Together with (i), After_$\$_n$ expresses that the next n letters are taken from the set $\{a, b\}$ and that they are followed by an infinite tail of $\#$.

We choose

$$\varphi_n := \text{Sing} \wedge \text{One\_\$} \wedge \mathbf{F}\,(\text{Match}_n) \wedge \mathbf{G}(\$ \to \text{After\_}\$_n).$$

Since the lengths of After_$\$_n$ and Match_n belong, respectively, to $\mathcal{O}(n)$ and $\mathcal{O}(n^2)$, the length of φ_n belongs to $\mathcal{O}(n^2)$. Clearly, we have $\mathcal{L}_\omega(\varphi_n) = L_n$.

(b) Take an ω-word of the form $\# w_1 \# \cdots \# w_k \# \$ \, w \#^\omega$, where all of $w_1, \ldots, w_k$ are of length n. The intuition is that, after reading the only occurrence of $\$$, the DRA must have stored in its state the set $\{w_1, \ldots, w_n\}$, since otherwise, after reading w it cannot decide whether it belongs to the set. Since there are 2^{2^n} sets of words over $\{a, b\}$ of length n, the automaton also needs at least this number of states.

Formally, for every set $S = \{w_1, \ldots, w_k\}$ of words from Σ_0^n, where w_i is lexicographically smaller than w_j for all $i < j$, let $w_S = \# w_1 \# \cdots \# w_k \# \$$. Let A be a DRA recognizing L_n. For the sake of contradiction, suppose that A has less than 2^{2^n} states. There must exist distinct sets S and T such that the state reached by A after reading w_S and w_T is the same. Moreover, we may assume w.l.o.g. that there is a word w that belongs to $S \setminus T$. Note that

A accepts w_S w $\#^\omega$ and hence w_T w $\#^\omega$. The latter does not belong to L_n, which yields a contradiction. ☐

Solutions for Chapter 14

☆ 🖳 **Exercise 188.** Give an $MSO(\{a,b\})$ sentence for each of the following ω-regular languages:

(a) Finitely many as: $(a+b)^*b^\omega$
(b) Infinitely many bs: $((a+b)^*b)^\omega$
(c) as at each even position: $(a(a+b))^\omega$

What regular languages would you obtain if your sentences were interpreted over finite words?

Solution:

(a) $\exists x\,\forall y\,((x<y)\to Q_b(y))$
(b) $\forall x\,\exists y\,((x<y)\wedge Q_b(y))$
(c) $\exists X : [\forall x\,(x\in X \leftrightarrow (x=0 \vee \exists y\,(x=y+2 \wedge y\in X)))] \wedge [\forall x\,((x\in X)\to Q_a(x))]$ where

$$(x=0) := \forall y\,\neg(y<x),$$

$$(x=y+2) := \exists z\,[(y<z \wedge z<x)\wedge(\forall z'\,((y<z' \wedge z'<x)\to(z'=z)))],$$

$$(z'=z) := \neg((z'<z)\vee(z<z')).$$

Over finite words, we obtain

(a) $(a+b)^+$
(b) $(a+b)^*b$
(c) $(a(a+b))^*$

☆ 🖳 **Exercise 189.** Let us revisit exercise 131 over infinite words rather than finite ones. Consider a formula $\phi(X)$ of $MSO(\Sigma)$ that does not contain any occurrence of predicates of the form $Q_a(x)$. Given two interpretations that assign the same set of positions to X, we have that either both interpretations satisfy $\phi(X)$, or none of them does. Thus, we can speak of the sets of natural numbers satisfying $\phi(X)$. This observation can be used to automatically prove some (very) simple properties of the natural numbers. Consider, for instance, the following "conjecture": every set of natural numbers has a minimal element.[3] The conjecture holds iff the formula

$$\text{Has\_min}(X) := \exists x\in X\,\forall y\in X\,(x\leq y)$$

is satisfied by every interpretation in which X is nonempty. Construct an automaton for $\text{Has\_min}(X)$, and check that it recognizes all nonempty sets.

---

3. We only proved the case of *finite* sets in exercise 131. Here, we handle finite and infinite sets.

Solution: After replacing abbreviations, we obtain the equivalent formula

$$\exists x \, [x \in X \wedge (\neg \exists y \, (y \in X \wedge y < x))].$$

The Büchi automaton for formula $\neg \exists y \, (y \in X \wedge y < x)$, where the encoding of x is at the top and the encoding for X is at the bottom, is as follows:

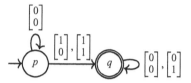

The Büchi automaton for $x \in X$ is as follows:

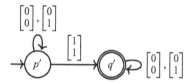

The intersection of the two automata is as follows:

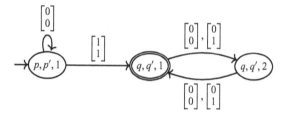

After projection onto X (second row), we get a Büchi automaton for Has_min(X):

In words, it recognizes all ω-words with at least one 1, which corresponds to nonempty sets.

☆ 🔲 **Exercise 191.** Let φ be a formula from linear arithmetic s.t. $\mathcal{V} \models \varphi$ iff $\mathcal{V}(x) \geq \mathcal{V}(y) \geq 0$. Give an NBA that accepts the solutions of φ (over $\mathbb{R}$), without necessarily following the construction presented in the chapter.

Solution: We provide the following automaton. The part on the left deals with edge cases where x or y begins with 1 but is equal to zero (e.g., $x = 1, 1^{\omega}$). The part on the right deals with the general case where both x and y begin with 0.

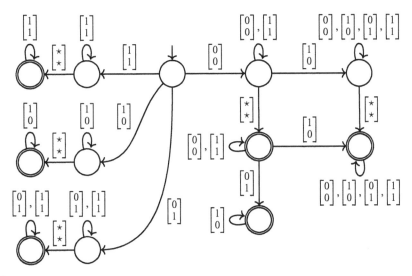

★ 🔲 **Exercise 193.** Linear arithmetic cannot express the operations $y = \lceil x \rceil$ (ceiling) and $y = \lfloor x \rfloor$ (floor). Explain how they can be implemented with Büchi automata.

Solution: Let us consider the case of $y = \lfloor x \rfloor$, where *both* numbers begin with 0 (there are other edge cases to consider, e.g., $x = 0 \star 0^\omega$ and $y = 1 \star 1^\omega$). If the fractional part of x is not 1^ω, then we can copy the integer part and set the fractional part to 0^ω. However, there exists a second representation of the resulting integer. For example, $0110 \star 010^\omega$ (6.25) becomes either $0110 \star 0^\omega$ (6.0) or $0101 \star 1^\omega$ (5.$\overline{9}$). If the fractional part is 1^ω, then the number is already an integer. We produce its two versions—that is, from $\mathrm{MSBF}(x) \star 1^\omega$, we produce $\mathrm{MSBF}(x) \star 1^\omega$ itself or $\mathrm{MSBF}(x+1) \star 0^\omega$. For example, $0011 \star 1^\omega$ (3.$\overline{9}$) becomes either $0011 \star 1^\omega$ (3.$\overline{9}$) or $0100 \star 0^\omega$ (4.0). The resulting automaton is as follows:

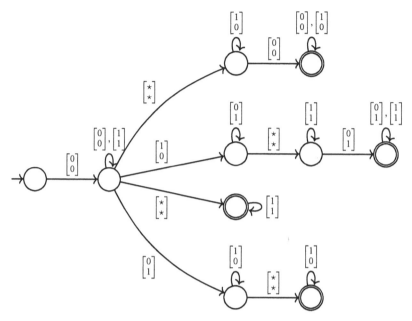

The reasoning is symmetric for negative numbers. For example, $101 \star 110^{\omega}$ represents -2.25, and its floor can be represented by $101 \star 000^{\omega}$ (-3.0) or $100 \star 111^{\omega}$ ($-4 + 0.\overline{9}$). Similarly, $110 \star 1^{\omega}$ represents -1, and its floor can be represented either by itself ($-2 + 0.\overline{9}$) or by $111 \star 0^{\omega}$ (-1.0).

⭐ ■ **Exercise 194.** Let c be an irrational number such as π, e, or $\sqrt{2}$. Show that *no* formula from linear arithmetic is such that $\mathcal{V} \models \varphi$ iff $\mathcal{V}(x) = c$.

Solution: For the sake of contradiction, suppose that there exists some formula from linear arithmetic such that $\mathcal{V} \models \varphi$ iff $\mathcal{V}(x) = c$. There exists a Büchi automaton $A = (Q, \Sigma, \delta, Q_0, F)$ for φ. Recall that a Büchi automaton always accepts at least one periodic word. Since A only accepts encodings of c, which is irrational, this is a contradiction.

More precisely, A accepts some word of the form

$$w_{k-1} \cdots w_0 \star x_1 \cdots x_m (y_1 \cdots y_n)^{\omega}$$

for some $m \geq 0$ and $k, n \geq 1$. Thus, c is rational as it can be expressed as a finite sum of rational numbers:

$$c = \sum_{\ell=0}^{k-1} w_{\ell} \cdot 2^{\ell} + \sum_{j=1}^{m} \frac{x_j}{2^j} + \sum_{i=0}^{\infty} \frac{1}{2^{m+i \cdot n}} \cdot \left(\sum_{j=1}^{n} \frac{y_j}{2^j} \right)$$

$$= \sum_{\ell=0}^{k-1} w_{\ell} \cdot 2^{\ell} + \sum_{j=1}^{m} \frac{x_j}{2^j} + \sum_{i=0}^{\infty} \frac{1}{2^{m+i \cdot n}} \cdot \frac{y_1 \cdot 2^{n-1} + \ldots + y_n \cdot 2^0}{2^n}$$

$$= \sum_{\ell=0}^{k-1} w_\ell \cdot 2^\ell + \sum_{j=1}^{m} \frac{x_j}{2^j} + \frac{y_1 \cdot 2^{n-1} + \ldots + y_n \cdot 2^0}{2^{m+n}} \cdot \sum_{i=0}^{\infty} \left(\frac{1}{2^n}\right)^i$$

$$= \sum_{\ell=0}^{k-1} w_\ell \cdot 2^\ell + \sum_{j=1}^{m} \frac{x_j}{2^j} + \frac{y_1 \cdot 2^{n-1} + \ldots + y_n \cdot 2^0}{2^{m+n}} \cdot \frac{1}{1 - (1/2^n)} \qquad (*)$$

$$= \sum_{\ell=0}^{k-1} w_\ell \cdot 2^\ell + \sum_{j=1}^{m} \frac{x_j}{2^j} + \frac{y_1 \cdot 2^{n-1} + \ldots + y_n \cdot 2^0}{2^{m+n} \cdot \underbrace{(1 - (1/2^n))}_{\neq 0 \text{ since } n \geq 1}},$$

where (*) follows from a geometric sum with $r = 1/2^n$.

Bibliographic Notes

Chapter 1. Automata Classes and Conversions

Regular languages have been extensively studied. Several textbooks are dedicated to this topic (and, more generally, to the theory computation), for example, [HMU07, Sip12, Koz97, And06].

Regular expressions were introduced by Kleene in [Kle51, Kle56] under the name "regular events." The equivalence laws of table 1.1 are folklore. Kleene already asked the question of finding an axiomatization—that is, a collection of equivalence laws such that any two equivalent regular expressions can be proved equivalent by applying a sequence of laws in the collection. Redko showed that no finite axiomatization consisting only of equivalence laws exists [Red64]. Salomaa gave a finite axiomatization containing the laws of table 1.1 and Arden's lemma [Ard61], an inference rule stating that if $r \equiv rs + t$, then $r = ts^*$. Regular expressions and their axiomatization are also the subject of a monograph by Conway [Con71]. The textbook by Hopcroft, Motwani, and Ullman describes extensions of regular expressions and applications to pattern matching and lexical analysis [HMU07].

DFAs and NFAs were introduced by Rabin and Scott [RS59]. Previous automata models had been defined by McCulloch and Pitts under the name "nerve nets" (this model inspired Kleene's work in [Kle51, Kle56]) and, according to [RS59], by Myhill in unpublished work. The Rabin–Scott model defines finite automata as a special class of Turing machines. It introduced many of the results presented in chapters 1–3 and much of the terminology and notations we use today. However, the paper is not written in an algorithmic style. For example, corollary 7.1 states: Given a finite automaton A, there is an effective procedure whereby in a finite number of steps, it can be decided whether $\mathcal{L}(A)$ is empty. The complexity is not discussed, and the algorithm is hidden in the proof.

The powerset construction is due to Rabin and Scott [RS59]. The construction that transforms regular expressions into NFA-ε is due to Thompson [Tho68]. Previously, McNaughton and Yamada presented an algorithm that directly transforms a regular expression into a DFA [MY60]. The same paper contains an algorithm to transform a DFA into a regular expression, although not the one given in the chapter using NFA-reg.

Exercises 5 and 7 were respectively inspired by Marijana Lazić and Peter Rossmanith. Alternating automata (exercise 22) were introduced by Chandra, Kozen, and Stockmeyer in [CKS81] and have become a popular model. Exercise 26 is borrowed from Abdulla, Bouajjani, and Jonsson [ABJ98]. Exercise 31 was inspired by Rupak Majumdar. Exercise 34 is due to Andrzej Ehrenfeucht and Paul Zeiger [EZ76]. Weakly acyclic automata (exercise 35) are inspired by Krötzsch, Masopust, and Thomazo [KMT17].

Chapter 2. Minimization and Reduction

The existence of a unique minimal DFA for a given regular language is shown in [RS59], where it is credited to unpublished work by Myhill and Nerode [Ner58]. Textbooks usually introduce the Myhill–Nerode equivalence relation on words. This equivalence relation has one equivalence class for each state of the canonical automaton, say q, containing all words leading from the initial state of the canonical automaton to q. Our residuals are defined differently; the residual for the state q is the set of words leading from q to the final states of the canonical automaton. Hopcroft's algorithm was presented in [Hop71]. The version of the chapter is taken from a paper by Knuutila [Knu01]. An extensive discussion of minimization algorithms is conducted by Berstel, Boasson, Carton, and Fagnot in [BBCF21].

The reduction algorithm for NFAs is actually an algorithm that constructs the unique minimal NFA that is strongly bisimilar to a given one. For the definition of strong bisimilarity, see, for example, the book by Milner [Mil89]. An efficient algorithm to construct this automaton was proposed by Kannellakis and Smolka [KS90], later improved by Paige and Tarjan [PT87]. The algorithm of Paige and Tarjan runs in time $\mathcal{O}(m \log n + n)$ for an NFA with n states and m transitions.

The characterization of the regular languages as those with a finite number of residuals (theorem 2.31) is similar to the one given by Rabin and Scott in [RS59]: a language is regular iff the Myhill–Nerode equivalence relation has a finite number of equivalence classes.

Exercise 50 was inspired by Thomas Henzinger. Exercise 53 presents Brzozowski's minimization algorithm for DFAs [Brz62]; for a generalization, see [BT14]. Exercise 54 is due to Salomon Sickert.

Chapter 3. Operations on Sets: Implementations

Rabin and Scott showed that the regular languages are closed under union, intersection, and complement, and in particular, they introduced the pairing construction [RS59]. Their approach is not algorithmic. The subsumption test for checking universality and inclusion of NFAs is due to De Wulf, Doyen, Henzinger, and Raskin [WDHR06]. Theorem 3.13 and proposition 3.14 showing that the universality and inclusion problems are PSPACE-complete for NFAs can be traced back to Meyer and Stockmeyer [MS72], although the results appear more prominently in Hunt, Rosenkrantz, and Szymanski in [IRS76]. Both papers reduce the membership problem for context-sensitive grammars (which is PSPACE-complete, but this terminology was not established at the time) to universality and inclusion of regular expressions.

The automaton from exercise 76 appears, for example, in [Vol08].

Chapter 4. Application I: Pattern Matching

Pattern matching (also called string matching) is a fundamental problem of computer science, for example, see [AG97, NR02]. Chapter 3 of [HMU07] contains a brief introduction to applications of regular expressions and finite automata to pattern matching. The chapter is influenced by David Eppstein's lecture notes for his course on the design and analysis of algorithms.[1] In the literature, algorithm *CompMiss* is known as the *Knuth–Morris–Pratt (string-searching) algorithm* [KJP77]. Different variants were independently discovered by James H. Morris, Donald Knuth, Yuri Matijasevich, and Vaughan Pratt.

Mohri presents in [Moh97] an automata-theoretic description of the Knuth–Morris–Pratt algorithm, related to, but different from, ours. Lazy automata are a (very) restricted case of two-way automata, introduced by Rabin and Scott [RS59] (see also exercise 88). In two-way automata, the reading head can move right, stay put, or move left. Rabin and Scott show that finite two-way automata have the same expressive power as finite (one-way) automata, that is, they precisely recognize regular languages.

Chapter 5. Operations on Relations: Implementations

Transducers are automata that transform finite input words into finite output words. Early definitions of transducers were introduced by Moore [Moo56] and Mealy [Mea55], known in the literature as Moore and Mealy machines, respectively. An early appearance of the term "finite transducer" is [Sch61]. The transducers defined in the chapter produce exactly one output symbol for each input symbol and are often called length-preserving transducers. More general transducers can also produce a (possibly empty) sequence of output symbol and also produce outputs on ε-input. For a modern introduction to finite transducers, going beyond this chapter, see, for example, [HK21]. For applications to language processing, see [Moh97]. Applications to program verification are discussed in chapter 7.

The Collatz function, also known as the $3n + 1$ function, is named after Lothar Collatz, who formulated the conjecture in 1937.

Exercise 98 was inspired by [Gul11].

---

1. See http://www.ics.uci.edu/~eppstein/teach.html.

Chapter 6. Finite Universes and Decision Diagrams

This chapter is very influenced by Andersen's introduction to reduced ordered binary decision diagrams (ROBDDs) [And98]. This model was introduced by Bryant as a data structure for the representation and manipulation of boolean functions [Bry86]. ROBDDs are extensively used in the field of formal verification, for example, in CTL model checkers such as NuSMV [CCGR99]. The observation that the ROBDD of a boolean function is very related to the minimal DFA recognizing its satisfying assignments (once a variable order is chosen) is folklore, but, to our knowledge, it has not been explicitly described in the literature.

Chapter 7. Application II: Verification

The approach to formal verification presented in the chapter is usually known as *model checking*, which consists of a systematic and exhaustive exploration of the set of reachable configurations of the formal model of the system. Dedicated books on model checking include [BK08, CGK$^+$18, CHVB18].

The application of automata-theoretic techniques to model checking was pioneered by Kurshan in the early 1980s. Kurshan led the development of COSPAN, a software system for the formal verification of coordinating processes [Kur95]. Kurshan used finite automata to formalize both the behavior of single processes and their specification and composed them by means of an operation similar to our asynchronous product. The idea of modeling program variables as processes that communicate with the control process appears in Milner's book [Mil89]; see also work on Petri net semantics of concurrent programs [Jen92, Bes96, Rei98].

Compositional verification is one of the *raisons d'être* of process algebras such as CSP [Hoa85] and CCS [Mil89]. The approach to compositional verification from the chapter is close to that of software like FDR [GABR14] or CADP [GLMS13]. Symbolic state-space exploration was proposed by Burch, Clarke, McMillan, Dill, and Hwanng [BCM$^+$92]. NuSMV [CCG$^+$02] is, for example, a well-known symbolic model checker.

The Lamport–Burns' mutual exclusion algorithm is taken from [Lam86]. The distinction between safety and liveness properties is due to Lamport [Lam77].

Chapter 8. Automata and Logic

The equivalence of $MSO(\Sigma)$ and regular languages is due to Büchi [B60], Elgot [Elg61], and Trakhtenbrot [Tra62]. The logic $FO(\Sigma)$ was first considered by McNaughton and Papert [MP71], who established its equivalence with star-free languages (see exercise 123). The algorithm that converts a formula of $MSO(\Sigma)$ into an equivalent automaton is the core engine of the MONA tool [HJJ$^+$95, KS99], a satisfiability checker for $MSO(\Sigma)$. MONA has been applied to the verification of hardware circuits [BK95].

Chapter 9. Application III: Presburger Arithmetic

The first decision procedure for Presburger arithmetic was given by Presburger in 1929 [Pre29]. The connection of Presburger arithmetic and automata theory was first established by Büchi in [B60], where he showed how to transform a formula φ into an automaton that encodes the set of solutions of φ.

It was shown by Cobham and Semenov that the subsets of integer vectors encodable by finite automata in any base $b \geq 2$ are those definable in Presburger arithmetic [Cob69, Sem77]. For a fixed base $b \geq 2$, the expressiveness extends slightly beyond Presburger arithmetic as one can test for powers of b [BHMV94].

The algorithmic manipulation of Presburger formulas through automata was considered by Wolper and Boigelot [WB95, Boi98]. Dedicated constructions for translating (in)equations into automata, as those presented in chapter 9, were presented in [BC96, WB00].

A column of Haase provides an overview on "the history, decision procedures, extensions and geometric properties of Presburger arithmetic" [Haa18].

Exercise 138 is known as the chicken nuggets problem or the Frobenius coin problem, after the mathematician Ferdinand Frobenius. In the coin version, the problem asks for the largest monetary amount that cannot be obtained using only coins of specified denominations.

Chapter 10. Classes of ω-Automata and Conversions

Automata on infinite words were introduced in the 1960s by several authors as a tool for solving decision problems in logical theories. In particular, Büchi used what we now call Büchi automata to give a decision procedure for monadic second-order logic on ω-words, a result discussed in chapter 14 [B62, BL69]. (Büchi's works were collected by McLane and Siefkes in [MLS90].)

Büchi automata, ω-regular expressions, and their equivalence, demonstrated in section 10.2.2.1, were introduced by Büchi [B62]. The determinization procedure for co-Büchi automata of section 10.2.3.1 can be traced back to Miyano and Hayashi [MH84], but the form shown in the chapter goes to Kupferman and Vardi [KV97, KV01]. The Rabin condition was introduced by Rabin in [Rab68], although for automata on infinite trees, a generalization of automata on infinite words. Theorem 10.18 is due to Safra [Saf88]. The proof of proposition 10.20 can be found in [Bok18], a paper by Boker containing an exhaustive analysis of the blowups involved in conversions between automata types. The Streett acceptance condition was introduced by Street in [Str81]; again, it was originally defined for automata on infinite trees. The conversion NSA → NBA is described by Choueka in [Cho74]. The parity condition was introduced independently by Mostowski [Mos84] and by Emerson and Jutla in [EJ91] under the name "chain Rabin condition." A proof of theorem 10.25 due to Piterman can be found in [Pit06, Pit07]. Muller automata were introduced by Muller in [Mul63]. McNaughton showed that every NBA has an equivalent DMA [McN66]. Proposition 10.20 is adapted from a similar result by Boker [Bok17]. Exercise 148 is inspired by Kupferman [Kup18].

For the reader interested in the theory of ω-automata, there exist excellent publications containing more advanced results. Thomas's chapter in the *Handbook of Theoretical Computer Science* presents a very clear account of the work of Büchi [Tho90]. The monograph by Perrin and Pin presents the connection with algebra and topology. The most extensive work is [GTW02], a monograph by multiple authors. Wilke's brief introduction to ω-automata for automata-theorists presents basic constructions one can use to implement operations like complementation or determinization [WS21]. Kupferman's chapter in the *Handbook of Model Checking*, and the chapter by Kupferman, Vardi, and Esparza in the *Handbook of Automata Theory* [Kup18, EKV21] are oriented toward the application of ω-automata to program verification.

Chapter 11. Boolean Operations: Implementations

The conversion "NGA $\rightarrow$ NBA" appears in [Cho74], where it is used with a slightly different purpose—namely, to implement intersection of NBAs. The first complementation procedure for NBAs, due to Büchi [Bü62], had a double-exponential blowup in the number of states. Sistla, Vardi, and Wolper presented in [SVW87] an improved construction with a $2^{\mathcal{O}(n^2)}$ blowup. The complementation procedure of section 11.3, with a blowup of $2^{\mathcal{O}(n \log n)}$, is due to Kupferman and Vardi [KV01]. An improvement with the same asymptotic blowup but a smaller constant in the $\mathcal{O}$-notation was presented by Friedgut, Kupferman, and Vardi [FKV06]. Schewe gave a construction that matches the lower bound of section 11.3.3 modulo a $\mathcal{O}(n^2)$ polynomial factor [Sch09]. Detlef Kähler and Wilke introduced a different construction in [KW08] that can be used to both complement Büchi automata and determinize them. The $2^{\mathcal{O}(n \log n)}$ lower bound of section 11.3.3 is due to Michel [Mic88]. The constant was improved by Qiqi Yan in [Yan08]. For a survey of these developments up to 2007, see [Var07], and for an experimental comparison of different algorithms, see [TFVT14].

Exercise 158 on automata with transition-based acceptance is inspired by the tool SPOT of Duret-Lutz et al. [DLF$^+$16] that offers translations into such automata. Exercise 162 is inspired by the work of Muller, Saoudi, and Schupp [MSS86] and Kupferman and Vardi [KV01] on weak alternating automata.

Chapter 12. Emptiness Check: Implementations

The introduction to depth-first search, at the beginning of section 12.1, particularly the parenthesis theorem and the white-path theorem, is taken from the chapter on elementary graph algorithms of Cormen, Leiserson, Rivest, and Stein's textbook on algorithms [CLRS22]. The nested-DFS algorithm of section section 12.1.1 is due to Courcoubetis, Vardi, Woper, and Yannakakis [CVWY90, CVWY92]. The improvement of section 12.1.1.2 is due to Holzmann, Peled, and Yannakakis [HPY96]. The algorithm and its use in the model checker SPIN [Hol04] is described in Holzmann's chapter of the *Handbook of Model Checking* [Hol18]. Gastin, Moro, and Zeitoun proposed a further improvement in [GMZ04] with slightly higher memory requirements. A version that incorporates the improvements of [HPY96, GMZ04] but without the additional memory requirements is Schwoon and Esparza's four-color algorithm presented in section 3 of [SE05]. SCC-based algorithms for Büchi emptiness are modifications of Tarjan's algorithm for the computation of the SCCs of a graph [Tar72]. The first such algorithms were proposed by Couvreur [Cou99] and Geldenhuys and Valmari [GV04]. Both of them are optimal in the sense explained in the chapter. The algorithm of section 12.1.2 is based on unpublished lecture notes by Schwoon. Emerson–Lei's algorithm in section 12.2 is taken from [EL86]. A comparison of several algorithms is presented by Ravi, Bloem, and Somenzi in [RBS00]. The modified algorithm of section 12.2.2 is due to Fisler, Fraer, Kamhi, Vardi, and Yang [FFK$^+$01].

Chapter 13. Application I: Verification and Temporal Logic

The classification of program properties into "safety" and "liveness" properties (already introduced in chapter 7) was introduced by Owicki and Lamport in [OL82]. A formal definition of these terms was given by Alpern and Schneider in [AS85]. Lamport–Burns' mutual-exclusion algorithm is described by Lamport in [Lam86].

Temporal logic was proposed as a formalism for the specification of program properties by Pnueli [Pnu77, Pnu81]. Readers interested on a compact survey on LTL and other temporal logics and their applications to program reasoning can consult the survey by Emerson in the *Handbook of Theoretical Computer Science* [Eme90]. The standard textbook on linear temporal logic and its application to specification of reactive and concurrent systems is the monograph by Manna and Pnueli [MP92]; a second volume by the same authors focuses on the verification of safety properties [MP95]. More recent monographs have also been authored by Kröger and Merz [KM08] and by Demri, Goronko, and Lange [DGL16]. Dwyer, Avrunin, and Corbett carried out a survey of specifications formalized in LTL and other temporal logics, and they compiled a set of useful property specification patterns [DAC99]. The *property specification language (PSL)* is an IEEE standard that extends LTL with regular expressions and syntactic sugar to ease specification and improve the expressive power. For introductions to PSL, the reader can consult the monographs by Cisner and Fisman [EF06]

A first translation of LTL to (generalized) Büchi automata is due to Wolper, Vardi, and Sistla [WVS83, VW94] (in fact, these papers translate an extension of LTL). The translation of section 13.3 closely follows unpublished lecture notes by Vardi. A more efficient construction yielding smaller automata was presented by Gerth, Peled, Vardi, and Wolper in [GPVW95] and implemented in SPIN [Hol04]. It is a tableau construction that produces a Büchi automaton, instead of a generalized one, and was improved further by Daniele, Giunchiglia and Vardi [DGV99], Etessami and Holzmann [EH00], and Somenzi and Bloem [SB00]. A new construction using very weak alternating automata as an intermediate step was given by Gastin and Oddoux [GO01]; it is also distributed with SPIN. Couvreur proposed in [Cou99] a construction similar to the one of [GPVW95], but yielding a generalized Büchi automaton with sets of accepting *transitions*, instead of accepting *states*; it always produces automata at most as large as those of [GPVW95]. Duret-Lutz and Poitrenaud provided a more efficient implementation of Couvreur's construction in the SPOT tool [DP04], further improved by Duret-Lutz in [Dur14]. This is essentially the construction implemented in SPOT 2.0 [DLF⁺16]. SPOT 2.0 offers an online translator from LTL formulas into different automata models that constitutes an invaluable tool for teaching LTL. The procedure for the automatic verification of LTL formulas described in section 13.4 was proposed by Vardi and Wolper in [VW86]. It is usually called the automata-theoretic approach to *model checking* (of LTL). The approach is described in Kupferman's chapter in the *Handbook of Model Checking* [Kup18] and, among other topics, in the monographs on model checking by Clarke, Grumberg, Kroening, Peled, and Veith [CGK⁺18] and Baier and Katoen [BK08]. The approach was implemented by Holzmann in SPIN [Hol04].

Exercise 179 is taken from [DAC99], adapted by Salomon Sickert. Exercise 183 is due to Schwoon. Exercise 187 is taken from Kupferman and Rosenberg [KR10].

Chapter 14. Application II: Monadic Second-Order Logic on ω-Words and Linear Arithmetic

Monadic second-order logic on ω-words was studied by Büchi across several papers [MLS90], and his successful attempt to finding a decision procedure for the logic led to the introduction of Büchi automata. Thomas's chapters in the *Handbook of Theoretical Computer Science* and the *Handbook of Formal Languages* give very clear introductions to this work and to its extension to monadic second-order logic on ω-trees [Tho90, Tho97].

The idea of using Büchi automata as a data structure for sets of real numbers can be traced back to Boigelot, Rassart, and Wolper [BRW98]. The algorithmics of this data structure were developed by Boigelot, Wolper, and others in several publications [WB00, BJW01, BJW05]. The sets of real numbers representable by Büchi automata were studied by Boigelot and Brusten [BB09]; Boigelot, Brusten, and Bruyère [BBB10]; and Boigelot, Brusten, and Leroux [BBL09]. The constructions have been implemented in the tool LASH (Liège Automata-based Symbolic Handler) [Las04]. Boigelot's chapter in the *Handbook of Automata Theory* is an excellent introduction to this work [Boi21].

Bibliography

[ABJ98]   Parosh Aziz Abdulla, Ahmed Bouajjani, and Bengt Jonsson. On-the-fly analysis of systems with unbounded, lossy FIFO channels. In *Proc. 10th International Conference on Computer Aided Verification (CAV)*, 305–318, 1998.

[AG97]   Alberto Apostolico and Zvi Galil, editors. *Pattern Matching Algorithms*. Oxford University Press, 1997.

[And98]   Henrik Reif Andersen. An introduction to binary decision diagrams. 1998.

[And06]   James A. Anderson. *Automata Theory with Modern Applications*. Cambridge University Press, 2006.

[Ard61]   Dean N. Arden. Delayed-logic and finite-state machines. In *Proc. 2nd Annual Symposium on Switching Circuit Theory and Logical Design (SWCT)*, 133–151, 1961.

[AS85]   Bowen Alpern and Fred B. Schneider. Defining liveness. *Information Processing Letters (IPL)*, 21(4):181–185, 1985.

[B60]   J. Richard Büchi. Weak second-order arithmetic and finite automata. *Mathematical Logic Quarterly*, 6(1/6):66–92, 1960.

[B̈62]   Julius R. Büchi. On a decision method in restricted second order arithmetic. In *Proc. International Congress on Logic, Method, and Philosophy of Science*, 425–435. Stanford University Press, 1962.

[BB09]   Bernard Boigelot and Julien Brusten. A generalization of Cobham's theorem to automata over real numbers. *Theoretical Computer Science*, 410(18):1694–1703, 2009.

[BBB10]   Bernard Boigelot, Julien Brusten, and Véronique Bruyère. On the sets of real numbers recognized by finite automata in multiple bases. *Logical Methods in Computer Science (LMCS)*, 6(1), 2010.

[BBCF21]   Jean Berstel, Luc Boasson, Olivier Carton, and Isabelle Fagnot. Minimisation of automata. In Jean-Éric Pin, editor, *Handbook of Automata Theory*, 337–373. European Mathematical Society Publishing House, 2021.

[BBL09]   Bernard Boigelot, Julien Brusten, and Jérôme Leroux. A generalization of Semenov's theorem to automata over real numbers. In *Proc. 22nd International Conference on Automated Deduction on Automated Deduction (CADE)*, 469–484, 2009.

[BC96]   Alexandre Boudet and Hubert Comon. Diophantine equations, Presburger arithmetic and finite automata. In *Proc. 21st International Colloquium on Trees in Algebra and Programming (CAAP)*, 30–43, 1996.

[BCM⁺92]   Jerry R. Burch, Edmund M. Clarke, Kenneth L. McMillan, David L. Dill, and L. J. Hwang. Symbolic model checking: 10^{20} states and beyond. *Information and Computation*, 98(2):142–170, 1992.

[Bes96]   Eike Best. *Semantics of Sequential and Parallel Programs*. Prentice Hall International series in computer science. Prentice Hall, 1996.

[BHMV94]   Véronique Bruyère, Georges Hansel, Christian Michaux, and Roger Villemaire. Logic and p-recognizable sets of integers. *Bulletin of the Belgian Mathematical Society*, 1:191–238, 1994.

[BJW01]   Bernard Boigelot, Sébastien Jodogne, and Pierre Wolper. On the use of weak automata for deciding linear arithmetic with integer and real variables. In *1st International Joint Conference on Automated Reasoning (IJCAR)*, 611–625, 2001.

[BJW05]   Bernard Boigelot, Sébastien Jodogne, and Pierre Wolper. An effective decision procedure for linear arithmetic over the integers and reals. *ACM Transactions on Computational Logic (TOCL)*, 6(3):614–633, 2005.

[BK95]   David A. Basin and Nils Klarlund. Hardware verification using monadic second-order logic. In *Proc. 7th International Conference on Computer Aided Verification*, 31–41, 1995.

[BK08]   Christel Baier and Joost-Pieter Katoen. *Principles of Model Checking*. MIT Press, 2008.

[BL69]   J. Richard Büchi and Lawrence H. Landweber. Definability in the monadic second-order theory of successor. *The Journal of Symbolic Logic*, 34(2):166–170, 1969.

[Boi98]   Bernard Boigelot. Symbolic methods for exploring infinite state spaces, 1998.

[Boi21]   Bernard Boigelot. Symbolic methods and automata. In *Handbook of Automata Theory*, 1189–1215. European Mathematical Society Publishing House, 2021.

[Bok17]   Udi Boker. On the (in)succinctness of Muller automata. In *Proc. 26th EACSL Annual Conference on Computer Science Logic (CSL)*, volume 82, 12:1–12:16, 2017.

[Bok18]   Udi Boker. Why these automata types? In *Proc. 22nd International Conference on Logic for Programming, Artificial Intelligence and Reasoning (LPAR)*, volume 57, 143–163, 2018.

[BRW98]   Bernard Boigelot, Stéphane Rassart, and Pierre Wolper. On the expressiveness of real and integer arithmetic automata (extended abstract). In *Proc. 25th International Colloquium on Automata, Languages and Programming (ICALP)*, 152–163, 1998.

[Bry86]   Randal E. Bryant. Graph-based algorithms for boolean function manipulation. *IEEE Transactions on Computers*, 35(8):677–691, 1986.

[Brz62]   Janusz A. Brzozowski. Canonical regular expressions and minimal state graphs for definite events. In *Proc. Symposium of Mathematical Theory of Automata*, 529–561, 1962.

[BT14]   Janusz A. Brzozowski and Hellis Tamm. Theory of átomata. *Theoretical Computer Science*, 539: 13–27, 2014.

[CCG$^+$02]   Alessandro Cimatti, Edmund M. Clarke, Enrico Giunchiglia, Fausto Giunchiglia, Marco Pistore, Marco Roveri, Roberto Sebastiani, and Armando Tacchella. NuSMV 2: An opensource tool for symbolic model checking. In *Proc. 14th International Conference on Computer Aided Verification (CAV)*, 359–364, 2002.

[CCGR99]   Alessandro Cimatti, Edmund M. Clarke, Fausto Giunchiglia, and Marco Roveri. NuSMV: A new symbolic model verifier. In *Proc. 11th International Conference on Computer Aided Verification (CAV)*, 495–499, 1999.

[CGK$^+$18]   Edmund M. Clarke, Orna Grumberg, Daniel Kroening, Doron A. Peled, and Helmut Veith. *Model Checking, 2nd edition*. MIT Press, 2018.

[Cho74]   Yaacov Choueka. Theories of automata on ω-tapes: A simplified approach. *Journal of Computer and System Sciences*, 8(2):117–141, 1974.

[CHVB18]   Edmund M. Clarke, Thomas A. Henzinger, Helmut Veith, and Roderick Bloem, editors. *Handbook of Model Checking*. Springer, 2018.

[CKS81]   Ashok K. Chandra, Dexter Kozen, and Larry J. Stockmeyer. Alternation. *Journal of the ACM*, 28(1):114–133, 1981.

[CLRS22]   Thomas H. Cormen, Charles E. Leiserson, Ronald L. Rivest, and Clifford Stein. *Introduction to Algorithms, 4th edition*. MIT Press, 2022.

[Cob69]   Alan Cobham. On the base-dependence of sets of numbers recognizable by finite automata. *Mathematical Systems Theory*, 3(2):186–192, 1969.

[Con71]   J. H. Conway. *Regular Algebra and Finite Machines*. William Clowes & Sons Ltd, 1971.

[Cou99]   Jean-Michel Couvreur. On-the-fly verification of linear temporal logic. In *Proc. Formal Methods, World Congress on Formal Methods in the Development of Computing Systems (FM)*, 253–271, 1999.

[CVWY90]   Costas Courcoubetis, Moshe Y. Vardi, Pierre Wolper, and Mihalis Yannakakis. Memory efficient algorithms for the verification of temporal properties. In *Proc. 2nd International Workshop on Computer Aided Verification (CAV)*, 233–242, 1990.

[CVWY92]   Costas Courcoubetis, Moshe Y. Vardi, Pierre Wolper, and Mihalis Yannakakis. Memory-efficient algorithms for the verification of temporal properties. *Formal Methods in System Design*, 1(2/3): 275–288, 1992.

[DAC99]   Matthew B. Dwyer, George S. Avrunin, and James C. Corbett. Patterns in property specifications for finite-state verification. In *Proc. International Conference on Software Engineering (ICSE)*, 411–420, 1999.

[DGL16]   Stéphane Demri, Valentin Goranko, and Martin Lange. *Temporal Logics in Computer Science: Finite-State Systems*. Cambridge Tracts in Theoretical Computer Science. Cambridge University Press, 2016.

[DGV99]   Marco Daniele, Fausto Giunchiglia, and Moshe Y. Vardi. Improved automata generation for linear temporal logic. In *Proc. 11th International Conference on Computer Aided Verification (CAV)*, 249–260, 1999.

[DLF$^+$16]   Alexandre Duret-Lutz, Alexandre Lewkowicz, Amaury Fauchille, Thibaud Michaud, Etienne Renault, and Laurent Xu. Spot 2.0—A framework for LTL and ω-automata manipulation. In *Proc. 14th International Symposium on Automated Technology for Verification and Analysis (ATVA)*, 122–129, 2016.

[DP04]   Alexandre Duret-Lutz and Denis Poitrenaud. SPOT: An extensible model checking library using transition-based generalized Büchi automata. In *Proc. 12th International Workshop on Modeling, Analysis, and Simulation of Computer and Telecommunication Systems (MASCOTS)*, 76–83, 2004.

[Dur14]   Alexandre Duret-Lutz. LTL translation improvements in Spot 1.0. *International Journal of Critical Computer-Based Systems*, 5(1/2):31–54, 2014.

[EF06]   Cindy Eisner and Dana Fisman. *A Practical Introduction to PSL*. Series on Integrated Circuits and Systems. Springer, 2006.

[EH00]   Kousha Etessami and Gerard J. Holzmann. Optimizing Büchi automata. In *Proc. 11th International Conference on Concurrency Theory (CONCUR)*, 153–167, 2000.

[EJ91]   E. Allen Emerson and Charanjit S. Jutla. Tree automata, mu-calculus and determinacy (extended abstract). In *Proc. 32nd Annual Symposium on Foundations of Computer Science (FOCS)*, 368–377, 1991.

[EKV21]   Javier Esparza, Orna Kupferman, and Moshe Y. Vardi. Verification. In *Handbook of Automata Theory*, 1415–1456. European Mathematical Society Publishing House, 2021.

[EL86]   E. Allen Emerson and Chin-Laung Lei. Efficient model checking in fragments of the propositional mu-calculus (extended abstract). In *Proc. Symposium on Logic in Computer Science (LICS)*, 267–278, 1986.

[Elg61]   Calvin C. Elgot. Decision problems of finite automata design and related arithmetics. *Transactions of the American Mathematical Society*, 98(1):21–51, 1961.

[Eme90]   E. Allen Emerson. Temporal and modal logic. In Jan van Leeuwen, editor, *Handbook of Theoretical Computer Science, Volume B: Formal Models and Semantics*, 995–1072. Elsevier and MIT Press, 1990.

[Epp90]   David Eppstein. Reset sequences for monotonic automata. *SIAM Journal on Computing*, 19(3):500–510, 1990.

[EZ76]   Andrzej Ehrenfeucht and H. Paul Zeiger. Complexity measures for regular expressions. *Journal of Computer and System Sciences*, 12(2):134–146, 1976.

[FFK$^+$01]   Kathi Fisler, Ranan Fraer, Gila Kamhi, Moshe Y. Vardi, and Zijiang Yang. Is there a best symbolic cycle-detection algorithm? In *Proc. 7th International Conference on Tools and Algorithms for the Construction and Analysis of Systems (TACAS)*, 420–434, 2001.

[FKV06]   Ehud Friedgut, Orna Kupferman, and Moshe Y. Vardi. Büchi complementation made tighter. *International Journal of Foundations of Computer Science*, 17(4):851–868, 2006.

[GABR14]   Thomas Gibson-Robinson, Philip J. Armstrong, Alexandre Boulgakov, and A. W. Roscoe. FDR3—A modern refinement checker for CSP. In *Proc. 20th International Conference on Tools and Algorithms for the Construction and Analysis of Systems (TACAS)*, 187–201, 2014.

[GJ79]   M. R. Garey and David S. Johnson. *Computers and Intractability: A Guide to the Theory of NP-Completeness*. W. H. Freeman, 1979.

[GLMS13]   Hubert Garavel, Frédéric Lang, Radu Mateescu, and Wendelin Serwe. CADP 2011: A toolbox for the construction and analysis of distributed processes. *International Journal on Software Tools for Technology Transfer*, 15(2):89–107, 2013.

[GMZ04]   Paul Gastin, Pierre Moro, and Marc Zeitoun. Minimization of counterexamples in SPIN. In *Proc. 11th International SPIN Workshop on Model Checking Software*, 92–108, 2004.

[GO01]   Paul Gastin and Denis Oddoux. Fast LTL to Büchi automata translation. In *Proc. 13th International Conference on Computer Aided Verification (CAV)*, 53–65, 2001.

[GPVW95]   Rob Gerth, Doron A. Peled, Moshe Y. Vardi, and Pierre Wolper. Simple on-the-fly automatic verification of linear temporal logic. In *Proc. 15th IFIP WG6.1 International Symposium on Protocol Specification, Testing and Verification*, 3–18, 1995.

[GTW02]   Erich Grädel, Wolfgang Thomas, and Thomas Wilke, editors. *Automata, Logics, and Infinite Games: A Guide to Current Research [outcome of a Dagstuhl seminar, February 2001]*, volume 2500 of *Lecture Notes in Computer Science*, 2002.

[Gul11]   Sumit Gulwani. Automating string processing in spreadsheets using input-output examples. In *Proc. 38th ACM SIGPLAN-SIGACT Symposium on Principles of Programming Languages (POPL)*, 317–330, 2011.

[GV04]   Jaco Geldenhuys and Antti Valmari. Tarjan's algorithm makes on-the-fly LTL verification more efficient. In *Proc. 10th International Conference on Tools and Algorithms for the Construction and Analysis of Systems (TACAS)*, 205–219, 2004.

[Haa18]   Christoph Haase. A survival guide to Presburger arithmetic. *ACM SIGLOG News*, 5(3):67–82, 2018.

[HJJ+95]   Jesper G. Henriksen, Jakob L. Jensen, Michael E. Jørgensen, Nils Klarlund, Robert Paige, Theis Rauhe, and Anders Sandholm. Mona: Monadic second-order logic in practice. In *Proc. 1st International Workshop on Tools and Algorithms for Construction and Analysis of Systems (TACAS)*, 89–110, 1995.

[HK21]   Tero Harju and Juhani Karhumäki. Finite transducers and rational transductions. In *Handbook of Automata Theory (I.)*, 79–111. European Mathematical Society Publishing House, 2021.

[HMU07]   John E. Hopcroft, Rajeev Motwani, and Jeffrey D. Ullman. *Introduction to Automata Theory, Languages, and Computation, 3rd edition*. Addison-Wesley, 2007.

[Hoa85]   C. A. R. Hoare. *Communicating Sequential Processes*. Prentice-Hall, 1985.

[Hol04]   Gerard J. Holzmann. *The SPIN Model Checker—Primer and Reference Manual*. Addison-Wesley, 2004.

[Hol18]   Gerard J. Holzmann. Explicit-state model checking. In *Handbook of Model Checking*, 153–171. Springer, 2018.

[Hop71]   John Hopcroft. An $n \log n$ algorithm for minimizing states in a finite automaton. In *Theory of Machines and Computations*, 189–196. Elsevier, 1971.

[HPY96]   Gerard J. Holzmann, Doron A. Peled, and Mihalis Yannakakis. On nested depth first search. In *Proc. DIMACS Workshop—The Spin Verification System*, 23–31, 1996.

[Hun73]   H. B. III Hunt. On the time and tape complexity of languages I. In *Proc. 5th Annual ACM Symposium on Theory of Computing (STOC)*, 10–19, 1973.

[IRS76]   Harry B. Hunt III, Daniel J. Rosenkrantz, and Thomas G. Szymanski. On the equivalence, containment, and covering problems for the regular and context-free languages. *Journal of Computer and System Sciences*, 12(2):222–268, 1976.

[Jen92]   Kurt Jensen. *Coloured Petri Nets—Basic Concepts, Analysis Methods and Practical Use—Volume 1*. EATCS Monographs on Theoretical Computer Science. Springer, 1992.

[KJP77] Donald E. Knuth, James H. Morris Jr., and Vaughan R. Pratt. Fast pattern matching in strings. *SIAM Journal on Computing*, 6(2):323–350, 1977.

[Kle51] Stephen C. Kleene. *Representation of Events in Nerve Nets and Finite Automata*. Technical Report RM-704, The RAND Corporation, 1951.

[Kle56] Stephen C. Kleene. Representation of events in nerve nets and finite automata. *Annals of Mathematics Studies*, 34:3–41, 1956.

[KM08] Fred Kröger and Stephan Merz. *Temporal Logic and State Systems*. Texts in Theoretical Computer Science. An EATCS Series. Springer, 2008.

[KMT17] Markus Krötzsch, Tomás Masopust, and Michaël Thomazo. Complexity of universality and related problems for partially ordered NFAs. *Information and Computation*, 255:177–192, 2017.

[Knu01] Timo Knuutila. Re-describing an algorithm by Hopcroft. *Theoretical Computer Science*, 250(1/2):333–363, 2001.

[Koz77] Dexter Kozen. Lower bounds for natural proof systems. In *Proc. 18th Annual Symposium on Foundations of Computer Science (FOCS)*, 254–266, 1977.

[Koz97] Dexter Kozen. *Automata and Computability*. Undergraduate Texts in Computer Science. Springer, 1997.

[KR10] Orna Kupferman and Adin Rosenberg. The blowup in translating LTL to deterministic automata. In *Proc. 6th International Workshop on Model Checking and Artificial Intelligence (MoChArt)*, 85–94, 2010.

[KS90] Paris C. Kanellakis and Scott A. Smolka. CCS expressions, finite state processes, and three problems of equivalence. *Information and Computation*, 86(1):43–68, 1990.

[KS99] Nils Klarlund and Michael I. Schwartzbach. A domain-specific language for regular sets of strings and trees. *IEEE Transactions on Software Engineering (TSE)*, 25(3):378–386, 1999.

[Kup18] Orna Kupferman. Automata theory and model checking. In *Handbook of Model Checking*, 107–151. Springer, 2018.

[Kur95] Robert P. Kurshan. *Computer-Aided Verification of Coordinating Processes: The Automata-Theoretic Approach*. Princeton University Press, 1995.

[KV97] Orna Kupferman and Moshe Y. Vardi. Weak alternating automata are not that weak. In *Proc. 5th Israel Symposium on the Theory of Computing Systems (ISTCS)*, 147–158, 1997.

[KV01] Orna Kupferman and Moshe Y. Vardi. Weak alternating automata are not that weak. *ACM Transactions on Computational Logic (TOCL)*, 2(3):408–429, 2001.

[KW08] Detlef Kähler and Thomas Wilke. Complementation, disambiguation, and determinization of Büchi automata unified. In *Proc. 35th International Colloquium on Automata, Languages and Programming (ICALP), Part I: Track A: Algorithms, Automata, Complexity, and Games*, 724–735, 2008.

[Lam77] Leslie Lamport. Proving the correctness of multiprocess programs. *IEEE Transactions on Software Engineering*, 3(2):125–143, 1977.

[Lam86] Leslie Lamport. The mutual exclusion problem: Part II—statement and solutions. *Journal of the ACM*, 33(2):327–348, 1986.

[Las04] The Liège Automata-Based Symbolic Handler (LASH). http://www.montefiore.ulg.ac.be/~boigelot /research/lash/, 2000–2004.

[McN66] Robert McNaughton. Testing and generating infinite sequences by a finite automaton. *Information and Control*, 9(5):521–530, 1966.

[Mea55] George H. Mealy. A method for synthesizing sequential circuits. *The Bell System Technical Journal*, 34(5):1045–1079, 1955.

[MH84] Satoru Miyano and Takeshi Hayashi. Alternating finite automata on ω-words. *Theorertical Computer Science*, 32:321–330, 1984.

[Mic88] Max Michel. Complementation is more difficult with automata on infinite words. *CNET*, 15, 1988.

[Mil89] Robin Milner. *Communication and Concurrency*. PHI Series in Computer Science. Prentice Hall, 1989.

[MLS90]   Saunders Mac Lane and Dirk Siefkes, editors. *The Collected Works of J. Richard Büchi*. Springer, 1990.

[Moh97]   Mehryar Mohri. Finite-state transducers in language and speech processing. *Computational Linguistics*, 23(2):269–311, 1997.

[Moo56]   Edward F. Moore. Gedanken-experiments on sequential machines. In *Automata Studies*, 129–153. Princeton University Press, 1956.

[Mos84]   Andrzej Wlodzimierz Mostowski. Regular expressions for infinite trees and a standard form of automata. In *Proc. 5th Symposium on Computation Theory*, volume 208, 157–168, 1984.

[MP71]   Robert McNaughton and Seymour A. Papert. *Counter-Free Automata*. The MIT Press, 1971.

[MP92]   Zohar Manna and Amir Pnueli. *The Temporal Logic of Reactive and Concurrent Systems— Specification*. Springer, 1992.

[MP95]   Zohar Manna and Amir Pnueli. *Temporal Verification of Reactive Systems—Safety*. Springer, 1995.

[MS72]   Albert R. Meyer and Larry J. Stockmeyer. The equivalence problem for regular expressions with squaring requires exponential space. In *Proc. 13th Annual Symposium on Switching and Automata Theory (SWAT)*, 125–129, 1972.

[MSS86]   David E. Muller, Ahmed Saoudi, and Paul E. Schupp. Alternating automata. The weak monadic theory of the tree, and its complexity. In *Proc. 13th International Colloquium on Automata, Languages and Programming (ICALP)*, 275–283, 1986.

[Mul63]   David E. Muller. Infinite sequences and finite machines. In *Proc. 4th Annual Symposium on Switching Circuit Theory and Logical Design*, 3–16, 1963.

[MY60]   Robert McNaughton and Hisao Yamada. Regular expressions and state graphs for automata. *IRE Transactions on Electronic Computers*, 9(1):39–47, 1960.

[Ner58]   A. Nerode. Linear automaton transformations. *Proceedings of the American Mathematical Society*, 9(4):541–544, 1958.

[NR02]   Gonzalo Navarro and Mathieu Raffinot. *Flexible Pattern Matching in Strings—Practical On-line Search Algorithms for Texts and Biological Sequences*. Cambridge University Press, 2002.

[OL82]   Susan S. Owicki and Leslie Lamport. Proving liveness properties of concurrent programs. *ACM Transactions on Programming Languages and Systems (TOPLAS)*, 4(3):455–495, 1982.

[Pin83]   Jean-Éric Pin. On two combinatorial problems arising from automata theory. In *Combinatorial Mathematics*, volume 17 of *Annals of Discrete Mathematics*, 535–548, 1983.

[Pit06]   Nir Piterman. From nondeterministic Büchi and Streett automata to deterministic parity automata. In *Proc. 21th IEEE Symposium on Logic in Computer Science (LICS)*, 255–264, 2006.

[Pit07]   Nir Piterman. From nondeterministic Büchi and Streett automata to deterministic parity automata. *Logical Methods in Computer Science (LMCS)*, 3(3), 2007.

[Pnu77]   Amir Pnueli. The temporal logic of programs. In *Proc. 18th Annual Symposium on Foundations of Computer Science (FOCS)*, 46–57, 1977.

[Pnu81]   Amir Pnueli. The temporal semantics of concurrent programs. *Theoretical Computer Science*, 13: 45–60, 1981.

[Pre29]   Mojżesz Presburger. Über die Vollständigkeit eines gewissen Systems der Arithmetik ganzer Zahlen, in welchem die Addition als einzige Operation hervortritt. In *Comptes Rendus du Ier Congrès des mathématiciens des pays slaves*, 192–201, 1929.

[PT87]   Robert Paige and Robert Endre Tarjan. Three partition refinement algorithms. *SIAM Journal on Computing*, 16(6):973–989, 1987.

[Rab68]   Michael O. Rabin. Decidability of second-order theories and automata on infinite trees. *Bulletin of the American Mathematical Society*, 74:1025–1029, 1968.

[RBS00]   Kavita Ravi, Roderick Bloem, and Fabio Somenzi. A comparative study of symbolic algorithms for the computation of fair cycles. In *Proc. 3rd International Conference on Formal Methods in Computer-Aided Design (FMCAD)*, 143–160, 2000.

[Red64]   V.N. Redko. On defining relations for the algebra of regular events. *Ukrainian Mathematical Journal*, 16:120–126, 1964.

[Rei98]   Wolfgang Reisig. *Elements of Distributed Algorithms: Modeling and Analysis with Petri Nets.* Springer, 1998.

[RS59]   Michael O. Rabin and Dana S. Scott. Finite automata and their decision problems. *IBM Journal of Research and Development,* 3(2):114–125, 1959.

[Saf88]   Shmuel Safra. On the complexity of ω-automata. In *Proc. 29th Annual Symposium on Foundations of Computer Science (FOCS),* 319–327, 1988.

[SB00]   Fabio Somenzi and Roderick Bloem. Efficient Büchi automata from LTL formulae. In *Proc. 12th International Conference on Computer Aided Verification (CAV),* 248–263, 2000.

[Sch61]   Marcel Paul Schützenberger. A remark on finite transducers. *Information and Control,* 4(2/3):185–196, 1961.

[Sch09]   Sven Schewe. Büchi complementation made tight. In *Proc. 26th International Symposium on Theoretical Aspects of Computer Science (STACS),* 661–672, 2009.

[SE05]   Stefan Schwoon and Javier Esparza. A note on on-the-fly verification algorithms. In *Proc. 11th International Conference on Tools and Algorithms for the Construction and Analysis of Systems (TACAS),* 174–190, 2005.

[Sem77]   A. L. Semenov. Presburgerness of predicates regular in two number systems. *Siberian Mathematical Journal,* 18(2):289–300, 1977.

[Sip12]   Michael Sipser. *Introduction to the Theory of Computation, 3rd edition.* Cengage Learning, 2012.

[Str81]   Robert S. Streett. Propositional dynamic logic of looping and converse. In *Proc. 13th Annual ACM Symposium on Theory of Computing (STOC),* 375–383, 1981.

[SVW87]   A. Prasad Sistla, Moshe Y. Vardi, and Pierre Wolper. The complementation problem for Büchi automata with appplications to temporal logic. *Theoretical Computer Science,* 49:217–237, 1987.

[Tar72]   Robert Endre Tarjan. Depth-first search and linear graph algorithms. *SIAM Journal on Computing,* 1(2):146–160, 1972.

[TFVT14]   Ming-Hsien Tsai, Seth Fogarty, Moshe Y. Vardi, and Yih-Kuen Tsay. State of Büchi complementation. *Logical Methods in Computer Science (LMCS),* 10(4), 2014.

[Tho68]   Ken Thompson. Regular expression search algorithm. *Communications of the ACM,* 11(6):419–422, 1968.

[Tho90]   Wolfgang Thomas. Automata on infinite objects. In *Handbook of Theoretical Computer Science, Volume B: Formal Models and Sematics (B),* 133–191. Elsevier and MIT Press, 1990.

[Tho97]   Wolfgang Thomas. Automata theory on trees and partial orders. In *Proc. 7th International Joint Conference CAAP/FASE: Theory and Practice of Software Development (TAPSOFT),* 20–38, 1997.

[Tra62]   B. A. Trakhtenbrot. Finite automata and logic of monadic predicates. *Sibirskij Matematiceskij Zurnal,* 3(1):103–131, 1962.

[Var07]   Moshe Y. Vardi. The Büchi complementation saga. In *Proc. 24th Annual Symposium on Theoretical Aspects of Computer Science (STACS),* 12–22, 2007.

[Vol08]   Mikhail V. Volkov. Synchronizing automata and the Černý conjecture. In *Proc. 2nd International Conference on Language and Automata Theory and Applications (LATA),* 11–27, 2008.

[VW86]   Moshe Y. Vardi and Pierre Wolper. An automata-theoretic approach to automatic program verification (preliminary report). In *Proc. Symposium on Logic in Computer Science (LICS),* 332–344, 1986.

[VW94]   Moshe Y. Vardi and Pierre Wolper. Reasoning about infinite computations. *Information and Computation,* 115(1):1–37, 1994.

[WB95]   Pierre Wolper and Bernard Boigelot. An automata-theoretic approach to Presburger arithmetic constraints (extended abstract). In *Proc. 2nd International Symposium on Static Analysis (SAS),* 21–32, 1995.

[WB00]   Pierre Wolper and Bernard Boigelot. On the construction of automata from linear arithmetic constraints. In *Proc. 6th International Conference on Tools and Algorithms for Construction and Analysis of Systems (TACAS),* 1–19, 2000.

[WDHR06] Martin De Wulf, Laurent Doyen, Thomas A. Henzinger, and Jean-François Raskin. Antichains: A new algorithm for checking universality of finite automata. In *Proc. 18th International Conference on Computer Aided Verification (CAV)*, 17–30, 2006.

[WS21]   Thomas Wilke and Sven Schewe. ω-Automata. In *Handbook of Automata Theory*, 189–234. European Mathematical Society Publishing House, 2021.

[WVS83]   Pierre Wolper, Moshe Y. Vardi, and A. Prasad Sistla. Reasoning about infinite computation paths (extended abstract). In *Proc. 24th Annual Symposium on Foundations of Computer Science*, 185–194, 1983.

[Yan08]   Qiqi Yan. Lower bounds for complementation of ω-automata via the full automata technique. *Logical Methods in Computer Science (LMCS)*, 4(1), 2008.

Index